THE NEW

STRATEGIC
BRAND
MANAGEMENT

THE *NEW* STRATEGIC BRAND MANAGEMENT

Creating and Sustaining Brand Equity Long Term

JEAN-NOËL KAPFERER

KOGAN
PAGE

London and Philadelphia

First published in France in hardback in 1992 and in paperback in 1995 by Les Editions d'Organisation
Second edition published in Great Britain in 1997 by Kogan Page Limited
Third edition 2004
Reprinted 2005, 2007
Fourth edition 2008

120 Pentonville Road
London N1 9JN
United Kingdom
www.kogan-page.co.uk

525 South 4th Street, #241
Philadelphia PA 19147
USA

© Les Editions d'Organisation, 1992, 1995, 1997, 2004, 2007, 2008

The right of Jean-Noel Kapferer to be identified as the author of this work has been asserted by him in accordance with the Copyright, Designs and Patents Act 1988.

ISBN 978 0 7494 5085 4

British Library Cataloguing-in-Publication Data

A CIP record for this book is available from the British Library.

Library of Congress Cataloging-in-Publication Data

Kapferer, Jean-Noël.
  New strategic brand management : creating and sustaining brand equity long term / Jean-Noël Kapferer. – 4th ed.
      p. cm.
  Includes bibliographical references and index.
  ISBN-13: 978-0-7494-5085-4 (alk. paper)   1. Brand name products–Management.   I. Title.
  HD69.B7K37 2008
  658.8'343–dc22

                                                          2007037849

Typeset by Saxon Graphics Ltd, Derby
Printed and bound in Great Britain by MPG Books Ltd, Bodmin, Cornwall

Contents

Figures

Tables

Preface to the fourth edition

Integrating brand and business

This is a book on strategic brand management. It capitalises on the success of the former three editions. As far as we understand from our readers worldwide (marketers, advertisers, lawyers, MBA students and so on), this success was based on six attributes which we have of course maintained:

▌ **Originality**. *Strategic Brand Management* is quite different from all the other books on brand management. This is due to its comprehensiveness and its unique balance between theory and cases. It also promotes strong and unique working models.

▌ **Relevance**. The cases and illustrations are new, unusual, and not over-exposed. They often represent business situations readers will relate to and understand more readily than over used examples using Coke, Starbucks, Cisco, Fedex, BMW and other great classics of most books and conferences on brands.

▌ **Breadth of scope**. We have tried to address most of the key decisions faced by brands.

▌ **Depth of treatment**. Each facet of brand management receives a deep analysis, hence the size of this edition. This is a book to consult.

▌ **Diversity**. Our examples cover the fast-moving consumer goods sector (FMCG) as well as commodities, business-to-business brands, pharmaceutical brands, luxury brands, service brands, e-brands, and distributors' brands – which are brands almost like the others.

▌ **International scope**, with examples from the United States, Europe and Asia.

This fourth edition is much more than a revision of the previous one. It is a whole new book for understanding today's brands and managing them efficiently in today's markets. Sixteen years after the first edition, so much change has happened in the world of brands! This is why this new edition has been thoroughly updated, transformed and enriched. Of course, our models and methodologies have not changed in essence, but they have been adapted to reflect current competition and issues.

This edition concentrates on internationalisation and globalisation (how to implement these in practice), on portfolio concentration (managing brand transfers or switches), on the creation of megabrands through brand extensions, on the development of competitive advantage and dominant position through an adequate brand portfolio, and on the efficient management of the relationships between the brand, the corporation and the product (the issue of brand architectures).

There are many other significant new features in this edition, which reflect the new branding environment:

▎ Because distributors' brands (often wrongly described as private labels) are everywhere and often hold a dominant market share, they need their own chapter. In addition, in each chapter we have addressed in depth how the recommendations do or do not apply to distributors' brands.

▎ Significantly, this edition develops its new section on innovation. Curiously, the topic of brands and innovation is almost totally absent from most books on branding. This seems at odds with the fact that innovation and branding has become the number one topic for companies. In fact, as we shall demonstrate, brands grow out of innovation, and innovation is the lifeblood of the brand. Furthermore, contrary to what is often said or thought, the issue of innovation is not merely about creativity. It is about reinventing the brand.

▎ This new edition is also sensitive to the fact that many modern markets are saturated. How can brands grow in such competitive environments? A full chapter on growth is included, starting with growth from the brand's existing customers.

▎ The issue of corporate brands and their increasing importance is also tackled, as is their relationship with classic brand management.

▎ We also stress much more than previously the implementation side: how to build interesting brand platforms that are able to stimulate powerful creative advertising that both sells and builds a salient brand; how to activate the brand; how to energise it at contact points; and how to create more bonding. We provide new models to help managers.

This book also reflects the evolution of the author's thought. Our perspective on brands has changed. We feel that the whole domain of branding is becoming a separate area, perhaps with a risk of being self-centered and narcissistic. Too often the history of a company's success or even failure is seen through the single perspective of the brand, without taking into account all the conditions of this success or failure. A brand is a tool for growing the business profitably. It has been created for that purpose, but business cannot be reduced to brands. The interrelationship between the business strategy and the brand strategy needs to be highlighted, because this is the way companies operate. As a consequence, we move away from the classic partitioning of brand equity into two separate approaches. One of these is customer-based, the other cashflow-based. It is crucial to remember that a brand that produces no additional cashflow is of little value, whatever its image and the public awareness of it. In fact, it is time to think of the brand as a 'great shared idea supported by a viable economic equation'. In this fourth edition, we try regularly to relate brand decisions to the economic equation of the business.

Today, every business now wants to have its own brand, not for the sake of possessing it, as one possesses a painting or statue, but to grow the business profitably. We hope this book will help readers significantly, whether they are working in multinationals or in a small dynamic business, developing a global brand or a local one.

Introduction:
Building the brand when the
clients are empowered

It is surprising to see how brands continue to stimulate interest although so many prophets and experts have recently claimed they have no future. Today, all business managers are supposed to have attended conferences on CRM, ECR, customer equity, relationship marketing, customer database management, e-relationships and proximity marketing: all these new tools criticise the old brand concept and focus on the most efficient techniques to serve the most profitable customers. They claim that conquering new clients is of no value any more: profitability will come from mastering databases and loyalty programmes. Despite this, managers keep on attending conferences on brand management. Why haven't they been convinced that brand management is an outdated tool? They have learnt that all these useful techniques soon lose their potential to create a lasting competitive advantage. The more they are diffused and shared, the more they become a standard, used by all competitors. What is customer equity without brand equity?

There are very few strategic assets available to a company that can provide a long-lasting competitive advantage, and even then the time span of the advantage is getting shorter. Brands are one of them, along with R&D, a real consumer orientation, an efficiency culture (cost cutting), employee involvement, and the capacity to change and react rapidly. This is the mantra of Wal-Mart, Starbucks, Apple and Zara.

Managers have also rediscovered that the best kind of loyalty is brand loyalty, not price loyalty or bargain loyalty, even though as a first step it is useful to create behavioural barriers to exit. Finally, A Ehrenberg (1972) has shown through 40 years of panel data analysis that product penetration is correlated with purchase frequency. In other words, big brands have both a high penetration rate and a high purchase frequency per buyer. Growth will necessarily take these two routes, and not only be triggered by customer loyalty.

In our materialistic societies, people want to give meaning to their consumption. Only brands that add value to the product and tell a story about its buyers, or situate their consumption in a ladder of immaterial values, can provide this meaning. Hence the cult of luxury brands.

Pro logo?

Today, every organisation wants to have a brand. Beyond the natural brand world of producers and distributors of fast-moving consumer goods, whose brands are competing head to head, branding has become a strategic issue in all sectors: high tech, low tech, commodities, utilities, components, services, business-to-business (B2B), pharmaceutical laboratories, non-governmental organisations (NGOs) and non-profit organisations all see a use for branding.

Amazingly, all types of organisations or even persons now want to be managed like brands: David Beckham, the English soccer star, is an example. Los Angeles Galaxy paid US$250 million to acquire this soccer hero. It expects to recoup this sum through the profits from licensed products using the name, face or signature of David Beckham, which are sold throughout the world. Everything David Beckham does is aimed at reinforcing his image and identity, and thus making sales and profits for the 'Beckham brand'.

Recently, the mayor of Paris decided to define the city as a destination brand and to manage this brand for profit. Many other towns had already done this. Countries also think of themselves in brand terms (Kotler *et al*, 2002). They are right to do so. Whether they want it or not, they act de facto as a brand, a summary of unique values and benefits. India had a choice between allowing uncontrolled news and information to act (perhaps negatively) on world public opinion, or choosing to try to manage its image by promoting a common set of strategic values (its brand meaning), which might be differentiated by market. Countries compete in a number of markets, just as a conventional brand competes for profitable clients: in the private economic and financial investments market, various raw materials and agricultural markets, the tourism market, the immigration market and so on.

It takes more than branding to build a brand

Companies and organisations from all kinds of sectors ask whether or not a brand could consolidate their business or increase its profitability, and what they should do to create a brand, or become a corporate brand. What steps should be followed, with what investments and using what skills? What are realistic objectives and expectations? Having based their success on mastering production or logistics, they may feel they lack the methods and know-how to implement a brand creation plan. They also feel it is not simply a matter of communication. Although communication is necessary to create a brand, it is far from being sufficient. Certainly a brand encapsulates in its name and its visual symbol all the goodwill created by the positive experiences of clients or prospects with the organisation, its products, its channels, its stores, its communication and its people. However, this means that it is necessary to manage these points of contact (from product or service to channel management, to advertising, to Internet site, to word of mouth, the organisation's ethics, and so on) in an integrated and focused way. This is the core skill needed. This is why, in this fourth edition of *Strategic Brand Management*, while we look in depth at branding decisions as such, we also insist on the 'non-branding' facets of creating a brand. *Paradoxically, it takes more than branding to build a brand.*

Today clients are empowered as never before. It is the end for average brands. Only those that maximise satisfaction will survive, whether they offer extremely low prices, or rewarding experience or service or performance. It is the end of hollow brands, without identity. The trader is also more powerful than many of the brands it distributes: all brands that do not master their channel are now in a B to B to C situation, and must never forget it.

Building both business and brand

Hit parades of the financial value of brands (brand equity) are regularly published in business, financial and economics magazines. Whatever doubts one may have on their validity (see Chapter 18), they do at least stress the essentially financial intentions behind building a brand. Companies do not build brands to have authors write books on them, or to make the streets livelier thanks to billboard advertising. They do it to grow the business still more profitably. One does not make money by selling products, but brands: that is to say a unique set of values, both tangible and intangible. Even low-cost operators need to compete on trust.

Our feeling is that, little by little, branding has been constructed as a separate field. There is a risk however of the branding community falling in love with its own image: looking at the considerable number of books published on brands, and at the list of most recent brand equity values, one could think that brands are the one and only issue of importance. Indeed branding professionals may become infatuated and forget the sources of brand equity: production, servicing, staffing, distributing, innovating, pricing and advertising, all of which help to create value associations and effects which become embedded in clients' long-term memory.

Looking at one of the stars of this hit parade, Dell, whose brand is valued so highly, one question arises: is Dell's success due to its brand or to its business model? It could be argued that it was not the Dell brand but Dell activities in a broader sense that allowed the company to announce more price cuts in 2006, putting Hewlett-Packard in a difficult position between two 'boa constrictors', Dell and IBM.

The brand is not all: it captures the fame but it is made possible by the business model. It is time to recreate a balance in accounting for success and failures. It is the end of fairy tales; let's introduce the time of fair accounts.

Throughout this new edition of *Strategic Brand Management*, we relate the brand to the business, for both are intimately intertwined. We regularly demonstrate how branding decisions are determined by the business model and cannot be understood without this perspective. In fact in a growing number of advanced companies, top managers' salaries are based on three critical criteria: sales, profitability and brand equity. They are determined in part by how fast these managers are building the strategic competitive asset called a brand. The goal of strategy is to build a sustainable advantage over competition, and brands are one of the very few ways of achieving this. The business model is another. This is why tracking brands, product or corporate, is so important.

Looking at brands as strategic assets

The 1980s marked a turning point in the conception of brands. Management came to realise that the principal asset of a company was in fact its brand names. Several articles in both the American and European press dealt with the discovery of 'brand equity', or the financial value of the brand. In fact, the emergence of brands in activities which previously had resisted or were foreign to such concepts (industry, banking, the service sector, etc) vouched for the new importance of brands. This is confirmed by the importance that so many distributors place on the promotion of their own brands.

For decades the value of a company was measured in terms of its buildings and land, and then its tangible assets (plant and equipment). It is only recently that we have realised that its real value lies outside, in the minds of potential customers. In July 1990, the man who bought the Adidas company summarised his reasons in one sentence: after Coca-Cola and Marlboro, Adidas was the best-known brand in the world.

The truth contained in what many observers took simply to be a clever remark has become increasingly apparent since 1985. In a wave of mergers and acquisitions, triggered by attempts to take up advantageous positions in the future single European market, market transactions pushed prices way above what could have been expected. For example, Nestlé bought Rowntree for almost three times its stock market value and 26 times its earnings. The Buitoni group was sold for 35 times its earnings. Until then, prices had been on a scale of 8 to 10 times the earnings of the bought-out company.

Paradoxically, what justified these prices and these new standards was invisible, appearing nowhere in the companies' balance sheets. The only assets displayed on corporate balance sheets were fixed, tangible ones, such as machinery and inventory. There was no mention of the brands for which buyers offered sums much greater than the net value of the assets. The acquiring companies generally posted this extra value or goodwill in their consolidated accounts. The actual object of these gigantic and relentless takeovers was invisible, intangible and unwritten: they were aimed at acquiring brands.

What changed in the course of the 1980s was awareness. Before, in a takeover bid, merger or acquisition, the buyer acquired a pasta manufacturer, a chocolate manufacturer or a producer of microwave ovens or abrasives. Now companies want to buy Buitoni, Rowntree (that is, KitKat, After Eight), Moulinex or Orange. The strength of a company like Heineken is not solely in knowing how to brew beer; it is that people all over the world want to drink Heineken. The same logic applies for IBM, Sony, McDonald's, Barclays Bank or Dior.

By paying very high prices for companies with brands, buyers are actually purchasing positions in the minds of potential consumers. Brand awareness, image, trust and reputation, all painstakingly built up over the years, are the best guarantee of future earnings, thus justifying the prices paid. The value of a brand lies in its capacity to generate such cashflows.

Hardly had this management revolution been born than conflicting arguments arose regarding the reality and the durability of brand equity. With the systematic rise in distributors' own brands it was argued that the capacity of brands had been exaggerated. The fall in the price of Marlboro cigarettes in the USA in April 1993 created panic on Wall Street, with the share prices of all consumer goods firms falling. This mini-Pearl Harbor proved healthy. At the height of recession we realised that it was not the brand – registered trademark – as such that created value, but all the marketing and communication done by the firm. Consumers don't just buy the brand name, they buy branded products that promise tangible and intangible benefits created by the efforts of the company. Given time, the brand may evoke a number of associations, qualities and differences, but these alone do not comprise the whole offer. A map alone is not the underlying territory.

In the 1990s, because of recession and saturated markets, the emphasis shifted from brands to customer equity. New techniques, based on one-to-one targeting, replaced the emphasis on classic media advertising. They could prove their effectiveness and targeted heavy buyers.

Just as some have exaggerated the overwhelming power of brands, so the opposition to brands has been short-lived. The value of brands comes from their ability continuously to add value and deliver profits through corporate focus and cohesiveness. Another question is, who is best placed to make use of brands? Is it the producer or the distributor?

You must be very wary as regards ideological preferences; for example, there are very few manufacturers' brands on the furniture market other than those of Italian designers, yet everybody talks about Habitat or Ikea, two distributors. They are seen as agents offering strong value-added style in the first case and competitive prices and youth appeal in the second.

With manufacturers integrating their distribution, and distributors thinking of themselves as brands, the world of brands is moving permanently, looking for new brand and business models, sources of sustainable advantage and added value for clients. We shall explore these new models that define the winning brands of today and tomorrow.

Part One

Why is branding so strategic?

1

Brand equity in question

Brands have become a major player in modern society. In fact they are everywhere. They penetrate all spheres of our life: economic, social, cultural, sporting, even religion. Because of this pervasiveness they have come under growing criticism (Klein, 1999). As a major symbol of our economies and postmodern societies, they can and should be analysed through a number of perspectives: macroeconomics, microeconomics, sociology, psychology, anthropology, history, semiotics, philosophy and so on. In fact our first book on brands was a collection of essays by eminent scholars from all these disciplines (Kapferer and Thoenig, 1989).

This book focuses on the managerial perspective: how best to manage brands for profit. Since brands are now recognised as part of a company's capital (hence the concept of brand equity), they should be exploited. Brands are intangible assets, assets that produce added benefits for the business. This is the domain of strategic brand management: how to create value with proper brand management. Before we proceed, we need to clarify the brand concept.

What is a brand?

Curiously, one of the hottest points of disagreement between experts is the definition of a brand. Each expert comes up with his or her own definition, or nuance to the definition. The problem gets more acute when it comes to measurement: how should one measure the strength of a brand? What limited numbers of indicators should one use to evaluate what is commonly called *brand equity*? In addition there is a major schism between two paradigms. One is customer-based and focuses exclusively on the relationship customers have with the brand (from total indifference to attachment, loyalty, and willingness to buy and rebuy based on beliefs of superiority and evoked emotions). The other aims at producing measures in dollars, euros or yen. Both approaches have their own champions. It is the goal of this fourth edition of *Strategic Brand Management* to unify these two approaches.

Customer-based definitions

The financial approach measures brand value by isolating the net additional cashflows created by the brand. These additional cash flows are the result of customers' willingness to buy one brand more than its competitors', even when another brand is cheaper. Why then do customers want to pay more? Because of the beliefs and bonds that are created over time in their minds through the marketing of the brand. In brief, customer equity is the preamble of financial equity. Brands have financial value *because* they have created assets in the minds and hearts of customers, distributors, prescribers, opinion leaders. These assets are brand awareness, beliefs of exclusivity and superiority of some valued benefit, and emotional bonding. This is what is expressed in the now classic definition of a brand: 'a brand is a set of mental associations, held by the consumer, which add to the perceived value of a product or service' (Keller, 1998). These associations should be unique (exclusivity), strong (saliency) and positive (desirable).

This definition focuses on the gain in perceived value brought by the brand. How do consumers' evaluations of a car change when they know it is a Volkswagen, a Peugeot or a Toyota? Implicitly, in this definition the product itself is left out of the scope of the brand: 'brand' is the set of added perceptions. As a result brand management is seen as mostly a communication task. This is incorrect. Modern brand management starts with the product and service as the prime vector of perceived value, while communication is there to structure, to orient tangible perceptions and to add intangible ones.

Later we analyse the relationship between brand and product (see page 39). A second point to consider is that Keller's now-classic definition is focused on *cognitions* (mental associations). This is not enough: strong brands have an intense emotional component.

Brands as conditional asset

Financiers and accountants have realised the value of brands (see Chapter 18). How does the financial perspective help us in defining brands and brand equity?

▮ First, brands are *intangible assets*, posted eventually in the balance sheet as one of several types of intangible asset (a category that also includes patents, databases and the like).

▮ Second, brands are *conditional assets*. This is a key point so far overlooked. An asset is an element that is able to produce benefits over a long period of time. Why are brands conditional assets? Because in order to deliver their benefits, their financial value, they need to work in conjunction with other material assets such as production facilities. There are no brands without products or services to carry them. This will have great consequences for the method of measuring financial value. For now, this reminds us that some humility is required. Although many people claim that brands are all and everything, brands cannot exist without a support (product or service). This product and service becomes effectively an embodiment of the brand, that by which the brand becomes real. As such it is a main source of brand evaluation. Does it produce high or low satisfaction? Brand management starts with creating products, services and/or places that embody the brand. Interestingly, the legal approach to trademarks and brands also insists on their conditional nature. One should never use the brand name as a noun, but as an adjective attached to a name, as for instance with a Volvo car, not a Volvo.

The legal perspective

An internationally agreed legal definition for brands does exist: 'a sign or set of signs certifying the origin of a product or service and differentiating it from the competition'. Historically, brands were created to defend producers from theft. A cattle brand, a sign burned into the animal's hide, identified the owner and made it apparent if the animal had been stolen. 'Brands' or trademarks also identified the source of the olive oil or wine contained in ancient Greek amphoras, and created value in the eyes of the buyers by building a reputation for the producer or distributor of the oil or wine.

A key point in this legal definition is that trademarks have a 'birthday' – their registration day. From that day they become a property, which needs to be defended against infringements and counterfeiting (see page 87 for defence strategies). Brand rights disappear when they are not well enough defended, or if registration is not renewed. One of the sources of loss of rights is degenerescence. This occurs when a company has let a distinctive brand name become a generic term.

Although the legal approach is most useful for defending the company against copies of its products, it should not become the basis of brand management. Contrary to what the legal definition asserts, a brand is not born but made. It takes time to create a brand, even though we talk about launching brands. In fact this means launching a product or service. Eventually it may become a brand, and it can also cease to be one. What makes a brand recognisable? When do we know if a name has reached the status of a brand? For us, in essence, *a brand is a name that influences buyers*, becoming a purchase criterion.

A brand is a name that influences buyers

This definition captures the essence of a brand: a name with power to influence buyers. Of course, it is not a question of the choice of the name itself. Certainly a good name helps: that is, one that is easily pronounceable around the world and spontaneously evokes desirable associations. But what really makes a name become a brand are the *saliency, differentiability, intensity* and *trust* attached to these associations. Are the benefits the name evokes (a) salient, (b) exclusive and (c) trusted?

We live in an attention economy: there is so much choice and opacity that consumers cannot spend their time comparing before they make a choice. They have no time and even if they did, they cannot be certain of being able to determine the right product or service for them. Brands must convey certitude, trust. They are a time and risk reducer. In fact where there is no risk there is no brand. We made this point in an earlier book (Kapferer and Laurent, 1995). The perceived risk could be economic (linked to price), functional (linked to performance), experiential, psychological (linked to our self-concept), or social (linked to our social image). This is why it takes time to build the saliency that is part of brand awareness, and this trust (trusted beliefs about the brand's unique benefits).

Brand power to influence buyers relies on representations and relationships. A representation is a *system* of mental associations. We stress the word 'system', for these associations are interconnected. They are in a network, so that acting on one impacts some others. These associations (also called brand image) cover the following aspects:

- What is the brand territory (perceived competence, typical products or services, specific know-how)?

- What is its level of quality (low, middle, premium, luxury)?

- What are its qualities?

- What is its most discriminating quality or benefit (also called perceived positioning)?

- What typical buyer does the brand evoke? What is the brand personality and brand imagery?

Beyond mental associations, the power of a name is also due to the specific nature of the emotional relationships it develops. A brand, it could be said, is an attitude of non-indifference knitted into consumers' hearts. This attitude goes from emotional resonance to liking, belonging to the evoked set or consideration set, preference, attachment, advocacy, to fanaticism. Finally, designs, patents and rights are of course a key asset: they provide a competitive advantage over a period of time.

In short, *a brand exists when it has acquired power to influence the market.* This acquisition takes time. The time span tends to be short in the case of online brands, fashion brands and brands for teenagers, but longer for, for example, car brands and corporate brands. This power can be lost, if the brand has been mismanaged in comparison with the competition. Even though the brand will still have brand awareness, image and market shares, it might not influence the market any more. People and distributors may buy because of price only, not because they are conscious of any exclusive benefit from the brand.

What makes a name acquire the power of a brand is the product or service, together with the people at points of contact with the market, the price, the places, the communication – all the sources of cumulative brand experience. This is why one should speak of brands as *living systems made up of three poles*: products or services, name and concept. (See Figure 1.1.)

When talking of brands we are sometimes referring to a single aspect such as the name or logo, as do intellectual property lawyers. In brand management, however, we speak of the whole system, relating a concept with inherent value to products and services that are identified by a name and set of proprietary signs (that is, the logo and other symbols). This system reminds us of the conditional nature of the brand asset: it only exists if products and services also exist. Differentiation is summarised by the brand concept, a unique set of attributes (both tangible and intangible) that constitute the value proposition of the brand.

To gain market share and leadership, the brand must be:

- able to conjure up a big idea, and attractive;
- experienced by people at contact points;
- activated by deeds and behaviours;
- communicated;
- distributed.

One of the best examples of a brand is the Mini. This car, worth US$14,000 in functional value, is actually sold for US$20,000. It is one of the very few car brands that gives no rebates and discounts to prospective buyers,

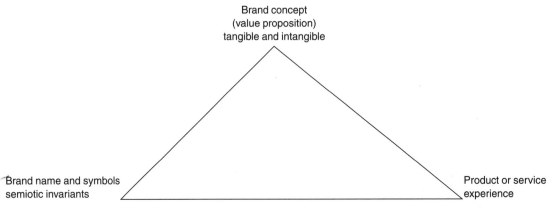

Brand concept
(value proposition)
tangible and intangible

Brand name and symbols
semiotic invariants

Product or service
experience

Figure 1.1 The brand system

who queue to get 'their' Mini. The Mini illustrates the role of both intangible and tangible qualities in the success of any brand. Since it is made by BMW, it promises reliability, power and road-holding performance. But the feelings of love towards this brand are created by the powerful memories the brand invokes in buyers of London in the 'Swinging Sixties'. The classic and iconic design is replicated in the new Mini – and each Mini feels like a personal accessory to its owner (each Mini is customised and different).

The brand triangle helps us to structure most of the issues of brand management:

▌ What concept should one choose, with what balance of tangible and intangible benefits? This is the issue of identity and positioning. Should the brand concept evolve through time? Or across borders (the issue of globalisation)?

▌ How should the brand concept be embodied in its products and services, and its places? How should a product or service of the brand be different, look different? What products can this brand concept encompass? This is the issue of brand extension or brand stretch.

▌ How should the product and/or services be identified? And where? Should they be identified by the brand name, or by the logo only, as Nike does now? Should organisations create differentiated sets of logos and names as a means of indicating internal differences within their product or service lines? What semiotic variants?

▌ What name or signs should one choose to convey the concept internationally?

▌ How often should the brand symbols be changed, updated or modernised?

▌ Should the brand name be changed (see Chapter 15)?

▌ Speaking of internationalisation, should one globalise the name (that is, use the same name around the world), or the logo, or the product (a standardised versus customised product), or the concept (aiming at the same global positioning)? Or all three pillars of the brand system, or only two of them?

Since a brand is a name with the power to influence the market, its power increases as more people know it, are convinced by it, and trust it. Brand management is about gaining power, by making the brand concept more known, more bought, more shared.

In summary, a brand is a shared desirable and exclusive idea embodied in products, services, places and/or experiences. The more this idea is shared by a larger number of people, the more power the brand has. It is because everyone knows 'BMW' and its idea – what it stands for – even those who will never buy a BMW car, that the brand BMW has a great deal of power.

The word 'idea' is important. Do we sell products and services, or values? Of course, the answer is values. For example, 'Volvo' is attached to an idea: cars with the highest possible safety levels. 'Absolut' conjures another idea: a fashionable vodka. Levi's used to be regarded as the rebel's jeans.

Differentiating between brand assets, strength and value

It is time to structure and organise the many terms related to brands and their strength, and to the measurement of brand equity. Some restrict the use of the phrase 'brand equity' to contexts that measure this by its impact on consumer mental associations (Keller, 1992). Others mention behaviour: for example this is included in Aaker's early measures (1991), which also consider brand loyalty. In his late writings Aaker includes market share, distribution and price premium in his 10 measures of brand equity (1996). The official Marketing Science definition of brand equity is 'the set of associations and behavior on the part of a brand's customers, channel members and parent corporation that permits the brand to earn greater volume or greater margins than it could without the brand name' (Leuthesser, 1988).

This definition is very interesting and has been forgotten all too quickly. It is all-encompassing, reminding us that channel members are very important in brand equity. It also specifically ties margins to brand associations and customers' behaviour. Does it mean that unless there is a higher volume or a higher margin as a result of the creation of a brand, there is no brand value? This is not clear, for the word 'margin' seems to refer to gross margin only, whereas brand financial value is measured at the level of earnings before interest and tax (EBIT).

To dispel the existing confusion around the phrase brand equity (Feldwick, 1996), created by the abundance of definitions, concepts, measurement tools and comments by experts, it is important to show how the consumer and financial approaches are connected, and to use clear terms with limited boundaries (see Table 1.1):

▌ *Brand assets.* These are the sources of influence of the brand (awareness/saliency, image, type of relationship with consumers), and patents.

▌ *Brand strength* at a specific point in time as a result of these assets within a specific market and competitive environment. They are the 'brand equity outcomes' if one restricts the use of the phrase 'brand equity' to brand assets alone. Brand strength is captured by behavioural competitive indicators: market share, market leadership, loyalty rates and price premium (if one follows a price premium strategy).

▌ *Brand value* is the ability of brands to deliver profits. A brand has no financial value unless it can deliver profits. To say that lack of profit is not a brand problem but a business problem is to separate the brand from the business, an intellectual temptation. Certainly brands can be analysed from the standpoint of sociology, psychology, semiotics, anthropology, philosophy and so on, but historically they were created for business purposes and are managed with a view to producing profit.

Only by separating brand assets, strength and value will one end the confusion of the brand equity domain (Feldwick, 1996 takes a similar position). Brand value is the profit potential of the brand assets, mediated by brand market strength.

In Table 1.1, the arrows indicate not a direct but a conditional consequence. The same

Table 1.1   From awareness to financial value

Brand assets ⟶	Brand strength ⟶	Brand value
Brand awareness	Market share	Net discounted cashflow attributable
Brand reputation (attributes,	Market leadership	to the brand after paying the cost of
benefits, competence,	Market penetration	capital invested to produce and run
know-how, etc)	Share of requirements	the business and the cost of marketing
Perceived brand personality	Growth rate	
Perceived brand values	Loyalty rate	
Reflected customer imagery	Price premium	
Brand preference or attachment	Percentage of products the	
Patents and rights	trade cannot delist	

brand assets may produce different brand strength over time: this is a result of the amount of competitive or distributive pressure. The same assets can also have no value at all by this definition, if no business will ever succeed in making them deliver profits, through establishing a sufficient market share and price premium. For instance if the cost of marketing to sustain this market share and price premium is too high and leaves no residual profit, the brand has no value. Thus the Virgin name proved of little value in the cola business: despite the assets of this brand, the Virgin organisation did not succeed in establishing a durable and profitable business through selling Virgin Cola in the many countries where this was tried. The Mini was never profitable until the brand was bought by BMW.

Table 1.1 also shows an underlying time dimension behind these three concepts of assets, strength and value. Brand assets are learnt mental associations and affects. They are acquired through time, from direct or vicarious, material or symbolic interactions with the brand. Brand strength is a measure of the present status of the brand: it is mostly behavioural (market share, leadership, loyalty, price premium). Not all of this brand stature is due to the brand assets. Some brands establish a leading market share without any noticeable brand awareness: their price is the primary driver of preference. There are also brands whose assets are superior to their market strength: that is, they have an image that is far stronger than their position in the market (this is the case with Michelin, for example). The obverse can also be true, for example of many retailer own brands.

Brand value is a projection into the future. Brand financial valuation aims to measure the brand's worth, that is to say, the profits it will create in the future. To have value, brands must produce economic value added (EVA), and part of this EVA must be attributable to the brand itself, and not to other intangibles (such as patents, know-how or databases).

This will depend very much on the ability of the business model to face the future. For instance, Nokia lost ground at the Stock Exchange in April 2004. The market had judged that the future of the world's number one mobile phone brand was dim. Everywhere in the developed countries, almost everyone had a mobile phone. How was the company still to make profits in this saturated market? If it tried to sell to emerging countries it would find that price was the first purchase criterion and delocalisation (that is, having the products manufactured in a country such as China or Singapore) compulsory. Up to that point, Nokia had based its growth on its production facilities in Finland. Nokia's present brand stature might be high, but what about its value?

It is time now to move to the topic of tracking brand equity for management purposes. What should managers regularly measure?

Tracking brand equity

What is a brand? A name that influences buyers. What is the source of its influence? A set of mental associations and relationships built up over time among customers or distributors. Brand tracking should aim at measuring these sources of brand power. The role of managers is to build the brand and business. This is true of brand managers, but also of local or regional managers who are in charge of developing this competitive asset in addition to developing the business more generally. This is why advanced companies now link the level of variable salary not only to increments in sales and profits but also to brand equity. However, such a system presupposes that there is a tracking system for brand equity, so that year after year its progress can be assessed. This system must be valid, reliable, and not too complicated or too costly. What should one measure as a minimum to evaluate brand equity?

An interesting survey carried out by the agency DDB asked marketing directors what they considered to be the characteristics of a strong brand, a significant company asset. The following were the answers in order of importance:

▌ brand awareness (65 per cent);

▌ the strength of brand positioning, concept, personality, a precise and distinct image (39 per cent);

▌ the strength of signs of recognition by the consumer (logo, codes, packaging) (36 per cent);

▌ brand authority with consumers, brand esteem, perceived status of the brand and consumer loyalty (24 per cent).

Numerous types of survey exist on the measurement of brand value (brand equity). They usually provide a national or international hit parade based just on one component of brand equity: brand awareness (the method may be the first brand brought to mind, aided or unaided depending on the research institute), brand preference, quality image, prestige, first and second buying preferences when the favoured brand is not available, or liking. Certain institutions may combine two of the components: for example, Landor published an indicator of the 'power of the brand' which was determined by combining brand-aided awareness and esteem, which is the emotional component of the brand–consumer relationship. The advertising agency Young & Rubicam carried out a study called 'Brand Asset Monitor' which positions the brand on two axes: the cognitive axis is a combination of salience and of the degree of perceived difference of the brand among consumers; the emotional axis is the combination of the measures of familiarity and esteem (see Chapter 10). TNS, in its study Megabrand System, uses six parameters to compare brands: brand awareness, stated use, stated

preference, perceived quality, a mark for global opinion, and an item measuring the strength of the brand's imagery.

Certain institutions, which believe that the comparison of brands across all markets makes little sense, concentrate on a single market approach and measure, for example, the acceptable price differential for each brand. They proceed in either a global manner (what price difference can exist between a Lenovo PC and a Toshiba PC?) or by using a method of trade-off which isolates the net added value of the brand name. Marketing directors are perplexed because so many different methods exist.

There is little more consensus among academic researchers. Sattler (1994) analysed 49 American and European studies on brand equity and listed no fewer than 26 different ways of measuring it. These methods vary according to several dimensions:

▌ Is the measure monetary or not? A large proportion of measures are classified in non-monetary terms (brand awareness, attitude, preference, etc).

▌ Does the measurement include the time factor – that is, the future of the brand on the market?

▌ Does the brand measure take the competition into account – that is, the perceived value in relation to other products on the market? Most of them do not.

▌ Does the measurement include the brand's marketing mix? When you measure brand value, do you only include the value attached to the brand name? Most measures do not include the marketing mix (past advertising expenditure, level of distribution, and so on).

▌ When estimating brand value do you include the profits that a user or a buyer could obtain due to the synergies that may exist with its own existing brand portfolio (synergies of distribution, production, logistics, etc)? The majority of them do not include this, even though it is a key factor.

▮ Does the measurement of brand equity include the possibility of brand extensions outside the brand's original market? In general, no.

▮ Finally, does the measure of brand equity take into account the possibility of geographical extension or globalisation? Again, most of the time the answer is no.

We recommend four indicators of brand assets (equity):

▮ *Aided brand awareness.* This measures whether the brand has a minimal resonance.

▮ *Spontaneous brand awareness.* This is a measure of saliency, of share of mind when cued by the product.

▮ *Evoked set*, also called *consideration set.* Does the brand belong to the shortlist of two or three brands one would surely consider buying?

▮ Has the brand been *already consumed* or not?

Some companies add other items like most preferred brand. Empirical research has shown that this item is very much correlated to spontaneous brand awareness, the latter being much more than a mere cognitive measure, but it also captures proximity to the person. Other companies add the item consumed most often. Of course this is typical of fast moving consumer goods; the item is irrelevant for durables. In addition, in empirical research the item is also correlated to evoked set. One should never forget that tracking studies dwell on the customer's memory. This memory is itself very much inferential. Do people really know what brand they bought last? They infer from their preferences, that logically it should have been brand X or Y.

Table 1.2 gives a typical result of a tracking study for a brand.

Table 1.2 Result of a brand tracking study

	Brand X	
	Japan	Mexico
Aided awareness	99%	97%
Unaided awareness	48%	85%
Evoked set	24%	74%
Consumed	5%	40%

There are two ways of looking at the brand equity figures in the table. One can compare the countries by line: although it has similar aided awareness levels, this brand has very different status in the two countries. The second mode is vertical, and focuses on the 'transformation ratios'. It is noticeable that in Japan, the evoked set is 50 per cent of unaided brand awareness, whereas it is 87 per cent in Mexico.

Although there is a regular pattern of decreasing figures, from the top line to the bottom line, this is not always the case. For instance in Europe, Pepsi Cola is not a strong brand: its market share is gained through push marketing and trade offers. As a result, Pepsi Cola certainly grows its business but not its intrinsic desirability. In tracking studies Pepsi Cola has a trial rate far higher than the brand's preference rate (evoked set). At the opposite end of the spectrum there are brands that have an equity far superior to their consumption rate. In Europe, Michelin has a clear edge over rival tyre brands as far as image is concerned. However, image does not transform itself into market share if people like the Michelin brand but deem that the use they make of their cars does not justify buying tyres of such a quality and at such a price.

Tracking studies are not simply tools for control. They are tools for diagnosis and action. Transformation ratios tell us where to act.

Goodwill: the convergence of finance and marketing

The 1980s witnessed a Copernican revolution in the understanding of the workings of brands. Before this, ratios of seven or eight were typical in mergers and acquisitions, meaning that the price paid for a company was seven to eight times its earnings. After 1980 these multiples increased considerably to reach their peak. For example, Groupe Danone paid $2.5 billion for Nabisco Europe, which was equivalent to a price:earnings ratio of 27. Nestlé bought Rowntree Macintosh for three times its stock market value and 26 times its earnings. It was becoming the norm to see multiples of 20 to 25. Even today when, because of the recession, financial valuations have become more prudent, the existence of strong brands still gives a real added value to companies. What happened between the beginning and the end of the 1980s? What explanations can be given for this sudden change in the methods of financial analysts? The prospect of a single European market certainly played a significant role, as can be seen by the fact that large companies were looking for brands that were ready to be European or, even better, global. This explains why Nestlé bought Buitoni, Lever bought Boursin, l'Oréal bought Lanvin, Seagram bought Martell, etc. The increase in the multiples can also be explained in part by the opposing bids of rival companies wishing to take over the few brand leaders that existed in their markets and which were for sale. Apart from the European factor, there was a marked change in the attitude towards the brands of the principal players. Prior to 1980, companies wished to buy a producer of chocolate or pasta: after 1980, they wanted to buy KitKat or Buitoni. This distinction is very important; in the first case firms wish to buy production capacity and in the second they want to buy a place in the mind of the consumer.

The vision has changed from one where only tangible assets had value to one where companies now believe that their most important asset is their brands, which are intangible (see Tables 1.3 and 18.2). These intangible assets account for 61 per cent of the value of Kellogg's, 57 per cent of Sara Lee and 52 per cent of General Mills. This explains the paradox that even though a company is making a loss it is bought for a very high price because of its well-known brands. Before 1980, if the value of the brand had been included in the company's earnings, it would have been bought for a penny. Nowadays brand value is determined independently of the firm's net value and thus can sometimes be hidden by the poor financial results of the company. The net income of a company is the sum of all the financial effects, be they positive or negative, and thus includes the effect of the brand. The reason why Apple lost money in 1996 was not because its brand was weak, but because its strategy was bad. Therefore it is not simply because a company is making a loss that its brand is not adding value. Just as the managers of Ebel-Jellinek, an American-Swiss group, said when they bought the Look brand: the company is making a loss but the brand hasn't lost its potential. Balance sheets reflect bad management decisions in the past, whereas the brand is a potential source of future profits. This potential will become actual profit only if it can meet a viable economic equation.

It is important to realise that in accounting and finance, goodwill is in fact the difference between the price paid and the book value of the company. This difference is brought about by the psychological goodwill of consumers, distributors and all the actors in the channels: that is to say, favourable attitudes and predisposition. Thus, a close relationship exists between financial and marketing analyses of brands. Accounting goodwill is the monetary value of the psychological goodwill that the brand has created over time through communication investment and consistent focus on

Table 1.3 Brand financial valuation, 2007

Rank	Brand	Value (US$ billion)
1	Google	66,434
2	GE	61,880
3	Microsoft	54,951
4	Coca Cola	44,134
5	China Mobile	41,214
6	Marlboro	39,166
7	Wal-Mart	36,880
8	Citi	33,706
9	IBM	33,572
10	Toyota	33,427
11	McDonald's	33,138
12	Nokia	31,670
13	Bank of America	28,767
14	BMW	25,751
15	Hewlett-Packard	24,987
16	Apple	24,728
17	UPS	24,580

Sources: Brand Z, Milward Brown

product satsifaction, both of which help build the reputation of the name.

What exactly are the effects of this customer and distributor goodwill?:

▌ The favourable attitude of distributors that list some products of the brand because of their rotation system. In fact a retailer may lose customers if it does not stock products of a well-known brand that by definition is present everywhere. That is to say, certain customers will go elsewhere to look for the brand. This goodwill ensures the presence of the brand at the point of sale.

▌ The support of wholesalers and resellers in the market for slow-moving or industrial goods. This is especially true when they are seen as being an exclusive brand with which they are able to associate themselves in the eyes of their customers.

▌ The desire of consumers or end-users to buy the product. It is their favourable attitude and in certain cases the attachment or even loyalty to the brand that is the key to future sales. Brand loyalty may be reduced to a minimum as the price difference between the brand and its competitors increases but attachment to the brand does not vanish so fast; it resists time.

The brand is a focal point for all the positive and negative impressions created by the buyer over time as he or she comes into contact with the brand's products, distribution channel, personnel and communication. On top of this, by concentrating all its marketing effort on a single name, the latter acquires an aura of exclusivity. The brand continues to be, at least in the short term, a byword for quality even after the patent has expired. The life of the patent is extended thanks to the brand, thus explaining the importance of brands in the pharmaceutical or the chemical industry (see page 108).

Brands are stored in clients' memories, so they exert a lasting influence. Because of this, they are seen as an asset from an accounting point of view: their economic effects extend far beyond the mere consumption of the product.

In order to understand in what way a strong brand (having acquired distribution, awareness and image) is a generator of growth and profitability it is first necessary to understand the functions that it performs with the consumers themselves, and which are the source of their valuable goodwill.

How brands create value for the customer

Although this book deals primarily with brands and their optimisation, it is important to clarify that brands do not necessarily exist in all markets. Even if brands exist in the legal sense they do not always play a role in the buying decision process of consumers. Other factors may be more important. For example, research on 'brand sensitivity' (Kapferer and Laurent, 1988) shows that in several product categories, buyers do not look at the brand when they are making their choice. Who is concerned about the brand when they are buying a writing pad, a rubber, felt-tip pens, markers or photocopy paper? Neither private individuals nor companies. There are no strong brands in such markets as sugar and socks. In Germany there is no national brand of flour. Even the beer brands are mostly regional. Location is key with the choice of a bank.

Brands reduce perceived risk, and exist as soon as there is perceived risk. Once the risk perceived by the buyer disappears, the brand no longer has any benefit. It is only a name on a product, and it ceases to be a choice cue, a guide or a source of added value. The perceived risk is greater if the unit price is higher or the repercussions of a bad choice are more severe. Thus the purchase of durable goods is a long-term commitment. On top of this, because humans are social animals, we judge ourselves on certain choices that we make and this explains why a large part of our social identity is built around the logos and the brands that we wear. As far as food is concerned, there is a certain amount of intrinsic risk involved whenever we ingest something and allow it to enter our bodies. The brand's function is to overcome this anxiety, which explains, for example, the importance of brands in the market for spirits such as vodka and gin.

The importance of perceived risk as a generator of the legitimacy of a brand is highlighted by the categories within which distributors' own-brands (and perhaps tomorrow's discount products) dominate: canned vegetables, milk, orange juice, frozen pizzas, bottled water, kitchen roll, toilet paper and petrol. At the same time producers' brands still have a dominant position in the following categories: coffee, tea, cereals, toothpaste, deodorant, cold sauces, fresh pasta, baby food, beauty products, washing powder, etc. For these products the consumer has high involvement and does not want to take any risks, be they physical or psychological.

Nothing is ever acquired permanently, and the degree of perceived risk evolves over time. In certain sectors, as the technology becomes commonplace, all the products comply with standards of quality. Therefore we are moving from a situation where some products 'failed' whereas others 'passed', towards one where all competitors are excellent, but some are 'more excellent' than others. The degree of perceived risk will change depending on the situation. For example, there is less risk involved in buying rum or vodka for a cocktail than for a rum or vodka on the rocks. Lastly, all consumers do not have the same level of involvement. Those who have high involvement are those that worry about small differences between products or who wish to optimise their choice: they will talk for hours about the merits of such and such a computer or of a certain brand of coffee. Those who are less involved are satisfied with a basic product which isn't too expensive, such as a gin or a whisky which may be unknown but seems to be good value for money and is sold in their local shop. The problem for most buyers who feel a certain risk and fear making a mistake is that many products are opaque: we can only discover their inner qualities once we buy the products and consume them. However, many consumers are reluctant to take this step. Therefore it is imperative that the external signs highlight the internal qualities of these opaque products. A reputable brand is the most efficient of these external signals. Examples of other such external indicators are: price, quality marks, the retail outlet where the product is sold and which guarantees it, the style and design of the packaging.

How brand awareness means value

Recent marketing research shows that brand awareness is not a mere cognitive measure. It is in fact correlated with many valuable image dimensions. Awareness carries a reassuring message: although it is measured at the individual level, brand awareness is in fact a collective phenomenon. When a brand is known, each individual knows it is known. This leads to spontaneous inferences. As is shown in Table 1.4, awareness is mostly correlated with aspects such as high quality, trust, reliability, closeness to people, a good quality/price ratio, accessibility and traditional styling. However it has a zero correlation with innovativeness, superior class, style, seduction: if aspects such as these are key differentiation facets of the brand, they must be earned on their own merit.

Table 1.4 How brand awareness creates value and image dimensions (correlations between awareness and image)

Good quality/price ratio	0.52
Trust	0.46
Reliable	0.44
Quality	0.43
Traditional	0.43
Best	0.40
Down to earth	0.37
Client oriented	0.37
Friendly	0.35
Accessible	0.32
Distinct	0.31
A leader	0.29
Popular	0.29
Fun	0.29
Original	0.27
Energetic	0.25
Friendly	0.25
Performing	0.22
Seductive	0.08
Innovative	0.02

(Base: 9,739 persons, 507 brands)

Source: Schuiling and Kapferer, 2004

Transparent and opaque products

At this stage it is interesting to remind ourselves of the classifications drawn up by Nelson (1970) and by Darby and Kami (1973).

These authors make the distinction between three types of product characteristics:

▮ the qualities which are noticed by contact, before buying;

▮ the qualities which are noticed uniquely by experience, thus after buying;

▮ credence qualities which cannot be verified even after consumption and which you have to take on trust.

The first type of quality can be seen in the decision to buy a pair of men's socks. The choice is made according to the visible characteristics: the pattern, the style, the material, the feel, the elasticity and the price. There is hardly a need for brands in this market. In fact those that do exist only have a very small market share and target those people who are looking for proof of durability (difficult to tell before buying) or those who wish to be fashionable. This is how Burlington socks work as a hallmark of chic style. Producers' brands do exist but their differential advantage compared to distributors' brands (Marks & Spencer or C&A) is weak, especially if the latter have a good style department and offer a wide variety at a competitive price.

A good example of the second type of quality is the automobile market. Of course, performance, consumption and style can all be assessed before buying, as can the availability of options and the interior space. However, road-holding, the pleasure of driving, reliability and quality cannot be entirely appreciated during a test drive. The response comes from brand image; that is, the collective representation which is shaped over time by the accumulated experiences of oneself, of close relations, by word of mouth and advertising.

Finally, in the market for upmarket cars, the feeling that you have made it, that feeling of fulfilment and personal success through owning a BMW is typically the result of pure faith. It cannot be substantiated by any of the post-purchase driving experiences: it is a collective belief, which is more or less shared by the buyers and the non-buyers. The same logic applies to the feeling of authenticity and inner masculinity which is supposed to result from smoking Marlboro cigarettes.

The role of brands is made clearer by this classification of sought-after qualities. The brand is a sign (therefore external) whose function is to disclose the hidden qualities of the product which are inaccessible to contact (sight, touch, hearing, smell) and possibly those which are accessible through experience but where the consumer does not want to take the risk of trying the product. Lastly, a brand, when it is well known, adds an aura of make-believe when it is consumed, for example the authentic America and rebellious youth of Levi's, the rugged masculinity of Marlboro, the English style of Dunhill, the Californian myth of Apple.

The informational role of the brand varies according to the product or service, the consumption situation and the individual. Thus, a brand is not always useful. On the other hand, a brand becomes necessary once the consumer loses his or her traditional reference points. This is why there is an increase in the demand for branded wine. Consumers were put off by too many small chateaux which were rarely the same and had limited production of varying quality and which sometimes sprung some unpleasant surprises. This paved the way for brands such as Jacob's Creek and Gallo.

A brand provides not only a source of information (thus revealing its values) but performs certain other functions which justify its attractiveness and its monetary return (higher price) when they are valued by buyers. What are these functions? How does a brand create value in the eyes of the consumer? The eight functions of a brand are presented in Table 1.5. The first two are mechanical and concern the essence of the brand; that is, to function as a recognised symbol in order to facilitate choice and to gain time. The following three functions reduce the perceived risk. The last three have a more pleasurable side to them. Ethics show that buyers are expecting, more and more, responsible behaviour from their brands. Many Swedish consumers still refuse Nestlé's

Table 1.5   The functions of the brand for the consumer

Function	Consumer benefit
Identification	To be clearly seen, to quickly identify the sought-after products, to structure the shelf perception.
Practicality	To allow savings of time and energy through identical repurchasing and loyalty.
Guarantee	To be sure of finding the same quality no matter where or when you buy the product or service.
Optimisation	To be sure of buying the best product in its category, the best performer for a particular purpose.
Badge	To have confirmation of your self-image or the image that you present to others.
Continuity	Satisfaction created by a relationship of familiarity and intimacy with the brand that you have been consuming for years.
Hedonistic	Enchantment linked to the attractiveness of the brand, to its logo, to its communication and its experiential rewards.
Ethical	Satisfaction linked to the responsible behaviour of the brand in its relationship with society (ecology, employment, citizenship, advertising which doesn't shock).

products due to the issue of selling Nestlé's baby milk to poor mothers in Africa.

These functions are neither laws nor dues, nor are they automatic; they must be defended at all times. Only a few brands are successful in each market thanks to their supporting investments in quality, R&D, productivity, communication and research in order to better understand foreseeable changes in demand. A priori, nothing confines these functions to producers' brands. Moreover, several producers' brands do not perform these functions. In Great Britain, Marks & Spencer (St Michael) is seen as an important brand and performs these functions, as do Migros in Switzerland, the Gap, Zara, Ikea and others.

The usefulness of these functions depends on the product category. There is less need for reference points or risk reducers when the product is transparent (ie its inner qualities are accessible through contact). The price premium is at its lowest and trial costs very little when there is low involvement and the purchase is seen as a chore, eg trying a new, cheaper roll of kitchen paper or aluminium foil. Certain kinds of shops aim primarily at fulfilling certain of these functions, for example hard discounters who have 650 lines with no brands, a product for every need, at the lowest prices and offering excellent quality for the price (thanks to the work on reducing all the costs which do not add value carried out in conjunction with suppliers). This formula offers another alternative to the first five functions: ease of identification on the shelf, practicality, guarantee, optimisation at the chosen price level and characterisation (refusal to be manipulated by marketing). The absence of other functions is compensated for by the very low price.

Functional analysis of brand role can facilitate the understanding of the rise of distributors' own brands. Whenever brands are just trademarks and operate merely as a recognition signal or as a mere guarantee of quality, distributors' brands can fulfil these functions as well and at a cheaper price.

Table 1.6 summarises the relationships between brand role and distributors' own-brands' market share.

How brands create value for the company

Why do financial analysts prefer companies with strong brands? Because they are less risky. Therefore, the brand works in the same way for the financial analyst as for the consumer: the brand removes the risk. The certainty, the guarantee and the removal of the risk are included in the price. By paying a high price for a

Table 1.6   Brand functions and the distributor/manufacturer power equilibrium

Main function of brand	Typical product category of brand	Power of manufacturers' brand
Recognition signal	Milk, salt, flour	Very weak
Practicality of choice	Socks	Weak
Guarantee of quality	Food, staples	Weak
Optimisation of choice, sign of high-quality performance	Cars, cosmetics, appliances, paint, services	Strong
Personalising one's choice	Perfumes, clothing	Strong
Permanence, bonding, familiarity relationship	Old brands	Strong but challenged
Pleasure	Polysensual brands, luxury brands	Strong
Ethics and social responsibility	Trust brands, corporate brands	Strong but challenged

company with brands the financial analyst is acquiring near certain future cashflows.

If the brand is strong it benefits from a high degree of loyalty and thus from stability of future sales. Ten per cent of the buyers of Volvic mineral water are regular and loyal and represent 50 per cent of the sales. The reputation of the brand is a source of demand and lasting attractiveness, the image of superior quality and added value justifies a premium price. A dominant brand is an entry barrier to competitors because it acts as a reference in its category. If it is prestigious or a trendsetter in terms of style it can generate substantial royalties by granting licences, for example, at its peak, Naf-Naf, a designer brand, earned over £6 million in net royalties. The brand can enter other markets when it is well known, is a symbol of quality and offers a certain promise which is valued by the market. The Palmolive brand name has become symbolic of mildness and has been extended to a number of markets besides that of soap, for example shampoo, shaving cream and washing-up liquid. This is known as brand extension (see Chapter 12) and saves on the need to create awareness if you had to launch a new product on each of these markets.

In determining the financial value of the brand, the expert must take into account the sources of any additional revenues which are generated by the presence of a strong brand. Additional buyers may be attracted to a product which appears identical to another but which has a brand name with a strong reputation. If such is the company's strategy the brand may command a premium price in addition to providing an added margin due to economies of scale and market domination. Brand extensions into new markets can result in royalties and important leverage effects. To calculate this value, it is necessary to subtract the costs involved in brand management: the costs involved in quality control and in investing in R&D, the costs of a national, indeed international, sales force, advertising costs, the cost of a legal registration, the cost

of capital invested, etc. The financial value of the brand is the difference between the extra revenue generated by the brand and the associated costs for the next few years, which are discounted back to today. The number of years is determined by the business plan of the valuer (the potential buyer, the auditors). The discount rate used to weigh these future cashflows is determined by the confidence or the lack of it that the investor has in his or her forecasts. However, a significant fact is that the stronger the brand, the smaller the risk. Thus, future net cashflows are considered more certain when brand strength is high.

Figure 1.2 shows the three generators of profit of the brand: the price premium, more attraction and loyalty, and higher margin. These effects work on the original market for the brand but they can be offered subsequently on other markets and in other product categories, either through direct brand extension (for example, Bic moved from ballpoint pens to lighters to disposable razors and recently to sailboards) or through licensing, from which the manufacturer benefits from royalties (for example all the luxury brands, and Caterpillar).

Once these levers are measured in euros, yen, dollars or any other currency they may serve as a base for evaluating the marginal profit which is attributable to the brand. They only emerge when the company wishes to strategically differentiate its products. This wish can come about through three types of investment:

▎ Investment in production, productivity and R&D. Thanks to these, the company can acquire specific know-how, a knack which cannot be imitated and which in accounting terms is also an intangible asset. Sometimes the company temporarily blocks new entrants by registering a patent. This is the basis of marketing in the pharmaceutical industry (a patent and a brand) but also of companies like Ferrero, whose products are not easily imitated despite their success.

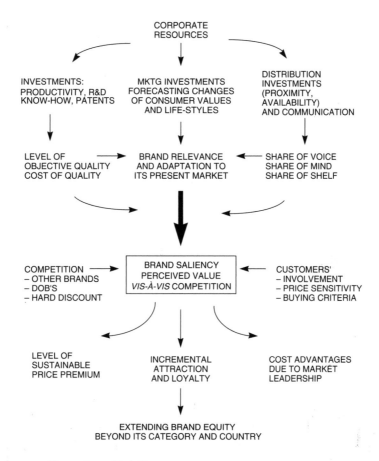

Figure 1.2   The levers of brand profitability

Patents are on their own an intangible asset: the activity of the company benefits from them in a lasting manner.

▌ Investment in research and marketing studies in order to get new insights, to anticipate the changes of consumers' tastes and life-styles in order to define any important innovations which will match these evolutions. Chrysler's Minivan is an example of a product created in anticipation of the demands of baby boomers with tall children. An understanding of the expectations of distributors is also needed, as they are an essential component of the physical proximity of brands. Nowadays a key element of brand success is understanding and adapting to the logic of distributors, and developing good relations with the channels (even though it is still necessary when valuing a brand to make a distinction between what part of its sales is due to the power of the company and what part to the brand itself).

▌ Investment in listing allowances, in the sales force and merchandising, in trade marketing and, naturally, in communicating to consumers to promote the uniqueness of the brand and to endow it with saliency (awareness), perceived difference and esteem. The hidden intrinsic qualities or intangible values which are associated with consumption would be unknown without brand advertising.

The value of the brand, and thus the legitimacy of implementing a brand policy, depends on the difference between the marginal revenues and the necessary marginal costs associated with brand management.

How brand reputation affects the impact of advertising

Brands are a form of capital that can slowly be built, while in the meantime one is growing business. Of course it is very possible to grow a business without creating such brand capital: a push strategy or a price strategy can deliver high sales and market share without building any brand equity. This is the case for many private labels or own-label brands, for instance. The volume leader in the market for Scotch whisky in France is not Johnnie Walker or Ballantines or Famous Grouse but William Peel, a local brand that aimed all its efforts at the trade (hypermarkets) and sells at a low price. It has almost no saliency (spontaneous brand awareness).

Now managers are being asked to build both business and brand value. Their salary is indexed on these two yardsticks: sales and reputation. One should not see them as separate, leading to a kind of schizophrenia. Chaudhuri's very relevant research (2002) reminds us that advertising and marketing are the key levers of sales. However, their effects on market share and the ability to charge a premium price (two indicators of brand strength) are not direct but are mediated by brand reputation (or esteem). In fact, as shown by the path coefficients of Figure 1.3, brand reputation is created by familiarity (I know it well, I use it a lot) and by brand perceived uniqueness (this brand is unique, is different, there is no substitute). Advertising does play a key role in building sales, but it has no direct impact on gaining both market share and premium price. This is most interesting: in brief, it is only by building a reputational capital that both a higher market share and price premium can be obtained.

Reputation also adds to the impact of advertising on sales. It is well known from evaluations of past campaigns that the more a brand is known, the more its advertisements are noticed and remembered. It is high time to stop treating brands and commerce as opposing forces.

Corporate reputation and the corporate brand

In 2003 Velux, which had become known as the number one brand for roof windows in the world, realised it needed to create a corporate brand. It felt that merely to compete through its product brand was not enough to

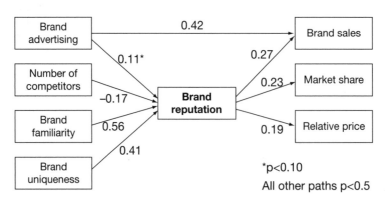

Figure 1.3 Branding and sales

Reprinted from the *Journal of Advertising Research*, copyright 2002, by the Advertising Research Foundation protect it against the growing number of me-toos all over the world. In addition, its brand equity was stagnating. When any brand reaches a level of 80 per cent of top-of-mind awareness in its category, part of its 'stagnation' is certainly due to a ceiling effect: there is not much room for improvement. However, the company felt that emotional bonding with its brand was not strong enough. Could the product brand alone improve the bond? The diagnosis was that it was high time to reveal 'the brand behind the brand' (Kapferer, 2000) and start building a corporate brand.

In fact many companies that based their success on product brands have now decided to create a corporate brand in order to make company actions, values and missions more salient and to diffuse specific added values. Unilever should soon develop some kind of corporate visibility, as Procter & Gamble does in Asia at this time and will probably do everywhere soon.

There is another reason that corporate brands are a new hot managerial topic: the defence of reputation. Companies have become very sensitive about their reputation. Formerly they used to be sensitive about their image. Why this change? Isn't image (perception) the basis on which global evaluations are formed (and thus reputation)? It is likely that the term 'image' has lost its glamour. It seems to have fallen into disrepute precisely because there was too much publicity about 'image makers', as if image was an artificial construction. Reputation has more depth, is more involving: it is a judgement from the market which needs to be preserved. In any case reputation has become a byword, as witnessed by the annual surveys on the most respected companies that are now made in almost all countries, modelled on Fortune's 'America's most admired companies'. Reputation signals that although the company has many different stakeholders, each one reacting to a specific facet of the company (as employee, as supplier, as

financial investor, as client), in fact they are all sensitive to the global ability of the company to meet the expectations of all its stakeholders. Reputation takes the company as a whole. It reunifies all stakeholders and all functions of the corporation.

Because changes in reputation affect all stakeholders, companies monitor and manage their reputation closely. Fombrun has diagnosed that global reputation is based on six factors or 'pillars' (Fombrun, Gardberg and Sever, 2000):

- emotional appeal (trust, admiration and respect);

- products and services (quality, innovativeness, value for money and so on);

- vision and leadership;

- workplace quality (well-managed, appealing workplace; employee talent);

- financial performance;

- social responsibility.

Since companies cannot grow without advocates and the support of their many stakeholders, they need to build a reputational capital among all of them; plus a global reputation, because even specialised stakeholders wish the company to be responsive to all stakeholders. There is a link between reputation and share performance.

As a consequence of this growth of the reputational concept, companies have realised they cannot stay mute, invisible, opaque. They must manage their visibility and that of their actions in order to maximise their reputational capital – in fact their goodwill, to speak like financiers. The corporate brand will be more and more present and visible: through art sponsorship, foundations, charities, advertising. As such it addresses global targets. The corporate brand speaks on behalf of the company, signals the company's presence. Now companies are also developing specialised corporate brands such as 'You' (the recruiting brand of Unilever), or specialised campaigns (such as semi-annual financial roadshows).

Corporate brands have therefore taken a new importance since they speak on behalf of the company, signal its presence and actions: in fact they draw the company's profile in the eyes of all those who do not have direct inter-actions with it. In our world people react more and more to names and reputations, to rumours and word of mouth. They do not see the headquarters or the factories any more. Often delocalised, corporations appear through the press, publicity, PR, advertising, financial reports, trade union reports, all sorts of communications, and of course their products and services. Managing the corporate brand and its communication means managing this profile. The methods to do so are not specific: they rely as do all brands on identity. They also rely on the markets.

What then is the difference between corporate brand methods and the product brand methods developed in this book? Companies do have an internal identity, core values that bear on the profile they wish to, or can, express outwardly. Companies and corporations are bodies with a soul (from the Latin, *corpus*). (They are enacted by people.) Product brands are more imaginary constructions, relying on intangible values which have been invented to fulfil the needs of clients. Ralph Lauren's or Marlboro's intangible values are pure constructions. It cannot be the same for companies. Reality leaves fewer degrees of freedom.

Second, since brand management is both identity and market oriented, corporate brands must tailor their profile to meet the expectations of multiple publics. The core value must be tailored for this global audience, which symbolically has to 'buy' the company, as a supplier, an employee or an investor. Managing the reputation of the name, through (among other methods) the commu-nication of the corporate brand, is aimed at making the company their first choice.

As to the very hot topic of the financial value of reputation, a conceptual distinction must be made: at the corporate level, this is called goodwill (the excess of stock value over book value). Now, the larger part of this goodwill is attributable to the financial value of the brand as commercial brand. This financial value is usually measured by the discounted cashflow method. This shows that the financial value of the brand, be it product brand or corporate brand, can only be traced through prospective sales (see Chapter 18).

How do corporate brands relate to product brands? The latter are there to create client goodwill, build growth and profits. In modern mature markets, consumers do not make a complete distinction between the product brand and the corporation: what the corpo-ration does impacts their evaluation of its brands, especially if they share the same name as the corporation or are visibly endorsed by the former. The issue of branding architec-tures with the four structural types of rela-tionship (independence; umbrella; endorsement; source or branded house) will be covered in Chapter 13. It has strategic implications in terms of the spillover effects (Sullivan, 1988) the organisation might or might not want to capitalise on, and in terms of bolstering confidence in the product (Brown and Dacin, 1997), if this is necessary, which is not always the case. For instance LVMH, the world's leading luxury group, remains separate from its 41 brands' commu-nication and marketing: they look inde-pendent. GM endorses its brands: it reveals the powerful and respected corporation behind its car marques. GE follows an umbrella strategy: GE Capital Investment, GE Medical Services. A classic strategy, in our world of global communication and synergies, is to use for the corporation the same name as its best brand. This is how BSN became Danone – just as 50 years earlier, Tokyo Tsuhin Kogyo became Sony. As we shall see, there are strong benefits in doing this.

A conceptual issue arises when one speaks, say, of Canon or Nike or Sony or Citibank. Are they corporate brands? Are they commercial brands? Since the company and the brand share the same name it is difficult to say. The answer is that they are both: it depends on the context and objectives and target of communication. Naomi Klein's book *No Logo* (1999) criticises Nike as a company, for all it tries to hide behind the attractive images and sports stars of its commercial brand (for the sweatshops in Asia, the delocalisation of manufacturing to developing countries, the lack of reactiveness to critics). To make it clear who speaks, the corporation or the brand, some companies have chosen to differentiate the logo of each source of communication: Nestlé's corporate logo is not that of Nestlé as a commercial brand (which itself is differentiated by product category).

The case is more acute still for service companies: can one differentiate Barclay's Bank or Orange as a brand and as a corporate brand? Since both share the same employees this is more difficult, although looking at the objectives and target of the communication should help. This is why the issue of brand alignment (Ind, 2001) has become so important: the corporation has to align on its brand values. Its whole business should be brand driven.

2

Strategic implications of branding

Many companies have forgotten the fundamental purpose of their brands. A great deal of attention is devoted to the marketing activity itself, which involves designers, graphic artists, packaging and advertising agencies. This activity thus becomes an end in itself, receiving most of the attention. In so doing, we forget that it is just a means. Branding is seen as the exclusive prerogative of the marketing and communications staff. This undervalues the role played by the other parts of the company in ensuring a successful branding policy and business growth.

Yet the marketing phase, which we now consider indispensable, is the terminal phase of a process that involves the company's resources and all of its functions, focusing them on one strategic intent: creating a difference. Only by mobilising all of its internal sources of added value can a company set itself apart from its competitors.

What does branding really mean?

Branding means much more than just giving a brand name and signalling to the outside world that such a product or service has been stamped with the mark and imprint of an organisation. It requires a corporate long-term involvement, a high level of resources and skills.

Branding consists in transforming the product category

Brands are a direct consequence of the strategy of market segmentation and product differentiation. As companies seek to better fulfil the expectations of specific customers, they concentrate on providing the latter, consistently and repeatedly, with the ideal combination of attributes – both tangible and intangible, functional and hedonistic, visible and invisible – under viable economic conditions for their businesses. Companies want to stamp their mark on different sectors and set their imprint on their products. It is no wonder that the word 'brand' also refers to the act of burning a mark into the flesh of an animal as a means to claim ownership of it. The first task in brand analysis is to define precisely all that the brand injects into the product (or service) and how the brand transforms it:

▌ What attributes materialise?

▌ What advantages are created?

▌ What benefits emerge?

▌ What ideals does it represent?

This deep meaning of the brand concept is often forgotten or wilfully omitted. That is why certain distributors are often heard saying – as a criticism of many a manufacturer's brand whose added value lies only its name – 'For us, the brand is secondary, there is no need to put something on the product.' Hence, the brand is reduced to package surface and label. Branding, though, is not about being on top of something, but within something. The product or service thus enriched must stand out well if it is to be spotted by the potential buyer and if the company wants to reap the benefits of its strategy before being copied by others.

Furthermore, the fact that a delabelled item is worth more than a generic product confirms this understanding of branding. According to the 'brand is just a superficial label' theory, the delabelled product supposedly becomes worthless when it no longer carries a brand name, unless it continues to bear the brand within. In passing, the brand has intrinsically altered it: hence the value of Lacostes without 'Lacoste', Adidases without 'Adidas'. They are worth more than imitations because the brand, though invisible, still prevails. Conversely, the brand on counterfeits, though visible, is in effect absent. This is why counterfeits are sold so cheaply.

Some brands have succeeded in proving with their slogans that they know and understand what their fundamental task is: to transform the product category. A brand not only acts on the market, it organises the market, driven by a vision, a calling and a clear idea of what the category should become. Too many brands wish only to identify fully with the product category,

thereby expecting to control it. In fact they often end up disappearing within it: Polaroid, Xerox, Caddy, Scotch, Kleenex have thus become generic terms.

According to the objective the brand sets itself; transforming the category implies endowing the product with its own separate identity. In concrete terms, that means that the brand is weak when the product is 'transparent'. Talking about 'Greek olive oil, first cold pressing' for example, makes the product transparent, almost entirely defined and epitomised by those sole attributes, yet there are dozens of brands capable of marketing that type of oil. Going from bulk to packaging is also symptomatic of this phenomenon. The weakness of fresh vacuum-packed food brands is partially due to the fact that their packaging, though designed to reassure the buyer – such as with sauerkraut in film-wrapped containers – only recreates transparency. Significantly, Findus and l'Eggs or Hoses do not just show their products, they *show* them *off*. This is the structural cause of Essilor's brand weakness, as perceived by the customers. They do not perceive how Essilor, the world leader in optical glass, transforms the product, nor its input, its added value. To them, glass is just glass to which various options can be added (anti-reflecting, unbreakable, etc). The added value seems to be created solely by the style of the rims (hence the boom in licensing) or the service, both of which are palpable and in the store. What is invisible is not perceived and thus does not exist in their eyes. However, the example of Evian reminds us that it is always possible to make a transparent product become opaque. The major mineral water brands have been able to exist, grow and prosper only because they have made the invisible visible. We can no longer choose our water haphazardly: good health and purity are associated with Evian, fitness with Contrex, vitality with Vittel. These various positionings were justified by the invisible differences in water contents. Generally speaking, anything adding to the complexity of ingredients also contributes to creating distance *vis-à-vis* the product. In this respect, Coca-Cola is doing the right thing by keeping its recipe secret. When Orangina was taken over by Pernod-Ricard, its concentrate was remixed into something even more complex. Antoine Riboud, the former CEO of Danone worldwide, expressed a similar concern when declaring: 'It is not yoghurts that I make, but Danones.'

A brand is a long-term vision

The brand should have its own specific point of view on the product category. Major brands have more than just a specific or dominating position in the market: they hold certain positions within the product category. This position and conception both energise the brand and feed the transformations that are implemented for matching the brand's products with its ideals. It is this conception that justifies the brand's existence, its reason for being on the market, and provides it with a guideline for its life cycle. How many brands are capable today of answering the following crucial question: 'What would the market lack if we did not exist?' The company's ultimate goal is undoubtedly to generate profit and jobs. But brand purpose is something else. Brand strategy is too often mistaken for company strategy. The latter most often results in truisms such as 'increase customer satisfaction'. Specifying brand purpose consists in (re)defining its *raison d'être*, its absolute necessity. The notion of brand purpose is missing in most marketing textbooks. It is a recent idea and conveys the emerging conception of the brand, seen as exerting a creative and powerful influence on a given market. If there is power, there is energy. Naturally, a brand draws its strength from the company's financial and human means, but it derives its energy from its specific niche, vision and ideals. If it does not feel driven by an intense internal necessity, it

will not carry the potential for leadership. The analytical notion of brand image does not clearly capture this dynamic dimension, which is demanded by modern brand management.

Thus, many banks put forward the following image of themselves: close to their clients, modern, offering high-performing products and customer service. These features are, of course, useful to market researchers in charge of measuring the perceptions sent back by the market and the level of consumer satisfaction. But from which dynamic programme do they emanate, which vision do they embody?

Certain banks have specified what their purpose is: for some it is 'to change people's relationship to money', while for others it is to remind us that money is just a 'means towards personal development'. Several banks have recently worked at redefining their singular reason for existence. All of them will have to do so in the future. The Amex vision of money is not that of Visa.

More than most, multi-segment brands need to redetermine their own purpose. Cars are a typical example. A multi-segment brand (also called a generalist brand) wants to cover all market segments. Each model spawns multiple versions, thereby theoretically maximising the number of potential buyers: diesel, gas, three or five doors, estate, coupé, cabriolet, etc. The problem is that by having to constantly satisfy the key criteria of each segment (bottom range, lower mid-range, upper mid-range and top range), ie to churn out many different versions and to avoid over-typifying a model in order to please everyone, companies tend to create chameleon brands. Apart from the symbol on the car hood or the similarities in the car designs, we no longer perceive an overall plan guiding the creative and productive forces of the company in the conception of these cars. Thus, competitors fight their battles either over the price or the options offered for that price. No longer brands, they become mere names on a hood or on a dealer's office walls. The word has thus lost most of its meaning. What does Opel or Ford mean?

What unifies the products of a brand is not their marque or common external signs, it is their 'religion': what common spirit, vision and ideals are embodied in them.

Major brands can be compared to a pyramid (see Figure 2.1). The top states the brand's vision and purpose – its conception of automobiles, for instance, its idea of the types of cars it wants, and has always wanted, to create, as well as its very own values which either can or cannot be expressed by a slogan. This level leads to the next one down, which shows the general brand style of communication. Indeed, brand personality and style are conveyed less by words than by a way of being

and communicating. These codes should not be exclusively submitted to the fluctuating inspiration of the creative team: they must be defined so as to reflect the brand's unique character. The next level presents the brand's strategic image features: amounting to four or five, they result from the overall vision and materialise in the brand's products, communication and actions. This refers, for example, to the positioning of Volvo as a secure, reliable and robust brand, or of BMW as a dynamic, classy prestigious one. Lastly, the product level, at the bottom of the pyramid, consists of each model's positioning in its respective segment.

The problem is that consumers look at the pyramid from the bottom up. They start with what is real and tangible. The wider the

Figure 2.1   The brand system

pyramid base is, the more the customers doubt that all these cars do indeed emanate from the same automobile concept, that they carry the same brand essence and bear the stamp of the same automobile project. Brand management consists, for its part, in starting from the top and defining the way the car is conceived by the brand, in order to determine exactly when a car is deserving of the brand name and when it no longer is – in which case, the car should logically no longer bear the brand name, as it then slips out of its brand territory.

As automobile history is made of great successes followed by bitter failures, major multi-segment brands regularly question their vision. Thus, after its smash hit models, the 205 and 405, Peugeot was somewhat perturbed, both internally and externally, by the series of setbacks with the 605 and the slow take-off of the 106 and 306. A basic question was then asked: 'Are Peugeots still Peugeots?' Answering it implied redefining the long-term meaning of the statement 'It's a Peugeot', ie the brand's long-lasting automobile concept.

Internal hesitation about brand identity is often revealed when searching for slogans. There is no longer a trend toward obvious and meaningless slogans such as 'the automobile spirit', which neither tell us anything about the brand's automobile ideal, nor help to guide inventors, creators, developers or producers in making concrete choices between mutually exclusive features: comfort and road adherence, aerodynamism and feeling of sturdiness, etc.

Permanently nurturing the difference

Our era is one of temporary advantages. It is often argued that certain products of different brands are identical. Some observers thus infer that, under these circumstances, a brand

is nothing but a 'bluff', a gimmick used to try to stand out in a market flooded with barely differentiated products.

This view fails to take into account both the time factor and the rules of dynamic competition. Brands draw attention through the new products they create and bring onto the market. Any brand innovation necessarily generates plagiarism. Any progress made quickly becomes a standard to which buyers grow accustomed: competing brands must then adopt it themselves if they do not want to fall short of market expectations. For a while, the innovative brand will thus be able to enjoy a fragile monopoly, which is bound to be quickly challenged unless the innovation is or can be patented. The role of the brand name is precisely to protect the innovation: it acts as a mental patent, by becoming the prototype of the new segment it creates – advantage of being a pioneer.

If it is true that a snapshot of a given market often shows similar products, a dynamic view of it reveals in turn who innovated first, and who has simply followed the leader: brands protect innovators, granting them momentary exclusiveness and rewarding them for their risk-taking attitude. Thus, the accumulation of these momentary differences over time serves to reveal the meaning and purpose of a brand and to justify its economic function, hence its price premium.

Brands cannot, therefore, be reduced to a mere sign on a product, a mere graphic cosmetic touch: they guide a creative process, which yields the new product A today, the new products B and C tomorrow, and so on. Products come to life, live and disappear, but brands endure. The permanent factors of this creative process are what gives a brand its meaning and purpose, its content and attributes. A brand requires time in order for this accumulation of innovations to yield a meaning and a purpose.

As shown in Figure 2.2, brand management alternates between phases of product differentiation and brand image differentiation. The

Figure 2.2   The cycle of brand management

typical example is Sony, whose advertising focuses on innovations when they exist, and on image in between.

Brands act as a genetic programme

A brand does in fact act as a genetic programme. What is done at birth exerts a long-lasting influence on market perceptions. Indeed revitalising a brand often starts with re-identifying its forgotten genetic programme (see Chapter 16).

Table 2.1 shows how brands are built and exert a long-term influence on customers' memories, which in turn influence their expectations, attitudes and degree of satisfaction.

In the life of a brand, although they may have been forgotten, the early acts have a very structuring influence. In fact they mould the first and long-lasting meaning of this new word that designates Brand X or Brand Y. Once learnt, this meaning gets reinforced and stored in long-term memory. Then a number of selective processes reinforce the meaning: selective attention, selective perception, selective memory.

This is why brand images are hard to change: they act like fast-setting concrete.

This process has many important managerial consequences. When going international, each country reproduces it. It is of prime importance to define the products to be launched in relationship with the image one wants to create in the long term. Too often they are chosen by local agents just because they will sell very well. They must do both: build the business and build the brand. Brand management introduces long-term effects as criteria for evaluating the relevance of short-term decisions.

Table 2.1   The brand as genetic programme

Early founding acts (past)	Memory (present)	Expectations (future)
First best-selling product	Brand prototype	Legitimate extensions for the future
First channel of distribution	Associated benefits	(what other areas of new products)
First positioning	Brand image	
First campaign	Brand competence and know-how	
First events		
First CEO		
Corporate visions and values		

New generations discover the brand at different points in time. Some discovered Ford through the Model T, others through the Mustang, others through the Mondeo, others through the Focus. No wonder brand images differ from one generation to another.

The memory factor also partly explains why individual preferences endure: within a given generation, people continue, even 20 years later, to prefer the brands they liked between the ages of 7 and 18 (Guest, 1964; Fry et al, 1973; Jacoby and Chestnut, 1978).

It is precisely because a brand is the memory of the products that it can act as a long-lasting and stable reference. Unlike advertising, in which the last message seen is often the only one that truly registers and is best recalled, the first actions and message of a brand are the ones bound to leave the deepest impression, thereby structuring long-term perception. In this respect, brands create a cognitive filter: dissonant and atypical aspects are declared unrepresentative, thus discounted and forgotten. That is why failures in brand extensions on atypical products do not harm the brand in the end even though they do unsettle the investors' trust in the company (Loken and Roedder John, 1993). Bic's failure in perfume is a good example. Making perfumes is not typical of the know-how of Bic as perceived by consumers: sales of ball pens, lighters and razors kept on increasing.

Ridding itself of atypical, dissonant elements, a brand acts as a selective memory, hence endowing people's perceptions with an illusion of permanence and coherence. That is why a brand is less elastic than its products. Once created, like fast-setting concrete it is hard to change. Hence the critical importance of defining the brand platform. What brand meaning does one want to create?

A brand is both the memory and the future of its products. The analogy with the genetic programme is central to understanding how brands function and should be managed. Indeed, the brand memory that develops contains the programme for all future evolution, the characteristics of upcoming models and their common traits, as well as the family resemblances transcending their diverse personalities. By understanding a brand's programme, we can not only trace its legitimate territory but also the area in which it will be able to grow beyond the products that initially gave birth to it. The brand's underlying programme indicates the purpose and meaning of both former and future products. How then can one identify this programme, the brand DNA?

If it exists, this programme can be discovered by analysing the brand's founding acts: products, communication and the most significant actions since its inception. If a guideline or an implicit permanence exists, then it must show through. Research on brand identity has a double purpose: to analyse the brand's most typical production on the one hand and to analyse the reception, ie the image sent back by the market, on the other. The image is indeed a memory in itself, so stable that it is difficult to modify it in the short run. This stability results from the selective perception described above. It also has a function: to create long-lasting references guiding consumers among the abundant supply of consumer goods. That is the reason a company should never turn away from its identity, which alone has managed to attract buyers. Customer loyalty is created by respecting the brand features that initially seduced the buyers. If the products slacken off, weaken or show a lack of investment and thus no longer meet customer expectations, better try to meet them again than to change expectations. In order to build customer loyalty and capitalise on it, brands must stay true to themselves. This is called a return to the future.

Questioning the past, trying to detect the brand's underlying programme, does not mean ignoring the future: on the contrary, it is a way of better preparing for it by giving it roots, legitimacy and continuity. The mistake is to embalm the brand and to merely repeat in the present what it produced in the past, like the new VW Beetle and other retro-innovations. In fighting competition, a brand's products must always belong intrinsically to their time, but in their very own way. Rejuvenating Burberrys or Helena Rubenstein means connecting them to modernity, not mummifying them in deference to a past splendour that we might wish to revive.

Respect the brand 'contract'

Brands become credible only through the persistence and repetition of their value proposition. BMW has had the same promise since 1959. Through time they become a quasi contract, unwritten but most effective. This contract binds both parties. The brand must keep its identity, but permanently increase its relevance. It must be loyal to itself, to its mission and to its clients. Each brand is free to choose its values and positioning, but once chosen and advertised, they become the benchmark for customer satisfaction. It is well known that the prime determinant of customer satisfaction is the gap between customers' experiences and their expectations. The brand's positioning sets up these expectations.

As a result, customers are loyal to such a brand.

This mutual commitment explains why brands, whose products have temporarily declined in popularity, do not necessarily disappear. A brand is judged over the long term: a deficiency can always occur. Brand trust gives products a chance to recover. If not, Jaguar would have disappeared long ago: no other brand could have withstood the detrimental effect of the decreasing quality of its cars during the 1970s. That is a good illustration of one of the benefits a brand brings to a company.

The brand contract is economic, not legal. Brands differ in this way from other signs of quality such as quality seals and certification. Quality seals officially and legally testify that a given product meets a set of specific characteristics, previously defined (in conjunction with public authorities, producers/manufacturers and consumers) so as to guarantee a higher level of quality and distinguishing it from similar products. A quality seal is a collective brand controlled by a certification agency which certifies a given product only if it complies with certain specifications. Such certification is thus never definitive and can be withdrawn (like ISO).

Brands do not legally testify that a product meets a set of characteristics. However, through consistent and repeated experience of these characteristics, a brand becomes synonymous with the latter.

A contract implies constraints. The brand contract assumes first of all that the various functions in the organization all converge: R&D, production, methods, logistics, marketing, finance. The same is true of service brands: as the R&D and production aspects are obviously irrelevant in this case, the responsibility for ensuring the brand's continuity and cohesion pass to the management and staff, who play an essential role in clientele relationships.

The brand contract requires internal as well as external marketing. Unlike quality seals, brands set their own ever-increasing standards. Therefore, they must not only meet the latter but also continuously try to improve all their products, even the most basic ones, especially if they represent most of their sales and hence act as the major vehicle of brand image; in so doing, they will be able to satisfy the expectations of clients who will demand that the products keep pace with technological change. They must also communicate and make themselves known to the outside world in order to become the prototype of a segment, a value or a benefit. This is a lonely task for brands, yet they must do it to get the uniqueness and lack of substitutability they need. The brand will have to support its internal and external costs all on its own. These are generated by the brand requirements, which are to:

▌ Closely forecast the needs and expectations of potential buyers. This is the purpose of market research: both to optimise existing products and to discover needs and expectations that have yet to be fulfilled.

▌ React to technical and technological progress as soon as it can to create a competitive edge both in terms of cost and performance.

▌ Provide both product (or service) volume and quality at the same time, since those are the only means of ensuring repeat purchases.

▌ Control supply quantity and quality.

▌ Deliver products or services to intermediaries (distributors), both consistently over time and in accordance with their requirements in terms of delivery, packaging and overall conditions.

▌ Give meaning to the brand and communicate its meaning to the target market, thereby using the brand as both a signal and reference for the product's (or service's) identity and exclusivity. That is what advertising budgets are for.

▌ Increase the experiential rewards of consumption or interaction.

▌ Remain ethical and ecology-conscious.

Strong brands thus bring about both internal mobilisation and external federalisation. They create their company's panache and impetus. That is why some companies switch their own name for that of one of their star brands: BSN thus became Danone, CGE became Alcatel. In this respect, the impact of strong brands extends far beyond most corporate strategies. These only last while they are in the making, after which they either vanish or wind up as pompous phrases ('a passion for excellence') posted in hallways. In any case, the corporate brand is the organisation's external voice and, as such, it remains both demanding and determined to constantly outdo itself, to aim ever higher.

Becoming aware that the brand is a contract also means taking up many other responsibilities that are all too often ignored. In the fashion market, even if creators wish to change after a while, they cannot entirely forget about their brand contract, which helped them to get known initially, then recognised and eventually praised.

In theory, both the brand's slogan and signature are meant to embody the brand contract. A good slogan is therefore often rejected by managing directors because it means too much commitment for the company and may backfire if the products/ services do not match the expectations the brand has created so far. In too many cases brands are seen as mere names: this is very evident in some innovations committee meetings, where new products are reallocated to different brands of the portfolio many times in the same meeting. One brand name or another is perceived as making no difference. Taking the brand seriously, as it is (that is, as a contract) is much more demanding. It also provides higher returns.

The product and the brand

Since the early theorisation on the brand, there has been much discussion on the relationship of brands to products. How do the concepts differ? How are they mutually interrelated? On the one hand, many a CEO repeats to his or her staff that there is no brand without a great product (or service), in order to stimulate their innovativeness and make them think of the product as a prime lever of brand competitiveness. On the other hand, there is ample evidence that market leaders are not the best product in their market. To be the 'best product' in a category means to compete in the premium tier, which is rarely a large segment. Certainly within the laundry detergent category, market leaders such as Tide, Ariel and Skip are those delivering the best performance for heavy-duty laundry, but in other cases it is the brand with the best quality/price ratio that is market leader. Dell is a case in point. Are Dell's computers the best? Surely not. But who really needs a 'best computer'? What would be the criterion for evaluation? 'Best' is a relative concept, depending on the value criteria used to establish comparisons and identify the 'best'. In fact the market is segmented: the largest proportion of the public, and even most of the B2B segment, wants a modern, reliable, cheap computer. Thanks to its build-to-order business model, Dell was able to innovate and become the leader of that segment. Co-branded 'Intel inside', it reassures buyers and surprises them by its astonishing price and one-to-one customisation: each person makes his or her own computer. Is Swatch the best watch? Surely not either. But in any case this is not what is asked by Swatch buyers: they buy convenience and style, not long-lasting superior 'performance', whatever this may mean.

It is time to look deeper into the brand–product relationship. Looking at history, most brands are born out of a product or service innovation which outperformed its competitors. A superior product/service was the determining factor of the launch campaign. Later, as the product name evolves into a brand, customers' reasons for purchase may still be the brand's 'superior performance image', although in reality that performance has been matched by new competitors. This has been the basis of Volkswagen's leadership and price premium: a majority of consumers keeps on believing that Volkswagen cars are the most reliable ones. The new Golf Five, launched in September 2003, 30 years after the first Golf, is 10 per cent more expensive than its two European rivals, the Peugeot 307 and the Renault Megane. This quality reputation is

crucial for Golf and for Volkswagen itself: this model used to represent 28 per cent of its sales and almost half its operating profit. When Golf 4 sales fell by 17.9 per cent over 12 months, Volkswagen's operating profit fell too, by 56 per cent.

As all tests and garage repair records demonstrate, Volkswagen quality has now been matched and even bypassed by Toyota, but for buyers, perception is reality. Brand assets are made of what people believe. As for rumours (Kapferer, 2004), the more people believe a rumour, the more strongly their belief is held. Why would so many people be completely wrong? It took 20 years for Toyota to shake the belief among US consumers that Volkswagen cars are the most reliable: it takes time to prove one's reliability. Often, to go faster it is best to target a new generation of drivers with an open mind.

Looking at competitive behaviour, it seems that brands alternate in their focus. They capitalise on their image, then innovate to recreate or nurture the belief of product superiority (on some consumer benefit), then recapitalise on their image, and so on (Figure 2.2). Sony's advertising is very typical of this pendulum behaviour: it alternates ads that introduce new products and pure image ads with no specific material content or superiority content. These latter ads maintain brand saliency (Ehrenberg *et al*, 2002).

Figure 2.3 summarises the product–brand relationship.

Suppose a consumer wants to buy a new car because of the birth of his or her fourth child. This major event creates a new set of expectations, some tangible, some intangible. The consumer wishes to buy a minivan, with two sliding doors, high flexibility within the cabin, and of course a reliable, secure brand, with credentials and some status. By looking at Internet sites, at magazines and visiting dealers, it is possible to identify those models with the requested visible attributes (size, flexibility, sliding doors). Now what about the invisible attributes, like the experiential ones (driving pleasure) or those one has to believe on faith, such as reliability? Obviously, these attributes do or do not belong to the brand's reputational capital. They cannot be observed. This is one of the key roles of brands: to guarantee, to reassure customers about desired benefits which constitute the exclusive strength of the brand, also called its positioning.

Psychologists have also identified the halo effect as a major source of value created by the brand: the fact that knowing the name of the brand does influence consumer's perception of the product advantages beyond what the visible cues had themselves indicated, not to speak of the invisible advantages.

Finally, attached to the brand there are pure intangible associations, which stem from the brand's values, vision, philosophy, its typical buyer, its brand personality and so on. These associations are the source of emotional ties, beyond product satisfaction. In fact, in the car industry, they are the locus of consumers' desire to possess a brand. Some brands sell very good products at fair price but lack thrill or desire: they cannot command a price premium in their segment. Their dealers will have to give more rebates (which undermine brand value and business profitability).

Figure 2.3 reminds us of the double nature of brands. People buy branded products or services, but branding is a not a substitute for marketing. Both are needed. Marketing aims at forecasting the needs of specific consumer segments, and drives the organisation to tailor products and services to these needs. This is a skill: some car marques offer minivans with sliding doors, some do not. However, part of the willingness to pay is based on a personal tie with the brand. Uninvolved consumers will bargain a lot. Brand-involved consumers will bargain less. Brand image is directly linked to profitability. In fact, in the Euromonitor car brand tracking study, measuring the image of all automobile brands operating in Europe, it has been said that a positive shift of one unit on the global opinion scale means there is 1 per cent less bargaining by customers.

Each brand needs a flagship product

A given brand will not be jeopardised by competitors offering similar products, unless there are large quantities of the latter. It is indeed inevitable for certain models to be duplicated in the product lines of different brands. Suppose that brand A pursues durability, brand B practicality and brand C innovation: the spirit of each brand will be especially noticeable in certain specific products, those most representative or typical of the brand meaning. They are the brand's

Figure 2.3   The product and the brand

'prototype' products. Each product range thus must contain products demonstrating the brand's guiding value and obsession, flagships for the brand's meaning and purpose. Renault, for instance, is best epitomised by its top minivans, Nina Ricci by its entrancing evening gowns, Lacoste by its shirts, Sony by its Walkmans and digital pocket cameras.

However, there are some products within a given line that do not manage to clearly express the brand's intent and attributes. In the television industry, the cost constraints at the low end of the range are such that trying to manufacture a model radically different from the next-door neighbour's is quite difficult. But, for economic reasons, brands are sometimes forced to take a stake in this very large and overall highly competitive market. Likewise, each bank has had to offer its own savings plan, identical to that of all other banks. All these similar products, though, should only represent a limited aspect of each brand's offer (see Figure 2.4). All in all, each brand stays in focus and progresses in its own direction to make original products. That is why communicating about such products is so important, as they reveal the brand's meaning and purpose.

The problem arises when brands within the same group overlap too much, with one preventing the other from asserting its identity. Using the same motors in Peugeots and Citroëns would harm Peugeot, built on the 'dynamic car' image. It is when several brands sell the same product that a brand can become a caricature of itself. In order to compete against Renault's Espace and Chrysler's Voyager, neither Peugeot or Citroën, Fiat or Lancia could take the economic risk of building a manufacturing plant on their own; neither could Ford or Volkswagen. A single minivan was made for the first four brands. Similarly, a Ford–Volkswagen plant in Portugal was set to produce a common car. The outcome, however, is that in producing a common vehicle, the brand becomes reduced to a mere external gadget. The identity message was simply relegated to the shell. So each brand has had to exaggerate its outward appearance in order to be easily recognised.

Advertising products through the brand prism

Products are mute: the brand gives them meaning and purpose, telling us how a

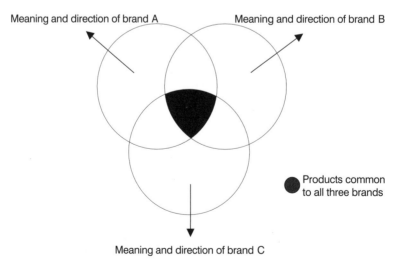

Figure 2.4   Product line overlap among brands

product should be read. A brand is both a prism and a magnifying glass through which products can be decoded. BMW invites us to perceive its models as 'cars for man's pleasure'. On the one hand, brands guide our perception of products. On the other hand, products send back a signal that brands use to underwrite and build their identity. The automobile industry is a case in point, as most technical innovations quickly spread among all brands. Thus the ABS system is offered by Volvo as well as by BMW, yet it cannot be said that they share the same identity. Is this a case of brand inconsistency? Not at all: ABS has simply become a must for all.

However, brands can only develop through long-term consistency, which is both the source and reflection of its identity. Hence the same ABS will not bear the same meaning for two different car-makers. For Volvo, which epitomises total safety, ABS is an utter necessity serving the brand's values and obsessions: it encapsulates the brand's essence. BMW, which symbolises high-performance, cannot speak of ABS in these terms: it would amount to denying the BMW ideology and value system which has inspired the whole organisation and helped generate the famous models of the Munich brand. BMW introduced ABS as a way to go faster. Likewise, how did the safety-conscious brand, Volvo, justify

its participation in the European leisure car championships? By saying 'We *really* test our products so that they last longer.'

The minivans that Peugeot, Citroën, Fiat and Lancia have in common has left only one role for the respective brands to play: to enhance its association with the intrinsic values of the respective's brand – imagination and escape for Citroën, quality driving and reliability for Peugeot, high class and flair for Lancia, practicality for Fiat. (See Figure 2.5.)

Thus brand identity never results from a detail, yet a detail can, once interpreted, serve to express a broader strategy. Details can only have an impact on a brand's identity if they are in synergy with it, echoing and amplifying the brand's values. That is why weak brands do not succeed in capitalising on their innovations: they do not manage either to enhance the brand's meaning or create that all-important resonance.

A brand is thus a prism helping us to decipher products. It defines what and how much to expect from the products bearing its name. An innovation which would be considered very original for a Fiat, for instance, will be considered commonplace for a Ford. However, though insufficient engine power may scarcely have been an issue for many car-makers, for Peugeot it is a major problem. It disavows Peugeot's deeply-

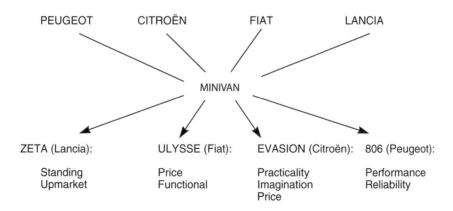

Figure 2.5 Brands give innovations meaning and purpose

rooted identity and frustrates the expectations that have been raised. It would be at odds with what should be called Peugeot's 'brand obligations'.

In fact, consumers rarely evaluate innovations in an isolated way, but in relation to a specific brand. Once a brand has chosen a specific positioning or meaning, it has to assume all of its implications and fulfil its promises. Brands should respect the contract that made them successful by attracting customers. They owe it to them.

Brands and other signs of quality

In many sectors, brands coexist with other quality signs. The food industry, for instance, is also filled with quality seals, certificates of norm compliance and controlled origin and guarantees. The proliferation of these other signs results from a double objective: to promote and to protect.

Certifications of origin (eg real Scotch whisky) are intended to protect a branch of agriculture and products whose quality is deeply rooted in a specific location and know-how. The controlled origin guarantee capitalises on a subjective and cultural conception of quality, coupled with a touch of mystery and of the area's unique character. It segments the market by refusing the certification of origin to any goods that have not been produced within a certain area or raised in the traditional way. Thus in Europe since 2003, Feta cheese has been a name tied to a controlled Greek origin. Even if Danish or French cheese-makers were to produce a 'feta' cheese elsewhere that buyers were unable to tell apart from the feta cheese made in Greece in the traditional way, their products can no longer lay claim to the name 'feta'.

Quality seals are promotional tools. They convey a different concept of quality, which is both more industrial and scientific. In this respect, a given type of cheese, for example, involves objective know-how, using a certain kind of milk mixed with selected bacteria, etc. Quality seals create a vertical segmentation, consisting of different levels of objective quality. The issue here is not so much to present typical characteristics as to satisfy a stringent set of objective criteria.

The legal guarantee of typicality brought by a 'certified origin' seal means more than a simple designation of origin, a mere label indicating where a product comes from, in that the latter implies no natural or social specificity – although it may mislead the buyer into thinking that there is one. Moreover, several modern cheese-makers deliberately mix up what is genuine and what is not, inventing foreign names for their new products that are reminiscent of places or villages in an effort to build their own rustic, parochial imagery.

It is interesting to see how European countries tried to reassure consumers during the 'mad cow crisis' in order to redress the 40 per cent drop in beef consumption:

▌ Although it is not legal under EU regulations, they reinstated designations of origin referring to a country (ie French beef). This did not prove fully reassuring since it was soon heard that French cattle could have eaten not only local grass but also contaminated organic extracts imported from the UK.

▌ Certifications of origin (ie Charolais beef) add typicality but cannot guarantee a 100 per cent safe meat.

▌ Seals of quality did not exist and had to be created but it would take years to promote them: however, unless full control of the entire cattle raising process is guaranteed, the output itself cannot be guaranteed.

▌ The crisis highlighted the need for meat brands. Since 1989, alerted by early warnings, McDonald's had indeed sought new suppliers in Europe, scrutinising the way in which each and every one raised and fed their cattle.

▌ Retailers like Carrefour have promoted their own signed contract with farmers.

Whether or not official indications of quality in Europe should still exist in 2010 is a bitter issue that is still being discussed among northern countries (United Kingdom, Denmark, etc) who believe that only brands should prevail, and southern countries (France, Spain, Italy) who support the idea of having official collective signs of quality co-existing with brands (Feral, 1989).

The northern European countries claim that brands alone should be allowed to segment the market and thus build a repu-tation for excellence around their names, thanks to their products and to their distri-bution and marketing efforts. These coun-tries tend to favour an objective concept of quality: it does not matter that the feta cheese that the Greeks prefer is made in Holland or that Smirnoff vodka is neither Russian nor Polish. The southern European countries believe for their part that collective signs enable small companies to use their ranking and/or their typical characteristics as promotional tools, since they do not have their own brands. As their products do not speak for themselves, their market posi-tioning is ensured by quality or certified origin seals. Clearly, behind the European debate on whether or not brands that have built their reputation on their own should coexist with official collective signs of quality lies another more fundamental debate between the proponents of a liberal economy on the one hand, and the partisans of government intervention to regulate it on the other.

From the corporate point of view, choosing between brand policy and collective signs is a matter of strategy and of available resource allocation.

Often, quality certificates reduce perceived difference. Distributors' brands can also receive them. Brands define their own stan-dards: legally, they guarantee nothing, but empirically they convey clusters of attributes and values. In doing so, they seek to become a reference in themselves, if not the one and only reference (as is the case with Bacardi, the epitome of rum). Thus, in essence, brands differentiate and share very little. Brands distinguish their products. Strong brands are those that diffuse values and manage to segment the market with their own means.

In handling the 'mad cow' crisis, McDonald's wondered whether they should rely on their own brand only or also on the collective signs and certificates of origin.

On an operational level, let us once again underline the fact that brands do not boil down to a mere act of advertising. They contain recommendations regarding the long-term specificities of the products bearing their name, such as attractive prices, efficient distribution and merchandising, as well as identity building through advertising. It is easier for a small company to earn a quality seal for one of its products through strict efforts on quality, than it is to undertake the gruelling task of creating a brand, which requires so many financial, human, technical and commercial resources. Even without an identity, the small company's product can thus step out of the ordinary, thanks in part to the legal indicators of quality.

Obstacles to the implications of branding

Within the same company, brand policy often conflicts with other policies. As these are unwritten and implicit, they may seem innocuous, when in fact they are a hindrance to a true brand policy.

Current corporate accounting, as such, is unfavourable towards brands. Accounting is ruled by the prudence principle: conse-quently, any outlay for which payback is uncertain is counted as an expense rather than valued as an asset. This is the case of investments made in communications in order to inform the general public about the brand's identity. Because it is impossible to measure exactly what share of the annual communications budget generates returns immediately, or within a specified number of years, the whole sum is taken as an operating expense which is subtracted from the financial year's profits. Yet advertising, like investments in machinery, talented staff and R&D, also helps build brand capital. Accounting thus creates a bias that handicaps brand companies because it projects an under-valued image of them. Take the case of company A, which invests heavily to develop the awareness and renown of its brand name. Having to write off this investment as an expense results in low annual profits and a small asset value on the balance sheet. This usually occurs during a critical period in the company's growth, when it could actually use some help from outside investors and bankers. Now compare A to company B, which invests the same amounts in machines and production and nothing whatsoever in either name, image or renown. As it is allowed to value these tangible investments as fixed assets and to depreciate them gradually over several years, B can announce higher profits and its balance sheet, displaying bigger assets, will project a more flattering image. B will thus look better in terms of accounting, when, in fact, A is in a better position to differentiate its products.

The principle of annual accounting also hinders brand policy. Every product manager is judged on his yearly results and on the net contribution generated by his product. This leads to 'short-termism' in decision making: those decisions which produce fast, meas-urable results are favoured over those that build up brand capital, slowly no doubt, but more reliably in the long term. Moreover, product-based accounting discourages product managers from putting out any addi-tional advertising effort that would serve

essentially to bolster the brand as a whole, when the latter serves as an umbrella and sign for other products. Managers thus only focus on one thing: any new expenditure in the general interest will be charged to their own account statement. For example, Palmolive is a brand covering several products: liquid detergent, shampoo, shaving cream, etc. The brand could decide to communicate only one of these products singled out as a prominent image leader, capitalising on image spillover reciprocal effects (Balachander, 2003). But the investment made would certainly be higher than could be justified solely by the sales forecast of that product. This new expenditure will in fact always be on the given product, even though its ultimate purpose is to collec-tively benefit all products under the umbrella brand.

In order to react against the short-term bias caused by accounting practices and the under-estimation of (corporate) value as shown in the balance sheets, some British companies have begun to list their own brands as assets on their balance sheets. This has triggered a discussion on the fundamental validity of accounting practices that emerged in the 'age of commodities', when the essential part of capital consisted of real estate and equipment. Today, on the contrary, intangible assets (know-how, patents, reputation) are what make the difference in the long run. Beyond the need for an open debate in Europe and the United States on how to capitalise brands, it has become just as important to find a way for companies to account for the long-term pros and cons of short-term brand decisions in their books. It is all the more compelling as brand decision-makers themselves rotate often, perhaps too often.

Even the way in which the various types of communication agencies are organised fails to comply with the requirements of sound brand policy. Even if an advertising agency has its own network of partner companies – in charge of proximity marketing, CRM, e-business and so on – and can thus promote itself as an integrated communications group, it remains the crux of the network. Furthermore, advertising agencies think only in terms of campaigns, operating in a short, one-year time frame. Brand policy is different: it develops over a long period and requires that all means be considered at once, in a fully integrated way.

It is clear that a company rarely finds contacts inside so-called communications groups who are actually in charge of strategic thinking and of providing overall recommendations rather than merely focusing on advertising or on the necessity to sell campaigns. Moreover, advertising agencies are not in a position to address strategic issues, such as what should be the optimal number of brands in a portfolio. As these affect the survival of the brands that are under their advertising responsibility, the agencies find themselves in the awkward position of being judge and jury. That is why a new profession has been created: strategic brand management consulting. The time had indeed come for companies to meet professionals with a mid-term vision who are capable of providing consistent, integrated guidelines for the development of brand portfolios without focusing on one single technique.

A high personnel turnover disrupts the continuity a brand needs. Yet companies today actually plan for their personnel to rotate on different brands! Thus, brands are often entrusted to young graduates with impressive degrees but little experience and the promotion they expect often consists of being assigned to yet another brand! Thus, product managers must achieve visible results in the short term. This helps to explain why there are so many changes in advertising strategy and implementation as well as in decisions on brand extension, promotion or discounts. These are in fact caused by changes in personnel.

It is significant that brands that have maintained a continuous and homogeneous image belong to companies with stable brand decision makers. This is the case for luxury brands: the long-lasting presence of the creator or founder allows for sound, long-term management. The same is true of major retailers where senior managers often handle the communication themselves or at least make the final decisions. As a means to alleviate the effects of excessive brand manager rotation, companies aim not only at incorporating brand value into their accounts, but also at creating a long-term brand image charter. The latter represents both a vital safeguard and an instrument of continuity.

Business organisation is sometimes an obstacle to building the brand. In 2001, the very high-profile Toshiba Corporation created a new and hitherto non-existent vice-president post: VP Brand. Significantly, the appointee was the existing VP of Research and Development. The fact that the world number one in laptops and a major player in the television, hi-fi and lo-fi sectors should create such a post demonstrates a strong awareness of an unfilled gap. Toshiba's products are undeniably excellent, and until now this has been the key to the success of Japanese companies in general, and Toshiba in particular. This is a company that enjoys a dominant position in a sector as cut-throat as the laptop industry. So what was it missing?

Worldwide studies had revealed that there was no 'magic' to the Toshiba brand. It could be compared to a colleague at the office whom you would regularly consult for advice, but would never invite home for dinner. It was a brand based on a single pillar: there was a strong rational component, but little by way of emotional appeal, intangible values and 'magic'. In short, it was no Sony, and could not command Sony's higher margins. A company can become a leader in the Toshiba mould through excellent products and prices, or a leader like Dell by dint of a distribution system with levels of efficiency that remain head and shoulders above any (known) competitor. But since the effect of competition is to erode perceived difference, other instruments are needed to attract customers and keep them loyal; to ensure that they remain customers of the brand. This desire is based on the need for security, and on intangible factors.

Up until 2001, there was no management of the Toshiba brand. The company's organisation was based on a branched structure, and thus no one was responsible for the cross-company resource that is the brand. The medical branch had one view of Toshiba, while the computer branch had another, and so on. There was no coordination or global brand platform, to say nothing of joint promotions between branches, of course. Horizontal initiatives (such as sponsorship) were rare, and commercial necessity dictated that the power lay with the distribution subsidiaries: the name of the game was to sell imported products, not to build a brand reputation. Local managers' remuneration packages were calculated on sales, not brand equity.

Another syndrome pertains to the relationship between production and sales. In the Electrolux group, for instance, production units are specialised according to product. Both mono-product and multi-market, they sell their product to the sales units who are, on the contrary, mono-market and multi-product (grouped under an umbrella brand). The problem is that these autonomous sales divisions, who each have their own brand, all want to benefit from the latest product innovation so as to maximise their division's turnover. What is missing is a structure for managing and allocating innovations in accordance with a consistent and global vision of the brand portfolio. As we will see later, there is no point in entrusting a strong innovation to a weak brand. Moreover, this undermines the very basis of the brand concept: differentiation.

Lastly, if words mean anything at all, communications managers should have the power to prevent actions that go against the brand's interest. Thus, Philips never succeeded in fully taking advantage of its former brand

baseline: 'Philips, tomorrow is already here'. In order to do so, they would have needed to ban all advertising on batteries or electric light bulbs that either trivialised the assertion, contradicted it, or reduced it to mere advertising hype. It would also have been possible to communicate only about future bulb types rather than about the best current sales. Unfortunately, nobody in the organisation had the power (or the desire) to impose these kinds of constraints. When the Whirlpool brand appeared, however, the managers from Philips actually created the organisation they needed for implementing a real brand policy: as it was directly linked to general management, the communications department was able to ensure the optimal circumstances for launching the Whirlpool brand, by banning over a three-year period any communication about a commonplace product or even a best-selling product.

Failing to manage innovations has a very negative impact on brand equity. Even though salespeople go up in arms when they are not given the responsibility of a strong innovation, it is a mistake to assign the latter to a weak brand, especially in multi-brand groups. When dealing with a weak brand, attractive pricing must indeed be offered to distributors as an incentive to include the latter in their reference listing. But since the brand's consumers do not expect this innovation (each brand defines its type and level of consumer expectations), the product turnover is insufficient. As for the non-buyers, such a brand is not reassuring. If the innovation is launched a few weeks later under a leading brand name, distributors will refuse to pay for the price premium due to a leader because they purchased it at a lower price just a while back from the same company. Thus, even with the strong brand, the sales price eventually has to be cut.

Breeding many strong brands, l'Oréal allocates its inventions to its various businesses according to brand potency. Innovation is thus first entrusted to prestigious brands sold in selective channels as the products' high prices will help cancel out the high research cost incurred. Thus, liposomes were first commercialised by Lancôme, the new sun filter Mexoryl SX by Vichy. Innovation is then diffused to the other channels and eventually to the large retailers. By then, the selective channel brands are already likely to have launched another differentiating novelty.

However, this process is affected by the fact that innovation is not exclusively owned by any one company; it quickly spreads to competitors, which calls for immediate reaction.

Along the same lines, when a producer supplies a distributor's brand with the same product it sells under its own brand, it will eventually erode its brand equity and, more generally, the very respectability of the concept of a brand. This simply means that what customers pay more for in a brand is the name and nothing else. When the brand is dissociated from the product it enhances and represents, it becomes merely superficial and artificial, devoid of any rational legitimacy. Ultimately, companies pay a price for this as sales decrease and distributors seize the opportunity to declare in their advertising that national brands alienate consumers, but that consumers can resist by purchasing distributors' own-brands. This also justifies the sluggishness of public authorities regarding the increasing amount of counterfeit products among distributors' own-brands. Finally, such practices foster a false collective understanding of what brands are, even among opinion leaders, which contributes to the rumour that nowadays all products are just the same!

3

Brand and business building

How do companies grow both the brand and business? What does it take to build a brand? What are the necessary steps and phases? In this chapter we address these questions with a particular emphasis on integration of efforts. Brand building is not done apart, it is the result of a clear strategy and of excellence in implementation at the product, price, place, people and communication levels. There are prerequisites before a brand can be built, and they need to be understood.

Are brands for all companies?

The brand is not an end in itself. It needs to be managed for what it is – an instrument for company growth and profitability, a business tool. Does branding affect all companies? Yes. Are all companies aware of this? No. For many industrial companies or commodity sellers, the concept of the brand applies only to mass markets, high-consumption products and the fast-moving consumer goods (FMCG) sector. This is a misconception. A brand is a name that influences buyers and prescribers alike. Industrial brands have their own markets: Air Liquide sells to industry, Somfy sells its tubular motors to window-blind installers and fitters, Saint Gobain Gypsum and Lafarge sell to companies and craftspeople in the construction and public works sectors, and the William Pitters company is famous among retailers for the quality of its trade relationships.

Nevertheless, these companies are affected by brands in a variety of ways:

▍ Stock-exchange-listed groups have to manage the widened recognition for their products. Their corporate brand is the vehicle for this recognition. Stock exchanges operate on anticipation. By definition an anticipation is not rational, but can be influenced by emotive factors.

▍ Worldwide groups should be asking themselves whether it might not be time to complete their transformation into worldwide buyers and distributors in order to consolidate their local operators under a single name.

▍ Chinese or Indian groups should be asking themselves how to get rid of the status of low cost supplies and take a larger part of the high margin segments in developed countries: to do so they need a global brand.

▌ Producers should be asking themselves whether the brand is a differentiating factor in any sector threatened by commoditisation. For this reason, it is noteworthy that BPB chose to retain the Placoplatre product brand – a local brand which had become synonymous with the product itself, and indeed a leader in its own markets. Similarly, it is significant that the industrial Air Liquide company asked Mr Lindsay Owen-Jones, the CEO of l'Oréal, to sit on its board of directors. Having worked its way through hundreds of product names and legal trademarks for these names, Air Liquide realised that it had still failed to create any real value. What it needed was to restructure its range of high-tech products under several mega-brands, as l'Oréal had done.

▌ Producers of intermediary goods should be asking themselves whether it might not be time to sell to their clients' customers, not through direct sales, but by instilling a brand awareness in these customers. In this way, Lafarge – a world leader in construction materials – invested several million euros on informing the general public about the advances made possible by its innovations, in order to create a demand for its products among people who would live in the flats or work in the offices built by its clients. In relationships with intermediaries and distributors, the brand is an instrument of power. Another typical example is Somfy, a world leader in motors for window blinds and openings for home use: this leadership has been earned through changing its OEM business model and refocusing the brand on the end user, just as Intel, Lycra, Woolmark and others have successfully done. After all, what do

you say to a window-blind dealer for whom the Somfy motor makes up 35 per cent of the product cost and who is threatening to source the part from China at half the price? Somfy fears being relegated to the role of a mere OEM player: hence its increasingly high-profile public 'Somfy powered' strategy.

Building a market leader without advertising

What does it take to build a brand? Brand definitions are innumerable (see the discussion on page 9), and almost every author in the field has his or her own. Although they can be useful, definitions tell us very little about how to build a brand. Definitions are static: they take the brand for granted. Building the brand is dynamic.

In general, in our executive seminars, when we ask attendees how to build a market-leading brand, typical answers include advertise, create an image, and develop awareness. They are mostly answers that focus on communication.

Instead of answering that question frontally, we shall look at an interesting case: how did an unknown Australian company, Orlando Wyndham, build the UK's leading bottled wine brand, Jacob's Creek? This brand is now the leader in volume and the leader in spontaneous brand awareness, with a very strong image. All that was achieved without mass-market advertising before 2000. It is most interesting also to note that between 1984 and 2000, the UK wine market doubled in size. What then was needed to create a successful wine brand in the UK mass market?:

▌ The first condition is to have enough volume. Addressing the mass market means being able to fulfil trade expectations. Multiple retailers hate to deal with companies that cannot provide sufficient supply if a product is a success. For a wine maker this means being able to rely on a very large supply source.

■ The second condition is to secure a stable quality. The first role of any brand is to reduce perceived risk: the consumer experience must be the same whenever and wherever the product is bought. (This is why branding services is tougher than branding tangible products: human variability works against this stability.) For a wine maker, it means mastering the art of blending, to make sure consumer expectations are not betrayed. Once consumers discover they like a specific wine taste, their repurchase indicates a willingness to reduce risk and re-find the same taste, the same pleasure.

■ For a mass-market brand, price is key: it must be mainstream. Everything must be done, at the back office level, to ensure higher productivity, and hence a lower production cost, while not altering the quality and taste.

■ It is essential to be end-user driven, and find the right taste for the particular market. Many UK consumers are not long-practised wine drinkers. Their tastes have been shaped by cold soft drinks and beer. This means that they prefer wines with a specific taste and in-mouth profile. In addition, if an organisation hits the right local expectations it can expect to obtain good publicity, medals and press coverage, thus reinforcing the trade support.

■ Another requirement is a national sales force. Wine is mostly chosen at the point of purchase. On-shelf visibility and point-of-purchase advertising are success factors. It is important to draw up national agreements with the major multiple retailers (in this case Sainsbury, Asda, Tesco and a few others) to achieve this, but even when these are in place a day-to-day check needs to be carried out, store by store, to make sure everything is in place. Only a national sales force can achieve this. In addition, an intensive wet trial phase is needed, to encourage customers to pause in wandering up and down the store aisles and taste the product. This too requires a national sales force.

These five steps to build a brand in the market may seem straightforward and easy to follow. Actually they are not. French wines could not meet the conditions, while New World wines, and Australian wines in particular, could. Let us examine why, for each condition.

Old World wines are based on one principle. The quality of the wine is totally dependent on natural factors: the specific type of soil, the sun, the climate, the air. As a consequence, hundreds of wines have been created, differentiated by the wine-growing area, or even specific vineyard, from which they come, and its unique characteristics. Each vineyard claims its soil is better than that of competitors, for example. As a consequence, the product is fragmented. For example, behind each of the 5,000 marques of Bordeaux wine there is a different grower, usually rather small. This prevents suppliers from responding to the first condition for building a brand: enough volume.

Old World wines have tried to secure their market leadership by transforming their wine-producing practices into laws. Producing a Burgundy or a Bordeaux wine means obeying these laws. What was intended as a quality control system has become a major block against innovating to address the competition from emerging growing areas.

If a wine is to be called a Pauillac, a Graves or whatever (these are subregions within Bordeaux), its producers are not permitted to mix the grapes from this region with grapes grown anywhere else, or only at a very small level. If one season is dry they cannot irrigate; nor can they add chemicals to moderate the differences in quality caused by differences in climate from year to year. Because they respect these laws, Old World wines have an inherent variability: they are the true produce of nature, more than the produce of man. There is much more variety of soils and variance in climate from year to year in Europe than in Australia, California or Argentina, and this too leads to differences between one Old World wine and another.

Branding means suppressing this variability: to secure the same taste from year to year, one must master the art of blending grapes coming from very different soils – and regions, if one of them is underproducing. Australia, as a relatively newly settled country without a long wine-growing tradition, had few laws governing wine producing; it could do it. It was not so for wine makers from Bordeaux or Burgundy.

The same holds true for getting the right quality at low production costs. French wine makers are not allowed to use mechanised harvesting: they are required to harvest by hand. They cannot irrigate, and so radically increase the productivity of their soils; they cannot make use of chemical additives. In France too, wine is stored in barrels as a rule. In Australia wine is kept in huge aluminium tanks, and wood cuttings are put in the wine: there is more wood surface in contact with the wine, which accelerates the process of giving the wine the right 'woody' taste. Time being money, this reduces production costs.

Point four concerns getting the right taste to appeal to the target market. New World wines have no tradition to respect: they started from the customer. They adapted their product to the taste of customers in emerging markets, used to drinking soft drinks and beer. Their wine had to be fruit-driven, very soft, very smooth, easy to drink for all occasions. Some varietals (types of grape) such as Chardonnay and Semillon Chardonnay could deliver such a taste. These were not the varieties that made the reputation of Bordeaux or Burgundy wines.

One other dimension of being client-driven is language. Marketing research showed that the English were still broadly an 'island race':

many of them are not well versed in European languages and the cultural traditions of Continental Europe. Unlike the maze of thousands of hard-to-pronounce wine names from Europe, Jacob's Creek is an English name, and the wording on the wine labels is written in English. Until recently French wines rarely provided any labelling information in English. Furthermore, Australia is part of the Commonwealth, and some English people identify more closely with it than with France.

In addition, each New World country has become associated with a small number of grape varieties. This means that consumers find it easier to forecast the taste of an Australian wine than of a French wine. The country of origin adds its own risk-reducing role to the brand.

Last but not least, the industry's organisation in the Old World is too fragmented. Individual growers cannot afford a dedicated sales force even in their homeland. Even when the wine is produced by cooperatives of growers, the coops tend to want to remain independent and refuse to join larger organisations, the only viable path to reaching the critical size to create a brand.

As a result, in the 16 years to 2001, Australian wines, led by Jacob's Creek, went from zero to a 16.9 per cent share by volume and a 20.1 per cent share by value of the British market. Meanwhile the market doubled in size. Interestingly, as is shown by the value share being higher than the volume share, price is not the main reason consumers choose Australian wines. The New World growers have succeeded in persuading customers to trade up, by offering higher quality brand extensions designed to appeal to former novice wine drinkers who are now willing to explore more complex wines.

Can Old World wines come back and stop their sharp decline? As long as they do not suppress their internally based regulations, their production laws, and do not encourage supplier concentration, they will not be able to fulfill the five conditions for building brands. Bordeaux and Burgundy cannot do it.

However, the Languedoc wine-growing region is the biggest in the world. As such it fulfils the first condition. In this region, which historically produced lower-status wine than Bordeaux and Burgundy, there are very few production rules to obey. The future is in the hands of Languedoc's growers if they can concentrate and meet customers' requirements, not only in the UK but also in Japan, Korea and other countries with a growing market for wine. They might also export their know-how and build brands where the future market is: China. This is why so many players are signing joint ventures with Chinese companies and authorities, to grow grapes in China and develop brands that have none of the Old World wine industry's self-imposed limitations.

What lessons can be drawn and generalised? New World wine brands have succeeded because they innovated, breaking with the competition's conventions for consumer profit. They have not stopped innovating and disrupting conventions. In Australia, Jacob's Creek recently introduced screw cap closures on its Riesling varieties, abandoning a sacred cow: cork closure. Riesling is more likely than wines from some other grape varieties to be affected by problems of cork quality, and half-bottles are especially vulnerable. Both consumers and the trade reacted favourably to this small but revolutionary innovation.

A second lesson is that a part of Jacob's Creek appeal was based on one enduring weakness of competition: it was not an elitist brand, and it had no snob value. It was approachable for everybody.

The product's quality–price ratio was excellent, attracting praise from experts and taste makers. This is an endless race: each year the brand continues to improve the quality, thus winning continuous publicity. Since it was the first of the major Australian wine exporters, Jacob's Creek benefited from the 'pioneer advantage', and became the symbol of Australian wine. Interestingly, Orlando

Wyndham, the company that owns the brand, is far smaller than some of its Australian competitors such as Hardy's, but all its energy and efforts were focused on this one single brand.

Many brands have developed by contact and retail without advertising: Google, Zara, Amazon. This is not the only brand-building model. Yellow Tail became the number one wine brand in the United States thanks to a huge advertising campaign, a fun personality and a price which strongly motivated its main distributor. In addition it was aimed at the wide field of non-experts in wine.

Brand building: from product to values, and vice versa

It takes time to build a really strong brand. There are two routes, two models for doing so: from product advantage to intangible values, or from values to product. However, with time, this two-way movement becomes the essence of brand management: brands have two legs.

Most brands did not start as such: their founders just wanted to create a business, based on a very specific product or service: an innovation, a good idea to start their business and open the distributors' closed doors. Through time, their name or the name of the product became a brand: well known and endowed with market power (the ability to influence buyers). It did not simply designate a product or a person, but little by little came to be associated with imagery, with intangible benefits, with brand personality and so on. Perception had moved upwards from objects to benefits, from tangible to intangible values.

As is shown by the upward-pointing arrow in Figure 3.1, most brands start not as brands but as a name on an innovative product or service. Nike started out as a meaningless name on a pair of innovative running shoes: if they had not been innovative no distributor would have paid attention to Phil Knight in the first place. With time, that name acquired awareness, status and trust, if not respect or liking. This is the result of all the communication and stars which accompanied the business building. Little by little an inversion takes place in the process: instead of the product building the brand awareness and reputation (the bottom-up arrow of influence), it is the brand that differentiates and endows the product/service with its unique values (the top-down dotted arrow). In fact at this time the brand determines which new products match its desired image. Nike is now in the phase of brand extensions: the brand has stretched from running shoes to sports apparel and now golf clubs.

Through time, brand associations typically move up a ladder (the vertical axis of Figure 3.1), from ingredient (Dove with hydrating cream) to attribute (softening), to benefit (protection), to brand personality, brand values and even mission (Apple or Virgin have a mission), at the very top intangible end.

Now this does not mean that, with time, brand management should not be concerned with material issues and differentiation any more. Brands are two-legged. Even luxury brands, bought for the sake of show, must give their buyers the feeling that they have bought a great product and that the price difference is legitimate. But material differentiation is a never-ending race: competitors copy your best ideas. Attaching the brand to an intangible value adds value and prevents substitutability. The Mercedes price premium is permanently explained by product-based advertising copy,

but also by PR operations that accentuate the unique status of the brand.

This first model concerns brands that started as a product. There exists a second model of brand building: many brands start as concepts or ideas. This is true of all licensed brands (Paloma Picasso perfume, Harry Potter products and so on) and of many fashion brands, spirits or cigarette brands. The Axe men's hygiene line started from an insight as well: teenagers feel insecure about their sex appeal.

This model also provides a reminder that even when launching a product brand (that is, a brand based on a product advantage) it is important to incorporate from the start the higher levels of meaning that are intended to attach to the brand in the longer term. The brand should not simply acquire them, by accumulation or sedimentation; they should be planned from the start and incorporated at birth. Incorporating this perspective from the start accelerates the process by which products become brands. This is why product launch and brand launch are not the same.

This is also why brand names should never be descriptive of the product. The first reason is that what is descriptive soon becomes generic, when competitors come into the market with the same product. Second, clients will soon learn what the business is about. Names should better aim at telling an intangible story. Amazon speaks of newness, force and abundance (like the River Amazon), and Orange says 'definitely non-technical', just as Apple Computers did 25 years earlier.

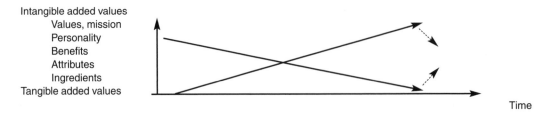

Figure 3.1   The two models of brand building through time

Finally, as is illustrated by the two dotted arrows of the graph, brand management consists of a permanent coming and going between tangible and intangible values. Brands are two-legged value producing systems. This means that having an excellent product is not enough in modern competition. (See for instance the Toshiba case, page 47). However, neither luxury nor image brands can afford to forget the functional realities of products.

Are leading brands the best products or the best value?

To create a brand is much more than simply marking a product or service, the necessary first step of brand differentiation. It is about owning a value.

It is often held to be a paradox that the number one brands are not the best products. Was the original IBM PC the best PC available at the time? No. Is Pentium the best chip? Who knows? Are Dell computers the best computers?

The paradox stems from the word 'best': best for whom, and at what? Let's take the analogy of a school class. Academic gradings are determined according to well-understood criteria: students who do well display qualities such as excellent memory, the ability to solve problems fast, to work accurately and to present their work well. These are the values of the schoolroom; and similarly, each market has values. To become number one in any market it is necessary to understand what the market values are. Of course, one cannot succeed without a good product or service. Those who try the product must like it enough to make repeat purchases, to refer others to it; the product must build brand loyalty. In the truck tyre market, Michelin is certainly the number one: it holds 66 per cent of the original tyre market (that is, the tyres the manufacturer supplies with the truck). But in the replacement market, the so-called 'after-

market', although Michelin is still the market leader, its share falls to 29 per cent. It looks as if Michelin is not as well oriented to the values of the buyers in this aftermarket, fleet owners and those who maintain their trucks.

In the spirits market, Bacardi is world number one; is it the best spirit? One could certainly argue that it is nothing of the kind: it has no taste, and in all blind testings it fares very poorly. So why does it sell in such volume? The source of its business is not experts deliberating over its taste, but casual drinkers and partygoers. They generally want a spirit that will blend well in a cocktail, and an ideal mixer should have a very neutral taste. This is exactly what Carta Blanca delivers; it provides 90 per cent of Bacardi's sales.

Branding starts from the customer, and asks, what does he or she value? Bacardi is certainly not the 'better', but it could be called the 'batter'. One of its key intangible added values is its personality, epitomised by its symbol: a bat. The first Bacardi factory in Cuba was full of bats. This became the brand's symbol, adding an enduring halo of mystery to it.

Another example can be found in the educational market. The Master's degree in Business Administration (MBA) is a passport to success. It was first introduced in US universities. To get their MBA, students at US universities need two years of intense work: one year to learn the fundamentals, and one year to specialise in a major field.

Insead is now a respected brand in the MBA market, and Europe's best-known MBA. However its MBA course lasts less than a year. This is the power of branding: a strong brand awareness acts as a quality cue. Because it created the MBA category in Europe, Insead soon benefited from the pioneer advantage: its name effectively became the local standard, because of the lack of competition. The French management school HEC created its MBA in 1969, while Insead had started in 1957. HEC and some other late entrants made another mistake: they delivered a genuine American-type MBA. The HEC MBA, which lasted two years, was arguably of too high quality for European corporate recruiters, and too long for European students.

Understanding the value curve of the target

Insead became Europe's best-known MBA by understanding the value curve of European human resources directors who hire young executives. In delivering an MBA based on the US model, premium schools such as HEC showed that they did not understand the local value curve. In Europe, recruiters do not really care how much time students have spent on campus: the extra salary one gets after having spent two years at Harvard, Stanford or Northwestern instead of less than a year at Insead is very small. One thing recruiters do value, however, is an intensive immersion in a truly international programme, in which students learn to work with 10 different nationalities. This mirrors the working context for which they are being hired. European companies tend to consider that they will really teach their recruits how to do business in-house, and that a fast academic introduction lasting less than one year will suffice. Finally, companies prefer to rely on continuing education, providing a regular stream of specialised company seminars, throughout their managers' working lives.

Since not all clients are alike, different brands can coexist in the same sector, because they address the value curve of different segments. This is why groups build brand portfolios. GM has a portfolio of car marques, as does the Volkswagen Group.

Breaking the rule and acting fast

The MBA example also illustrates another issue: to build a brand one must quickly reach the critical size to create barriers to entry (such as top-of-mind awareness). By breaking the two-year rule, Insead was able to produce twice as many graduates as a US school of the same size, and so to reach the critical size of alumni who act as its referees within companies in half the time. Recently it made a strategic move by doubling the number of graduates produced per year, thus accentuating its market share and increasing its productivity (the number of students per professor). It also decided to capitalise on its now well-known brand to open a branch in Asia.

Many lessons should be drawn from the above examples:

▌ The first is that all brands start by being non-brands, with zero awareness and image. However, they were based on an innovation that succeeded. Starting a brand means finding a disrupting innovation.

▌ Second, creating a market is the best way to lead it. This is the well-known pioneer advantage. However, to be able to create a market, one must break free from the conventions and codes that create herdism in the marketplace.

▌ Third, time is an essential ingredient of success. The winners start first and move fast so as to rapidly create a gap from the incoming competition.

▌ Fourth, it is important to reach the critical size rapidly, to reinforce that gap from the competition. This creates more resources for advertising, communication and word of mouth.

Fifth, a brand is not a producer's brand or a retailer's, as is often heard in marketing circles: it is the customer's brand. A brand epitomises values, but as we know, value lies in the eyes of the beholder, the customer. It is essential to be market focused and ask, what is the value curve of the target? Then comes the question how to address this value curve better than the existing competition. The best way is to create a disruption (Dru, 2002), to break the conventions of the market.

Comparing brand and business models: cola drinks

It is interesting to compare a number of brand and business models within the same category. This illustrates how one cannot understand market leadership simply in terms of brand image. Structural factors such as production costs, the type of competition, and the trading structure of the sector need to be incorporated into the analysis. Why not take as a field for analysis the very symbolic one of colas? Colas as a commodity have succeeded remarkably in 'decommoditisation', unlike other soft drinks. They are also the market in which the largest brand in the world, Coca-Cola, operates.

What is a soft drink? In a material sense it consists of water, flavourings, a sweetening agent and carbonate. In the fruit juice market, brands are having a hard time: in Germany, hard-discount labels hold more than 50 per cent of the market. The same process is taking place in the UK and all over Europe, where unlike in the United States, distribution is very concentrated and discount labels do not mean poor-quality products. The problem faced by brands is how to differentiate a product like orange juice that seems generic. In addition, the raw cost of orange juice is high: this creates pressure on the margins, and as a consequence on the level of advertising

Table 3.1 Consumer price (in euros/litre) of various orange-flavour drinks in Europe

Brand	Price
Hard discount Carrefour Standard	0.25
Orange juice	0.70
National brand	0.84
Sunny Delight	1.08
Tropicana	2.45
Tesco Finest	2.50

budget affordable, when selling prices are under pressure from retailer own-labels and unbranded generic products.

In the fruit juice market, there are not many ways of finding a favorable economic equation. Tropicana follows a premium price strategy, based on permanent product innovations (freshly collected oranges for instance) and a premium image. These are value innovations, increasing the price paid by consumers per litre. It is the premium market leader, and a global brand, but in each country it is a small player in volume.

As always, Procter & Gamble followed a high-tech approach to differentiate its product. It introduced Sunny Delight as a competitor in the fruit juice market although it has almost totally artificial ingredients (there is only 5 per cent orange in it, for legal reasons). These created a taste and texture that beat all the competitors using natural fruit juice. It also added vitamins to appeal to mothers. Thanks to its name, its colour (orange, and variants for the different flavours) and logo (a round sun), Procter & Gamble created an innovative product, which was reminiscent of orange juice and was certainly thought by some consumers to be orange-based. Its artificial chemical formula is patentable, which creates a barrier to entry and prevents it from being directly copied. Most important, it is priced high, whereas its raw material cost is far lower than that of natural orange juice.

Coca-Cola is an opaque product: almost black, mysterious, with a secret formula, it created from the start the conditions, both real and psychological, of a product that is not fully substitutable. Also, since it is an invented rather than natural product, the brand became associated with the product, which can be described by no other name. It has since become the reference product for an entire genre of cola drinks. Benefiting from the pioneer advantage, throughout more than a century the Coca-Cola brand has pursued one single objective, now on a worldwide scale: to continue to grow the cola category. It was in competition first with sodas in America, then with other soft drinks, and now with virtually all other types of drink, including water in Europe or tea in Asia.

Coke's brand essence is 'the refreshing bond between people everywhere'. In making its brand the number one drink in the world, it benefited from being made from a syrup that is easy to transport at low cost, with high efficiency (that is, it can be highly concentrated, so many litres of Coca-Cola are produced from a single litre of concentrate) and remarkably high resistance to temperature and time (it can be stored for a long time, anywhere, unlike most fruit-based soft drinks). It is definitively a great physical product. In addition, the tuning of its acidity/sweetness ratio is optimal so customers can drink many glasses or cans in a row without being satiated. The cola syrup itself is very cheap to produce, thus allowing high margins and as a consequence high marketing budgets to reinforce its top-of-mind position (a key competitive advantage in this low-involvement category, where the buying decision is based on impulse). It is resold to bottlers at five times its production price, so profit can be located at the company level and pressure can be exerted on bottlers/distributors to pursue a high-volume strategy if they want to be profitable.

To grow the business through the expansion of the category, the strategy rests on three facets, which are always the same:

availability, accessibility, attractiveness, in that order. Most people focus on communication, but the key of Coke's domination is in these three levers:

▌ Availability, the distributive lever, comes first. 'Put Coke at arms' reach'. The aim is for people to find Coke everywhere: bars, fast-food restaurants, canteens, retailers, vending machines in streets and public places, refrigerators in offices, classrooms soon.... An essential point to appreciate is that building both the business and the brand image is tied to the active presence on premises. On-premise presence gives status to a drink, and creates consumption habits. In addition, unlike multiple retailers (Wal-Mart, Asda, Ika, Carrefour, Aldi and the like), which do not sell one brand exclusively, but their clients have the choice, on-premise customers do give exclusive rights, thereby granting a local monopoly to the brand. This is why Coke makes global alliances with McDonald's and other synergistic organisations. One condition of this type of exclusive deal is that the supplier provides, and the outlet agrees to stock, its full portfolio of soft drink brands. The goal is to create a barrier to entry to any soft drink competitor.

As part of competing on availability, one should not forget access to the bottlers: in many countries there are few good bottlers, and eventually one only. Controlling this bottler is a sure way to prevent competition entering the country. Conversely, it is a way to push competition out, as when the Venezuelan bottler that had formerly handled Pepsi decided to work for Coke. Within a day, Pepsi operations in Venezuela were closed.

▌ Accessibility is the price factor: 'In China, in India, sell Coke at the price of tea'. This is made possible by the low cost of syrup production, its easy transportability, and also the volume-based strategy. Economies of scale create another pressure on the competition, if not a total barrier to entry. Having located the profit at the company level (exactly as Disney Corporation does through licensing royalties, while some of its foreign entertainment parks are not profitable), the Coca-Cola Corporation can afford to have its local companies lose money for the sake of rapidly growing a high per capita consumption rate. In addition, to push competition out of the market (whether it is defined as cola drinks or more widely), the company exerts a high-price pressure on the whole market. For instance, it seems that specific prices on Coke are granted to trade distributors if they give preference to the company's other brands, such as Fanta, Minute Maid and Aquarius. This is why the Coca-Cola Company is now being sued by the European authorities on charges of anti-competitive manoeuvres.

▌ Attractiveness is the third factor: it is the communication issue. Although Coke's advertising is conspicuous, non-media communication (relationship, proximity, music and sports sponsorship, and on-premise communications) represents the main part of the budget. Share-of-mind domination is made possible, let us remind, by the low production cost. Last but not least, Coke's image is not that of a product but of a bond: it delivers both tangible promises (refreshment) and intangible ones (modernity, dynamism, energy, American-ness, feeling part of the world) which make it so special, much more now than its secret formula.

Coca-Cola's main challenger worldwide, Pepsi-Cola, is following exactly the same brand and business model. Its differentiation is based on the fact that it was introduced more recently than Coke, and did not create the category. As a challenger, its brand image and market grip are lower. It challenges the leader on three facets: price, product and image:

▌ Price: it is a dime cheaper than Coke, at consumer level, but this creates a higher pressure profitability.

▌ Product: since it is not the referent, Pepsi is more daring and permanently works on the product to beat Coke on palatability and taste (the 'Pepsi challenge'). Its formula is actually preferred to Coke in most blind tests. It pushed Coca-Cola Corporation to make the 'marketing blunder of the century' launching New Coke in 1985 to replace the classic Coke, the water of the United States. More innovating by necessity, it practised line extensions such as Diet Pepsi well before Coke.

▌ Image: Pepsi is younger than Coke. Capitalising on the only durable weakness of Coke, its advertising positioning makes Pepsi the choice of the new generation. Pepsi's essence is 'the soft drink for today's taste and experiences'.

To secure a presence for Pepsi-Cola on premises and circumvent the barriers to entry created by Coke, the Pepsico Company had to diversify into restaurants and fast-food chains.

Other rivals to Coke have had an even harder time. In February 2000, Richard Branson of Virgin admitted defeat in its war against Coca-Cola and Pepsi in the United States, less than two years after he rode into New York's Times Square in a tank to launch his challenge. On reviewing the brand and business model that is common to both Coke and Pepsi, it is easy to understand why Virgin Cola failed everywhere but in the UK, its domestic base. Even there it won less than 5 per cent of the market. Brand is not enough.

Virgin Cola bought the Canadian company Cott's, which was able to make a very good syrup: it makes the cola sold under Loblaw's

President's Choice private label. It proposed a cheaper price than Coke or Pepsi. But Virgin Cola never got the distribution, it never accessed the consumer. Branson's whole idea was to save on advertising and thus make a cheaper price possible by taking advantage of the Virgin umbrella brand. Unlike the two world-leading carbonated soft drink companies, which both follow a product brand policy (one brand per type of flavour), Virgin's only brand asset is its core brand, which has been extended to all types of category (see Chapter 12), and in the process gained extensive worldwide awareness. As well as a low volume of advertising and selling a large volume on promotion, Virgin had a small sales force, a sure handicap for trade marketing and store-by-store direct relationships. Finally, Virgin Cola was not able to work in the market without a full portfolio of soft drinks to support it. This is necessary to access the on-premise consumption sector, and is also the only way to make a true national sales force economically possible.

As a rule, extension failures are immediately attributed to some image-based reason that it is impossible for the brand to extend to the new category. The brand and business perspective shows us that this explanation is superficial. It was not the Virgin brand that was the source of the failure, but the fact that Virgin could not compete on the same brand and business model as its two Goliath competitors. Fairy tales are one thing, but most of the time David gets killed.

Virgin Cola failed to get enough distribution: in Europe, for instance, it never entered the main multiple retailers. It was not sold sufficiently in the fashionable bars and restaurants. To do better in distribution terms it would have needed a real sales force and a real portfolio of brands and products. Arguably it should have looked for alliances with soft drink manufacturers looking for a branded cola.

Without advertising, the cola was mostly sold on a promotional basis. It is questionable whether that creates the basis for a long-term preference. Also, Virgin wanted to be perceived as the anti-Coke cola. However throughout the worldwide market this role already belonged to Pepsi. Finally, is the Virgin brand image that strong among the young generation outside the UK?

What other brand and business model could exist in this sector? At this time, two alternative models are surviving: ethnic colas and colas dedicated to trade. In its edition of Sunday 12 January 2003, the *New York Times* published an article, 'Ire at America helps create the Anti-Coke'. This announced the creation of Mecca Cola by a young Tunisian-born entrepreneur. He targeted it at the Muslims of France and soon of other countries. This brand had two strengths. The first was immediate goodwill in the Muslim community: its identity is based on a real feeling of community and resentment against what is felt as an imperialist drink and brand. The second was an immediate presence in the specific channel of distribution held by this community, innumerable small convenience stores that open long hours.

It is too early to judge its success, since this will only be evidenced by long-term durability. However, sales are skyrocketing. Interestingly, other colas have burgeoned, based on the same approach: they capitalise on religious, ethnic or geographical feelings of community and identity. For instance there are Corsica Cola and Breiz'h Cola (sold in Brittany), aimed at two regions with strong identity and even independentist movements. This model can be reproduced elsewhere: Irish cola? Scottish cola? In the era of globalisation, regional identities are revived to resist what is perceived as a loss of essence, soul, and quality of life. Such attempts access local distribution or the local stores of national multiple retailers. No store owner or manager wants to take the risk of hurting the local feelings of the community living around its store.

Monarch Beverage Company has created an interesting alternative brand and business model. It is totally trade oriented, thereby securing access to modern distribution, worldwide. However it is not simply providing cola for retailers own labels. This is a true branding approach.

The problem for multiple retailers is to get free from the grip of Coke and Pepsi. Unfortunately, with some exceptions (Sainsbury's Cola in the UK, President's Choice Cola in Canada), market shares of own labels remain very small. This is probably because compared with the real thing, private labels look like faked cola. Parents who buy own-label colas to save money risk being criticised by their children. Private labels have no image in a category that has been decommoditised by brand image. Coke's identity encapsulates the American dream, authenticity and pleasure. Pepsi has the same associations, although to a lesser extent, and also means youth. Own-labels create no such value in the eyes of the young heavy consumers. They create bad will.

The Monarch Beverage Company was created in Atlanta, USA, by two former Coca-Cola marketing VPs. With the help of a former Coca-Cola chemist, it knew how to produce a good cola syrup. Most important, instead of focusing on the end-consumer (the mistake of Virgin) and running the risk of having no access to mass distribution, it focused on the customer problem: to increase the share of its own label with profit. Even if they were given away free, own-label colas would not be consumed: they lack authenticity, a reassurance on quality and taste, and fail to deliver the right intangible values. Monarch has created a portfolio of brands, all looking American (like 'American Cola'), and coming from a true American company based in the Mecca of colas, Atlanta, close to Coca-Cola's own headquarters. These brands, owned by Monarch, are granted under licence to multiple retailers. Each mass multiple retailer therefore has its own brand, different from its competitors', for its operations worldwide. Carrefour for instance has American Cola. The syrup is made by Monarch to match each retailer's specifications. The company provides the brand and the product; it leaves its customers totally free to manage their own bottlers, prices and promotion. No national sales force is needed: negotiations are carried out at the corporate level, with the category global manager.

This in-depth comparison of alternative brand and business models has illustrated the benefits of enlarging the perspective on competitive strategies, beyond communication and brand image. Brand leadership is gained through the synergy of multiple levers within a viable economic equation. Thus is the true condition of brand equity.

4

From private labels to store brands

Each day brings fresh news of the expansion of distributors' brands. On 28 November 2006, Carrefour launched its mobile phone range under its own brand, while praising the capabilities of its Orange network, aiming to turn it into a tool for creating customer loyalty that would itself be profitable and a channel for growth. The offer was carried by the 218 hypermarkets under the Carrefour name, visited by one million clients every day.

This is not an isolated phenomenon. Distributors' brands are on the rise every-where, and now dominate the market in many so-called mass consumption categories. For example, in France the market for self-service packaged ham is 400,000 tonnes a year. The hard-discount circuit alone, without national brands, sells 100,000 tonnes. In large and medium-sized stores 300,000 tonnes are sold, of which two-thirds, or 200,000 tonnes, are 'low-cost products' under the store brand. There are only 100,000 tonnes remaining for the major brands: Fleury Michon, Herta (Nestlé), Madrange, Sara Lee, etc. In Germany, 45 per cent of organic products are sold under distributors' brands (Jonas and Roosen, 2006).

Having been restricted for so long to the mass consumption sector, distributors' brands are now part of the competitive environment in all sectors: even the mass prestige products store Sephora has undertaken a voluntary policy of own-name products over the past three years. Distributors' brands are also found in automobile equipment (the Norauto tyre is the biggest seller in France), agricultural cooperatives, pharmacy groups and so on. For so long merely the cheapest products, they have now become innovators which are quick to offer consumers products that keep pace with the latest trends in society (organic farming, fair trade, exoticism, gourmet dishes and so on), following in the footsteps of the Monoprix and Sainsbury's brands. In many cases, these have become inseparable from the store: thus Picard stores sell only the distributor's brand. Clients go to Picard and buy Picard. The Body Shop, now part of the l'Oréal family, sells only its own distributor's brand. Gap began life as an exclusive retailer of Levi Strauss, stocking jeans in all sizes, but changed its strategy when discount arrived in the United States. Now Gap only sells... Gap, an action that seems to have inspired Decathlon. Other examples include Ikea,

Habitat, Roche and Bobois, Crate & Barrel and William Sonoma. Marks & Spencer's has done the same since its inception.

In the B2B sector, distributors' brands and low-cost products are also present: it is true that Asian companies are competing to supply them. Thus a Facom key for a mechanic costs €10, but only €3 if made in Taiwan. Bubbendorf, the famous blind maker, now has the tubular motors for the electric automation of its blinds manufactured in Asia. Until recently, it installed automations by Somfy, the market leader: now it is its main competitor. In the office furnishings market, Office Depot and Guilbert have based their success on distributors' brands: apart from the so-called obligatory products (certain Pentel products, Stabilo Boss, Post-It, Staedtler, Dymo, Bic) they sell only the products of their own brand. And is there not something paradoxical about the way that the same big companies that complain about the rise of distributors' brands, then buy the Niceday brand from their Guilbert supplier instead of buying major branded products? In short, they are criticising consumers for doing what they are themselves doing: managing their spending.

Evolution of the distributor's brand

Academic studies have until recently failed to pay sufficient attention to distributors' brands. With the producer's brand being considered as the only point of reference, distributors' brands were thought of as 'non-brands', attracting price-sensitive customers. Moreover, the distributor's brand has been even less extensive in the United States than in Europe. In fact, in the United States, with the exception of Wal-Mart, no distributor dominates: distribution is regional, and the national brands still have power in the distribution channel. This is why distributors'

brands have long been perceived in the United States as low-cost, low-quality alternatives, an assessment that failed to take the full measure of the phenomenon.

It is revealing that the latest book published in the United States about distributors' brands (Kumar and Steenkamp, 2007) chose 'private label' and not 'trade brands' as its title: the notion of 'private label' categorises the distributor's brand as a thing apart, and not using the word 'brand' therefore fails to account for the true reach of distributor's brands. They are indeed brands in the eyes of consumers, who are now loyal to them, even if, as will appear, they are not brands like the others. However, this situation has recently changed, as can be seen from a recent interview with Russ Klein, the executive director of 7-eleven, the store that invented the convenience store concept some 79 years ago, He attests, 'Private label has changed to the point where retailers are using it as the premium brand in some cases' (quoted in *Marketing Management*, July–August 2006). Tesco is an example of this.

At Tesco, the number one distributor in Britain, a survey of the fruit juice aisle is revealing: far from being a product, the distributor's brand is in reality a segmented range, from the lowest possible price (Tesco Value), priced at €0.33 per litre, to €1.84 for the top of the range, under the label 'Tesco Finest'. Tropicana's product, by the way, is sold at €1.62 per litre.

In fact, distributors are well schooled in distributors' brands. They:

▪ allocate the majority of their shelf space to them, eliminating all weaker brands;

▪ have segmented their portfolio of distributors' brands in order to meet the different expectations of their clients (a far cry from the 'Soviet' own brand, signalling the absence of choice) without forcing them to identify with the shop name (Wal-Mart named its men's clothing range George);

segment their range in order to cover not only different price levels, from the cheapest to the highest price on the entire shelf, but also the emerging needs known as 'trends' (such as Tesco Fair Trade, Tesco Organic and Tesco Healthy Eating).

The distributor's brand, managed with strength and ambition, in this way contributes to the store's reputation. However, as we shall discover below, the brand issue for the distributors has shifted: the question now is to turn the store itself into the brand.

Throughout the world, the distributor's brand is often becoming the only true competitor to the producer's brand, when it is not the shelf leader in volume. Too many brand managers have not yet accepted this reality: their brands are in a minority. Their enemy is not the other 'big' brand, but the distributor's much cheaper products, with an increasingly comparable quality level. To make things worse, on hypermarket and supermarket shelves we find the producer's brand, the distributor's brand and now the lowest-price products, 60 per cent cheaper. This further heightens the urgency to act (Quelch and Harding, 1996) and position the major producer's brand firmly and squarely on its pillars of differentiation: innovation and quality on the one side, and emotional added value on the other.

Distributors' brands occur in all countries, from the richest and most developed to developing countries. In Eastern countries, low-cost products and hard discount are growing rapidly. However, the hard discounters were also a bolt from the blue for mass distribution in the highly developed countries of Western Europe: their growth in France stabilised only this year. And yet these are rich countries.

The distributor's brand is thus not a phenomenon linked to low income. In Switzerland – which has one of the highest per capita incomes in the world – the leading food brand is Migros, well ahead of Nestlé. This is hardly surprising, as Migros is a dominant

distributor: every village has its own Migros store. Migros – without exception – sells only Migros products. The citizens of Germany, Europe's most powerful country, enjoy their luxury cars, but they buy most of their food from the Aldi and Lidl hard discounters, which also – almost without exception – sell only exclusive private-label products. It is hard to imagine that the Germans would buy poor-quality goods. Loblaw's, a Canadian chain, has built its reputation on its President's Choice brand. The story is the same at Carrefour, Albert Heijn in Holland and Ika in Scandinavia.

Distributors now manage their brand portfolios as part of an overall vision for the category and for the store. They have to choose their 'brand mix' for each category segment, and make a decision with regard to the type of brand to offer: producer's or distributor's brand? The latter may offer either ranges of economical products, a value-for-money line (often in the distributor's own name) or own brands (private labels) offering more flexibility in terms of positioning – perhaps even genuinely premium positioning.

It is true that within the meaning of the catch-all term 'distributor's brand' there are distinctions to be made between very different realities. Two axes give structure to all the distributor's products or brands: the level of value added, and the relation to the store (see Figure 4.1).

In terms of added value, at the bottom of the scale are the low-cost products, hastily designed by mass-distribution multiple retailers to counter the breakthrough of the so-called 'hard-discount' German stores (Aldi and Lidl) and their French counterpart (Ed). These products are the result of a minimalist conception of quality: low-cost sardines have the legal right to be called sardines, but make no pretence at anything more. Their low price is obtained through the purchase of the cheapest sardine lots in fish auctions the world over. Low-cost gingerbread contains

Figure 4.1   Relative positioning of the different distributors' brands

not one gram of honey. This should not be confused with the business model of the hard discounters such as Aldi and Lidl, which established precise quality specifications with industrialists, aiming to obtain decent quality despite the rock-bottom prices, via economies of scale pushed to the extreme: the manufacturer recruited will produce only one reference, in astronomical quantities. At the other extreme of added value, we find products such as Tesco Finest, for example fresh fruit juices made less than three days earlier and with a limited shelf life (without preservatives) and Monoprix Gourmet, which, as its name suggests, offers products with high experiential value. In the United States and Canada, the President's Choice line from Loblaw's aims high in terms of quality, as its name suggests.

In terms of nominal relationship to the store, a distributor's brand may either carry the name of the store or its own name: one or the other. Thus, at Carrefour, there are 'Carrefour products', Tex (for textiles) and BlueSky. Of course, intermediate situations do exist, where the store endorses its own products: all Auchan products aimed at children are signed *Rik et Rok*, but the Auchan logo is clearly visible on the front of the packaging.

We thus arrive at the matrix shown in Figure 4.1. The store does not impose its name

directly:

▌ when its insufficient reputation is a handicap for product sales;

▌ when the badge function of the consumption does not fit the presence of a generalist distributor (for example wine or textiles);

▌ when the level of added value of the products is too low and could reflect negatively on the store: for example, at Carrefour low-cost products are labelled No. 1 or Eco, without any mention of Carrefour.

Why do Leclerc hypermarkets have no store brand with their name? I organised a seminar on this theme with the managers of this group, and it appears that this has to do with the company's culture and its historical legacy. Leclerc was conceived and grew up as a discounter of major brands. Signing its products Leclerc would not fit with this vision of the company's *raison d'être*. Nevertheless, customers have clearly realised that *Marque Repère* (Marker Brand) is Leclerc's distributor's brand. In this regard it is interesting to note that this brand is itself named 'brand', and uses at its second name the ontological function of any brand: to serve as a reference marker.

Other terms are used to denote the forms of distributors' brands:

▌ The **own brand** or **private label** is a distributor's brand that has its own name and does not generally refer to the company's name (for example Miss Helen for cosmetics at Monoprix, or Jodhpur for textiles at Galeries Lafayette).

▌ The **counter brand**: this word designates a distributor's brand, generally a private label, created to divert clientele from a particular big brand, by slavishly imitating all its distinctive traits in order to play on client confusion and the psychological principle according to which everything that looks very much alike is in fact very similar. Thus each company creates its counter brand to Ricoré – Calicoré, Incoré, etc – with packaging similar in all respects, placed just next to the national brand on the shelf.

▌ The **positioning brand**: these are ranges that, far from being content with offering the best quality/price ratio, position themselves on trends or in the premium segment. Take for example the Monoprix brands, such as Monoprix Bio (organic), Monoprix Equitable (fair trade), Monoprix Gourmet.

Certain stores use their name in all segments: Figure 4.1 shows how the highly respected British company uses its name Tesco both for low-cost products (Tesco Value) and for the top of the range (Finest) and niches and trends (Tesco Healthy Eating). Capitalising on a single name makes the customer's job easier, and profits the store, but of course means that high standards must be achieved in all segments, even at low prices. French stores prefer not to run the risk to their reputation, and do not use their name on the cheapest products.

Are they brands like the others?

The big brands have long regarded distributors' brands with condescension, and would deny their new type of products the sacred title of 'brands'. That would call their historic hegemony into question, a kind of *lèse-majesté*: until now, the big brands have led the field and dominated it. For them, stores were distributors, a revealing term, since it refers more to logistics and transport than to a talent for composing an overall offer, for stage-managing the shelves, for business through optimisation of the upstream and downstream. This is why, moreover, stores insist on being called retailers. The rise of the distributor's own brand (DOB) is all the harder to accept since it signifies the end of a particular type of marketing (see page 139): it therefore leads to questions that go far beyond the problems of gaining market share, of which companies have not yet taken the full measure.

In order to answer the question of the exact nature of the distributor's brand, we can examine either their management, or their status among buyers.

Is the distributor's brand managed like a manufacturer's brand?

From a managerial point of view, distributors' brands are, broadly speaking, brands like any other. They have all the features of a brand (thinking of a particular target, selecting a principal competitor whose clients they will attempt to steal, defining an offer and a price, setting themselves up with packaging and communication) but in addition they have to respond to two different constraints simultaneously. They have to find their place in the distributor's marketing mix, in which they now represent a key component of identity, differentiation and loyalty generation (although the effect on customers' loyalty to the store has not yet been proven: see

Corstjens and Lal, 2000). And they generally use price as the driving force behind their own marketing mix, even when, exceptionally, they are positioned in a premium segment.

For this reason, management of these brands does not have the same autonomy as a producer's brand. Their image positioning is based on that of the company. As for their price positioning, it is generally relative, set between the two client benchmarks of the big brand prices and hard-discount product prices.

In formal terms, the distributor's brand often takes on the form of the umbrella brand: Carrefour products, or Auchan or Tesco products. Admittedly, there are also private labels that make no reference to the store but present themselves as isolated, thematic brands. The hypermarket chain Intermarché has its own boats and factories: it sells seafood under the Captain Cook brand, and its processed meats under the name Monique Ranoux. Carrefour sells a range of over 100 regional products under the brand *Reflets de France* (Reflections of France).

To concentrate on the store brand, also known as the banner, since it capitalises on the reputation of the store's name to define a tangible offer at the product level, it typically covers a large number of products, or even shelves: through its extension, it brings a service of practicality to the customer, who can find it by passing from shelf to shelf. It functions like a common factor, a decisional marker across the store.

The manufacturer's brand, on the other hand, signifies competence: its extension is therefore necessarily more limited (see Chapter 13). Fleury Michon, the French specialist in processed meat and fresh delicatessen products, would not dream of selling jam. The maker's mark has a trade, an expertise, and a *savoir-faire* that underpin its progress, materialised through innovations.

This does not mean that a distributor's brand may serve as an umbrella for anything and everything. We shall see (in Chapter 13)

that this should be carried out based on a category that creates reputation (the prototype) first and foremost for those products that are considered to be close to each other, because they are either complementary or substitutable. Bringing everything together under the umbrella of a name is not an end in itself: the brand is there not to save money, but to create value for customers. From this point of view, it is revealing that the big supermarkets develop a portfolio of umbrella brands, in order to cover the whole scope of their offer while also seeking the level and type of client involvement (Kapferer and Laurent, 1988). At Monoprix Miss Helen is the feminine beauty and hygiene brand, just as at Wal-Mart George is the male clothing brand. In contrast, Monoprix aims to associate its name with emerging consumer trends: organic, sustainable development, gourmet, openness to the world, healthy eating, etc in the form of 'line brands', as does Tesco (healthy choice, organic, sustainable development etc).

This cross-cutting status of the distributor's brand explains the difficulty of managing the store brand entirely like a brand. In fact, there is no brand without positioning: thus at Carrefour First Line was the brand of the most recent progress in television, hi-fi, white goods and computing, at the cheapest price. Among the big distributors, it is still often the purchasers and not the marketers who have the power. The former, and this is their key strength, react by seizing opportunities (an exceptional lot of goods here, filling a gap in the range there), and by optimising the difference between the purchase and the sales price.

The marketing viewpoint is to install the necessary brand coherence, which goes far beyond the logo, in all the aisles. The brand must not depart from its positioning, its platform (same price range, same level of technology, etc). These two points of view are on a collision course. Often the store brand is asked to put its name to products that are not entirely in line with its positioning in order to avoid having to create an individual marque for them. Moreover, the distributor's brand is subject to the vagaries of sourcing. To return to First Line, this brand never took off, since easy as it is to imitate the top-of-the-range Bonne Maman jam, it is difficult to offer high-definition plasma screens at low prices. There are simply no suppliers in the high-tech market to deliver such products. This is why at the end of 2005 Carrefour decided to put an end to First Line, and retained only its lowest-price brand, BlueSky.

It is impossible to talk about brands without touching on the question of innovation. In fact, the function of the national brand, the big brand, is to supply progress through innovation, change, fashion, design and so on. This requires marketing expertise – long-term thinking on the expressed, or latent and unconscious, expectations of future clients. They also have the expertise of the major industrialists. Thus in 2006, Fleury Michon, in accordance with its brand charter, launched hams without preservatives, since these are the future, even if today's customer is not aware of it. To be a brand is to be a leader, to look far into the client's future. Eliminating the chemical preservatives implies replacing them with natural preservatives: it took three years of R&D to find bouillons to carry out the same preservative function. Some years previously, during the mad cow crisis, Fleury Michon was able to innovate in offering ham steaks. It is also the brand of turkey ham, and other unusual products.

Does the distributor's brand also innovate? No, since it does not have the means to do so. Its business model assumes light marketing – in order to reduce the costs linked to the dozens of product heads –and the fact that it follows quickly in the wake of what is already working, that is the innovations of the successful manufacturers, by copying them to within a few details. In fact, the product specifications of subcontractors tasked with manufacturing a distributor's brand product are up to 80 per cent defined by the characteristics of the successful product to be imitated. If Henkel invents tablets to replace washing powder, the DOB must then manufacture identical tablets. According to the stores, the remaining 20 per cent of the specifications will be a way of providing differentiation linked to the store's own values. However, in order to be able to appear quickly on the shelves with an identical offer at a 30 per cent lower price, it is necessary to economise on marketing and R&D: the distributor's brand business model is that of copying, of imitation taken to the maximum.

A common riposte is that distributors' brands were the first to introduce such and such an innovation in terms of packaging: for example, turning shampoo bottles upside down, in accordance with their actual position in the bathroom. However, the distribution brand, by the very construction of its economic model, does not seek to innovate: its price is obtained through turning the efforts and investments of the manufacturer's brand to its advantage, profiting from its strong position in the relationship, which means that the manufacturer needs the store far more than the store needs the manufacturer. Upon the launch of new food, hygiene and maintenance products, the mass distribution stores today request immediate access to the same innovation for their own brand.

The examples most often given to prove that distributor's brands can innovate are *Reflets de France* and *Escapades Gourmandes* (Gourmet Escapades). We know that this revolutionary concept consists of revitalising the production of 100 regional recipes, having them produced by SMEs in these regions, and bringing them together under the same brand, sold in all the Carrefour Group's stores. From this point of view, *Reflets de France* is a true brand: an innovative concept, a target, a price positioning maintained for all products, a strong graphic identity, a high level of taste quality and an imaginary quality (nostalgia).

This example shows that, when the distributor behaves like a true brand, it opts for own brands, or becomes the store of the brand and not the brand of the store. For example, Gap, which was the exclusive seller of Levi's, began to introduce its DOB, and progressively ceased to sell anything but its own store brand products. However, it was then necessary to clearly define a brand concept, the store becoming the place where the brand was expressed and experienced. Gap defined the concept as anti-fashion. Decathlon does the same. It is symptomatic that in order to accentuate its status as a designer/manufacturer with its own stores, Decathlon gave up its store brand (there are no longer any Decathlon products) in order to organise everything under what it called 'passion' brands: that is, a portfolio of private labels. We present below this interesting case of a distributor becoming a designer.

Consumer relationships with distributors' brands

Let us now look at the question (are distributor's brands truly brands?) from the angle of the consumers themselves. For consumers in mature countries, distributors' brands are perceived as genuine brands, with their attributes of awareness and image always combined with an attractive price.

When asked the classic awareness question ('What are the yoghurt or bicycle brands that you know, even if only by name?'), consumers name Asda or Decathlon. When asked if they intend to buy them (general client opinion) or buy them again (behavioural loyalty), the scores are just as high. It is no accident that on the majority of mass-consumption shelves, lowest-price products and distributors' brands hold the dominant market share. Over time, some distributors' brands are able to achieve the typical brand effect, as shown by Table 4.1, which looks at the United Kingdom, for many years a leader in this field. According to the Brandz study, the consumer's proximity to

the brand moves from a feeling of presence (awareness, recognition) to a feeling of relevance (it's for me) to the perception of performance and a clear advantage, and ultimately to a genuine affective attachment. It is interesting to note that two distributors' brands have made it into the top 10 of English brands studied by Brandz: Marks & Spencer and Boots.

We might say, of course, that there is an affective transfer from the store to its products, a halo effect. Boots and Marks & Spencer are highly respected and historic stores in the United Kingdom, having created a relationship of reciprocal trust and esteem with their clientele over time. However, this halo effect is precisely the lever on which the distributor's brand is counting.

Table 4.1   Brand attachment: the 10 winning brands

1. Gillette	57	7. Nescafé	39
2. BT	56	8. Heinz	39
3. Pampers	53	9. Kellogg's	39
4. Marks & Spencer	42	10. Boots	37
5. McDonald's	42	11. Colgate	32
6. BBC	40	12. Royal Mail	32

Source: Brandz (UK).

Research carried out by one of our HEC doctoral students on the sources of engagement with the brand, depending on whether it is a producer's or a distributor's brand, throws brand-new and unprecedented light on the matter. C Terrasse (Terrasse and Kapferer, 2006) worked on four product categories, in order to compare engagement with the Carrefour brand with that for the big brand in the same category. Engagement with the brand means more than repeat purchase. Panel data has long shown that distributor products obtain repeat purchase rates (behavioural loyalty) as high as those of the big brands, or even higher. The same is true for engagement: the declared levels of engagement are high in both cases, for both DOBs and national brands.

Engagement – personal involvement with the brand – measures a strong relationship with the brand, meaning that if the brand were not there, the client would prefer to wait than buy an alternative. For the consumer, there is no substitutability. The reverse is indifference, or sensitivity to the slightest rise in price. This engagement comes from two sources. The first is attachment, measured here as a strong perception of proximity (the customer feels a closeness with the brand), and the second, satisfaction linked to a perception of difference in product performance.

As Table 4.2 demonstrates, what engagement with the store brand does is essentially to create closeness with the store. The reverse is true for the manufacturer's brand: their 'fans' are fans because of a strong experience of the product's superiority.

C Terrasse's doctoral thesis also examines the consequences of engagement with the brand. In theory, the more people are engaged with the producer's or distributor's brand, the less they will seek variety when shopping in this aisle, and the less sensitive they will be to the price. This is exactly what happens with the big brand: repeat purchase of the identical product results directly from the client's engagement with the brand and its reductive effect on two key factors of disloyalty (enjoying variety and being sensitive to price). For the store brand, engagement with Carrefour certainly influences the repeat purchase, and certainly diminishes the appeal of variety, but does not make the client insensitive to the price. This means that the repeat purchase of the distributor's brand is always contingent on the price: it is highly conditional. These shelves are now seeing the advent of lowest-price products. The repeat purchase rate of the

distributor's brand, although high, is essentially false loyalty (Kapferer and Laurent, 1996): the customer is always sensitive to the price, and keeps an eye on price differences on the shelf. It is not an absolute brand.

Nevertheless there is an interesting difference in the way a distributor's brand works, compared with the manufacturer's brand. As C Levy's research (in Levy and Kapferer, 1996) on the impact of distributors' brand trials on attitudes showed, the satisfaction created by a distributor's brand increases the credibility of all the distributors' brands, at least in terms of attitude. If a customer tastes Carrefour chocolate biscuits, which compete with the segment leader Pepito, and finds them to be excellent, it increases the possibility that they will also buy Tesco chocolate biscuits.

This is why distributors' brands have difficulty creating loyalty to the store, as is often observed in studies: admittedly they create repeat purchasers within the store, but they do not appear to offer discriminating reasons, or even overriding reasons for visiting one store over another. Nor does an examination of the reasons for purchase in people on the border of the two 'regular customer' zones find them appearing as the number one criterion. The distributor's brand therefore plays less of a role in differentiating itself from the competition than the manufacturer's brand, which works only for itself. These results have been shown again in very recent analyses (Szymanowski, 2007).

This does not mean that all distributors' brands are perceived to be equal: the image of the store (quality, cleanliness, popular or elitist character, and so on) reflects on everything that bears its name, therefore firstly on the distributor's brand.

Table 4.2 Determinants of attachment to distributors' and producers' brands

	Carrefour brand	Big brand
Satisfaction linked to perceived product superiority	0.161	0.539
Attachment, perceived proximity with the brand or store	0.601	0.236

Source: C Terrasse/J-N Kapferer, 2006 (correlation coefficients)

Why have distributors' brands?

In 2006, at the world's number one distributor Wal-Mart, out of a turnover of US$285 billion, 40 per cent was made from distributor's brands. This percentage is 60 per cent at Tesco, the fourth-largest distributor in the world, 35 per cent at Metro, but 90 per cent at Aldi, the king of the hard discounters. In the field of sports products, it is 51 per cent at Decathlon. Why do distributors come to set up their own brands, to the point that – like Gap or Picard – they eventually sell nothing else?

For an answer to this question, we should not look to the consumer, who is only too happy to have finally found a cheaper product. In reality, the true economic motor of the unstoppable growth of distributors' brands lies with the industry: the distributors and producers themselves.

In the mass consumption sector, the early distributors' brands are almost always born of a conflict between the distributor and the producer. Dissatisfied with the poor treatment it receives, the distributor has its goods produced elsewhere, in order to plug a gap, and sells them either under its own name or under a private label. The atmosphere of conflict persists, particularly since – in Europe for example – brands now typically depend on a very small number of distributor clients (four) for 60 per cent of their sales. Procter & Gamble makes 16 per cent of its worldwide turnover (US$51 billion) from a single client: Wal-Mart. In some sections the concentration is even higher: Decathlon accounts for more than 10 per cent of Nike's sales in Europe. Furthermore, these distributors' brands parallel the worldwide development of distributors, leading them to match the expectations of quality products at lower prices that are prevalent in emerging countries (Brazil, Eastern Europe, Russia, India and so on).

Consumers are selective. They decide in which categories they are the most tempted to buy distributors' brands: those in which they have a low degree of involvement (Kapferer and Laurent, 1995). Remember that brands exist wherever customers perceive a high risk in purchasing. Conversely, where they see no risk, they are tempted by the distributor's brand, particularly if they consider that distributor to have a good reputation and an image of quality. For example, the butter category is now dominated by distributors' brands. Three-quarters of all the processed meat sold in self-service stores in France is low-cost or distributors' brand products, but the same is not true of new food products, such as low-fat butters and unsalted hams, which suggests product development is a source of concern, and consumers need the reassurance of a well-known brand name. In all cases where the consumer expects superior performance (cosmetics, for example), the producer's brand carries the day. The same is true wherever the product has assumed the status of a symbol or 'badge': again, the distributor's brand fails to make an impression, except where it has become itself a declaration of self (the Gap is the anti-fashion).

Now, emboldened by satisfactory past experiences, consumers are taking the plunge: there are distributors' brands for PCs, €120 bicycles, hi-fis and domestic appliances. Consumers may want a Sony or Samsung television for their living room, but in the kitchen or in a child's bedroom they are less involved: they may be tempted by a BlueSky (Carrefour's low-cost hi-fi brand). The same is true for home computing. Dell is a product assembler, and sells under its distributor's brand. However, its products are guaranteed 'Intel inside'.

In reality, the distributor's brand is based on supply, not demand. Whenever distribution is concentrated, and the size of the domestic market makes it economically possible, there is no other way of increasing return on investment (ROI), as we shall analyse below. On the one hand, in the previously independent retail sector, as trade concentration progresses, the first step is to buy in bulk to reduce purchasing costs. Next, a collective commercial store name is applied (for example Bureau +, Qualipage). But if there is to be a collective name, there must also be a collective range: this forms the heart of the store's product range. The last step is a logical one; the distributor's brand – which only represents a small part of the offer to begin with – can only grow. It is an integrating factor.

Bear in mind that growth in distribution is achieved over time, through the elimination of competing channels or forms of commerce, followed by the competitors themselves. In this way, in Europe, small traders have vanished altogether in many categories, having been swamped by the supermarkets and the hard discounters; this was how the distributors first started to grow. Having reached the end of this path, distributors have turned to the international market and cost reductions: hence the fashion for cost-cutting techniques such as efficient consumer response (ECR) mode and trade marketing. The final stage is the distributor's brand as a means of improving ROI.

Finally, we should not forget what the major distributors sometimes call upstream marketing. The distributor's brand makes it possible for large stores to present themselves as objective allies of local and regional SMEs against the multinationals, since it is the SMEs that manufacture the distributors' brands.

Everyone knows that mass distribution does not always have a good image. The crushing of small businesses has contributed in large measure to the desertion of town centres, and of complete suburban zones: society as a whole is paying a steep price for this. In their eagerness to position themselves as the cheapest, the major players in distribution and their massive bulk buying have launched themselves on the world like hunting dogs, driven by a single idea: to always find it cheaper and import it as quickly as possible. This quest – with the approval of consumers

only too happy to save money in the short term – has led to the downfall of companies, entire sectors and towns, leaving thousands of workers unemployed. This social cost has passed largely unnoticed. The salaries in mass distribution are among the lowest in the country: the store owners are rich, but the prospects for salary increases for a cashier over 10 years are minimal, a situation dictated by the price war.

What has society gained from this frenetic competition between the major distributors? Conscious of the collateral damage for society, mass distributors make use of two levers to give themselves a clear conscience. Either, like Carrefour, they flatter national pride, since the company has exported itself worldwide (although this does not create more jobs in France), or like Leclerc, they present themselves as the defender of SMEs, the majority suppliers of distributors' brand products. Having been crushed by the multinationals, SMEs will be saved by mass distribution. We know that this is provisional, since this preference for SMEs derives from the refusal of the major industrial groups to produce DOBs. Where they do so, there are no SMEs. Now the question for all boards of directors of the major industrial groups is: why leave this market to the SMEs?

The financial equation of the distributor's brand

In a competitive market, the distributor's brand is a logical stage in the growth of a distributor. It satisfies the need to maintain ROI once all other approaches have been exhausted. Alternatively, it may have been the key differentiating component from the outset (as in the case of Ikea, Starbucks, Body Shop and so on).

Let us look again at the principle of ROI, in order to understand why the distributor's brand is an advisable step at a certain stage in a distributor's growth.

Net margin   = Gross margin – Costs

Stock rotation = Sales per square metre/
                 Investment per square
                 metre

ROI   = Net margin × Stock rotation

What does a distributor do when it wants to increase ROI from 20 per cent to 22 per cent (an increase of 10 per cent of the current ROI)? Suppose that this is a major distributor with a net margin of 2 per cent and a stock rotation of 10 per cent. Two possible options are available: either to increase sales by 10 per cent per square metre (giving a rotation of 11), or to increase net margin from 2 per cent to 2.2 per cent through selling private labels and demanding even more price concessions from brand producers, or a share of the profits from their advertising/promotional campaigns (which ultimately amounts to the same thing).

This second option – increasing the net margin – is a much easier way of increasing ROI: everyone knows how hard it is in a mature market to increase turnover per square metre. This is why all distributors are choosing, or will choose, the distributor's brand if they wish to make optimal profits. In fact, the first lever for improving ROI arises from the fact that the margin on DOBs is better than that on national brands (Ailawadi and Harlam, 2004).

The second reason for introducing a distributor's brand relates to the increase in negotiating power with the manufacturer. Not only does the distributor improve its margins on the DOB, it also receives better margins from makers of national brands, who wish to persuade it not to go further.

A third effect on distributor profitability induced by the introduction of DOBs relates to the increase in the number of innovations launched by the maker. Distributors receive listing fees on these products. Moreover, they are rarely low-price innovations (Pauwels and Srinivasan, 2004).

Finally, distributors hope that their distributors' brands will contribute to increasing loyalty to the store itself. In theory, these are products that can only be found there. Research carried out at HEC (by the author in 1998) demonstrates that this effect has not yet been proven. Among the reasons for loyalty to a store, the distributor's brand is almost never cited, except for stores that have developed distributors' brands with strong added value (Monoprix, Tesco) and have acquired a reputation of their own.

Why will distributor's brands increase still further in future?

Other parameters also explain why those distributors with distributors' brands will promote them still further: the hard-discount circuit. This form of commerce, based on a low-cost type of business model, saw remarkable growth between 1995 and 2006, offering prices 30 per cent lower than those of distributors' brands, close to home, with a new store opening every day in the town or shopping centre. It appears that the turnover per square metre of this form of distribution is now falling, or has at least stabilised since 2006: this is due to the lowest-price products that the bigger stores have had to learn to introduce onto their aisles en masse, in order to keep clients in the store. Now their unitary margin is lower.

In France, this has been compensated for by the goldmine of the Galland law: the backroom (deferred) margin of major brand products could not be passed on to the client – only the volume markdowns. This suppressed price wars among the brands, and even made it easier for prices to go up. This backroom margin, repaying the services of distribution, could amount to 40 per cent of the price charged.

Since 2006, a new circular has suppressed these negative effects of the Galland law: the distributor may reinject what it gained in backroom margin (above a 20 per cent threshold) in order to bring down retail prices. Since stores can no longer protect these margins, it is up to the DOB to protect them. That haven of non-comparability, the distributor's brand, is the only remaining path to recovering financial health. This is why the number of DOB references can only increase on all shelves.

How far can the distributor's brand go?

What is the optimum distributor's brand for a store? What fraction of sales, of the aisle, and of the shelf should it represent? The answer depends largely on the store's strategy – itself a function of the competitive situation and the margin provided by the producers of branded articles, in comparison with that offered by the distributor's brand.

Take Decathlon, for example. This store began, like many others, as a simple distributor of brands. Over time, the store's mission (to allow access to the pleasure of sport for the maximum number of people) proved easier to carry out through a greater control over product design and production planning, even purchasing the raw materials, although production is still subcontracted. Little by little, the Decathlon brand took control of aisles where brands were weak. However, it is forced to cohabit with well-known brands in sections such as running, tennis, skiing, and golf. Having become aware that a single, uniform brand harmed the desirability of the store itself and therefore the number of visitors, Decathlon abandoned its single brand in 1998 and exchanged it for a portfolio of passion brands. Today these brands represent more than 50 per cent of turnover. The store's deep desire is to become a major producer of sports brands, and therefore to always push its specialised brands through sport. Decathlon still needs major brands in certain sections, but less so in others. If its brands become genuine brands, it will have reached its objectives, following the

example of Gap, which passed from the status of a simple store to that of a store brand and finally to that of a pure brand with its own stores. This change was itself the consequence of an evaluation of the future profitability of the textile market for a brand distributor, at the moment of the opening of discount textile stores in the United States.

The part devolved to DOBs is therefore not the result of an optimisation, but the fruit of a voluntary strategy. Research has nevertheless analysed the impact of the increase in the DOBs' share of the offer on the frequency (measured as the average number of purchases per week in relation to the number of references offered) (Ilec, April 2006). For a small supermarket, the frequentation index is continually decreasing: it is 140 when the DOB offer is situated between 8 and 18 per cent of the overall offer, and 79 per cent when it reaches the segment between 47 per cent and 57 per cent of the offer. For a large supermarket, the same is true. For a small hypermarket (under 6,000 square metres), the frequentation index also falls as the share of DOBs increases, but over 20 per cent of DOBs, the frequentation index rises once more: it increases from 87 per cent to 99 per cent for a DOB offer rate of 22 to 29 per cent. For large hypermarkets, the frequentation index rises with the DOB range! The best frequentation (index 125) is found with an average DOB rate of 19 per cent, then the frequentation index falls again for any increment in the presence of DOBs.

The three stages of the distributor's brand

Once the decision has been taken, there are three stages in the business growth of distributors' brands: oblative, imitative and identity.

The first stage is known as reactive or oblative: historically, it results from the refusal of sale by the major industrialists. This is how many own-brand products are born. However, it is also strengthened through identifying gaps in the ranges of the major producers. A category management approach quickly identifies those segments where something should be offered to the client, but where the major brands have nothing to offer, since it is not their strategy. These gaps need to be filled.

The second stage is imitative: here, the distributor examines its competitors' distributor's brand ranges, and sets about imitating them, producing the same products typically supplied by its other competition. By means of this emulative method, the distributor's brand core offer is constructed, created from all the references common to all the distributors' brands. We should add that this is also typically a phase during which the distributor, for lack of investment in its own distributor's brand identity, chooses to imitate, trait for trait, the packaging of the brand products that it is targeting (generally the category leader). The objective of this copycat approach is clear: a deliberate intent to take market share from the big brands by allocating more space to one's own distributor's brand, a similar copy, and to increase the average price of the big brands in order to attract clients to the distributor's brand (Pauwels and Srinivasan, 2002).

This imitative or 'copycat' approach borders on trademark infringement, and sometimes gives rise to court cases by the outraged and wronged producers, complaining of either an infringement of their brand rights, or unfair competition (see page 270), or economic parasitism. A visit to the aisles of mass distribution is enough to note the striking similarity between the copy and the brand packaging. In most cases, however, disputes – arising from the overzealousness of the designers – are resolved amicably. Furthermore, the distributor takes refuge in the fact that the issue is not brand codes, but rather category codes. The real aim of this approach (the imitation of the essential attributes of branded product packaging), which dominates mass distribution, is to cause confusion,

profiting from the average attention span of the shopper in the aisle. Through lack of attention, the consumer may take the distributor's brand instead of the major brand product.

The InVivo company has actually calculated that, for mass consumption products, in hypermarkets, consumers spend 7 seconds on each purchase: speed matters to them. When there is intentionally strong resemblance between the packaging, a hurried buyer with an average attention span can be confused.

Our research into the imitation of brand packaging (trade dress) by distributor's brands (Kapferer, 1997; Kapferer and Thoenig, 1992) has shown that the unconscious recognition factors in the aisle were, in decreasing order of importance:

1. Colour.

2. Packaging shape.

3. Key designs.

4. Name, typography and so on.

This is exactly what distributors' brand products copy: Ricoré's packaging is yellow, and so Calicoré's. There is an image of a small Mexican on Pepito, the leader in biscuits for children. There is a very similar character on *Rik and Rok*, Auchan's children's brand, and so on.

As our results (shown in Table 4.3) demonstrate, where the private label copy/original product pairs are placed in decreasing order of resemblance, the stronger the perceived resemblance in trade dress, the more the consumer infers that the producer of the two products is one and the same – and the more confidence the copy inspires.

Another study has shown that the discovery of a quality distributor's brand created a less positive attitude towards to the leading brand. J Zaichowsky and R Simpson (1996) conducted consumer trials with Lora Cola, a distributor's brand imitating the appearance of Coca-Cola cans. The taste of the product

Table 4.3   How copycat resemblance influences consumers' perceptions

Rank of packaging resemblance	They are made by the same manufacturer (%)			I trust the private label (%)
	Definitely	Probably	Total	Yes
1 Panzani/Padori (pastas)	39	41	80	78
2 Martini/Fortini (spirits)	30	31	61	56
3 Amora/Mama (ketchup)	21	46	67	62
4 Ricore/Incore (coffee)	16	17	33	38

Source: Kapferer (1995a)

was manipulated in such a way that one section of consumers would find it very good, while others would find it bad. Among the latter group, the Coca-Cola evaluation, measured twice (before and after trying Lora Cola) did not change (5.41 versus 5.71). However, it did fall significantly in the case where the consumers liked the taste of the copy (falling from 5.67 to 5.22, or a drop of –0.45).

The third stage is the identity stage: the distributor's brand is used to capture market share from competitors. It becomes a genuine instrument of strategic differentiation, expressing the identity, values and positioning of the store itself. It should generate loyalty not just to itself (through its effect on the share of requirements), but also – more challengingly – to the store.

During this stage, the brand's power and management is no longer in the hands of the purchaser alone. The purchaser strives for an optimal mix of purchase and resale conditions. Making the brand into an instrument for shaping identity and positioning presupposes genuine marketing strategy, and also the construction of a range that reflects the brand's ability to communicate the distributor's own values and identity. Here, the trick is to effect the shift from purchase driven by confusion to one driven by preference.

In this situation, the distributor's brand holds key positioning importance, since its content and products express the values of the

(distributor's) store. To this end, it offers one or more components of added value, based on the ingredients, packaging, traceability, concept and so on.

This is generally the point at which brands appear for which the main sales argument is no longer price, but the concept itself. It is true that often they have no equivalent among the branded producers, for a simple reason: these are specialised by category, product or trade. For example, what producer could construct an umbrella brand around the concept of 'Pleasures of yesterday', bringing together more than a hundred of the best products from every region of the country, along with rediscovered recipes and method of manufacture? Nestlé would be incapable of doing this, as it does not produce oils, jams, biscuits and the like. The same is true of Unilever, Philip Morris and Danone. Carrefour, however, can: all it needs to do is promote the concept among small regional companies in each country where it operates.

The case of Decathlon

Few stores reveal as much about modern distribution as Decathlon and the key role that its own brands play in its growth. In a recent article, Anglo-Saxon academic research notes that the share of shelf space given over to distributor's brands among US distributors is less than among European distributors (Corstjens *et al*, 2006). The US distributors allocate shelf space according to a simple short-term profit equation. It is true that in the United States distributors' brands have a poor reputation, and are all considered 'sub-brands'. They do not allow for positioning of the store or the loyalty generation through attachment to the store. The situation is different in Europe and Canada, where, very early in their brand history, distributor's brands had a combative vocation: fighting not to launch a price war, but to offer the consumer genuine value. Just think of Migros, the dominant chain in Switzerland, which does not sell products by Nestlé, the world's leading food company with its headquarters in Switzerland, but rather Migros products. In this case, the long-term strategic dimension takes precedence in decisions on shelf space allocation: this is the best way to get consumers to try the product, and therefore to begin a cycle of loyalty generation.

In our view, the main difference between the approaches of the distributors themselves in the United States and in Europe is that, in the United States, it is a question of selling the store's brand alongside the big brands, whereas in Europe it is a question of making it the store of the brand, with a few other brands alongside it. Decathlon has now become a designer of brands that controls its own distribution. This is what differentiates it from the sports section of Wal-Mart or Sports Unlimited. Even its lowest-price products are labelled as 'best-price technical' products, to remind us that the ethics of sport forbid sacrificing everything for money: there is a threshold below which a football is no longer a genuine football in terms of quality and security. Others might sell it anyway, in order to maintain the image of always having the lowest price, but not Decathlon.

This process, which transformed the store into a brand, may also be illustrated by Gap. The Decathlon ideal is the same as Gap's – to reduce its main manufacturer brand (in this case, Nike) to 10 per cent of sales in the running department. This is already the case

in the camping department: all the rucksacks, sleeping bags, and tents are private label products. In order to succeed, Decathlon needs to do much more than buy and sell: it needs to innovate, design, establish its own production plans, and choose its own partners. This is why Decathlon is now the world's fifth largest producer of sports goods. Its business model is the integration of design/production/distribution.

Decathlon began life 30 years ago as a simple discount store. It sold all branded products, and only branded products, in all sports. Today, more than 55 per cent of its turnover is made on store brands, although, in accordance with its company culture, Decathlon never speaks of store brands, only of passion brands. The word 'passion' here is not a slogan, but a true understanding of the brand in sport. The sports brand is built first internally; it is a true culture. Then it is carried outward by those who are passionate about it.

Moreover, few stores take their own brands as seriously as Decathlon does. Decathlon shows how the organisation must be able to adapt to the brand, rather than the reverse. Finally, Decathlon enacts its brand policy worldwide, which is all the more challenging since Decathlon dominates its original market, France, by some distance, but is only just making its debut in China, where its products are produced, and has pulled out of the United States. It has 340 stores.

Decathlon's vocation is to give as many people as possible access to the pleasure of sport. The key values are vitality, truth, fraternity and responsibility. It is a low-cost operator, but one that has always favoured product quality over selling at the lowest possible price. Loyalty is not generated through prices, but through client satisfaction. At the same time, it is the best way of defending the chain against the entry of discounters from the food sector, such as Wal-Mart Sport. This policy is a success: in the bicycle sector, for example, not only is

Decathlon the brand that first comes to mind for French consumers, but in addition it is also the one that is necessarily taken into account when making the next purchase, with a consideration score double that of the first producer's brand (Raleigh or Peugeot Cycles).

The store was founded in 1976 by Michel Leclerq. It quickly took the distributor's brand option, capitalising on the strong name awareness of the Decathlon company, and its dominant distribution. Decathlon seeks the development of the largest possible number of its clients through sport. The store is positioned on the hedonistic side of sport, and designs very comfortable products, aimed at wellbeing, with emphasis on safety. It is a diffuser of pleasure.

The components of its success in France were like those of any store: the quality of its store sites, the range (that is, the choice of goods for 60 sports under the same roof), unprecedented low prices, remarkable computerised logistics that avoid stock breakdowns by supplying stores once or twice daily, young, helpful and competent salespeople, and finally the freedom to choose, with aisles so well constructed that customers could easily dispense with the salesperson. The defeat suffered in the United States also hinged on the fact that the majority of these success factors could not be implemented in the discount chain acquired, first among them being the site quality. Secondly, the US discount store was renamed Decathlon before the stores could be 'Decathlonised'. It is not easy in the United States, a country with low unemployment, to find passionate and motivated young people, genuinely attached to their store.

In 1999 in France, after 23 years of uninterrupted growth, for the first time in its history its turnover per square metre fell. The diagnosis was simple: the policy of a single brand, Decathlon, strongly emphasised in all its stores, together with its dominance of the national market, created a monopolistic situation and a 'Soviet-like' brand. Whether on the beach, on the ski lift, while hiking in the forest, everyone wore Decathlon-branded products. Customers increasingly got the impression of a lack of choice.

The strength of distributors, often family-type businesses, is their ability to take decisions quickly, and to enact radical changes. These are enacted in order to produce tangible, measurable results, allowing them to take the necessary corrective measures. This is what Decathlon did:

▪ It abandoned nearly 25 years of store brand policy, in France and abroad, to move towards a portfolio of brands segmented by sport. In order to create these brands, it began with the observation that there were 60 sports under Decathlon's roof. For each brand to reach critical mass and justify its overheads, a shortlist of 17 was drawn up, combined into seven finally. Then it was decided to increase this number, since modern sports are 'tribes' that cannot easily be brought under the same tent in the name of 'critical mass'. Thus Domyos was separated into roller sports and running. Tennis and golf were also separated, having previously been united under the common brand Inesis.

▪ These brands are autonomous, decentralised business units, with dedicated teams. Their goal is for each to become recognised leaders in its sport. Now three-quarters of the operational budgets are spent on the brands, with one quarter remaining for transverse tasks. Decathlon abandoned its historical organisation at Villeneuve d'Ascq in order to turn these brands not into labels on products, but forces for creative proposals at the best prices, based on passionate men and women. At Decathlon, semantics are crucial: these brands are named passion brands, not as a slogan or an advertising gimmick but as a profound reality, first internally, and then externally.

These brands need to be located close to where the sports are practised, so that the internal teams can live them out, and local opinion leaders can play a role in their creation: Tribord by the sea, Quechua in the mountains. They communicate independently of one another. For example, *Chulanka* is Quechua's magazine, distributed in stores: it circulates 2 million copies. This is the highest circulation of any of the mountain magazines.

The 15 brands are named passion brands because they are each entrusted to a passionate manager, who creates and carries them, with a dedicated team, on autonomous sites, with a genuine business plan and a high degree of autonomy. In the stores, the salespeople are also passionate. In time, the goods may be distributed beyond the flagship Decathlon store. In December 2006, Decathlon announced a historic agreement with independent ski equipment hire stores in the mountains. This very lucrative market had previously been locked up by the manufacturer brands. This will make it possible for skiers and snowboarders to try Quechua products in the stations themselves. The internet will be the medium for hiring: clients can reserve in advance and at low prices.

In order to build these passion brands, with imaginary qualities that are weaker than those of the major brands, the only thing that matters is product innovation and quality levels. This is why the Decathlon Group also invests in ingredient brands that lend credibility to the offer, becoming technological labels themselves. It is a question of prying open the vicelike grip on costs exerted by the technological brands such as Lycra, Goretex and Coolmax. For this reason, the ingredient brands of the Decathlon group are also autonomous business units, seeking to increase their opportunities outside the Group.

Decathlon's challenge is international. Decathlon is currently the 10th largest sports distributor in the world: the margin of progression is still strong. The brand policy described above is global. Decathlon's strength was built in France, progressively (over 30 years) using a different model – that of the single brand (Decathlon) which was also the name of the store. This contributed to creating enormous communication synergies.

The country manager's situation, for example in China, Hungary or the United States, will be very different. The start-up will be implemented with the passion brands: in China they represent 70 per cent of the range. However, the store is not known there, and will not have 20 years to build recognition. Therefore the pricing policy must be more discount-based. The name Decathlon, however, should no longer in theory be visible on the products, since they all now stem from one of the passion brands. The principle of the passion brand, as with any brand, is in fact autonomy. Only the back office cuts across all brands. This consideration, a pragmatic one at the international level, explains the maintenance of a 'Decathlon creation' brand inside the product, in order to establish the link between the store and its brands.

Factors in the success of distributors' brands

As always, the rise of a new brand is also the result of the actions (or lack of action) taken by the competition. For example, distributors' brands have strong market share in the cosmetics sector in Germany. The reverse is true in France, and yet both are among the more highly developed countries. Setting aside any possible differences between the two countries' relative conceptions of beauty, one explanation lies in an analysis of the competition. In France, l'Oréal has dragged all other brands into a war fought on scientifically proven performance, supported by colossal advertising budgets. In Germany the leading national brand is Nivea, which relies much more on empathy, softness and a close relationship than on the rational approach of proven results. We believe this explains why distributors' brands have found it easier to make inroads there: consumers have not perceived them to be all that different from Nivea.

Hoch and Banerji (1993) have analysed the factors behind distributor's brands' market share.

These are:

- the size of the potential market: the distributor opts for long production runs;

- the high margin in the sector;

- the low advertising expenditure;

- the ability to achieve quality (few or no patents);

- consumers' price sensitivity.

However, these authors also maintain that market fragmentation does not appear to constitute a barrier to the growth of distributors' brands.

Conversely, it is known that a factor that does affect the penetration of distributors' brands is the rate of innovation in a sector (measured by the share of new products in companies' turnover): it forces product ranges to be continually renewed, and is associated with a large amount of advertising. In fact, it is also the most natural reaction by producers confronted with distributors' brands: to increase their rate of innovation.

As has been observed, most of the factors mentioned above are linked to management deficits among the producers: insufficient rate of innovation, high margins, low advertising. When the brand is treated as a 'cash cow', the door is opened to distributors' brands. Moreover, many brand companies are willing to manufacture distributors' branded products. For example, the tyres at Norauto (a

chain of stores selling spare parts and services to motorists) are manufactured by the Michelin Group; it is inconceivable that they should be low-quality products.

In this way, the success of distributors' brands is linked to a supply effect (by strong promotion on distributors' shelves and the creation of 'me-toos' that ape big-brand products) but also by a lack of competitiveness from high-profile brands, which are too used to high margins, and do not innovate.

Lastly, this penetration depends on the specific range and category. It is strong in basic products, but no longer unique to them. Kapferer and Laurent (1995) linked the attractiveness of distributors' brands to consumers' degree of involvement, either in an enduring sense (interest in the product) or as a temporary feeling at the moment of purchase (Is the purchase a risky one? Does it have badge value? Will it give me pleasure?). It is therefore hardly surprising to find that the categories listed in Table 4.4 are those in which DOBs have the highest penetration.

Note that studies on distributors' brand customers have shown that their penetration has now reached all segments of the population. Nevertheless, there is a core target of people in reduced financial circumstances who have a low sensitivity to quality. In C Lewi's thesis at HEC (Lewi and Kapferer, 1996), even though they were given a biscuit that was objectively poor (in the light of results in blind tests), 18 per cent of these people decided to buy it anyway because it was cheap. Furthermore, these are the people who least noticed the difference in flavour.

Garretson's (2002) and Ajawadi's (2001) works provide an interesting new path for study: according to these authors, customers who resist distributors' brands are those who link price with quality. For these people, the price is the measure of the quality. It should be added here that hard discount itself finds its most frequent shoppers, and those whose average basket is fullest, among families with several teenagers still living at home.

Table 4.4   In which sectors do big brands resist trade brands and where are they defeated?

Sector	Big-brand share (%)	Sector	Big-brand share (%)
Make-up	99	Cookies	4
Hair colourants	98	Frozen vegetables	6
Baby food	96	Garbage bags	15
Chewing gums	92	Cotton wool	21
Shaving products	90	Fruit juice	23
Insecticides	89	Kitchen paper	25
Deodorants	89	Ham	26
Floor washing products	88	Pasta	35
Cola	82	Soft-drink concentrates	36
Tea	81		
Soups	81		
Beer, cider	80		
Laundry detergent	79		

Source : TNS sofres, 2007

Optimising the DOB marketing mix

The notion of a distributor's brand is therefore heterogeneous, offering the store a range of possibilities for getting its overall offer across. Research has analysed how each type of distributor's brand was able to increase its market share to the detriment of the leading brands of the segment, and also to reduce the price differential between the two, thereby boosting profitability (Levy and Kapferer, 1998). More than 500 mothers, in a simulated store, were presented with a choice between the leader in chocolate biscuits (Pepito by Lu/Danone group) and a distributor's brand. This choice varied from one customer to the next according to four criteria:

▌ presence or absence of the store name itself in the brand name (DOB or private label);

▌ whether there was a 'copycat' of the Pepito packaging, or clearly differentiated packaging;

▌ objective quality of the distributor biscuit (established through blind tests): identical or markedly inferior to Pepito;

▌ level of price difference with Pepito: index 50, 65 and 80.

The combination of these variables makes it possible to reproduce any form of distributor's brand currently active on this market. The key findings of this research were:

▌ The quality of the distributor product has a strong and positive impact on the intention to purchase the distributor product. It increases from 16 per cent when the product tasted is inferior to Pepito, to 34 per cent when it is equal.

▌ The store's reputation also has a bearing on the intention to purchase. When the store name is masked (private label strategy), the average intention to purchase is only 20 per cent. It increases to 30 per cent once the name is known.

It is the interactions, however, that prove most interesting in practice, as Table 4.5 demonstrates. Each line refers to a different form of distributor's brand:

▌ The first line concerns a DOB that carries the store name, therefore bringing its reputation into play, and packaging that is not a copy of Pepito's. It is acting like a true brand (reputation and differentiation and quality). What do we observe? This is where the demand for the distributor product is strongest (38 per cent). Furthermore, it is the strongest even though the price difference is less (20 per cent cheaper): therefore the profitability is maximal. Interestingly, the demand does not increase when the price is lowered (35 per cent cheaper); on the contrary, it decreases to 28 per cent when the price is lowered still further (50 per cent cheaper), probably as a result of the anxiety that this price arouses in mothers (this is a product for children, after all). The moral is that the DOB is most dangerous to national brands, and also most profitable, when it behaves most like a true brand.

▍ The second line shows a store brand copy: this is the most common form of a distributor's brand in the food departments of superstores. Here the demand only increases if the price decreases. Although it also reaches 38 per cent of pure demand, this time it is only at a rock-bottom price (50 per cent cheaper): profitability is therefore not as good as with the previous line.

▍ The third line is what is known as a 'counterbrand': the store name is absent, and the product is marked by an unknown brand (that is, a private label). Furthermore, its only option is to slavishly copy the packaging of the leader, in order to create confusion and allow clients to think that there is a similarity between the products, since the packaging is so alike. Demand follows an inverted U-shaped curve, with the best intention to purchase scores for the distributor product (31 per cent of intentions) at the intermediate price level (35 per cent cheaper).

▍ In the fourth line the store is unknown but the packaging is different from the leader's. Here the distributor's brand resembles a small, unknown brand, and the client has no point of reference for evaluating it. It is therefore not surprising that price is the only motivator: demand grows as the price falls. This is typically the case for lowest-price products, created to counter the products on the hard-discount circuit.

What can we draw from this analysis? When the distributor's brand behaves like a true big brand, it reaps the benefits (market share and profitability): however, it must have the will and the means to do so. Not everyone can be Decathlon or Tesco.

The real brand issue for distributors

As has been shown above, the distributor's brand is not a brand like the others. It is subject to three conditions: it must express the values of the store, position itself in relation to the big brands, and finally deliver a 'plus' compared with low-cost products. It is therefore more like a quality label attached to a price. To increase its financial results, it is certainly possible to increase its share of the shelf and have the goods appear in great

Table 4.5 Percentage of consumers who intend to buy the distributor's product

Brand and packaging type	Price gap from segment leader		
	−20%	−35%	−50%
Store brand (not copycat)	38	38	28
Store brand (copycat)	17	28	38
Private label (copycat)	26	31	27
Private label (not copycat)	21	24	31

numbers, which can give the impression of a Soviet store. It is better, however, to increase the client's preference for it. How?

Table 4.5 indicates how a better purchasing and promotion policy can contribute to this. Above all, however, it is necessary to sell it through greater brand strength. Since the distributor's brand carries the store name, value must therefore be created through the store itself, its positioning and its identity. Too many stores are devoid of meaning: they are businesses and nothing more. The hypermarket, like a cathedral, must decide which god it serves: the generic god of the consumer society, or an intimate desire on the part of the distributor to modify its relationship with its clients? For example, Carrefour venerates rationalism: its entire crusade is aimed at the enlightenment of the audience.

Remember that a big brand is built through the intangible: it is embodied in the tangible, and forms the basis of a durable relationship, a community of values among its clients. The first task that the store should set itself during this work is to identify its project, its vision: what in its customers' lives does it want to change? Although it will be necessary to compete on price, on choice and on service, it will also require an internal energy: this is found through the vision and the battle that the store takes as its own. What is the battle for most stores? When an organisation does not have critical mass, it is necessary to compensate through goodwill, and therefore through the power of the brand.

Once this has been defined, it must be implemented through 360 degrees, and not only through the distributor's brand products. For example, what service innovations will embody it in stores, and also beyond? It is these that will spark off word of mouth, turn customers into ambassadors and carry the brand's point of view.

In comparison to the weight and inertia of the multinationals, which can only innovate once they have confirmed that the innovation will be profitable because it can be

implemented worldwide, distributors must innovate more reactively. Of course technological innovation is beyond them. But customers do not expect it of them: on the contrary, it is their job to render customers' lives more pleasant, even more liveable. This is achieved through recognising that the customer segments are fragmented and that it is therefore necessary to adapt the distribution brand to this variety. Second, the distributors must be ahead of the curve on trends: it is up to them to lead in terms of ecology, organic produce, fair trade and so on. These are all profound movements that destabilise the status quo. The risk is much less for distributors: the distributor's brand should be segmented to fill these niches. This is how a close affective relationship is forged: client by client.

The brand-store must go further, into personal service. Remember the remarkable phrase of Howard Schultze, the founder of Starbucks. Asked about the success of Starbucks, which will soon have more outlets worldwide than McDonald's, he replied: 'We are not in the business of coffee serving people, but of people serving coffee.' Starbucks does not sell coffee to people – it is at their service, and serves them coffee, of good quality, in recyclable cups, using fairtrade coffee beans, in a peaceful, calm environment and with genuinely happy staff. It is easy to understand why Starbucks had no need to advertise: its customers took care of that. It is time to stop talking about 'distributors'; the ambition now should be to place 'life centres' at the customers' disposal, facilitating and stimulating places where they can also do their shopping.

'The tail does not wag the dog', as the proverb goes (it is the other way around). The real issue is to turn the store itself into a brand. Among distributors, the brand manager is no longer there to manage DOBs, but to ensure the coherence of all the brand project's activities. This presupposes that there is a brand project, with a vision, a mission, strong values that are felt internally, and implementation well beyond the store itself and the private label products.

Competing against distributors' brands

We are frequently asked, how is it best to compete with distributors' brands, which are – as their market share attests – the number one competitor of the big brands? Procter & Gamble Europe has long believed that it was competing against Unilever, Henkel or Colgate, old friends which share the same business model, the same cultural references, and even the same HEC MBA's. The consumer sees things differently. Moreover, it has been shown that an excess of price-based promotions created sensitivity to price and led consumers to try distributors' brand products, itself a preliminary step to trying low-cost products. There are different levels of response to the question above, some tactical, others involving a revision, not of the brand, but of the business model.

A precondition: do not tolerate brand imitations

In developed countries, brands fall victim to unfair competition on the part of distributors' brand products, in the form of imitations of their distinctive symbols. This imitation is anything but accidental, as the design and packaging agencies recruited for the purpose well know. The national brand product is used as a brief, not for what to avoid – according to good brand principles – but what the rival should most resemble. This is where competitors increase their 'me-too' product's chances of success, by closely imitating – albeit with a few differences – the characteristics of the targeted brand product, as well as its distinctive marks. To be considered as an unfair threat, the imitation must be likely to cause confusion in a consumer of average attentiveness.

Imitations can come either from competing producers, or from the product's own distributors – and the response must vary depending on the individual case. Most big companies would in fact be reluctant to take action against their distributor if they believed that one of its distributor's brand products, placed alongside one of their own branded products, was imitating it too closely and constituting an act of unfair competition. It is true (see page 78) that the second phase in the implementation of a distributor's brand policy is generally to imitate the targeted market leader on a shelf by shelf, reference by reference basis. It can even be the case that distributors' brands within a given group copy one another. Bicycles sold by Auchan superstores have borne an extremely close resemblance to a best-seller at Decathlon (the 'be-twin'): the two stores form part of the same group.

Actual legal proceedings against the distributor are rarer still. Big companies, many of whose products are stocked by the distributor, fear a Pyrrhic victory and prefer to build up a dossier with the aim of avoiding legal action and resolving disputes amicably. The dossier consists of a form of proof that could be produced as legal evidence if required, for it is in fact possible to devise a scientific approach to prove illegal imitation. Two methods exist.

The first works on the legal definition: the imitation is illegal if it is likely to create confusion in a consumer of average attentiveness. There are two techniques capable of demonstrating such a risk of confusion, without actually asking customers directly whether they would be confused by the copycat (an invalid method). The first is the use of a tachistoscope, which 'flashes' a picture of the copy at consumers, first at high speed, then at slower speeds. They are then simply asked to describe or name what they have seen (Kapferer, 1995b), and the number of times the copy is mistaken for the original is measured. The second method is to start with a computer-degraded image of the copy, and to build it up, step by step, using computer software. Consumers indicate what they think they can see on the computer screen (Kapferer, 1995a). These two techniques produce a working imitation of consumers of average attentiveness, either by limiting the length of their exposure to the product, and then increasing it (the tachistoscope) or by presenting low-resolution pictures (computer method) and steadily increasing the resolution. Using the first method, we have found confusion scores of 40 per cent.

The second approach ignores the legal concept of confusion. Indeed, although they pay lip service to it in their rulings, judges do not truly use the concept of confusion. Rather, they concentrate on excessive manifest resemblance. They pay more attention to resemblances and less to differences (as advanced by the imitator's lawyer). Objective proof of an excessive resemblance can be obtained by asking one group of consumers to describe the original, and then asking an identical group of consumers to describe the copy. An analysis is made of which aspects were mentioned first, second, third and so on, for each of the two products, and the level of agreement between the aspects stated first by each group.

Once these results on the reality of the prejudice have been obtained, contact with the distributor must be made at a high managerial level in order to emphasise the seriousness of the matter. Furthermore, this is the level at which long-term interests are best appreciated. The distributor needs big brands, a dynamic aspect to its store shelves, the value innovations the brands bring to the category and the margins they give the distributor. The manufacturer needs the distributor to gain access to the customer. At lower managerial levels, the producer–distributor relationship is more antagonistic. The outcome of such contact is the modification of the trade dress or packaging of the distributor's disputed products.

In general terms, brand management must plan for these phenomena and put the brand in a position to be able to defend itself strongly. Thus, in order for a brand colour to be defensible, the brand itself must also defend it internally. For example, the brand's product lines are very often segmented: this leads to the use of different colours to identify each segment. In this way, the ability to claim that the brand is characterised by a particular colour is reduced. Thus, if a Coke label is red, and a Diet Coke label is silver, red is no longer the colour of the Coca-Cola brand: after all, when producing their own colas, distributors always start by producing red packaging.

In general terms, the brand must become a moving target through innovation and regular modifications to its packaging and its characteristic components. However, it must always be remembered that the aim of these modifications is to bring more value to the consumer. The difficulty that this permanent movement creates for copies is a secondary effect.

On the design front, the brand must accentuate and radicalise the signs of its own individuality, in order to be able to defend them better, and at the same time make them recognisable to consumers of average attentiveness. It is significant that the often-imitated Bailey's goes as far as to print the word 'Original' twice on its front label: 'Original Irish Cream' and 'Bailey's the original'.

Re-communicating the risks

Asian imports, DOBs and discount products enter first into the categories with low perceived risk. A first reaction is to remind people of the risks, to regenerate involvement in the category. For example, in 2005 one book became the talk of France, despite its size and its forbidding cover, which showed two nutritionists (Cohen and Serog, 2006). The whole press talked about it, and television devoted time to it. In fact, this book revealed a truth that big distribution would much prefer to keep hidden: the lowest-price products are not good for your health. The drastic reduction in price is made by forcing through awkward compromises, where client health and pleasure hardly enter into the equation. All that matters is the price. This is where we learnt that low-cost gingerbread contains no honey, and so on.

Bic did something similar in 2006 among tobacconists. The brand is known as the leader in disposable cigarette lighters, disposable razors, ballpoint pens and so on. It practises a single umbrella brand policy: everything is sold under the same name, Bic. It is essentially a company based on its sales force. In Europe, the disposable lighters division, strengthened by its market share, lived on its reputation and spent nothing on advertising. This prudent budgeting, however, had a drawback: for years, there had been nothing to communicate to customers why they should prefer a Bic lighter. In fact, until then, in service stations and tobacconists, there had been nothing but Bic. In 2004 Chinese products arrived, under the PROF brand, which retailers bought 50 per cent cheaper than Bic and sold for the same price as a Bic lighter. The increased margin for the retailers was such that they now sold nothing but PROF. Moreover, Chinese products were more fun and their decorations changed three times a year. The end consumers made no complaint – they were happy to find something new on the shelves, with more enter-taining products.

The decision was made to recreate the perceived risk. Chinese lighters are in fact dangerous: for example, they can explode if left on the rear shelf of a car. This does not happen with Bic lighters, which are products of remarkable quality. The problem is that in marketing, perception is reality. By not communicating the advantages of the product, Bic had admittedly made savings, but it had weakened the brand and paved the way for Chinese imports, chosen by the trade, which was unconscious of the considerably higher safety of a Bic and the danger of Chinese lighters. Bic created a magazine for its distributors in order to put the word out, and remind them of their legal responsibility if a Chinese lighter sold by one of them were to cause physical harm to a client. At the same time, it took action to raise the level of the criteria for approval for sale on European territory.

Price reductions

Faced with a decrease in their market share, producers are conscious that their brand no longer justifies the price differential that it offers on the shelf. It is tempting to reduce the price in order to restore the lost balance of perceived value and price.

This approach is logical, but carries several drawbacks. There is nothing easier than lowering prices. What will they do when an even cheaper Asian competitor appears? Lower them again – taking the money from which budget? Should it not be a question of recreating value by increasing quality and price? Also in many stores, the consumers do not even walk past the big brands: for them, the brand is too expensive by definition! They would not even notice the reduced price. The anticipated effect on sales would misfire. The price, and therefore the margins, would be decreased without benefiting from superior volumes.

An interesting study (Pauwels and Srinivasan, 2004) showed that the premium brands should not fear DOBs, since the market is segmented. On the contrary: statistical analysis showed that, after the introduction of DOBs, their sales became less price-dependent, and their turnover increased. The intermediate brands, on the other hand, saw their price sensitivity increase and their sales fall.

Several conclusions emerge at this stage. First, the era of systematic price increases upon the launch of new products is over. It is necessary to place price at the heart of the innovation, and move on to a value analysis.

The non-premium big brands should take care to create a ladder enabling them to increase penetration through a product at an accessible price, and then practise trading up, once the client is aware of the quality of the brand's products. The difficulty, it must be admitted, is the reaction of distributors, since these mini or economy-priced products compete directly with their DOBs, whose strategic role in their margins has already been discussed.

Thus, having bought all Colgate Palmolive's washing powders, Procter & Gamble decided to use Gama as a 'fighting brand'. In the second quarter of 2006, the price of Gama was reduced by 25 per cent, from €6.65 to €4.95 per 27-measure tub (Ariel is priced at €10). Gama became an 'everyday low price' brand, at a price lower than some DOBs. The goal was to bring hard-discount purchasers back into the superstores, since studies showed that they were particularly attracted by the cheapest washing powders. Sales increased by 54 per cent in four months, increasing market share from 3 per cent to 5.4 per cent.

The effect of price reductions on leader brands cannot be guaranteed: thus, in order to combat the products of the hard-discounter Aldi, Always (Procter & Gamble's feminine hygiene brand) lowered its prices in Germany, moving from an index of 240 to 197, with Aldi's index at 100. Aldi's market share remained stable at around 45 per cent. Always' market share moved from 21.7 per cent to only 24.7 per cent. It was a failure. The same tactic was successful, however, for Pampers: by moving from index 131 to 116, the market share jumped from 31.1 per cent to 42.2 per cent, and Aldi's product fell from 53.9 per cent to 45.9 per cent. A significant difference between these two cases is the far smaller difference in price for Pampers than for Always. Is it really worthwhile for premium brands to lower their prices?

Facing the low-cost revolution

It would be hard to underestimate the rise of hard-discount and lowest-price ranges as a fundamental phenomenon in mature societies. Offering a reduced range or a pared-back service at an unbeatable price, hard discount is more than just a price – it is a business model. It also represents a new attitude towards consumption, and heralds a crisis for added value. It throws marketing itself into question, and thus brands too. This is why no organisations should consider themselves safe from this phenomenon.

Even in the country that invented the hypermarket, and where this form of commerce is now dominant, hard discount has succeeded in capturing nearly 12 per cent of market share (in value) over 15 years. Given that in food products, the price gap between discounters and the leading brands varies between 30 per cent and 50 per cent, it can be seen that this represents between 18 per cent and 24 per cent by volume. And of course – depending on the category – these figures may be even higher. For example, in the pre-packed cold meats (ham) market, the hard discounters' market share by value is of the order of 16.5 per cent.

Hard discount is more than just a price. It is a new way of doing business, with its own specific retailers: German (Lidl and Aldi) or French (Ed, Leader Price). At present, the most recent European panel figures suggest that 62 per cent of households shop at a hard-discount food store. The phenomenon will reach a limit, however, reflecting the segmentation of the market: in food products, a threshold of 20 per cent in value market share should be expected. In the DIY sector, the major retailers have created separate hard-discount-style retail brands. The phenomenon now also extends to textiles: the classic discount stores were well known, but now new hard-discount retailers are emerging.

All these figures show that hard discount cannot simply be turned into a phenomenon that targets only lower-income groups. Hard discount is a necessity for the poorest in society, but also an opportunity for the better-off. It offers an alternative way of living: consumers can do the daily shop close to their home, in 10 minutes, thanks to the simplification offered by a reduced range of goods, freeing buyers from the torments of too much choice. Hard discount does not represent a return to asceticism, but to realism. Among consumers who could afford to buy elsewhere, it attests to a desire to simplify, to un-complicate, and to retake control. It will exert strong pressure on brands with low added value, the average brands, which do not possess a strong enough dream value. Hard discount advocates a form of intangible value: the return to a kind of simplicity for people who are not limited to it through a lack of resources. Hard discount is a search for purification of one's life, de-pollution, and liberation from imposed constraints.

This is a genuine challenge for the major brands, as this growing form of distribution excludes them in favour of the discounters' own products. For the major brands, this further erosion of their accessibility on store shelves compounds the problem created by the amount of space already set aside for distributors' brands in the hypermarkets and supermarkets. Indeed, even retailers' brands are coming under threat from this increasingly cut-price competition, which attracts clients to another store. This is why they have been strengthened, which will make them even more of a danger to the major brands as well. In fact, in 2007, the distributor's brand is now typically 35 per cent cheaper than the national brand. As it increases in quality, however, its competitiveness also increases.

The hard-discount phenomenon is set to spread. Everyone will look for a way to increase their purchasing power in an ultimately painless way, by making shrewder purchasing decisions in respect of a portion of their consumption. This will affect telephone communications, the internet, transport,

petrol, clothing and other areas. No company is immune to this phenomenon, because the competition has changed: consumers have become highly versatile, situation-driven and pragmatic. They are quite capable of shopping both at a hard-discount store and at Harrods on the same day.

Modern competition is thus expanded competition: it is no longer restricted to peers, identical brands or similar channels. Like the modern consumer, it is open and all-embracing. In the process of experimenting with new channels, consumers are bound to find themselves re-evaluating brands and their added value.

What should our answer to this be? We would argue that it involves heeding the implicit message in this new form of range, while remaining true to oneself, by copying what may be copied from this competitor, while increasing one's own strength. The brand must retaliate with a different intangible factor and value system: product performance on the one hand, or the emotive experience of the store on the other. Hypermarkets have no choice, either. Their own brands exist only in relation to the producer brands that innovate, create and nurture markets, reveal tendencies, and also participate in the consumer society.

Remember that a brand can justify its existence only through the innovations it offers. The majority of brands are born of innovation, and innovation continues to be the brand's oxygen: it has a stimulating, euphoric effect in promoting a sense of wellbeing, pleasure, *joie de vivre* and hedonism. However, this intangible factor will have to start earning its keep. This begins with respecting the customer: an intangible benefit that is not rooted in a tangible superior quality will be weakened, and will contribute to the brand's excess. There are plenty of cheap polo shirts, but only one Lacoste. A Lacoste shirt lasts 10 years and, furthermore, adds distinction. This point has to be reinforced repeatedly. This raises the question of the visibility of brand communication, governed by the advertising dogma of the USP: how, and through which media, to promote the product. Thankfully, the internet offers many opportunities.

This new brand responsibility comprises service, citizenship, and sustainable development, which is transmitted through client service via a call centre or over the internet, but also through the services such as taking in worn-out electrical appliances, which indicate the brand's high degree of social responsibility. The brand must adopt ethical principles and demonstrate that consumption is not a synonym for inefficient waste, pollution and exploitation – themes to which society is becoming increasingly sensitive. Even Nike has had to make changes in the wake of the revelations in Naomi Klein's book *No Logo* (1999). The mega-brand, with its iconic status among the young, may well have invented concept upon concept, but its social conscience left much to be desired, a fact that is particularly unacceptable in a flourishing company.

It would be a mistake to believe that hard discount will become the norm. In France, Cristalline spring water, sold at a price three times cheaper than Evian, does not control 100 per cent of the market, and Evian is still the leader by value. However, it will grow, until it reaches its threshold – and in so doing it may lead to a re-evaluation of attitudes and behaviour. As is always the case in our modern societies, contradictory tendencies appear, coexist and learn to live together – but what they cannot do any longer is ignore each other.

An examination of the specific strategies of companies and brands to combat hard discount reveals the following themes, all of which capitalise on the enduring weakness of hard-discount.

What link is there between Ryanair, Virgin Express, and Asda or Aldi? They are all so-called low-cost companies. How have the traditional competitors responded? Through the introduction of a new, lowest-price product offer to its existing range. The brand must create a stepped price range, with accessible products that make it possible to experiment with and to discover the brand. Furthermore, this contradicts the discounters' arguments, since they wish to stereotype all manufacturer brands as 'expensive'.

In air travel, for example, Air France has shown that the famous bait-and-switch prices of the low-cost companies (€20 flights from Paris to London) applied only to a few seats and time slots. Conversely, Air France's promotion of its lowest prices, and of reduced prices in the case of reservation long in advance, has also demonstrated that its price range is much wider than the low-cost companies had claimed. The SNCF (French national rail) created e-TGV to reduce prices. Thanks to yield management and process optimisation, Air France and British Airways can also offer a quota of seats at very low prices. These may be obtained by booking far in advance, reserving over the internet, and so on. In this way, the SNCF's e-TGV puts Marseilles only a €20 journey away from Paris.

The superstores have offered products even cheaper than the hard discounters, but under specific brands (the No. 1 brand at Carrefour, for example). This reduces the temptation to look elsewhere by capitalising on the hypermarket's traditional strength, 'one-stop shopping'. The difference in terminology is revealing: 'low-cost' is a business model; 'even cheaper product' was the result of an emergency action.

For 50 years Aldi and Lidl have been designing an efficient business model in order to provide a quality product at the lowest price, based on the elimination of all unnecessary costs, and on a new vision: long-term agreements with suppliers, dedicated factories with a common design, not to mention a store concept without flourishes, with a greatly reduced range of goods. If Aldi's fruit juice is still the market leader in Germany, it is because it is good: its quality/price ratio is unbeatable.

Conversely, the lowest price products at Carrefour, sold under a brand that (significantly) makes no reference to Carrefour, were created in haste to block the client drain, and obtained through increased pressure on suppliers, and therefore on the quality of constituents. Thus the fruit juice at this price will only have perhaps the legal minimum required amount of fruit juice. This is why hard discount, unlike the hypermarket's lowest price range, satisfies its clients.

At the communications level, it is necessary to constantly recreate the perceived risk, by revealing the invisible and the unspoken aspects of 'low cost'. Perceived risk is a key lever of brand sensitivity (Kapferer and Laurent, 1995). The book written by two nutritionists was therefore a timely arrival in 2005. It showed that drastic price-cutting on food products was bound to negatively affect the intrinsic quality of the products. Thus, low-cost gingerbread contained not a single gram of honey. Low-cost ham contained high levels of chemicals. Low-cost chicken is raised in the worst conditions and barely has time to grow up (40 days), and so on. In the air travel sector, a degree of doubt will inevitably remain regarding the maintenance, the quality of the equipment, and the heavy usage of the airplanes.

The brand must react to attacks on price by playing its trump cards: innovation and creating desire. In order to see off the challenge of the cheapest possible industrial chicken, the brand must offer halal chicken, organic chicken, regional chicken, and so on. To oppose the cheapest possible yoghurt, it must offer one that does you good: Actimel, Danacol, Bio-Activia. To oppose a €5 cafetière in Carrefour, imported from China, it must offer Nespresso, or Senseo by Philips, or Krups. To oppose the cheapest MP3 player, it must offer the iPod and its continual innovation (images, nano, mini, access to iTunes, iPhone, and the like).

Value innovations are low volume, at least initially. Without volume there can be no strong brand, since it is volume that creates the financial resources for R&D, marketing, communication and so on. It is therefore first of all necessary to innovate on pillar products, those products that achieve the volume and the margin, and are essential to the distributor. In short, faced with supermarket shelves where space is at a premium due to the introduction of low-cost products, and in order to retain clients who might be tempted by the vista of hard-discount stores, it is important to remember that an essential reference remains essential only when supported through innovation and communication.

It is also vital to track the costs that do not carry added value, even imitating the best practices of the low-cost competitors. Thus Air France is constantly reducing the time clients must wait before they can board, via machines that deliver boarding cards: this also helps to economise on personnel. The same is true for the growing use of the internet to book and to pay. For low-cost companies, as is well known, everything is done at a distance.

Finally, the brand must react through a specific business model. Air France adopted the hub-style business model: it allows any traveller from the French regions to travel to Paris on an Air France flight and to make use of very convenient international connections (with short waiting times), not to mention the immediate transfer of baggage, and moving within a single terminal. All these added values discourage the internal traveller from flying to Paris with a low-cost company, then being forced to change airports or terminals, without guaranteed immediate connections to international flights – not to mention the air miles.

Should manufacturers produce goods for DOBs?

One of the questions all company managers ask concerns the opportunity to work for distributors' brands. This question is even more urgent today, since with the shrinking of the shelf space allocated to branded industrialists, their economic model is under threat. How can they maintain the volumes that create profitability?

Those industrialists in favour of producing DOB goods advance the following arguments:

- It relieves the burden of fixed costs.

- It allows them to benefit from economies of scale.

- It may be intrinsically profitable, since there is no need for marketing, communication, or sales force.

- If they do not do it, their competitors will.

In contrast, those who oppose it are right to argue that it will undermine the long-term legitimacy of the company's own brands, since the industrialist will not be capable of producing a bad product. For a while the product Olympia manufactured for Carrefour was superior to the comparable product of the brand itself. An examination of the figures in the cheese sector also shows that the most profitable cheese maker is Bel, which sells only branded products (Laughing Cow, Mini Babybel, Leerdammer, etc).

Rather than drawing up a pointless balance sheet for and against, it is worth turning to research in this case. HEC has carried out several specific studies on this important theme for companies in all sectors, under the direction of M Santi (Santi, 1996). The selected criterion is operational profitability compared with turnover, and the sample comprised 167 cases drawn from numerous mass-consumption sectors. What does this research have to teach us?

- The profitability level is maximal when the policy is the result of a voluntary strategy (9 per cent) and not an opportunistic reaction to a short-term demand (5.19 per cent) or a survival strategy (6.53 per cent).

- The profitability level also depends on the underlying motivations: it is at its highest when the company is seeking to create a genuine partnership with distributors, in order to defend already strong brands (7.90 per cent). If the brands are weak and the DOB manufacturing approach is an attempt to save them, the profitability in the sample is less (3.50 per cent).

- The profitability is maximal if this is the dominant or even exclusive activity of the industrialist (7.51 per cent).

- The profitability is maximal if the market is not a commodity market (7.64 per cent).

- The profitability is weakened by the fact that the industrialist does not make a distinction between its brand and the distributor's brand it is producing: this is an important point, since many industrialists distinguish between the two only through the packaging, in order to make the most of the economies of scale and long production runs.

- The profitability is better when the manufacturer works with distributors that promote quality.

What can we draw from this HEC research data? Whether or not to manufacture distributor's brand products is a strategic choice, and should be analysed as such.

Should they do it? Refusal to do so is clearly the result of a long-term vision: Procter & Gamble, Gillette and l'Oréal all invest too much in research to wish to share the benefits they reap from it. They reserve the first fruits for their own brands, within a structured portfolio.

Which companies should do it? There is no correlation between any classic company description and profitability in DOB production: rather, profitability is linked to the manner in which it is implemented.

In which segments should they operate? The least commoditised possible, those where there is still innovation.

Which distributors should they work with? Here, too, selectivity in the choice of distributors proves to be rewarding in terms of profitability over turnover.

5

Brand diversity: the types of brands

What becomes of these brand principles in specific markets? It is worth asking the question, given the disparities between markets as varied as industry, business-to-business (B2B) and medical prescription on one side, and the world of service and luxury on the other. Are internet brands controlled using the same levers? What should we think of the emergence of the brand in sectors such as fresh produce, previously the domain of generic products or a variety resulting from nature and regional tendencies? Finally, we should examine these new extensions of the brand domain: countries, towns, educational establishments, and also television programmes and sporting heroes.

These questions on the adaptation of brand principles to specific sectors are raised by sector managers themselves, since they all recognise the trans-sectoral validity of brand logic, its points of application, and the brand activation modes, which are bound to differ according to the different markets. This chapter is dedicated to these differences.

Luxury, brand and *griffe*

Recently there has been a surge of interest in luxury brands. It is true that they are the polar opposite of low cost: here, the company has complete freedom to fix its prices – as high as possible. How much does a bottle of Royal Salute cost in a Shanghai disco? The answer is €1,000. This is why financial groups have been set up to relaunch luxury brands – the world number one, LVMH, was born from the talent of its founder, B Arnault, who acquired a fading star, Dior, at a low price. Then he got his hands on Vuitton, now the world's leading luxury brand in terms of financial value.

But what is luxury? How is it different from premium brands, such as Victoria's Secret lingerie, Callaway golf clubs, Belvedere vodka or Nespresso coffee? These brands are typical of trading up, as consumers move up the range. Admittedly there is a little of luxury's ingredients in these brands (better quality, selective distribution, emotive value), but luxury is elsewhere. Let us return to its etymology. The word 'luxury' derives from the Latin *luxatio*, meaning distance: luxury is

an enormous distance. There is a discontinuity between premium and luxury.

To return to the essence of luxury, it is
customers' desire to mark their difference. The
first luxury manager was King Louis XIV of
France. Aristocracy is now dead, but it has
been replaced by the power of money.
Everywhere in China, in Russia, in the United
States and in Dubai, recent fortunes grant
more than unlimited purchasing power: they
grant power, pure and simple. This is the heart
of luxury: giving men and women of power
the privileges that accompany it. For power
must be shown off in our democratic societies.
Once upon a time, the mere name of the
noble marked the unbridgeable distance
between him or her and an ordinary person.
Nowadays, the frontier still exists and it must
be marked.

Russian oligarchs, Chinese billionaires and
Wall Street's golden boys do not buy Victoria's
Secret or Belvedere vodka for their partners.
They want Dior, la Perla, Elit by Stolichnaya or
Krug's le Clos du Mesnil, which has deposed
Dom Perignon. Luxury, like power, is a quest
for the absolute.

The luxury business model aims to outgrow
this niche in order to exploit the fundamental
mechanism described by R Girard: desire born
of imitating a model. Luxury brands know
how to create more accessible product lines
for those who wish to introduce a little luxury
into their lives, to enliven their daily grind
from time to time. These are luxury's 'day
trippers'. This created the luxury business.

What does luxury mean to consumers?

Luxury can vary as widely as East from West.
Everyone can see where it is, but it is
constantly on the move. Luxury is relative.
For a modest individual, luxury is eating in a
good restaurant once a year. For one of the
City's golden boys, it is buying a Ferrari with
your annual bonus. For Bill Gates, it is playing
tennis with the world number one or buying a
Picasso.

Our research has delved more deeply into
the notion of luxury among consumers. There
are profound differences between people
questioned on their concept of luxury.
Analysis of the traits that – in their minds –
define luxury reveals four concepts of luxury,
each with its most representative brand(s)
(that is, those that are judged the best
example of the type of luxury by interviewees)
(Kapferer, 1998).

The first type of luxury, according to this
international sample of affluent young executives with high purchasing power, is the
closest to the general hierarchy, the average
emerging from our studies. It gives prominence to the beauty of the object and the
excellence and uniqueness of the product,
more so than all the other types. The brand
most representative of this type of luxury is
Rolls-Royce, but Cartier and Hermès also show
these characteristics. The second concept of
luxury in the world exalts creativity, the
sensuality of the products. Its luxury 'prototypes' are Gucci, Boss and J-P Gaultier. The
third vision of luxury values timelessness and
international reputation more than any other
facets. Its symbols are Porsche, with its
immutable design, Vuitton and Dunhill.
Finally, the fourth type values the feeling of
rarity attached to the possession and
consumption of the brand. In their eyes, the
prototype of the brand purchased by the
select few is Chivas.

We also find Mercedes in this category:
this might seem curious, given the recent
diffusion of Mercedes – now more than
1,300,000 vehicles sold worldwide each year.
However, our study dates from 1998, when
Mercedes produced only 700,000 cars per
year, and its dynamism and product attractiveness were called into question. This is
what led to the revolution we all know about
(multiplication of models, introduction of
aesthetics, the A class, the M class and so
on). Its presence as a symbol of this fourth
type of luxury testifies to the brand's
problems. Only a few years ago, its only

Table 5.1 Consumers' four concepts of luxury

Consumer group	Type 1	Type 2	Type 3	Type 4
What defines luxury (percentage giving each answer):				
Beauty of an object	97	63	86	44
Excellence of the products	88	3	9	38
Magic	76	50	88	75
Uniqueness	59	10	3	6
Tradition and savoir faire	26	40	40	38
Creativity	35	100	38	6
Sensuality of the products	26	83	21	6
Feeling of exceptionality	23	23	31	31
Never out of fashion	21	27	78	19
International reputation	15	27	78	19
Produced by a craftsperson	12	30	9	3
Long history	6	7	16	13
Likeable creator	6	7	10	13
Belonging to a minority	6	3	2	63
Very few purchasers	0	3	2	69
At the cutting edge of fashion	0	17	36	31
Typical luxury brands of this type according to interviewees:	Rolls-Royce Cartier Hermès	Gucci Boss Gaultier	Vuitton Porsche Dunhill	Chivas Mercedes

Source: Kapferer (1998b)

potential market was among those looking for the luxury, not of a sensory pleasure, but of status, the badge of belonging in a class with money and a desire to flaunt it. We should add, however, that in China, India, Brazil and Russia, it is the very expensive and status-loaded Mercedes S Class that sells. These are *de facto* inaccessible cars.

Two different approaches to luxury brand building

The only real success is commercial, yet there are many roads to this destination. An examination of 'new luxury' brands such as Ralph Lauren, Calvin Klein and DKNY proves that it is possible to become an overnight success in the luxury market without the long pedigree of a Christian Dior, Chanel or Givenchy. True, these newer brands have not yet demonstrated their ability to endure and survive beyond the death of their founders, but their commercial success

is evidence of their attractiveness to customers the world over. We need to distinguish between two different business models for brands. The first includes brands with a 'history' behind them, while the second covers brands that, lacking such a history of their own, have invented a 'story' for themselves. It comes as no surprise that these companies are US-based: this young, modern country is a past master in the art of weaving dreams from stories. After all, both Hollywood and Disneyland are American inventions.

Furthermore, the European luxury brands – rooted as they are in a craftsperson-based tradition predicated upon rare, unique pieces of work – place considerable emphasis on the actual product as a factor in their success, while the US brands concentrate much more on merchandising, and the atmosphere and image created by the outlets dedicated to their brand, in the realm of customer contact and distribution. What we see is the creation of a dichotomy between 'history' and the product on the one hand, and 'stories' and distribution on the other. Let us examine and compare these two brand and business models in more detail.

The first brand and business model may be represented by the luxury pyramid (see Figure 5.1). At the top of the pyramid, there is the *griffe* – the creator's signature engraved on a unique work. This explains what it fears most: copies. Brands, on the other hand, particularly fear fakes or counterfeits. The second level is that of luxury brands produced in small series within a workshop: a 'manufacture' in its etymological sense, which is seen as the sole warrant of a 'good-facture'. Examples include Hermès, Rolls-Royce and Cartier. The third level is that of streamlined mass production: here we find Dior and Yves Saint Laurent cosmetics, and YSL Diffusion clothes. At this level of industrialisation, the brand's fame generates an aura of intangible added values for expensive and prime quality products, which nonetheless gradually tend to look more and more like the rest of the market. Hence its name equals mass prestige.

In this model, luxury management is based on the interactions between the three levels. The perpetuation of *griffes* depends on their integration in financial groups that are able to provide the necessary resources for the first level, and on their licensing to industrial groups able to create, launch and distribute worldwide products at the third level (such as P&G, Unilever and l'Oréal). Profit accrues at this level, and is the only means to make the huge investments on the *griffe* pay off. These investments are necessary to recreate the dream around the brand. Reality consumes dreams: the more we buy a luxury brand, the less we dream of it. Hence, somewhat paradoxically, the more a luxury brand gets purchased, the more its aura needs to be permanently recreated.

This is exactly how the LVMH group operates. The model is best explained in the actual words of Bernard Arnault, the CEO of LVMH, the world's leading luxury group, which owns 41 luxury brands. What are the key factors in the success of its brands? Arnault (2000: p 65) lists them in the following order:

- product quality;
- creativity;
- image;
- company spirit;
- a drive to reinvent oneself and to be the best.

Figure 5.1   The pyramid brand and business model in the luxury market

Writing earlier in his book with reference to Dior, the ultimate luxury brand, he notes, 'Behind Dior, there is a legitimacy ... roots ... an exceptional evocative power ... a genuine magic, to say nothing of its potential for economic growth' (p 26).

As we can see, in this pyramid model, with its base which expands to feed the brand's overall cashflow (through licensing, extensions and a less elective distribution system), there must be a constant regeneration of value at the tip. This is where creativity, signature and creator come in, supplying the brand with its artistic inventiveness. Here we are in the realm of art, not mere styling. Each show is a pure artistic event. Unlike the second brand and business model (as we shall see), it is not a question of presenting clothing which will be worn in a year's time. As Arnault puts it, 'One does not invite a thousand guests to watch a procession of dresses which could be seen on a coat hanger or in a show room' (p 70); 'most competitors prefer to show off mass-produced clothing on their catwalks, or indulge in American-style marketing. We are not interested in working this way' (p 73); and 'Marc Jacobs, John Galliano and Alexander McQueen are innovators; fashion inventors; artists who create' (p 75).

The creativity of the signature label, at the tip of the pyramid, is at the heart of the business model: within a few years of the arrival of John Galliano at Dior, sales had increased four fold. Never before had Dior been talked about so much worldwide. Dior was back at the centre of world artistic creation for women.

The disadvantage of this model – and after all, every model has a disadvantage – is that the more accessible secondary lines are entrusted to other designers, and the further away you move from the tip of the pyramid, the less creativity there is. In this model, there is a strong danger that brand extensions will show little of the creativity of the brand itself: they will merely exploit its name.

The second brand and business model may have originated in the United States, but we should also include the likes of Armani and Boss in this category, which is characterised by its flat, circular, constellation-like model. At the centre is the brand ideal, while all manifestations of the brand (its extensions, licences, and so on) are around the edge, at a more or less equal distance from the centre. Consequently, these extensions are all treated with equal care, since each of them brings its own individual expression of this ideal to its target market. Each portrays the brand in an equally important way, and plays its own part in shaping it. For example, Ralph Lauren's home textile extension (bed sheets, blankets, tablecloths, bath towels and so on) is a complete expression of the patrician East Coast ideal and its values: indeed, the tactic of merchandising the range in the corners of department stores aims to create an idealised reconstruction of a room in a house.

This second model can include brand 'places' such as The House of Ralph Lauren – superstores which not only stock the entire brand range and its various collections and extensions, but are also specifically designed to give flesh, structure and meaning to the brand ideal. Ralph Lifshitz, Ralph Lauren's founder, built his brand on an ideal: that of American aristocracy, symbolised by Boston high society. Ralph Lauren's flagship stores are three-dimensional recreations of this fanciful illusion (Figure 5.2).

The same model is also used by brands such as Lacoste, created in 1933 in the days of tennis champion René Lacoste, a Davis Cup winner along with his friends 'Les Mousquetaires', and nicknamed 'The Crocodile' for his tenacity. Ever since then, the brand's values, which are encapsulated in his famous *chemise* (meaning 'shirt': the word itself is important), have been upheld by the Lacoste family and a collection of partners, their licensed producers and distributors. Lacoste thus has a certain authenticity and a genuine history, yet at the same time follows this second business model.

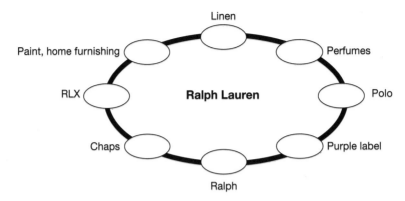

Figure 5.2   The constellation model of luxury brands

Indeed, the creation of this model has nothing to do with chance: it is an economic necessity for any brand which continues to be sold at an accessible price point. There is no way of sustaining an exclusive distribution network with an average purchase of around €65 or US$75 – that is, the price of a Lacoste shirt – or US$60, the price of a Ralph Lauren polo shirt. The economics only become feasible with multiple extensions. Following our model, this can be done in two ways. The first is horizontal product extension to increase brand recognition, providing that elusive access to large-scale advertising budgets, and breaking into different distribution channels or different locations inside the same department store. This increases the perceived presence and status of the brand.

The second is vertical product extension to increase average till prices. Today, for example, Lacoste has segmented its product range into three groups – sport, sportswear and Club – yet has steered clear of formal wear, which is outside the brand's sphere of legitimacy. This segmentation makes it possible for customers to wear Lacoste in a variety of situations: sport, leisure and 'dress-down Friday wear'. At the same time, the average product price is increasing according

to the particular segment: the high-quality materials used in a Club jacket explain why. Of course, the product ranges of all Lacoste's extensions are arranged around this same segmentation.

Ralph Lauren uses a similar model: its recent Purple Collection features Italian-made outfits produced from quality materials, and a price tag to match: €3,000 per outfit.

This brand extension policy makes matters easier for distributors, who have come to understand that the rate of return increases as the physical sales area expands. Each store can now offer a rich assortment of products which are no longer mere accessories, but extensions in their own right – and in so doing, can increase the value of the average shopping trip.

It should be noted that 'pyramid-based' brands face a rather perverse problem. If they create too many accessible extensions, they reduce the profitability of the sales outlets. In a Chanel boutique, it makes more sense to spend 10 minutes selling a customer a Chanel bag – given the margin it offers – rather than a perfume or a product from the Chanel Precision range. Clearly, the extension policy is inseparable from the distribution policy.

History-based and story-based luxury

An examination of luxury brand strategies shows two brand construction models. The first is based on product quality taken to the extreme, the cult of product and heritage, History with a capital H, of which the brand is the modern embodiment. The second is American in origin, and lacking such a history of its own, does not hesitate to invent one. Ralph Lifshitz became Ralph Lauren, taking on the traits and character of the Great Gatsby, a direct descendant of the ultra-chic Bostonian high society. (See Figure 5.3.) These newcomer brands also grasped the importance of the store in creating an atmosphere and a genuine impression, and of making the brand's values palpable there. America invented Disney and Hollywood – both producers of the imaginary.

The psychology of counterfeiting

Counterfeiting is on the increase. It is now a global business, involving organised groups, and forming part of Mafia activity as a result of the profits that it offers at the margin of intellectual property and trademark protection laws. It has also found a new distribution channel through the internet and its marketplace sites such as e-Bay. However, if there is a market, there must be customers.

In Asia, the phenomenon relates to local culture. Everyone knows the extent of counterfeiting in China. There is no trademark protection. Traditionally, Chinese culture praises those who share and vilifies people who keep things only for themselves. Faithfully reproducing the master's work is praised in traditional Chinese education and pedagogy. Furthermore, in the monopolistic

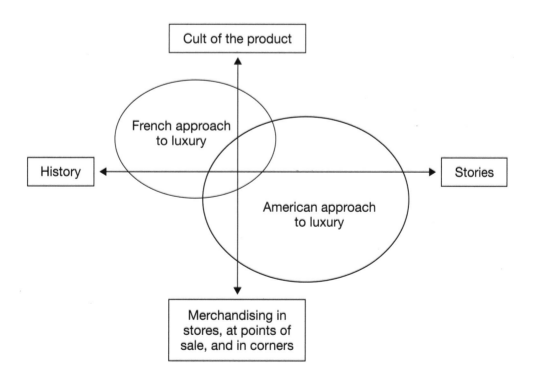

Figure 5.3 History-based and story-based approaches to luxury

economy that dominated the Chinese mentality for 50 years, even the notion of property did not exist, and it was common to see all Chinese factories carrying the same name. Let us add that only the counterfeits are accessible to local consumers. In these countries, everyone wants to show their neighbours that they have finally arrived. Everyone has heard about the Western brands, but very few actually know them: they do not realise they are buying a fake. Research has confirmed this point (Lai and Zaichkowsky, 1999): local consumers choosing a counterfeit or an imitation do so because they are not familiar with the original.

Western consumers know perfectly well which is the original: they play with imitations and counterfeits (McCartney, 2005). Our qualitative research of this phenomenon reveals five motivations:

▌ The feeling of getting a bargain, since everyone knows that luxury and Nike products are manufactured in factories in the developing world. These consumers deny the difference in quality between the original and the copy, when they are both produced in China, as is the case for some Vuitton products. These are highly discriminating shoppers. They only buy Vuitton bags 'identical' to the original, admiring the quality of the copy: it is this quality, together with the price, that makes it 'a real bargain' and enables them to carry the copy every day, under the gaze of friends who will not know the difference. The purchaser of a very good imitation Bulgari watch, a close semblance to the genuine one she already owns, will not hesitate to give it to one of her children for their 15th birthday.

Revealingly, purchasers sometimes own a true original themselves: this is what qualifies them as experts, and gives status to the copy chosen for its close resemblance. They know what they are talking about.

▌ The idea of brightening up functional items: fake Ralph Lauren polo shirts, even if they are approximate copies, are good enough for doing household chores, gardening or washing the car, for example.

▌ Certain consumers willingly buy the counterfeit, since they cannot or will not pay the higher price for the original. They find it superfluous or exaggerated to buy a Ralph Lauren polo shirt at €60, since they are not strongly involved with the brand.

▌ There is also a 'moral' motivation among some purchasers of counterfeits: they are scandalised by the price of the original, arguing that since it was manufactured in a south-east Asian factory the cost price must be tiny. For these purchasers, it is only right and proper: since this brand is practising daylight robbery, judging by a comparison of its sales price with its cost price, stealing from it in return is morally justified.

▌ An original gift: rather than bringing home a cheap Thai souvenir that will go straight into a drawer, they bring their friends a typical product of the country, a beautiful imitation, a counterfeit that can barely be distinguished from the original. This present always surprises the recipient, and sparks conversations on the good or bad quality of the counterfeit. Finally, it is certain to be used. However, this type of gift is becoming risky, since European customs consider the traveller who brings home such gifts to be a receiver of stolen goods.

The fight against counterfeiting

Counterfeiting is the identical, trait-for-trait imitation of the brand and its identifying components: it is clearly illegal, with no need to prove that the consumer is confused. Perpetrators should be reported and prosecuted. However, longer-term action is necessary in certain countries where it is more than tolerated, even acceptable:

- Collective action at the level of the Foreign Ministry or Ministry of Justice. This involves inter-state relationships.

- Collective sensitisation efforts, for example at the World Trade Organization (WTO) level, to develop local legal systems.

- Advertising of the original brand in the country in question. It is necessary to familiarise people with the 'true brand' so that they can distinguish it from the fakes.

- Advertising on counterfeiting in tourists' countries of origin. Action among Western consumers in their country of origin is educational: they must be reminded that counterfeiting is linked to Mafià groups and laundering drug money. It is also juridical: bringing home a counterfeit makes someone an accomplice and is therefore a crime, punishable by law.

This fight is shifting continually, and requires tact and a highly developed strategic sense. A typical case is *Lacoste* v *Crocodile Garments*. In November 2003, Crocodile Garments announced at a press conference in Hong Kong that it had signed an agreement with the Lacoste shirt brand. In fact, the Crocodile Garments company had registered a crocodile symbol – a strict imitation of the Lacoste crocodile, but facing to the left instead of the right – in Hong Kong back in the 1970s, and had been exploiting this brand and the 'Crocodile' store chain, not only in Hong Kong but also in Singapore and now in China. With the law on its side, Lacoste took the matter before the relevant courts in Singapore and China. However, although the judgements were always favourable, they remained unheeded on the ground.

In the meantime, hundreds of other counterfeits sprang up in China, including Cartelo International with over 600 boutiques. Lacoste and Crocodile Garments came to a pragmatic and wise agreement. The latter company could see that China was coming

under strong pressure from all quarters to respect the WTO's rules: eventually it would take punitive action against the counterfeiters. This is why the agreement signed stipulated the cessation of legal action against it, with Crocodile Garments moreover becoming Lacoste's licensee in Hong Kong. In exchange, Lacoste insisted that the counterfeit crocodile must take a more rounded shape, be contained in a circle and cease to be coloured green, like the famous original crocodile of 1933. By signing this agreement, the two companies formed a common front against a hundred other local counterfeiters.

Service brands

There is no legal difference between product, trade or service brands. These are economic distinctions, not legal ones. By focusing only on branding *per se*, ie on signs only, the law does not help us much to understand either how brands and the branding process work or what the specific characteristics among the various players are.

Service brands do exist: Europcar, Hertz, Ecco, Manpower, Visa, Club Med, Marriott's, Méridien, HEC, Harvard, BT, etc. Each one represents a specific cluster of attributes embodied in a quite concrete, though intangible, type of service: car rental, temporary work, computer services, leisure activities, hotel business or higher education. However, some service sectors seem to be just entering the brand age. They either do not consider themselves as being a part of it yet or have just started becoming aware that they are. This evolution is fascinating to watch, as it highlights all that the brand approach involves and reveals the specificities of branding an intangible service.

The banking industry is a fine example. If bank customers were asked what bank brands they knew, they probably would not know or understand what to answer. They know the names of banks, but not bank brands. This is significant: for the public, these names are not brands, identifying a specific service, but corporate names or business signs linked to a specific place.

Until recently, bank names designated either the owner of the corporation entrusted with the customers' funds (Morgan, Rothschild) or a specific place (Citibank) or a particular customer group. Name contraction often signals that a brand concept is in formation. Thus, for example, Banque Nationale de Paris has become BNP. Some observers consider this as just a desire to simplify the name, as per the advertising principle 'what's easy to say is easy to remember', as short signatures make it easier to identify the signer. Such abbreviations have definitely had an impact; however, they seem to reduce the whole branding concept to a mere part of the writing and printing process solely within the realm of communication.

As they are contracted, these bank names come to represent some kind of contract instead of a mere person or place. In order to become visible, this contract may take the form of specific 'bank products' (or standard policies in the insurance industry). But these visible and easy-to-imitate products are not the explanation and justification for why they have decided to build a true brand. They are merely the brand's external manifestation. Banks and insurance companies have understood the key to what makes them different: the relationships that develop between a customer and a banker under the auspices of the brand.

Finally, one aspect of service brands that contrasts with product brands is that service is invisible (Levitt, 1981; Eiglier and Langeard, 1990). What does a bank have to show, except customers or consultants? Structurally, service brands are handicapped in that they cannot be easily illustrated. That is why service brands use slogans. No wonder: slogans are indeed vocal, they are the brand's *vocatio*, ie the brand's vocation or calling. Slogans are a commandment for both internal and external relations. Through a slogan, the brand defines its behavioural guidelines, and these guidelines give the customer the right to be dissat-

isfied if they are transgressed. Claiming to be the bank with a smile or the bank who cares is not enough. These attributes must be fully internalised by the people who offer and deliver the service. The fact that humans are intrinsically and unavoidably variable is definitely a challenge for the brand approach in service industries.

This is why brand alignment has become so important if the whole organisation is to 'live the brand' (Ind, 2001). Brand alignment is the process by which organisations think of themselves as brands. The brand experience in the service sector is totally driven by what happens at points of contact, where customers meet the company's staff, salespeople and so on. This is true of Starbucks as well as of Citibank or HSBC. It is also crucial at Dell. This company is actually not a computer manufacturer but a service company, identifying each client's need and assembling the product to fit it. There is hardly any R&D investment at Dell. All the efforts are concentrated on the customers and organising the company by customer segment to better listen and react. People are essential in this process, not machines.

Branding in the service sector entails a double recognition. Within the company, people must recognise the brand values as their own. The internalisation process is crucial. It means explaining and justifying these values to each cell within the company. It also means stimulating the self-discovery of how these values might modify everyday behaviour. At the client level it also means that clients recognise these values as those to which they are attracted.

One point must not be overlooked. Brand management in the service sector means not only delivering a differentiated experience but ensuring that the resulting satisfaction will be attributed to the right brand. This is why the design and branding of all contact points are so important. Places of business, call centres, websites and the like must all convey the brand. Just posting one's logo on the front door is not enough.

The human component of the service brand

In services, there is no difference between the internal and the external. In other words, it is what is behind the brand that makes the brand. Thus, on a return flight from Tokyo to Paris, customers of the airline are in contact with its staff for 14 hours at a time. It is the attentive personnel who carry the brand, not a few seconds of stealth advertising. This is what makes passengers forget the frustration of the delays that build up from the beginning, disrupting executives' best-laid plans. What has built Starbucks' worldwide reputation, if not the politeness of its employees? For products it is quite the opposite: Evian is visible in bottles, in shops and in advertising. We never see the factory or the workers.

The first consequence of this is that the service brand is constructed internally. Orange is built up through hours and hours of training all staff how to behave in an Orange way, according to Orange's codes and values. This concerns all points of contact with the customer, in the store, from the call centre or over the internet. The second consequence is that employees cannot be expected to treat customers well if they are not happy themselves. In order to create the relaxed, warm atmosphere that characterises Starbucks, its founder Howard Schultz innovated by responding to the worries of many part-time staff: with good health insurance cover, for example.

Another essential distinction between services and products is that the 'factory' is in the store. The location for the service production (or serviduction, as the late lamented E Langeard called it) is also the place of its consumption: post office, hospital or restaurant. This is why it is so important to take care of the little details, since they lead to expectations and feelings. The rise of architectural and interior design expresses the desire for greater control over the impressions produced by the immediate environment on what is known as the customer experience, and therefore customer satisfaction.

Since service is carried out by people, their variability is a risk for the brand. The brand promises regular and dependable quality – hence the importance of defining strong behavioural norms, supported by plenty of training (McDonald's and Disney are models of this type). The alternative is to keep the personalised connection between customers and the agents themselves, who found a lasting relationship, based on mutual recognition. However, this second approach conflicts with the need to move staff around.

Service, process and recruitment brands

In the services sector, in order to carry out the primary function of any major brand (guaranteeing the same quality of service), the brand is necessarily linked to the setting up of internal and customer-facing processes. To take the example of accounting and audit consultancies, to be 'Mazars' is to differentiate oneself from the big international agencies, the famous 'big four' who are all Anglo-Saxon, and therefore offer a different culture. However, it is still necessary to homogenise the internal processes, to provide more regularity and the client experience. The brand is not only a common seal linking profoundly independent agencies in order to give an impression of size, but the sharing of the same concept of the profession. In services, it is important to make the intangible tangible – hence the importance of common processes.

Naturally, this has an impact on what is commonly known as the employer brand, since the raw material of service is the personality and competence of the people. For the employer brand, the task is to develop its reputation among executives or students of the top universities, based not on better salaries, but on shared values.

Brand and nature: fresh produce

Many mass-consumption food product brands were born through the disappearance of fresh produce in bulk. Sweetcorn, peas and gherkins were all canned, giving birth to Green Giant, Saupiquet, d'Aucy, Amora, Bonduelle and so on. Findus was the first brand to freeze vegetables. Fleury Michon produced plastic-wrapped ham. The big brands were therefore born through providing progress and practicality, precisely connected to the removal of the vagaries of fresh produce and the drawback of its perishable nature.

Innovation in fresh produce

We are present at a major event among small retailers in the traditional markets themselves: the emergence of fresh produce brands. A stroll past market stalls, or very early in the morning at Rungis, the world's biggest wholesale market, is enough to show this. Although they are a minority in number and market share, their innovative approach is clear: they have inserted themselves into the mounting campaign against poor eating habits, which advises people to eat fresh fruit and vegetables daily. Fresh produce, however, has an intrinsic variability derived from the vagaries of nature: some customers prefer more regularity and certainty. Here we find the essence of the brand, the suppression of perceived risk – here the qualitative risk of pleasure and taste.

This is what the Saveol tomato brand, the Philibon melon brand from Guadeloupe and the Gillardeau oyster brand, to mention but a few of the best known, have done: it is the sign of a true brand policy. It would be wrong to assume that these brands are products of communication: as always, everything began through product-related innovation. They are based on flavour, and the shape that makes a food item either more practical or more interesting.

The Saveol brand is the banner under which dozens of tomato producers have joined together, united by a single desire to create a superior and different product, to respect the same innovative production processes while eliminating insecticides (replaced by lady-birds), and to invent a true range of flavourful products, in previously unseen forms suitable for different types of consumption (cherry tomatoes, olive tomatoes, etc). This policy of innovation is accompanied by mass-media communication: Saveol's objective is for its name to be the tomato brand spontaneously cited by half the population by 2010.

Philibon, the melon from Guadeloupe, guarantees exceptional flavour all year round.

Mr Gillardeau is the creator of an eponymous brand that has become omnipresent in restaurants in just a few years. The brand guarantee relates to the qualitative aspect of Gillardeau oysters, with guaranteed taste and flesh all year round, everywhere in the world. Gillardeau has built its brand through the restaurant trade, which has then rebounded into a reputation among the general oyster-eating public. The market insight on which the brand is based comes from an understanding of the problems faced by restaurateurs, who wish to ensure a strong, risk-free experience for their customers. Top-of-the-range restaurants made Gillardeau a success, since these restaurants want to avoid any possible problem or disappointment with their oysters: they are committed to the pursuit of perfection. However, its market also contains the small quality brasserie, which by only offering Gillardeau oysters can reassure customers, who habitually mistrust the provenance of the oyster basket.

Furthermore, Gillardeau was able to implement a selective and controlled distribution policy, ensuring exclusivities at the wholesaler level, so that it knows exactly where it is sold and where it is not. Control over its own distribution is the first condition of the premium brand.

Wine brands

Wine may also be considered as the application of a brand to a living product. The majority of new wine consumers in France, and more particularly in other countries, justifiably expect no surprises from wine: they expect to find the same pleasurable taste each time, as with Coca-Cola. The major American successes of Yellow Tail, and also Two Bucks Chuck (wine priced at US$2, as its name suggests) and the Australian Jacob's Creek, are a specific response to this expectation.

These wines have brushed aside the old-world wines, since they were designed entirely on the basis of the expectations of the modern (generally Anglo-Saxon) customer and of the distributor. They are the answer to the B to B to C world in which we are now living (see page 152). The key components of their success are these:

- the ability to supply mass distribution in quantity (therefore reaching critical mass in production terms: an end to the patchwork of small independent cooperatives, and the emergence of big capitalist groups);

- a fruity, easy to drink flavour, designed to please consumers who generally drink beer or soft drinks, with priority given to white wine served chilled;

- maintaining the taste of the wine from year to year, thanks to the blending of different sources;

- the lowest production costs, thanks to legitimate innovations in productivity, which make it possible to reap higher margins, capable of largely financing their distributors;

- investment in the brand, rather than the region, so as not to be limited in quantity, and above all to generate loyalty to a single name: the brand's own;

- logical grape variety: remember that modern customers are not brought up on wine;

- the capacity to create a national sales force to visit all points of purchase and carry out promotions at point of purchase (brand visibility means the product will be picked up);

- investment in communication to cause the brand to emerge in spontaneous awareness, and therefore set itself apart from the thousands of small wine brands;

- the capacity for regular innovation, in order to make waves in the press and achieve good scores from juries, or in wine magazine categories;

- labels written in English, since the wines hail from California, or Australia or New Zealand, or even from South Africa.

There is nothing to say that we will never see international brands for French wine, other than the classic grands crus. B Magrez has provided an example, creating the generic Bordeaux brand Malesan 15 years ago, followed since then by Baron de Lestaque. It is true that there are more than 3,000 Bordeaux wines named 'château', and the unevenness of the taste quality and the low prices have undermined the confidence once placed in the 'château' label. Malesan owes its success to its ability to supply in quantity a product that customers like, for every day, and therefore at an accessible price. The first condition for a table wine brand is the existence of production capacity able to meet the expectations of mass distribution: from this point of view Languedoc-Roussillon, the world's largest vineyard, offers genuine opportunities and the necessary flexibility for adapting supply to demand, rather than the other way around.

Pharmaceutical brands

Some might be surprised to hear talk of pharmaceutical brands, since the role of a drug's constituents, and therefore of the intimate link of the active ingredients with the success of the drug, seems to defy any other element. Nevertheless, doctors do not prescribe products, but brands, where the generic product is not available. Science comes to us not in the form of the international scientific denomination of the chemical compound, but in the form of its brand name: Zantac, Tagamet, Clamoxyl, Prozac, Viagra and so on, not to mention medicines sold without prescription, which fall under classic marketing (Malox, Aspro, Doliprane and so on).

The medical environment is characterised by several factors that outline how and why 'brand building' is specific to it:

▊ All prescribers are known, put on file and stored on a database, some even visited directly several times a year (if they represent large volumes). In each country, there are a limited number of doctors, specialists and so on. It is therefore a closed environment. Each laboratory has one or more sales forces, known as medical delegates, who personally meet with all the doctors in order to inform them of the progress of the medicines they are tasked with promoting.

▊ The available information is almost complete. Through doctors' panels and pharmacists it is possible to know which doctor is prescribing what, and in what quantities, for what conditions, together with which other drugs, and so on.

▊ In this market, it is possible to model demand in an econometric fashion, due to the completeness of the information. Each laboratory is aware of the pressure it exerts on each doctor (measured by the number of visits, the time of the visit, the number of calls, time spent on the internet, etc). Since

they also know the effect on sales through medical prescription, it is possible to establish a mathematical function linking inputs with outputs, causes with effects.

▊ The subject is highly scientific. Even if 'business to consumer' communication is now sometimes permitted under certain stringent conditions, the end client has little say in the final prescription decision, although this does not mean no say at all. In fact, a general public medical culture has grown up in our ageing, over-informed societies: all mass-media magazines regularly talk about advances in the treatment of this or that ailment. Without citing the drug prescribed by name, they talk of active ingredients. The internet has also considerably increased the general public's level of awareness – nowadays, although people respect their doctor, they also have their own opinion. Furthermore, general practitioners wish to generate loyalty in their clientele: they listen to their clients.

▊ Prescription is increasingly influenced by the final payer: this is particularly true of generic drugs. Aware of the enormous and growing black hole of health spending, public authorities have exerted pressure for a compulsory switch to generic drugs, where possible. The pharmacist has even been given the right of substitution: if a generic exists, the pharmacist has authority to substitute it for the brand-name drug indicated by the doctor. If the patient refuses, he or she will receive a smaller reimbursement from their mutual fund.

▊ It is a market where, given the short lifespan of patents – 20 years – the day and year of the generic drug's launch can be predicted. Brand-name drugs attempt to delay this date, the signal for their programmed decline, which may be slower or faster depending on the country:

– for example, through patenting of original medicinal forms;

- or through continual modifications to the product, in order to extend the patent's duration of protection;

- or through hyper-segmentation of the range and the dosages, in order to make the generic drug less profitable;

- or through a lowering of prices at the end of the product's lifecycle to make the switch less attractive.

Public authorities, however, tend to oppose these manoeuvres, because the pressure on public health finances demands drastic savings.

We should also note that certain countries, such as Thailand in February 2007, have decided to bypass intellectual property rights by authorising the manufacturing and storing of generic forms of two famous anti-AIDS drugs, while they are still under patent protection. The Thai government invokes the argument of protecting its population: these two drugs are too expensive and therefore not accessible. AIDS is causing devastation in Thailand. Note that France did the same when it was a question of building stocks to protect the French population against the risk of anthrax, in the case of a chemical terrorist attack.

▪ It is an increasingly regulated market. Given its low margins, if too many generic producers offer the same product, they will struggle to turn a profit. Thus, in some countries, the state gives one leading generic producer leave to market even before the expiry of the patent, or to enjoy a temporary monopoly.

▪ It is a market where counterfeits now flourish. In fact, the active ingredients of drugs can be bought at very low prices in India or China. It is therefore easy to manufacture counterfeits. To date they have been sold via the internet, at the internet user's own risk. However, they are now finding their way into pharmaceutical channels.

Case study: How branding affects medical prescription

Brands create value both for the company and to those that decide to use them. This is done by a dual quest of differentiation on tangible dimensions but also on intangible dimensions. This quest is often not simultaneous: most brands start as the mere name of a product innovation. Once they achieve success, they are copied and the intangible dimension created by the communication of brand identity creates a form of protection: products may be similar but consumers choose one brand instead of another. This is the effect of habit, of proximity, of leadership and pioneering aura, and essentially of the need for reassurance. However, protections do not last: there is a need to recreate a material differentiation by innovation that delivers tangible benefits through improved products or services.

Very few sectors demonstrate the value of branding as much as the pharmaceutical sector. This sector is dominated by the ideology of progress through science. Those prescribing drugs are rational and make what they perceive as the best choice for the patient. Normally this should imply a product-driven market, in which brands are a forbidden word.

Recent research has shown however that medicines have a personality, as do all brands. By 'personality' we mean that both generalist doctors and specialists find it possible to attribute human personality traits to medicines. Not only did they not refuse to answer questions about brand personality, but statistical data analysis showed that some of the personality traits they ascribed to drugs were correlated with prescription levels (Kapferer, 1998).

When looking at Table 5.2, you will see that the anti-ulcer medicines that are most prescribed are described as more 'dynamic' and 'close' than other forms of medication. A

Table 5.2   Brand personality is related to prescription levels

| | Personality score (1 to 3) of highly prescribed vs less prescribed medical brands | | | | | |
| | Anti-hypertension | | Antibiotics | | Anti-ulcer | |
	Low P	High P	Low P	High P	Low P	High P
Dynamic	2.01	2.20+++	2.17	2.37+++	2.10	2.46+++
Creative	1.87	1.92	1.81	1.93+	2.03	2.22+++
Optimistic	2.02	2.21+++	2.00	2.23+++	2.22	2.31
Prudent	2.13	2.11	2.08	1.98	2.08+++	1.90
Hard	1.58+++	1.39	1.70+++	1.45	1.56+++	1.31
Cold	1.67+++	1.45	1.72+++	1.40	1.60+++	1.33
Caring	2.04	2.11	2.01	2.09	2.03	2.09
Rational	2.28	2.23	2.38	2.27	2.23	2.15
Generous	1.85	1.95	1.87	2.02+++	1.93	2.02
Empathetic	1.88	2.09+++	1.90	2.02++	1.99	2.01
Close	2.06	2.09	2.16	2.25	2.08	2.13
Elegant	1.97	1.97	1.99	2.04	1.92	2.03
Class	2.01	2.04	1.87	1.94	1.93	2.20+++
Serene	2.10	2.12	2.12	2.25+	2.20	2.11
Calm	2.15	2.07	2.16+	2.04	2.12+++	1.90

Source: Kapferer (1998)

(+++ level of statistical significance)

product, an active ingredient cannot be dynamic or close; a brand can. Thus brands of drugs do have a mental existence and influence in the minds of the prescribers.

Interestingly too, Table 5.3 shows that although they recognised the products themselves as being totally identical and saw two brands as fully similar in the functional benefits they delivered, respondents prescribed one three times more frequently than the other. However the chosen one was endowed with significantly more 'status' than the less chosen one. Status is an intangible dimension created by impressions of leadership) of presence, of proximity to the doctors, of intensity of communication. It is created by marketing once the drug has been developed. Once created, this serves as competitive edge against 'me-too' products, at least before a new drug replaces the existing one as market leader.

This example illustrates the fact that even in the high-tech sector, brands are a psychological reality, which operate even in the context of rational decision makers who are

disposed to make optimal rational decisions. Choice is always a risk: products increase the range of choice, and thus of perceived risk. Brands make choice easier by reducing the likelihood of choosing alternatives to the market leader.

The choice of the English word 'likelihood' here is interesting because it implies both a statistical concept (probability) and the mediating process by which alternatives are being more chosen (they are more 'likeable'). Branding is thus a consumer-oriented response to the problem of decision making in opaque and dense choice environments. Brand spontaneous awareness and positioning (linking to a need) are short cuts that are very helpful for decision making. Brands do create a decisional bias: as such they facilitate choice and reduce perceived risk (Kapferer and Laurent, 1988).

These examples illustrate the relationship between the product and the brand: there is a natural interaction between them. Brand mission determines what products or services should be created. These innovative products

Table 5.3   The brand influence in medical prescription

| | Category: anti-ulcer | |
	Brand A	Me-too
Product image		
Efficient	2.9	2.9
Rapid	2.7	2.7
Prevents recurrence	2.7	2.7
No side-effects	2.7	2.6
No anti-acid	2.6	2.6
Low cost	1.4	1.4
Brand status		
It is a reference product	3.7+++++	3.1-----
High reputation	3.8+++++	3.3-----
Superior quality	3.3	3.1
Major product	3.7+	3.6-
Prescription	6.7+++++	3.3-----

Source: Kapferer (1998)

endowed with a value-adding identity create attractiveness, and encourage trials, repeat sales and loyalty despite incoming copies and low-cost alternatives. However, new disruptive innovations may shift clients' value curves, hence change their preferences. This means that the brand cannot be defended only through intangible values: even the much admired Jaguar brand went broke and had to be bought by Ford to enable it to regain the capacity to make high-quality and high-tech cars for today's exacting new affluent consumers.

Prescription therefore typically follows a 'two-steps flow of influence' model. Communication with leaders creates status and reputation, which then makes it necessary for people to be informed about this brand that everyone is talking about: familiarity with the product follows this desire created by its reputation. (Figure 5.4)

Tomorrow, for certain chronic illnesses, it will be even easier to carry out direct to consumer (DTC) information advertising, mentioning the laboratory and the active ingredients of the drug, but not the brand.

Today, the role of the internet in the dissemination of information to patients, who know more on the subject than their general practitioners do, and interrogate them about the new brands and compounds, is being measured. When updating this research, the patient's own point of view should be included as a new lever in medical prescription. Thanks to the internet, patients arrive at their doctor's office already well informed: they have heard about this treatment or that drug on a blog, a forum, a website, in a women's magazine and so on. Doctors need to generate loyalty among their clientele and are reluctant to act against the patient's wishes, even if they can. For chronic illnesses, the patient's feelings on the unpleasantness of the treatment also play a part. Price should also be integrated as a new lever: in fact, the preoccupation with reducing health expenditure is now shared by doctors themselves.

In another of our studies, we showed how certain facets of the laboratory's image can directly influence medical prescription. This is why, in today's global drug marketing, it is

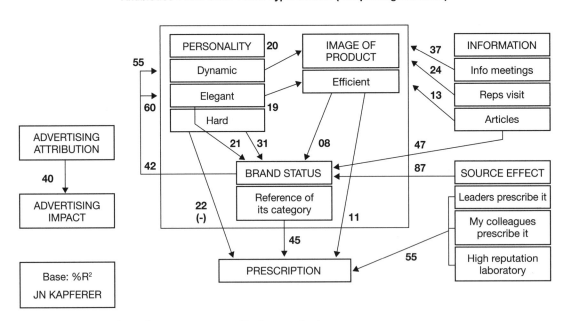

Figure 5.4   How brands impact on medical prescription

first necessary to establish the laboratory's credibility, one country at a time. In this way it can then enjoy the source effect.

Becoming aware of the intangible

The research outlined above shows that the intangible factor is also present in medical brands, and in this they are brands in the fullest sense. Big brands inspire confidence, and have an attractive personality. However, big brands sometimes possess an intangible dimension that escapes the laboratory, in both senses of the word: due to its rationalist culture, it is not aware of it, and also it does not control it.

Prozac is a major brand. Its reputation has in many ways transcended the context of a medical environment. In fact, more than simply a drug, it is a cultural revolution. By launching Prozac, Lilly did more than launch a new anti-depressant: without knowing it, it overturned Judeo-Christian ideology. Could it

be that man was no longer born to suffer? Prozac owes its diffusion to the fact that it is now possible, even apart from genuine depression, to smooth over emotional traumas (divorce, relationship breakdown and so on). It now seems that forces in the service of this ideology have chosen it as a target. Those sects that exploit the fragility of individuals in distress to recruit members have even attacked this drug by any means possible. Clearly, it is the intangible factor that drives the emotion.

The laboratory brand

In a second piece of research, we investigated the importance of the laboratory's own image in medical prescription. Of course the characteristics of the brand-name drug outweigh everything else, as they should, but the image traits of the laboratory appear in fifth place, in particular the laboratory's perceived competence in the field, and its ability to hear and respond to information from doctors (highly reactive services and call centres, consultation, the type of medical delegates, and so on) is also significant. They wish to know 'the brand behind the brand'. This means that in the worldwide launch of a new drug, it is first necessary to establish confidence in the laboratory itself among opinion leaders and prescribers, country by country.

The business-to-business brand

Managers working in the B2B domain regularly complain of the lack of theorisation on B2B brands. They are rarely found in academic works on brands, where most examples are drawn from mass-consumption brands, generally food products with low involvement (yoghurts, soft drinks and the like). This is why, in this book, we have purposely used different examples and introduced a genuine variety of sectors, in order to establish the relevance of the models proposed as a tool for decision making.

Is B2B different?

Is B2B really different? For us, the B2B argument is used as a standard, reflecting above all the need for recognition of the sector for a world that receives very little attention. The seminars we run for B2B companies clearly show what their principal request is: models are attractive, but need to be demonstrated and illustrated in a B2B context. Moreover, the notion of B2B itself is illusory: it does not reflect a homogeneous reality. For example, the so-called 'Soho' market (small office, home office) functions at a purchasing level very close to the mass or general public markets. We can observe a concentration of distribution under international names such as Office Depot or Staples, which subsequently create their own brand products and substitute them for the producer's brands wherever possible. In contrast, the high-voltage electrical equipment

market, based on invitations to tender, is entirely different in nature. Another difference is linked to the question of whether the company buys personalised, made-to-measure products or solutions, or service, or just a cost? Finally, can we really place the purchase of silicons from Dow, bleach from Arkema, oxygen from Liquid Air, and customer relationship systems such as those from SAP or Sage on the same level?

One thing is certain: there are indeed B2B brands. If we define the brand as a name with power, a name considered by industrial players as an indispensable reference in conjunction with a particular need, there are plenty of examples.

First, the B2B world has its product brands: for example, the building trade buys Giproc or Pregipan plasterboards, Sikkens or Levi's paint, Agilia cement, Daikin air-conditioning, Legrand or Hager electrical equipment, Technal or Wicona aluminium and so on. The automobile sector, although under constant pressure on prices, is conscious of equipment brands such as Sekurit for windscreens and Gefco for logistics requirements: the transport upstream and downstream of supply chains of industrial production. Note that these product brands are often names of former companies that, once acquired by a group, cease to be companies and become brand ranges in a catalogue. This is the case for Giproc – now owned by Saint Gobain – and Merlin Gerin at Schneider Electric. Of course these names alone do not ensure sales and loyalty generation, but they contribute strongly to it.

Next, studies also show the influence of corporate reputation. This is composed of awareness and the image of power, commercial dynamism, innovation and ethics. It influences the selection of a company in weighty decisions – weighty because of both their financial total and the length of the commitment. There is a high degree of correlation between the recognition and image of a company and the readiness to 'strongly consider this company for any future tenders', or even to refuse to do so. Of course this does not mean that it is the only factor affecting the choice: in fact, in an industrial environment, consideration does not equal selection, and the tangible components of the tender and the price will of course weigh heavily. It does prove, however, that the name of these companies has acquired the power of a brand as a result of the specific reputation they have built through their expertise and their skill in communicating it. To be considered on the mental, or even the official, 'shortlist' is one of the major benefits of a brand – that is, the reputation that is attached to it. When the brand no longer possesses this power, entire sectors fall to the principle of the lowest bidder, where only the price per kilo or per tonne counts. The function of a brand policy is precisely to avoid this.

Is there no difference, then, between B2B brands and B to B to C brands? In our view there is one essential difference: pressure on costs. B2B purchasing generally forms part of the cost price of another product. A truck or a set of tyres for an articulated lorry is part of the price of transport, which will consequently affect the sale price of products transported by road. In fact, freighters are demanding ever lower prices from transporters, who increasingly view their truck or tyre purchases from an accounting, even a financial, perspective. This leads to a constant B2B pressure towards commoditisation. This difference has a major effect on three facets of the brand: the brand function, the brand weight, and the brand's point of application.

Functions of the industrial brand

In our research on sensitivity to brands, with Professor G Laurent (Kapferer and Laurent, 1995), the brand's role as a reducer of risk quickly became apparent. This is not enough in many mass consumption markets: consumers no longer see any risk there. In

B2B, very often the products and services play a part in the composition of the products sold, making them components of customer satisfaction and therefore reputation. The Lafarge signature is important for concrete, just as the word Siemens is important for turbines. Of course, concrete could be considered a commodity, where suppliers have shifted the competitive playing field towards services. In the choice of concrete, however, engineering consultancies issuing invitations to tender are sensitive to the risks linked to failures in building infrastructure. This may not be a question of an individual suburban dwelling in Calcutta in India, but of a new council housing office, or a planned new skyscraper in Berlin.

In B2B, every ingredient forms an integral part of the offer that the purchasing company makes to its own clients. Its reputation depends on them. This is why car manufacturers, with their mechanical background, buy Bosch, the specialist in electrical equipment. They know that the weak link in today's cars is not the mechanics, but the electronics. The company 'covers itself' by buying from the top name in the sector for its clients downstream. Furthermore, nowadays it is the equipment makers that provide the innovations. Automobile brands are designers and builders. This is why in B2B it is so important for a brand to worry about the clients of its clients. This is where the big brand's function as a guarantor of quality comes in.

This is its first, even its predominant function in B2B, as the level of perceived risk rises. However, this is not its only function: the B2B brand is also an instrument of pride. It can add an intangible dimension that also increases the brand's potential to attract and earn loyalty. For example, the American company ITW (International Tool Works) has always spurned umbrella, multi-sector brands. It sells equipment and tools to carpenters, electricians and plumbers, taking care to offer them a brand for each trade. Thus Stihl is dedicated to carpenters alone. This differentiation makes it possible to capitalise on each profession's conviction that it is different, and its desire to mark that difference: tool brands either help or hinder this.

One of the problems causing the fall in sales of Black & Decker – a multi-market umbrella brand – is that it sells both to the general public, through major stores, and also to professionals, forgetting the brand's intangible function as an instrument of self-expression for professionals. In the same way that wearing Nike is a source of comfort, but also of a symbolic association with the world of Olympic or baseball heroes, buying Stihl is a way of saying, 'I am with the carpenters, the professionals.' Black & Decker has destroyed part of its intangible value by extending the umbrella so far, lumping the professionals together with the general public. It is reacting, but too late, by launching a new brand dedicated to professionals alone, De Walt.

When the IBM PC was the best-selling PC, everyone was in agreement that the product was average, or in any case far from being the best. However, in 1981 it was reassuring to company IT directors who were uncomfortable with this new market (of personal computing), since it came from their supplier of larger systems: the giant IBM. For users, the IBM seal offered them the satisfaction of saying to themselves (mentalisation) or communicating to others (self-reflection) that they must be serious executives, since they had an IBM. The recent transfer of IBM to Le Novo (a Chinese company) reflects how much the PC market has been commoditised. The perceived risk in the purchase has shifted from the assembler of the PC to the components themselves (Intel, AMD), which now become parameters of choice, and the operating system (Windows Vista). Hence the struggle for component manufacturers to build themselves up as brands: that is, as major choice criteria. They do this through co-branding and major financial involvement in the communications budgets of their partner assembly brands.

The weight of the industrial brand

An enduring suspicion regarding the real weight of the brand in industry decisions relates to the questioning methods used in the sector – surveys with direct questions are used. Thus, during a study on the factors involved in the choice of a maritime transporter for major shippers (such as the industrialists Saint Gobain for glass, and Michelin for tyres), the five main criteria given by logistics directors were price, dates and times, reliability, capacity for last-minute delivery, and the availability of information throughout the journey. The brand is the last criterion named. In contrast, when an indirect questioning method is used, of identifying choice factors – by varying the parameters of maritime companies' offers and examining the impact on the shippers' choices – we see that reputation (or in other words, the brand) becomes a key factor, if not the principal factor.

There is nothing irrational in this, as too many people in the industrial sector experience it or say it. How, in fact, can one know in advance whether everything will go well before and during maritime transport? None of us are soothsayers. We must therefore make hypotheses: a well-known brand is not well known by accident. It carries in itself the quasi-certainty – subjective but based on experience – that everything will go well, or better than it otherwise would.

It would be wrong to suggest that reputation (and therefore the power of the brand) is the number one criterion in all B2B selling. Guilbert, the office furnishings distributor, delivering direct to companies, owes its profitability to its product policy. Guilbert sells first and foremost its remarkable service to companies. Products come second, with Guilbert attempting as far as possible to substitute its own products for branded products: in fact, the latter are now in a minority. It retains only a few Scotch products, for example, and not all of them: it offers adhesive tape under its own NiceDay brand. Of course, it is sometimes still obliged to offer Stabilo Boss, Bic Crystal and Post-Its, and the Dymo label printer, but that is all. And yet all the brands deleted from its catalogue are well known. Today, however, this is not enough. The end users – secretaries, managers or employees – do not even notice that the product they find on their desks is not the true Post-It, but a cheaper distributor's brand copy. A strong brand is a brand with indispensable products or with strong intangible added value (reassurance or pride).

What makes a product indispensable? The patents that protect it, the communication that makes its name the key reference in the category among users themselves (downstream, therefore the professional buyers) and prescribers (upstream), and of course the innovation that maintains this status as the key reference and gives it an advantage over distributors' copies and low-cost Asian products imported by the distributors. This innovation may relate to the products, but also to the services provided to intermediaries, installers and distributors. A brand is more than a timely product. It is a mutual, long-term dedication of one business to another.

This shows us that among industrial distributors, and now in B2B, there is an obsession with substituting brands, as Carrefour has done since 1967 in the mass market. A study among wholesalers of electric heating indicated that they had in stock three electric water heaters: the first because 'everyone asks for it', the second because 'people ask for it', and the third for its price. Saying that 'people ask for it' clearly reveals that in the industrial sector, the brand is a prescription. All of the brand's B2B marketing should focus on the distributor's clients, or the professional buyer's clients within the company. If this prescription is not created, for example through a dedicated sales force, then the brand enters into a downward spiral through the distributor and the buyer, who only thinks about the price. Legrand's great

strength is that it has understood this: Legrand has made its brand such a 'must' for electricians that to Legrand, wholesalers are merely stockists. It needs them only for this stock function.

The corporate and the brand

One of the characteristic traits of the B2B brand is that it has a double nature. It may be the company itself, or the products and ranges, or a combination of the two. However, the level of risk is such that the reputation of the source and of the company is most often called into play.

At Air Liquide, the brand is the corporate name for the sale of commodities with little differentiation: the prestige attached to this leading company cannot overcome a price handicap, but where prices are the same, it will add its guarantee of seriousness and regularity of provision. It may even be enough to justify a small price difference. In order to move away from the 'commoditised' market, Air Liquide has developed and co-created specialised lines, together with its clients, such as for example the gas brand Aligal, intended for the preservation of fresh produce in plastic packaging. These innovations carry a name that refers back to the corporate name through its prefix (Al) and specifies the destination market. At Gaz de France, the range of prices and associated services has been promoted under the Provalis name, in order to de-commoditise it.

Industrial B2B companies often believe that they can manage without the corporate brand reputation, and that only the product reputation matters. This is an error that passes unnoticed until the day that financial analysts signal undervaluing on the stock exchange arising specifically from the absence of a brand. This is the case with Sage. Sage is rather like Europe: an economic giant, but a political dwarf. Sage is one of the giants of management software for companies, but it is not recognised as such. It is true that the company has grown through external growth, buying companies that became product names within its product portfolio (of management software). With a turnover of €1.4 billion, Sage is an expert in marketing products and remarkably successful at selling them. Its competitors in this market are SAP, which turns over €8 billion, Oracle, which turns over €4 billion, and Microsoft, which turns over only €0.7 billion but has the highest growth rate in the software market for SMEs. These figures suggest to the stock market that a consolidation is on the cards: it awaits a takeover bid for Sage, which appears to show a lack of dynamism, due to its low recognition as the key actor in the sector. The stock market wants Sage to demonstrate that it has the capacity for organic growth.

Divided by market, Sage allows its divisions to run their own autonomous communications: the largest divisions therefore communicate the most. These are the ones that are active on the historically best-known major markets (accounting, pay and human resources). They therefore drag Sage's image down, to the detriment of the new markets, which show promise for future organic growth, but where sales are still small. The failure to take into account the reputation needs of the parent brand itself, Sage, makes it a weak brand. It is a portfolio of products and clients, but not a brand. For any development of legislation or regulations relating to the SME, governments consult Microsoft or SAP, not Sage: Sage is not perceived as a genuine actor in its sector.

Its reputation is less than that of its products. Significantly, there are only 200 links leading to its website, whereas it has more than 300 licensed distributors – a sign that to them, Sage is not a necessary reference.

It appears that, having neglected to organise themselves and to invest in order to create a reputed and recognised crossover brand, companies suffer the consequences at a given point in their growth. Organisation by product and by market creates sales, but also

silos: worried about the figures in their annual evaluations, nobody works on the collective reputation, which costs money without bringing short-term benefit.

The activation points of the B2B brand are different

The B2B brand is a relational brand. Other than in commodities markets, people do not buy a product, but rather a supplier, with a view to durable joint development. Wholesalers themselves do not just stock a brand – they represent it, and are thus committed to it. They therefore expect it to behave like a brand, with a guarantee, innovation, services with added value, development of markets through communication, and activation of networks. The carriers of the brand are both products and the consultation of commercial delegates, their reactions and the quality of their follow-up and service.

Facom's reputation was built on a fleet of trucks that visited garages, not to sell, but to explain the products and listen to the garage mechanics, their comments and requests, from 7 am when the workshop opened. This is how the spread of lowest-bidder tenders, where the only things that matter are the price and the regularity of provision, can be avoided. In contrast, by going ever further afield, to China, Vietnam or Bangladesh, in search of the unknown supplier who can offer an even lower price, buyers reject the concept of the brand, which represents safety. Here, the first consideration is how to produce more cheaply, even to the point of taking risks for the downstream client. By chartering dubious transporters, petroleum companies expose the coasts of Brittany to the serious risks with which we are all familiar.

The B2B brand is a prescription

Lastly, the B2B brand focuses on prescribers. The decision to buy within a company always involves not one, but several people. The brand is therefore built up through identifying the key prescribers: the architect, the research offices, the consultancies, the technical departments and so on, all the way to the final client. Thus Legrand does without wholesalers, except for logistics, since it carries out permanent promotional campaigns among electricians and the general public, to let them know about innovations so that they can demand them from their electrician. All the success of Lycra, the brand that de-commoditised generic elastane fibre, consisted of working first of all with those who acted as guides and opinion leaders for the entire textile sector: the luxury and premium brands. When they developed common applications, the innovations made were noticed by the entire sector. In the meantime, Lycra had acquired a precious aura to justify a price much higher than generic fibres. Tactel followed the same approach to constructing its brand, through co-creation and the decision to target leaders with strong prescriptive power.

Multi-brand groups specialise their brands according to their business model, which is linked to prescription. The Norwegian Norsk Hydro group, a leader in aluminium applications, has three brands in Europe for aluminium profiles intended for construction: Wicona, Technal and Domal. The first is aimed at large projects, and therefore capitalises on the prescriptions of architects, design offices and engineering consultants. Technal uses the final customer as the lever of prescription on the installers themselves. Domal aims at small companies directly.

Moving away from a commoditised market

The risk of commoditisation is the sword of Damocles for B2B. Of course there are niches where the level of perceived risk ensures positional income, as with companies specialising in the analysis of aviation fuel quality, but these are exceptions. For the world leader in

industrial paints, Akzo Nobel, the brands have a single objective: to bring value to the client in order to move away from competition on price. Therefore it pursues a policy of global brands, each dedicated to a target, according to a global segmentation built on painters' expectations.

A market is commoditised when the actors have not worked hard enough on it. The brand is not a miraculous answer, but the name that takes a genuine marketing approach of creating value for a dedicated target. It is therefore necessary first of all to analyse the clients, to understand them – to go beyond the machine-gun volleys of surveys that show the client only cares about price. All markets are segmented, even the low-cost markets. Everything depends on what is offered alongside the price.

Thus any chemical company will claim that the silicones market is a purely commoditised market. In reality, as with many other industrial markets, there are four segments:

- those clients who want innovation in order to be able to innovate themselves for their clients;

- those clients who want to improve their efficiency and productivity;

- those clients who want to reduce the total production cost;

- those clients who want the lowest possible price.

Three segments here are sensitive to price, and would probably put this criterion in first place in an opinion poll with direct questions. However, a more in-depth investigation might show the client's problem with its own client, downstream: this is where we find fertile soil for the added value that must be created. If we consider the fourth segment lost, it is necessary to concentrate on segments two and three.

This is what Dow does: it has created a business known as Xiameter, separate from

Dow's core business, aimed at the cost-oriented segment. Then began the work on the value curve of the Xiameter offer. It is necessary in fact to stop talking about the product, but to envisage the delivery of silicones as the creation of value for the client. If you wish to offer a low price, but also value alongside it, it is important to analyse the facets that the client is likely to neglect (and therefore reduce them to zero) in order to maximise those of which the client expects most. This innovation, known as 'value innovation' since it redefines an attractive value curve previously unseen in the sector, makes it possible to innovate in the price segment (see Chapter 9 on value innovation). Of course, in the case of Xiameter, everything was carried out via the internet, which made it possible to set prices according to stock levels, rather like yield management of prices in air and TGV travel.

The internet brand

How do internet brands function, the purely online brands such as Google, eBay and Amazon? What are the specific mechanisms of their growth, seemingly so rapid while it is taking place? We now have the benefit of distance to guide our analysis. The first phase of the internet, which led to the speculative bubble, was that of prophets rather than profits, business plans rather than proven use. We know what happened to the thousands of investors who believed in an El Dorado without effort. Nevertheless, the end of the beginning was not the beginning of the end. While investors turned away from the internet as quickly as they had first picked it up, campus students, researchers and managers continued for their part to make increasing use of it. We now have a phenomenon that has restructured our society, and will remake our way of life, redefine our expectations and our impatiences. The process is underway, since the

billions of users who have tried it are asking for more. With Web 2.0, the internet is becoming the first interactive and interpersonal mass media: the rise of blogs is the clearest signal, as is the rise of sites such as MySpace and YouTube.

The pure internet brands, also known as e-brands or dot.coms, have begun the new century in a very different context from that in which they were born. Only the best from that first period remain: Amazon, Google, eBay, MySpace. We must learn from them and from others how the online environment creates very specific conditions, which are themselves transforming traditional brand management.

The customer makes the brand

One of the reasons that so many internet start-ups in the first period never took off, implicating so many investors in their collapse, was that they only thought about their flotation on the stock exchange, offering considerable prospects for increases in value. The paradox, as we know, is that they still had very few loyal customers, very little income, and were far from covering their running costs. The majority of those companies that boasted of their high spontaneous awareness scores were strangely silent about their sales. We experienced a period where valuation preceded value.

Logically, it is the value created by the customers that is the only basis for serious valuation. It is true that the e-brands of this internet era innovated by creating a way of functioning that was aimed more at investors than at consumers and value creation. The dominant logic aimed to bring together a significant pool of several million euros in order to invest quickly in an offline advertising campaign, essentially on prime-time television, in order to create interest in another pool, which would be immediately reinvested in advertising. The spontaneous awareness thus created gave rise to curiosity, causing people to click on the icon and visit the page, but above all it impressed investors, sure that they were getting their hands on one of tomorrow's winners.

This was neither B2C, nor B2B, but B2I, business to investors. The goal was to achieve the initial public offering (IPO), and flotation on the stock exchange, as quickly as possible. Sadly, how many start-ups confided in us, off the record, that the initial clicks were from curious surfers who did not buy anything? It is true that the internet has its aficionados, young and ultra-curious, in search of the latest innovations – but consequently also disloyal and fickle. Since it was born from dozens of internet reviews, not to mention supplements in the ordinary press and magazines, each new campaign thrilled editors, since it gave them something to talk about. These start-ups were surfing on a rumour effect, not on reality. Rumours will always run out of steam in the end.

During that same period, for the brands that have survived, the eBays, Amazons, Googles and Intuits, their delighted customers were continually talking about them, essentially on the internet, chat rooms, e-mail, forums and the like. One of the surest predictors of company growth is what is known as the NPS (net promotion score) (Reichheld, 2006). This is the difference between the percentage of people who would recommend the brand to others around them (known as promoters) and those who would criticise it to those around them (known as detractors): the score is 40 per cent for eBay, one of the strongest. We are indebted to Jeff Bezos for the following quote: 'Our users would tell us what was wrong during the day, and we would work overnight to improve the system.' As for the boss of Inuit, he reminds us that on Web 2.0, it is useless to invest in advertising campaigns, since it is satisfied customers who do the work: it is necessary to invest in ways to satisfy them, day after day.

This is the specificity of the Web 2.0 internet brands: 'brand building', construction of the affect and attachment to the brand, is much faster, since the company can receive immediate feedback from its clientele, segment by segment, person by person, and immediately make the changes that will increase satisfaction, to the great surprise of the people in question, who notice the improvements for themselves day by day.

The internet brand is both experiential and relational. It is experiential, because each person forms their own idea by visiting personally, by living the experience. One only has to visit Google to be impressed by what a simple click can obtain, time after time. It is a typical process of loyalty generation through the systematic distribution of gratifying experiences to the user.

It is relational, because the great strength of the internet is its ability to learn from each individual, one to one, and to demonstrate what it has learnt to that same individual. Amazon is the model here: the user only has to go online to see that he or she is recognised, and welcomed with good, personalised news (new books chosen for him or her, based on recent purchases).

To this is added the positive effect of 'network externalities'. eBay has benefited from these, as has Kelkoo: the more visitors there are to an auction site, the greater the chance that the sellers will find a better buyer able to offer a better price, and likewise the greater the chance that the visitors will find a seller with the product they have always wanted, but had despaired of ever finding. It is a giant virtual car boot sale, like the Paris flea market or the Portobello market in London, except that it is transparent: the user can tell immediately who is offering what. Visitors to eBay have all the more reason to revisit the site, since it continues to grow – not to mention the fact that by returning to the same site, users have no need to relearn how to use it. They already have their bearings, even when they are not recognised, spotted and greeted like a dear friend. These are all factors that create, if not a barrier to leaving or to visiting rival sites, at least a mechanical propensity to revisit. Of course the service is high quality, and is always improving, to adapt to clients that are becoming more sophisticated and whose demands are growing. Like any brand, the internet brand must continually create value for each fragment of its clientele, almost one to one.

The internet is also a mass medium of affinity: users can immediately communicate with their friends and community how satisfied they are with a particular site, and what they have just found or experienced there. Electronic word of mouth, or 'word of mouse', finds an accelerator out of all proportion to usual word of mouth, hence the recent notion of the 'viral rumour'.

Virtual closeness and psychological closeness

What is a brand? Fundamentally it is a name (and its associated symbols) that has a lasting influence on purchasing behaviour. What is a big brand? A name that is also linked with emotion by a very large number of potential purchasers. A big brand has no effect without an emotive relationship. It is this attachment, or commitment, that generates the desire to pursue the relationship, from the purchaser's point of view, which translates to loyalty to the brand. The value of a brand is measured by its capacity to create a personal tie of loyalty with the consumer, at a particular price level.

Are the pure internet brands brands like any other? Studies show that closeness is still lacking for many brands. This might appear paradoxical at a time when the internet is presented as the alpha and omega of personalisation. However, those are the facts. When asked, consumers are hesitant to say of dot.coms, 'This is a brand I feel close to', as if the relationship of repeat visits had not yet been translated into a genuine intimacy and

complicity. Do we visit Kelkoo, a price search engine, or Price Minister because we prefer Kelkoo or Price Minister? Or simply because they are the only names that immediately spring to mind, so that we click on them, and then click on them again, using the economy of effort represented by a favourites list?

For some analysts, this lack of closeness is structural: the pure dot.com brands will always lack the sensory, physical and palpable dimension without which there can be no genuine closeness. What is left of these brands once the screen is switched off?

For other analysts, it is a temporary phenomenon. Relational closeness is built over time, through repeated and extended use. Thus Yahoo! began as a search engine, and then extended its services to local weather forecasts and many other services. In doing so, it is penetrating more deeply into the internet life of individuals.

Brands such as eBay took four years of silent work to progressively refine their concept and their services: they made little use of advertising, but much more of word of mouth of satisfied pioneers, then early adopters and finally customer-ambassadors. Their reputation was built through interactions with enthusiastic surfers, who had the feeling of being listened to, which in addition to their recommendation also had the effect of lending these brands an emotive dimension and closeness.

The closeness and complicity are those of shared values and emotions – hence the phenomenal success of a site such as MySpace or YouTube, both bought by Google for a king's ransom for that reason. Amazon, for example, is a genuine brand in the sense that it carries values that extend beyond the product. It has moved beyond the marketplace by offering on its site a new way of interacting with other people on the subject of books, and now many other products as well. It symbolises more than the new economy – it prefigures a new society and a new era.

How does the internet brand communicate?

The brand's first medium is its name, in this case its domain name. Two schools of thought clash on this subject. The first is afraid of generalism, a disease that we have often shown and castigated: wishing to describe the service, all actors end up with names that are very, if not too, similar. The purpose of a brand name, as with a domain name, is not to describe but to distinguish. According to this first school of thought, a site for small online advertisements or online auctions should under no circumstances call itself 'e-auction', but rather 'eBay', for example (which is indeed the name of the world leader). There are in fact many competitors seeking to use the generic term 'auction', which will quickly create confusion in the market for consumers. In fact, the leading European online auction site was called e-bazar, which did not describe the service but brought a touch of added value (the word bazaar invokes spontaneous mental associations of profusion, excitement, merchandising, human relationships, amusement, as with the Great Bazaar in Istanbul). The word 'bazaar' immediately brings added values and emotive resonance.

The second school of thought states that the appropriation of a service also occurs through the appropriation of its name. We should add that the strategy of appropriation is not limited to the name, but involves a temporal advance and the exploitation of this advance at the online and offline communication levels. Thus the leading brand in price comparison is named Kelkoo. To a French-speaking audience, it sounds like *'quel coût?'* (What price?), with a touch of modernity and impertinence in the spelling. Note, however, that for Swedes, Germans, Spaniards and Italians, Kelkoo is a purely connotative name, which is evocative but means nothing. By lucky chance, it still retains positive mental associations (in Germany, for example, the sound of the word Kelkoo evokes 'calcu-lation', and in Italy it evokes something funny).

The example of the first internet portal dedicated to women in France is also revealing: what could be more descriptive than the domain name aufeminin.com? The choice of this name met three objectives: to find an explicit name to make a quick impact, a name with potential to become a brand (therefore with emotional depth), and of course a name available on the internet (it was bought from the owner) and also able to be registered as a trademark. Add a fourth, implicit criterion that must characterise all internet brands: its potential to be immediately internationalisable. In fact, aufeminin.com became enfemenino.com in Spain, alfeminile.com in Italy, and go.feminine.de in Germany. From the point of view of this fourth criterion – internationalisation – a non-descriptive name is easier to use, but has the disadvantage in the country of origin of not being direct enough, if directness is the objective.

After the name comes the home page, the brand's lobby. Google's example is revealing. Few places on the Web have been thought through as carefully as this almost virgin, all-white page. Paradoxically, the more Google becomes in reality an ogre, a hydra that wants to buy and swallow up everything around it, to become the number one mass medium in the world, the more important this page becomes. It hides the tentacular dimension of the Google company via a very pared-back, limpid, serene brand design, an advertisement for a world where everything is simple, beautiful and easy. One only needs to insert a word in the search box and await the miracle. The home page is certainly a key application point for the internet brand: Orange's home page resembles a bazaar. It is like being on the Paris metro: far from the desired personalisation, it is full of competing advertisements that manifestly have nothing to do with the individual.

Then the brand communicates through its ergonomic qualities, its arborescence, its complication or the ease of moving through the site itself – not to mention the background, the ability to move customers to the point that they wish to return to the site, knowing that there will always be something new for them. There can be no brand without regular good news for customers and visitors!

Country brands

Among the most spectacular extensions of the notion of a brand, we find countries. There is no shortage of symbols: in New Delhi, more than 100 people work full-time on 'Brand India' and on the implementation of a global communications programme 'Incredible India', with the goal of modifying behaviour towards this infinitely varied country by working on people's perception of it and even giving it a positioning. Books such as *Rebuilding Brand America* (Martin, 2007) or *The Marketing of Nations* (Kotler, 1997) mark how countries have become symbols, words charged with emotion, and sources of influence over the actions of people who, for the most part, have never visited them. In fact, countries are associated with snippets of history, recent or more distant, imaginary elements, the personality traits of their inhabitants, key competences and accomplishments. The reputation of certain countries is based more on their history; for others it is based more on their accomplishments. This is why companies and their commercial brands shape the country brand itself through their success, and sketch out the international stereotype of their key competence. The reputation of its universities also creates the country brand.

The country's evocative power

Countries are therefore names with brand power: they have the power to influence through the spontaneous associations they evoke, for good or ill, and through the emotions that they stir up. This brand power (influence) is nevertheless linked to specific contexts: Italy is the great cultural brand, a sign of quality and creativity in the fashion market, for example. The United States has a wider effect: we voluntarily 'consume' the US brand and its affective evocations when we buy Coca-Cola (the water of America), jeans (the clothing of America), American cinema from Hollywood, American hamburgers, when we smoke Marlboro cigarettes, the metaphor inhaled from American Westerns, and when the whole world accepts the dollar as the base of international exchanges. However we no longer buy their cars, ill suited to the era of expensive and soon to be scarce petrol.

As with all strong global brands, the country brand encapsulates a myth, a stereotype that boosts its own attractiveness through an emotive resonance. The United States, a country built by immigrants, encapsulates worldwide the mythology of liberty (hence the famous statue of that name) and the self-made man, the accomplishment of success through hard work and effort. In fact, in the DNA of American identity, we find immigrants fleeing their miserable living conditions in their home countries in Asia and Europe, who have rebuilt their life in this new promised land.

The country brand combines information at all levels: from political to social to cultural to economic to tourist, from the past to the present, real and imaginary, in complete syncretism. Managing the country brand entails working specifically on the salience of these different facets, burying some (by saying nothing) and making others more visible.

With globalisation, we learn snippets of information and glean impressions of the whole world, even the most distant countries. These perceptions are malleable when they are not anchored as stereotypes, or based on striking personal experience. Thus the image of Korea has evolved among elites and opinion leaders through the emergence of Korean cinema, recognised at film festivals such as Cannes and Venice, an original type of cinema at a time when the resurgence of the great Japanese masters is still dawdling. Korea has ceased to be a 'hollow' brand, a shadow of Japan or hidden by its giant neighbour China: it is transmitting meaning. At the same time, abandoning its policy of commoditised products at the lowest prices, thanks to high technology but also to strong investment in design, Samsung is penetrating the United States and Europe in the dynamic and highly visible market of mobile telephony. In short, the 'Korea' brand is nurtured by successful *Korean* brands, and those in turn benefit from the umbrella of their country's image, which is undergoing a positive transformation, therefore acting like a collective federating brand. We can see how much the country brand and the 'Made in ...' brand interact – for it is also necessary to mention the 'Made in ...' brand.

The 'Made in ...' stereotype

We have known for a long time how much the words 'Made in Germany' create value in the automobile industry and industrial equipment worldwide. In just 10 years, 'Made in Australia' has become a symbol of value in the current wine market, through daily and relaxed usages. The words 'Made in Korea' have moved from a devaluating status (second-rate copies) to a symbol of respected quality between 1990 and 2002. The biggest question for the Western world today hinges on whether 'Made in China' has the ability to follow the same positive trajectory in the same short time frame.

Marketing research itself has set up 'country of origin' as a specific, rich and prolific field, demonstrating how much countries are associated with attributes, competences, real or imaginary representations that combine to create relevant value (or not). This research

teaches us that the 'country of origin effect' is not uniform. It varies:

- according to the sector (France for perfumes, Germany for machine tools);
- according to the consumer (national stereotypes have more influence for novices and laypersons: professional buyers and experts rightly move beyond them to seek partners and new suppliers for their own company);
- according to the level of perceived risk attaching to the decision, its individual or collective nature (the need to prove to others that the choice is a reasoned one).

To recapitulate the paradigm of research into persuasion (Kapferer, 1990), the words 'made in country X' act as a sign of specific qualities and faults, but also like any source of communication. If it is a credible source, it relieves the receiver of the need to look too deeply into it, and lowers his or her resistance to persuasion. If it is not credible, it has the same effect on information handling: it will remain superficial but here will lead directly to rejection.

The country brand is managed

In order to create a perception of value, it is necessary to give content to the perception that one seeks to create of the country, a perception profile that will be unique to this country, that can be attributed to it and that will drive behaviour both internally (in the country) and externally (abroad). The country brand is by nature a collective, federalising brand: it needs to distribute its power and its content to its daughter brands, specialised by market. The Incredible India brand is in fact varied according to whether India is seeking to attract tourists (the Visit India daughter brand), industrial investment in high-tech or services, or positive attitudes at the political or cultural level, and so on.

As with any other brand, the country brand must have an international dispersal if it is to influence the entire world. This dispersal is carried by ambassadors, the country brand's 'flagship products': products that it exports (for example Bollywood cinema), acknowledged expertise in IT and mathematics, past and present political figures (Gandhi), the cultural identity (spirituality, castes and so on), the geographic (demography), politics (leader of the developing world), and tourist identities (Rajasthan).

The country brand is in competition with other countries: it must be seen, perceived to be different, credible and attractive. The country brand must therefore have a positioning based on its identity, on which it is promoted abroad: perceived values, perceived history, perceived competence and the accomplishments that prove it make the brand. The problem with the France brand today occurs largely because its ambassadors hail from its history (Louis XIV, Napoleon, De Gaulle), its values embodied by the 1789 Revolution, its culture (the chateaux of the Loire, Impressionism, gastronomy, etc), but its influence is decreasing and the giants of its global industrial success (Bouygues, Vinci, Lafarge, Alstom, Thales, Veolia, Suez and so on) are unknown, or are not attributed to France. There remain luxury, l'Oréal, perfumes, Danone and tourism. Even its wine is no longer influential. Furthermore, the televised images of recent events in the suburbs have shown that France as a country can no longer live up to its own values in today's reality. Under these conditions, choosing a positioning is not easy. However, if one wishes to be perceived, one needs to know how to define oneself. Positioning is a battle of perceptions. By not choosing, one leaves the construction of one's image to others, to the competition, by default.

The considerable difficulty for the country brand is internal. In fact, a country does not have the same levers of power and authority that enable a company to transform itself from the inside out in order to bring itself into line with the values it promotes in its advertising. Bringing words and objects into conformity and coherence is difficult in a democratic country. An early-morning arrival from Tokyo or Shanghai into Roissy-Charles de Gaulle airport, despite the fact that it is managed by a public body (ADP, Airports of Paris), is enough to note the poor image given to foreign visitors as the first contact with our country, before they join the interminable queue to have their passports checked, for lack of personnel to welcome them. The country brand proves itself through the facts – but it can also be weakened through them.

Thinking of towns as brands

Have towns and cities themselves become brands? Yes – take as evidence the struggle that pitted London against Paris for the organisation of the 2012 Olympic Games. Paris's technical dossier seemed to be superior, but even the name of London is more attractive nowadays than that of Paris. In other words, the product was perhaps better but the intangible components of the London brand made the difference with the international jury. What are these intangible associations that make it different, that create its international fame and its attractiveness? To say 'London' is to spontaneously evoke a group of value-bearing notions such as multiculturalism, the intermingling of different nationalities, economic dynamism, liberty, today's cultural abundance, and youth. It is the unsurpassed brand image of London that makes it influential.

Why introduce the concept of the town brand?

Today, all municipalities will perforce have to turn to brand concepts in order to manage their town more efficiently and contribute to its growth. Two structural factors lead them towards this. The first is the growth in the number of large transnational actors with large sums of money designated for site regeneration. These are the actors that the town must convince – for example the World Bank, the European Union or regional development funds. Second comes the movement towards decentralisation and delegation of power at the local level. It is no longer a question of the municipality lobbying Paris, but rather of it fending for itself with its own budget.

How can the experience of Danone or Coca-Cola be useful in the management or development of these complex entities known as towns? Is there not something incongruous in linking a town's ambition to develop, and the means it uses to do so, with these concepts issuing from the commercial sphere, and marketing, a discipline imported from the Anglo-Saxon world? Is not everything against it?

The fact that the question is even raised today reveals not a 'mercantilisation' of society, or a 'privatisation' of public affairs, but an awareness that every organisation, and by the same token every town and even every country, must make sure of its own growth and development, attract resources, people, energies and means to itself. In order to attract them, it must convince them and seduce them – hence the brand logic.

Mayors know that they are in competition with other towns on various markets: they must therefore know how to sell themselves. By creating a good reputation for their town they give themselves a voice. Like brands, towns need to grow: they therefore need to attract new resources (people, workers, companies, finances and so on). Like any brand, they must also be able to define where their unique attractiveness lies, or what is known as positioning.

Some towns have had to reposition themselves. This is the case when an economic crisis flattens their traditional expertise. Once all the textile factories of famous brands such as Dim, Well, Aubade, Olympia and Kindy have moved away, what will be left to the town of Troyes? This is also what happened to

the great mining town of Bilbao, in the Basque country of Spain, a sombre town that suffered the demise of its mining industry. Like the phoenix, however, it has risen from the ashes, under the impulsion of a global flagship product: the fantastical Guggenheim Museum that was built there, bringing with it a great cohort of modern art lovers and tourists, giving the town a new lease of life.

Implications of the town brand notion

In order to treat a town as a brand, first of all it is necessary to respecify what 'brand' means. A brand is a name that has a power, a power to influence. This power has nothing to do with the name itself, with its euphony, its rhythm or its pronunciation, but is concerned with what it means in the mind of the audience. A brand is therefore a known name with which the audience spontaneously associates positive, attractive and unique values, both tangible (the advantages of living or working there) and intangible (the town's style and heritage, etc).

The further away one moves from objects, from reality, and therefore from the towns themselves, the more they are known through the prism of their meaning and reputation. Managing a town's communication like that of a brand means becoming aware of the need to define that meaning precisely, and then undertaking all necessary actions to build that perception among the strategic audiences on which the town will depend for growth and influence. In fact, at the same time, other towns and other countries will be polishing up their own meanings and their resources to attract and seduce the same audiences. Some will retort that the decisions of these latter are taken on the basis of dossiers, analyses and well-founded comparisons – but let us not deny the capacity of reputations and images to influence so-called rational evaluation processes: the example of the Olympic Games being awarded to London is a pertinent reminder.

Turning a town into a brand therefore means building perceptions among strategic audiences, turning it into a unique and attractive destination, for companies, individuals, or cultural or educational organisations that might think of moving there. Perception has to be built. In order to do this, awareness vectors and image vectors are required. The cycling race between Paris and Roubaix each year is an awareness vector for Roubaix, but hardly a good image vector: the talk is all of bicycles, mud, and the hell of the north. In contrast, the presence there of leading European mail-order companies (La Redoute and Damart) could be a strong image vector. A reputation can also be destroyed: a crisis relayed by the media is enough to create far less positive associations that tarnish the image the town is seeking to build.

Would a town then be managed like Coca-Cola or Pepsi? At this point it is necessary to remember the specific qualities of a town, and therefore the limits of the above comparison. Commercial brands are often artefacts: they invent a reality that they turn into an image, for example linking a blend of coffee to an imaginary explorer named Jacques Vabre, who is supposed to have travelled around the Earth. This imaginary aspect is sold to the consumer as much as the product itself. However, it is completely independent of the thousands of men and women working for Kraft, the company that produces Jacques Vabre coffee, and of the reality of the company. This, moreover, is why brands are bought and sold, passing from one company to another.

A town, on the other hand, is first and foremost a human, local and immovable reality (which is not to say that it is unchangeable), anchored in history, culture and its ecosystem. It can and should be altered to adapt to evolution, to the economic and social needs of the present day. However, the brand cannot be built without it. It must be reckoned with. The construction of the brand should first of all involve a consensus among the town's key actors.

These actors, who often defend specific points of view, issues or communities, must forget their own preserve to an extent. For example, increasing the attractiveness of a town externally, in order to ensure its development, consists of defining what the town wants to become the reference for. The brand logic is that of the 'customer': why choose number two if you can have number one? Thinking like a brand means choosing the advantage that the town wants to symbolise.

It is therefore necessary to distinguish between two types of argument, or attractive element, for the town brand: positioning and reassuring. The first will be the driving force, the lever of influence of the town, its perceived uniqueness and its attractiveness. This choice is crucial, since it defines in the long term the ground that the town is determined to dominate in the perception of the target audiences. The second type is there to reassure: for example infrastructure, crèches, schools, the existence of a dynamic town centre and so on.

How does the town choose its positioning, this long-term, mobilising, attractive differentiation strategy? By digging deep into its own DNA, its identity. A town is a living and complex social body, which has its own genes. There is everything to be gained, not by reproducing the past and what the town once was, but by reinventing it on the basis of the values, competences and ideals that have moved it throughout its history. This is why it is necessary to dig into the town's soil, identify its genes, beyond the vicissitudes of recent history, in order to define its identity kernel. This retrospective study is the necessary prelude to selecting the positioning that will project the brand into its future.

A concrete example: the town of Roubaix

The town of Roubaix, in the north of France, carried out such a historical study before re-founding its identity. What shape does its originality take, its motivation, the basis for its reinvention and projection into the open economic and social world of the 21st century? Before we imagine this, however, it is prudent to remember what is at issue: the branding process is part of an ambitious revitalisation programme for the 'poorest town in France', to quote the words of its dynamic mayor, who was referring to the average amount of local tax paid per inhabitant. It is also a town with a high rate of immigration and therefore of unemployment. It was therefore a question of making it attractive once again, with the stated aim of revitalising its old, preserved town centre, which had been deserted, rather than recreating it in the suburbs, as has been done in so many other towns. Therefore it was necessary to develop in parallel a cultural offer, a demand for public spaces, and a renewed commercial offer. To do so, Roubaix needed brands and companies. What identity would contribute to this goal nowadays?

The first question in any work on branding is to rediscover the design, the brand's DNA. What appears to be the design of this northern French town? The town's genetic patrimony provides the key components. It was always a textile town. During the period when it did not belong to France, in 1469, it was one of the first free trade zones created, thereby affirming its destiny as a great merchant town, which had also been granted the right to weave fabrics. Roubaix is associated with the spirit of enterprise. All the big families in textiles, and then in mass distribution, started here: the Mothes, the Lepoutres, the Mulliezes, the Paulets, the Prouvosts, and even the Arnaults, who moved from textiles to luxury goods.

Other than weaving, it is also the town of cross-fertilisation: a pioneer in commercial exchanges, the town was at the heart of international exchanges within Europe. This is where the deep truth and the forgotten times of Roubaix are to be found: it is the French town for textiles, for creation, fashion, mass distribution, but also today of its most advanced version: mail order. La Redoute (based in Roubaix) is the foremost seller of female garments in France. It now takes more orders over the internet than through the post. We can clearly see the sketching out of a legitimate territory of competence and influence that the municipality can activate. This positioning is the source of coherence of present and future activities to be carried out locally, in the same way as the communications that diffuse them.

As with any brand, the town has its slogan: 'Fashion loves Roubaix'. This encapsulates the profound truth of the town brand: a textile town, a town of creative entrepreneurs, and a town of good business. It is aimed both 'internally', at the community itself, an active partner in its own development and reputation, and at federalising all so-called external activities. Strong perceptions can only be built if all these activities converge on a single direction and a single meaning.

As for the products that represent renewal vectors, embodying the town's mercantile and fashion vocation, they include the opening of the 'La Piscine' museum (housed in the historic swimming baths), the arrival of the Edhec business school in Roubaix, the installation of a MacArthur Glen brand centre of 17,000 square metres that brings customers to Roubaix from 50 kilometres around, including from Belgium, the rehabilitation of factories to create a fashion and creative quarter, and so on.

Universities and business schools are brands

Nowadays, the dynamism of a country is judged not by its history, its monuments or its cuisine, but by its brands, in particular those that spell attraction, modernity and intellectual power. The report submitted to the French prime minister in November 2006 did not disagree: the name of any country is now attached to the image of its centres of intellectual excellence, its universities, its research centres, its innovative companies, its design centres, its hi-tech and hi-touch brands – or the lack thereof.

Working on the France brand means asking questions about the foundation of its reputation tomorrow, as a great country of the 21st century: that is, as the transmitter of a living, contemporary culture, therefore capable of attracting students from around the world, not only to study philosophy and literature, art history or sociology, as they once did, but to study economics, business, management, high and new technologies.

Higher education institutions are now also engaged in a brand war. Revealingly, there are now global comparisons on the quality of universities and business schools – a sign that the market is now global and the evaluators are not French. The same is true for wine. In Europe, the *Financial Times* draws up the ranking of 55 European business schools. Its 2006 ranking is shown in Table 5.4.

Table 5.4   The top ten European business schools

1   HEC Paris (France)
2   London Business School (UK)
3   IMD (Switzerland)
4   Instituto de Emprese (Spain)
5   Iese (Spain)
6   ESCP-IAP (France/Germany/Spain/Italy)
7   RSM Erasmus University (Netherlands)
8   Cranfield School of Management (UK)
9   Bradford/Tias Nimbas (UK/Netherlands/Germany)
10   Insead (France)

Source: Financial Times, 4 December 2006.

The challenge that European universities must meet is considerable. Their resources are so small that they do not even appear in worldwide evaluations. Like Oxford, the Sorbonne is a true brand, whose reputation has been built over centuries and diffused worldwide. Its excellence in literary studies is well known, carried by the excellence of its professors. However, an objective analysis of the service that each student receives illustrates that in terms of teaching, as with any brand, the intangible components are not enough. Major financial resources are required to bring today's teaching up to the standards of global excellence in education. This will be the great challenge for Europe brand: to give its universities the financial resources to shine internationally. If the state cannot do it, then companies must, and therefore it is necessary to change the relationships between companies and the university. This is why the big business schools everywhere have already acquired the status of global brands.

Every country has its star brands: the United States has Harvard and MIT for example, the United Kingdom has Oxford and Cambridge, and China has Tsing Hua; in France, HEC and Insead are brands. Of course the United States also has other excellent business schools, as global comparative rankings continue to demonstrate. However, only some of these have additional emotive value, strongly linked to intangible components, the vague feeling of entering into more than simply a university or school, but into a very exclusive and global club.

It is striking to see how globalisation poses new problems for educational institutions, which were previously sheltered from it. Like it or not, they must now think like global brands, and give themselves the resources to do so. What is a brand, if not a name with strong influence and power to attract – since their market at least is global? Reputation is the inevitable attraction vector: an aura attached to a name able to bring the world's students and major executives to Europe to round off their education at great expense.

It is therefore necessary to know how to export our qualifications, if Europe wishes to remain in the hunt as a great country. However, globalisation requires a complete revision of our certainties, practices and habits. It is now necessary to think globally in order to remain number one.

This global market is now revealed by global judges, who have drawn up their evaluations as objective rankings. In the international evaluation by the *Financial Times*, considered the reference on business schools the world over (as summarised in Table 5.4), HEC Paris occupies the top European spot, just above the London Business School, IMD in Switzerland and the two Spanish business schools. Insead is the tenth-ranked European business school. In worldwide terms, HEC is now 18th, even ahead of the Kellogg Business School (Northwestern University). This evaluation by the *Financial Times* is based on a multi-criteria analysis objectifying the performance parameters of each business school, its ability to deliver added value to its students on all programmes, and to executives who go there to improve their competencies.

These new evaluating authorities define the objective criteria for their judgements: they measure the true added value for each business school. In so doing, they impact the products and the processes.

The discreet but systematic rise of HEC Paris on the world stage is slower than many executives would have liked. The university or school brand is built through its products: it does not flood the media with big promotional campaigns. On the contrary, its ambassadors are the quality and success of its students, hence the importance of selection and the critical mass of the number of former students, and publications by professors in the best scientific management journals, as a way of durably impacting managerial thinking. Professor Philip Kotler has made Northwestern known as a global marketing Mecca, and Michael Porter has strengthened the status of Harvard Business School. Another contribution comes from the reputation of international pedagogical engineering missions by the biggest groups, and the ongoing training of executives worldwide.

Two strategies compared: penetration or skimming off

Reasoning like a brand also leads to drawing inspiration from brand management. From this point of view, we know that to grow in a market, there are two main strategies: creaming off or penetration. It is interesting to compare the rapid penetration strategy of Insead with the strategy of creaming off the best followed by HEC Paris.

Founded in 1959, Insead chose the strategy of rapid market penetration, capitalising on the fact that in Europe at the time, the MBA was not a concept that was either known or practised. Only the fortunate few pursued their studies through an MBA at Harvard or Stanford. In the best business schools in the United States, the country that created the MBA, it takes two years to obtain this prestigious qualification. The first year of the MBA is used for learning management in general, and the second is necessary for specialisation and further study, structured individual projects and so on.

For a teaching institution, the rapid penetration strategy consists of acquiring a high market share as quickly as possible, by multiplying the number of students and thereby obtaining a large body of alumni, capable of lobbying within companies to influence their recruitment. As the notion of the MBA was still nebulous in Europe at that time, Insead decided to deliver its MBA after only one year, which enabled it to produce twice as many graduates as the true Harvard-style MBA, which takes two years. As a further consequence of this rapid penetration strategy, the school considerably increased its class size: it now has 440 students per year. Finally, another campus was created in Singapore, to create even more Asian graduates.

The result of this very coherent strategy is that the Insead brand acquired international recognition, and its 'educational product' is ranked in tenth place among the business schools of Europe by the *Financial Times* in 2006. Compare this strategy to that of HEC Paris, now ranked number one among European business schools.

Beginning 10 years later in the race towards internationalisation, HEC followed a strategy of creaming off the best, as this brand required. When you are the guarantor of excellence in your own country, you cannot do otherwise. This is why the HEC MBA was based on the model of the best American MBAs: two years were required to deliver quality teaching and to train high-level managers. The size of the first classes was also reduced: the selection of the best students is an integral part of brands of excellence. Dedicated MBA professors created a unique level of teaching and team spirit. Little by little, the reputation for quality spread. Furthermore, HEC, through its relationship with the Chamber of Commerce, is closely linked to the world of business. The result of this highly coherent strategy, dictated by the desire to maintain the brand equity attached to HEC, is that a worldwide name awareness remains to be constructed, but the experts (Human Resources directors, CEOs, the *Financial Times* and the like) have recognised the superior quality of the product.

Thinking of celebrities as brands

It is common to talk about brands as we talk about people. We will see, furthermore, that one of the facets that make up the singularity and the identity of a brand is its personality, its character. This derives from an increasingly anthropomorphic conception of the brand. This is one of the consequences of the need to pursue so-called relational marketing: that is, worrying less about the imminent sale than about establishing an enduring relationship between the customers and the brand. We form relationships with people, not products – hence the notion of brand personality, as if we were describing the profile of a friend. To communicate this, the brand may sometimes associate itself with a genuine personality, someone who brings their own attractiveness and incarnates the brand's values. Michael Jordan and Tiger Woods are the prototypes of this practice: where would Nike be without them? L'Oréal Paris, whose personality is glamour, is represented by what they call the 'dream team', a team of Hollywood stars and global top models who appear in all its advertising.

Conversely, some celebrities became genuine brands and were managed as such. By brand, we mean a name capable of generating enthusiasm, fans and customers. Think for example of James Bond or Harry Potter, virtual celebrities whose spin-off products create genuine, profitable and durable business. The failing perfume house Coty rebounded by developing a new business model: creating perfumes for stars (Alain Delon, Celine Dion), just as others, upon leaving HEC, hit on the brilliant idea of offering to create a perfume for Salvador Dali (to their great surprise, he accepted, and it is one of the best-selling perfumes in Japan).

Picasso is not only the name of a famous painter, but also a brand. The company set up by his heirs, with its headquarters on the Place Vendôme in Paris, works constantly to prevent the name falling into the public domain. In order to prevent this, it must be in proven and meaningful commercial use. This is why, 10 years ago, the company went around the car manufacturers and offered them the licence to the Picasso name. Citroen accepted: the name increased the perception of novelty and creativity of its new model, which would go on to successfully challenge the Renault Scenic in the segment it created.

The newest development is that sports stars, for example, are becoming brands. Not all of them – far from it – but some of them. Michel Platini has not become a brand, nor has Thierry Henry, nor Zinedine Zidane, nor George Best, nor Roger Federer, despite being the world number one in tennis. In contrast, the lyrical poet-footballer Eric Cantona could have become one, as his too-rare excursions into cinema show.

Among the great footballers, perhaps David Beckham, previously of Manchester United and Real Madrid, best represents the notion of a celebrity becoming a brand (Milligan, 2004). It is well known in football that celebrities make a profit for their clubs. If Manchester United has 17 million fans in Asia, imagine the number of spin-off products that could be sold to them as objects of their cult.

How can we recognise that a celebrity sportsperson has become a brand? It happens when his or her national or global influence emanates as much from personality as from sporting prowess. One of the key phrases in understanding what a brand is runs thus: 'the brand is everything that makes a product much more than a product'. Sportspeople become brands when not only does the product (the sport at which they excel) place them above the rest (making them super-products), but they are also intrinsically interesting and attractive away from the stadiums and the rugby or football pitches, in their daily lives. Some great sportspeople, such as Zidane, never make this step: they refuse to accept that their public life is also the field for expression of who they are, and a source of their influence. Celebrity-brands are loved for what they do, but also for what they are, how they live and what they represent (the myth that they embody).

In this, the celebrity-brand becomes a life-style brand, a mediator of new behaviours offered to the audience. Think of the influence that André Agassi has over how American and European adolescents dress or cut their hair. David Beckham's Mohican haircut legitimised this controversial hairstyle in schools. By putting himself forward with his children, he broke the male stereotype in the United Kingdom and promoted acceptance of the 'metrosexual' sensibility. By marrying a Spice Girl, he also added a touch of complexity to his image, moving it further from the stereotype of the pure footballer.

In managerial terms, knowing that they are a brand leads such people to managing themselves as such, or even taking on an agent who will be better placed to do so. The essential requirement is to preserve the brand value, doing nothing that would destroy even a little of its attraction. The goal is for the brand to outlive the sportsperson – since all champions have to retire in the end. Thus, far from accepting all commercial contracts, however lucrative, it is important to know how to say no to some of them. What products should they create under their name: perfume, clothing or...?

First of all it is necessary to understand the driving forces of their own brand. Each person who becomes a celebrity-brand should ask:

▮ What are my values?

▮ What are the facets of my identity?

▮ What role do I play for the audience?

▮ What myth do I embody?

▮ What are my recognition signs?

Thinking of television programmes as brands

Pop Idol is more than a programme, it is a brand. Where does the biggest part of the profits for TF1 (France's leading television channel) come from? Not from the commercial breaks that it sells to advertisers, but what are known as spin-off products from programmes. *Ushuaia*, the channel's flagship programme dedicated to nature and ecology, became a cult programme, attracting millions of loyal viewers each week. It also turned its star presenter into a celebrity, a defender of the planet's threatened biodiversity, its ozone layer, its temperature, its inexhaustible marine resources and so on.

Ushuaia was thus a name loaded with

emotive values and with power. It was of interest to industrialists. TF1 created a specialised department to capitalise on licences from programmes viewed as brands. *Ushuaia* met l'Oreal's urgent need for a shower gel brand for the supermarkets. It was also of interest to sellers of camping equipment and the like.

However, not all programmes are suited to becoming commercial brands. To do so, their values must be able to transmute metaphorically into products. Thus *Thalassa* is a cult programme dedicated to the sea, sea dwellers, ships and so on, which has appeared on French television every Friday evening for more than 20 years. It has a loyal audience at 8.45 pm who would not miss it for the world, and its audience share is strong and stable. However, to date, this devotion has not created a flourishing business. What could be sold under its name?

Star Academy (*Pop Idol* outside France) is the opposite example: it is the flagship programme among adolescents, who talk of nothing else and make systematic use of telephone voting (a major source of revenue for the TF1 channel), which increases their level of involvement. Their obsession needs other consumables to express their burning devotion. There is now a major magazine (the second-biggest adolescent magazine in readership terms), as well as many licences and spin-off products.

Disney's business model is based on the profits created by movies which must become brands and lead to a huge stream of licenced products. Disney would not produce a film, such as *Men in Black*, that although a great movie created no profit flow from licences.

Part Two

The challenges of modern markets

6

The new rules of brand management

What is actually new in strategic brand management? Since the 1990s companies have been well aware that brands are an asset, and that consequently they should always be reinforced and nurtured by tangible innovations and intangible added values.

The 10 key principles of strategic brand management are known:

▌ Capitalise on a few strategic brands, which all convey a big idea, a vision, and are driven by the desire to change the customer's life. No brand should be without a strong intangible component. ,

▌ Nest all variants and sub-brands under these mega-brands, to nurture them.

▌ Act as a leader and be passionate about increasing the standards of the category.

▌ Sustain all brands by a constant flow of innovations (product, service etc) in line with their positioning.

▌ Create direct ties with your end customers to deepen the link and the attachment, especially in markets where the trade pushes its trade brands. In fact the main

competitor of many a so-called strong brand is now the trade brand.

▌ Deliver personalised services.

▌ Reward customers' involvement to make them become active promoters of your brand, not simply loyalists. Word of mouth is indeed the real sign of success: when customers become active ambassadors because they feel passionate about the brand – as a result of what it did to them and the community of values. Reichheld (2006) has shown that the rate of promoters among the customer base is directly correlated to the growth rate of the company or the brand.

▌ Encourage communities that share your values.

▌ Quickly globalise the brand and its products.

▌ Be ethical: big is not beautiful any more, and consumers have become cynical about size. Do not only adopt rapidly the perspective of individual benefits, also take into account collective benefits (recyclable products, organic ingredients, ethical and sustainable trade, helping the poor, etc).

If the brand principles given above have remained constant, their implementation has had to adapt to new markets, new customers, media and technological realities, and the effects of globalisation on costs.

First of all, let us state that one traditional manner of building brands is now defunct, or in any case has lost its reference status. This was elevated to a dogma by Procter & Gamble (P&G) in the last century, at the time of the arrival of mass marketing, made possible by large superstores, motorways and television. I learnt it myself at the beginning of my career, when I moved to P&G. In short, in this model of 'brand building', everything followed from a superior product, which responded better than the competition to a need expressed by customers. Then distribution was set up, and then a large promotional campaign was done in order to promote trial, prior to re-purchase and loyalty formation. This approach corresponded to the state of the market, of customers and of technology. It is no longer suitable for today's world. Proof of this is that it has not prevented the rise of distributors' own brands, cheaper copies, and in particular the discount and hard discount sectors.

This model of brand building, of constructing and defending the brand over time, runs into four stumbling blocks today:

▮ Are there durable, meaningful differences between products these days?

▮ Is there still a large amount of shelf space available for brands in the big superstores or with wholesalers, which are now pushing their own products?

▮ Are there still mass media, taking into account the fractioning of the audience?

▮ Are there still loyalists? The rise in the rate of promotions makes customers more sensitive to price, less faithful, more opportunistic. The case of mobile telephones is a typical one. In France, as everywhere in Europe, 13,800,000 sales were made in 2006 by the dominant mobile operators (Orange, SFR, Bouygues, etc). Of these 10,225,447 were to clients who had just given up their contract with one of these operators! It is true that the multiplication of advertising on lower and lower charges can only lead to disloyalty. Moreover, benchmarking and copying smooth over the differences.

Everywhere, cheaper alternatives to the major brands now hold significant market shares, even majority shares in mass-consumption goods. This is true of both consumer and industrial products: many B2B brands complain at the substitution of their products by cheaper Chinese imports in client companies, not to mention the generalisation of the practice of using inverse auctions as a method of selecting suppliers. Here, only the price counts.

Let no one be deceived: even if everyone thinks of Danone when the yoghurt market is mentioned, Danone is in a minority on the shelves at Carrefour. Even if Fleury Michon is the name that comes to mind in terms of processed meat products, distributor-brand, low-cost hams hold the dominant market share. Of course it is possible to argue that distributor brands are also brands, and that in fact to speak of the decline of brands is deceptive: the reality is that a new type of brand is replacing other brands on the shelves and in customer choices. Danone yoghurts replaced Nestlé's; Carrefour yoghurts replace Danone's. Tesco Finest is replacing Tropicana, and so on.

We showed in Chapter 4 that if distributor brands are brands, they are not brands exactly like the others, since their positioning is always relative. They are structurally positioned between the cheapest products and the major brands. They are therefore relative brands. Do they have a financial value in themselves? No.

On the other hand, the rise of products on the hard discount circuit, unbranded products and Chinese imports clearly demonstrates that the traditional brand no longer responds to the needs of all buyers. It has ceased to be universal. The market is segmented by price, and different types of operators excel in each price segment. The ability of brands to be present in each segment is a challenge. Nevertheless, for example, Bic does indeed try to occupy the bottom-of-the-range segment, although it is apparent that there are now much cheaper ballpoint pens and disposable lighters than Bic produces.

The pre-eminence of price in the factors determining consumer choice shows that a certain type of marketing has reached its limit, as has the habitual manner of managing brands.

The limits of a certain type of marketing

This was forged by P&G, the inventors of marketing for mass-consumption products. Since I began my career in this company, I have experienced it. Traditionally, at P&G the brand is a superior product. Everything begins with the product and hinges upon it. It must prove its worth all alone: brutally, this company only launches mass-consumption products if they can speak up for themselves and 'make the difference' in use. Hence the importance of 'blind tests' in this sector. In these tests clients must judge the product without seeing the brand, so that they are not biased in their perception by recognition of it. With Pampers, the baby must be drier; Always must absorb better; Ariel must wash better, and the difference must be visible to the naked eye; Sunny Delight, an orange-flavoured drink but without real oranges, must taste infinitely better on the tongue, and so on. Note that in its luxury products division (licensed Boss and Lacoste perfumes, etc) P&G uses different rules, since the notion of a 'superior' perfume makes very little sense.

In and of itself, the principle that a brand begins with a great product remains a pillar of the great brand. Laughing Cow has an organoleptic quality superior to other soft cheeses. In business to business, Facom mechanic's keys are the benchmarks in the market.

But the model begins to seize up when it continues ad infinitum: then we reach the zone of diminishing returns. The cost of marginal improvement becomes increasingly high. Making a Michelin tyre safer than it already is involves considerable investments in research and development, which must be absorbed either over very large product runs (hence the notion of a global product) or over smaller, more expensive runs.

This one-dimensional strategy reaches its limits: there comes to be an imbalance between the additional cost of marginal progress, and the customer's perceived needs. In fact, with traffic jams and rising petrol prices, the majority of car owners use their car in town, for short journeys. Safety remains an essential function of a tyre, but the notion of differentiation on safety loses its market relevance if you continue to seek more and more safety. Moreover, although the higher price is perceptible, the safety increment remains invisible. It is then necessary to change the client benefit.

This product development model still seems to work for certain brands: Gillette is a typical example. After the single-blade close-shave razor came the two-blade razor for an even closer shave, then three blades, then the roller, then vibrating razors. Gillette is a past master in the art of planned obsolescence in its products.

It is no accident that P&G took over Gillette in 2004. These two companies share basically the same product culture, and the same mode of innovation: always more. To achieve this, P&G is now prepared to look beyond its own walls for the innovations of tomorrow: in university laboratories, in start-ups and so on. For the majority of companies, however, the model no longer functions.

Figure 6.1   Limits of traditional marketing

In fact the incremental improvements are no longer perceptible or meaningful; on the other hand, the increase in price is. Consumers can thus make considerable savings (typically 35 per cent) by buying distributor brand products with an equivalent degree of functional satisfaction. The loss in terms of function is minimal compared with the economy achieved.

This reasoning is also true for truck tyres. This is why, although the market share of Michelin Trucks at first tyre mounting is 65 per cent in Europe and the West, it falls by 50 per cent in the second-mounting market, when it comes to replacing the tyres (although Michelin remains the leader).

The reasoning is the same in food: what does an even better albacore tuna at Saupiquet mean? Tesco Finest sells indistinguishable albacore tuna. What does an even crustier gherkin from Amora mean? A cul-de-sac has been reached.

The consumer can find comparable and cheaper alternatives, since distributor brands have made up their disadvantage. Consumers have realised this. There is no technological barrier in most mass-consumption goods. Bear in mind that the first explanatory factor of brand sensitivity in the client is the thought, 'There is a difference.' Admittedly this is a thought, the client's belief: it can therefore be influenced by advertising and recognition. Nevertheless, for frequently consumed products, it is modified through use. With experience, consumers see no difference, except for the price. Hence the systematic rise in all European studies of the opinion that 'distributor brands are a better price/quality choice than major brands'. Agreement with this opinion is at 59 per cent in France, 57 per cent in Germany, 55 per cent in Britain, 54 per cent in Italy and so on. This is made easier by the fact that nowadays the majority of large groups supply distributor brands. Some do so openly: the strategy of the Lactalis Group is to dominate the camembert market in two ways; via the President brand itself, and via distributor brand products. Other large industrial companies do the same without admitting it, by delivering to front companies that in turn supply the major distributors.

Since the specifications of the distributors are sometimes highly ambitious, the distributor brand product, although cheaper, can be superior to the brand product. Everyone knows of the case of the famous shoemaker, none of whose own brand products is the equal of the product it makes for Carrefour. In this way, companies reduce the objective distance between branded and unbranded products. Outsourcing to China produces the same result: Chinese factories quickly learn to match Western standards.

The weakness of the idea of 'best product' is that it is often defined without taking the customer's point of view – that is, without considering the use to which it will be put. This is its greatest shortcoming. Take the example of DIY: given that an electric drill will, on average, be used for a few seconds per year in a normal household, what point is there in buying a Bosch-branded one? In functional terms it makes no sense. On the other hand, if the consumer picks a cheaper alternative, the immaterial satisfaction of owning 'a Bosch' will be frustrated: this is a key aspect of the strong brand. Bosch enjoys the values associated with its country of origin (Germany), which make the buyer proud.

The brand that has not built in elements of intangible added value (trust, pride, emotion, attachment, or familiarity capital) is copiable and may be damaged by an attack on price. This is what preserves Coca-Cola; despite its contribution to the rise in obesity. Of course it has a great taste, but it is also has massive distribution (a Coke should always be within reach) and a unique intangible capital made up of joie de vivre, youth and friendship, coloured by Americanness.

Fundamentally, at P&G the brand is in fact the name of a superior product. Was the IBM PC superior? Was it the best PC? In the experts' opinion, no. But it was the best-seller of its era. It was broadly sufficient for the uses it was put to. It also had a unique intangible value that forced the preference in the serious world of business: it was known as 'IBM', the company that was considered by all to have founded modern information technology (even if it was Sperry Univac who invented the first computers). The brand suggested a high 'perceived quality'.

About brand equity

The economic press regularly gives figures on the financial value of brands. The Coca-Cola brand might have been worth US$67 billion, Microsoft US$60 billion, Mercedes US$22 billion, Marlboro US$21 billion, Louis Vuitton US$17 billion, Google and Dell US$12 billion and Zara US$4 billion in 2006. These figures are estimations: that of the future ability of the brands to generate a profit surplus entirely based on their name – that is, on all the values with which the name is associated in the mind of the public worldwide.

Other study institutes therefore regularly publish the measurements of the associations consumers make with the names of these brands. For example TNS measures the recognition of brands, their evocative power, their perceived quality, their rate of declared use and the stated desire to buy the brand again in future. Brandz measures the rate of presence in the customer's mind, the perceived feeling that the brand is relevant (to the customer), that it is effective, that it offers advantages, and finally a sense of attachment to it. Others measure empathy scores, familiarity, perceived difference and stature scores. Brands have never been examined in such detail, nor have so many different measurements been published. It is true that the news for certain brands is not good: something seems to have been damaged recently between the public and the major brands.

Let us examine the recent retrospective data published by TNS (in 2006) based on 300 brands of all sectors (see Table 6.1). TNS measures both attitudes (familiarity with the brand, evocative power, and perceived quality) and declarative behaviours (past and future use).

Table 6.1   Evolution of brand indicators over 10 years

	Brand awareness	Evocation	Superior quality	Declared use	Declared re-use (intention)
2005	88	61	52	22	11
2002	89	66	58	27	15
1997	86	61	56	28	18

Source: TNS, 2006, based on 300 brands of all sectors. The figures are percentages of a French sample of category consumers

What do we notice here? The basic contract of brands has been eroded between 1997 and 2005: the perception of genuinely superior quality has decreased, whereas the richness of evocation has remained stable. In fact, the most notable absence in these types of study, which focus only on major brands, is the distributor brand. Now manufactured by the same companies as are responsible for traditional major brands, they have reduced the quality gap first objectively, and then, with time and experience, subjectively.

We can also note that the ratio of intention to repurchase the brand is deteriorating: in 1997 it was 64 per cent (18/28), but it was no more than 50 per cent (11/22) in 2005. It is as if the link between customers and the brands they use was stretching, or as if they have become 'shoppers', and have learnt to optimise their choices in-store. After all, what use is there in shopping in-store, if not to take advantage of the special offers and novelties of the moment? And now, in-store, the landscape has changed considerably: the shelf reflects the distributor's strategy, and no longer purely that of the brand manufacturer.

According to Interbrand, a design agency also involved in estimating the financial value of brands, the leading global brand remains Coca-Cola. However, even this mythical figure is suffering from erosion of the strong link with its audience that once characterised it. The TNS figures in Table 6.2 bear witness to this.

In the case of Coca-Cola and Danone in particular, two star brands, there has been little erosion of the brand image itself. But on the other hand behaviour and intentions are both retreating: the strength of consumers' conviction that they will buy the same again is weaker. This strengthens our diagnosis that brands are built in-store, and destroyed in-store. What does having a good image matter, if customers are less likely to keep buying the brand as a result?

This question will be analysed later. It must also be recognised that these measures, while useful, only measure the health of brands among themselves, rather than their resistance to new competition. This is why so

Table 6.2   Evolution of brand capital for Coca-Cola and Danone (in France, %)

	Brand awareness	Brand evocation	Superior quality	Declared use	Declared re-use (intention)
Coca-Cola					
2005	99	75	62	45	26
2002	98	77	67	52	34
Danone					
2005	99	83	83	66	32
2002	99	85	87	72	40

Source: TNS

many managers are disappointed: there is nothing wrong with their brand equity indicators, but there is a problem with their behaviour panel indicators.

At this stage it is necessary to make a fundamental distinction between three aspects:

▨ Brand assets (awareness, image, consideration as a whole), also known as brand equity from a customer point of view.

▨ The strength of the brand, which integrates the distribution parameter: market share, price premium, numerical distribution of store presence, weighted distribution (by size and global category sales of each store), growth and so on.

▨ Brand equity in the strict sense of the term: that is, the current financial value of the flow of future profits attached to the brand itself (the potential future contribution linked to the name in the current distribution context). This flow is largely dependent on the brand's weight in the purchasing decision: people may believe that Total is a superior quality brand, but may not take brand into account in their choice of service stations, basing their decision more on proximity or price.

If there is a link between these three facets, it is no longer a strict one: many brands that have genuine brand capital among clients have low brand strength. For example, Lafuma has a great reputation in France, but is nowhere to be found: this brand does not meet the objectives of the dominant distributor in its sector, Decathlon. Why are Nestlé dairy products throwing in the towel in France and selling their factories to Lactalis? Because the price premium of the Nestlé brand does not enable it to sell enough yoghurts and ultra-fresh products: without sufficient volume there can be no marketing communications, and distributors are no longer interested. Of course it would be possible to lower prices, but then the profitability would suffer, since it is rare to gain in volume and cumulative margin what is lost through dropping the price. Nestlé prefers to step back from the market and put its free capital to more profitable uses.

The current emphasis on measuring brand equity from the customer's point of view alone has its limits: it neglects the true playing field, which is distribution, and its own decision-making factors such as its actors (the shoppers). It is fine to measure preferential choices in interviews, but in-store the

Figure 6.2 From brand values to brand value

distributor's brand is omnipresent and weighs more on decisions than it does in interviews. Moreover, the shopper is sensitive to price differences shown on the labels.

Financial brand equity, the expected future revenues due to the brand itself, will certainly depend on the brand's assets (ability to make itself desired, even preferred), but will also depend also on its ability to transform this desire into an effective choice on the shelves, with a price differential, a premium (brand strength). This is illustrated in Figure 6.3.

In the wine sector, many are questioning the real financial value of wine brands: in fact, they may have a good image, but on the shelf customers will be tempted by novelties, incited to do so by distributors who promote new and unknown brands, perhaps of New World wines. In addition, once customers have been introduced to wine via one brand, they like to discover others. Is this not a market governed by disloyalty, linked to the pleasure of discovery?

The new brand realities

The new brand management is the fruit of the adaptation of companies to their new environment. What are its facets?

The rise of the shopper

Studies like the one discussed above, on brand equity and image capital, measure indicators that have a certain short-term inertia, whereas choice behaviours are more versatile and malleable. Despite the higher brand assets of Coca-Cola and Danone (awareness, evocation, perceived superior quality), behaviour is changing. This translates into a fundamental change: the rise of the shopper.

Everyone knows of Procter & Gamble – the company that invented marketing and dominates the mass-consumption markets. What has its managing director, A Laffley, been repeating incessantly to all its teams for two years? Think about the shopper! This is a sign that the shopper might have been forgotten in the daily reflexes of management; that people have concentrated their studies too much on consumers and forgotten to understand this slightly different concept: the part of themselves that, in a shop, wanders around, scrutinises, hesitates, then decides. The shopper is now the focus of all the attention at P&G. This is not an isolated phenomenon.

A revolution is taking hold of life-styles in our modern societies: what we call 'shopping' has become one of the three favourite

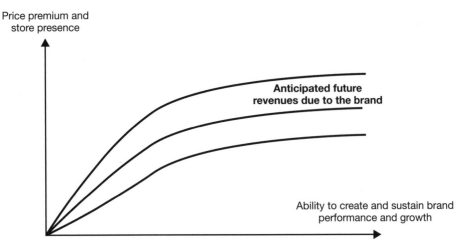

Figure 6.3   Brand equity

pastimes at a time when television consumption is systematically decreasing, as is reading. Everywhere, in Western cities as in Asia, we like to visit shopping centres; we like to wander through arcades, malls, brand shops, factory shops. Asian tourists visiting France expect only one thing after the obligatory visits to the Eiffel Tower and the Louvre: a visit to the shops. Airports have become more than 'air malls': they are 'air fashion malls'.

The French language is deceptive here: it uses the phrase 'faire ses courses' where the English use the phrase 'to go shopping'. The French has retained the dimension of speed, of counting time, which is in fact very appropriate for the kind of 'duty' shopping carried out in supermarkets. Modern working people have even less time than before: buying groceries and household consumables is something that must be done quickly, therefore shoppers rush through the aisles of the supermarkets and hypermarkets. Hence the well-known figures of the average time spent choosing a mineral water, a washing powder or a shampoo. This is counted in seconds:10, 12, 16, no more.

To realise the modern frenzy of shopping, it is necessary to keep in mind the expression 'to do the shops', in the same way that one 'does' a painting or a museum.

It is interesting to see that marketing shows little interest in the shopper. Marketing talks only of consumers. The two are very different, like two faces of the same coin. It is always consumers who are consulted in telephone surveys and on the internet. It is consumers who are scrutinised in focus group meetings, where everyone is collectively liberated, the comfortable chairs and canapés helping this process. The *consumer* writes the list of products and brands to buy. It is the *shopper* who decides on the spot whether to take this or that. It is the shopper who has now become so eclectic, and who passes from a large, gleaming store to a discounter or a bazaar in the same afternoon. As a result, shopping has

become exciting, surprising, full of emotions, the key being the possibility of doing business, enjoying oneself at the same time by wandering through places designed for the pleasure of – the shopper.

There is a tendency to confuse the concepts of the consumer and the shopper. In the B2B sector, they are two separate entities: the user and the purchaser. Each has different criteria and objectives, hence they also have conflicts of interest. The rise of the shopper is general: shopping is therefore no longer a race, a chore, but a way to exercise one's talent and to gain money by spending less of it. The *consumer* may declare a liking and respect for Michelin, but the *shopper* will leave a car at a Norauto garage and pick it up with tyres from Norauto.

Today's shopper may be also a businessman or woman. He or she enjoys brands and good business. For all the industries that have adopted the cycle of fashion as the economic engine of annually renewed client desire, the reduced-price brand outlets represent an opportunity – to sell last season's unsold stock rather than slash the prices at discount traders or even in factory shops. Moreover, these sales deliver a true brand message, since they take place in branded shops, where the brand can be expressed through the service and the staff in addition to the product and prices. Hence the importance of staff training, so that each contact with the shopper is an opportunity to leave a positive, durable memory trace. The brand is built through contact.

Shops, like internet sites, in fact become complete destinations for an afternoon full of what is called 'retail-tainment', that is, the fusion of 'retail' and 'entertainment'. In mass consumption, the internet, the proliferation of shopping centres, factory shops and brand centres convey a single fact: shopping is not necessarily a chore, but a leisure activity. People can simultaneously find pleasure, excitement, and an opportunity to go out as a group and to do business. Shopping takes on the air of a safari, where people seek deals, and good deals. Through their internet search behaviour, or in the aisles, clients now set their own price; they are not subjected to a price offering. They can decide whether to pay the higher price on the ticket, and be certain that they have found the latest thing, and in the right size, or wait for the sales, but take the risk of not finding the desired product, or finding it only in the wrong size.

Markets are fragmenting, and volumes too

Traditional marketing also stumbles on the pitfall of market fragmentation. The mass market is dead, even though we continue to speak of 'mass-consumption products'. It is enough to look at the figures: even for a product as global as Diet Coke, in this country 8 per cent of purchasers represent 40 per cent of its volume and more than half of its profits. What product can boast a penetration rate higher than 20 per cent?

Nowadays we no longer talk about segments, but rather fragments. The segment remains a valid notion at a macroeconomic level: in the car trade, there are the segments B1, B2, M1, M2 and so on. These are divisions of the car market according to the range level. The car makers create a platform corresponding to each segment, on the basis of which they will in reality build different models, themselves divided into highly differentiated versions, each aimed at a specific fragment. You might think this is nothing new: haven't car makers always broken down their basic model into multiple peripheral versions (coupe, cabriolet, estate)? What is new is that there is no longer a basic model. Peugeot initiated this strategic approach and uses it for each launch. Thus the 207 is launched in seven versions, all highly specialised according to the life-style fragment they are aimed at; but there is no more talk of a basic version.

Ralph Lauren has created more than 10 subbrands or daughter brands targeted according

to the time of day and week – more or less casual or elegant – and according to sex and age. Nevertheless, this does not fragment the brand, since it has a highly compact central kernel, a very clear identity, symbolised by Mr Lauren himself and created in any Ralph Lauren shop.

The signs of fragmentation are everywhere: 10 years ago, a best-selling book sold around 350,000 copies. Nowadays, even the winner of France's prestigious Goncourt prize only sells 250,000. Fragmentation poses an acute problem for the 'product brands'. They are typical single product specialities: Nutella, Mars, M&Ms, Orangina and Boursin are examples. That is, it is a very specific product that has a name, and this name belongs to only the one product (the inverse of this being the umbrella brand, which covers numerous products, such as Nivea or Legrand). Numerous groups have based their strategy precisely on a portfolio of specialities, so their brands are product brands.

It was a winning strategy until now: the volumes of each brand made it possible to justify a sufficient advertising budget to give the brand visibility and to unleash sales. With the fragmentation of the market, and therefore of volumes, the brand no longer has access to the major media, for example television, which contributed to building its success. The distributors, hypermarket and supermarket chains, become aware of this and realise that the brand is not in such good health, or is investing less in its future. In time many brands, despite being well known, no longer have an advertising budget anywhere near large enough. They concentrate their action on in-store sales promotion, a disguised special offer price, in order to support the turnover without which even their presence on the shelf is under threat. They no longer invest in their brand capital: that is, in the future.

How can companies escape from this snare created by market fragmentation? The product brand cannot do so with any great ease. To modify a speciality is to change that speciality. Is a Boursin cheese without garlic still Boursin? No. Another solution is to bring together several previously disjointed, separate specialities, each with its own identity, under a common umbrella. For example the Berchet group, owner of toy brands such as Berchet and Charton, thought of bringing them together under an umbrella name 'SuperJouet' and promoting that. The Bongrain group brought together many of its brands under an umbrella of 'Weight Loss and Pleasure'.

A different tactical approach, chosen by groups that opt to maintain their presence on television at any cost, is to adopt a short format for ads (10 seconds instead of the classic 30 seconds). This maintains the frequency of the brand appearances, even with a reduced advertising budget. It is also necessary to buy the advertising at the last minute in order to optimise costs, and communicate during empty slots of the day or night, when the home is typically deserted by the 'homemaker under 50', and broadcasting time is therefore much less expensive. Moreover, in this ageing country, this home-maker no longer corresponds to the core target. The limitation of the exercise is that the short slots can only provide awareness. It is difficult to build the intangible quality of the brand, the true bulwark of brands, through this creative format.

Media fragmentation

Every day a typical American has a choice between 7,000 hours of television. The 32 per cent of households equipped with a TiVo can not only watch their chosen television programmes 'a la carte', pre-recorded and available exactly when they choose, but also cut out all the commercial breaks. As for young people, they spend hours every day on the internet. It is understandable. In 2006, Google bought MySpace for the fabulous sum of US$900 million. This site enables millions

of people to introduce themselves to each other. Some months later Google bought YouTube.com for more than US$1 billion. This site is the home for the spontaneous production of video clips by millions of internet users. The goal is to provide the public with My Google TV, the first totally a la carte television service.

In short, normal advertising communications now face a real problem in reaching their targets. People channel-hop, they get up during commercial breaks, they are online or on the phone or on their PlayStation. In France and in Europe as a whole, you might think the situation has not yet gone so far – but it has. The audience monitoring figures from Mediamétrie demonstrate this: 50 per cent of media consumption is interactive.

France is at the forefront in making ADSL (broadband) generally available, even in the furthest reaches of the countryside. What is known as Web 2.0, the second internet revolution, is the true one. The first was a revolution of promises and visionaries. The technology existed; it was going to change our lives. Sadly, it was slow and the content was missing. Hence the disappointment and the bursting of the dot.com bubble. In the meantime, young people continued to consume the internet, to create exchanges between themselves, to turn it into their preferred mode of communication. They are the ones who shape its content (via MySpace, YouTube and the rest), not to mention the ability to have the world on demand.

Everyone can see how a youth clothing brand such as Quiksilver or a sportswear brand such as Nike could form part of the advertising of tomorrow: on the internet, the brand will be highly customised thanks to the information collected on each internet user connected to MyGoogle TV, (for example, or YouSpace). The advantage is less clear, however, for Herta delicatessen products, or for Saupiquet tuna. This is why television channels are trying to remain faithful to their etymology. What is a television channel? It is simply a link. Television is no longer the 'mad woman in the attic': it still has to re-demonstrate its ability to be an audience aggregator. This involves the production of successful series, of talk shows that mirror today's society, where everybody is telling their life story to somebody, like a case study to be discussed collectively among households.

Sport is an ideal means for reuniting the exploded audience around an intense emotional ceremony. We may also see a return to soap operas: the name dates back to the 1930s, when soap brands financed programmes themselves, precisely in order to attract the audience and justify their advertising. This seems all but certain. What is known as the convergence of Vine and Madison, a term taken from Vine Street in Los Angeles, where all the film actors' agents are concentrated, and Madison Avenue in New York (the avenue for advertising agencies), announces that we are moving towards brand communication in a different form from the classic 30 seconds (Donaton, 2004). This is a question not of 'product placement', with which we are familiar (placing the brand in the story, such as Peugeot in *Taxi 1, 2, 3* and *4*), but of inventing a new form of brand expression.

With technology, the consumer has seized power

Technology is the consumers' friend: this is why they have adopted it. In fact, it has modified their relationship to manufacturers, to controlled or official information, and therefore to political cant. This revolution has an impact on brand management, which must also integrate this freedom technology.

Some key figures are useful to depict the new world that brands inhabit:

- More mobile phones are sold worldwide than televisions.

- The premier digital camera brand is not Canon or Fuji but Nokia.

- 80 per cent of Koreans have a mobile phone with a digital camera.

- More than 15 per cent of internet users visit blogs.

- Nearly 20 per cent of internet users give their opinions on internet sites dedicated to the evaluation of products and services by the clients themselves.

- Three months after the appearance of a consumer comment on the bikeforum.com site from someone who was amused at having been able to open a lock with a Bic ballpoint, and the circulation through the blogosphere of an amateur film proving this could be done, the Kryptonite company, which had spent 30 years building its reputation in the United States on safety, incurred a loss of US$10 million recalling all the vulnerable locks on the market. The same was true for Apple following the creation of the site Appledirtysecret.com, revealing the shortcomings of the iPod battery. Blogs start conversations, and the traditional media pick up on them.

- With a click on priceminister or kelkoo, you can find out where to buy cheaper.

- With a glance at epinions.com, you can find out what other people are thinking.

All traditional marketing was founded on the asymmetry of power in the manufacturer's favour. Customers found it hard to become well informed, and therefore based their buying decisions on the familiarity of the brands, small distributors were grateful to the major brands for letting them deliver their goods, and competition was waged by every means except on price. This is over: the consumer has never had so much power.

This is also true of B2B clients:

- They are rare, and know it. They like to be seduced by a mass of brands that are often neighbours.

- They are informed: today everything is known. They can search online to find out what is thought about such and such a product by looking on e-pinion sites, consulting their sector community and so on. They can easily find the best vendor sites where the product is sold for less. The frontiers of the company and the brand are now porous. This is why IBM prefers to authorise certain key people in the company to create their own blogs, which open it up to the flow of questions, and at the same time make it possible to gain familiarity with what is being said.

- They can form blocs, and exert pressure on the company through collective internet action, their virtual community and e-lobbying. The impact of iPoddirty secret.com, which alerted all fans to the battery problems of the first iPod, is well known.

- They have acquired a communicative, participative, interactive culture. This leads to new opportunities for brands, which will cease to work as before – 'for customers but without them'. Nowadays involvement is at stake: the more customers or prospective customers are involved, the more they nurture a genuine engagement with the brand.

The goal of any brand is to make each customer a member, part of a virtual club of which he or she is not the centre, but where the customers' preoccupations, and their interests, are at the club's core. It is necessary to go beyond the notion of technical, relational marketing, which is admittedly useful, but which, like any technique, bypasses the essential. The more customers feel listened to,

involved, required not to purchase but to act as advisors, the more a genuine link, a genuine community will be created around and with the brand.

Web 2.0 has set the seal on client or consumer power. The internet is no longer visionary or prophetic: it is easy, practical, abounding in services and information or games. Blogs have become the truth of the market, the true consumer magazine, while the brand websites, and in particular consumer magazines on glossy paper, are the 'official' truth. (see also Figure 8.3.)

The era of the choice economy

Every 10 years or so, it is claimed that consumers have changed. Nothing of the sort has happened. It is the choice that has changed. It is the information that has changed, as a result of the technology made accessible to everyone. Previously, the range was restricted to a few 'me-toos' from similar competitors. Marketing was the art of making war while avoiding a price war.

Today consumers have the choice of an economy brand. They are confronted with considerable price differences for products, none of which are poor quality. By dint of manufacturing everything in China or Romania, the differences between branded and unbranded products are reduced. Moreover, the internet renders the offer transparent. This is the end of one of the brand's previous levers of power: a lack of familiarity on the part of customers with the available choice, leading them to favour the recognition factor of the brand. Blogs now give back to the markets the function they had lost: that of genuine discussion between consumers, as in the marketplaces of yore. Cold hypermarkets had killed all discussion: blogs initiate discussions and the media then diffuse them.

What, then, is left to the true brands? Two things: product innovation and the intangible factor. Consumers today look at brands as products: it is necessary to prove their advantages in order to justify the price premium. At the same time, in the era of the mass society, there is a demand for personalisation, for services, and also for social differentiation through image. At its extreme, it is a search for the superlative life through the intangible, pure image and luxury.

Another facet of the choice economy is what Alderson has called 'the long tail model'. The editor-in-chief of *Wired* magazine was the first to draw attention to the fact that the internet would put paid to the hit parade. It is because physical shops existed that hit parades of songs, or books, had to be created. It is highly expensive to stock books or CDs, and it is better to stock only a few, with a high turnover. However, if music and books are downloaded, the cost of transport and stocking becomes nil. From this point of view any song, any book, even the least well known, now has the same ease of access as a hit. The hit parade is therefore no longer necessary to the economy. Perhaps it is still necessary to society. We have seen it, indeed, with sites like Myspace or YouTube, where spontaneously created music circulates over the internet. As the slogan says, 'the world is now on demand': likewise with Google, everything is now accessible.

The era of the ego-economy is possible: people creating their own programming via iPod and iTunes are the demonstration of this. Hence the success of these alternatives. This is how to manage products successfully now: by multiplying the accessories. There are several thousand possible accessories for an iPod! Mini has based its advertising on 'make it your Mini', as has Dell.

The power of communities

Nowadays it is no longer consumers who build brands, but communities. It was New York's gay community that made Absolut a success, whereas that of Los Angeles made a success of Bombay Sapphire. It was the

community of designers and creative people who supported Apple in its lowest periods.

Today in the United States the talk is all of 'community marketing'. Marketing plans are highly differentiated according to whether they are addressed at African-Americans, Chinese-Americans, or Americans of Hispanic or Puerto Rican origin.

What does the notion of community add to the notion of segment? Why not simply talk about the Chinese or Puerto Rican segment? A segment is a marketing abstraction designating people with the same profile or the same expectations. In contrast, a community is a living group, daily weaving new links through communication, exchange and participation. A community exists, lives, grows and has an identity. A segment is defined and measured: it agglomerates. The community expresses, and brings together.

The power of communities is admittedly not new: the cases of Absolut and Bombay Sapphire prove it. However, the internet has given a new perspective; communities are beehives of communication. The internet is their medium, as are mobile phones. The power of communities therefore ceases to be a sociological abstraction, or a recuperation technique: it becomes a true lever, if the brand knows how to put itself at the community's disposal. For example:

- Telephone brands invest in services to be supplied to communities of football fans, or of a particular football team (Manchester United has several million devotees).

- Danone, via the 'Danone and you' website, puts itself genuinely at the service of mothers of young families.

- The aluminium extrusion brand Technal has created a new profession, that of the aluminium worker, and places itself at its service.

- The La Roche Posay brand stakes the centre of its communication activity on the effective involvement of the dermatological community.

▦ Quiksilver, Oxbow and Billabong strongly involve and become involved in the world of true surfers.

▦ Nike has created true niche marketing by becoming involved in the streets, with rappers or with the different tribes within each sport.

The limits of mono-distribution

Coca-Cola's strength is its multitude of distribution channels. Danone's weakness is its mono-distribution; the bigger stores are over-represented in its turnover. It is possible to follow a strategy associating the brand with a single distribution channel: this is the very basis of the l'Oréal group's success. L'Oréal, however, has turned its brands into indispensable brands in their sector. This is no longer the case for the Wal-Marts, Carrefours, Tescos, Targets, Dias and so on. In fact the major stores are now promoting their own brands, by providing them with a shelf space greater than their market share. This reduces by the same amount the visibility of branded products. As everyone knows, if a brand is not highly visible on the shelf, it is as if it had never been distributed.

Now in traditional marketing, in addition to a superior product, it is necessary to have enlarged distribution. In mass-consumption goods, visibility on the shelf is vital. Of course, fanatical clients will come looking for a brand that is not readily visible, but the others, the majority, will not make the effort. In order to escape this bottleneck, it is necessary to know how to compensate for weakness on the shelf by means of faster turnover. This is capable of bringing an overall margin to the distributor that makes the branded product attractive. This supposes that the brand owner has a star product in its range, a leading light on the shelf, an indispensable reference. On the

processed meat aisle for example, it would be Herta Knackis, or Herta pate, or Label Rouge ham from Fleury Michon.

One solution to this problem is to exit the shelf, and to move towards the client through promotion, through putting oneself forward. This is the strength of Ferrero. This discreet Piedmontese family company is a model of growth and serenity in the mass-consumption field. Its well-known European brands are Nutella, Kinder, Mon Cheri, Rocher, Tic Tac and Duplo. Kinder is a brand systematically highlighted in hypermarkets. It is a question of moving towards the client, rather than expecting the client to come to the shelf. Thanks to its extensive range, Kinder can economically create massive aisle-end displays, or autonomous displays installed far from the core shelf. Moreover, while most mass-consumption brands are reducing investment in their sales force, encouraged to do so by mass distribution and its centralised management logic, at Ferrero they understand the importance of constantly watching over the total visibility of their products, whether they stand out on the shelf and so on.

The other solution pursued by all brands is the diversification of distribution circuits. Thus we find soft drinks on sale in bakers' shops, on trains and so on. In the same vein, certain brands have attempted to re-enter the hard discount distribution circuit, from which they had been excluded almost by definition by the founders of the concept – the German chains Aldi and Lidl. It was still necessary to have a product that could not be substituted and to insert themselves into the need for differentiation of one of the actors. This is currently the case.

A non-substitutable product is a product for which, if it is not in-store, the client does not buy anything else in its place: this is the case for mini Babybel cheese and Kinder Surprise candies, for example. From this point of view, offering such goods on the hard discount circuit could prove interesting for the distributor, since it offers customers a genuine service but does not tread on the toes of their own products. On the other hand Lidl, number two in the market, which consequently has higher costs than Aldi, needs to find a source of profit through a few brand references, in order to remain competitive on price with the market leader Aldi in terms of essential products.

We have entered the B to B to C phase

The first edition of Philip Kotler's seminal book *Marketing Management* in 1971 dwelt on the revolution of B to C: the marketing share of the end client. Thirty years later, new realities have arrived and this notion must be amended. In many sectors, we have passed from B to C (business to consumer) marketing to B to B to C. We need to integrate the whole chain into the discussion, and ask ourselves what added value we bring to it.

The brand that does not have the luxury of independent distribution of its own must first of all consider the manner in which it will help the distributor/retailer to reach its own objectives. It is the distributor that must be convinced first of all. What is the use of a 'major brand' if it does not appear on the shelf, like all the other brands that have disappeared, not because clients no longer like them, but because they are no longer strategic for the distributors or retailers?

In a rolling market, for low-cost products such as toilet paper, or paper for other uses, an examination of a supermarket shelf might lead us to ask where the 'major brands' (Lotus, Kleenex, Charmin, Trèfle) have gone. They have all been replaced by Carrefour, Tesco, Sainsbury and other distributor brands There remains only one manufacturer brand, Okay, positioned on its price/quality ratio. The Portuguese brand Renova, however, managed to retain this market. This SME first conquered its domestic market, then Spain, and now European mass distribution. Its entry

into mass distribution was based on a double diagnosis of the distribution:

This shelf does not earn money: it is necessary to give it value through innovation.

This shelf is typically threatened by hard discounters.

Renova therefore did not arrive as a product but as a new partner for each distributor/retailer, primed with a double offer. At the top of the range it offered hydrated paper and soft paper, and at the bottom of the range, the ability to maximise offers (12 for 8, 24 for 18). This promotional range was presented pre-packaged on wheeled stands.

In *The Devil Wears Prada*, Meryl Streep asks where her Jarlsberg is. This is the name of a famous Norwegian cheese, not dissimilar to Emmental. Its market share in the United States, where it has been sold for at least 40 years, is considerable. What was the key to its success? The fact that its roundels only weigh 10 kg, whereas the Swiss ones weigh 30 kg, so it is easier and more economical for stockists. It is through understanding the trade's expectations that Jarlsberg has made allies.

Everyone has heard of the phenomenal success of Yellow Tail, the Australian wine, in the United States. Nobody doubts that it is a good product, suited to the market, at a good price. Still, this was a wholly unexpected success. The Australian maker, Casela, however, had had two good ideas, typical of a good B to B to C understanding of the market. First, it gave shares to the US distributor, which motivated it to promote the product everywhere in the US specialised distribution sector, and second, it fixed the price at a level that allowed it to pay these same distributors even more than the competition.

The indisputable fact that brands that no longer have their own distribution circuits are in fact engaged in B to B to C marketing is not given enough recognition. It is time that the distributor ceased to be considered as a 'distributor'. This word stems from the vocabulary of logistics, like stockist, dispatcher or wholesaler. A distributor is above all a retailer with its own differentiation strategy, and therefore its own brands. It is necessary to envisage it as a partner, and to start from its key problems, which are the same as those of the brand: the differentiation of its name, creating loyalty to its name, and profitability. It is concerned with the profitability of its own company, not of Danone or l'Oréal.

There is no point, therefore, in multiplying the studies on brand awareness or brand equity at the final client level if the brand is no longer referenced in the supermarket. Bic suffered the same misadventure in Europe in tobacconists and service stations: they have no need for Bic lighters, and prefer Chinese lighters that are more fun, cheaper to buy and sold at the same price. The 'strength' of Bic in the European market was in fact an illusion: for lack of other competitors, Bic was the only one to be found. For the past five years, however, Chinese competition has arisen, with a differentiated offer that has seduced retailers, so they no longer sell only Bic lighters. Bic, enjoying its position of near-monopoly, preferred to make profits rather than strengthen its brand among end clients (by telling them for example how a Bic lighter was better, and much safer), and the end customers saw no reason to complain when Bic lighters disappeared from the shelves.

Brand or business model power?

Yellow Tail offered more than a new brand, however: in the United States, it provided a new business model based on distribution. This was the number one problem to be resolved in the United States, bearing in mind that there are three levels of distribution there, as opposed to only two in Britain. The revolution was the business model. In Britain,

where Yellow Tail arrived years after Jacob's Creek, its strategy did not work. It was Jacob's Creek that enjoyed the pioneer effect with *its* new business model.

Easyjet and Ryanair are more than just new and reassuring brands at low prices. They offer a radically different business model, that the regular airlines are unable to copy, since it is so widely opposed to their own model. This is why British Airways failed with its subsidiary, Buzz (it was perceived as a subsidiary however independent it actually was). In contrast, British Airways exploits to the fullest the structural advantages of the 'hub' business model, which offers great flexibility to international travellers.

The fundamental lesson to be learnt here is that the brand is not a self-sufficient asset. By itself, it can do nothing: it is therefore conditional. It only produces its effects in interaction with the business model that supports it. This is the case for all successful new entrants: Dell, eBay, Google, Zara and so on.

Take textiles as an example. Everyone emphasises the extraordinary rise of the Zara brand worldwide, providing high fashion at low prices. To make this possible, however, it was in the mode of management that Zara really innovated. It managed to destabilise all those low-price competitors, such as Promod and Kiabi, that ran on different business models and therefore were not able to adapt. Zara is based on the fast turnover of small stocks of each item. The shortage of each garment is organised as a system of desirability promoting regular customer return to the shop. It treats the shop as a theatre stage, does no advertising, and has a remarkable system for eliciting qualitative information on the latest customer expectations. On the other hand, unlike its competitors Zara does not manufacture its clothing in China, in which case it could expect only two deliveries per year. It needs greater flexibility, which can only be obtained through a swarm of dedicated SMEs producing goods close by.

In mass consumption goods, it is notable that German-style hard discounters offer a better quality/price ratio than cheap products launched by the supermarkets in an attempt to resist them. This is due to their business model: the Germans launched on the basis of long-term agreements with reputable manufacturers, who could then invest in the production of a very restricted number of products. This therefore reduces the cost price, but the products remain of good quality. The supermarkets for their part are resistant to anything that ties them to a single supplier in the long term; their business model is based on being able to permanently exert pressure on their sources, and change them at the first opportunity. There is a fundamental difference between buying merchandise at the lowest price, wherever it may come from, and creating an industrial and logistical system to produce a product of acceptable quality at half the price, from reliable suppliers.

It is therefore time to recognise that the great novelty of the 1990s was the appearance of radically different business models, opening the market to previously unknown and innovative actors. The brands already in place proved no barrier to their entry, since the newcomers' business models completely overturned the range available. They provided value innovations. The brand is an active conditional: it depends on the quality of its business model. Now, to struggle in ultra-competitive circumstances, it is therefore necessary to become more strategist than marketer: that is, to integrate the brand into an original and effective business model.

The error of Virgin Cola in the United States and Europe was to believe that its brand would be enough, and to opt for roughly the same business model as Coke and Pepsi, without the resources and practices that it implies. In the field of mass-consumption goods, modern marketing is no longer B to C. Virgin believed in the consumer. However, it was the distributors that wanted none of it. The product was distributed only through Monoprix and Auchan in France, for example,

and that was not sufficient to make the operation profitable. Virgin's brand capital is not self-sufficient.

Other brands, such as Red Bull, have sought to bet on distribution channels in competition with the supermarkets in order to either loosen the stranglehold, or bypass it. The great good fortune of ready-to-wear clothing brands with their own points of sale is not accessible to many mass consumption product brands. They nevertheless seek to use other circuits as levers of prescription, even of sales. Thus, Roquefort Papillon owes the durability of its premium image to the fact that it was launched exclusively in cheese shops at the time when the market leader, Société, was betting on mass distribution. In order to create a shampoo brand today, it is best to begin from a hairdressing label and create a complete range under licence in this name, sold in major shops: this business model was created by J Dessanges for l'Oréal. It has since been taken up by J C Biguine, J F David and others. At l'Oréal, every brand in fact has a different business model.

Building the brand in reverse?

In the traditional model of brand construction, the work is done in stages: first the product, then the distribution, and finally the marketing communication. The problem is that, during the second and third stages, that is to say late in the process, it becomes clear that there is not enough money for advertising, not to mention that there are increasing doubts about its efficiency, if not its effectiveness. This then harms the credibility of the proposal made to the distributor. In fact, mass distribution sells access to display space and 'associated services' dearly – in the form of pre-margin and post-margin – which further eats into the advertising investment.

Perhaps it is time to review the process itself? C Boutineau, managing director of Bongrain for many years, suggested the concept of the brand in reverse. He is right. Rather than falling at these two hurdles, would it not be better to begin with the hurdles and build brands constructed to overcome them (that is, contagious brands)?

First of all, could not rumour and word of mouth come to the rescue of the brand, taking up the slack left by the faltering budgets? Since my team's work on the effectiveness of word of mouth and rumours (Kapferer, 1987, 1991 etc) has become internationally known, this question is regularly asked of us, and constitutes a frequent theme for management seminars. In reality, in order to make a brand contagious – that is, to transform its first clients into spontaneous, zealous ambassadors – it is necessary to conceive the brand in this manner from the beginning. You need to make it contagious, not through a viral marketing artifice, but intrinsically, through the idea that it represents or the experience it provides.

It is at the moment of conception of the product or service itself (of choosing a name, a packaging and so on), that it is necessary to inject the power of contagion, and not at the end, when it is too late. The keywords of contagion are strong idea, strong experience, interactive direct relationship, emotion and opinion leaders. It is interesting to note that in order to relaunch Converse, Nike did not use an advertising blitz. On the contrary, it favoured intimate, community media, and the direct involvement of customers, whose works contributed to the online Converse Gallery.

When the US marketing manager of BMW was asked how he planned to reach his sales objectives, he claimed he already had the means to make them: the simple rise of current clients up the range. His role, he added, was to make sure that young Americans dreamt about BMW when they fell asleep each night. This long-term marketing strategy led him to use the internet to carry long and very original films, created at his request by famous directors with the

maximum creative freedom. These films circulated on the web and reached their intended addressees a thousand times better than any mass advertising campaign. It was even better that everyone to whom they were passed knew which of their friends were BMW fans, or at least fans of beautiful cars.

Japan Tobacco has become a leader in the launching of new brands, such as Sakura, without advertising. It has access to a mega-database (bringing together several million Japanese smokers), and this makes it possible to send a high-quality boxed set, such as only the Japanese can do, to very precise segments. This presents the universe of the Sakura brand, and encourages them to try the product. Nespresso has also used reverse brand building.

In the automobile sector, Toyota launched its Xion brand to young people without mass advertising. Mini did the same thing. Swatch, less so.

Pernod Ricard excels in its ability to build brands with very strong foundations, thanks to the emphasis placed initially not on advertising, but on direct relationships with the bar trade, where its products are consumed, and where numerous, repetitive and very well-managed events leave a durable emotional trace on customers, at the same time as they understand the new product, and how to use it. In order to stage-manage a brand, it must have a base: it needs to embody an idea, a strong idea.

The power of passions

The brand is everything that makes a product more than just a product. It is in this that the brand differentiates and makes itself incomparable: it renders the competition uncompetitive. Of course, this process often begins with a new and highly innovative product. This is the basis, for example, of medical brands, or high tech, or fashion. Dell is a distributive innovation. In mass consumption, Sunny

Delight was a great product launched by Procter & Gamble. With the help of chemistry, it was possible to give an incredible taste experience without the need for real orange juice (although orange is included in the recipe, in those countries where it is in competition with Orangina). However, copies quickly arrived on the scene: under distributor brands, for example. What makes the brand incomparable then ceases to be exclusively the product or the service, but the idea that accompanies it: the intangible.

This is why the major brands are all brands that have a vision, that are not culturally empty. They are based on an intimate and personal 'big belief' (Edwards and Day, 2005), which they make real through their products, services, customer relations and marketing communications. This strong idea, which energises all the brand's activities, is communicative: it is the source of all conscious or unconscious adherences. In its day, Benetton was far more than sweaters in all the colours of fashion; it was the brand of tolerance and openness to all the colours of the world. Admittedly, perhaps 50 per cent of clients entering a Benetton store saw nothing but sweaters like any others, in a similar colour. This is normal: the aspirational capital of a brand is not built through the whole of its purchasers, but on a very small part. Then the mechanism of social contagion will get under way.

Today the brand must aim to be more than a 'preference' and reach the level of passion. To do this, it must itself be passionate. All entrepreneurs would like to change the world in their own way: they tap into this energy to make it contagious, a source of passion in others. For Biotherm, truth is found in water, and in plankton. For l'Oréal, women's happiness can only be found in science and its ability to turn back the years. Toyota puts product quality above all else. If Nissan expects first and foremost a low price from its suppliers, Toyota never mistakes its own priorities: obsessive quality comes before everything.

In marketing, consumer modelling focuses on the idea of preference. This stems from the fact that for many academic researchers, fundamentally a brand is a product with a name. It is true that if people are forced to choose between two products, they do indeed express a preference based on the attributes of these products. Apple's iBook is preferred to a Toshiba Tectra because it is more attractive, has more exciting colours, and makes it possible to do this or that more easily – and moreover it is an Apple. An iPod is more than an MP3 Walkman with specific characteristics.

To own an Apple is an affirmation of self. Its users engage with their self-concept and their internal image, in relation to others. In the same way, driving a Volvo truck or owning a fleet of Volvo Trucks is not the same thing as driving or owning an Iveco. Too many brands only aim at preference via product or service characteristics. Are not great brands, however, a big idea that is made real in products and services and attention to the customer? The whole identity process is aimed at identifying this big idea, or essence of the brand, and then transforming it into effective behaviour. Fundamentally, therefore, it is the intangible that must guide the tangible.

Beginning with the strong 360° experience

If managers think of the brand in a 'top down' manner, beginning with its essence and its values, then moving towards the tangible, its concrete activation, consumers proceed in the opposite manner. They begin with the tangible and the perceived. Everything begins with the concrete experience: I only believe what I see and feel.

I am indebted to my colleague at Columbia University, B Schmitt, for bringing my attention to the experiential dimension of the brand (Schmitt and Zhang, 2001; Schmitt, 2003). The brand is lived, felt, touched or heard: this goes without saying in the airline industry. Our impression of Air France or

Singapore Airlines is built during the 12 hours of the flight from Paris to Tokyo or Singapore, through contact with the onboard staff: they are the brand during those hours. The Air France brand, however, is also tied up in the treatment of customers in telephone contacts with reservations, by ground hostesses, when things go well, and when they go badly and there are delays. Understanding the perceptible dimension of the brand makes us forget the product alone, in order to take into account the sum total of the client experiences on contact with the brand. Michelin is not just tyres, nor is Citroen just cars, or Nivea just a range of hygiene and care products. The Michelin brand is built experientially through its sites, its advertising, its news on such and such a strike at Clermont Ferrand, the town where its headquarters are located, Formula 1, but also through the Michelin Guide and the friendly Michelin Man that organises events during the holidays.

Brands that are only products must add an experiential dimension that will involve the client. Involvement is the prerequisite for engagement with the brand: that is, a true affective loyalty and not a repeated purchase for the sake of gaining miles or points. How can this experiential dimension be created?

▮ Putting on l'Oréal make-up is a true ritual, using little tubs and pots which are beautifully thought-out and decorated.

▮ Danone gives personalised health advice on its 'Danone and you' website.

▮ Car makers are now highly attentive to the experiential elements (door noises, softness of the leather, position of the armrests and so on).

▮ Complaint handling is increasingly practised in advance. Scripts are prepared so that the response reduces the negative effect, or even leaves customers satisfied, and so surprised by their good experience that they become ambassadors for the brand.

▮ Champagne makers offer visits to their cellars where the mystery of creation can be felt.

▮ Société Roquefort constructs its cellars as 3D shows in stone in order to accentuate the perceptible visitor experience.

▮ The fabulous ascension of the Pernod Ricard group stems from its progress into experiential territory. The core of brand investment goes on organising events in bars, cafes, hotels and discos, based around the brand's values, its history and its imagined qualities.

▮ The Fedex brand has identified that the delivery person who comes to pick up the sealed envelopes or delivers them is the key personality in the Fedex experience for companies. To this is added the ergonomy of the website for tracking letters and parcels, the call centres and so on.

▮ Sponsorship is also a perceptible experience: visually associating the brand with an event, a sporting team or the like.

▮ Donations to good causes can demonstrate the brand is not insensitive to the world around it.

Finally, everyone will have noticed the tendency of brands to create a brand universe for themselves in increasingly large sites, designed as experiential places, where the client feels the brand 120 per cent. Louis Vuitton opened its two biggest shops in the world in Tokyo on 31 August 2006, and in Shanghai in 2005. On 19 May 2006, a riot took place on Fifth Avenue in New York at the opening of the Apple Megastore, beneath a giant glass cube, opposite Central Park. Open day and night, clients can find all their iPod accessories here, and enter into discussion, not with salespeople, but with Apple experts, all of them very young, and able to answer all technical problems.

Every Ralph Lauren shop could be Ralph Lauren's own house, with mahogany furniture, carpets, sofas, armchairs, pictures and photos, all aimed at creating a fake 'true' history (not everyone can be Lacoste). Remarkably, this perceptible Ralph Lauren ambience is also reproduced in the simple corners of the brand.

Tomorrow, just as there is a first division and a second division in football, these new brand cathedrals will sort the major brands from the small brands.

Beginning with the shop

All the exemplary cases of recent success, those that are praised to the skies worldwide in management seminars and symposia, are brands that have integrated distribution into their value offer. This is the case with Starbucks, Zara, Amazon, Dell, l'Occitane, Sephora and so on: they are all equally brands and distributors. We go to Zara in order to buy Zara.

It is interesting to note that Starbucks, Zara, Amazon and Google, to mention but a few, did not bother with advertising. On the contrary, they invested in training, men, women, architecture, the sensory contact, ergonomy, touch and the like.

It is revealing that all the stars of modern management, presented in all the management seminars, are brands whose shops are a source of enjoyment for the shopper: through the environment, choice, atmosphere and so on. We were already familiar with Galeries Lafayette, FNAC, the Virgin Megastore, IKEA and Nature and Discoveries, but we must now add Sephora, the Apple Store, the Nike Store, and the new-look factory shops that have consequently become destinations in themselves for a busy afternoon of what is now known as 'retail-tainment'.

What is the impact on brands? The brand today is built through retail. What use is recognition if the brand is not to be found in distribution, or even if it passes unnoticed or does not create a value-added shopper expe-rience?

Now all product brands audit their sales points in order to turn them into experiential and sensory levers in five dimensions. These are also crucial links for customer relationship managers (CRMs), who must connect to the customers' preferred points of sale if the relationship is to be converted into sales.

The company must be more human, more open

We are indebted to Franklin D Roosevelt for the quotation 'We have nothing to fear but fear itself.' In fact, one of the reasons that people had not explored the unknown seas before the great explorers of the sixteenth century did so was the fear of this unknown. It was thought that there were chimeras lurking there. The same is true of genetically modified organisms in France today: fear dominates thought and action.

For brands, a new reality is making itself felt: the technology is there, it will expand, and it has already been adopted by the customers themselves. It must therefore be used, and made into a friend. It is under-standable that brands fear technology: it profoundly changes all consumers' habits, and above all gives them power.

Recall certain inescapable facts:

▪ More mobile phones are sold worldwide than televisions. Does the brand's media strategy take this into account?

▪ In developed countries, the under-35s spend more time on the internet than watching television.

▪ In the United States, Americans spend more time on video games than at the cinema.

▪ More than 15 per cent of people who use the internet read blogs.

If during the first internet revolution there

were only prophecies, Web 2.0 makes its mark because the internet works, is used everywhere and makes money. The characteristics of our world can be summed up in four words: on demand, interactive, collaborative.

▮ Nowadays everything is provided on demand. With Google, everyone finds what they are looking for. On iTunes, people can find the tune they have been seeking for years without success. On tomorrow's television, we will no longer ask what a channel is showing this evening, but say, 'I'd like to see a Clint Eastwood film. Where is one being shown?'

▮ Nowadays the audience have developed a taste for interactivity: they no longer wish to be passive. They want to participate actively, give their opinion on everything and read the opinions of others. Blogs and forums help them to do so.

▮ The new generation is collaborative: they help one another, and remain switched on in order to continually seek the opinions of others. The blogosphere is a world of collaboration. Everyone's opinions on everything are exchanged, circulated, and diffuse like viruses.

For marketing, things have now come full circle. Marketing was born from the end of physical markets. The merchant and marketplace discussions between customers were replaced by self-service and television advertising. Now with the internet and 3G mobiles, other people's opinions are accessible about everything. The brand no longer has the monopoly on communication. Wishing to control everything, it must now compound with consumer, or customer, power, the power to broadcast another truth: their own. It is the end of broken product promises. It is the end of unethical or non-citizen brands.

The internet and blogs have revived conversation with an unequalled power: rumour and word of mouth now have a weapon of mass diffusion. The conversations, however, are also the best way of getting to know each other better, and of appearing human. They are a way of bringing down the barricades of mutual ignorance. The image of Microsoft in the United States has changed a great deal since Robert Scoble, a Microsoft employee, created his blog in 2004, attracting the visits and participation of nearly 3,500,000 people. Robert Scoble believed that Microsoft's image was too far removed from what he experienced within the company: it was not the ogre, the demon that others described it to be. He was not a communications director, or a public relations or marketing manager. He did know how to create a community around his blog, a trust connection. Since then companies have come to understand the value of these spontaneous corporate ambassadors: they give the company a human face, and build a trust network with the community they create.

Experimenting for more efficiency

When we talk of the impact of technology, we too often mention high-tech companies. Personally, I wonder each time: what does this mean to the managers of Fleury Michon, a company from Pouzauges in the Vendée, the French number one in superior-quality ham and fresh pre-cooked meals? We can dream for a moment or two, but does all of this have a genuine connection to their business, and the difficulty of maintaining that number one position, faced with distributor brands that instantly copy all good ideas, and hard discount products that are twice as cheap? Should they continue with the traditional television spots promoting their Red Label ham slices? Are there not two worlds? Should we be asking ourselves whether the homemaker is really high-tech?

It is true that it is easy to escape into the technological dream and Silicon Valley.

However, we need to recall that since 2003, Coca-Cola has reduced its television advertising investment by 10 per cent and brought a wholesale innovation in terms of media. Thus it competes with iTunes in Spain and in Britain with the mycokemusic.com website. Coca-Cola invests in the domain of video games, and product placement. Its media plan still follows its clients closely: the mobile phone has become the major point of contact.

Returning to Fleury Michon: if the penetration of its fresh, vacuum-packed ready-cooked meals is 10 times less than that of its ham, should the company run television advertisements for those products? Would it not be better to be referenced on all the important female-oriented websites, or work on micro targets such as:

▢ parents of students who do not have time to cook meals in their college rooms;

▢ children of grandparents who no longer have the energy to cook their meals every day;

▢ partners or spouses who are going away and wish to leave high-quality meal solutions;

▢ singletons of all ages.

How can they be involved, induced to participate, affected?

Nowadays market share is built through an aggregate of niches, of distinct groups. Technology has finally made it possible to reach these targeted groups at low cost. It is not a question of replacing 100 per cent of television advertising with a 0 per cent television budget from one day to the next: even Apple, the queen of Silicon Valley, has not done so. It is, however, time to experiment and see whether the returns on each euro invested are not better here than there.

For example, at Google, the 70/20/10 rule is used to describe three types of investment:

▢ 70 per cent of investment relates to current pillar products, best-sellers, in order to strengthen them;

▢ 20 per cent relates to experiments to test new ways of marketing, and promote these products along the way, due to technological progress: this is a matter of seeking efficiency;

▢ 10 per cent is spent on projects that have no relation to current business.

Coca-Cola has been reducing the share of television investment in its marketing budget for some time. Since television is no longer the preferred medium of young people, but has been replaced by the mobile phone, it is necessary to adapt and to test other modes of communication. Coca-Cola is constantly experimenting: in Spain and Britain it has launched mycokemusic.com, in competition with iTunes, thanks to an alliance with a major player in the telephony sector. Coca-Cola has also invested in space in video games, product placement, proximity events and street marketing, in addition to its B52s of sports and music sponsorship.

The enlarged scope of brand management

Brand management itself is much influenced by the revolution that has shaken marketing theory and practice: a shift from a mere transactional perspective to a relational perspective. This has led theorists to ask new questions, and propose new working methods, new modes of thinking, new tools, which often claiming to be substitutes for the former 'old' ones.

From transaction to relationships

Traditionally marketing focused on consumer behaviour: it aimed at influencing choice. Its focus was on understanding purchase, and the choice criteria that prompted it, whether they were tangible or intangible, product-based or image-based. Its tool for influencing demand was the marketing mix, with its sacred four Ps: product, price, place and publicity. Marketing research aimed at identifying the attributes that predict purchase, and its typical statistical tool was a multi-attribute model. Segmentation is another key concept of transactional marketing: recognising that transactions are facilitated when expectations are higher, and the mass market has been segmented into groups, or types with similar expectations. Then brands could be profiled and created to meet each set of expectations.

Because competition is fierce, imitation rapid, and consumers sometimes seemed overwhelmed by these very tightly tailored proposals and brands, the focus of marketing has moved from conquering clients to keeping them, from brand capital to customer capital. The new buzz words of good efficient brand management are share of requirements, shared loyalty and CRM. The focus is on building lasting relationships through time, and on post-purchase activities, all of which is subsumed under the term 'relationship marketing'. The focus of research has moved from predicting choice to classifying the different types of relationships consumers have with brands (Fournier, 1998), or the different types of interactions companies engage in with their clients, beyond selling a product or service (Rapp and Collins, 1994; Peppers and Rogers, 1993).

It should be noted that relationship marketing is a financially driven concept. Customers are still segmented, but the distinctions are behavioural. In traditional marketing, segmentation is aimed at maximising the value created by the brand or company for its customers. In relationship marketing, segmentation is based on the value a customer brings to the company: only profitable customers should receive repeated attention. Hence the concept of lifelong customer value. Internet technology has created the means to meet this demand for more and more efficiency in tracking, analysing, servicing and selling to each one of these important customers.

Of course, these two approaches are complementary. The best loyalties are not based on mere calculus and loyalty cards: they are internalised as voluntary loyalty, as brand commitment. On the other hand, weak brands need to start somewhere. Behavioural loyalty programmes create the conditions for deepening the customer–brand relationship, and create emotional connections between consumers and the brand.

From purchase to satisfaction and experiential rewards

Another consequence of this shift towards post-purchase phenomena is the focus on product/service satisfaction. How does what the product/service delivers match the expectations of the consumer? How can this satisfaction be raised, improved relentlessly? In this process the conditions of the consumption situation need to be taken into consideration. A product is always consumed in a context. The nature of this context affects the degree of satisfaction that the customer reports, through the notion of a 'rewarding experience'. In fact all marketers have known for a long time that food served in a pleasant atmosphere is judged to taste better than food eaten in unpleasant surroundings. Philip Kotler (1973) has coined the term 'atmospherics' to point out this facet of consumption, the experiential facet. Today, stores such as Niketown and the House of Ralph Lauren are typical applications of this experiential concept (Kozinets, 2002). As early as 1982, a pioneering paper by Holbrook and Hirschman insisted on the necessity of providing modern consumers with fantasies, feelings and fun in their experiential consumption. Schmitt (1999) has coined the term 'experiential marketing' to refer to 'how to get customers to sense, feel, think, act and relate to your company and brands'.

Bonding through aspirational values

Beyond functional and experiential rewards, brands must now also be aspirational. It is through their intangible values that they help consumers to forge their identities, at a time when inherited identities are weaker. The famous and elusive 'customer bonding' is based on product satisfaction, on a rewarding consumption experience (which includes the tailoring of proactive services even for products). It cannot exist if the brand values do not fit the consumers' values. All brands have to be somehow aspirational. Beyond materialistic and hedonistic satisfactions, they say, 'We understand each other, we share the same values, the same spirit.' This is why it is so important to specify these non-product-based values. Visions and missions are the typical source of these values.

It is therefore possible to plot the extension of the scope of brand management on a two-dimensional matrix (Figure 6.4). The horizontal axis refers to the time perspective of the relationship sought (from immediate transaction to repeat purchase to long-term commitment), while the vertical axis refers to the depth of customer bonding. It has three tiers: product satisfaction, experiential enchantment and aspirational intimacy, or the sharing of deep values. At the intercept, it is possible to position the new tools and behaviours of modern brand management.

The importance of communities

How many fans does the Manchester United football team have all around the world? Five million in the UK and 50 million elsewhere in the world? Most of these will never see the team play in the flesh, but they watch real-time television showings or connect to webcasts of the team's matches on the internet. They consume merchandise such as T-shirts. In the Old Trafford stadium, UK fans drink only Manchester United Cola. This is a real community; thanks to it, the team can hire the most expensive players, such as Wayne Rooney. The income from the merchandise sold by association with the most famous players virtually covers their enormous wages and transfer fees.

Figure 6.4   The extension of brand management

Traditionally, in consumer research consumers were seen as individuals, who were eventually aggregated into market segments. Most multi-attribute models aiming at predicting purchase made that implicit assumption, for they were based on individual responses. One could argue that consumers are not isolated individuals: they belong to groups, tribes or communities, either stable or transient, durable or situational. In fact, the brand acquires meaning not through a summation of individual evaluations, but after a collective screening made of conversations within the reference groups, the community, where opinion leaders can play a determining role.

Along with advertising, new forms of behaviour have emerged through which brands are *enacted*, that is, they eventually 'live' their values with consumer communities in a non-commercial environment. Classical examples of this are the Michelin-sponsored races around the world, or the Harley-Davidson rally where management and bikers meet once a year. The modern brand also animates communities created around itself or a topic (parenthood for Pampers, rock music for Jack Daniel's). Internet sites, 'fanzines', hotlines, brand clubs and events, are the classic tools to implement this new attitude and share the brand values through servicing or animations. The brand becomes 'mediactive', it helps its customers get in touch with each other, on the net or in reality through specific events. Building *brand communities* is now part of the scope of brand management (Hagel, 1999). For consumers, getting together and sharing experiences is another form of reward. Feather (2000) has identified four drivers of e-communities: they can be interest-based, transaction-based, relationship-based or fantasy-based. Each one determines a specific type of site, of content, of interaction between the brand and this very involved public; it goes beyond mere purchasing and looks for interactions with the brand and other customers. The customers are driven by the rewards of community interaction and transaction.

Activating the brand at contact

Most of our thinking about the role of advertising in supporting brands is based on the *'big bang model'* (Kapferer, 2001). At a time when there were few channels available, the core media could really be called mass media. But attention is scarce and fragmented now, because there is such a diversity of available media channels, not to mention the internet. The power and energy of the massive gross rating point (GRP) campaigns is fragmented. Down in the marketing channels, this energy arrives weakened. This is why it is necessary to recreate energy at contact. All brands must be concerned with the energisation of their value-transmitting chain, including prescribers, VIPs, opinion leaders, professionals, early triers, involved consumers and of course distributors. A brand that existed only on shelves and on television would seem remote and lack depth. One does not create relationships at a distance.

As a consequence, all brands now must think of their activation plan:

▍ Acting within communities (like Vittel mineral water, which has developed partnerships with local sports clubs where consumers train).

▍ Acting on premises, at the point of the consumption, creating memorable collective experiences.

▍ Acting with prescribers (that is, those who recommend the brand to a user further down the channel), to foster their cause.

▍ Acting with virtual communities created around the brand. The brand must become a medium between the people in the community, real or virtual, and provide more than products. It must provide real services.

Licensing: a strategic lever

Licences are a rapidly growing phenomenon (Warin and Tubiana, 2003), demonstrating an awareness of two facts. First, although brands are a form of capital, they still have to produce revenue. Second, this type of partnership enables the brand to acquire abilities or distribution that it had previously lacked, and so to be extended yet further. However, there is still an image problem with licences, which explains why they have experienced slower growth in some countries than others. English-speaking countries, for example, have extensively exploited this concept. Yet in numerous other countries, licences are still restricted only to the luxury sector, sport and so-called 'derivative' products – knick-knacks from every sector that this pejorative name implies. Furthermore, the current trend among luxury brands for announcing – as Gucci has done – that they are to cut the number of their licences has served to strengthen this negative aura around the licence. For some brands, such action has merely been a case of correcting the licensing excesses into which they had fallen, as part of a drive to recreate the rarity (and perhaps even quality) of their brand. Gucci was a typical example of this.

In reality, licences have now become a truly magnificent opportunity for improving business volume, brand capital and profitability. Why was this not the case before?

First, brand managers have now realised they need to focus on relationships. Beyond the product itself, the brand must forge links with its customers – and its best customers in particular – which are based on a rapport and mutual understanding. The products we currently refer to as 'derived' should really be renamed as 'customer relationship products'. For example, one initiative taken by Orangina has been to rebuild its relationship with the young people and teenagers who had increasingly been abandoning the product in the face of Coca-Cola's relentless encroachment.

Second, today's brand is community focused, as in, 'Tell me which community you belong to, and I'll tell you who you are.' In other words, the choices the brand makes in terms of promotional agreements reveal the community to which it belongs and whose tastes it shares. The decision by the Suze apéritif company to launch an annual limited edition, teaming up with J-C de Castelbajac in 2001 and Christian Lacroix in 2002, is an illustration of this principle, and has positioned Suze as the drink for lovers of arts and literature, revitalising a fundamental aspect of the product which this character brand had ignored for too long.

Third, the brand builds its status through its extensions. The one-product brand has had its day, and the brand is viewed no longer as a product, but rather as a concept. Once created, a concept develops and strengthens itself via extensions. Under this approach, the company acknowledges that the brand extension calls for industrial, logistical or commercial skills that the company itself probably does not possess in the short term. However, there are many other companies that do have the required resources, and can place them at the immediate disposal of the brand.

The strength of the brand is also linked to its geographical extension. Production and distribution licences are necessary in order to understand and penetrate continent-sized countries such as China and India. The product range of a luxury ready-to-wear brand such as Lacoste in Japan or Korea has to take into consideration the physical size of its customers and the specific sports they play. The local licensee is in the best position to develop an extension to the collection which improves the brand's local relevance, while creative and quality control remain in the hands of the talented licence holder.

In sectors eroded by the dictates of concentrated large-scale distribution, the licence provides an opportunity to release some of the pressure. This applies to any sector in which companies have failed to create brands based on strong, intangible values, for this is the one thing that the distributor brands are incapable of copying. The principle operates across the most diverse categories, from spectacle frames to men's footwear. It also applies to SMEs that, lacking the finances to create their own brand, manufacture and distribute under licence. This is how Weight Watchers has expanded its world distribution.

However, it would be a mistake to see licences as nothing more than a godsend to SMEs crushed by the excessive demands of concentrated large-scale distribution. They also represent an opportunity for multinationals making a late entry into a marketplace already dominated by other firms. Creating a new brand makes the risk of competition too great. A better strategy is to use a ready-made one, thus circumventing the barriers to entry. This is what l'Oréal did with *Ushuaia*, a shampoo brand that has taken the name of a very famous French television programme on Channel 1 based on the Earth, the environment and its preservation. The licence owned by Channel 1 enabled l'Oréal to compete with Unilever and Henkel in the shower gels market, in which it had previously had no presence.

Lastly, the case of the J Dessanges hairdressing and beauty chain provides an illustration of a remarkable use of licensing in its strategy to increase its prestige, status and desirability still further. By using l'Oréal as its licensee to distribute a full range of large-scale distribution products, this upper range or even luxury chain not only created an exceptional source of profits, but also strengthened its brand via the licence. The whole of France is familiar with, and is now able to buy, products from the J Dessange Professional Range (which are, it should be said, the most expensive on hypermarket and supermarket shelves), while at the same time dreaming of one day being able to afford visits to the hairdressing salons, whose spiralling prices are driven by their luxury strategy. After all, in the West, luxury derives its desirability from being well known to all, yet affordable by very few; and Dessange would not have been as desirable without this licence. It is worth pointing out that the company has launched a second, cheaper hairdressing salon brand (Camille Albane) at the same time as releasing a line of large-scale distribution products named 'Camille Albane'. Here, the licence will serve as a motor to accelerate recognition and image, since the number of Camille Albane salons is still small. Hence its low profile.

Ultimately, the very nature of a brand can change as a result of its licences. Cacharel is an example of a licence that went on to become the true centre of gravity of a brand. Cacharel started out as a woman's ready-to-wear brand in the 1970s, positioned to appeal to romantic women. A perfume licence was subsequently granted to l'Oréal, with the launch of Anaïs Anaïs, a worldwide best-seller, followed by Loulou and Eden. In the last five years, four perfumes have been launched to appeal to today's young clientèle: Noa, Nemo, Gloria and Amor Amor. For l'Oréal, the problem with the Cacharel licence is that it is built on nothing: the ready-to-wear business has since vanished into obscurity. This is precisely the opposite of the Armani and Ralph Lauren licences. However, for Cacharel, the situation is very different: thanks to the recognition generated by advertising and the worldwide distribution of its perfumes, the company is in a position to consider other licences for its brand. In this way, it plans to increase its royalties from €7.6 million to €12 million over five years (*Les Echos*, 7 July 2003). Cacharel has become a de facto perfume brand and is exploited through various other licences (household linen, lingerie, sunglasses, fine leather goods, scarves): an original business model.

As we can see, the licence can take many forms in the question of how to manage the brand over time: at launch, or during the growth, reinforcement, maturity or relaunch phases. It provides a source of accessible, creative solutions, taking competitors by surprise. It is truly a tool for increasing brand competitiveness.

No such discussion would be complete without considering the fiscal element of the licence, by which many multinationals have shifted profits from their local subsidiaries back to the head office through the mechanism of royalties paid in remuneration for the use of brands, logos, artwork and so on. For example, it is common knowledge that Disneyland Paris is a commercial success but a financial disaster. More than 12 million visitors a year queue up to get into the park, yet given the scale of the initial investment and interest rates, and thus the venture's current liabilities, the project could only start to turn in a profit if the banks were to write off their debts. Despite this, Disney Corporation still draws annual royalties for the concession of its brands and trademarks (all of the Disney characters) to Disneyland Paris.

Yet good fiscal administration knows that licensing may be a way to siphon profit out of a country and pay less taxes: it demands proof that a genuine service is being provided. If royalties are being paid, they should reflect real and tangible added value. Thus a holding that requires its subsidiaries in other countries to pay royalties for the use of a company name and logo may find itself required to produce evidence of the value of the service provided to the subsidiary through the use of this name and logo. Paradoxically, it may be the holding itself that ought to pay for such a service. The holding's name is often unknown to consumers; yet if it is listed on a stock exchange, a visible profile is essential. Unless the holding chooses to produce its own advertising (such as the LVMH group's sponsorship programme), such visibility can only be created further downstream, by appending its name to all its subsidiaries' products.

How co-branding grows the business

Products that have two creators, and advertise the fact through double branding, are on the increase: for example Inneov by Nestlé and l'Oréal, the first nutritional pill to prevent hair loss, launched in pharmacies in November 2006. We are already familiar with Danao, by Danone and Minute Maid. Philips created a revolution with its Coolskin razor with a moisturising cream, entrusted to Nivea worldwide – a fact that appears on all the razor's packaging, and in advertising. Everyone knows the 'Intel Inside' signature that appears on all computers that use Intel, and in their advertising.

The rise of co-branding is symptomatic of our era, with its culture of networking and partnerships. It is also the result of a desire to remain within the company's key competences, to the point of looking elsewhere for those competences that are missing. It therefore merits an in-depth discussion.

Why this rise in co-branding?

Co-branding is fundamentally a response to the need for continual growth. However, whereas yesterday companies would have sought at any price to acquire the new competences that were missing and restricting their ability to innovate, today they seek to find a partner with which to co-create. This is the era of alliances, partnerships and the networked economy, where each party retains its specialisation and its key competence, and utilises those of others to the fullest extent. In the pursuit of growth, it is not long before we encounter the difficulty in reconciling this with maintaining the brand's specificity and the company's expertise.

In the West, the brand is the name for a specific expertise or state of mind (in Asia, the brand is far less specialised). When trying to grow, the brand can reach the limits of its own identity and its specificity: it therefore has need of an ally to fill the gaps where it is not competent or legitimate. When this ally is competent but not legitimate, the partnership does not give rise to co-branding. For example, Weight Watchers needed the industrial and distribution competences of Fleury Michon in order to develop a genuinely qualitative range of vacuum-packed ready meals. However, this was not mentioned anywhere on the packaging. In fact, not only is the Weight Watchers brand sufficient for diet disciples, its 'marriage' with Fleury Michon, the epicure's brand, suggestive of French-style good living, is unclear and even contradictory.

In contrast, when the two images complement one another, both brands strongly endorse it. Thus, in order to please the youth of today, increasingly seduced by computer games and consoles, Lego decided to add an electronics line to its products. However Lego not only has no industrial competence in this field (which can always be subcontracted), crucially its brand image would not lend credibility to the new products. The signature of a brand with a strong reputation in electronics among young people would remove this obstacle. Mattel had already worked with Compaq to create a line of interactive, high-tech toys.

We can see therefore that several strategic questions arise on the subject of co-branding:

▧ Will the visible alliance of two brands create a favourable impression among clients?

▧ Is there a high degree of complementarity between the two brand images that will create value?

▧ Is there a good 'fit' between these two brands, given the perceived status of each? As with any successful marriage, of course there must be complementarity, but also a common vision and shared values.

▧ Will the innovation be attributed to both partners, or only to one of them?

Typical situations that lead to co-branding

▧ Co-branding is necessary to increase the chances of success for a brand's extension beyond its original market. Thus, as a strongly child-centred brand, Kellogg's explicitly marked its new range of cereals for health-conscious adults with the Healthy Choice brand, already well-known in this segment. Danone and Motta pooled their competences and their images to launch Yolka, a yoghurt ice cream. This was also the case for a refrigerated fruit juice from Minute Maid/Danone, and as mentioned above, the Mattel-Compaq interactive toy.

▧ Co-branding is also necessary when the brand's image makes it difficult to communicate with a particular target. In that case, it needs an intermediary, someone to open doors for it, another brand that has the ear of this target and can therefore act as a relay. When Orangina, primarily thought of as a child's drink, wanted to boost its sales by targeting adolescents, the biggest consumers of soft drinks, its childish image was a handicap. It created a partnership with NRJ, the most popular radio station among young people, and a jeans brand, Lee Cooper. Orangina cans were co-branded NRJ and Orangina.

▧ Co-branding makes it possible to develop a product line that is often sold in a separate distribution channel. The goal, in addition to selling to a previously reluctant clientele, is to nurture certain traits of the brand's identity kernel. Thus, in order to create a relationship with 'creative' young women, Tefal developed a range of specific products internationally with the young, unconventional, up-and-coming and very media-friendly British chef,

Jamie Oliver. This line is sold worldwide. The partnership between Jamie Oliver and Tefal is that of two – admittedly different – actors who nevertheless share the same vision: a taste for simplicity, pleasure and conviviality. The marketing positioning of this product line will be just below the top of the range: it will only be found in selective channels.

▍ Co-branding makes it possible to move up a level. In food products, it is difficult for a known brand to move up a level, and therefore up in price, to become a mass-market brand. It needs a credibility link. This is why all pre-cooked meals, even distributors' brands, have created lines that are co-endorsed by a famous chef: Ducasse, Troisgros, Robuchon and so on.

▍ Ingredient brands are also a way to send the client a message about the product's superior quality, and to lift it above the more ordinary copies, thereby justifying its higher price. Diam's, by Dim, displays the Lycra logo. The same goes for Goretex, Woolmark, Tactel, and for Nutrasweet in the food sector. In B2B, the practice is also on the increase: the 'Intel Inside' brand is exhibited by all computer assemblers that use Intel chips and agree to say so in their communications, in return for which Intel pays half of its clients' advertising expenses.

For the distributor Decathlon, which creates its own brands, co-brands are strategically valuable since they boost the perceived technicality of the products of its passion brands, which are still relatively unknown to the end customer. All of Damart's structure and profitability is based on an ingredient brand, Thermolactyl. This brand, which is owned by Damart, designates a generic fibre that retains heat (rhovilon): this gives Damart the appearance of exclusivity. While many other distributors offer warm underwear, only Damart has Thermolactyl!

▍ Co-branding is also a response to the fragmentation of the market and the emergence of communities. Take, for example, the telephone and internet brand Orange. How can it grow? It can sell wholesale to virtual operators, the mobile virtual network operations (MVNOs), which will act as discounters (for example Carrefour, Darty and so on). In this first phase, the Orange brand name disappears: customers believe they are buying their internet services from Carrefour. It may also propose an association with those brands that already have a captive audience, and offer specific value-added content aimed at this audience. For example, loyal customers of Fnac (a rival of Virgin Megastores) can buy Fnac telephone packages: these clearly show the Orange logo. They offer more than just a price – that is, services and contents aimed solely at Fnac customers. Orange reassures them, and manages the whole business.

Orange does likewise with football clubs, creating subscriptions in the club's name, associated with Orange's: fans benefit from ad hoc content, with a strong football focus. When their club wins, they also win promotions, the opportunity to send free SMSs, or to 'chat' with the star players. Orange has also negotiated exclusive mobile phone retransmission rights for certain major competitions. In this way, Orange has succeeded in adapting to market fragmentation.

On the internet, co-branding also has a role to play. This is normal: online brands reference one another, in order to mark a community of values, interests and audiences.

▍ Co-branding, in the form of licences, was one way to boost sales for car models at the end of their life-cycle, when the product itself no longer has the value of technical novelty. New value was added by customising the car in the style of a famous designer or couturier. Prominent examples include the Peugeot 205 Lacoste and the Citroen Bic. This approach is now used at the beginning of the life-cycle, in order to put a sociocultural stamp on the vehicle and emphasise its positioning: Twingo Kenzo illustrated the car's central proposition, that 'It's up to you to invent the life that goes with it', and strengthened its creative aspect. The Citroen Picasso was also a response to the desire to strengthen Citroen's positioning as an innovator, competing against the Renault Espace. For the Picasso family themselves, this maintains the brand status of their surname, and prevents it from falling into the public domain through lack of commercial use.

Co-branding sometimes aims to provide a buzz around the brand among opinion leaders, to create an image. This is the case with the specially designed products Mark Newson has created for Tefal. In the same way, to give itself a fashionable, stylish touch, Adidas has entrusted designer Stella McCartney with the task of developing a co-branded product line. The brand is effectively seeking to have a presence on the style market and not only the technical market. This approach of co-branding with a creator is prevalent in the sportswear sector: Puma has done likewise. H&M caused a riot by launching a limited series by Karl Lagerfeld: customers were queuing up outside from midnight.

Finally, co-branding is the visible – confidence-inspiring – sign of a brand union. Skyteam is the airline alliance formed around Air France and KLM, in order to standardise their loyalty programmes and enable travellers to increase their air miles still further – an additional defence against the low-cost airlines.

Co-branding, alliances and partnerships

The modern world is a world of alliances and partnerships between groups, companies, brands and so on. Co-branding is the symbol of an alliance that neither party is seeking to hide (unlike subcontracting, for example).

An analysis of company strategies since 1990 saw certain forms of behaviour, such as alliances, undergo considerable growth, and even saw new, hybrid forms emerge – hence the creation of new concepts and terms to capture them. One of these is 'coopetition' – an alliance with a competitor.

Before we proceed, let us give some definitions. An alliance is indeed a strategic decision, with long-term implications, aiming to bring together complementary competences in order to develop innovative processes and products/services, and finally new markets. It is therefore distinct from a simple partnership, which is limited both in time and in the scope of the cooperation. As for the neologism 'coopetition', it refers to alliances involving two mutually competitive companies. Thus it is coopetition when PSA and Toyota create a common manufacturing unit together in Slovenia, to produce the same small car model. It is a partnership when PSA carries out various cooperation and exchange projects with Ford on diesel engines. It is also a partnership when, in order to exist in this gigantic country, Evian entrusts its US distribution to Coca-Cola. It is apparent that this agreement may be called into question at any time. It is also a partnership when Nestlé entrusts Krups with the European development of a coffee maker that uses Nespresso, the famous and vastly expensive top-of-the-range coffee capsules. Tomorrow, or in another part of the world, Krups could be replaced by another famous brand.

Alliances are nothing new. Think back to Ariane, Airbus and Concorde – all projects on such a scale that even at the planning stage nationalism, competition and sensitivities had to be forgotten in order to fuse cutting-edge competences in a meta project that no single company, or even single country, could achieve alone.

In strategic terms, an alliance is an alternative to acquisition and fusion. This latter is a common type of company growth, buying out key competences or market shares through the sacrosanct critical mass. All of the following companies are the result of fusions or acquisitions: Novartis, Aventis, Vinci, Vivendi, Aviva, Arcelor, Entenial and Sony-Ericsson. An analysis of the components of the success or – as it is admitted nowadays – lack of success of fusions and acquisitions

between companies is not relevant to this section. As for the alliance, it preserves the cultures, identities and legal forms of the companies that come together in a common, large-scale project.

In terms of visibility, the members of alliances are not always clearly identified. This is the case when a new name and often a new collectively managed structure are created for the project in question: Airbus Industries, Eurocopter, Thalys, Eurostar or Arianespace. However, it is sometimes the case that the parents are clearly identified by their names and logos. In fact, many products are clearly endorsed by both creators: Philips Alessi, Samsung B&O and so on.

Table 6.3 Strategic uses of co-branding

How	Sources of growth Increasing frequency per customer	Enhancing proximity to a target	Enhancing perceived quality	Creating a new market

Same product	Co-branded
	loyalty cards
	– Air France AMEX
	– Smiles
		Image strategy
		– Orangina
		  Lee Cooper cans
		– Orangina
		  Kookaï
			Component
			co-branding
			Collective
			(Intel/Lycra)
			– Proprietary
			  (Damart)	

Line extension/
variant
		Limited series
		– Peugeot 205
		  Lacoste
		– Renault Clio
		  Kenzo
			Endorsement
			– Weight Watchers
			  by Fleury Michon
			– Max Havelaar
			  and coffee brands	

New full line		Co-creation
		– Tefal line
		  designed by/for
		  Jamie Oliver
		– Philips–Alessi
		– Hilfiger–Thierry Henry		

Value
innovation/
disruption
				Co-creation
				– Danoe
				  (Minute Maid–
				  Danone)
				– Nespresso–
				  Krups

7

Brand identity and positioning

A brand is not the name of a product. It is the vision that drives the creation of products and services under that name. That vision, the key belief of the brands and its core values is called identity. It drives vibrant brands able to create advocates, a real cult and loyalty.

Modern competition calls for two essential tools of brand management: 'brand identity', specifying the facets of brands' uniqueness and value, and 'brand positioning', the main difference creating preference in a specific market at a specific time for its products.

For existing brands, identity is the source of brand positioning. Brand positioning specifies the angle used by the products of that brand to attack a market in order to grow their market share at the expense of competition.

Defining what a brand is made of helps answer many questions that are asked every day, such as: Can the brand sponsor such and such event or sport? Does the advertising campaign suit the brand? Is the opportunity for launching a new product inside the brand's boundaries or outside? How can the brand change its communication style, yet remain true to itself? How can decision making in communications be decentralised regionally or internationally, without jeopardising brand congruence? All such decisions pose the problem of brand identity and definition – which are essential prerequisites for efficient brand management.

Brand identity: a necessary concept

Like the ideas of brand vision and purpose, the concept of brand identity is recent. It started in Europe (Kapferer, 1986).The perception of its paramount importance has slowly gained worldwide recognition; in the most widely read American book on brand equity (Aaker, 1991), the word 'identity' is in fact totally absent, as is the concept.

Today, most advanced marketing companies have specified the identity of their brand through proprietary models such as 'brand key' (Unilever), 'footprint' (Johnson & Johnson), 'bulls' eyes' and 'brand stewardship', which organise in a specific form a list of concepts related to brand identity. However, they are rather checklists. Is identity a sheer linguistic novelty, or is it essential to understanding what brands are?

What is identity?

To appreciate the meaning of this significant concept in brand management, we shall begin by considering the many ways in which the word is used today.

For example, we speak of 'identity cards' – a personal, non-transferable document that tells in a few words who we are, what our name is and what distinguishable features we have that can be instantly recognised. We also hear of 'identity of opinion' between several people, meaning that they have an identical point of view. In terms of communication, this second interpretation of the word suggests brand identity is the common element sending a single message amid the wide variety of its products, actions and communications. This is important since the more the brand expands and diversifies, the more customers are inclined to feel that they are, in fact, dealing with several different brands rather than a single one. If products and communication go their separate ways, how can customers possibly perceive these different routes as converging towards a common vision and brand?

Speaking of identical points of view also raises the question of permanence and continuity. As civil status and physical appearance change, identity cards get updated, yet the fingerprint of their holders always remains the same. The identity concept questions how time will affect the unique and permanent quality of the sender, the brand or the retailer. In this respect, psychologists speak of the 'identity crisis' which adolescents often go through. When their identity structure is still weak, teenagers tend to move from one role model to another. These constant shifts create a gap and force the basic question: 'What is the real me?'

Finally, in studies on social groups or minorities, we often speak of 'cultural identity'. In seeking an identity, they are in fact seeking a pivotal basis on which to hinge not only their inherent difference but also their membership of a specific cultural entity.

Brand identity may be a recent notion, but many researchers have already delved into the organisational identity of companies (Schwebig, 1988; Moingeon and Soenen, 2003). There, the simplest verbal expression of identity often consists in saying: 'Oh, yes, I see, but it's not the same in our company!' In other words, corporate identity is what helps an organisation, or a part of it, feel that it truly exists and that it is a coherent and unique being, with a history and a place of its own, different from others.

From these various meanings, we can infer that having an identity means being your true self, driven by a personal goal that is both different from others' and resistant to change. Thus, brand identity will be clearly defined once the following questions are answered:

▌ What is the brand's particular vision and aim?

▌ What makes it different?

▌ What need is the brand fulfilling?

▌ What is its permanent nature?

▌ What are its value or values?

▌ What is its field of competence? Of legitimacy?

▌ What are the signs which make the brand recognisable?

These questions could indeed constitute the brand's charter. This type of official document would help better brand management in the medium term, both in terms of form and content, and so better address future communication and extension issues. Communication tools such as the copy strategy are essentially linked to advertising campaigns, and so are only committed to the short term. There must be specific guidelines to ensure that there is indeed only one brand forming a solid and coherent entity.

Brand identity and graphic identity charters

Many readers will make the point that their firms already make use of graphic identity 'bibles', either for corporate or specific brand purposes. We do indeed find many graphic identity charters, books of standards and visual identity guides. Urged on by graphic identity agencies, companies have rightly sought to harmonise the messages conveyed by their brands. Such charters therefore define the norms for visual recognition of the brand, ie the brand's colours, graphic design and type of print.

Although this may be a necessary first step, it isn't the be all and end all. Moreover, it puts the cart before the horse. What really matters is the key message that we want to communicate. Formal aspects, outward appearance and overall looks result from the brand's core substance and intrinsic identity. Choosing symbols requires a clear definition of what the brand means. However, while graphic manuals are quite easy to find nowadays, explicit definitions of brand identity *per se* are still very rare. Yet, the essential questions above (ie the nature of the identity to be conveyed) must be properly answered before we begin discussing and defining what the communication means and what the codes of outward recognition should be. The brand's deepest values must be reflected in the external signs of recognition, and these must be apparent at first glance. The family resemblance between the various models of BMW conveys a strong identity, yet it is not *the* identity. This brand's identity and essence can actually be defined by addressing the issue of its difference, its permanence, its value and its personal view on automobiles.

Many firms have unnecessarily constrained their brand because they formulated a graphic charter before defining their identity. Not knowing who they really are, they merely perpetuate purely formal codes by, for example, using a certain photographic style that may not be the most suitable. Thus Nina Ricci's identity did not necessarily relate to the company's systematic adherence to English photographer David Hamilton's style.

Knowing brand identity paradoxically gives extra freedom of expression, since it emphasises the pre-eminence of substance over strictly formal features. Brand identity defines what must stay and what is free to change. Brands are living systems. They must have degrees of freedom to match modern market diversity.

Identity: a contemporary concept

That a new concept – identity – has emerged in the field of management, already well versed in brand image and positioning, is really no great surprise. Today's problems are more complex than those of 10 or 20 years ago and so there is now a need for more refined concepts that allow a closer connection with reality.

First of all, we cannot overemphasise the fact that we are currently living in a society saturated in communications. Everybody wants to communicate these days. If needed, proof is available: there have been huge increases in advertising budgets, not only in the major media but also in the growing number of professional magazines. It has become very difficult to survive in the hurly-burly thus created, let alone to thrive and successfully convey one's identity. For communication means two things: sending out messages and making sure that they are received. Communicating nowadays is no longer just a technique, it is a feat in itself.

The second factor explaining the urgent need to understand brand identity is the pressure constantly put on brands. We have now entered an age of marketing similarities. When a brand innovates, it creates a new standard. The other brands must then catch up if they want to stay in the race, hence the increasing number of 'me-too' products with similar attributes, not to mention the copies produced by distributors. Regulations also cause similarities to spread. Bank operations, for example, have become so much alike that banks are now unable to fully express their individuality and identity. Market research also generates herdism within a given sector. As all companies base themselves on the same life-style studies, the conclusions they reach are bound to be similar as are the products and advertising campaigns they launch, in which sometimes even the same words are used.

Finally, technology is responsible for growing similarity. Why do cars increasingly look alike, in spite of their different makes? Because car makers are all equally concerned about fluidity, inner car space constraints, motorisation and economy, and these problems cannot be solved in all that many different ways. Moreover, when the models of four car brands (Audi, Volkswagen, Seat and Skoda) share many identical parts (eg chassis, engine, gearbox), for either productivity or competitiveness purposes, it is mainly brand identity, along with, to a lesser extent, what's left of each car, which will distinguish the makes from one another.

Diversification calls for knowing the brand's identity. Brands launch new products, penetrate new markets and reach new targets. This may cause both fragmented communications and patchwork images. Though we are still able to discern bits and pieces of the brand here and there, we are certainly unable to perceive its global and coherent identity.

Why speak of identity rather than image?

What does the notion of identity have to offer that the image of a brand or a company or a retailer doesn't have? After all, firms spend large amounts of money measuring image.

Brand image is on the receiver's side. Image research focuses on the way in which certain groups perceive a product, a brand, a politician, a company or a country. The image refers to the way in which these groups decode all of the signals emanating from the products, services and communication covered by the brand.

Identity is on the sender's side. The purpose, in this case, is to specify the brand's meaning, aim and self-image. Image is both the result and interpretation thereof. In terms of brand management, identity precedes image. Before projecting an image to the public, we must know exactly what we want to project. Before it is received, we must know what to send and how to send it. As shown in Figure 7.1, an image is a synthesis made by the public of all the various brand messages, eg brand name, visual symbols, products, advertisements, sponsoring, patronage, articles. An

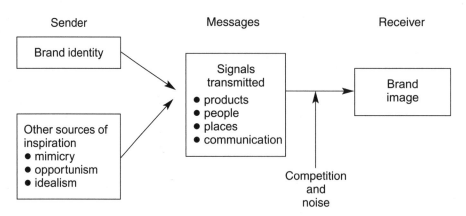

Figure 7.1   Identity and image

image results from decoding a message, extracting meaning, interpreting signs.

Where do all these signs come from? There are two possible sources: brand identity of course, but also extraneous factors ('noise') that speak in the brand's name and thus produce meaning, however disconnected they may actually be from it. What are these extraneous factors?

First, there are companies that choose to imitate competitors, as they have no clear idea of what their own brand identity is. They focus on their competitors and imitate their marketing communication.

Second, there are companies that are obsessed with the willingness to build an appealing image that will be favourably perceived by all. So they focus on meeting every one of the public's expectations. That is how the brand gets caught in the game of always having to please the consumer and ends up surfing on the changing waves of social and cultural fads. Yesterday, brands were into glamour, today, they are into 'cocooning'; so what's next? The brand can appear opportunistic and popularity seeking, and thus devoid of any meaningful substance. It becomes a mere façade, a meaningless cosmetic camouflage.

The third source of 'noise' is that of fantasised identity: the brand as one would ideally like to see it, but not as it actually is. As a result, we notice, albeit too late, that the advertisements do not help people remember the brand because they are either too remotely connected to it or so radically disconnected from it that they cause perplexity or rejection.

Since brand identity has now been recognised as the prevailing concept, these three potential communication glitches can be prevented.

The identity concept thus serves to emphasise the fact that, with time, brands do eventually gain their independence and their own meaning, even though they may start out as mere product names. As living memories of past products and advertisements, brands do not simply fade away: they define their own area of competence, potential and legitimacy.

Yet they also know when to stay out of other areas. We cannot expect a brand to be anything other than itself.

Obviously, brands should not curl up in a shell and cut themselves off from the public and from market evolutions. However, an obsession with image can lead them to capitalise too much on appearance and not enough on essence.

Identity and positioning

It is also common to distinguish brands according to their positioning. Positioning a brand means emphasising the distinctive characteristics that make it different from its competitors and appealing to the public. It results from an analytical process based on the four following questions:

- A brand for what benefit? This refers to the brand promise and consumer benefit aspect: Orangina has real orange pulp, The Body Shop is environment friendly, Twix gets rid of hunger, Volkswagen is reliable.

- A brand for whom? This refers to the target aspect. For a long time, Schweppes was the drink of the refined, Snapple the soft drink for adults, Tango or Yoohoo the drink for teenagers.

- Reason? This refers to the elements, factual or subjective, that support the claimed benefit.

- A brand against whom? In today's competitive context, this question defines the main competitor(s), ie those whose clientele we think we can partly capture. Tuborg and other expensive imported beers thus also compete against whisky, gin and vodka.

Positioning is a crucial concept (Figure 7.2). It reminds us that all consumer choices are made on the basis of comparison. Thus, a product will only be considered if it is clearly

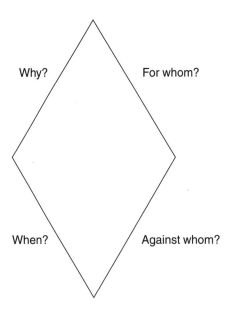

Figure 7.2   Positioning a brand

part of a selection process. Hence the four questions that help position the new product or brand and make its contribution immediately obvious to the customer. Positioning is a two-stage process:

▌ First, indicate to what 'competitive set' the brand should be associated and compared.

▌ Second, indicate what the brand's essential difference and *raison d'être* is in comparison to the other products and brands of that set.

Choosing the competitive set is essential. While this may be quite easy to do for a new toothpaste, it is not so for very original and unique products. The Gaines burger launched by the Gaines company, for instance, was a new dog food, a semi-dehydrated product presented as red ground meat in a round shape like a hamburger. Unlike normal canned pet foods, moreover, it did not need to be refrigerated, nor did it exude that normal open-can smell.

Given these characteristics, the product could be positioned in several different ways, for example by:

▌ Attacking the canned pet food market by appealing to well-to-do dog owners. The gist of the message would then be 'the can without the can', in other words, the benefits of meat without its inconveniences (smell, freshness constraints, etc).

▌ Attacking the dehydrated pet food segment (dried pellets) by offering a product that would help the owner not to feel guilty for not giving meat to the dog on the basis that it is just not practical. The fresh-ground, round look could justify this positioning.

▌ Targeting owners who feed leftovers to their dogs by presenting Gaines as a complete, nutritious supplement (and no longer as a main meal as in the two former strategies).

▌ Targeting all dog owners by presenting this product as a nutritious treat, a kind of doggy Mars bar.

The choice between these alternative strategies was made by assessing each one against certain measurable criteria (Table 7.1).

The firm ended up choosing the first positioning and launched this product as the 'Gaines burger'.

What does the identity concept add to that of positioning? Why do we even need another concept?

In the first place, because positioning focuses more on the product itself. What then does positioning mean in the case of a multi-product brand? How can these four questions on positioning be answered if we are not focusing on one particular product category? We know how to position the various Scotch-brite scrubbing pads as well as the Scotch videotapes, but what does the positioning concept mean for the Scotch brand as a whole, not to mention the 3M corporate brand? This is precisely where the concept of brand identity comes in handy.

Second, positioning does not reveal all the brand's richness of meaning nor reflect all of its potential. The brand is restricted once reduced to four questions. Positioning does not help fully differentiate Coca-Cola from Pepsi-Cola. The four positioning questions thus fail to encapsulate such nuances. They do not allow us to fully explore the identity and singularity of the brand.

Worse still, positioning allows communication to be entirely dictated by creative whims and current fads. Positioning does not say a word about communication style, form or spirit. This is a major deficiency since brands have the gift of speech: they state both the objective and subjective qualities of a given product. The speech they deliver – in these days of multimedia supremacy – is made of words, of course, but even more of pictures, sounds, colours, movement and style. Positioning controls the words only, leaving the rest up to the unpredictable outcome of creative hunches and pretests. Yet brand language should never result from creativity only. It expresses the brand's personality and values.

Creative hunches are only useful if they are consistent with the brand's legitimate territory. Furthermore, though pretest evaluations are needed to verify that the brand's message is well received, the public should not be allowed to dictate brand language: its style needs to be found within itself. Brand uniqueness often tends to get eroded by consumer expectations and thus starts regressing to a level at which it risks losing its identity.

A brand's message is the outward expression of the brand's inner substance. Thus we can no longer dissociate brand substance from brand

Table 7.1   How to evaluate and choose a brand positioning

- Are the product's current looks and ingredients compatible with this positioning?
- How strong is the assumed consumer motivation behind this positioning? (what insight?)
- What size of market is involved by such a positioning?
- Is this positioning credible?
- Does it capitalise on a competitor's actual or latent durable weakness?
- What financial means are required by such a positioning?
- Is this positioning specific and distinctive?
- Is this a sustainable positioning which cannot be imitated by competitors?
- Does this positioning leave any possibility for an alternative solution in case of failure?
- Does this positioning justify a price premium?
- Is there a growth potential under this positioning?

style, ie from its verbal, visual and musical attributes. Brand identity provides the framework for overall brand coherence. It is a concept that serves to offset the limitations of positioning and to monitor the means of expression, the unity and durability of a brand.

Why brands need identity and positioning

A brand's positioning is a key concept in its management. It is based on one fundamental principle: all choices are comparative. Remember that identity expresses the brand's tangible and intangible characteristics – everything that makes the brand what it is, and without which it would be something different. Identity draws upon the brand's roots and heritage – everything that gives it its unique authority and legitimacy within a realm of precise values and benefits. Positioning is competitive: when it comes to brands, customers make a choice, but with products, they make a comparison. This raises two questions. First, what do they compare it with? For this, we need to look at the field of competition: what area do we want to be considered as part of? Second, what are we offering the customer as a key decision-making factor?

A brand that does not position itself leaves these two questions unanswered. It is a mistake to suppose that customers will find answers themselves: there are too many choices available today for customers to make the effort to work out what makes a particular brand specific. Communicating this information is the responsibility of the brand. Remember, products increase customer choice; brands simplify it. This is why a brand that does not want to stand for something stands for nothing.

The aim of positioning is to identify, and take possession of, a strong purchasing rationale that gives us a real or perceived advantage. It implies a desire to take up a long-term position and defend it. Positioning is competition-oriented: it specifies the best

way to attack competitors' market share. It may change through time: one grows by expanding the field of competition. Identity is more stable and long-lasting, for it is tied to the brand roots and fixed parameters. Thus Coke's positioning was 'the original' as long as it competed against other colas. To grow the business, it now competes against all soft drinks: its positioning is 'the most refreshing bond between people of the world', whereas its identity remains 'the symbol of America, the essence of the American way of life'.

How is positioning achieved? The standard positioning formula is as follows:

> For ... (definition of target market)
> Brand X is ... (definition of frame of reference and subjective category)
> Which gives the most ... (promise or consumer benefit)
> Because of ... (reason to believe).

Let us look at these points in detail.

The target specifies the nature and psychological or sociological profile of the individuals to be influenced, that is, buyers or potential consumers.

The frame of reference is the subjective definition of the category, which will specify the nature of the competition. What other brands or products effectively serve the same purpose? This is a strategic decision: it marks out the 'field of battle'. It must not under any circumstances be confused with the objective description of the product or category. For example, there is no real rum market in the UK, yet Bacardi is very popular. This is because it is perfectly possible to drink Bacardi without realising that it *is* a rum: it is the party mixer *par excellence*.

Another example illustrates the strategic importance of defining the frame of reference. Objectively speaking, Perrier is fizzy mineral water. Subjectively, however, it is also a drink for adults. Seen in the light of this field of reference, it acquires its strongest competitive advantage: a slight natural quirkiness. As we can see, the choice of the field of competition should be informed by the strategic value of that field: how big, how fast growing, how profitable? But it also lends the brand a competitive advantage through its identity and potential. Perceived as water for the table, Perrier has no significant competitive advantage over other fizzy mineral waters, even though this market is a very large one. However, when viewed in relation to a field of competition defined as 'drinks for adults', Perrier becomes competitive again: it has strong differentiating advantages. What are its competitors? They include alcoholic drinks, Diet Coke, Schweppes and tomato juice.

The third point specifies the aspect of difference which creates the preference and the choice of a decisive competitive advantage: it may be expressed in terms of a promise (for instance, Volvo is the strongest of all cars) or a benefit (such as, Volvo is the 'safety' brand).

The fourth point reinforces the promise or benefit, and is known as the 'reason to believe'. For example, in the case of the Dove brand, which promises to be the most mois-turising, the reason is that all of its products contain 25 per cent of moisturising cream.

Positioning is a necessary concept, first because all choices are comparative, and so it makes sense to start off by stating the area in which we are strongest, and second because in marketing, perception is reality. Positioning is a concept which starts with customers, by putting ourselves in their place: faced with a plethora of brands, are consumers able to identify the strong point of each, the factor that distinguishes it from the rest? This is why, ideally, a customer should be capable of paraphrasing a brand's posi-tioning: 'Only Brand X will do this for me, because it has, or it is ...'

No instrument is entirely neutral. The above formula was created by companies such as Kraft–General Foods, Procter & Gamble, and Unilever. It is designed for businesses that base competitive advantage on their products,

and works perfectly for the l'Oréal Group which, with its 2,500 researchers worldwide, only ever launches new products if they are of demonstrably superior performance. This fact is then promoted through advertising.

There are cases where the brand makes no promise, or where the benefit it brings could sound trivial. For example, how would you define the positioning of a perfume such as Obsession by Calvin Klein in a way that clearly represented its true nature and origi-nality? It would be wrong to claim that Obsession makes any specific promise to its customers, or that they will obtain any particular benefit from the product apart from feeling good (a property which is common to all perfumes). In reality, Obsession's attrac-tiveness stems from its imagery, the imaginary world of subversive androgyny which it embodies. In the same way, Mugler appeals to young people through its inherently neo-futuristic world, and Chanel stands for timeless elegance.

What actually sells these perfumes is the satisfaction derived from participating in the symbolic world of the brand. The same is true of alcohol and spirits: Jack Daniel's is selling a symbolic participation in an eternal, authentic untamed America. To say that Jack Daniel's is selling the satisfaction of being the finest choice would be a mere commonplace, like the tired old cliché that customers are satisfied at having made a choice that set them apart from the masses (a classic benefit stated by small brands attempting to emphasise their advantage over large ones).

Faced with this conceptual dilemma, there are three possible approaches. The first of these is to define positioning as the sum of every point that differentiates the brand. This has been Unilever's approach: the 60-page mini-opus known as the Brand Key, which explains how to define a brand across the entire world, starts with the phrase: 'Brand Key builds on and replaces the brand positioning statement ...'. There are eight headings to Brand Key:

1.   The competitive environment.

2.   The target.

3.   The consumer insight on which the brand is based.

4.   The benefits brought by the brand.

5.   Brand values and personality.

6.   The reasons to believe.

7.   The discriminator (single most compelling reason to choose).

8.   The brand essence.

Fundamentally, therefore, this collection forms the positioning of a brand. However, the concept that most closely resembles positioning in the strict sense of the word is referred to here as the 'discriminator'. McDonald's also adopts a similar reasoning (see Figure 7.3). Larry Light defends the idea that positioning is defined when this chain of means–ends is completed (this is a parallel concept to the 'ladder' – moving from the tangible to the intangible):

My position is that two tools are needed to manage the brand. One defines the brand's identity, while the other is competitive and specifies the competitive proposition made at any given time in any given market. This is the brand's unique compelling competitive proposition (UCCP). Thus the tool called 'brand platform' will comprise, first, the 'brand identity', that is to say, brand uniqueness and singularity throughout the world and whatever the product. Brand identity has six facets, and is therefore larger than the mere positioning. It is represented by the identity prism. At its centre one finds the brand essence, the central value it symbolises.

Second, the brand platform comprises 'brand positioning': choosing a market means choosing a specific angle to attack it. Brand positioning must be based on a customer insight relevant to this market. Brand positioning exploits one of the brand identity facets. Positioning can be summed up in four key questions: for whom, why, when and against whom? It can be represented in the form of a diamond, the 'positioning diamond' (see Figure 7.2, page 176).

In positioning, the brand/product makes a proposition, plus (necessarily) a promise. The proposition may additionally be supported by a 'reason to believe', but this is not essential. Marlboro presents its smoker as a man – a real man, symbolised by the untamed cowboy of the Wild West. No support is offered for this proposition; no proof is necessary. It is true because the brand says so. And the more often it is repeated, the more credible it becomes.

In this way the brand's proposition, which forms the basis of the chosen positioning at a given moment in a particular market, may be fuelled by various 'edges' contained within the brand's identity:

Figure 7.3   The McDonald's positioning ladder
Source: L Light

- a differentiating attribute (25 per cent moisturising cream in Dove, the smoothness and bite of Mars bars, the bubbles of Perrier);

- an objective benefit: an iMac is user-friendly, Dell offers unbeatable value for money;

- a subjective benefit: you feel secure with IBM;

- an aspect of the brand's personality: the mystery of the Bacardi bat, Jack Daniel's is macho, Axe/Lynx is cool;

- the realm of the imaginary, of imagery and meaning (the American Wild West for Marlboro, Old New England for Ralph Lauren);

- a reflection of a consumer type: successful people for Amex;

- 'deep' values (Nike's sports mentality, Nestlé's maternal love), or even a mission (The Body Shop, Virgin and so on).

A few introductory remarks should be made at this juncture.

What is the connection between identity, essence and positioning? Clearly, for existing brands, positioning derives from identity. But it exploits a specific aspect of identity at a given point in time in a given market and against a precise set of competitors. Consequently, at the level of global brands, a unified identity can generate various angles of attack for different markets. For example, Bacardi favours its Carta Blanca white rum product in Northern Europe – a market that consumes very little rum – and thus places its confidence in the party spirit that surrounds the Cuba Libre cocktail drink. However, in its Southern European market it chiefly promotes its mature brown rums, with an almost gastronomic promise.

For 50 years, Mars was little more than a chocolate bar. The essence of Mars is energy; its positioning is as a meal substitute in the UK and as a revitalising snack in Europe.

It is this degree of freedom between identity, essence and positioning that enables a brand to change over time while still remaining itself. Thus, over time (40 years), Evian has changed its slogan and baseline on several occasions, symbolising a change in its angle of market attack: for indeed, the market itself has changed. It has become increasingly saturated with competing brands, the original consumers have aged, and low-cost brands have carved out a significant share. On each occasion, these changes have led to a re-examination of the most compelling advantage, the angle of market attack. There has thus been a shift from 'water for babies' to the purest of waters, water from the Alps, well-balanced water, and now the water of youth (this time round, the campaign is worldwide). However, each positioning has remained true to the essence of the Evian brand, which is more than any other water distinguished by its origins, its composition, its first campaign (babies) and so on. Evian is about life itself.

What is the connection between the positioning of the brand and the positioning of its products? It is true that today's brands are increasingly based on multiple products: Dove was born as a soap in the United States, but now encompasses shampoos, shower gels, moisturising cream, deodorants and so on. The essence of Dove is 'Femininity restored'. But Dove is being launched in a market via one or more products that have to fight for their own space amid a host of competitors: hence when Dove soap was launched, its positioning was: 'Dove is a premium beauty bar for the mature women, worried about their skin, which won't dry your skin like soap because it contains one quarter moisturising cream.'

This example is a good illustration of how the product's positioning promotes a consumer attribute or benefit, while the parent brand specifies the 'terminal value' that this attribute and benefit enables the consumer to reach. When a brand consists of multiple products, care should be taken to ensure that their respective positioning converges on attaining the same core value (that of the parent brand). If this is not the case, either the product requires repositioning, or the question should be asked whether it is part of the right brand at all.

Table 7.2 illustrates the link between the essence of the l'Oréal Paris parent brand and the positioning of its products such as Elsève and Studio Line.

The six facets of brand identity

In order to become 'passion brands', or 'love marks', brands must not be hollow, but have a deep inner inspiration. They must also have character, their own beliefs, and as a result help consumers in their life, and also in discovering their own identity.

What is brand identity made of? Many ad hoc lists have been proposed in the brand literature, with varying items. One of the sources of this diversity is their lack of theoretical basis. By being too analytical, some of these tools get their users into a muddle.

In fact, leaving the classical stimulus–response paradigm, modern brand communication theory reminds us that when one communicates, one builds representations of who speaks (source re-presentation), of who is

the addressee (recipient re-presentation), and what specific relationship the communication builds between them. This is the constructivist school of theorising about communications. Since brands speak about the product, and are perceived as sources of products, services and satisfactions, communication theory is directly relevant. As such it reminds us that brand identity has six facets. We call this the 'brand identity prism'.

The identity prism

Brand identity should be represented by a hexagonal prism (see Figure 7.4):

1. A brand, first of all, has physical specificities and qualities – its 'physique'. It is made of a combination of either salient objective features (which immediately come to mind when the brand is quoted in a survey) or emerging ones.

   Physique is both the brand's backbone and its tangible added value. If the brand is a flower, its physique is the stem. Without the stem, the flower dies: it is the flower's objective and tangible basis. This is how branding traditionally works: focusing on know-how and classic positioning, relying on certain key product and brand attributes and benefits. Physical

Table 7.2   Sub-brand and master brand positioning

	Elsève Nutri-céramides	Revitalift	Studio Line	l'Oréal
Target market	Women with dry and brittle hair	Women aged over 45	Men and women under 35	All adults, men and women
Market segment	Shampoo	Skin care products	Hair styling products	Beauty and hygiene products
Positioning	Nourishes and repairs damaged hair (consequence)	Reduces wrinkles and firms the skin (consequence)	Enables you to create the hairstyle of your choice (consequence)	Enhances consumers' self image ('because you're worth it')

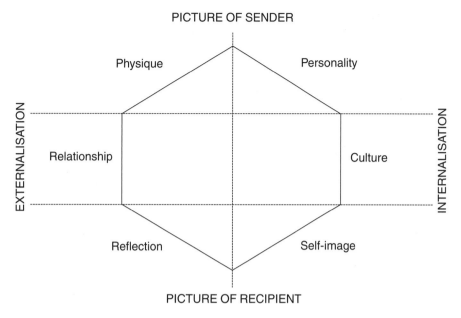

Figure 7.4   Brand identity prism

appearance is important but it is not all. Nevertheless, the first step in developing a brand is to define its physical aspect: What is it concretely? What does it do? What does it look like? The physical facet also comprises the brand's prototype: the flagship product that is representative of the brand's qualities.

That is why the small round bottle is so important each time Orangina is launched in a new country. The bottle used today is the same as it has always been. From the beginning, it has served to position Orangina, thanks to its unique shape and to the orange pulp that we can actually see. Only later was it marketed in standard family-size PET bottles and in cans. In this respect, it is also quite significant that there used to be a picture of the famous Coca-Cola bottle on all Coke cans. It is true that modern packaging tends to standardise brands, making them all clones of one another. Thus, in using the image of its traditional bottle, Coca-Cola aims to remind us of its roots.

There are several delicate issues regarding Coke's physical facet. For example, is the dark colour part of its identity? It is certainly a key contributor to the mystery of the brand. If it belongs to the brand's kernel, key identity traits, then there could never be any such thing as colourless Crystal Coke, even though there is such a thing as Crystal Pepsi. Likewise, would grapefruit Orangina in the classic round bottle be possible?

Many brands have problems with their physical facet because their functional added value is weak. Even an image-based brand must deliver material benefits. Brands are two-legged value-adding systems.

2. A brand has a personality. By communicating, it gradually builds up character. The way in which it speaks of its products or services shows what kind of person it would be if it were human.

    'Brand personality' has been the main focus of brand advertising since 1970.

Numerous American agencies have made it a prerequisite for any type of communication. Ted Bates had to come up with a new USP (now, the unique selling personality), while Grey had to define brand personality. This explains why the idea of having a famous character represent the brand has become so widespread. The easiest way of creating instant personality is to give the brand a spokesperson or a figurehead, whether real or symbolic. Pepsi-Cola often uses this method, as do all perfume or ready-to-wear brands.

In the prism, brand identity is the personality facet of the source. It should not be confused with the customer reflected image, which is a portrayal of the ideal receiver.

Thus, brand personality is described and measured by those human personality traits that are relevant for brands (see page 110 for an application). Since 1996, academic research has focused on brand personality, after Aaker's (1995) creation of a so-called 'brand personality scale'. However, despite its wide diffusion among scholars, this scale does not measure brand personality in the strict sense, but a number of intangible and tangible dimensions that are more or less related to it, and that correspond in fact to other facets of a brand's identity (Azoulay and Kapferer, 2003). Recent empirical research (Romaniuk and Ehrenberg, 2003) has corroborated this. For instance, computers or electronic equipment were the categories most associated with the 'up to date' trait, as ice creams were associated with the 'sensuous' trait, and energiser drinks with 'energising'. These data demonstrate that this scale is not measuring personality: a lot of its traits instead measure a physical facet of the brand, while some others relate to the cultural facet of the identity prism, thus creating conceptual confusion in the field. This is because Aaker's conceptualisation of brand personality is inherited from the old habit of advertising agencies of describing as 'brand personality' in their creative briefing and copy strategy everything that was not related to the product's tangible benefits.

3. A brand is a culture. There is no cult brand without a brand culture. A brand should have its own culture, from which every product derives. The product is not only a concrete representation of this culture, but also a means of communication. Here culture means the set of values feeding the brand's inspiration. It is the source of the brand's aspirational power. The cultural facet refers to the basic principles governing the brand in its outward signs (products and communication). This essential aspect is at the core of the brand. Apple was the product of Californian culture in the sense that this state will forever symbolise the new frontier. Apple was not interested in expanding geographically but in changing society, unlike the brands of Boston and the East Coast. Even in the absence of Apple's founders, everything carried on as if Apple still had some revolutionary plan to offer to companies and to humankind. This is a source of inspiration for Apple's original products and services.

Major brands are certainly driven by a culture but, in turn, they also convey this culture (eg Benetton, Coca-Cola, IBM, etc). The cultural facet is the key to understanding the difference between Adidas, Nike and Reebok or between American Express and Visa. In focusing too heavily on brand personality, research and advertising have neglected this essential facet (we will also notice this with retailers: the leading ones are those who not only have a personality, but also a culture). Mercedes embodies German values: order prevails. Even at 260 km/h, a Mercedes has perfect handling. Even though the surrounding landscape may be whizzing by, the Mercedes remains stable and unperturbed. Symmetry governs this brand: the three-box bodywork is a strong physical characteristic of Mercedes. The brand symbol set at the nose-tip of every Mercedes further epitomises this spirit of order.

Countries of origin are also great cultural reservoirs for brands: Coca-Cola stands for America, as does IBM, Nike or Levi's. In other cases, however, they are ignored: thus, Mars is a worldwide brand like Shell. Canon and Technics deny their Japanese origin whereas Mitsubishi, Toyota and Nissan emphasise it. One of the bonuses for Evian exports is that it actually represents a part of French culture. However, this is not the only factor adding to their value. When Americans buy Evian, they are not just paying for the cultural facet but for all six aspects of these brands, starting with the basic consumer benefit: Evian quenches thirst and promotes health. American style food is McCain's cultural and symbolic reference; for Jack Daniel's, it is the authentic untamed America.

Culture is what links the brand to the firm, especially when the two bear the same name. Because of its culture, Nestlé has not succeeded in conveying the image of a fun and enjoyable food brand. Indeed, its image cannot be fully dissociated from that of the corporation, which is overall perceived as austere and puritan. The degree of freedom of a brand is often reduced by the corporate culture, of which it becomes the most visible outward sign.

Brand culture plays an essential role in differentiating brands. It indicates the ethos whose values are embodied in the products and services of the brand. Ralph Lauren is WASP; Calvin Klein's minimalism expresses a different set of values.

This facet is the one that helps differentiate luxury brands the most because it refers to their sources, to their fundamental ideals and to their sets of values. Culture is also the basis for most bank brands: choosing a bank means choosing the kind of relationship with money one wishes to have. Even though their services are identical (physical facet), the Visa Premier and the American Express Gold cards do not belong to the same cultural system. The American Express Gold card symbolises dynamic, triumphant capitalism. Money is shown, or even flashed about. Visa Premier, on the contrary, represents another type of capitalism, such as the German kind, making steady, quiet progress. Money is handled discreetly yet efficiently, neither gingerly nor flamboyantly.

4. A brand is a relationship. Indeed, brands are often at the crux of transactions and exchanges between people. This is particularly true of brands in the service sector and also of retailers, as we shall see later. The Yves Saint Laurent brand functions with charm: the underlying idea of a love affair permeates both its products and its advertising (even when no man is shown). Dior's symbolises another type of relationship: one that is grandiose and ostentatious (not in the negative sense), flaunting the desire to shine like gold.

Nike bears a Greek name that relates it to specific cultural values, to the Olympic Games and to the glorification of the human body. Nike suggests also a peculiar relationship, based on provocation: it encourages us to let loose ('just do it'). IBM symbolises orderliness, whereas Apple conveys friendliness. Moulinex defines itself as 'the friend of women'. The Laughing Cow is at the heart of a mother–child relationship. The relationship aspect is crucial for banks, banking brands and services in general. Service is by definition a relationship. This facet defines the mode of conduct that most identifies the brand.

This has a number of implications for the way the brand acts, delivers services, relates to its customers.

5. A brand is a customer reflection. When asked for their views on certain car brands, people immediately answer in terms of the brand's perceived client type: that's a brand for young people! for fathers! for show-offs! for old folks! Because its communication and its most striking products build up over time, a brand will always tend to build a reflection or an image of the buyer or user which it seems to be addressing

Reflection and target often get mixed up. The target describes the brand's potential purchasers or users. Reflecting the customer is not describing the target; rather, the customer should be reflected as he/she wishes to be seen as a result of using a brand. It provides a model with which to identify. Coca-Cola, for instance, has a much wider clientele than suggested by the narrow segment it reflects (15- to 18-year-olds). How can such a paradox be explained? For the younger segment (8- to 13-year-olds), the Coca-Cola protagonists embody their dream, what they want to become and do later on when they get older (and thus freed from the strong parental relationship), ie an independent life full of fun, sports and friends will then become true. Youth identifies with those heroes. As for adults, they perceive them as representatives of a certain way of life and of certain values rather than of a narrowly defined age group. Thus, the brand also succeeds in bringing 30- or 40-year-old consumers to identify with this special way of life. Many dairy brands positioned on lightness or fitness and based on low fat products project a sporty young female customer reflection: yet they are actually purchased in the main by older people.

The confusion between reflection and target is quite frequent and causes problems. So many managers continue to require advertising to show the targeted buyers as they really are, ignoring the fact that they do not want to be portrayed as such, but rather as they wish to be – as a result of purchasing a given brand (or shopping at a given retailer's). Consumers indeed use brands to build their own identity. In the ready-to-wear industry, the obsession to look younger should concern the brands' reflection, not necessarily their target.

All brands must control their customer reflection. By constantly reiterating that Porsche is made for show-offs, the brand has weakened.

6. Finally, a brand speaks to our self-image. If reflection is the target's outward mirror (they are ...), self-image is the target's own internal mirror (I feel, I am ...). Through our attitude towards certain brands, we indeed develop a certain type of inner relationship with ourselves.

In buying a Porsche, for example, many Porsche owners simply want to prove to themselves that have the ability to buy such a car. In fact, this purchase might be premature in terms of career prospects and to some extent a gamble on their materialisation. In this sense, Porsche is constantly forcing to push beyond one's limits (hence its slogan: 'Try racing against yourself, it's the only race that will never have an end'). As we can see, Porsche's reflection is different from its consumers' self-image: having let the brand develop such a negative reflection is a major problem.

Even if they do not practise any sports, Lacoste clients inwardly picture themselves (so the studies show) as members of an elegant sports club – an open club with no race, sex or age discrimination, but which endows its members with distinction. This works because sport is universal. One of the characteristics of people who eat Gayelord Hauser health and diet products is that they picture themselves not just as consumers, but as proselytes. When two Gayelord Hauser fans meet, they can strike up a conversation immediately as if they were of the same religious obedience. In promoting a brand, one pledges allegiance, demonstrating both a community of thought and of self-image, which facilitates or even stimulates communication.

These are the six facets which define the identity of a brand as well as the boundaries within which it is free to change or to develop. The brand identity prism demonstrates that these facets are all interrelated and form a well-structured entity. The content of one facet echoes that of another. The identity prism derives from one basic concept – that brands have the gift of speech. Brands can only exist if they communicate. As a matter of fact, they grow obsolete if they remain silent or unused for too long. Since a brand is a speech in itself (as it speaks of the products it creates and endorses the products which epitomise it), it can thus be analysed like any other speech or form of communication.

Semiologists have taught us that behind any type of communication there is a sender, either real or made up. Even when dealing with products or retailers, communication builds an image of its speaker or sender and conveys it to us. It is truly a building process in the sense that brands have no real, concrete senders (unlike corporate communication). Nevertheless, customers, when asked through projective techniques, do not hesitate to describe the brand's sender, ie the person bearing the brand name. Both the physique and personality help define the sender thus built for that purpose.

Every form of communication also builds a recipient: when we speak, everything seems as if we were addressing a certain type of person or audience. Both the reflection and self-image facets help define this recipient, who, thus built, also belongs to the brand's identity.

The last two facets, relationship and culture, bridge the gap between sender and recipient.

The brand identity prism also includes a vertical division (see Figure 7.4). The facets to the left – physique, relationship and reflection – are the social facets which give the brand its outward expression. All three are visible facets. The facets to the right – personality, culture and self-image – are those incorporated within the brand itself, within its spirit. This prism helps us to understand the essence of both brand and retailer identities (Virgin, K-Mart, Talbott's).

Clues for strong identity prisms

Identity reflects the different facets of brand long-term singularity and attractiveness. As such it must be concise, sharp and interesting. Let us remember that brand charters are management tools: they are necessary for decentralised decision making. They must help all the people working on the brand to understand how the brand is special, in all its dimensions. They must also stimulate creative ideas: they are a springboard for brand activation. Finally, they must help us to decide when an action falls within the brand territory and when it does not.

As a consequence, a good identity prism is recognisable by the following formal characteristics:

▎ There are few words to each facet.

▎ The words are not the same on different facets.

▎ All words have strength and are not lukewarm: identity is what makes a brand stand out.

Too often, in our consulting activity, we notice just the opposite:

▎ Facets are filled up with image traits that derive from the last usage and attitude study. Let us remember that identity is not the same as image. The question is, which

Polo

From casual to formal, always comfortable

Social distinctiveness Exclusive

Ralph Lauren = Success

Self confident

WASP
Boston elitism
American
Luxury

They are comfortable, young men of good social standing, nice, rich: Ideal son-in-law

I belong to my time
I am fashionable
I am the elite

Shirt 12x12

Soft, airy
Crocodile
Colours

Valorisation
Accessible

Lacoste = Chic

Well balanced
Authentic
Serene

Aristocratic ideals
Sophistication and simplicity
Sport and classicism
Individualism

They are non-conspicuous men and women having real class

I am discreetly elegant
I am always correct
although casual

Figure 7.5   Sample brand identity prisms

of these very many image items does the brand want to identify with?

▌ There is a lot of redundancy between facets, the same words being used many times. This should not be possible. Although related, each facet addresses a different dimension of brand uniqueness.

▌ Most of the words are looking for consensus, instead of looking for sharpness. Consumers do not see the strategies, nor do they see the brand platforms. They do experience the brand by its creations, or at contact, or in its places. To produce ideas, creative people need flesh: an identity with soul, body, forms, a real profile, not an average excellent profile, where nothing really stands out.

Sources of identity: brand DNA

How can we define a brand's identity? How can we define its boundaries, its areas of strength and of weakness? Anyone in charge of managing a well-established brand is perfectly aware that the brand has little by little gained its independence and a meaning of its own. At birth, a brand is all potential: it can develop in any possible way. With time, however, it tends to lose some degree of freedom; while gaining in conviction, its facets take shape, delineating the brand's legitimate territory. Tests confirm this progression: certain product or communication concepts now seem foreign to the brand. Other concepts, on the contrary, seem to be perfectly in tune with the brand, as it both endorses and empowers them, by giving them greater credibility.

Brand image research does not provide any satisfactory answer to these questions. Neither do the purchasers when asked to say what they expect from the brand. Generally, they haven't a clue. At best, they answer in terms of the brand's current positioning. Thus, in the USA, and the UK, there are only very few purchasers of Saab cars: the brand is not widespread though it is expanding its market distribution network. That is why English or American owners see their Saab as unusual rather than foreign. When asked what they expect from the brand, they are, indeed, likely to answer that Saab must continue to design unusual, unique cars. In doing so, they expect that the brand will reinforce their own unusuality and uniqueness which they, as the only few marginal Saab buyers, most definitely want to demonstrate. Obviously, however, if Saab focused exclusively on such self-centred expectations, its market share would most certainly remain restricted: the economic future of the Saab automotive division would then be under threat.

Consumers and prospects are often asked what their ideal brand would be and what attributes it would need in order to get universally approved. This approach fails to segment properly the expectations and thus to produce any definition other than the average brand ideal. It is typical for consumers to expect banks to provide expertise and attention, availability and competence, proximity and know-how. These expectations are also ideal in the sense that they are often incompatible. In pursuing them, such brands may lose their identity and regress to the average level. In seeking at all costs to resemble the ideal brand described by the consumers (or industrial buyers), brands thus often begin to downplay their differences and look average.

The mistake is to pursue this market 'ideal': it's up to each brand to pursue an ideal of its own. Commercial pressure naturally requires

a firm to stay attuned to the market. Of course no brand envies the destiny of Van Gogh, who lived a life of misery and became famous only after he died. Nonetheless, present brand management policy must be reappraised, because unfortunately it still assumes that consumers are the masters of brand identity and strategy. Consumers are actually quite incapable of carrying out such functions. Firms should, therefore, begin to focus more on the sending side of brand marketing and less on the receiving side.

Trying to define the specifics of a brand's substance and intrinsic values naturally requires an understanding of what a real brand is all about. A brand is a plan, a vision, a project. This plan is hardly ever written down (except for the few brands which have a brand charter). It can therefore only be inferred from the marks left by the brand, ie the products it has chosen to endorse and the symbols by which it is represented. Discovering the essence of brand identity, ie of the brand's specific and unique attributes, is the best way to understand what the brand means overall. That is why identity research must start from the typical products (or services) endorsed by the brand as well as on the brand name itself, the brand symbol if there is one, the logo, the country of origin, the advertisements and the packaging. The purpose of all this is to semiologically analyse the sending process by trying to discover the original plan underlying the brand's objectives, products and symbols. Generally, this plan is simply unconscious, neither written anywhere, nor explicitly described. It is simply enacted in daily decisions. Even creators of famous brand names (Christian Lacroix, Yves Saint Laurent, Calvin Klein or Liz Claiborne) are not conscious of it: when asked about the general plan, they are indeed unable to explain it clearly, yet they can easily say what their brand encompasses and what it does not. Brand and creator merge. We have shown (p 95) that, paradoxically, a luxury brand does not really begin to exist until its creator dies. It then shifts from body and instinct to plan and programme.

In conducting research on brand identity, it may well be that we discover several underlying plans. The history of a brand indeed reflects a certain discontinuity in the decisions made by different brand managers over time. Thus Citroen changed when it was purchased by Michelin, and later by Peugeot. A lot of its cars have left no print, although they reached a high level of sales. Rather than attempt the impossible task of making sense of all its products, brand managers must choose the sense that will best serve the brand in its targeted market and focus only on that one. Finally, when dealing with a weak brand, we might not discover any consistent plan at all: in this case, the brand is more like a name stuck on a product than a real player in the field. This situation is very similar to the initial stage of brand creation: the brand has great latitude and almost infinite possibilities, even though it has already planted the seeds of its potential identity in the memory of the market.

The brand's typical products

The product is the first source of brand identity. A brand indeed reveals its plan and its uniqueness through the products (or services) it chooses to endorse. A genuine brand does not usually remain a mere name printed on a product, ie a mere graphic accessory added on at the end of a production or distribution process. The brand actually injects its values in the production and distribution process as well as in the corollary services offered at the point of sale. The brand's values must therefore be embodied in the brand's most highly symbolic products. This last sentence calls for some attention. Cognitive psychology (Kleiber, 1990; Rosch, 1978; Lakoff, 1987) has taught us that it is easier to define certain categories by simply showing their most typical members than by specifying what product features are required to be considered a member of those categories. As stated in this example, it is difficult to define the 'game' concept, ie to

specify the characteristics which could help us identify when we are in a game situation and when we are not. For abstract categories, made of heterogeneous products, the difficulty is even greater. In this case, brands can serve as examples only if they are not exclusively attached to one specific product. What is Danone? When does a product deserve to be named Danone and when does it not? The same holds true for Philips or Whirlpool.

Consumers can easily answer this question: they are indeed able to group products in terms of their capacity to typically represent and perfectly exemplify a large spectrum brand. This is shown in Table 7.3, which ranks Danone's most typical products against Yoplait's, according to the consumers' point of view. The most representative product is called the 'brand prototype', not in the sense of an airplane or car prototype, but rather in that of the best exemplar of the brand's meaning. In this respect, in Europe Danone has two prototypical products: plain yoghurt (natural) and the refrigerated dessert cream, Danette. The cognitive psychologists around Rosch (1978) claim that prototypes actually transfer some of their features to the product category (Kleiber, 1990). In other words, if there were no definition of Danone, the public would probably be able to come up with one anyway, by taking a close look at the features of Danone's most representative products. This is what we call prototype semantics. It is true that each brand spontaneously brings to mind certain products – some more than others – and actions as well as a certain style of communication. These prototype products are representative of the various facets of brand identity. According to some cognitive psychologists, such products may convey brand identity, but above all they generate it. In fact, when questioned on Danone's brand image, consumers are more likely to answer in terms of Danone's prototype products.

Historically, it is quite significant that Danone became famous with its plain

Table 7.3   The most typical products of two mega-brands

Products	Danone	Yoplait
Danette – dessert cream	9.33(1)	4.04
Plain yoghurt (natural)	9.16(2)	8.93(1)
Fruit yoghurt	8.64(3)	8.39(5)
Whole milk yoghurt	8.55(4)	8.88(2)
Liquid yoghurt	8.54(4)	8.51(4)
Whipped yoghurt	8.44(6)	6.76
Petit fromage frais	8.13(7)	7.98
Fromage frais	8.11(8)	8.66(3)
Chocolate/coffee delight with whipped cream	8.07(9)	7.6

Key: grading from 0 to 10 (rank in parentheses if grade >9)

Source: Kapferer and Laurent (1996)

yoghurt, a product which had previously been sold in pharmacies as natural medication. That is where Danone's health image originated. And it is now revived by the creation of the Danone Foundation. But the duality of prototypes has also contributed to soften Danone's image: Danette cream dessert signifies hedonism, pleasure and opulence. Danone's brand identity is thus dual: both health and pleasure (Table 7.3). As such it captures the largest share of the market. It leaves the smallest shares to brands that do not provide this balance to consumers: they offer either diet brands or sweet confectionery brands.

If this theory holds, another question comes to mind: just what is it, in a typical product, that conveys meaning? A brand's values only convey meaning if they are at the core of the product. Brand intangible and tangible realities go hand in hand: values drive reality, and reality manifests these values.

For example, the essence of Benetton's brand identity is tolerance and friendship. Colour is more than an advertising theme. It is both the symbolic and industrial basis of the brand. Using a technical innovation, dyeing sweaters at the last minute, Benetton could stay ahead of its competitors through its capacity to meet the latest fashion require-

ments, ie the new colours of the season. Saying it is not enough though: the toughest part is doing it, and they did. Unlike their competitors, Benetton innovated by dyeing pullovers after they were made and not before, which helped save lots of precious time. By delaying their decision on the final colours, they were indeed better prepared for the whims of fashion and last-minute changes. If summer turned out to be magenta, Benetton could immediately react and fulfil expectations. However, although it is an essential physical facet of Benetton's brand identity, colour is not just a question of physique (in the identity prism): the colour element also impacts on the other facets of the prism, especially the cultural (which has sometimes made brands look like religions), a key facet when a brand markets to youth.

Colour does not merely serve to position the brand (the colourful brand); it is the outward sign of an ideology, a set of values and a brand culture. In its very slogan 'United Colours of Benetton', as in its posters showing a blond and a black baby, the brand expresses its inspiration and its idealistic vision of a united world in which all colours and races live together in harmony. Colour then ceases to be a mere feature distinguishing the manufacturer. It is a banner, a sign of allegiance. Colour is celebrated by the youth who wears it. Brotherhood and cultural tolerance are the brand's values. That is why the provocative style of Benetton's recent advertising was so disturbing: it was at odds with the brand's past identity.

Orangina is the case of a brand in search of identity, substance and psychological depth. For years Orangina has been represented by both a certain physique and a unique product: a fizzy orange soft drink. What makes it really stand out is that the orange pulp is purposely left in the liquid. This feature was so crucial to the product that an orange-shaped bottle was designed especially for it and its advertising focused on the need to shake the bottle well in order to disperse the pulp and experience the unique and best-tasting flavour of Orangina. The brand further developed its own personality through its TV advertising, which was done in a jumpy, video-clip style so popular among young people. The last stage in this process consisted of conveying the full meaning of the brand and, to do this, the brand/product relationship had to be reversed. Until then, Orangina was merely the name of a soft drink containing orange pulp. Thus, adopting a modern style does not change the structure of this relationship. Today, the basic question is asked the other way around: what are the values that a soft drink containing orange pulp could serve to embody? Coca-Cola's leadership among 13- to 18-year-olds cannot be understood on the basis of physique and personality only. Coca-Cola is a brand that vows an allegiance to the all-American cultural model. Pepsi-Cola embodies the values of the new generation, as does Virgin in the UK, hence its ability to challenge Pepsi's second place in terms of cola market share with its own Virgin Cola. Orangina must find its own source of inspiration as well as the set of values that its product will embody. This search for identity is based on our fundamental axiom of brand management: the truth of a brand lies within itself. It is not by interviewing consumers or consulting oracles of sociocultural trends that

the brand will discover itself. Roots last, trends don't. They indicate the present direction of the wind, the energy that pushes consumption.

The values that Orangina has conveyed since the beginning are: spontaneity, humour and friendliness. Orangina is a healthy, natural drink, a mixture of pulp and water. It symbolises sunshine, life, warmth and energy. All combine latently to give a typical taste and feeling of the South (underlying it all, there is a common model: the Southern model). The word 'model' reminds us that a strong brand is always the product of a certain culture, hence of a set of values which it chooses to represent. In the case of Orangina, Southern values seem to be a potent alternative to the North. Living in the South means both looking at the world and experiencing it in a different way.

The Lacoste shirt now only represents 30 per cent of the company's world sales. It is nonetheless a core product, since it conveys the brand's original values. This shirt was indeed designed at a time when tennis was still being played in long trousers and shirts with rolled-up sleeves. In 1926 (Kapferer and Laurent 2002), René Lacoste asked his friend André Gilliet to make a 'false' shirt: something that would look like a shirt (so as not to shock the Queen at Wimbledon), yet would be more practical, ie airy (hence the cotton knit), sturdy and with straight sleeves. Thus right from the beginning, and by accident, René Lacoste's shirt came to embody the individualistic and aristocratic ideal of living both courageously and elegantly. Whatever the occasion, a Lacoste is always appropriate: perfectly suited to the person who, overall, cares to respect proper dress codes, but not in very minute detail. Lacoste is neither trendy nor stuffy: it is simply always appropriate.

All major brands thus have a core product in charge of conveying the brand's meaning. Chanel has its gold chain, Chaumet its pearls and Van Cleef a patented technique of setting stones in invisible slots. These features do not merely characterise the products, they actually embody the brands' values. Dupont, on the other hand, does not seem to have much at stake: it certainly endorses superb lighters, but beyond them is there any dynamic brand concept in evidence? In terms of ready-to-wear clothing, 501 jeans are at the heart of the Levi's brand and of the carefree and unconventional ideology it represents. (On this point, it is significant that the product most frequently worn with a Lacoste shirt is a pair of jeans.) Conversely, brands such as Newman suffer from never having created a real core product, one exclusive to the brand which conveys its very identity.

These examples serve to illustrate a key principle for brand credibility and durability: all facets of brand identity must be closely linked. Moreover, the brand's intangible facets must necessarily be reflected in its products' physique. This 'laddering' process is illustrated by the Benetton case (Table 7.4). Likewise, Lacoste's identity prism can neither be dissociated from the story behind its famous shirt nor from the values of its emblematic sport, tennis.

The power of brand names

The brand's name is often revealing of the brand's intentions. This is obviously the case for brand names which, from the start, are specifically chosen to convey certain objective or subjective characteristics of the brand (Steelcase or Pampers). But it is also true of other brand names which were chosen for subjective reasons rather than for any apparent objective or rational ones: they too have the capacity to mark the brand's

legitimate territory. Why did Steve Jobs and Steve Wozniak choose Apple as their brand name? Surely, this name neither popped out of any creative research nor of any computer software for brand name creation. It is simply the name that seemed plainly obvious to the two creative geniuses. In one word, the Apple brand name conveyed the exact same values as those which had driven them to revolutionise computer science.

What must be explained is why they did not go for the leading name style of that period, ie International Computers, Micro Computers Corporation or even Iris. The majority of entrepreneurs would have chosen this type of name. In deciding to call it Apple, Jobs and Wozniak wanted to emphasise the unconventional nature of this new brand: in using the name of a fruit (and the visual symbol of a munched apple), was it taking itself seriously? With this choice, the brand demonstrated its values: in refusing to idolise computer science, Apple was in fact preparing to completely overturn the traditional human/machine relationship. The machine had, indeed, to become something to enjoy rather than to revere or to fear. Clearly, the brand name had in itself all the necessary ingredients to produce a major breakthrough and establish a new norm (which all seems so obvious to us now). What worked for Apple also worked for Orange. This name reflected the founders' values, which materialised into user-friendly mobile phone services. Similarly Amazon conveys strength, power, richness and permanent flow.

The brand name is thus one of the most powerful sources of identity. When a brand

Table 7.4   Brand laddering process: the Benetton case

▨ Physical attribute: colour and price.

▨ Objective advantage: the latest fashion.

▨ Subjective advantage: the brand for young people who want to be 'in'.

▨ Value: tolerance and brotherhood.

questions its identity, the best answer is therefore to thoroughly examine its name and so try to understand the reasoning behind its creation. In so doing, we can discover the brand's intentions and programme. As the Latin saying goes: *nomen est omen* – a name is an omen. Examining the brand name thus amounts to decoding this omen, ie the brand's programme, its area of legitimacy and know-how as well as its scope of competence.

Many brands make every effort to acquire qualities which their brand name fails to reflect or simply excludes altogether. 'Apple' sounds fun, not serious.

Other brands simply proceed by ignoring their name. The temptation for a brand to just forget about its name is caused by a rash interpretation of the principle of brand autonomy. Experience indeed shows that brands become autonomous as they start to give words specific meanings other than those in the dictionary. Thus when hearing of 'Bird's Eye', no one thinks of a bird. The same is true of Nike. Mercedes is a Spanish Christian name, yet the brand has made it a symbol of Germany. This ability is not only characteristic of brands but also of proper nouns: we do not think of roofing when talking of Mrs Thatcher. Thus, strong brands force their own lexical definitions into the glossaries: they give words another meaning. There is no doubt that this process takes place, but the time it requires varies according to its complexity.

A name – like an identity – has to be managed. Certain names may have a double meaning. The purpose of communication then is to select one and drop the other. Thus, Shell naturally chose to emphasise the sea-shell meaning (as represented in its logo) rather than the bomb-shell one! Likewise, the international temporary employment agency, Ecco, has never chosen to exploit the potential link with economy suggested in its name. On the other hand, it does use its name as a natural means to reinforce its positioning in the segment of high quality service: its

advertising cleverly plays upon the theme of duplication – those stepping in from Ecco will of course perfectly duplicate and echo those stepping out of the company.

Generally speaking, it is best to follow the brand's overall direction as well as its underlying identity, whenever possible. All Hugo Boss is entirely contained in that one short, yet international, name – Boss: it conveys aggressive success, professional achievement, conformity and city life. Rexona is a harsh name all over the world because of its abrupt R and its sharp X: thus it implicity promises efficiency.

Brand characters

Just as brands are a company's capital, emblems are a brand's capital equity. An emblem serves to symbolise brand identity through a visual figure other than the brand name. It has many functions such as:

- To help identify and recognise the brand. Emblems must identify something before they signify anything. They are particularly useful when marketing to children, since the latter favour pictures over text, or when marketing worldwide (every whisky has its own emblem).

- To guarantee the brand.

- To give the brand durability – since emblems are permanent signs – thereby enabling the company to capitalise on it. Thus Hermès' legendary horse is the common emblem of 'Equipage', 'Amazone' and 'Calèche'.

- To help differentiate and personalise: an emblem transfers its personality to the brand. In doing so, it enhances brand value. But it also facilitates the identification process in which consumers are involved.

Animal emblems are often used to perform this last function. Animals symbolise the brand's personality. It is quite significant, in this respect, that both the Chinese and Western horoscopes represent human characters by animals. The Greek veneration of animals reflected their conception of a certain spiritual mystery. The animal is not only allegorical of the brand's personality but also of the psychological characteristics of the targeted public. Wild Turkey symbolises the independent mind and free spirit of the drinker of this particular bourbon. The red grouse, symbol of Scotland and a rare bird, has been chosen as the emblem of Famous Grouse whisky in order to reflect the aesthetic ideal of its consumers.

Emblems epitomise more than one facet of brand identity; that is why they play such a crucial role in building identity capital. The world of whisky is filled with wild, rare, untameable animals that symbolise the natural, pure and authentic character of this alcohol. The associated risk perceived by the customer is thus reduced. They also demonstrate, as we saw above, the brand's personality: the red grouse is known for its noble gait and carriage; the wild turkey is a stubborn and clever bird symbolising independence in the US. These animals also represent the brand's value and culture facet, either because they are geographical symbols (the grouse for Scotland, the wild turkey for the USA) or because they refer to the brand's essence itself.

Many other brands have chosen to be represented by a character. A character can, for example, be either the brand's creator and endorser (Richard Branson for Virgin) or an endorser other than the creator (Tiger Woods for Nike). It can also be a direct symbol of the brand's qualities (Nestlé's bunny rabbit, Mr Clean, the Michelin bibendum). Some characters serve to build a certain relationship and an emotional, prescriptive link between the brand and its public (Smack's frog, Esso's tiger). Others, finally, serve as brand ambassadors: though Italian, Isabella Rossellini embodied the type of French beauty that Lancôme promises to all women.

Such characters say a lot about brand identity. They were indeed chosen as brand portraits, ie as the brand's traits, in the etymological sense. They do not make the brand, yet they define the way in which the brand brings to reality its traits and features.

Visual symbols and logotypes

Everybody knows Mercedes' emblem, Renault's diamond, Nike's swoosh, Adidas' three stripes, Nestlé's nest, Yoplait's little flower and Bacardi's bat. These symbols help us to understand the brand's culture and personality. They are actually chosen as such: the corporate specifications handed over to graphic identity and design agencies mainly pertain to the brand's personality traits and values.

What is important about these symbols and logos is not so much that they help identify the brand but that the brand identifies with them. When companies change logos, it usually means that either they or their brands are about to be transformed: as soon as they no longer identify with their past style, they want to start modifying it. Some companies proceed otherwise: to revitalise their brands and recover their identity, they milk their forlorn brand emblems for the energy and aggressiveness they need in order to be able to change. Just as human personality can be reflected in a signature, brand essence and self-image can be reflected in symbols.

Geographical and historical roots

Identity is born out of the early founding acts of a brand. Among these one finds products, channels, communications and also places.

The identity of Swissair is intimately associated with that of Switzerland. The same is true of Air France abroad or of Barclay's Bank. Outside of the United States, the Chrysler brand represents the cars of the New World. Certain brands naturally convey the identity of their country of origin. Others are totally international (Ford, Opel, Mars, Nuts). Others still have made every possible effort to hide their national identity: Canon never refers to Japan, while Technics has adopted an Anglo-Saxon identity though the company is Japanese.

Some brands draw their identity and uniqueness from their geographical roots. It is a deliberate choice on their part. What advantage did Finlandia expect to gain, for example, by launching a premium vodka? As its name suggests, Finland is the country where the earth ends – a cold, austere, unspoilt, remote land, where the sun scrapes the ground. This spontaneous vision both feeds and supports the creation of an extremely pure water and vodka.

Brands can benefit from the values of their native soil. Apple has thus adopted the Californian values of both social and techno-logical progress and innovation. There is a touch of alternative culture in this Californian brand (which is not true of all Silicon valley brands, such as Atari). IBM epitomises East coast order, power and conservatism. Evian's symbolism is linked to the Alps, or rather to the image of the Alps, as projected by the company. Roots are crucial for alcoholic drinks too: Glenfiddich means Deer Valley, Grouse is the fetish bird of Scotland. The Malibu drink, on the contrary, has never defined its origin: only recently has its advertising specified that its home was the Caribbean.

The brand's creator: early visions

Brand identity cannot be dissociated from the creator's identity. There is still a lot of Richard Branson in Virgin's brand identity. Inspired by its creator, Yves Saint Laurent's brand identity is that of a feminine, self-assured and strong-minded 30-year-old woman. The YSL brand celebrates the beauty of body, of charm, of surrender to romance, and is flavoured with a hint of ostentatious indecency. Paloma Picasso's flaming Mediterranean looks permeate her perfume products and explain

why she is so successful in South America, in the US Sun Belt (Florida, Texas, California) and in Europe (Spain, France, Germany). The relationship between a brand and its creator can last far beyond the death of the creator. Chanel is a good example of this: Karl Lagerfeld does not try to imitate the Chanel style, but to interpret it in a modern way. The world is changing: the brand's values must be respected, yet adapted to modern times. The same holds true for John Galliano and Dior, or Tom Ford for Gucci.

When its creator passes away, the brand becomes autonomous. The brand is the creator's name woven into a set of values and a pattern of inspiration. Thus, it cannot be used by another member of the creator's family. This was confirmed in court in 1984 when Olivier Lapidus, son of the founder of the Ted Lapidus ready-to-wear brand, was refused the right to use the word 'Lapidus'. Even blood kinship thus does not entitle one to use brand name equity in the same sector.

Advertising: content and form

Let us not forget that it is advertising which writes the history of a brand, retailer or company. Volkswagen can no longer be disso-ciated from the advertising saga that helped it develop. The same is true of Budweiser and Nike. This is only logical: brands have the gift of speech and they can only exist by commu-nicating. Since they are responsible for announcing their products or services, they need to speak up at all times.

When communicating, we always end up saying a lot more than we think we do. Any type of communication implicitly says some-thing about the sender, the source (who is speaking?), about the recipient we are appar-ently addressing and the relationship we are trying to build between the two. The brand identity prism is based on this hard fact.

How is this implicit message slipped between the lines and conveyed to us? Simply through style. In these times of audio-visual media, a

30-second TV ad says just as much about the style of the brand sending the message and of the recipient apparently being targeted as about the benefits of the product being announced. Whether or not they are managed, planned or wanted, all brands acquire a history, a culture, a personality and a reflection through their cumulative communications. To manage a brand is to proactively channel this gradual accumulation of attributes towards a given objective rather than just to sit and wait to inherit a given brand image.

Yet what is inherited can also be a boon. Volkswagen tightly controls its marketing, but entirely delegates its communications to its agency. Thus all Volkswagen cars are launched under the same name, no matter what the country. However, the Volkswagen style is definitely a legacy of the advertising genius, Bill Bernbach: indeed, he succeeded in making the entire DDB network follow the stylistic guidelines which he had defined. It is thus through the memorable VW Beetle campaigns that both the brand's specific style and scope of communication began to take shape.

Both in its advertising films and spots, the VW brand has always freely played with the motifs of both the cars and the logo. The brand's style of expression is one of humour and humour only, as shown in its attitude of self-derision, false modesty and impertinence towards competitors as well as in the use of paradox. Volkswagen's advertisements have thus built a powerfully intimate relationship with the public. They appeal to consumers' intelligence, reflecting the image of the pragmatic people who prefer functional features to fancy ones.

The paradox of Volkswagen is that it has always managed to speak of a quite prosaic product in an almost elitist, yet friendly and humorous style. This has enabled Volkswagen to introduce minor modifications as major developments. The selling points put across in the adverts are based on facts and on certain values, which the brand has always conveyed,

such as product quality, durability, weather-resistance, reliability, reasonable prices and good trade-in value.

But this advertising style, though created outside the Volkswagen company, was not just artificially added to the brand. Who could possibly have created such a monstrous car with an insect name (the Beetle), which so completely defied the trends in the US automobile world at the time? It could only have been an extremely genuine, honest creator, with a long-term vision. To encourage its own customers to buy, the brand had not only to flatter their ego and intelligence but also to acknowledge them for breaking away – if only this one time – from the stylistic clichés of North American cars. In a tongue-in-cheek style, the brand manages to convey its values and its culture. The Volkswagen style *is* Volkswagen, even though it was created by Bernbach.

Brand essence

Many companies and advertising agencies use the phrase 'brand essence'. The analysis of this practice reveals that it stems from a desire to summarise the identity and/or the positioning. Some would say that the essence of Volvo is security (its positioning), others would say that the essence of Volvo is 'social responsibility' (a high-order typical Scandinavian value), from which is derived the desire to build the most secure as well as recyclable cars. Similarly, some speak of Mars' essence as 'bite and smoothness, with caramel and chocolate', others as 'vitality and energy'. In essence, the concept of 'brand essence' asks in an atemporal and global way: what do you sell? What *key value* does the brand propose, stand for? No more than three!

Part of the discussion lies in the notion of value: some speak of benefit, others of higher order ideals, such as those revealed in a classical means–ends questionnaire called 'laddering' (see the Benetton example, page

193). In fact it is possible that for some brands, essence is intimately tied to the product experience, whereas it is not true for others.

Let us look at an example. What is Nivea's essence? To answer one needs to first specify Nivea's identity. As we have seen in this chapter, we should look to the prototype to find the key values of any brand. In Nivea's case, this is Nivea cream and its characteristic blue box – the means via which the brand gains entry to each country, and thus the brand's underpinning factor. More than a mere product, Nivea cream in its round box constitutes one of the first acts of love and protection that a mother performs for a baby. After all, doesn't everyone remember the typical scent, feel, softness and sensuality of this white cream, reinforced by the Nivea blue? The blue box is thus the brand's true foundation in all senses:

▌ It is the first Nivea product people encounter in their life, from the age of four.

▌ It bears the Nivea values.

▌ It constitutes the first sales of Nivea in every country where the brand is established.

So what is the significance of this blue colour and this flagship moisturising cream, the cornerstones of the whole edifice?

Remember that blue is the favourite colour of more than half the population of the western world, including the United States and Canada. It is the colour of dreams (the sky), calm (the night), faithful, pure love (the Virgin Mary has been depicted in blue since the 12th century), peace (UN peacekeepers) and the simple, universal appeal of blue jeans (Pastoureau, 1992). The cream's whiteness is the white of purity, health, discretion, simplicity and peace (a white flag). As for the moisturising cream itself, it adds water to the skin, an essential injection of a human aspect to one's natural environment.

This reveals the values of the brand. Nivea's philosophy penetrates to its very core: a view of life founded on human coexistence, and containing strong moral values such as confidence, generosity, responsibility, honesty, harmony and love. In terms of competence, it stands for safety, nature, softness and innovation. Lastly, it sells itself as timeless, simple and accessible, at a fair price. And this is the way in which the Nivea brand itself is identified worldwide. Even if at any given moment, within a particular group, segment or country, these values are not perceived, they remain the values that form the basic identity of the brand. What does Nivea sell in essence? Pure love and care.

Other examples of brand essence directly derived from the early prototype of the brand are:

▌ masculine attractiveness (Axe/Lynx dual brand);

▌ untamed America (Jack Daniel's);

▌ family preservation (Kodak);

▌ love and nutrition (Nestlé);

▌ sign of personal success (Amex).

Do we need the brand essence concept? It has a managerial utility: trying to summarise the richness of an identity. As such it is easier to convey. Its inconvenience is that the meaning of words is highly culturally specific. Thus a word as simple as 'natural' does not evoke the same things in Asia and in Europe, and within Europe there are huge differences between southern countries and northern countries. As such, to understand a brand one really needs the full identity prism, where words acquire their meaning in relationship with others.

Practically, the brand essence can be written in the middle of the brand identity prism or on the top of the brand pyramid, relating essence, values, personality and attributes (see page 199).

Both identity and positioning are summarised in the brand platform. When the brand carries multiple products, each of them expresses the values with its own weighting, and has a position that competes against specific brands (see Chapter 11).

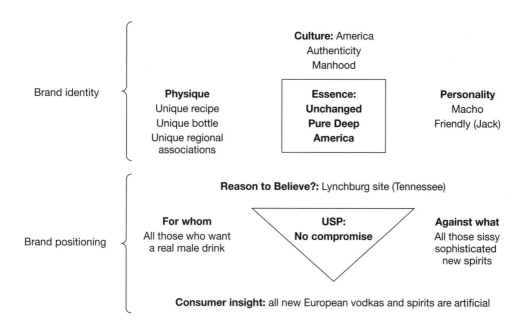

Figure 7.6   Example of brand platform: Jack Daniel's

Part Three

Creating and sustaining brand equity

8

Launching the brand

When they came into being, all the major brands examined so far – Nike, Lacoste, Amazon, Orange, l'Oréal, Nivea, Ariel – were of course also new brands. Over the years, and often by intuition, chance or accident, they became major brands, leading brands, powerful brands.

Since at one point they were all necessarily new, we might ask ourselves what the established brands have or have done that the others don't have or have not done.

Launching a brand and launching a product are not the same

Marketing books devote chapters to the definition of new products, but none to the launching of new brands, except for an occasional word or two on how to choose the name of a new product. This confusion between product and brand is an enduring problem. Most famous brands, rich in meaning and values, started out as the ordinary names of innovative products or services, different from those of competitors. These names were generally randomly chosen, without any prior study or analysis: Coca-Cola reflected the contents of the new product; Mercedes was the name of Mr Daimler's daughter; Citroën was a family name; Adidas is a spin-off of Adolphe Dassler; likewise Lip of Lippman and Harpic of Harry Picman. The new product had to be given a new name so that it could be advertised. Advertising was then put in charge of presenting the advantages of the new product as well as the benefits which consumers could expect from it.

After some time, new products usually get copied by competitors. They then get replaced by new, higher quality products, which often benefit from the fame of the existing product name. However, although products change, brands stay. In the beginning then, advertisements will boast the merits of the new, initial product, say X. But, since all products naturally become obsolete over time, X will soon come to announce that it's about to update and upgrade itself by lending its name to a higher quality product. And that's how a new brand comes to life. From then on, it is no longer advertising that will sell the products, but the brand itself.

Over time, the brand will gain greater autonomy and part with its original meaning (often the name of the company founder or of a specific feature of the product) by developing its own way of communicating (about the products), of addressing the public and of behaving. Few British people think of 'clean' when saying 'Kleenex' and few French think of the lotus leaf when saying 'Lotus'. The product name has become a proper noun, meaningless in itself, yet loaded with associations that have built up through experience (of the products and services), word-of-mouth and advertising. Advertising gives us hints of who the X who is now communicating really is: what is its core activity, its project, its cultural reference, its set of values, its personality, and whom is it addressing? Over time, the meaning of X has changed: it is no longer the mere name of a product, it is the very meaning of all products X, present and yet to come. The famous brand, X, is now the purveyor of values, from which its own endorsed products can benefit (as soon as they enter production).

In terms of brand creation, there is only one simple lesson to be learnt from this: if the new brand does not convey its values from the very start, ie as soon as it is created and launched, it is quite unlikely that it will manage to become a major brand.

On an operational level, this means that in launching a new brand, knowing its intangible values is just as important as deciding on the product advantage.

A successful launch requires that the new brand be treated as a full brand, right from the very start – not as a mere product name presented in advertising. Launching a new brand means acting before the product name becomes a brand symbol, with a much broader and deeper meaning than previously. Modern management must show results a lot sooner. From the very beginning, the new brand must be considered in full, ie endowing it with both functional and non-functional values. Creating a brand means acting straightaway as if it is a well-established brand, rich in meaning. This entails a few fundamental principles.

Defining the brand's platform

Unlike the product launch, the brand launch is, from the very start, a long-term project. Such launch will modify the existing order, values and market shares of the category. It aims at establishing a new order and different values and at impacting on the market for a long period of time. This can only be achieved if people are convinced of the brand's absolute necessity and are ready to give it all they have. In order to keep staff, management, bankers, clients, opinion leaders and salespeople mobilised for the long term, the company must be driven by a real brand project and a true vision. The latter will indeed serve to justify, internally and externally, why the brand is being launched and what its essential purpose is.

Creating a brand implies first drafting the brand's programme, which underlies the brand identity and positioning. Presenting the brand in a programmatic format (Table 8.1) is fruitful. It indicates where the brand stems from, where it draws its energy, what big project lies behind the brand. This is useful as a step in the brand thinking process itself, before the brand identity prism and brand positioning are defined.

Many brands no longer know why they exist, so they would be quite unable to answer questions such as those in Table 8.1 defining the brand programme. Such questions reflect a philosophy at the opposite of niche tactics. Only those who are driven by a grand project within can actually set out on the long journey of brand making.

Of course, this brand project will have to be transformed into 'strategic image traits'. In the car industry, we realise that Peugeot cannot be defined by simply a few of its features, such as dynamism, reliability and aesthetics. These image traits do help differentiate Peugeot from Volkswagen, which is rather positioned in terms of reliability and comfort. However, each brand reflects its own fundamental automobile project and its own philosophy. As a result, Volkswagen speaks of cars, Peugeot of automobiles. Finally, without any industrial, marketing or commercial expertise, or any financial means, a project is just a wish.

The preliminary definition of brand identity is not the same for company-named brands as for brands that have their own name. Many companies nowadays act as brands. Alcatel is both company and brand, as are Siemens, Toshiba, Du Pont, Philips and IBM. On the other hand, Audi is one of Volkswagen's brands, as Persil is one of Henkel's and Dash one of Procter & Gamble's. Companies become aware that their name is actually a brand when they notice that the purchaser and user are just as important as the financial analyst in the markets in which they operate.

On an operational level, creating a brand with no direct reference to the firm offers a greater degree of freedom: everything is possible, which does not automatically mean that everything is relevant or easy. What it does mean is that we can create the brand's identity entirely from scratch.

In the case of company-named brands, the brand becomes the major spokesperson for the company. There must therefore be a relationship between brand identity and corporate identity. Brand identity has less freedom than in the previous case. The company-named brand is indeed the company's external showpiece: it is the messenger telling the company story to a larger audience. It is therefore vital for the company to identify with this brand as well as fully support this new spokesperson (which is different from the institutional spokesperson, the CEO). That is why we observe that company-named brands have the same culture as the companies from which they emanate (see Figure 8.1).

Now the brand is here to sell to customers, while the corporation itself has other stakeholders and markets (see Chapter 13). This is why, although they share the same name, and thus strongly interact, it is important to differentiate for instance Nestlé as a corporate brand and Nestlé as a commercial brand. To help

Table 8.1 Underlying the brand is its programme

1. Why must this brand exist?
    What would customers be missing if the brand did not exist?
2. Vision.
    What is the brand's vision of the product category?
3. Ambition.
    What does the brand want to change in people's lives?
4. What are our values?
    What will the brand never compromise on?
5. Know-how.
    What is the brand's specific know-how? Its unique capabilities?
6. Territory.
    Where can the brand legitimately provide its benefit, in which product categories?
7. Typical products or actions.
    Which products and actions best embody, best exemplify the brand's values and vision?
8. Style and language.
    What are the brand's stylistic idiosyncrasies? Its semiotic invariants?
9. Reflection.
    Who are we addressing? What image do we want to render of the clients themselves?

differentiate these two sources, the company itself has created two different visual symbols for each of its two facets. The same holds true also for Danone, which has created a specific symbol for Danone as corporation (a small child looking at a star in the sky), different from the geometric form of the Danone brand logo. Even if they did share the same graphic identity (as do Shell, BP and Total), the distinction remains to be made. The corporation is not the brand but is nourished by the brand (and vice versa).

Nestlé as a brand could never assume a fun and exuberant or greedy and permissive identity. This is because it bears the same name as the company, whose identity is none of these. Even though the public does not know this company, the Nestlé brand is nevertheless strongly influenced by the overall Nestlé corporate identity. Final acceptance of a new brand's identity is a company prerogative. And if the latter cannot identify with the new brand, the brand identity will be modified in order to be in tune with that of the company. This does not mean that the two perfectly coincide, but that there is a bridge between them.

Such a bridge is usually easier to build by means of the cultural facet (see Figure 8.1). There is a theoretical reason for this: a company coins its identity by focusing on one or two key values (Schwebig, 1985). These are the values which feed the brand, give it the company's outlook on the world and the impetus to transform the product category. This 'source-value' gives meaning to the brand. Underlying Peugeot's rigour and quality, there has always been the corporate determination to offer more than a strictly functional product: a car which drivers could truly enjoy.

Over time, this relationship between brand and company is switched around. The company's outward image is reflected inside and becomes far more effective in mobilising the workforce than all of the other here-today-gone-tomorrow 'company projects'. In order to take advantage of this positive feedback, many companies have traded in their old name for one of their leading brand names. Tokyo Tsuhin Kogyo, for instance, has thus become Sony Inc; Tokyo Denki Kagaku adopted the name of its famous brand TDK. Likewise, BSN became Danone throughout the world.

The identity of strong brands reminds us that identity is not just a matter of functional attributes. That is why choosing a new brand's symbolic references is just as important as choosing its product references. Apple is steeped in the Californian high-tech and 'counterculture' imagery. Toshiba promoted its products, but never wove them into any particular symbolic reference. The brand has no aspiration and no vision of its own either for the product category or for the microcom-

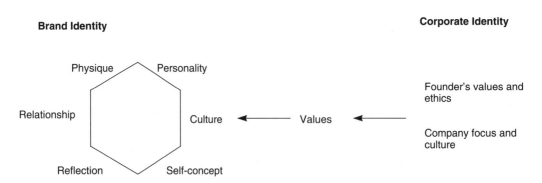

Figure 8.1 Transfer of company identity to brand identity when company and brand names coincide

puter industry as a whole. Mitsubishi sells cars, but is not a brand in the full sense: we cannot perceive its values, its source of inspiration, its project, where it is heading and where it is taking us. It is just a name on a car, to which is attached the reassurance provided by the size of the industrial super group, Mitsubishi. For non-Japanese people, Mitsubishi means little beyond Japan and a giant conglomerate. Imported Korean cars have only their price and quality to rely on. They are not yet real full brands, with both tangible and intangible values.

The process of brand positioning

By what practical process can a brand platform be defined that will maximise the chances of a successful brand launch? This concerns local brands but also global ones with the big challenge of finding a strong global identity, and eventually a global positioning (if not, one that can be tailored to different markets). There are five phases to this process: understanding, exploring, testing, strategic evaluation and selection, and implementing or activating the brand:

1. *The understanding phase* is about identifying all potential added values for the brand, based on its identity, roots, heritage and prototypes, as well as its current image. This is a self-centred approach: a brand's truth lies within itself. However, in order to detect which area of potential is most likely to be profitable for the business, an analysis of customers and competition is required. Markets are also analysed for this reason, as well as developments among consumers looking for 'insights' – consumers' aspirations or dissatisfactions on whom the brand can build. Lastly, the aim of analysing the competition is to identify opportunities, gaps, exploitables and areas of interest. The tool for this is perceptual mapping,

for in marketing the fight is over perceptions. Perceptual maps do produce a remarkably synthetic model of the mind of the consumer – the psychological battlefield.

2. *The exploration phase* is about suggesting scenarios for the brand. Finding the brand platform is not something that can be done in one fell swoop: it takes an iterative approach, using repeated eliminations and adjustments. For example, what would the possible scenarios be for a brand such as Havana Club? This is the only rum produced in Cuba, an island famous for the quality of its sugar cane (and thus its rum), and seeks to promote this quality on a worldwide scale. Going back to our four questions– against whom? why? for when? for whom? – we can identify four major scenarios, each of which uses its own approach to express the full richness of the imagery evoked by Cuba and its capital Havana, which have remained authentic and intact over time (see Table 8.2). Note that these four scenarios do not each rely on the same product. As is the case with many brands, preferences can differ from one country to another. For example, in the case of rum, some countries consume only white rum, while others consume only dark rum. Evidently not all of these countries could be penetrated using the same product. This has a strong impact on positioning, as the competition faced by a white alcohol will not be the same as that facing a dark rum. In one case, Havana Club will try to take market share away from gin and vodka, while in the other it will be up against whiskies, malts and brandies. Within the white alcohols sector, the question concerning the competition needs to be asked again: are we targeting the leader or not?

It all depends on the subjective category and the targeted competitors: to define oneself as rum is already to have specified the nature of the competition. In the UK, however, there is no rum market – despite the fact that Bacardi sells very well there. But to drink Bacardi, do you necessarily have to be aware that it is a rum? It is – thanks to Cuba – perhaps the very epitome of the party cocktail drink.

The angle of attack will differ depending on whether the target is Bacardi (the world leader), mixers and quality rums, or dark spirits in general (whiskies, brandies and so on).

3. *The test phase* is the time when scenarios are either refined or eliminated. It requires consumer studies to evaluate the credibility and emotive resonance of each scenario. What are being tested at this stage are ideas and formulations, but certainly not whole campaigns.

4. *The strategic evaluation* takes the form of a comparison of scenarios based on criteria, followed by the economic evaluation of potential sales and profits. The latter is conducted in 'bottom-up' fashion, through the summation of sales and contribution of forecasts from each country in question and so on.

Let us look again at some of the 11 criteria for evaluating positioning (see page 177). The second of these raises the question of the strength of the 'consumer insight' on which it is based. Is there a genuine business opportunity here? The fifth is a reminder that all positioning has to target a weakness in the competition – and indeed, a long-term weakness. Positioning itself is a durable decision. So you might ask the question, how do you find your competitor's long-term weakness? Paradoxically, through its very

Table 8.2 Comparing positioning scenarios: typical positioning scenarios for a new Cuban rum brand

| | White mixer | | Dark straight | |
	A	B	C	D
	Better-tasting mixer than the leader	Experience Cubania	The 'absolute' rum	An original spirit
Against whom?	The leader	All mixers	Premium rums	Whiskies, cognac
Why?	'Taste'	'The Cuban drink'	'The best rum'	'Be different'
When?	Cocktail/mixed	Night/mixed	Home/bars/straight	Home/after dinner
To whom?	25/40 Spain, UK, Canada, Germany Bacardi drinkers	16/30 Urban/B in Europe and Canada, non-rum drinkers	25/40 Urban/heavy rum drinkers in Canada, Spain, Italy, UK	30/45 Urban heavy spirit drinkers in Europe, Canada, Asia
Product priority	White	White/3 yrs	Anejo (dark)	7 yrs (dark)
Pricing	–10 % vs leader	Par with leader	Premium	Par with whiskies
Communication	Mass media	2-step marketing	2-step marketing	2-step marketing

strength (Neyrinck, 2000). For example, what is the long-term weakness of the world leader, Bacardi? It is the very fact that it is the world leader. To sell in such quantities, you have to sell at low prices, and thus produce everything locally. Bacardi may have been born in Cuba; but its rum no longer comes from Cuba, for a variety of commercial and economic reasons.

To evaluate a positioning, one must always take the trade into account. For example, in the world of shampoo, would a positioning of the 'for men' type constitute good positioning? The answer would seem to be 'yes' when judged by certain strategic evaluation criteria. It achieves differentiation and it represents a 'customer insight' (a genuine purchasing motive). But adopting the philosophy of the retailer leads us to a different conclusion. Retailers such as Wal-Mart, Carrefour and Asda tend to have a special men's section for hygiene and cosmetics products. This would immediately attract those arguing for this positioning. But it tends to be women who buy for men, and these women tend to choose for their men a shampoo from their own section. Thus, in terms of sales potential, it makes more sense to leave the product in the normal shampoo section. If it were put in the men's section, sales would fall by 50 per cent. Furthermore, let us suppose that the brand was in the men's section, at which point the 'for men' positioning stops being a source of differentiation, since that section contains nothing but products and brands for men only!

5. The fifth phase is that of *implementation and activation* once the platform has been chosen and drawn up. This new term clearly expresses the fact that today, a brand's values must be made palpable and tangible; and the brand must therefore transform them into acts at 360°.

This is all about defining the brand's marketing strategy, functional objectives and campaign plan. Will it be mainly mass-media advertising, or mainly proximity marketing? How will the brand be activated? Here again, choices will be determined by the competitive environment. Consider the example of Dolmio – the European leader in Italian sauces – whose marketing strategy cannot be the same for both the UK and Ireland. In the UK, Dolmio controls a mere 20 per cent of the market, while in the latter it is the comfortable leader with 50 per cent. Furthermore, far more proximity marketing can be carried out in a country with a small population than in a very large country. Activation is the phase during which strategy becomes behaviour and tangible actions, thus transcending mere advertising and promotion. (See Figure 8.2.)

Determining the flagship product

In launching a new brand, companies have to be extremely careful in choosing which product or service to present in their first campaign and how to speak about it, even more so if the overall brand is particularly ambitious. This 'star product' should be the one that best represents the brand's intentions, ie the one that best conveys the brand's potential to bring about change in the market. Likewise, in terms of name, only those products that best support the overall project should prominently bear the brand name. On the less typical products, the brand name should intervene far less, serving only to endorse the product.

Not all products of a brand equally represent it. Only those which truly epitomise the brand's identity should be used as support in a launch campaign. Ideally, this identity must be visible. The major car manufacturers are well aware of this. Car design must be the outward expression of the brand's long-term design. The choice of the brand's best

Brands are built by the sum of delights at each contact point and by their coherence

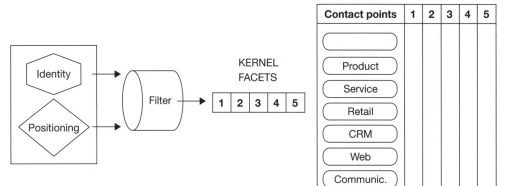

Figure 8.2   From brand platform to activation

exemplar may conflict with short-term business objectives. The product that would sell the best might not be representative of the brand identity to be fostered. In this situation the long term should determine the short term, since it is evident that without business there is no brand.

Brand campaign or product campaign?

Volkswagen has never produced communications about anything other than its products. Since the beginning, its ads have consistently reflected a deliberate choice of graphic style – that of purity: hence, the motif of a car on a white background. So, even if the brand treats the rational arguments aloofly, humorously, impertinently or paradoxically, the car remains the 'hero' of the ad. Sony occasionally launches so-called 'brand campaigns', which aim to emphasise the brand's slogan. Whenever a brand is created, there are two alternative strategies: to communicate the brand's meaning either directly, or by focusing on a particular product. Which path is followed depends on the company's ability to select one product which will fully convey the brand's meaning. It is no wonder that Volkswagen took the second

option. The Beetle plainly demonstrated the genius of an original artist, an outsider, and obviously represented a different car culture.

In launching its brand in Europe, Whirlpool, the white goods world leader, decided to forbid any product ad for three years. It wanted to create a thrill around its name that no product campaign would have created, through a very imaginative and symbolic campaign.

The reason banks prefer brand campaigns is quite logical. As service companies, they have nothing tangible to show the potential customer. They can only symbolise their values and their identity. They also encapsulate the essence of their identity in slogans, in this way hoping to make up for their lack of visible products.

Brand language and territory of communication

Today's vocabulary is no longer just verbal, it may even be said to be predominantly visual. In this multimedia era, in which only a few split-seconds' attention are spent on advertisements in magazines, pictures are far more important than words.

A territory of communication does not

appear from nowhere, nor can it be arbitrarily assigned to the brand. Brand language allows brands to freely express their ideology. Not knowing which language to speak, we merely repeat the same groups of words or pictures over and over again, so that the whole brand message eventually becomes clogged. There is such a great urge to create unity, resemblance and a common spirit among the different campaigns that in the end they all seem merely to repeat one another. Each specific campaign message thus gets obliterated by an excessive concern to find the missing code!

The code is always rather artificial whereas language is natural: it conveys the personality, culture and values of the sender, helping the latter either to announce products and services or to charm customers.

Brand language finally serves as a means of decentralising decisions. Thanks to the use of a common glossary of terms, different subsidiaries worldwide can adapt the theme of their messages to local market and product requirements and yet preserve the brand's overall unity and indivisible nature. Brand identity must reconcile freedom with coherence, a task which expression guides (also called brand charters) are meant to facilitate. These should not merely address issues such as the position of the brand name on the page and so on. They must also specify the following:

▨ dominant features of style;

▨ the audio-visual characteristics such as a gesture, a close-up of a customer's face, a jingle;

▨ the graphic layout or narrative structure codes, and the brand's colour codes;

▨ the principles determining if and how the brand – and its signature, if it has one – can be used in some circumstances.

Such cases must indeed be anticipated and defined in the expression guide.

Choosing a name for a strong brand

Manufacturers make products; consumers buy brands. Pharmaceutical laboratories produce chemical compounds, but doctors prescribe brands. In an economic system where demand and prescription focus on brands, brand names naturally take on a pre-eminent role. For if the brand concept encompasses all of the brand's distinctive signs (name, logo, symbol, colours, endorsing characteristics and even its slogan), it is the brand name that is talked about, asked for or prescribed. It is therefore natural that we should devote particular attention to this facet of the brand creation process: choosing a name for the brand.

What is the best name to choose to build a strong brand? Is there anywhere a particular type of name that can thus guarantee brand success? Looking at some so-called strong brands will help us answer these usual questions: Coca-Cola, IBM, Marlboro, Perrier, Dim, Kodak, Schweppes… What do these brand names have in common? Coca-Cola referred to the product's ingredients when it was first created; the original meaning of IBM (International Business Machines) has disappeared; Schweppes is hard to pronounce; Marlboro is a place; Kodak, an onomatopoeia. The conclusion of this quick overview is reassuring: to make a strong brand, any name can be used (or almost any), provided that there is a consistent effort over time to give meaning to this name, ie to give the brand a meaning of its own.

Does this mean that there is no need to give much thought to the brand name, apart from the mere problem of ensuring that the brand can be registered? Not at all, because following some basic selection rules and trying to choose the right name will save you time, perhaps several years, when it comes to making the baby brand a big brand. The question of time is crucial: the brand has to conquer a territory of its own. From the very start, therefore, it must anticipate all of its potential changes. The brand name must be chosen with a view to the brand's future and destiny, not in relation to the specific market and product situation at the time of its birth. As companies generally function the other way around, it seems more than appropriate to provide some immediate information on the usual pitfalls to avoid when choosing a brand name, and also to give a reminder of certain principles.

Brand name or product name?

Choosing a name depends on the destiny that is assigned to the brand. One must therefore distinguish the type of research related to creating a full-fledged brand name – destined to expand internationally, to cover a large product line, to expand to other categories, and to last – from the opposite related to creating a product name with a more limited scope in space and time. Emphasis, process time and financial investments will certainly be different in both cases.

The danger of descriptive names

Ninety per cent of the time, manufacturers want the brand name to describe the product which the brand is going to endorse. They like the name to describe what the product does (an aspirin that would be called Headache) or is (a biscuit brand that would be called Biscuito; a direct banking service called Bank Direct). This preference for denotative names shows that companies do not understand what brands are all about and what their purpose really is. Remember: brands do not describe products – brands distinguish products.

Choosing a descriptive name also amounts to missing out on all the potential of global communication. The product's characteristics and qualities will be presented to the target audience thanks to the advertisements, the sales people, direct marketing, articles in

specialised periodicals and the comparative studies done by consumer associations. It would thus be a waste to have the brand name merely repeat the same message that all these communication means will convey in a much more efficient and complete way. The name, on the contrary, must serve to add extra meaning, to convey the spirit of the brand. For products do not live forever: their life cycle is indeed limited. The meaning of the brand name should not get mixed up with the product characteristics that a brand presents when it is first created. The founders of Apple were well aware of this: within a few weeks the market would know that Apple made micro-computers. It was therefore unnecessary to fall into the trap of names such as Micro-Computers International or Computer Research Systems. In calling themselves Apple, on the contrary, they could straightaway convey the brand's durable uniqueness (and not just the characteristics of the temporary Apple-1): this uniqueness has to do more with the other facets of brand identity than with its physique (ie its culture, its relationship, its personality, etc).

The brand is not the product. The brand name therefore should not describe what the product does but reveal or suggest a difference.

Taking the copy phenomenon into account

Any strong brand has its copy or even its counterfeit. There is no way out of this. First of all, manufacturing patents end up being public one day. So what is left to preserve the firm's competitive advantage and provide legitimate recompense for investing in research and development and innovating? Well, the brand name. The pharmaceutical industry is the perfect example: today, as soon as patents become public, all laboratories can produce the given compound at no R&D cost and generic products start flooding the market. A brand name that simply describes the product and the product's function will be unable to differentiate the brand from copies and generic products entering the market. Choosing a descriptive name boils down to making the brand a generic product in the long run. That is exactly how the first antibiotics got trapped: they were given names indicating that they were made from penicillin – Vibramycine, Terramycine, etc.

Today, however, the pharmaceutical industry has become aware that the name is in itself a patent which protects the brand from copies. This name must therefore be different from that of the generic product: in becoming distinctive and unique, it also becomes inimitable. The Glaxo-Roche laboratory, for instance, discovered an anti-ulcer agent which it called 'ranitidine'. Yet the brand name is 'Zantac'. Their competitor, Smith, Kline and French, also identified an anti-ulcer agent called 'cimetidine', but sold it under the Tagamet brand name. This naming policy is a good hedge against copies and counterfeits. Doctors are under the impression that Vibramycine and Terramycine are the same thing. Tagamet, though, seems unique, as does Zantac. The inevitable generic products that will eventually take advantage of the cimetidine or ranitidine patents will not use the Tagamet or Zantac names.

An original name can protect the brand since it reinforces the latter's defence against all imitations, whether they be fraudulent or not. The perfume name Kerius, for example, was considered as a counterfeit of Kouros: in litigation, legal experts do not judge counterfeit in terms of nominal or perfect similarity but in terms of overall resemblance. Thus Kerius became Xerius, while another cosmetics company had to pull out the products it had just launched under the name, Mieva because of Nivea. Descriptive names fail to act as patents. A brand called Biscuito would be very little protected: only the 'o' could be protected so as to prevent someone from naming a product 'Biscuita'! Even Coca-Cola was unable to prevent the Pepsi-Cola name! Quickburger,

Love Burger and Burger King have similar names, whereas McDonald's name is inimitable.

Distributors' own brands have greatly taken advantage of descriptive brands' scarce protection. Planning to win over some of the leading brands' customers, distributors have chosen names for their own brands that are very similar to those of the strong brands to which they refer: this way, consumers are likely to easily mistake one for the other. Ricoré by Nestlé has thus been copied by Incoré, l'Oréal's Studio Line by Microline, etc. Because the packages look alike (Incoré is in a yellow can like Ricoré's, with a picture of a cup and table setting also like Ricoré's ...), consumers get all the more confused as they only rely on visual signs to find their way through the store aisles. As a matter of fact, recent research has shown that confusion rates are often above 40 per cent (Kapferer, 1995 (see also page 79)).

The way in which the pharmaceutical industry has been handling the copy problem is extremely promising in terms of the long-term survival of all brands. By creating at the same time a product name (that of a specific compound) and a brand name, they have avoided the Walkman, Xerox or Scotch syndrome. These proper nouns now tend to become common names, merely used to designate the product. In order to overcome such risk of 'generism', companies must create an adjective-brand (the Walkman pocket music-player), not a noun-brand (a walkman). When creating a brand name, it might therefore also be necessary to coin a new name for the product itself (in this case, the pocket music-player).

Taking time into account

Many names end up preventing the brand from developing naturally over time because they are too restrictive:

▌ 'Europ Assistance' hinders the geographical extension of this brand and has also facilitated the creation of Mondial Assistance.

▍ Calor etymologically (meaning 'heat' in Latin) refers to heating appliance technology (irons, hair-dryers), and thus excludes refrigerators, The Radiola brand never managed to impose itself in the field of household appliances: its brand name was much too reminiscent of one specific sector.

▍ As time goes by, Sport 2000, the sporting goods distributor, seems less and less modern and futuristic.

▍ The non-fat yoghurt name, Silhouette, was too restrictive in terms of consumer benefit: slimness for the sake of slimness does not necessarily prevail anymore. This is why Yoplait decided to change the name to Yoplait fat-free, after having invested over 20 million dollars since 1975 in advertising the first brand name.

Thinking internationally

Any brand must be given the potential to become international in case it should want to become so one day. Yet many brands still discover quite late that, if such is their desire, they are limited by their name: Suze, the bitter French aperitif wine, almost literally means sweet in German. Nike cannot be registered in certain Arab countries. The Computer Research Services brand name causes problems in France, as does Toyota's MR2. In the United States, the almighty CGE name cannot be protected against the famous GE (General Electric) brand name. Prior to internationalising a brand, one must ensure that the name is easy to pronounce, that it has no adverse connotations and that it can be registered without problems. These new requirements explain why there is so much interest in the 1,300 words which all seven major languages of the European Union have in common. It also explains the current tendency to choose abstract names which, having no previous meaning, can thus create their own.

Making creative 360° communications work for the brand

In the world of mature countries, advertising is a challenge: it is costly, and its results are not always measurable. They are, however, measurable at the time of the brand's launch, at which time it quickly becomes apparent whether the public's demand and attitudes – as well as those of the trade – have changed.

The cost factor raises questions as to the appropriateness of advertising. There are sectors where launches are unthinkable without advertising: the FMCG sector, for example. But even in this case, it all depends on the precise category. The UK's current number one wine, Jacob's Creek (an Australian brand) was launched in the country in 1984, and its first large advertising campaign was in 2000. The brand has since stopped advertising, and now sponsors the *Friends* television programme. The brand's success was built on an excellent, multiple-award-winning product, trade support, public relations, plenty of in-store promotions, and encouraging consumers to try it at the point of sale, to say nothing of on-site promotions. It also develops product placement, a real lever to create and maintain the 'cool factor' of a brand.

Top-of-the-range brands also work on winning the long-term support of opinion leaders, capitalising on word of mouth. In the world of the internet, ebay – the only start-up company to have been profitable from the start, making it the internet's real success story – operates only through online referral and public relations.

When advertising is needed to give a boost to sales and business, the familiar old maxim springs to mind, 'Half of my advertising budget is wasted – but I don't know which half.' Actually, we believe that this half can easily be identified. Wasted advertising is advertising that:

▌ is not sufficiently creative, and so will not be seen;

▌ misses its target, so will not be seen by the right people;

▌ will be seen in places with no stores, where there is no distribution system in place.

These three points are the true causes of the waste; and the first of them is the most important. The question it raises is not so much the quality of the advertising agency as that of the client/advertiser. An advertiser can make a major contribution to the creativity of its agency – and thus to the quality of the campaign – in two ways: through the quality of its brief, and by the ability to take creative risks.

To achieve a leap of creative genius, a great creative idea, the brand proposition must be incisive, not bland. What can a creative person do with a brand proposition coming from a typical McKinsey-style brand consultancy output, such as 'Brand X is the ultimate (whisky for instance)'. There is a real problem with the tools and consulting companies that excel in analytics but produce no ideas. Because of the reduction in the demand for strategic consulting, most of the big consulting companies have reoriented their staff. They want now to accompany the client all through the executional process. However, analytical people, recruited for data processing skills, produce thick and exhaustive reports and a mass of matrices, but a dearth of actionable ideas.

The mistake is to think one can rely on the agency to transform as if by a miracle the bland proposition into a great creative concept. It just does not happen this way.

The second condition for a creative leap is to realise that the advertising target must be radicalised. It cannot be a simple description of those who will buy, but should provide their

reflection. If advertising is to break out of the clutter, it must not present plain people. Think of the Budweiser advertising saga 'Wazzup': by choosing quite radical characters in the commercials, the brand showed strong signs of modernity, of reinvention and of reinvolvement of the public. This was a challenge for this mainstream popular brand, which all Americans have known almost since they were born.

Building brand foundations through opinion leaders and communities

Unless one wants to position the brand in a niche at the very high end, high market shares and sales will come from a mass market positioning. However, paradoxically in order to influence the mass of the market, the people less involved with the brand, the 'switchers', a brand must be carried by a smaller group of opinion leaders. Consumer behaviour relies too much on an individual approach to consumer choice, using the paradigm of a person deciding in a social vacuum. But everyone belongs to a network, a group, a tribe. Building a brand means getting closer to these groups, which are mediators of influence (see Figure 8.3).

Proximity to opinion leaders

In all groups there are influencers, also called opinion leaders. The concept of opinion leadership is not new, but its significance has been hidden by an over-reliance on advertising. In fact, to build a brand one of the first questions to ask is, what group(s) will carry the brand? Here we do not speak of the market segment, but of the group(s) who will influence the market segment. A brand alone cannot convince. It needs relayers, committed relayers. Modern taste makers belong to tribes: micro-ethnic, cultural and geographical groups. These groups need proper identification and a programme of continuous direct relationship.

They must experience the brand, its values, and eventually interact with it. The brand must understand them, and present itself as being on their sides, sharing the same values.

Who are these influencers? Who are the opinion leaders? The two concepts need to be distinguished. Recent research (Valette Florence, 2004) suggests that opinion leaders combine three necessary traits. They are perceived as experts, are endowed with charisma and have a desire to be different from others, and have a high social visibility. Not all experts are opinion leaders: they are influencers, as are salespeople or prescriptors.

Influencers can be professionals. Canson would not have succeeded without the close ties that it is permanently weaving with the teacher community. Pedigree (pet food) relies on professionals too. L'Oreal relies on hairdressers, La Roche Posay on dermatologists.

They can be hobbyists. T-fal, positioned as tools for the successful cuisine, develops ties with cookery schools and with all the professionals engaged in developing a high level of skill in cuisine.

They can be the persons most involved in the category: all consumers are not equal. Some are more involved, more interested in all that concerns, not the product itself, but the need. They read more, use the internet much more, participate in chats and forums. For instance, mothers with more children play an influencing role.

Opinion leaders are to be found in specific community groups. We stress the word 'groups' because one should now speak of trend-setting tribes. As a result, the goal is to interact not with a sum of individuals, but with pre-organised groups, be they formal or informal. These groups can be met at specific places. Groups are organised, so it is easier to organise events with them. Salomon is obsessed with increasing the level of interaction with surfer groups all around the world, for they are trend-setters. Absolut Vodka succeeded because it came to be available at all the parties of the New York gay community. Bombay Sapphire gin did the same in Los Angeles.

To reach these groups, direct contact is needed and virtual intimacy on the net is necessary. One does not create strong ties at a distance. The goal is show that the brand is becoming part of their world, by means of participating in occasions that show the brand and group share the same values, in some way or another. Eventually the brand should be creating these occasions.

Creating a hard core of ambassadors

As soon as the brand is launched the reflex must be of creating a hard core of supporters, involved in the brand. Clarins, a very small cosmetic company when it started in 1954, facing giants such as Estée Lauder and l'Oréal, was extremely innovative in that respect, but it went unnoticed up to the point when market research showed to its competitors that the small brand was getting bigger, and that it experienced a high rate of loyal and even fanatical clients: with each product there was an invitation to write to the company and to Mr Courtin, its founder. One-to-one and CRM were already there, far before these became 'musts' for management.

There are many frameworks that have shown how consumers can be segmented on a dimension of closeness of the relationship to the brand. Typical segments range from hell to paradise, with a mix of behavioural and emotional dimensions:

1. Those consumers who dislike the brand, even hate it. It is really not part of their world.

2. Those who are not consumers because they consider the brand is underperforming on a sought attribute.

3. Those who simply are not consumers, without a specific reason (simply the brand has nothing salient to their eyes to induce trial).

4. Those who would like to buy but cannot (no availability, no accessibility, price problem).

5. Those who buy from time to time, switching between brands.

6. Those who buy more often.

7. Those buyers who are involved, engaged with the brand, its ambassadors.

As soon as the brand is launched everything must be done to create and identify consumers in segments 6 and 7, the heavy buyers and the involved consumers.

Asking for identification is a sure way to build the precious database that will enable the organisation to give VIP treatment to these forerunners: specific tips, a specific code number on the website, specific invitations, specific offers, PR events and online sales.

There is another way of creating a hard core of supporters. It can be summed up in one key phrase formulated 50 years ago by Paul Ricard: *faites-vous un ami par jour* (make a friend every day). Of course, this is easy to say if you

happen to be – as Ricard was – the man who created what is now the world's second-largest spirits group. But the phrase deserves closer examination:. He did not say 'make a customer every day', but 'a friend'. Service, free gifts, responsiveness, personalised relationships, attentiveness and the sharing of enthusiasm at small and large gatherings alike are the rungs on this upward ladder.

Creating word of mouth, buzz

Status is not granted by oneself: it is given by opinion leaders, experts, and the press. Virgin, although it is one the very few brands known throughout the world, hardly spends a dime on advertising. However, everybody has heard of Virgin, or will hear about it. Paradoxically Richard Branson, the founder of the Virgin galaxy, is not an extrovert. However, he knew that by seeking publicity he could avoid spending a lot money on advertising – money he did not have in any case.

Branson has become a man of public relations: he knows how to create events that will become widely broadcast and diffuse the buzz.

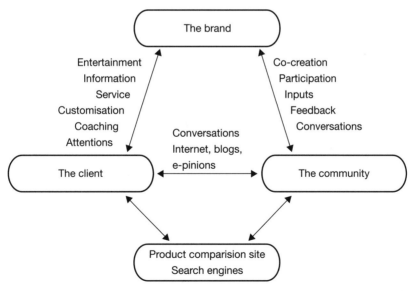

Figure 8.3   Consumer empowerment provides opportunity for bonding

Word of mouth should not however be seen as an alternative to advertising. Advertising is surely not dead. Brands have two feet: shared emotions and renewed products.

Advertising remains a fantastic tool to shape these common, shared imageries, or to create instant knowledge of an innovation.

How can one create the buzz, this modern, fashionable word for word of mouth, or positive rumours (Kapferer, 1991, 2004)?

The first approach is to make plenty of time for the press and media. Naturally, it is a good idea to recruit a specialist agent, but journalists will be flattered to be welcomed by managers themselves. This is where the work of making friends should begin: it is crucially important to know how to assist a journalist (for whom, as we all know, time is in short supply). We should also remember that everyone deserves attention, from the big-name television reporter to the freelancer from the small trade journal. The high-powered editor of the future is sure to be lurking among the dozens of freelancers you meet.

The second approach – which should become a discipline – is to do nothing without considering the press fallout. As the adage goes, every dollar you spend on public relations requires another to promote the fact. A buzz has to be activated and energised: it does not always start on its own.

The third approach is always to look for the difference and disruption in everything (Dru, 2002). It is said that in the world of PR, it has all been done before. This means that your job is to surprise, because surprise is what gets people talking.

This is why brands create their own events, engage in street marketing, tie up with celebrities, invest in sport or music sponsorship and so on.

9

The challenge of growth in mature markets

Brand management is a challenge in mature markets. How to build the business where consumers have their needs amply fulfilled, face considerable choice, become price-sensitive and find allies in multiple retailers who want a larger share of the added value created by brands?

Drawing from multiple cases and models, we look at the main strategies that can be followed to find growth in no-growth markets.

The first, short-term strategy is to build on existing clients. Customer relationship management (CRM), database management and relationship marketing have not emerged so forcefully in the panoply of modern brand management without a compelling reason. It is necessary to get still closer to the consumer, one's own consumers, who may be faced with too much choice. Seducing new customers seems too costly (Reichheld, 1996).

The second one is to carry out more research. What needs, or lacks of satisfaction or untapped uses can be better met? For instance, packaging and design innovations, although not spectacular, are able to provide incremental sources of share, especially if they

are differentiated according to the distribution channel.

However, for the long term, the two main options are to explore foreign markets and to innovate. We turn to these strategies now.

Growth through existing customers

The first source of growth is to be found among the existing customers of the brand. There are growth opportunities to be searched, evaluated and exploited. This is too often overlooked by managers who wish to move quickly to some hot brand extension.

Building volume per capita

Brand management over time is the permanent pursuit of growth. One way of achieving this is to move from a pattern of low-volume use to a pattern of potentially higher-volume use. For example, Bailey's Irish Cream – a worldwide spirits brand created in 1974 – suffered from a serious restriction to its growth. Its consumption was highly seasonalised, and sales mostly took the form of Christmas and New Year presents. It was consumed mainly by little old ladies, partaking on their own as a sort of sugary treat. It was taken neat in small measures, on account of its sweet taste. If it was to grow in volume, things had to change. The brand's future also depended on its ability to compete outside its category (narrowly defined as Irish cream liqueur). A major campaign was thus launched around the concept of Bailey's on ice. The creative idea was to communicate how the sensuousness of Bailey's allowed you to connect to your friends and family. The intention was to encourage groups of people to drink Bailey's on the rocks (which in fact increases the desire for another glass). A creative media campaign backed this new positioning, exploring how to link the brand to the key sensual moments in the media. For example, Bailey's sponsored *Sex and the City*.

But most important were the on-premise implications of the campaign. Drinking Bailey's on ice required a normal-sized glass, not a liqueur glass as before. The marketers had to persuade the trade to take the campaign seriously. They designed a new Bailey's glass for bar chains, 6,000 ice consumer kits, 4,000 large-measure POS kits, and 16,000 optics to deliver a suitable measure of Bailey's for drinking over ice. As a result on-trade sales grew from a low 46,000 cases in December/January 1989 to 107,000 in December/January 1996. It had become more hype, young and trendy to drink Bailey's on ice.

In the United States Jack Daniel's – suffering from its stereotypically 'macho' image – attempted to increase its per capita volume. To do this, the brand needed to create an association with parties (a consumption situation which has a galvanising effect on volume). The brand created a micro-marketing plan specifically for this purpose, 'The Jack Daniel's occasion'. The exemplar for this was the barbecue people enjoy around the back of their car after arriving at a sports event a few hours early. The brand developed specific paraphernalia and specific advertising designed to promote use in this context, which was placed in sports magazines.

Coca-Cola is a best practice exemplar in terms of increasing consumption per capita. Its goal is to bring consumers around the world closer to the consumption rate of American consumers, who drink 118 litres per person per year. Its first key strategic lever is not to use a cost-plus price fixing method, but to target the price of the most popular drink in each country: the price of tea in China, for instance. Because this put a strain on the profitability of local bottlers, the aim is to achieve a quick hike in sales. Profitability is guaranteed to the Coca-Cola Company itself, because it receives the difference between the cost of production of the cola syrup and its resale price (five times as high) to the bottler.

The second key lever is to gain local monopolies. 'Local' in this context means as close as possible to a thirsty person's impulse to drink. Ideally the product should be at an arm's reach, via automatic machines or small refrigerators, everywhere: in hotels, universities, hospitals, and also in bars and cafeterias, for on-premise consumption.

The third lever is to adapt pricing to the consumption situations, so that an identical litre of Coke is sold at very different prices according to when and where it is bought.

Last but not least, specific marketing plans are devoted to specific situations such as lunch and dinner, breakfast and evenings. In many countries consumers drink tap water, bottled water or mineral water. They do this by habit and also for health reasons: consuming too many sugary drinks leads to obesity and other health problems, which are being faced by many Americans at present. Coca-Cola's plan is to modify local customs, starting with children and young people whose habits are yet to be formed. Hence the global alliance with McDonald's, a key social change agent and a chain of which young people are heavy users. Similarly, Coke has another alliance with Bacardi, the world's leading spirit drink. It is significant that advertisements for Bacardi Carta Blanca show a 'Cuba Libre' cocktail, which is made up of rum and Coke.

Building volume by addressing the barriers to consumption

Branding is too obsessed by image, and not obsessed enough by usage. Even though Coca-Cola is held up as the paragon of good brand management, if we are honest we have to acknowledge that it took almost a century for its managers to address perhaps the most important reason for its non-consumption: it is perceived as an unhealthy drink containing too much sugar.

Certainly the Coca-Cola Company has realised the growth of fitness and health as purchase motivations, in a country where baby boomers were ageing. It launched Tab in 1963, just after Diet Royal Crown Cola and just before Diet Pepsi. However, Diet Coke was launched as late as 1983. It soon became the leader in its category, and what the company calls 'the world's second soft drink'. Later would come caffeine-free Coke, caffeine-free Diet Coke, Cherry Coke, Vanilla Coke, Coke and Lemon. Each of these products was an answer to a consumer problem. Some

consumers wanted to drink as much Coke as possible but were prevented from doing so by Coke itself. Some could not have any more sugar, while others could not take caffeine.

Thus, there were huge opportunities for increased consumption per capita among Coke's own clients. They were probably heard, but never listened to. Identifying the barriers of consumption and relieving them was a service not only to clients but also to profitability: aspartame (the sweetening ingredient in Diet Coke) is less costly than sugar.

In the Coke example, the reasons for consumer's limited consumption were known, but the company was deaf. It confused the brand with the product. By claiming 'Coke is it', it had made Coke symbolise one product and only one, period.

In the task of growing volume through higher consumption per capita, identification of what blocks consumption is not always obvious. Research is needed. One way to do it is to segment the clientele according to the strategic matrix shown in Figure 9.1.

This matrix segments customers according to two dimensions, both related to behaviour. The first is the household's share of requirements (among 100 occasions to purchase, how many times is the specific brand bought?), and the second is the household's

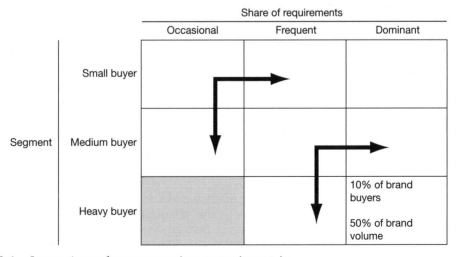

Figure 9.1   Increasing volume per capita: strategic matrix

level of consumption (is it a small, medium or heavy buyer?).

This creates eight cells (not nine because one of them is theoretically possible but empirically empty), and each household can be allocated to one of these cells. Of course this matrix can be used for any type of purchase, or purchaser, including companies in B to B markets. Each cell represents a percentage of the total number of households, and a percentage of the total volume sold of the category and of the brand. These figures are important in themselves. The key segment is the bottom right of the matrix, which represents high-consumption households that allocate the highest part of their requirements to the brand. For instance, in Europe households in this cell consume 70 per cent by volume of Coke Light, but only 48 per cent by volume of Coke. These two figures highlight how a single innovative product can release the barriers that prevent people from consuming more.

The brand manager's task is to move as many people as possible progressively in the direction of this bottom-right cell. This can be done, starting from other cells and going vertically or horizontally. But it is first necessary to understand the very specific circumstances and motivations of consumers in each cell. To increase a specific type of behaviour requires behavioural segmentation, then an in-depth understanding of those in each of these behavioural segments. Who are they? Why don't they consume more? Is it a taste problem, a satiety problem, a price problem, a format problem, a packaging problem, an insufficient variety of line extensions, a distribution problem? It is very rarely an image problem, because those being considered here are already clients. In modern markets we know from panel data that even for loyal customers, the brand's share of requirements is never 100 per cent. It is sometimes no more than 40 per cent. However, managers lack information on why these consumers choose other brands 60 per cent of the time.

The result is a new marketing mix, often involving specific product improvement, higher experiential benefits, range extensions (formats, taste and so on), designed to target each behavioral segment.

Growth through new uses and situations

Like it or not, every product is consumed within a particular situation. This is one of the four aspects of the positioning diamond (see page 76). Customers are looking for solutions to problems related to highly specific situations. For example, different things are expected of a car depending on whether it is intended primarily for town use, town use plus other short trips, or fairly long trips. The growth of a brand is thus often a matter of tackling new situations of use, knowing that these situations may well include the same customers, as it is possible for one person to consume the same product in several different situations. For many companies, the situation of use is now the one real criterion for segmentation, rather than the characteristics of the users themselves. A product is always consumed in a particular situation – and it is this situation that defines the brand's competitive set. The situation is the brand's true battleground. Each situation is associated not only with a different subset of competitors, but also with expectations, needs, volumes, and growth and profitability rates.

It is understandable that brands should seek to grow by breaking into high-growth-rate consumption situations in which their attributes give them a high degree of relevance. Such a movement often requires the launch of a new product or line extension.

This is why Mars launched the mini-Mars bar, a new product designed for consumers of the brand aged over 35 who were reducing their consumption of chocolate bars. This new product also changes Mars' positioning: in terms of its physical size, it is a 'sweet'. The

Figure 9.2   Segmenting by situation

situation into which it now fits is that of 'indulgence', rather than a meal substitute or re-energiser.

In the United States, Captain Morgan is a rum brand with a masculine personality: it is the rum of 'fun and adventure'. To achieve growth, the market was segmented according to the situations of use. Seeking to gain a foothold in the so-called 'partying' segment – a large group of friends indulging in noisy partying, dancing and drinking – the company launched Captain Morgan Spice. It then targeted the so-called 'lively socialising' segment – a smaller group of friends getting together for a cocktail – but the first attempt was a failure. Captain Morgan Coconut Rum suffered too much from the Captain Morgan umbrella name and its highly characteristic values. In the latter use situation, the key is to address a more feminine, elegant, romantic set of values, rather than some sort of macho ritual. This is why the second test product to be launched was Parrot Bay, a product merely endorsed by Captain Morgan.

Growth through trading up

A classic growth strategy is trading up. Customers may wish to receive an upgraded service or product from the brand. Gift packs and 'special series' capitalise on collectors' motivations. Larger formats have a built-in attractiveness too.

Extending the range can also be a way to increase profitability. Thus if it costs €3 to produce a litre of three-star cognac (that is, cognac aged for 3 years), €4.5 for a VSOP (4 to 5 years), €15 for an XO (30–35 years) and €21 for a litre of *Extra Vieux*, the customer trade-up is very profitable, as consumer prices are around the €15, €30, €60 and €150 mark respectively, according to the type of cognac.

Line extensions: necessity and limits

Today, most new product launches are range or line extensions. Shelves are replete with line extensions. As the examples we have given have demonstrated, extending the range is a necessary step in the evolution of a brand through time. Just as living species only survive if they adapt through evolution to their environment and seek to extend their ecological realm, the brand, which historically is designated by a single product (like Coca-Cola or McCain French fries) breaks up into sub-species. The extension of the line or range (we will address the difference between the two concepts later) typically takes on the following shapes:

- Multiplication of formats and sizes (typical in cars but also in soft drinks).

- Multiplication of the variety of tastes and flavours.

- Multiplication of the type of ingredients (for example Coca-Cola with or without sugar, with or without caffeine, types of motors in the Ford Escort).

- Multiplication of generic forms for medicine.

- Multiplication of physical forms such as Ariel in powder, liquid or micro formula.

- Multiplication of product add-ons under the same name, corresponding to a same consumer need in what is called line extension. Thus, Basic Homme by Vichy comprises a line of toiletries including shaving foam, soothing and energising balm, deodorant, and shower gel.

- Multiplication of versions having a specific application. For example, the Johnson company transformed its successful spray polish, Pliz, which was a mono-product brand for a long time, into a range called Pliz 'Classic', which offered products specialised for the type of surface. In doing so it also seized the opportunity to reduce its brand portfolio. Favor, a weak brand, became Pliz with beeswax especially for wood. Shampoo brands multiply endlessly, with varieties suited to different types of hair and scalp condition.

Line or range extension must be distinguished from brand extension, which is a real diversification towards different product categories and different clients. It is a highly sensitive and strategic choice that will be addressed in a separate chapter. Why does Yamaha brand both motorcycles and pianos? Line and range extensions represent 85 per cent of new product launches in consumer goods. It is the most common form of innovation in these markets.

Range extension naturally follows the logic of marketing and of even finer segmentation to better adapt the offer to the specific needs of consumers, needs that never stop evolving. At its beginning, we may recall, each brand was a unique product, in both meanings of the word: it is different and there is only one form of it. This was, for example, the case with the famous Ford: everyone could have it in the colour of their choice, as long as it was black. It was the same with the Coca-Cola and the Orangina bottle. With time, the brand becomes less narrow-minded, and acknowledging differentiated expectations, decides to respond to them. As the American advertising for Burger King, the competitor of McDonald's, says, 'Have it your way' (whatever way you like it, with or without sauce, onions, etc). Again, taking the example of Coca-Cola, while retaining its identity (the dark colour, cola taste, and other physical and symbolic attributes of the brand), the company was able to extend the power of attraction of its brand by allowing people who up until then were reluctant to try the product to indulge in Coke. The multiplication of versions (with or without sugar, with or without caffeine) increased the number of potential consumers. We therefore see that range extension can reinforce the brand by widening its market and its customer base. A variety of formats has the same effect. In the world of soft drinks, the launch of a new format may be considered the same as launching a new soft drink. Indeed, each new format allows the brand to enter a new usage mode.

In so doing, the brand proves itself to be full of energy and sensitivity. It recognises the different expectations of the public and responds to them. It follows the evolution of consumers and changes with them. Club Med was thus able to widen its offer beyond the simple Robinson Crusoe lodge to keep or attract families, then people in their forties seeking more comfort, and finally older people, children of the baby boom. The range extension is a token of the brand's attentive and caring character. Extending the brand range thus makes the brand interesting and friendly and maintains through these successive mini-launchings a strong visibility. From this point of view, instead of trying to force New Coke on Americans and make them give up the original flavour, the Coca-Cola Company would have done better to have launched the New Coke as an extension alongside the classic Coke!

Range extension is a way of revitalising many failing brands, by making sure they move closely to meet the expectations of today's customers. What saved Campari was the launching onto the market of a 'flanker' product: Campari Soda. Martini would have fallen by the wayside if it had not been for the launching of Martini Bianco, more in touch with the new modes of alcohol consumption. Smirnoff made a step towards customers who were not used to the strong taste of vodka by launching Smirnoff Mule and Smirnoff Ice in small individual bottles.

These motives may be worthy of praise, but the current proliferation of range extensions to be observed in all consumer goods markets results from frantic competition and from the new psychology of organisations.

In these markets there is a strong relationship between market share and the number of facings, ie the share of shelf space taken up. This is not surprising: the customer involvement in these products is average if not low and the number of impulse buyers (when the choice of brand is done on-site) never stops growing. It is, therefore, in the brand manager's interest to take up the most shelf space possible because it will attract even more attention from the customer, especially if a shelf is not extendible and competitors get pushed out. In many markets, demand is no longer growing and DOBs also occupy a share of the shelf, so the brand manager tries to position his product as 'captain of the category' by presenting a unique offer and so dominating the shelf reserved for national brands.

Distributors have an ambivalent attitude towards range extensions. On the one hand they oppose what is now considered hyper-segmentation, the proliferation of range extension. But as each brand tends to offer the same extensions, this creates bottlenecks because of the obsession each brand has to gain access to maximum distribution. This fight for ever-reducing shelf space strengthens the power of distributors and puts them in a position to ask for increasing amounts of money as a listing fee (Chinardet, 1994).

The problem is that the turnover of extensions, because of their novelty and their price premium, is often lower than that of the original product. When the distributor realises this (if he ever does), he withdraws the extension and awaits the offer of other brands, along with any kind of listing fee that might come with it.

Criticised by, but at the same time popular with distributors, range extensions are appreciated by product and brand managers. First of all, the amount of time needed for development is shorter than that needed for the launching of a new brand. The costs are less than those for the launching of a new brand (they are estimated to be one-fifth), and sales forecasts are more reliable. In the short term at least, it seems an almost automatic way of gaining market share and thus creating observable results that can be attributed to the actions of the manager in a relatively short time span. This counts for quick promotion within the company, or on another brand in another country. Few managers are willing to take the risk of launching a new brand, but would rather extend the range.

The proliferation of product extensions produces insidious negative effects that are not immediately measurable or measured.

First of all, because of small production runs and the increased complexity of production, logistics and management, extensions are more expensive to produce, the cost of which puts up the higher wholesale and retail price. According to Quelch and Kenny (1994), compared to an index of 100 for the cost of production of a mono-product, the corresponding production cost index of differentiated products in a range is, for example, 145 in the car industry, 135 for hosiery and 132 in the food industry. Moreover, in companies which do not take into account direct costs (eg raw materials, advertising), many costs are considered as common to the entire range and are allocated to different products within it according to sales. The bestsellers therefore attract more of the costs than range extensions, which makes the profitability of the latter rather illusory.

Second, non-controlled extension weakens the range logic. The first to find problems with this are the salespeople: the salesforce of Ariel or Dash, used to promoting the brand against Skip, had to undertake within a few months a complete cultural revolution. They had to promote Ariel in powder, in liquid and in micro formula formats all together and without ever explaining that one was superior to the other, or what advantages one format has in comparison to the others. The more extensions multiply, the more the specific positioning of each extension becomes subtle. This is accentuated by the fact that extensions are added without withdrawing the existing versions. Organisations always have a good reason for not cancelling this or that version. The thought of losing the odd customer here and there rules the notion out. This thinking overlooks the fact that product withdrawals should also be managed to gently propel customers towards newer, better versions.

The range logic is also lost on the shelf: indeed, the distributor is reluctant to take on the whole range. He will shop around and take only part of a range, which undermines the consistency of the range on the shelf.

Finally, brand loyalty might be undermined by a proliferation of extensions. The hyper-segmentation of shampoos according to new hair needs, leads the customer to take into account more needs in his/her choosing process. The brand is but a feature in an ever longer list of criteria. This result was verified empirically by Rubinson (1992).

In reaction to the proliferation of extensions, Procter & Gamble eliminated within 18 months 15 to 25 per cent of the product extensions that were not achieving a sufficient turnover. In the sector for cleaning products, the growth of new multi-usage products (all-in-one) is on the same principle of simplification. Economies of scale apply all the more since the product is designed for the worldwide market. The extreme strategy of counter-segmentation is applied by hard-discounters: there is absolutely no choice and products are generally only available in a single version with no variety. Thus, there will only be one type of diaper, whatever the weight or the gender of the baby, in contrast to Phases (boy or girl) by Pampers. On the other hand, because of this it will be 40 per cent cheaper than, say, Pampers.

Quelch and Kenny (1994) recommend four immediate actions for better management of range extensions:

- Improve the cost accounting system to be able to catch the additional costs incurred by a new variety all along the value chain. This enables the real profitability of each one to be assessed.

- Allocate resources more to high-margin products than to extensions that only appeal to occasional buyers.

- Make sure that each salesperson can sum up in a few words the role of each product within the range.

- Implement a new philosophy where product withdrawals are not only accepted but encouraged. Some companies only launch an extension after having cancelled another with a low turnover. This withdrawal does not have to be brutal, but can be done gradually so that clients turn to other products within the range.

Growth through innovation

When Moulinex was asked why its results were bad, executives answered that the company had only offered 10 per cent innovation when the average in the industry was 26 per cent.

Innovation, source of growth and competitiveness, does not come easy. Here too, there are no miracles. The firms that innovate most, such as Procter & Gamble, l'Oréal and Gillette, devote on average 3.2 per cent of their sales to research and development. Is there a lesson here for the food companies competing against DOBs and price leaders? The giants in the food industry spend much less in comparison on R&D: Unilever devotes 1.8 per cent of its sales to R&D, Nestlé 1.2 per cent, Kraft General Foods 0.8 per cent and Cadbury-Schweppes 0.4 per cent (Ramsay, 1992).

As a consequence, own-label products account for 62 per cent of the 4,600 new product launches in the British food and drink market. In the chilled sector, own-label product launches represent 79 per cent of the 2,188 introductions! Retailers' brands do act as real brands.

Innovation does not have to mean a technological breakthrough. Gillette is an extreme case: the Sensor required 10 years in research and led to 22 patents, the Sensor Excel 5 years and 29 patents, Sensor Plus Pour Elle 5 years and 25 patents. Many innovations can be linked to the service brought by the brand, in its packaging for example.

The head start that Evian took over Contrex and Vittel lies mostly in the micro-services which it was able to provide the customer with first. This service, although not spectacular or linked to advertising, allowed a gain

of 0.5 per cent in market share, which, given the volumes involved, is gigantic. Evian was thus the first to withdraw the metal capsule which sealed the bottle, which the consumer ripped off more often than not. That year, its sales jumped by 12 per cent when the market only grew by 7 per cent. The brand was also the first to introduce the handle which made the six-bottle pack carryable, the compactable bottle and so on.

On low-involvement products, incremental innovations are much appreciated by the consumer, the distributors amplifying the move if competitors do not react quickly – distributors prefer novelty.

In order to de-commoditise milk and to curb the surge of hard discounters, the milk brand Candia multiplied its innovations, giving each its own specific name to accentuate the differentiation and allow for strong advertising support: Viva (milk with vitamins), Grand Milk (enriched milk), Grand Life Growing (for children), Future Mother (ie for pregnant women). These 'daughter brands' of Candia stemmed the advance of hard-discount products and enabled distributors to work with high-margin and high-turnover products. These were not major technological innovations, but were add-ons of vitamins, minerals and so on to respond to the expectations of demanding customers. In doing so, Candia made the whole category advance forward. Actually, nowadays Viva is rarely bought for its vitamins but for the brand and for what it stands for (a dynamic life-style, full of life, of youth). This product, which at first was advanced or premium, becomes the basis of milk, the reference. Candia was thus instrumental in enhancing the reference level for milk. The premium becomes a standard.

Creating desire in saturated markets

With a few exceptions (telephony, the internet, the need for clean water, safety, entertainment and so on), volumes in most markets are stable, or even on the decline. People who eat two yoghurts a day will not be induced to increase their consumption to four or six. People will only wash their hair a certain number of times a day. There is a limit to the number of cars any country can tolerate. The future therefore lies with 'value innovations', to use a phrase coined by Chan and Mauborne (2000). These are innovations that create a new value curve by suppressing some benefits and boosting others, at an unprecedented level. RyanAir and Nespresso are classic examples.

Traditionally, market growth is achieved by lowering prices and the associated extension of distribution channels, which move towards the mass market or even – like Dell – direct marketing. Reduced prices introduced by Japanese, Korean and now Chinese brands have allowed anyone to have a television or coffee maker at home. Large retailers have democratised this progress, making low-margin products compatible with the economic equation of high throughput. But where do you go from there?

The average coffee-maker price is €30. Would they become more desirable if sold at €28? What about 25, or 20? In many categories, the motor of growth is no longer price, but desire – and desire is created through the innovation of value.

The crisis in the Japanese economy would be much worse if it were not for the remarkable rate at which Japanese companies innovate, and the civic responsibility of Japanese consumers, who consume and renew their products as a matter of duty – thus providing collective support for the economy.

A source of competitive advantage

In Europe and the United States, what innovation has revived the coffee-maker market? Nespresso – an original concept offering access to the best-quality coffee at home at a price of around €400, thanks to a partnership between Nestlé and Krups. And what innovation has done the same for vacuum cleaners? Dyson, the €300 bagless vacuum cleaner, which has enabled the company to take 30 per cent of the UK market – which was previously assumed impregnable, as it was controlled by the majors (Hoover, Electrolux, Philips).

Which firm is currently Europe's number two automobile manufacturer, just behind Volkswagen? The answer is not Ford, GM, Renault-Nissan or even Fiat. It is PSA, the group that jointly controls the Peugeot and Citroën brands. How is this possible? Between 1987 and 1997, the company's annual sales rose from 1,952,474 to 2,077,965 vehicles, representing a growth of 6.4 per cent in 10 years. Sales figures soared between 1998 and 2002, rising from 2,247,121 to 3,262,146 vehicles – a growth of 38 per cent in four years. The new CEO, J M Folz, had identified lack of innovation as the key factor behind the group's stagnation (Folz, 2003). Between 2000 and 2004, PSA launched 25 new models and body shapes spread across its two brands, driven by restated brand values and a renewed understanding of today's markets and customers.

Only innovation can slacken pressure on costs: it generates desire and a temporary monopoly. However, modern competition is all about non-durable but constantly repeated advantages, and sometimes allows new segments to be opened in which the innovating firm becomes the market standard. This fact is important for mass retailers.

What mass retailers want

Mass retailers are on the lookout for innovations that create value rather than just move market share from one brand to another. They expect the creation of new categories or segments that will dynamise sales and margins.

Innovation is brand oxygen

Where would Apple be without the iPod or iTunes? A brand will only survive in the long term if it can demonstrate its relevance with regard to the latent or expressed changing needs of a market which is in a state of constant evolution. It is through these new products and their associated advertising that this relevance is repeatedly demonstrated. Even brands whose success and business model are built on a single, durable product have been forced to change in order to survive and grow. Even Nivea, with its traditional little blue box, has had to take the path of innovation in a market where dreams are fed by the hope offered by each new development. Even Lacoste, despite its association with the legendary 12 × 12 René Lacoste shirt – a sign of sporting elegance and distinction since 1933 – now holds two shows a year to present its new collections in its three segments of sports, sportswear and 'dress-down' Friday wear. The same is true of Bic, whose worldwide success had until recently been based on a business model founded on two principles (one single brand, and single-product factories). Surely everyone is familiar with the Bic crystal ballpoint pen, disposable razor and cigarette lighter? Yet this model has had to be modified: the world has changed. Competition has come in the form of even cheaper ballpoint pens from China, but also from the Japanese Mitsubishi group, with ballpoint pens that are priced at above the €1-mark but are attractive, innovative and practical: they create value. Bic has now found itself forced to become creative too, and even to make modifications to its business model to outsource a portion of its new products – an approach which hitherto had been unthinkable.

The virtuous cycle of innovation

What managerial conclusions can be drawn from the above points? As Figure 9.3 shows, the brand can be managed in two ways.

Brand management is thus a balance between preservation, renewal, extension and growth of the prototype on the one hand, and on the other the creation of new products and services to capture new circumstances of use and new customers, and to open new segments. The first part maintains, feeds and consolidates the brand base, while the second opens bridgeheads into the future, carrying what will tomorrow become the brand's new prototype.

Figure 9.3 Brands' dual management process

The effect of innovation on sales

Innovation does not merely work for itself: it benefits the brand in terms of both image and sales. It is what is known as the spillover effect, that is, the effect that advertising for one product has on the sales of another product in the brand. This effect, which is well known to companies, has been confirmed by marketing research (Balachander and Ghose, 2003). Examining the sales of Dannon in the United States, the authors observed that advertising for a new Dannon product also had an effect on the sales of the prototype flagship product – the existing product most commonly identified with Dannon (which they wrongly name the 'parent brand' – strictly speaking, this term should refer only to Dannon itself, and not its products). Most importantly, this effect is three times greater than the effect that the prototype's own advertising has on its own sales (a 14.4 per cent rise in the probability of choosing the flagship product following advertising for the new product, compared with a mere 5.7 per cent following its own advertising).

There are several possible explanations for this phenomenon. The first – advanced by the authors themselves – is derived by reasoning. Since the prototype/flagship is strongly associated with the brand in consumers' memories, the stimulation of the brand name through the promotion of a new product produces a feedback effect which activates a path leading to the cornerstone product, the prototype. We believe there is another explanation. Every new product draws in new consumers distinct from those already consuming the established products. In so doing, they re-evaluate their overall perception of the brand, and are thus more tempted to explore its other hitherto ignored or undervalued products, and the brand's flagship best-seller in particular. Innovation reframes the brand's image and feeds it with the new tangible and intangible attributes brought by this innovation. This is typically the case in the automobile sector, where the Peugeot 206 was named Europe's best-selling car of 2002. It has brought consumers to the brand who until then would never have thought of buying a Peugeot, but are now even considering buying higher-end models such as the Peugeot 307, 407 or 607. Innovation is the force that removes barriers to a brand's image – and the feedback effect modifies this image in a lasting way.

Disrupting markets through value innovation

It is well known that markets grow by the reduction of unit prices: this is how the computer became a household necessity, mobile phone sales skyrocketed, and so on. In mature markets, the goal is no longer to increase the market in volume, but to increase it in value. There are obvious limits to usage for most products: nobody wants to shampoo their hair four times a day. The main question is really how to make the consumer willing to pay more. This added value will then be shared between the distributor and the producer.

The goal of all brands is to look for value innovations, an unprecedented bundle of attributes that shifts the preference function of consumers (Chan and Mauborne, 2000). 'Value innovation' consists in sacrificing some attributes (by suppressing them) in order to raise valued attributes to an unprecedented level. The best example is the Accor Formule 1 hotel chain created in 1985. This became the fastest-growing hotel chain in Europe. How did Accor, Europe's leading hotel group, achieve this?

The first point was in the identification of an 'oilfield', a source of growth nobody had thought of before, or that previously could not have been served profitably. Many people never go to a hotel, because they cannot afford it. This is true of students, young couples, families, workers – a huge potential market. When they travel they tend to stay with friends or family. This matches their price expectations (it is free for them) but creates a number of disutilities (lack of privacy, obligation to eat and spend time with their hosts, lack of freedom and so on). An analysis of the value curve of this very competition (staying at friends or parents) reveals what bundle of attributes will move consumer preferences. The solution is still to be very accessible pricewise but to offer all the guarantees of a clean, safe, quiet, practical hotel.

How to do that profitably? How to base the brand on a valid economic equation? Only by sacrificing an attribute. The disruptive nature of the Formule 1 innovation was in suppressing some of the features that all previous players in the hotel market had held to be essential, such as ensuite bathrooms. In Formule 1 there were no baths or toilets in the individual rooms, but collective ones at the end of each hall, auto-washed and disinfected after each usage.

Formule 1 succeeded in tapping a hidden need, and also adopted a successful development strategy. This strategy consisted in quickly reaching the critical size (250 units) to be able to cover the country (that is, initially, France). Customer approval was transformed

into loyal behaviour (which was only possible if they found a Formule 1 hotel wherever they went), and it was also possible for the brand to access television advertising, hence reaching the status of top-of-mind brand leader for the whole hotel category.

This brand did not meet the same success in all countries. In the UK for instance, land costs and the difficulty of finding good hotel locations prevented the fast development of the chain, and hence access to the critical size, essential in the brand and business-building model.

The breakthrough brought about by Virgin Atlantic did not reside in its price or in the logo, but in the ability to create a different in-flight experience through a number of innovations that have now been widely copied. In addition Virgin offered business-class travellers a full service before and after the flight itself, adding new benefits to the Virgin experience. They could be picked up at their offices by chauffeurs in Volvo cars and driven to the airport. In addition they were offered access to a shower room after landing, to get ready for their business day. This not only attracted new clients but stimulated a higher frequency rate among all clients.

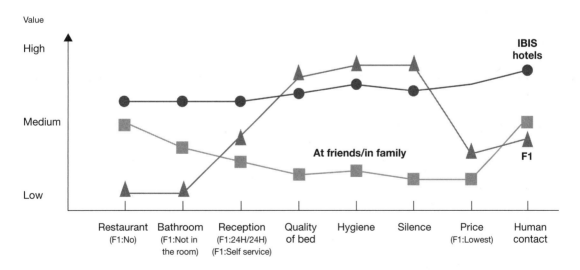

Figure 9.4   A disruptive value curve: Formule 1 hotels

Another case illustrates the concept of value innovation: ballpoint pens. What made the success of Bic, which launched the ballpoint pen on a commercial scale in 1950? Mastering quality at a low price. The prototype is the Cristal model, the all-time best-seller. It encapsulated the values of the brand: reliability, an excellent quality/price ratio and durability. Competition certainly came from lower-priced pens, with a lower quality, sold by discount chains or as distributors' brands. However the real challenge for Bic came from Pilot and Sanford, which introduced a lot of value innovations (ink gel, ink points, ink balls, more colours, better grip, new more sensual materials) at around five times the price of a Bic. When they encountered these products, which delivered experiential added values, closing the gap with classical ink pens, and provided a permanent thrill by frequently introducing new collections – as did Swatch, Gap and Zara in different fields – consumers were seduced. To survive, Bic had to change part of its business model, introducing variety to match what now emerged as very fragmented needs, thanks to an outsourcing policy, which had until then been forbidden within the Bic Group. Innovations now represent 25 per cent of each year's sales.

Increasing experiential benefits

Anyone who has visited a Nike Town cannot forget this experience. The same holds true for the House of Ralph Lauren, for Ikea and for Virgin Megastores. These places embody all the brand values in 3D, and in addition they deliver a memorable sensual experience. In developed countries, people have met their needs, and are now looking for exciting experiences. This creates a new source of growth: increasing experiential benefits.

The concept of experiential marketing has not emerged by chance over the past few years (Schmitt, 1999; Hirschmann and Holbrook, 1982; Firat and Dholakia, 1998). Consumers in developed countries and mature markets try to build thrills into their existence. This is

why, for instance, they love to patronise thematic restaurants and amusement parks, and want to discover New World wines. Through these consumptions, their minds and senses are stimulated. They live differently through the product.

Swatch has based its success on the delivery of repeated experiential benefits to each of its clients, through collections, design and a general sense of fun. Garnier, one of the mass-market global brands of the l'Oréal Group, has defined itself as a full experiential brand: this is apparent in everything from the touch and colour of the packagings to the internet site and the importance of street marketing in its brand building (with the creation of Garnier-owned buses, travelling around the country in Germany as well as in Shanghai). This also means that everything needs to change faster, to maintain the thrill: product lines, advertising, promotions, the contents of internet sites and so on.

In this respect, service acquires more and more importance, even for product brands. This can take the form of making the brand 'mediactive', a mode which favours communications among members of a virtual community through consumer magazines, forums and chatlines, FAQs and other communication devices. It can also be achieved simply through levels of service, such as the call centres created by Pampers and by Nestlé Infant Food to answer specific questions about babies.

Managing fragmented markets

Customisation is also a response to the slackening of desire among those who have become blasé. In the Maslow chain, individualisation comes high in the ladder. Everything that creates an ability to tie the brand and its products to the singularity of each client is to be looked for, within an economically favourable equation, of course. One quarter of the revenues of Harley-Davidson comes from accessories. They enhance the experience of both bike riders and non-riders, and meet these needs for individualisation.

Customisation has its limits in terms of cost and profitability. Segmentation can circumvent them. It is very interesting to analyse the Ralph Lauren range, which takes seriously the issue of market fragmentation (Table 9.1). Actually there are no fewer than 10 ranges within the Ralph Lauren empire, from the very expensive Purple Collection (with jackets price ranging from US $2,000) to the more inexpensive Polo Jeans and RLX. Each label provides a full range of products and line extensions. This policy has a number of advantages:

▓ It creates a built-in coherence that distributors might not match without guidance.

▓ It allows the distributor to allocate specific labels to specific stores and locations.

▓ It matches the inclination of consumers to feel different in the morning, afternoon and evening, while continuing to wear Ralph Lauren clothes.

▓ It increases the perception of rarity, of exclusivity, a feat for a brand that in fact is more and more diffused.

The car industry has also discovered the virtues of range fragmentation. It is not certain that consumers would want a fully personalised car. The number of alternatives available would make the choice a chore. However, they do expect to be able to choose between prepackaged variations on the same model. This is why modern car-makers increase the level of involvement of consumers with their cars by planning in advance the line extensions that target specific highly conspicuous targets, or valued life-styles. The sales of a new model are in fact made by the addition of segmented offers.

Mercedes decided to address the fragmentation of needs. It sold 700,000 cars in 1995, and has now reaches 1,250,000 a year. Meanwhile the number of models has made a leap, reaching 23 in 2005.

Nike's success can be explained the same way (Bedbury, 2002). It offers an increasingly broad array of niche products (a sign of mass customisation), thereby creating relationships with subsets of the market, with fragments. Being more involved with a product tailored to them, customers are ready to pay more. Nike now produces a number of collections even for a single sport. Also to maintain the thrill, product life cycles have been shortened from one year to three months.

As a whole, all these examples demonstrate the need for greater innovation in all aspects of the marketing mix, from product, channel and store to communication to match the fragmentation of demand.

Table 9.1   Addressing market fragmentation

Ralph Lauren's situation brands, 'portraying core life-style themes'

Ralph Lauren Collection (Purple Label, etc)

Polo Ralph Lauren	Polo Sport Ralph Lauren	Rlx Polo Sport	Polo Golf Ralph Lauren	Polo Jeans Ralph Lauren
Ralph Lauren	Ralph Lauren Collection	Ralph Lauren Sport		

Ralph, Ralph Lauren
Lauren, Ralph Lauren
Chaps, Ralph Lauren
Ralph Lauren, Children's Wear
Ralph Lauren, Home

Growth through cross-selling between brands

Is the brand perspective sometimes detrimental to growth? This provocative question has been raised by Accor Hotels, the number one European hotelier. Even though it had built a portfolio of strong brands, it wondered if, for growth purposes, it was not time to adopt a consumer orientation. With its complete portfolio of zero to four-star brands (Formule 1, Motel 6, Etap, Ibis, Novotel, Mercure, Sofitel and Suit'hotel), it realised that single-chain loyalty cards were causing its clients to defect to the competition.

This is because a businessperson travelling during the week does so at the company's expense, and his or her family cannot afford to stay in the same hotel at weekends. Although they were all Accor hotels, a loyalty card for Novotel (the three-star brand) conferred no benefits at Etap (one-star) or Formule 1 hotels. Seeing things from the client's point of view led to the planning not of product brands, but of a horizontal brand – Accor Hotels itself – as a loyalty vehicle. This allowed the client to be kept within the whole portfolio of the group's brands.

Seeing that Nivea enjoyed high levels of loyalty because of its umbrella branding architecture(all is Nivea), l'Oréal Paris decided to become a truly horizontal brand with a greater importance than that of its daughter brands (such as Elsève, Plénitude and Elnett). The aim of this mother brand was to increase cross-loyalty between the daughter brands.

Analysing its client database, Unilever calculated that 78 per cent of the most valuable consumers (MVCs) of Skip were also MVCs for Unilever products in general. This was also true of 76 per cent of MVCs for Sun, 69 per cent for Dove, 66 per cent for Lipton Ice Tea, and 63 per cent for Signal. Ultimately, this posed the question of a horizontal Unilever brand – a tricky issue in an organisation founded on a variety of unrelated product brands, in a 'house of brands' architecture.

However, in the short term there was an opportunity to be exploited: for example, to tell Skip's MVCs about the group's other products. Hence the creation of group CRM, not only for this reason, but also as a way of shouldering fixed costs collectively.

The key questions with regard to CRM are those concerning the single-brand or multi-brand approach. Consumer magazines such as *Danoe* and *Living Magazine* (Unilever), and their Procter & Gamble equivalents, illustrate the multi-brand approach and customise each mailshot to a great extent, deciding what coupons and new products will be offered to which customers. These magazines place a strong emphasis on cross-selling. This does not stop each brand from conducting its own relationship-based programme, for example, by organising conferences on issues relevant to customers, either face-to-face or through forums on the brand's website. Other channels also exist to enable such contact: for example, call centres providing real consumer services.

Growth through internationalisation

If domestic markets are mature, brands should look for better markets. This is why all brands look eastward, towards the Eastern European countries and Russia, and towards India and China. The two-digit growth markets of tomorrow are there. We address these issues in our chapter on globalisation. Brazil and Argentina should also qualify as growth markets once the Argentinian financial crisis is over. Finally, brands meeting sophisticated needs can find in North America the wanted source of growth.

For instance, Evian water has since 1991 faced an unprecedented challenge in its home country: the emergence of low-cost bottled water, sold at a third of Evian's price. These waters are not 'mineral water', with a guaranteed proportion of mineral ingredients in them, but 'spring water'. (Another category is 'purified water', such as Coke's now famous Dasani, Dannon water and Nestle Aquarel. These brands are mostly sold in North America and in emerging countries, and hardly at all in Europe.) While Evian is still the leader in value share, the volume-share leader is a low-cost brand, Cristaline.

It is easy to see how difficult it is to have to suddenly justify a major price gap. In 1972, four brands represented 80 per cent of the 2 billion litre bottled water market, and Evian was the leader with 653 million litres. Since then 17 major competitors have entered the market, and in 2003 the four main brands represented only 40 per cent of what had grown to be a 7 billion litre market. Evian's annual sales volume is now 793 million litres. The brand succeeded in growing its sales in value through three strategic actions:

- Permanent innovations in the format, packaging and handling of the packs. All these apparently tiny improvements gain significance when one has to shop for water.

- Systematic repositionings of the brand, from generic health and nature to equilibrium and now to the concept of eternal youth, while remaining within the brand's identity.

- Extending the brand. As early as 1962, Evian was a pioneer in brand extension. In response to hospital requests it introduced a spray to vaporise water on the faces of patients and babies. In 2001 Evian Affinity, another brand of facial spray, was launched in alliance with Johnson and Johnson. Two years after its launch it had become the number five brand by sales in the sector of mass market facial cosmetics. It now plans to launch in other countries such as Japan and Korea. This extension is consistent with the repositioning of Evian less as a water than as a source of health and beauty.

To make the business of Evian far more profitable, a simple calculus shows that a litre of water can be sold at a double price in developed countries such as the UK, Germany, the United States, Canada and Japan: there is a growing demand for healthy bottled drinks that is in reaction to the overconsumption of soft drinks, and the obesity syndrome attached to it. The real *un-cola* is not Sprite or Seven Up: it is Evian. Despite transportation costs, selling Evian in the United States delivers a high margin. The main problem is to access consumers and to justify the price premium in a market where Nestlé and Coca-Cola Corporation have established cheaper brands of purified water. This is why an alliance was needed with Coca-Cola to distribute Evian in North America in every outlet and vending machine.

Today, export represents 50 per cent of Evian sales. In each country the brand's role is to create the market for mineral water (not simply purified water), in order to build the business and become its referent, the brand with a fashionable, premium positioning.

10

Sustaining a brand long term

Many apparently modern and up-to-date brands have actually been with us for a long time: Coca-Cola was born on 29 May 1887, American Express in 1850, the Michelin bibendum appeared in 1898, Whirlpool in 1911, Camel in 1913, Danone in 1919, Alka-Seltzer in 1931, Marlboro in 1937 and Calvin Klein in 1968, to name a few. These are the brands that have survived – others have disappeared from the market even if their names do ring a bell.

The perennial appeal of some brands reminds us that, although products are mortal and governed by a more or less long life cycle which can be delayed but not avoided, brands can escape the effects of time.

Many great and well-known brands have disappeared, others are struggling. Why do some brands last throughout time and seem forever young, whereas others do not?

Time is but a proxy variable, a convenient indicator of the changes that affect society as well as markets, subjecting the brand to the risk of obsolescence on a double front – technological and cultural. With time, technological advances become more widely available and new cheaper entrants arrive that destabilise the balance of added value of established brands, forcing them into a never-ending cycle of constant improvement. For instance, the sudden growth of Daewoo in the car market is due to the fact that this conglomerate had access to GM assembly lines which were already 'obsolete' although they were just a few years old and were sold by GM at a low price. With the passing of time, consumers either become more sophisticated and expect customised offers, or become blasé and prefer a simplified and cheaper offer. Time also marks the cultural evolution of values, mores and consumer habits. As time goes by, current clients grow older and a new generation emerges which has to be won over from scratch all over again. Finally, time also wears down the signs, the words, the symbols and the advertising campaigns of brands.

Changes in the retail sector have far-reaching consequences. Take, for example, the rise of hard-discount in Europe, originating in Germany – where it has already become the leading form of retail, and is now getting close to a 20 per cent market share in Europe. In response to this, to pre-empt the risk that clients will desert them, hypermarkets have created low-price product ranges and – in order to avoid harming their store brand – have widened the price gap with the big brands. Stronger and stronger brands are needed to support this price differential, which has grown suddenly. In Japan, too, the retail sector is changing: in the wines and spirits market, bars have seen their market share fall from 32 per cent to 30 per cent, small independent stores have slipped from 14 per cent to 10 per cent and liquor stores are down from 34 per cent to 28 per cent. They have all lost share to the supermarkets, which have grown from 20 per cent to 32 per cent. Unlike the three first-named outlets, which offered little choice but could provide recommendations, supermarkets present a wide range – but in self-service style, with no recommendations. This change has come as a blow to all wines that formerly relied on a push strategy via in-store recommendation: it gives an advantage to Australian and US wines, which rely entirely on the brand's high profile.

Brands associated with a particular distribution channel are thus subject to the vagaries of the channel with which they are so closely linked. In terms of hygiene and beauty, the chemist's store channel is constantly losing ground to the hypermarkets and supermarkets. Indeed, the supermarket and hypermarket brands are improving their performance: Pond's, Olay, Bioré, l'Oréal Paris, Nivea, and so on. This makes the channel more and more attractive, and increases the pressure on other distribution channels. There are two possible responses to this, the first of which is to strengthen brands in the threatened channel and thus increase their attractiveness. This is the approach taken by the likes of Eucerin (Nivea), La Roche Posay and Vichy. The other approach is that of the twin channel, taking advantage of the reputation acquired in the chemist's store to sell the product in the supermarket. This is the Neutrogena option, tempting from the point of view of sales growth, but potentially threatening to brand equity. After all, sales may increase, but what will happen to the brand's reputation?

Is there a common feature of the seemingly everlasting nature of some brands? For convenience, one could say that an understanding of the brand logic, addressed in a previous chapter, offers the best bulwark against a brand slipping into decline and disappearing. A general definition also sums it up: 'to defend an added value that is constantly undermined by competition'. The following sentence epitomising the problem is attributed to Antoine Riboud (former CEO of Danone worldwide): 'I do not believe in the overpowering might of brands, but I believe in work.' A brand is not a once-and-for-all construction, but the aim of a constant effort to reconstruct the added value. The current product has to be continuously adapted to meet changing demand while at the same time the new concepts of the future have to be invented that will sustain the growth of the brand.

An analysis of the numerous brands that have survived the crises and lasted down the years may point to the key success factors of this virtuous spiral and is the purpose of the present chapter.

Is there a brand life cycle?

Curiously, the concept of brand life cycle is absent from most books on branding, as a review of their indexes shows. Does that mean that, unlike products, brands do not have a life cycle? In practice however the question whether brands have a life cycle is pervasive in a number of legal disputes. For instance, in 2002 LVMH, the world leading group for luxury brands and goods, sued the famous consulting group Morgan Stanley for having expressed the opinion that the Louis Vuitton brand (born in 1854) was now a 'mature brand', a judgement that carried implicit and explicit consequences for financial analysts and their clients, stock investors. Maturity is a typical phase of the product life cycle, the third after launch and growth, and just before decline. To describe a brand as in its maturity does indeed imply it is not far from decline, and so could hurt its reputation and the LVMH stock valuation.

The product life cycle does exist. Historical evidence proves it. All products (by which we mean the bundle of physical attributes) have an end. The problem is that the concept of product life cycle was mostly developed in hindsight. It is easy to reconstruct now the product life cycle of nylon, of transistors, of mainframe computers, of minicomputers, of word processing machines and so on. These products were replaced by more efficient solutions. Microsoft killed Wang: word processing software was a better solution than dedicated hardware. Looking at aggregate sales figures of the whole nylon industry, one finds the typical pattern: a birth and launch phase, a growth phase, a maturity phase and a decline. Maturity is signalled by a plateau, a levelling of sales.

As an after-the-fact concept, the product life cycle model is always correct. But as Popper showed us in the philosophy of science, concepts and theories that cannot be falsified are not thereby right. In practice, managers are never at their ease as to where they stand in the product life cycle. Should they interpret any stabilisation of sales as an evidence that the maturity phase has been reached, and make appropriate marketing decisions. Instead, they might argue that the decline was only due to weakened marketing, and that more work to identify and correct the causes of this stabilisation would make sales grow again. The routes to product growth recovery are multiple:

▌ through line extensions to capture the short-term new tendencies of the market and increase brand visibility;

▌ through distribution extensions to make the brand more available wherever customers are;

▌ through a reduction in the price differential from cheaper potential substitutes;

▌ through permanent 'facelifts' or innovations to deliver more value to customers and recreate perceived differentiation;

▌ through repositioning, and renewed advertising or communication in order to adapt the value proposition to the present competitive conditions.

A brand is not a product. Certainly it is based on a product or service: Nike started as a pair of sneakers, Lacoste as a shirt, l'Oréal as a hair dye. But as these examples imply, brands start from one product then continue to grow from multiple products. Louis Vuitton started as a luggage maker for the aristocracy: since then, it has become a full luxury brand covering many product categories. Recently the creative designer Mark Jacobs was hired to create the first Louis Vuitton clothing line. There should be perfumes soon. The brand keeps on surfing new products and their intrinsic growth. As such, has this process an end? Do brands managed in this way reach a levelling-off stage much later if ever?

One thing is sure. Brands that are not managed in this way, but remain attached to a single product, or even a single version of a product, are subject to the product life cycle. We all know of brands that in fact designate a very specific product: Marmite (that peculiarly English savoury spread), Xerox (photocopiers), Polaroid (instant cameras), Wonderbra and so on.

Certainly, brands such as Ariel or Skip are not growing any more in the heavy-duty low-suds detergent market. Their market share hovers around 11 to 12 per cent in Europe. They do try to create disruptions through regular innovations, but these are soon imitated, so this has become a yard-by-yard 'trench war'. Their growth will come from two sources. The first is geographical: the Russian market and all the former communist countries remain to be conquered, as does Asia (although this will be done by Tide, the equivalent of Ariel in the United States). The second is brand extensions. Why should Ariel be satisfied by just being the co-leader of the detergent market? Shouldn't it redefine its scope, its mission, as fabric care as a whole?

Of course, it can be said that once all countries of the world have been conquered and all possible extensions made, then a levelling-off in aggregated sales will unmistakably take place. This long-term prediction is as certain as J M Keynes's famous comment: in the long run we are all dead. But for practical purposes, in the short and middle term, sources of growth can always be found: it only requires more work.

In any case the emerging overriding rule of accounting for brand value (see Chapter 18) has given a clear answer to the question of the practical existence of a brand life cycle. Brand values should not be amortised for the single simple reason that no sure forecast can be made about their span of life. To amortise over 5, 10 or 40 years one needs such forecasts. The accounting standards and norms that are coming to be accepted worldwide dispel the notion of a brand life cycle as an operating concept (rather than a historical explanation).

Nurturing a perceived difference

Brands should always be 'good news'. A brand is the name that progress takes to gain access to the market. The progress marked by the inclusion of enzymes in detergents is called Ariel or Skip or Tide. The progress in convenience coffee is called Nescafé. But progress does not stop. The latest level of quality or performance is quickly integrated by the market and becomes a standard. Before long it can be found in DOBs. Continuous, but from now on selective, innovation is the brand's fate. This also applies to products with a strong intangible added value: the cologne brand Eau Jeune (literally Young Water) can only survive if it launches new versions

capable on each occasion of moving with the times. This applies just as much to stylish brands and to fashion designers as to luxury brands that have to renew constantly not their art but their products. Luxury must move with the times lest it become embalmed.

The exceptional longevity and leadership of Nescafé on the market can only thus be explained. Created in 1945, the brand has never stopped innovating, either by little imperceptible touches which when put together have produced an instant coffee whose taste is ever improving, or by major technological breakthroughs which helped recapture some of the 900 aromas that build a 'coffee taste'. The product has never stopped developing either in taste or in convenience (glass packaging replaced iron in 1962), or in its ecological considerations (the introduction of refills), or by its look. To signal the technical breakthrough and the progress made by lyophilisation, Nescafé took on the aspect of small grains under the name 'Special Filter'. In 1981, more aromas were recaptured, which was signalled by the creation of a real product range (Alta Rica, Cap Colombie), and new advertising focusing on South America. Later, a new manufacturing process called 'full aroma' was able to capture even better the aroma of freshly roasted coffee. Innovation and advertising are the two pillars of the long-lasting success of this brand. This incremental process never ends.

The leadership of Gillette follows the same pattern. Thirty-seven per cent of the sales of this multinational are accounted for by products that have been launched in the five previous years. In launching new products when the previous ones are barely established, Gillette keeps ahead of the pack, justifying a comfortable price premium and putting DOBs on short allowance (18 per cent volume on the disposables segment alone). Figure 10.1 demonstrates this well: there is a strict linear relationship between the innovation rate in a product category and the penetration of

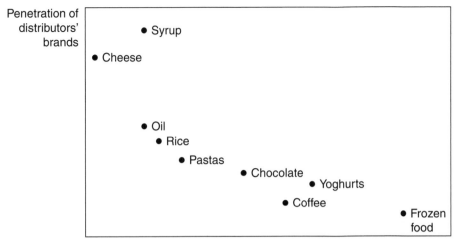

Figure 10.1 Innovation: the key to competitiveness

DOBs. When brands get lazy, cheaper copies can take a share of the market. It is significant that each year in the Lego catalogue out of 250 product references, 80 are new. In many sectors, the minute the innovation rate of a company goes down, it starts losing ground.

With their massive presence in distribution and daily presence on the table or in commercials, brands have become familiar, friendly and close, a source of empathy, even of loyalty and attachment. To maintain the strength of brands, it is vital to nourish the two pillars which make the relationship with the brand: one cognitive, the other emotional. Innovation serves precisely this purpose. It enables the brand to differentiate itself objectively and to draw once again the market's attention.

With time, it is noticeable that perceived differences erode faster than the emotional relationship. The liking persists even though we can see that the brand no longer has a monopoly over performance. A study conducted by the American agency, Young & Rubicam, is a reminder of this psychological fact. The survey, called Brand Asset Monitor and conducted on 2,000 brands worldwide,

situates them against two facets of their relationship: cognitive and emotional (bearing in mind the fact that during the growth of the brand, the first facet precedes the second). The customer learns through communication and distribution the existence of a brand before grasping its difference, which then leads to its pertinence. In the meantime, the seeds of familiarity and esteem have been sown, reminding us that prompted brand awareness precedes spontaneous awareness and that the latter is correlated with the emotional evaluation. The brands that come to mind spontaneously, as they belong to this group, also happen to be our favourite brands.

As shown by Figure 10.2, the decline of a brand, however, begins with a slide in the level of perceived difference between it and the competition and, in particular, with the opinion leaders of the product category. The esteem and the emotional ties are still alive and well, but the consumer realises that the quality gap has been bridged between the brand and its competition. He still likes it but may now become disloyal!

The benefit of this study is to underscore that

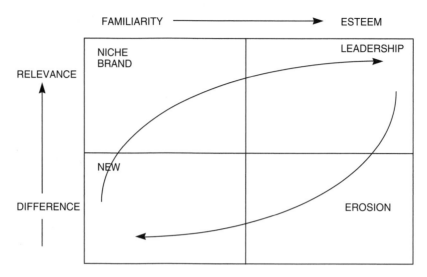

Figure 10.2 Paths of brand growth and decline

the drop in differentiation signals the beginning of the decline, however strong the liking score may be. Unfortunately, many leaders are no longer considered as the qualitative reference of their branch. We like Lotus, Kleenex, brands that we have known since childhood, but we no longer think that they are the sign of superior product quality. They will have to refocus on the product to regain their leadership. The Coke vs Pepsi duel in the United States is a good example of this. One often reduces the struggle between the two giants to a battle of advertising budget size. Actually, Coca-Cola's philosophy lies in the so-called 3A principle: Availability, Affordability and Awareness. Coca-Cola must be within reach everywhere, cheap and on one's mind. Another phrase sums up Coca-Cola's ambitions: 'To be the best, cheapest soft drink in the world' (Pendergrast, 1993). What is exactly the strategy deployed by Pepsi-Cola? As it could not compete in the communication, sponsoring, animation and promotion race it focused on product and price. Pepsi-Cola has always tried to improve its taste to fit as best it could the evolution in the taste of the American public. This is what founded the very aggressive advertising campaigns from 1975 onwards, such as the 'Take the Pepsi challenge', where surprised customers

found they preferred the taste of Pepsi in a blind test. Moreover, Pepsi has always sought to be a couple of cents cheaper than Coca-Cola. The strategy proved effective: we know it forced Coca-Cola to change its formula in 1985 so as not to take the risk of being surpassed in taste. This was the famous episode concerning New Coke.

How do you preserve the superior image of a brand, this capital of perceived difference?

▌ One way is to renew the product regularly, to upgrade it to the current level of expectation. This is why Volkswagen introduced the Golf, then Golf 2, 3, 4, 5 and 6. Detergent manufacturers make minor adjustments every two years or so, and make major changes in their formula every five years. This is how Ariel and Skip maintain their qualitative leadership, making them both the two most expensive brands and the leaders on the market. Moreover, for want of financial means, DOBs cannot keep up in the R&D race, a race which can become an obsession.

▌ A second way is to integrate new and emerging needs while holding onto the same positioning. In doing so, any car brand, even if it is not specifically positioned on safety as is Volvo, must from now on show that it is equally concerned with security and even the environment.

- A third way is to constantly confirm one's superiority by extending the line. A brand of shampoo treating hair loss should rapidly propose line extensions covering the different needs of people suffering from this problem – creams, lotions and so on. These extensions demonstrate the concern of the brand to address as best it can the different aspects of the problem on which it focuses and to affirm its leadership by becoming the reference linked to the need.

- The fourth way lies in adapting to one's own customers who themselves change and become more experienced. Line extensions should propose new products adapted to their more sophisticated needs, to prevent them from trying the competition.

Jacob's Creek is a good example of this. Over 20 years, from 1984 to 2004, the UK became a wine-drinking country. Consumption per capita was raised from a low 7 litres per person per year to more than 21 litres. This was the result, as ever, of three converging forces:

- Multiple grocers realised that this new category was very attractive. They wished to made it a 'destination category'.

- Consumers travelling in Europe or Australia tried wine and wished to pursue the experience back home.

- New players understood the UK consumer better than existing competition did, and the New World wine makers understood them best of all. Jacob's Creek introduced its first two varieties in 1986 (a dry red and a dry white): it is now the UK's number one bottled wine brand (see page 52).

New drinkers are fast learners. Thanks to the magic of wine, they want to flex their newly acquired wine appreciation muscles and explore the category. Soon they wanted to discard their former simplistic brands in search of new experiences. This consumer maturity was soon perceived as a potential threat by Jacob's Creek, which it met by introducing gradual line extensions. A permanently renewed top range of special limited series was designed to keep up with opinion leaders' expectations (Parker's wine guide, wine buffs, restaurants), and a number of sub-brands based on more complex grape varietals were designed to keep customers and at the same time demonstrate the competence of the brand, as a true leader should. Jacob's Creek extended its line upwards: prices in 2004 ranged from a basic £4.59 to £6.99 for sparkling wine and even £8.99 for a rare reserve Shiraz.

In the banking sector, credit cards are constantly launching extensions to satisfy a customer base which, over time, is becoming more affluent and expects increasingly high-performance service and insurance products. After Visa came Visa Premier, followed by Visa Infinite. With their very low cost but high perceived value, innovations generate revenue for the entire chain, starting with the broker and continuing to the bank which promotes the product to certain segments of its clientèle, thus increasing the profitability of each customer. In addition, it produces a feeling of exclusivity among carriers of the most expensive cards, a feeling which is destroyed by the spread of so-called 'standard' cards. This is the typical American Express strategy.

Investing in communication

In 2002, the Danone group undertook a significant move. It decided to increase significantly (by over 20 per cent) the media budget of its strongest brands. Since then, their share of voice and market leadership have increased. Similarly the whole l'Oréal success story is based on two pillars: research and advertising.

Communication is the brand's weapon. It alone can unveil what is invisible, reveal the basic differences hidden by the packaging which often looks the same among competitors, especially when this similarity is precisely the impression sought by DOBs to create confusion. It alone can sustain the attachment to the brand, by promoting intangible values, even if this loyalty is eroded by many in-store promotions. Advertising is a result of the rise of self-service distribution and reductions in the numbers of salespeople. It is the necessary consequence of investments in R&D that have to pay off ever faster and therefore need an ever bigger public. That this has to be repeated over and over is the proof that there is a confusion in people's minds about the legitimacy of advertising, even within marketing teams, and is why we will use numbers to back our statements.

As Figure 10.3 demonstrates, there is a linear relationship between the penetration of DOBs and the extent of advertising expenditure in a market, measured in percentage of sales spent on advertising. Advertising is a barrier to entry. However, upon examining the product categories, it becomes clear that the categories with a high investment in advertising are also those that invest in innovations and renovations, which are perfect opportunities for re-establishing the saliency of the brand in the public consciousness. It is the conjunction of these two factors (innovation and advertising) that produces added value.

The role of advertising in defending and sustaining the brand capital is shown by Table 10.1. With the exception of jam, where there is much consumption by children and the idealised reference to home-made jam favours small brands, advertising is quite efficient. Once more, we may notice that the categories that invest heavily in advertising are also

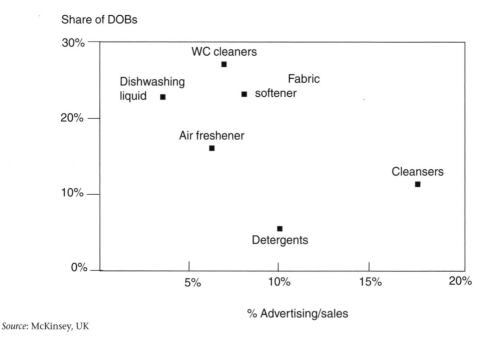

Source: McKinsey, UK

Figure 10.3 Penetration of distributors' brands and advertising intensity

Table 10.1 Advertising weight of trade brands' penetration

	Advertising sales ratio %	Trade brand market share %
Cereals	10	15
Detergents	8	11
Coffee	8	13
Jam	7	47
Butter	5	6
Soft drinks	5	20
Tea	5	26
Yoghurts	2	39
Cider	2	36
Fish	0.7	26
Wine	0.5	61

Source: McKinsey, UK

those that regularly innovate and strongly differentiate their products.

No one is free from price comparisons

Even if innovation and advertising do increase added value, loyalty at all costs does not exist. Customers can be both sensitive to the brand but disloyal to it, estimating that the price of the brand goes beyond the price span that they are willing to pay for the product category, and beyond the brand premium that seems reasonable to them given the added satisfaction which is expected. Distributors also have the same attitude.

During years of economic growth, the biggest brands were tempted to regularly increase their prices to maximise the overall profit accruing from a strong price premium and a large batch of loyal clients. For financial directors concerned about showing ever-increasing profits, what does a price increase of a few pence or cents per unit represent? For the market, however, it now has the utmost importance. In April 1993, one of the most famous brands, Marlboro, noting a slump in

sales, was the first to put into reverse this inclination by unilaterally lowering its prices in the United States. Wall Street reacted badly, thinking the bell was tolling for brands: on that day the stocks of all consumer goods companies dropped significantly. More than a year later, in August 1994, Marlboro's market share reached unprecedented heights (29.1 per cent), seven points more than in March of 1993 just before the famous 'Marlboro Friday'. In France 10 years ago, Philip Morris decided to bring down the price of Chesterfields from 11.60F to 10F at at time when competitors were preparing to pass on to customers the 15 per cent tax increase imposed by the government. Within two months the sales of Chesterfields jumped by 300 per cent. The market share of the brand went from less than 1 per cent to 12.2 per cent in two years. It became, in a year, the favourite cigarette for young people (71 per cent of buyers were under 25).

One may recall that Procter & Gamble significantly reduced the price of its brands in the United States in accordance with its brand-boosting programme, thanks to the allocation of part of the savings accruing from an impressive programme to increase industrial productivity, marketing and sales. These price reductions were part of the EDLP (Every Day Low Price) policy which put an end to the myriad of micro-promotions.

These price reductions show that the brand has to stay within the core of the market if it wants to continue. This was discovered by European car manufacturers after first the Japanese and now the Korean invasion: they forced all car OEM (original equipment manufacturers) suppliers to reduce their prices by 20 per cent. Portable computer manufacturers also know that they must both innovate and reduce their prices. Indeed, the price premium that pays for the superior added value is a differential concept. It says nothing of the standard, the reference level of the brand with which it is to compare. But nowadays in many markets this standard is falling in absolute value. If hard-discounters spread through Europe as they have in Germany, they can impose in certain sectors their own levels of price and quality as the standard that the branded products have to reckon with when setting their price levels. If brands leave their price premiums unchanged, they will not be able to hold their ground.

The preceding argument is *a fortiori* valid if the price premium is higher than the perceived added value of the brand. The brand then gets into a niche at a high-end segment of the market and watches its volume drop. As is shown in Figure 10.4, the latent savings unexploited by industrialists could represent up to 30 per cent of costs. It is true that part of the benefits linked to the product are sometimes not valued by customers or that the upgrade in production costs is not worth it in the customers' eyes. There is more to be gained by suppressing these costs and finding a new price competitiveness again. Besides, trade-off analyses demonstrate that the logic of 'bigger and better' can be counterproductive if it entails an increase in price. Beyond a certain performance threshold, utility slumps. There are also acceptable price thresholds: the rule for home computers is to always give the client more as long as the retail price does not go beyond the US$2,000 barrier.

The analysis carried out by OC&C has, however, two limits. First, it neglects, as do most economic analyses, the perceived value of the reputation and image of the brand: a brand does not only bring a product benefit.

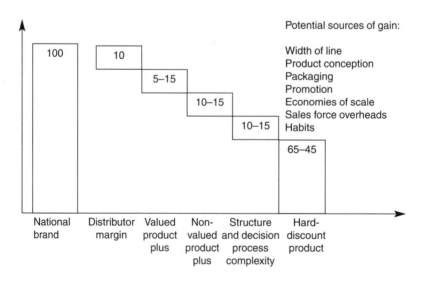

Figure 10.4 Sources of price difference between brands and hard-discount products

Second, it is not obvious that price leaders set the standard price that will be the reference for customers when they compare prices. It all depends on the level of involvement of the customer and of the perceived difference! For years, low-priced colas existed but attracted no consumers. Only recently have the Sainsbury's and Virgin colas been able to challenge Coca-Cola. Creating a large shelf space for price-leader detergents will not in itself create a significant sales volume: the quality reference is set by Skip and Ariel. Customers know they are not getting the same quality when, for want of buying power, they fall back onto secondary brands and *a fortiori* on unknown brands. At the other end, the Viva milk created by Candia, far from being perceived as a premium product, has become the milk that all milks should be like, the standard for milk, both modern and advanced. There are indeed other price-leader milks, but they are considered ordinary and lacking in character.

Any price decrease, if it does occur, should not therefore be conducted in comparison with the cheapest product of the category but with the products in the same segment aiming at the same need. The so-called 'trammel-hook analysis' (Degon, 1994) demonstrates empirically that the brands which are successful are most of the time those that have the lowest price within their own segment. To return to the Chesterfield case in France, the brand was withdrawn as early as 1988 from the declining segment of upmarket Virginia cigarettes (Marlboro, Stuyvesant, Rothmans) to be positioned in the segment just under it, that of 'popular Virginia cigarettes' (Lucky Strike, Gauloises Blondes). By pricing its pack at €1.5, it became the cheapest alternative within this segment and quickly became the leader. Since then, the brand has had to increase its price due to budgetary constraints from the government, but has kept this price positioning.

As a conclusion, a decrease in price has never in itself solved the problem of making

sure a brand lasts. It does not increase added-value but reduces costs. Moreover, a decrease in price on the part of the leader has important consequences in the long term: it will jeopardise the profitability of the whole sector for 20 years to come. The leader should instead aim either to retrieve the standard of quality that the customer knows he is leaving behind if he chooses a cheaper product, or to enlarge the market. But to do this the company must invest: lowering prices too much will make financing this effort impossible.

Branding is an art at retail

Where marketing is concerned, he who is in contact with the end-user often has a decisive edge. This is a major handicap for manufacturers who are not in control of their distribution network. It may be an illusion to consider that you can bypass supermarkets to sell significant food brands, but this is not the case for many other outlets. Selective distribution is such an example. The evolution of European Union law on selective distribution networks has substituted qualitative criteria for the old quantitative criteria linked to minimum volume quotas.

In the case of Levi's, the brand is quite selective in its distribution. While not permitting the sale of its products to supermarkets, Levi's expects its retailers to respect five criteria:

▌ the first one has to do with the offer range: the latter must comprise quality clothing and only brands that are recognised by the customer where jeans are concerned (therefore no price-leader or anonymous jeans);

▌ the environment must be as high quality as the offer;

▌ product ranges that could alter the image of Levi's must not be found close by;

▌ the service must be in tune with the brand

and the staff must be adequate and competent in the field of clothing;

▌ last of all, the shop must be part of a fixed construction (not a market stall) with adequate space reserved for jeans and capable of attracting youths aged 15 to 25.

Through this mastery of the channel, Levi's is, in fact, controlling its image and preserving its brand capital. A brand cannot be narrowed down to its advertising and to its products, it involves the customer in the purchasing act and even thereafter. This is also the strength of Benetton, Ikea, Häagen Dazs and Louis Vuitton. Coca-Cola itself does indeed have to contend with competitors in supermarkets and even with copies from distributors. But the reputation of a soft drink is enhanced by its distribution in cafés, hotels, restaurants and nightclubs. Moreover, the Coca-Cola company offers a wide range of non-colas that make it an exclusive distributor at the sales outlet. Hence, where there is Coca-Cola there usually is neither Pepsi Cola nor any product from Cadbury Schweppes.

Creating entry barriers

This last example draws attention to the importance of entry barriers in sound brand management: offering a full portfolio of brands helps the Coca-Cola Company extend its dominance, outlet by outlet. The bar owners and restaurant operating companies are satisfied: they can offer their clients a full range of famous soft drink brands, and in addition they often receive bonuses from Coca-Cola for providing full exclusivity to the whole Coca-Cola portfolio. (This was the source of lawsuits in Europe by the other soft drink companies.)

By focusing exclusively on the consumer's psychology, brand analysis has overlooked the crucial role of the management of the offer itself, which can make it impossible for competitors to enter on the market. This is one of the key questions in the analysis of the financial value of a brand, of the present value of its future profits. The impenetrability of the market is the best warranty for the latter, and the example of Black & Decker is quite revealing.

Why are there hardly any DOBs in the drilling machine market? Because Black & Decker makes it economically impossible for them to enter the market. DOBs sprout up when one or more of the following conditions are fulfilled:

▌ there is a high volume in the market;

▌ there is little product innovation;

▌ brands are expensive;

▌ customers perceive little risk;

▌ customers make their choice essentially according to the visible characteristics of the product;

▌ technology is accessible at low cost.

Much to the contrary, the market for drills is small, and moreover is cut up into many segments. Black & Decker drives the market and makes it develop at a fast technological pace. In addition, Black & Decker has globalised its production: each plant produces one single product for the worldwide market. The production cost level thus becomes unbeatable, and as Black & Decker is not overkeen to increase its retail price, it does not leave much room for copycats to manoeuvre. Lastly, the customer feels safe when buying such a well-known and ubiquitous brand.

What are the main sources of entry barriers?

▌ The cost of the factors of production is the most important, which leads to a long-lasting competitive advantage. This is the strategy of Dell, and also of Decathlon, the world's fifth largest sports goods retailer and eleventh largest producer. Decathlon may become for some sports the European number one manufacturer far ahead of any others because of the economies of scale accruing from its products developed at a European level.

- Mastering technology and quality is a key success factor for Procter & Gamble, Gillette, l'Oréal and 3M. Turning down any offer to yield an iota of their know-how to DOBs, these companies keep for themselves their main added-value leverage. This is what enables them to constantly innovate and to remain the reference of the market in terms of quality. Kellogg's even goes to the extent of indicating on its boxes that it does not supply DOBs.

- Domination through image and communication is Coca-Cola's mainstay, although it does not hinder a K-Mart or a Sainsbury brand cola from borrowing as much as possible the distinctive signs of Coke and selling at a lower price. In hard times, sensitivity to price is exacerbated. But as a worldwide brand, Coca-Cola had access to the sponsoring of the Olympic Games in Atlanta and was able to pass on the benefits to bottlers worldwide. This is also the weapon of Nike, Reebok and Adidas. Domination as a result of their fame and image is not solely a result of the titanic size of these companies' budgets. Focusing all their communications on the name itself and applying a brand extension logic beyond the initial segment, many brands are thus able to dominate in brand awareness.

- Quickly using up all the aspects of a promising concept through range extension is a method that hinders the entry of competitors. In the United States, and in Europe, the Snapple brand is surfing on the wave of so-called 'New Age' drinks and offers a wide variety of tea-based soft drinks. Dim, as we have seen, was quick to offer under one hosiery brand name a wide range of products covering different needs

and satisfying distributors' and customers' expectations. In the agricultural market, it is possible to count the different kinds of Decis (the leader in insecticides) according to the type of plant, thus reinforcing the worldwide leader status of this brand.

- Putting a name on a product in itself yields a uniqueness of offer and an added value that competitors will lack. All the giants of the chemical industry produce elastane, a fibre that makes stockings and foundation garments soft and shiny. On the other hand, only Du Pont de Nemours had Lycra, a fibre whose name in itself is used as a sales ploy by Du Pont and by all lingerie brands. Actually, Lycra was the trademark used by Du Pont to sell elastane. It is not the name in itself which added value to the fibre: it is 10 years of worldwide communication about the glamour linked to the Lycra name which gave the brand its exclusive attractiveness. The same strategy applies to Gore-Tex and Coolmax.

- Controlling the relationship with opinion leaders is one of the key success factors for a brand looking to the future. Canson, a school-supplies brand which is part of the Arjomari-Wiggins group, provides an illustration. What is more natural than a sheet of tracing paper or drawing paper for a schoolchild? However, despite the share of supermarket shelf space given to DOBs' drawing and tracing paper, only that of Canson sells. For more than 20 years the brand has developed a close relationship with teachers, for instance organising drawing competitions between classes on a national level. The long-lasting presence of Canson on a child's shopping list for school supplies is due to the excellence of what is now called relationship marketing. The main asset of Canson is its loyal teachers within the public education system.

- Controlling distribution is also a major handicap for new entrants. McDonald's will soon have 1,000 restaurants in France, and Quick, the second largest burger chain, will have 350. This sheer number closes the hamburger market off to competition. Mass-distribution brands also freely use this barrier to entry: by imposing their own brand on the shelf, they thus exclude manufacturer's brands. The ice-cream maker Häagen Dazs does indeed control the market of upmarket ice creams through the provision of a high-quality ice cream and through a well-managed word-of-mouth campaign from opinion leaders, but most of all through its own exclusive refrigerator present in all supermarkets and hypermarkets.

The last barrier to entry is based on legality. The brand must defend its exclusive image against counterfeit products, models or signs. It should not hesitate to defend the exclusive character of its distinctive signs against imitations and distributors' copycat brands. The latter, under the pretence that these are signs of the category, actually try to make their brands benefit from the value of signs developed by the leading brand. The imitations of Coca-Cola try to get as close as possible to the red that Coca-Cola has with time associated with its quality. Beyond the deliberate sought-after confusion, which leads the customer, if he or she is not careful, to mistake the copy for the original, the similarity between the signs induces a perception of equivalence (Kapferer, 1995). Just as Dior, Chanel and Cartier invest heavily in lawsuits against counterfeiter networks, the brands must sue imitators or, at least, state to them that they will tolerate no imitations or copying. From this point of view, the brands which from the start chose non-descriptive signs withstand the test of time and imitation better. The Orangina label is blue: it is not a generic colour and protects this orange-flavoured soft drink brand well.

Defending against brand counterfeiting

As soon as a brand starts to enjoy success, it is imitated: copies appear and multiply. The competitive advantages offered by innovation are short-term only, and this is why today's brand is built on the continual flow of innovation. Ideas, concepts and products can all be the subject of imitation. For example, shortly after the launch of a peach-flavoured low-alcohol drink named Carlton, targeting the top end of the range, lower-cost competitors such as Claridge began to appear. Competition is even more intense where it applies to intellectual property: this includes patents and designs, but also trade dress, and even trademarks (the name or pictorial image of the brand). This imitation stems from producers and retailers whose imitation of the leader is the first step towards building a store brand (see page 79).

It also comes from counterfeiting. Top-of-the-range brands such as Nike and Adidas, as well as various luxury brands, are directly targeted in this way. The markets and bazaars of foreign countries are filled with fake Cartier watches and Ralph Lauren polo shirts. No sooner has a Dior or Chanel fashion show finished than Asian factories begin to reproduce their designs, introducing them into parallel distribution channels even before the brand itself has sent out stock. More dangerous still is the practice of counterfeiting medicines or automobile spare parts, which can often deceive customers and potentially put lives at risk. Lastly, we have already discussed protection against brand imitations conducted by the brand's own retailers (see page 87).

Intellectual property must be defended and extended (for example, Harley-Davidson has patented the characteristic sound of its engines, as has Porsche). It is not our intention here to cover in a few lines a subject as important and strategic as trademark laws, particularly since, with the advent of globalisation, it is becoming obvious that not all countries have the same sensibilities when it comes to counterfeiting. In China, South-East Asia, Morocco and Italy, a considerable number of micro-companies make a living in this way. It is always more or less directly linked to money laundering, and sometimes receives covert government protection. Such divergent attitudes allow brands that could not legally exist in the West (or any country that upholds intellectual property laws) to become established. Everyone in Singapore, Hong Kong and Shanghai is familiar with the Crocodile store chain, an obvious imitation of the world-famous Lacoste brand, whose symbol since 1933 has been its famous crocodile. The Asian store chain has exploited lax local brand laws to position itself in Lacoste's slipstream: it even goes so far as to boast in its slogan, 'Enter the legend'.

The basic precautions to be taken in order to avoid losing protection rights for one's brand are well known. For example, never use the trademark as a noun, but as an adjective: in other words, we should say a Budweiser beer, not just a Budweiser. Let us also add that if a brand colour is to be protected, it too requires protection within the company. Brand product lines are frequently segmented, which leads to the use of different colours to identify each segment. As a result, it becomes harder to maintain that a brand is characterised by any one single colour.

How should the brand respond to counterfeiting and imitation? First, we should identify the difference between the two types of attack. Counterfeiting is the identical, trait-for-trait imitation of the brand and its identifying components: it is unlawful in the most direct sense, and there is no need to provide evidence of customer confusion. It simply needs to be identified, and legal action taken. However, longer-term work is necessary in a number of countries where it is more than simply tolerated, and indeed often accepted:

- Joint action aimed at the Ministries of Foreign Affairs and Justice. This works at the level of inter-state relationships.

- Collective information programmes to improve local laws directed at, for example, world trade organisation.

- Advertising for the original brand in the country in question. The extent of the phenomenon of counterfeiting in China, where there are no laws over brands, is well known. Chinese culture traditionally praises those who share, and condemns those who do not. Faithful reproduction of the master's work is a virtue in traditional Chinese education and teaching. Lastly, in the communist economy that dominated the Chinese way of thinking for 50 years, the notion of property itself did not exist, and it was common for all Chinese factories to go under the same name. We should add that counterfeits are the only financially accessible option for local consumers. Lastly, in these countries, after years of deprivation in terms of consumption, people are keen to show their neighbours they have finally 'made it'. Western brands are familiar to all, but very few actually have first-hand experience of them: they are unaware that what they are buying is a fake. Research has confirmed this point (Lai and Zaichkowsky, 1999): local consumers who choose a counterfeit or an imitation do so because they lack knowledge of the original.

- Counterfeit-related advertising in tourists' countries of origin. Western consumers are well aware which products are the originals: imitations and counterfeits are a game for them. Our own qualitative research of the phenomenon reveals five underlying motives for them to buy a counterfeit:
  - The sense of having obtained a bargain. After all, everyone knows that luxury goods and Nike products are made in third-world factories. Such consumers

deny there is any difference in quality between the original and the copy: they are therefore getting a bargain. This makes them very discriminating buyers: they will only buy copies of Vuitton bags that are 'identical' to the original, and they admire the quality of the copy. It is this quality, combined with the price, that makes it 'a real saving' and enables them to wear or carry the copy on a daily basis, even while with friends, who will not spot the difference. A buyer of a fake Bulgari watch – which is of very good quality compared with the genuine article he himself wears – will not hesitate to give it to one of his sons as a fifteenth-birthday present.

Revealingly enough, the buyers themselves often own the original product. This is what qualifies them as experts and lends status to the copy chosen for the quality of its resemblance. They know what they are talking about.

- The desire to put a little sparkle into everyday life. Fake Ralph Lauren polo shirts may be only approximate copies, but they are good enough for tasks such as housework, gardening or cleaning the car.
- An original present. Instead of going to Thailand and bringing back cheap knick-knacks as gifts which will immediately be hidden away in a drawer, a tourist buys friends what is these days a typical item from that country: a good imitation, a counterfeit scarcely distinguishable from the original. It will always surprise the recipient and lead to conversations about how well made (or not) the counterfeit is; furthermore, it is bound to be used.
- Some consumers willingly buy counterfeits because they cannot or will not pay the price differential for an original. They consider it ridiculous and pointless to pay €60 for a Ralph Lauren polo shirt, because they are not sufficiently involved.

- Lastly, some buyers of counterfeits are motivated by 'moral' considerations. They believe that the price of the original is scandalously high because, considering that it was made in a South-East Asian factory, the cost price of the product is actually infinitesimally small. They consider their actions as just retribution: given that the brand itself has committed theft by selling at a price way above its cost price, it is legitimate to steal it in return.

Preventive action with Western consumers in their country of origin takes the form of education. It needs to be pointed out that counterfeiting is linked to Mafia-style networks and the laundering of drug money. There is also a legal side: a consumer bringing back a counterfeit product is an accomplice, and is thus committing a crime punishable by law.

Brand equity versus customer equity: one needs the other

There is a debate about what is most important: customer equity or brand equity. This is a rather vain dispute. Loyalty bought through loyalty cards, rebates and gifts is a cost. Certainly it creates returns, but brands also need to nurture true love. On the other hand, CRM does help brands to demonstrate that they love customers and want to help them, and assist them quickly and efficiently. Both aspects interact.

Even luxury brands have created customer databases so that the travelling shopper is recognised in any shop of any city. CRM also lets companies make sales propositions by e-mail, in a way that is very customised and matches the customer's personal profile.

The financial value of a brand is a function of the amount of its future expected return and of the degree of risk on these returns. A brand can only be strong if it has a strong supply of loyal customers. This established fact led to a revolution in the practice of marketing, under way since the beginning of the 1980s: the major concern is loyalty and its related factor, client satisfaction. Leaving behind an approach which implicitly concentrated on conquering clients away from the competition, firms now do all they can to keep their own clients. This is to be expected at a time when, as a result of the abundance of offers, buyers tend to jump from one brand to the next, from one manufacturer to the next. Rather than zero defaults, the aim is zero defections.

A lifetime client at British Airways brings on average £48,000 to the company in revenues. Thus under no circumstance should one customer be lost. It is the same for Carrefour where a loyal client brings £3,550 in annual sales. Besides, loyal clients are more profitable. According to a study from the Bain company, a household spends €330 per month in the supermarket to which it goes most often, 85 in the second most frequent and 22 for the one where it only goes occasionally. And not only do loyal clients spend more, but their expenditure grows with time, they become less sensitive to price and they are the source of positive word-of-mouth reports concerning their favoured supermarket or brand. Moreover, they are five times less costly to contact than non-clients. That is why, also according to Bain, by lowering the defection rate of clients by 5 per cent, benefits go up 25 to 85 per cent. The example of Canal Plus is significant: this pay-TV channel benefits from an unprecedented loyalty rate: 97 per cent of its 6 million clients are loyal to it. Bearing in mind that a yearly subscription costs €310, if the loyalty drops by as little as 1 per cent, it would mean €11 million less in annual revenues!

All strong brands are currently establishing loyalty programmes. Nevertheless, a cautionary remark is necessary: no programme of this kind will make up for a service that is not adapted or sufficient. The actions required to keep loyal customers have two aims: the first is defensive, to give the customer no reason for leaving the brand or the company; the other is offensive, to create a personalised relationship with the client, the basis of a more intimate and therefore more involving bond, what Americans call 'Customer bonding' (Cross and Smith, 1994).

The essential part of the defensive side is the identification of the causes of disloyalty and dissatisfied clients. Thus, dissatisfaction linked to the food provided induces, because of disloyalty, a loss in revenue amounting to £5 million pounds at British Airways. The dissatisfaction linked to bad seating costs close to £20 million! Paradoxically enough, the company seeks to get as many voiced dissatisfactions as possible. Indeed, the worst thing is a silent dissatisfied client who, saying nothing to the company representatives, spreads negative rumours among his relatives, colleagues and friends. And there are statistics to prove that a dissatisfied client who is well treated becomes a real proselyte, and even more loyal into the bargain. When asked if they will fly with British Airways again, the rate is 64 per cent 'yes' among those that have never contacted the complaints office. It is, however, 84 per cent among those who have. The treatment of complaints with diligence, care and respect becomes a key lever in customer loyalty.

Seeking client satisfaction implies adding a touch of management spirit where spirit of conquest reigns exclusively. This is why l'Oréal Coiffure is nowadays a company with a conquering as well as an innovative and entrepreneurial spirit. It launches new products one after the other. Hairdressers like the l'Oréal products and l'Oréal knows their product needs well. Unfortunately, this led the firm to somewhat overlook the management spirit: some deliveries were wrong, stockouts occurred, discounts were unevenly granted, etc. The firm responded well to sophisticated needs but somewhat forgot some of the more down-to-earth needs. The hairdresser who put in an order on Tuesday for a tube of light golden brown colouring for a client coming on Friday could not be sure it would be there on time. He could not always count on the company. That is why even when its product launchings were successful, and even if customers were attracted, the sales of l'Oréal Coiffure stagnated for a while. When focusing on client satisfaction, the product alone is not sufficient if the basic service is deficient.

When going over to the offensive, a brand must become a landmark of personal attention. More emphatically, Rapp and Collins (1994) talk of becoming a 'loving company', interested not in the client but in the person. This marks the end of anonymous marketing: attention has to be customised if it is to be efficient. But it has to be acknowledged that even if the terminology of market studies distinguishes between big, medium and small customers, up until recently few companies had developed programmes designed specifically for big customers, who as a rule are also the most loyal. But the loyal client wants to be recognised. He or she therefore has to be identified, a direct bond has to be established and he or she should be the focus of special attention. This is why what is commonly called relationship marketing (McKenna, 1991; Marconi, 1994) uses databases, customers' clubs and collective events, which unite the best customers of the brand. Moreover, realising that a brand that does not have direct contact with customers becomes further and further out of reach – literally as well as figuratively – many brands have stepped out of mere television advertising and off the shelves to establish a direct relationship with customers. Nestlé offers to its customers a dietician, reachable by phone. Six days a week, Nintendo helps out 10,000 children who are stuck in a video game. As long ago as 1992, IBM France created an assistance hotline working around the clock seven days a week all-year-round. Treating clients as friends instead of accounts is the basis to a long-lasting relationship.

In their efforts to increase brand loyalty, brand companies have realised that they have to care about their customer equity or market share. In other words, these companies should focus not only on augmenting brand preference as a mental attitude, but also on increasing brand usage, especially among the best customer prospects: the heavy buyers. Recent findings, for example, recognise that mass market brand profits come not from the mass market, but from the top third of category buyers. Furthermore, a brand's greatest potential for additional profit rests on its ability to increase share in this high-profit, heavy-buyer category (Hallberg, 1995).

Unfortunately, advertising misses the mark with these prime prospects. Instead, it reaches mostly non-buyers or small-quantity buyers. On the other hand, promotions *do* touch the high-profit segment. That is, frequent buyers are more likely to encounter price promotions, coupons, rebates, etc. However, promotions over-sensitise consumers to price and tend to decrease brand loyalty in the high-potential, high-profit segment.

As a consequence, most mega-brands are now experimenting with database marketing on a grand scale. The database marketing concept is two-fold:

- All marketing actions should target the prime segment more effectively. The goal is to increase this segment's rate of brand use.

- Effective targeting requires companies to identify each of these customers or households, almost nominally. As a consequence, a by-product of all promotional activities should be a database, ultimately comprising 100 per cent of the high-profit customers.

At this time Procter & Gamble's database in the USA holds more than 48 million names. Danone's database in France holds 2 million names. Nestlé is building its own in each major country, as is Unilever. And this ignores all the broker-created databases for rental to smaller companies.

The function of these selective databases is to deliver customised offers to specific targets, to bring the store shelf to the home (thus decreasing impulse buying and distributors' power), and to promote a 'private image' among loyal and heavy-user customers. Generally, these customers are more involved in the brand, so they deserve recognition and special treatment. They also merit specific information to nourish brand image and equity. These activities constitute the nurturing of a 'private image', as opposed to a broader, general public image.

Many consumers hold very favourable attitudes *vis-à-vis* particular brands. Nevertheless, their loyalty is insufficient to inhibit switching within a repertoire of brands. These customers are potential loyals only if a tailor-made programme is devised to increase the rate of purchase of a particular brand. On the other hand, some repeat buyers are actually pseudo-loyals: they do not hold strong attitudes regarding the brand. Perhaps, for instance, they buy the brand because of its price or availability. To increase their brand preference, these buyers require a reinforcement of their choice and an increased perception of the brand's superiority. Finally, active and committed loyals should be induced to try more and more new products, whether line or brand extensions. Figure 10.5 illustrates Sony's situation, where committed loyals comprise 19 per cent of Sony's entire customer franchise. The potential loyals represent 4 per cent, and the pseudo-loyals 35 per cent. Each group deserves a specific marketing proposition.

The customer demand for dialogue

Although most brands claim to put customers' needs first, this does not extend to creating a dialogue with them. Advertising does not count as dialogue. Neither does a relationship with a seller with clear marketing intentions, and neither do satisfaction questionnaires: they may be very useful in obtaining feedback on perceived quality, but a series of questions does not constitute a dialogue. Do consumer magazines provide a dialogue? Once again, no. And the same is true of direct marketing mailshots from sellers inviting consumers to see or try out a new product, and the like.

Source: Sofres, Megabrand system

Figure 10.5   Brand capital and customer capital: matching preferences and purchase behaviour

Why do we say 'customer demand'? Because customers want to be valued, listened to and heard, and not merely as an averaged-out statistic in a market segment, but for themselves as individuals. Furthermore, the new internet firms, with their ability to amass 'intelligent' information (which learns from the most recent call, person by person) and use this information in future contacts, have made them accustomed to a responsive reaction and a listening ear.

A relationship with a brand automatically creates a need of this kind. Take banks and insurance companies, for example. Once the customer has initially been won over, the brand–client rapport will last for years. There are bound to be problems along the way, but if these are managed well, the result may be lasting loyalty. The problem is that they are often not managed well, and negative word of mouth can be the only means of retribution available to customers who feel ignored, or treated with contempt. Indeed, the retailer is not only the brand's best ally when things are going well; it can also become its worst enemy when problems arise. It is the enemy of the brand because it is perceived as the enemy of the customer. We believe that at such a time, the customer should have direct access to the brand itself, its ultimate recourse.

Saturn – the recent automobile brand created in the United States by GM as a response to Japanese brands – was a pioneer in customer relations. Following the example it set, every new buyer – whether large or small – should be given the name and telephone number of a brand employee who can if necessary be contacted by the customer in the event of unresolved problems. This is the real one-to-one relationship, and is what customers expect above all else when problems occur. The brand cannot delegate crisis management to third parties.

Without becoming the enemy of its own selective network, the brand must assume a benevolent 'the buck stops here' attitude, eager to find a solution for the customer. After all, the customer has bought a brand, not a retailer. Furthermore, what is the point in conducting customer intimacy operations and public relations exercises if, the minute a real need presents itself, the brand suddenly becomes distant and fails to return the customer's calls? The 'boomerang' effect is the only possible outcome here.

This demand for dialogue explains why brands seem as real media themselves. They create blogs, sites, forums not to sell but to let their customers and advocates or detractors speak freely together. They also outsource the many call centres to provide a really quick and relevant answer to all incoming demands.

Is relational marketing profitable?

Customer relations are certainly a good idea, but are they profitable? Here again, we must reconcile the brand (the creation of value) with the economic equation. Convincing statistics abound with regard to the profitability of loyal customers. However, studies also show that most customers who become disloyal to a brand were previously very satisfied with the brand: their requirements have simply changed. Another way of looking at these figures is to conclude that the customers' attachment – their desire to stay with the brand – cannot have been especially high to start with. This is where relational marketing comes in.

Attachment to a brand is evidence of a customer's desire to stay in a lasting relationship with the brand. This attachment is characterised by loyalty, which is a behavioural measure of repeat purchasing. Loyalty may be a consequence of attachment, but it can also be generated by means of bonuses and so-called 'loyalty cards'. Attachment to a brand is a one-dimensional concept of varying strength. Its opposite state is detachment, indifference and non-involvement.

Attachment is a different thing altogether from satisfaction. This is why attachments can be mainly rational (a desire to continue the relationship with the brand because it meets the buyer's implicit requirements, albeit without generating any real emotional involvement). Conversely, some customers remain very attached despite considerable dissatisfaction with the product or service (the Harley-Davidson/Jaguar syndrome).

Research has identified six sources of attachment. As we shall see, each of these points to specific levers for managerial action:

▌ Attachment based on the hedonistic satisfaction conferred by the use of the products and by the quality of the interaction with the brand's representatives (network, call centre and so on).

▌ Attachment based on the quality of the relationship established by the brand: appreciation of the individual and his or her uniqueness, personal recognition, ethical behaviour.

▌ Attachment based on shared values which affect the consumer; a shared vision.

▌ Attachment based on the increased self-image generated by the brand through its image, advertising, rallies, behaviour and so on.

▌ Attachment based on the pleasure of a lasting relationship. The brand has often played a part in the development of individuals, their family and their children. In a sense, it has become a part of the life of individuals and their 'clan'.

▌ Attachment based on the brand's association with people to whom the customer is emotively linked. Managers have little power to influence this particular factor, but it is real nonetheless ('Proust's madeleine syndrome') (Heilbrunn, 2003).

Many different types of behaviour result from attachment. A relational brand must respond to them in order to feed attachment:

▌ a desire for rituals and participation therein, like a community;

▌ a desire for information;

▌ a desire for participation in the life of the brand and company;

▌ a desire for shared creation and involvement in the process of creating new products;

▌ a desire to be heard;

▌ a desire for community;

▌ a desire for intimacy;

▌ a desire for customer involvement with the brand: evangelising, prescribing and acting as an ambassador for the brand;

▌ automatic repeat purchasing (loyalty in the strictest sense of the word).

Customer relations increases the effectiveness of brand promotion. An offer is never perceived as 'touting for business' when it arrives at the right moment! Only a relationship with – and deep understanding of – customers, informed by an awareness of their recent requests, can transform what is usually perceived as commercial harassment into an impression of genuine service. There is thus no real contradiction between increasing client profitability and nurturing a relationship. A fan will be delighted to be able to download historic advertising for the brand. A young mother will be pleased to receive child-related ideas, services or products from the many brands aimed at parents and children. It all boils down to the timeliness of the offer.

How can this synergy be achieved if there is no information; no ongoing relationship with the customer; no means of listening to that customer's needs and being able to store and update the information thus received through a variety of media (e-mail, text messaging, telephone, fax, post)? As we can see, well-targeted, relevant business offers that come at just the right time create satisfaction because of the service they provide and the understanding they demonstrate of the client's needs. They are thus one of the key ways of creating attachment.

Having said this, we should not deny the power of the service in creating loyalty and repeat purchases. For example, Courtepaille – the European high-quality fast-food restaurant chain – has no loyalty programme. Certainly, the customer will find very few other restaurants with such friendly service and hearty fare at prices of under €10. But margins are so tight that the benefit of a loyalty card is still uncertain: happy customers will come back anyway.

Such examples are rare: in mature countries, bad brands scarcely exist any more. The competition is divided between very good brands and merely good brands. An in-house engineer will say that his or her product is the best: the customer and retailer will not see things in this way. However, the brand will have played a successful part in influencing preferences if it has been able to draw alongside the customer and promote a relationship based on service, communication and community – a source of affective involvement.

Segmenting loyalty programmes

Does this mean that the concept of loyalty is outdated? The conceptual explanation above clearly shows that loyalty behaviour (automatic repeat purchasing) continues to be relevant because it concerns information of critical importance to the company: it is based on observation. Even so, there may be many reasons behind a lack of loyalty (as we have seen above), which should be linked to the level of satisfaction.

The modern nature of competition is such that the issue is no longer 'or', but rather 'and'. It is therefore essential to avoid neglecting strategies for increasing loyalty (repeat purchases) that operate at the strictly behavioural level. They have an immediate

effect: they raise the brand's share of requirements and create an exit barrier – as has been shown by airlines and store-card promotional offer coupons. In the sphere of commodity sales, given the competition from low-cost sources, loyalty cards are – along with service – an essential component of the economic equation. In petrol stations, for example, nearly 40 per cent of petrol by volume is sold to customers with loyalty cards.

However, the real aim is to shift clients from behaviour towards attitudes. In traditional marketing – symbolised by the AIDA (attention, interest, desire, action) model – purchase follows desire, and thus attitudes. Given the number of competitors, and the degree to which products resemble one other, the priority is now to stand out from the herd. Creating a well-known, high-profile brand with emotive impact is one way of doing this. Another way is to introduce a surprising, tempting innovation. A third way is to provide direct purchasing and repeat purchasing incentives. However, this last approach has meaning only if it creates long-term value: that is, if behaviour initially motivated by the lure of an incentive is subsequently transferred to the brand and its products or services. Repeat purchasing is the customer's way of giving the brand a unique chance to prove itself.

In terms of loyalty management, Accor, the European hotel sector leader, offers an interesting and rare example. A hotel chain's profitability is based on the occupancy rate in its hotels, and particularly in cases where prices are tight, such as the budget hotel sector. Accor has a strong presence here, with a brand portfolio which covers all segments: zero-star (Motel 6, Formule 1), one-star (Etap hotels), two-star (Ibis), three-star (Novotel and Mercure) and four-star (Sofitel), not forgetting the new luxury Suit'Hotels segment. However, despite its customers' sensitivity to price, Accor charges for its loyalty cards. It has created an entire range of cards, each addressing a different client segment and governed by its own precise terms of use, acting as a replacement for single-brand cards. An additional service is being offered to customers by allowing them to move freely between the various brands of the group as dictated by their own wishes, budget and situation. This is the competitive advantage of having a portfolio of brands.

The premier card is Accor Hotels Favourite Guest, an individual card sold at the high price of €270/year. It offers significant advantages to customers, and is therefore aimed at 'heavy stayers' who spend more than 20 nights a year in a hotel. It offers guaranteed reservation up to three days prior to the stay date, as well as immediate reductions and loyalty points – and can be used at Ibis, Mercure, Novotel and Sofitel hotels.

The second card is targeted at lighter users who spend an average of 13 nights a year in hotels, and costs €45 a year. To make it more attractive in terms of points earned, it is a combined payment and loyalty card thanks to a partnership with Amex.

This left the loyalty of 'small users' to be secured. An ordinary free card would be of no benefit here, since a quick calculation shows that it would take a customer who spends three nights a year in a hotel 15 years to earn enough points for a free night. One option might have been to take part in a Smiles-type frequent buyer programme – that is, a card allowing the user to accumulate points at a large number of sales outlets of all kinds (department stores, hypermarkets, supermarkets, specialist stores such as Delheze and Kaufhof and so on). But how much benefit does such a programme actually bring to the individual brand? None. Naturally, the aim of loyalty is to increase the brand's share of requirements, but also to feed its own values. The Total petrol company positions itself on its service, and so the main thrust of its loyalty programme is to provide access to additional quality service (such as Total Assistance breakdown cover); points are a secondary consideration.

It is for this reason that, with its so-called 'small-user' clients in mind, Accor joined forces with a number of partners, each of which shared the same client philosophy and operated in the same line of business (journeys and travelling) to create the Accor Compliments Mouvango card. This improved the services offered to customers and allows points to be accumulated more quickly than would have been possible if they had visited hotels even five or six nights a year. This partnership has its own brand – Mouvango, the sign displayed by partners to show that the card is accepted. It includes restaurants, Total service stations, Carlson-Wagons Lits, travel agencies and so on. Total's version is called the Club Total Mouvango card, and so on. As we can see, the brand remains pre-eminent among all partners in this scenario, for it is here that the customer contact and relationship exists: Mouvango is an exclusive additional service to sweeten this relationship.

From the product to attentions: from the client to the VIP

Segmentation leads rapidly to the realisation that not all customers carry the same sales potential. It is also true that not all customers have the same interest in an involvement with the brand and becoming its ambassadors. A brand cannot survive without loyal followers and ambassadors, especially if it has premium positioning in its segment: there are women who will spurn all washing powders other than the top-dollar Tide or Ariel brands. This is even more true in high-involvement markets such as automobiles and cosmetics.

Such markets have traditionally been driven by a product-oriented approach: this is why l'Oréal, the world leader, relies totally on research. The goal of its 1,000 PhD-holding researchers is to invent new products which will inspire dreams of beauty and youth among women of all ages and all countries. The l'Oréal Group's flagship brand, l'Oréal

Paris, only discovered relational marketing fairly recently, in 2002 – the date when it launched its first advertising campaign aimed at building a relational database as a way of offering services to women. The same is true of the luxury brand Lancôme, which took its first steps in this direction in South America at a time when a brutal economic recession had had a colossal impact on purchasing power. It was essential to retain existing customers and thus enable the business to survive. Clearly, it was not enough merely to expound the virtues of the products themselves: this was necessary, but insufficient under such circumstances. This is why Lancôme's local teams reacted by innovating – not with new products, but with the attention it paid its customers. This example is even more pertinent in that it involved retailers, and thus also created a trade relationship tool which generated business.

Lancôme instructed its authorised retailers to distribute a small smart card – the Lancôme beauty card – and to use equipment that would store the client's last few transactions when the card was presented. This was a revolutionary approach, since the retailers believed that a client record was their own property. In order to 'earn' the card, the client had to make an initial purchase of US $100. All subsequent purchases – regardless of the store, as long as it was a participant in the scheme and had an electronic recorder – would earn points. These points could be exchanged for Lancôme products, lingerie, jewellery and famous-name bags. Cards were also given to journalists and top fashion models. Once a database had been created, it became possible to create campaigns targeting VIPs, who are generally also big spenders, making repeated visits to their local sales point.

The company's first act was to produce and mail to these clients a woman's beauty magazine, paid for by advertising (from airline, jewellery, lingerie and similar companies). 'Sneak preview' announcements were also made of new products, and specific samples were provided, along with access to a dedicated, interactive MyLancôme.Vip website. The VIP card was accepted in selected restaurants and shops. Lastly, selective invitations to public relations events and fashion shows, offering meetings with leading figures, were issued regularly.

The database also becomes a tool for building a relationship between the brand and the sales outlets, for coordinating the promotion of new products, or performing a 'diary' function (reminding store clients of key dates – such as birthdays – appearing in the database, and prompting post-purchase calls). The aim of this is not only to make customers visit sales outlets, but also to enable them to be recognised as special and unique – receiving personalised attention to increase the pleasure of their visit. A VIP wants to be recognised as such.

Sustaining proximity with influencers

Today, mass targets have disappeared. Statistics should not create an illusion. What might appear to be mass targets are in fact made up of an aggregation of smaller ones, of micro targets. Even if mass advertising campaigns are still used, what is needed for a brand is a shared image, a collective bonding tool within societies. To develop the brand over time entails improving the brand's relationship with each of the strategic micro targets. These strategic targets are made of more involved customers, or those who are currently non-customers but have the potential to become involved. Once involved they can act as influencers. They can re-energise a brand image that is weakened by the deleterious effects of time.

This is critical for sustaining the equity of mature brands, facing new entrants. Such brands run the risk of losing contact with the trend-setting groups in a society. The risk is that they will be perceived as yesterday's brand. Recreating contact with trend-setting 'tribes' or micro-groups is of paramount importance even for brands that are not involved with fashion in any direct sense. Otherwise they run the risk of becoming just another supermarket brand.

Ricard provides a good example of best practice in its long-term engagement in recreating lost ties with critical groups. It is a historical leader in the aniseed-based alcoholic drinks sector, which comprises the fifth largest spirits sector in the world. It has introduced relational programmes aimed at three groups: women, those of high socio-economic status (SES), and young people. Ricard faces competition both from spirits such as whisky, vodka, gin, rum and tequila, and thus from world-famous brands such as Johnnie Walker, J&B, Absolut, Bacardi and Cacique, and from fashionable modern brands of beer. Finally, it is 40 per cent more expensive than the distributors' brands and other low-cost brands of aniseed drinks. Part of its resistance to these massive attacks has been to remain close to its core clients and to invest in reconquering proximity with the trend-setting groups, those most attracted and seduced by international competition.

Women may like the taste of Ricard but they did not like its image. They perceived it as a male, popular brand, not a sign of good manners. As a response, Ricard runs very specific adverts in trendy women's magazines, and sponsors events involving women. The brand sponsors literary events where new female writers are promoted. It is a major organiser of St Catherine's Day, a promotional event for national design schools. It continues to try out specific relational operations such as a cooperation with Mod's Hair, a youth-oriented hairdressing franchise. Typically, this involves the hairdresser's customers being offered a Ricard to drink while waiting in the salon in the summer. The new format RTD – ready to drink – is very useful for this purpose.

High-SES people of all sexes and ages are

addressed through Espace Ricard, an art gallery, open to the latest forms of painting, thus creating a proximity with the most advanced artists and art lovers. In addition, advanced designers are regularly asked to redesign the basic 'tools' that accompany a drink of Ricard, a carafe and an ashtray. The world-famous designers Garouste and Bonetti did the latest versions.

To gain proximity to young people interested in music and sport, Ricard has developed three long-term actions supported by a specific budget allowance. One is creation of the Paul Ricard car racing circuit, compatible with F1 international racing standards, and now the most modern and safe circuit in France. It hosted most of the major international car races, until a law was introduced preventing sports sponsorship by alcoholic drink brands. It was then sold but the name has been retained.

The second innovation is the Ricard Live Music Tour, providing the largest free music events in Europe, featuring famous rock stars. It has attracted more than 1 million people each year, and its name has become synonymous with quality music and concerts. The company has gained unique know-how in organising open concerts in the middle of major cities and synchronising sales events around them to maximise synergy. Each concert attracts a great deal of free publicity.

The third youth-oriented initiative is the organisation of 1,000 integration parties (for students just going up to university) and graduation parties each year. The targets for these are the top business and engineering schools, since their students will be the elite of tomorrow.

Of course, it is not possible to remain a popular brand without also maintaining a proximity to core consumers, existing heavy buyers and the engaged segment (see the segmentation scheme Figure 9.1). Locally, at the micro level, pétanque contests are still sponsored by the brand in Provence (the birthplace of the brand) and elsewhere. In summer, a squadron of Ricard 'fire girls' runs onto major beaches and offers sunbathers free drinks. For image management purposes, each brand needs to decide which of its many PR activities should receive publicity.

Nine lessons can be learnt from this example:

▌ Because change is permanent, and new competition is always coming in and can be very seductive, the brand's profile is always threatened over time. It must be nurtured and proximity eventually reconquered.

▌ No brand can stay apart from trend-setting tribes in its sector.

▌ Proximity and strong ties can only be built at points of direct contact.

▌ Strong ties need to be continuous: this is not a 'coup' policy, but a continuous decision.

▌ This activity must be supported by a strong investment.

▌ It must be done by courageous people. Trend-setting groups are not waiting to be approached by a currently unfashionable brand, and sometimes they will look down on its promoters.

▌ Again, targeting is key.

▌ Again, creativity and disruption are of paramount importance, to surprise and create a buzz.

▌ Finally, this is the occasion for creating selective publicity, deciding which of these ties should be most squarely in the spotlight.

Should all brands follow their customers?

Regularly, the same question arises: should the brand aim at its existing customers or at its future buyers? Should it try to maximise its present customers' satisfaction or should it think of the new generation?

For sure, the global mantra of management today is to focus on existing customers. They are the most profitable source of cashflow. This is why all companies and brands invest in building up large customer databases, CRM software, and undertake in-depth surveys on customer satisfaction with the product or service. This leads to necessary improvements, and in theory it increases customer loyalty. We write 'in theory', for all automobile surveys show that 60 per cent of the consumers who did not buy the same brand on their next purchase were very satisfied with their former brand. Why then did they change? Because consumption is situational. New situations create new expectations: this is called 'value migration'. New generations too develop a new set of values and expectations.

Existing customers are essential for short and medium-term growth and profitability, but listening too much to existing customers is the main reason companies do not innovate enough. Professor Christensen has shown that the main reason companies disappear is that disruptive innovations transform the market and rapidly make their products or services obsolete. What prevents these companies, which are often adjudged to be excellent, from innovating? Arguably they are too well managed (Christensen, 1997). Well-managed companies select the innovations that please their clients and that provide good profitability forecasts with a high degree of certainty. Disruptive innovations are just the contrary: they are not well perceived by current customers, and nothing can be said with certainty about their profitability. But disrupting the market is how the minicomputer made mainframe companies obsolete, then the PC did the same for the minicomputer and so on.

Collins and Porras (1994) have reminded us of the power of the 'and'. Most of us keep on asking questions about alternatives: should the brand do this or do that? It is a mistake.

We must do both. Brands must think of their present clients as the immediate source of growth, but they must also look to the future generation.

At present Smirnoff has 60 per cent of the UK vodka market. For most managers, this would be a good reason to be satisfied. Instead, the management of Smirnoff innovated to react to new entrants such as Absolut and Finlandia. Most importantly, it invented a vodka for the new generation, who were not interested in drinking vodka as their parents did, but could be persuaded to drink it outside pubs, not from a glass but straight from the bottle, like a beer. This is called dual management: already thinking of the emerging trends, new behaviours and customers, those who will be dominant tomorrow. Brands have targets: when their customers do not fit the target any more, they should be transferred to another brand. If not the brand will be expanded but also diluted.

Reinventing the brand: Salomon

The problem with brand management over time is how to deal with change. Customers change; society values change; and competitors change too. Few examples illustrate the challenges of change as well as the case of Salomon, the world winter sports leader with 30 per cent of its sales in Japan, 30 per cent in Europe and 30 per cent in North America.

In 1995, in an executive committee long-term planning meeting, a hypothesis emerged that established a scenario for the future, in which it was probable that the young teenagers who were giving up skiing to take up snowboarding would never go back to skiing and the other traditional winter sports that had established the reputation of not only Salomon but also Rossignol, Kneissl, Dynamic and others. On the basis of this prediction, it was decided to present a full range of snowboards at the forthcoming professional winter sports world exhibition. However, the stand remained bereft of visitors throughout the exhibition: visitors (who were all retailers) walked past without even stopping. For a company ruled by technical innovation, (for example, Salomon's safety bindings are world leaders), it was a major shock. Meanwhile, Salomon's overall sales shrank from €442 million in 1993/94 to €437 million in 1994/95, €396 million in 1995/96, and then €365 million in 1996/97 – a lower figure than in 1992/93. It should be said that between 1994/95 and 1995/96, world snowboard sales doubled while ski sales fell by 16 per cent.

The diagnosis was a shock, too. Salomon was perceived as an anti-model by new generations of anti-conformist, rebellious 'snow surfers' worldwide, who were opposed to the values prevalent in alpine skiing and in the sporting system in general. After all, a brand is always more than just a name. It is a point of view about a category, a vision, a set of values. As a pillar of the Olympic ideal and the Winter Games, and the first choice of the world's top ski teams, Salomon was becoming the symbol of a world from which the snowboarding community wanted to distance itself, standing as it did in total opposition to its values. Indeed, what are the typical values of traditional winter sports in which all participants ski along wide avenues of well-packed snow? What are the Olympic values if not individuality, competition, beating competitors, shaving off hundredths of a second, order and hierarchy? By contrast, snowboarding – which is after all a direct descendant of surfing – is about getting together in groups, going off-piste and enjoying unique snow sensations centred on the values of fun, groups, friendships, anarchy, freedom, pleasure and a disdain of competition.

Breaking with traditional values, snowboarders form tribes with very well-defined dress codes, in sharp contrast to the traditional clothing of the piste skier. Surfboarders generally shun the reds, whites and blues of traditional ski suits in favour of fluorescent colours straight out of the Timothy Leary psychedelic movement. Furthermore, snowboarding is a combination of sport and music: participants always wear their personal stereos on the slopes. This makes it more than just a sport: it is a sect.

Salomon's very future was at stake. The diagnosis was that there was no question of creating a new, dedicated snowboarding brand: to do so would ultimately be to sign a death warrant for Salomon and entomb it within the practices of yesterday. Surgery was required on the brand itself in order to bring about a profound change in its identity. Winter sports are not a segment or an activity, but instead represent a fundamental shift in western society. Therefore, no winter sports brand can afford not to play a part. A brand identity overhaul was thus set in motion.

The second part of the diagnosis was that Salomon should continue to maintain a presence in the ski and snowboard markets. The former market was the source of its current revenue; the latter would generate the revenue of the future. This left the brand with no choice: a dual marketing approach was needed. However, there is no room for schizophrenia within a brand. There is room for only one value system to be attached to any given name. When it comes to values, a brand cannot serve two masters. The answer was thus to reduce the values gap between skiing and snowboarding, bringing the former increasingly closer to the values of surfing: fun, sensations and pleasure.

This is where concept and product innovation came in. Salomon invented parabolic skis, freeride skis, X-screams skis and improved mini-ski technology. All of these new products offered new sensations and delivered the snowboarding feel without the snowboard. By means of these innovations, Salomon achieved an effective reduction of the distance between skiing and snowboarding or snowblading. Salomon thus dragged skiing out of its traditional mould – a

case of the category leader changing along with the category as the key to its survival.

But the hardest work was yet to be done. How was the firm to make up its lost ground in the opinion-leading teenage target market to which it remained the anti-model and very epitome of tradition? Of course, it could already count on the democratisation of the snowboard and snowblade. Assuming that this process continued, reaching increasing numbers of less radical people, the assets of the Salomon brand could offer them reassurance. However, the world of sport is dominated by fashions and by opinion leaders, who saw brands such as Quiksilver as the real stars.

Three radical decisions were taken to bring the brand closer to its reticent (or even hostile) targets: listening to customers, the creation of Salomon Stations, and a strategic extension into rollerskating.

Listening to customers became Salomon's main method of conducting market research. Young people were sent out to spend time alongside – and learn to understand – surfers and young teenagers on the US West Coast, since they are opinion leaders. Using this ethnographic method of participatory observation, they could feed back continuous information on forthcoming trends, expectations, key words and so on.

Another step was the creation of Salomon Stations, friendly places right at the heart of winter sports towns, offering a listening environment at the bottom of the pistes. The exercise was not about selling products, so as to avoid competing with local retailers, but rather about stimulating dialogue in a relaxed setting, thus furthering the values and practice of the sport. However, considering the significant set-up costs and times, another approach was needed: this took the form of brand stretching into the rollerskate and inline skate market.

This strategic extension was triggered by a simple observation: young people only spend one month a year playing winter sports. If Salomon is to become their brand, they must be approached during the preceding 11 months – and snowboarders are one and the same group as the die-hard rollerskaters found in town and city streets the world over. Furthermore, with regard to the actual roller-skates, Salomon's technical expertise could offer a significant advance over the performance of existing roller skates in two key areas: comfort and safety. As a world leader in mountain shoes and safety bindings, Salomon alone had the means to take a significant forward step through innovation. This led to the 1999 launch of a new range of roller skates whose performance characteristics were widely acknowledged.

The third strategic decision was based on an observation: in snowboarding, 'software' is just as important as hardware. It was not enough merely to be a manufacturer of products, however technically excellent. What was needed was the introduction of design, colour and hyper-modern codes capable of attracting young people brought up in the culture of tag graffiti and comic books. Most importantly, a plan was needed for marketing the 'software', extremely modern clothing ranges which would reflect the changes within the brand. Hence the purchase of the Bonfire textile brand, which enjoyed a high profile among surfers – and, more importantly, enlisting the help of Adidas in 1997 to assist in these changes. After all, who better than Adidas to master the balance between aspirational hi-tech and textiles and sportswear, worn by the young and not-so-young alike, immersing them in the crucible of worship of sport (and thus of the body)? Furthermore, there is great profitability in textiles, which are sports derivatives. Until then a family company which had been founded by Georges Salomon, Salomon discovered in Adidas the financial resources and expertise to assist in the transformation of its identity and business model.

The same strategy continues today: in a nautical twist, Salomon is now entering the surfing market. This is the result of a redefinition of its identity and business: it has moved from a product-based definition (mountain shoes and safety bindings for skis) to an identity based on the activity itself (winter sports) and on values (sensations and pleasure). It has developed from a cyclical business threatened by the vagaries of the climate ('Will it snow this year?') to a permanent business with its grass roots in the tarmac roads of New York and Oslo. Tomorrow, they will also be in the waves of Australia, California and the South of France. This product extension also satisfies the goal of profitability: it will enable the follow-up launch of a complementary textile range. After all, a textile range in this sector needs legitimacy, of the sort that is conferred by the equipment. The extension into surfing has no other aim than to provide this legitimacy.

Lastly, on the communication front, Salomon developed a relational marketing system and created communities. It initiated the Salomon X-Adventure ski trek in Europe, the United States and Japan, created 'free-ride' stages and offered a host of 'challenges' for inline skaters and snowbladers. It also put an end to superficial sponsoring. Now the champions, and opinion leaders for young teenagers, are more than just a brand vehicle – they are co-creators with Salomon.

What can we learn from this? A brand can only survive change if it is constantly re-earning its relevance among target groups of which it may have had little understanding. Paradoxically – as has been shown by Christensen (1997) – in their quest for 'good' management, companies often become slavishly devoted to understanding their existing client base. In the process of satisfying their own customers better and better, brands become these customers' hostages and neglect the weak signals of social or technological change. Considering that this change generally takes the form of a break with existing habits and products, it is rejected by the brand's existing customer base. The brand then works harder and harder to please a clientèle that does not represent the future, thus becoming an anti-model for innovators and tomorrow's customers.

The necessary process of winning customers over again takes time and requires a systematic, coordinated, focused approach which involves all areas of the company. It implies an internal revolution – at the management, organisation and identity levels.

It starts with a redefinition of identity. What parts of the old identity do you keep? What do you change to help in coping with changes in society and the rise of all the new sports that were still unknown 10 years ago?

Salomon's slogan – which defines its business and field of competence – is now 'freedom action sports', which applies equally to the mountains, the town – and in future, the sea too. This shows the path followed by the brand over time:

▌ In 1950, its identity was based on a product – the 'binding' safety fastening, an essential component.

▌ In 1980, the brand's entire identity, skills and value system could be summed up as skiing.

▌ In 1990, its identity became focused on mountains, with the introduction of hiking boots and the like.

▌ In 2000, the brand expanded its target and field of competence to a particular area, a conceptualised sport: freedom action sports. It became a specialist multi-sport brand, serving this concept and its underpinning values. What are these values? Freedom means unrestricted sensations and 'my style'; action means energy, gravity and the environment as a playground; and sports suggests gliding, adventure, riding and so on.

To equip itself against competitors and changes among consumers, distribution channels and competition, the brand continues to capitalise on its historic skills: its unique know-how in working with professionals to design pure, simple, unique, innovative products.

It has had to acquire new skills in order to communicate with – and indeed, enter into a genuine relationship with – a new generation of young sports enthusiasts worldwide.

Salomon has thus widened its target to young people and teenagers, tomorrow's trend leaders. Activating this identity implies a long-term commitment and substantial human and financial resources dedicated to:

1. Product innovation (brand extensions play a strategic role here). For this purpose, Salomon sets aside 7 per cent of its turnover for research and registers 80 patents per year. The company has also reduced its product-to-market timescales to one year for composite products and two years for mechanical products (bindings). In addition, opinion leaders are involved at an early upstream stage in the creative process, and surfers can contact the brand via the internet to influence research into new products.

    Furthermore, Salomon's product range marketing is no longer segmented simply into the old three categories of age, sex and skiing ability: a fourth category has now been added (the type of sensation sought after).

2. The brand's role as an engine for moving 'old-fashioned' but still majority activities (such as skiing) towards something more modern via new sensation-based products, and in so doing narrowing the gap that exists within both the brand and winter sports as a whole. In addition, snowboarding has become an Olympic event, and Salomon has been able to forge a link with Edgar Grospiron, an emblematic figure in winter sports.

3. Offering a complete range of experiences via challenges, competitions, ski treks and so on, and also via sportswear ranges.

4. Communication that has at last become more interactive, guerilla-styled and street-focused.

5. Proximity to the customer; perhaps even a direct relationship in locations devoted to the brand, during events and the like.

The commercial and financial results reflected the radical effort which had gone into adapting to this change: sales rose from €390 million in 1997 to €435 million in 1998, and €500 million in 1999. The company reversed its 1997 deficit to move back into profit in 1998. Bought out for 1.2 billion dollars by Adidas – 40 times its profit in a sector where the average multiple was just 20 – the Salomon group was keeping its promises. However, because global warming makes future snow levels uncertain, Adidas decided to sell Salomon to the Finnish sports group Amer, which already owned Atomic skis and Wilson tennis rackets.

11

Adapting to the market: identity and change

The only way a brand can grow is through movement. You cannot expect growth and lack of change. The brand is continually looking to create new markets, new segments in which it can become the reference and above all the market leader. It was said, for example, of the Twingo that Renault had invented 'the car that hadn't existed' (Midler, 1995). According to this plan the brand's image is, like its environment, in perpetual evolution. To fail to evolve is to appear to be shackled by the present, to have a dated and immobile image.

Mercedes could have repeated its famous sedans indefinitely, while always improving them, since they were the global image of what a luxury car should look like, to the point at which the Japanese Lexus copied their contours exactly. Meanwhile customers had changed. Those at the edge of leading opinion, who influence the opinion of 90 per cent of the rest, had changed their lifestyle and their points of reference. They were no longer wedded to sedans, but were looking for niche designs of car to suit them. The brand's hopes went into the Class A, the 'little Mercedes': a break with what had been the brand's contract with its customers. It represented a disruption, but not an incoherence or a contradiction. Mercedes could not afford to confine itself to a conception of a car that was becoming a minority taste. Its mission of offering the most reliable cars in the world needed to adapt itself to the requirements of the world.

Only radical change is visible. Otherwise, according to the psychological principle of 'perceptual assimilation', what we see is based on our preconceptions. Accordingly, brands should not hesitate to push their boundaries far from their original prototype. The frontiers of the brand's territory are made always to be pushed back, in the directions of products, geography and meaning. If, in order to manage the brand in the medium term (three to five years) there is a need for tools that fix its limits (such as the prism of identity), it is necessary to review them regularly, to adapt to changing circumstances, and indeed to prompt change. Equilibrium for a brand in a world in perpetual movement does not consist of staying static, but of introducing movement, of fighting a continual battle.

The luxury US brands surprise us, because they have an air of incoherence. Calvin Klein went from the provocation of Obsession to the idealism of Eternity. Ralph Lauren jumped from the Boston WASP image of Polo to the Safari ambience of 'Out of Africa'. In reality one product does not follow on neatly from the previous one, in the sense of a repetitive coherence that continues the same concepts to infinity, leading the brand inevitably down a path of decline. These products are signs of a brand in movement. Calvin Klein is not either Obsession or Eternity. It is both, a brand both more complex and more open than others had imagined. Renault comprises both the Megane and the Espace. The future belongs to brands that are able to handle this type of 'and', and to abandon the dichotomous choice of the 'or'.

This is also the message that Collins and Porras conveyed in their *Built to Last* (1994). Chanel surprised us in launching Coco and associating it with Vanessa Paradis. There was an incoherence, a break with the image it had conveyed through its previous figurehead, Carole Bouquet. But this kind of radical move does more to ensure the long-term survival of the brand in an era when it is faced with competition from American and Italian designers who know how to seduce the young.

The paradox is that at the same time, the brand only develops on the basis of a certain permanence, or perhaps a duration. The key concept of the brand's identity carries within itself the necessary continuity of 'identification': the meanings and expressions of the brand. We should not forget that the brand is a point of reference: it indicates a proposition, certain values. That is its first function. To create and build up a point of reference, the brand needs to have a clear sense of itself, a direction. A certain amount of continuity is also essential to the construction and development over time of the brand.

The parallel pursuit of these two require- ments (identity and change) leads us to view the brand from two angles: the timeless angle of its basic meaning and identity, and the offensive, disruptive angle of its new develop- ments. This is the theme of this chapter.

Bigger or better brands?

What are the main characteristics of Western markets? For us the most important thing is that needs are satisfied. This has considerable consequences.

First, growth will be found in Asia, Russia and Brazil. Second economic growth will rest on sustained consumption only if consumption itself can be stimulated. This means that brands will have to stimulate desire. This has great implications for brand management. Brands should now deliver experiences, and one of the first is to surprise their consumers.

Another key factor of mature markets is the wish to consume better. Globalisation is now a reality for consumers. They are aware that first-world companies have their products made in China or Brazil, that underdeveloped countries will only be able to develop if trade is more equitable, that some companies are more ecology-conscious than others. These considerations have no impact on consumers when their main problem is to fulfil their basic needs. Maslow reminded us that higher-level needs become important when lower-level ones are satisfied. This means that modern consumers do not want bigger brands, but better brands. Sustainable development is here to stay. It is no fad. Perhaps many companies now mention sustainable development in their corporate annual reports purely because their competitors do so, or because they feel forced to do it. Meanwhile their competitors have realised that sustainable development and fair trade are sources of competitive edge. Today intelligence is moral intelligence.

From reassurance to stimulation

Certainly the key concept of brand management is identity: we have been stressing it since 1990, when the first edition of this book was published. 'Identity' means that the brand should respect its key values and defining attributes. However, there is a point where too much repetition of the same creates boredom. Too much predictability is a drawback in modern markets. (Table 11.1.)

This is why the role of modern brands is to stimulate the consumer to have new experiences. The role of the brand in providing reassurance and generating trust is not dead, far from it: but it needs to be used to encourage the consumer to take more risks, explore new behaviours, try new unexpected products. In order to do so, disruptive innovations become very important. To grow through time while keeping its identity, the brand should continue differently.

To this end there is a need for new research tools. Why are all companies now listening to forecasting consultants, trend spotters? Because they need to think now about what consumers are not thinking about today, but will think about tomorrow. Classical marketing research analyses sources of satisfaction and dissatisfaction with the product or service or brand. The outcomes can be used to prompt immediate and continuous improvements. But can disruption come from this type of marketing research? Satisfaction is always linked to customers' existing values and goals. Research is needed also to spot how these values and goals will change, leading to new insights.

Brand management needs a set of boundaries. This is called brand identity, which covers how the brand defines itself, its values, its mission, its know-how, its personality and so on. A clear sense of identity is necessary, for the brand meaning to be reinforced by repetition. On the other hand market fragmentation, competitive dynamism and the need for surprises call not for reinforcement but for diversification. As ever, brand management will act as a pendulum, going from an excess of sameness to an excess of diversity. There is nothing wrong with this. The same holds true of the local/global dilemma, or the ethics versus business dilemma.

Another consequence is the need to know the identity of the brand. More precisely, what is its kernel, the attributes that are necessary for the brand to remain itself, and what are the traits that can show some flexibility? If all the attributes of the brand belong to its kernel, that is to say, they are all necessary to its identity, its ability to change will be hampered. How can a brand surprise customers, evolve, adapt to new uses, situations and markets, if it is too rigidly defined? Peripheral attributes can change, or be present in some products but not in others. Eventually, innovations introduce new peripheral attributes, which may become

Table 11.1   From risk to desire: the dilemma of modern branding

Brand = capital	Brand = impulse
Capitalise	Surprise
Repeat	Diversify
Sameness	Variety
Identity	Change

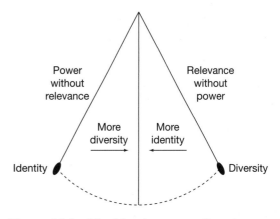

Figure 11.1   The identity versus diversity dilemma

incorporated into the kernel at some point in time. This is how brands evolve through time, how innovations have an impact on their identity. Peripheral traits act as the key long-term change agents within brands (Abric, 1994; Michel, 2000). The tools to identify the traits held by consumers as kernel traits of a brand are presented below but their use is not sufficiently widespread.

The brands that ultimately last are those that are able to surprise their customers, and the customers of tomorrow in particular. This sums up the challenge facing modern brand management in a nutshell. Far from seeking to capitalise on its past – and thus to repeat itself – the brand should surprise, and promote change. This is what should be termed the 'exploratory function', which plays an epistemic role for the brand (Heilbrunn, 2003). But how can you know what will surprise the customers of tomorrow?

Market studies provide a good understanding of today's customers; or at least, of the expectations they express. So much needs to be done to improve customer satisfaction. How long ago did readers receive a satisfaction questionnaire from their bank? Their car dealers? Their telephone company?

To surprise customers, you need to take a long-term view – hence the growing use of trends in brand management. Trends are hypotheses relating to change that occurs within small groups in our societies, but could potentially create a tidal wave among the general public. These trends are established on the basis of combined information regarding the demographic, technological, social and cultural future of our societies.

We thus need to define three levels of vision: long, medium and short term. Car concepts in the automobile sector, for example, are governed by long-term considerations. Decisions regarding models that are already part of the seven-year production plan are considered as medium term.

Consistency is not mere repetition

Brand messages and slogans are bound to evolve. Evian was, initially, the water of babies, then of the Alps, then the water of balance, later the water of balanced strength, and now a source of youth. These changes in positioning occurred over a long time period: they demonstrate the evolution of the consumer's attitude towards water, the maturation of the market and the evolution of competitive position. The functions and representations of water are not fixed: they depend on external factors linked to urbanisation, industrialisation, rediscovering nature, discovering pollution, new representations of the body, health and food hygiene. Positioning is the act of relating one brand facet to a set of consumer expectations, needs and desires. As these needs change through time, the brand is obliged to follow suit. However, Evian's identity remained consistent throughout these repositionings.

But within a brand's lifetime these changes in positioning should not happen too often, about every four or five years. However, the brand's means of expression can move faster to integrate with the evolution of fashion: new speech modes, new signs of modernity and new looks. It is essential that the brand is perceived as up to date although such necessary adjustments and changes make the brand run the risk of a loss of identity.

To retain their identity while changing, brands often stick to their communication codes, that is their fixed visual and audio symbols. This is undeniably a factor that contributes to a brand and what it represents being recognised. Even when not named, Coke commercials can be picked out: their music and their style are unique. But the style itself is subject to obsolescence. Continuing with it could prove fatal to the brand.

Unfortunately, it has to be acknowledged that brands have a hard time parting with their communication codes, even when they feel it is necessary. This is to be expected: they are afraid of losing their identity. But this reluctance is largely due to the fact that brand management concepts are essentially static. Time is not taken into account when it is a key parameter in markets. In that sense, the concept of 'communication territory' is a vision that clings to the ground: it has to do with all the visible signals that the brand uses to communicate its definition and what it represents. However, an identity that defines itself only through signs is subject to an alteration of their meaning. The brand is indeed recognised, but no longer in control of its meaning.

Brand and products: integration and differentiation

How, specifically, does a brand function? How are the relationships expressed between the brand and the products or services it sells? What are the consequences? What is brand coherence?

To borrow an expression from G. Mischel (2000), the brand is fundamentally a system that integrates and differentiates. The brand is first of all a tool of *integration*: it is a tool of coherence, by bringing together under its name a range of products and services, each of which must carry the central brand values. A product or service that is not representative of the brand must not carry the brand name. The brand is an explicit normative system: the brand's central values must be known internally and by everyone who has to set the brand in process. They are incumbent on them: we should therefore expect to find them in the products, services and communications. Admittedly, a Toyota at the bottom of the range does not have all the qualities of a top of the range model, but it should embody all the central values of Toyota (for example, exemplary reliability and an excellent quality–price ratio). This is why there cannot

be many central brand values. In the fact-finding mission for Peugeot and Citroen, the recommendation was for three per brand: dynamism, aesthetics and value for Peugeot, self-expression, comfort and inventiveness for Citroen. France, as is well known, is in crisis because she can no longer be run while respecting the three central values she set for herself: liberty, equality and fraternity. Too many tacitly accepted decisions or social factors contradict one of these values.

The brand is also a tool of *differentiation*: its name sets all its products apart, through their common tangible and intangible values. Because it carries the logo of Danone, whose central value is active good health, Danette, although it is sugary and rich, appears much healthier than a Mars or Lion bar, typically associated with obesity, or a creamy Mont Blanc dessert.

Like any well-managed brand, Virgin has explicitly stated its brand values: this is what is known as a brand platform. Virgin has six central values, those that belong to its identity kernel. They are 'fun, good quality/price ratio, quality, innovation, challenge, and brilliant client service'. This is its brand contract: as such it is non-negotiable. In fact, in everything that Virgin does, we can find these six ingredients. Hence the brand inspires respect, even if many of its attempts fail. These values are necessary because they help internally to decide whether a decision, action, product or service is 'Virgin enough' to be put on the market to face the competition. Naturally, depending on the products within a range, not everything will represent the brand values with the same relative intensity. A Virgin soft drink will have a lot of 'fun', but even Virgin Atlantic Business Class needs to have a little 'fun' about it, because otherwise it would not be Virgin, and because this is what differentiates it from the business classes of competing airlines.

These brand values are not invented: they are present from the first product that the brand produces. This is the founding product or service that carries the meaning of a word previously unknown on the market (the brand name). Its commercial success confirms the relevance of these values, and this is strengthened by the extension of the range, which then constitutes the 'core business'. Later, the brand will extend into other businesses, segments and markets, but always under the name of the same values, integrating the whole and differentiating it from the competitors in each market or segment. Andros, an SME from the Lot region of France, based in Biars, began by developing a mass-distribution jam business. That became its core business. Then its competence in fruit and the trust attached to its name led it to penetrate other segments: compotes (against the Materne brand) and now fruit juices (against Tropicana, Joker and other brands).

Brand values and segment expectations

The brand's products must therefore all embody in their way all the central values of the brand, hence the necessity of restricting

these in number to avoid creating paralysis. The brand is built through the coherence it imposes on everything it does, and which will be therefore lived experientially by the client.

If there are too many central brand values to maintain, the brand cannot evolve.

It is therefore necessary to differentiate between so-called 'central' values, that is, those values that are non-negotiable, and those known as 'peripheral' values, which may be present here but not there, in one market segment but not in another. In fact, the brand's products, since they are each in competition in their particular segment with different competitors, should have specific 'pluses' that do not emanate from the brand's central values. Thus Nivea sun cream must be hypo-allergenic, which is highly coherent with Nivea's central value (taking care of oneself), but also add scientific reassurance (not a central value for Nivea), since it is in competition with sun creams from the giants in active cosmetics (the l'Oréal and Estée Lauder groups), which have established science as the dominant code of this market of protecting the skin from sun damage.

Figure 11.2   The double role of brands integration and differentiation
Source: Michel, 2000

At the operational level, in order to manage a brand, the first thing to do is to specify clearly what is part of the brand's kernel (its central values and traits) and what could be variable, since it is peripheral, specific to each segment. This sorting must be explicit (written in a brand platform and diffused via an intranet), and should deal not only with the fundamental values, but also the personality traits of the brand and its tangible aspects. It is notable that Virgin included its 'fun' side (a personality trait) in the central facets of the brand identity.

The exercise of sorting out what is negotiable or even variable, adaptable, must equally involve the physical aspects of the client experience. For the Novotel brand, for example, it is necessary to specify whether its blue colour is negotiable or not, and also the appearance of the reception area in each hotel, the arrangement of the rooms, their furnishings and the level of service. Within a single country, even a region, the client experience cannot fluctuate: this is the effort that must be undertaken in order for the brand to become a benchmark of the quality it wishes to symbolise in an exemplary manner, and on which its reputation will be built. The answer is much less obvious from one continent to another. In fact, the Novotel on Broadway is in competition with other hotels with American standards, in the same way that the one in Bangkok on the banks of the Chao Praya is in competition with the mythical Hotel Oriental: it must be brought up to Asian standards, the highest in the world. Nevertheless, within the portfolio of Accor Group hotels, the hierarchy is always respected: the Bangkok Novotel does not offer the same level of services as the Bangkok Sofitel.

For service brands, rendering the client experience invariable is a challenge: Air France, with its 15,000 employees, has more difficulty homogenising its in-flight services than, for example, Lufthansa or Singapore Airlines. From one flight to the next, the service delivered is variable, since the company's young stewards and stewardesses show a degree of heterogeneity.

Figure 11.3 provides a reminder that there must also be a physical brand signature, experiential and perceptible. It cannot be reduced to an intangible. Concretely, what must be the physical signature of all Martell cognacs, in comparison with all Hennessy cognacs? What is the physical signature of Lancôme compared with that of Estée Lauder products? It is up to the R&D researchers at Lancôme or the cellar masters in the case of Martell to answer: customers do not have this acuity of judgement.

Specialist brands and generalist brands

Is the Renault brand managed the same way as the BMW brand? Is the Galeries Lafayette brand managed in the same way as IKEA? Is the Samsung brand managed in the same way as Sony? The generalist brand offers a broad range under its one name, aimed at covering the needs of all segments of its market sector. It is ecumenical and open. Its business model is that of capitalising on customers' durable values: by attracting young people via Clio or Twingo, Renault hopes to win their loyalty and therefore later on to sell them a larger model corresponding to the evolution of their life cycle and the needs that follow from it.

The specialist brand is excluding. It sets itself a particular target market segment, of which people either are or are not part, and builds its range according to that single target. For example, BMW targets people looking to buy a car for more than €20,000.

But a brand is a brand: to manage the brand is to undertake a 360° approach to coherence, to create the perception of a differentiated offer, carrying added values, tangible and intangible. The brand is built, in fact, through the coherence of everything it undertakes. The foundation of this coherence

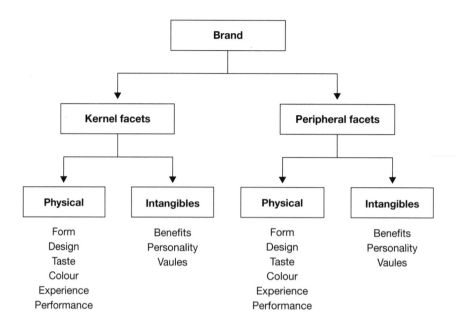

Figure 11.3   Differentiate what is variable from what is non-negotiable in the brand identity

is the 'brand kernel identity', that is, the necessary facets of the brand, those that define its singularity over the long term. Building a brand is first of all a matter of defining very clearly, explicitly and publicly what about the brand is non-negotiable, and what must therefore be transparent in everything it does. This preliminary work, called the brand platform, is necessary to help weigh up the daily decisions within the company and know how to say no. Among these questions we find, for example:

- When is a car no longer a Renault?

- When are client relationships no longer managed sufficiently in the Renault way?

- What should the welcome at a Renault dealership be like?

- When does a loyalty programme not carry enough of the values and personality of the Renault brand?

Given the Renault values, but also its still poor recognition and reputation worldwide, should Renault continue to invest in Formula 1? We know that Michelin answered no to this question from 2007: in fact, the governing body of Formula 1 wished to have only one tyre manufacturer for all the cars, so that the attention would be placed more on the competition between the different motors than between the different tyres. Nothing is further from Michelin's deepest values than a competition without competitors.

At this point, a difficulty arises: the generalist business model is based on the widest range, aimed at all market and customer segments. The specialist model is the reverse: it chooses its segments and therefore its customers. The generalist brand is open and adaptive; the specialist brand is exclusive. The generalist brand must therefore adapt to the rules of each of its market segments in order to succeed there. But how can you introduce brand coherence if you must also adapt to the segments?

The temptation, for the generalist brand, is to define such general and bland brand values that they thereby cease to define a singular offer in each segment. The generalist brand then becomes simply a recognised name, a label of quality and no more, but with no aspirational power. In the stores, the salespeople take note: clients are in a hurry to discuss the size of the discount. They do not nurture any strong intrinsic desire to finally possess 'a Renault' or 'an Opel'. In short, the generalist brand becomes, to use an analogy, a belt from which the models are hung, rather than a pole of attraction expressed by the models. This is why the generalist promotes models ('the Golf', 'the Quashquai'), whereas the specialist promotes itself ('a BMW'). The generalist turns its models into brands themselves, each with its own personality: not so the specialist. Every BMW is a BMW.

Confronting the risk of the markets becoming humdrum, and therefore of the price-only reasoning that threatens them on the front line, the generalist brand must be boosted with an intrinsic value that is more than the sum of its models. Contrary to the natural catch-all tendency of the generalist, there is a need to give it an exclusive meta-value, a positioning: that is, the power to say no. Being selective means losing short-term turnover, but increasing long-term desirability.

The most instructive comparison is between Samaritaine and Galeries Lafayette. As department stores in Paris, and therefore subject to very high overheads, these two entities had the same enormous requirements in terms of daily visits, since only a fraction of visitors will buy anything. The neutral point is very high. Samaritaine reacted like a store, and closed down. Galeries Lafayette, under the impulsion of P Houzé, reacted like a brand: it took a lead over its competitor Printemps. In 2006, the owner of Printemps,

the PPR group, preferred to sell it on to an Italian group.

Samaritaine's mistake was not to have understood that faced with the many forms of competition in the city centre, but also in the suburbs, it was necessary to focus, to refocus, and to make a choice. It needed to give consumers a greater and more aspirational reason to visit Samaritaine first. Faced with Zara, H&M, C&A and its other competition on Paris's Boulevard Haussmann, Galeries Lafayette centred itself on a meta value that became the guiding principle of all its daily decisions. Galeries Lafayette saw itself as a 'temple of fashion'. To achieve this, from 2000 onwards it pursued a systematic policy of not renewing contracts with all those brands that in its view were not sufficiently in line with its positioning. This was a brave decision in commercial terms: it is easy to imagine the nervousness of the salespeople and shareholders, facing a loss of turnover with no guarantee that this would ever be compensated.

Whereas the now-defunct Samaritaine claimed, 'You can find everything at Samaritaine' – that is, refused to do the work of selecting its range under the auspices of a positioning, and continued to think only in terms of breadth and depth of range – Galeries Lafayette made known both internally and externally that you would no longer find everything at Galeries Lafayette: only fashion would exist there, whatever the department. Exit the toy and book department, and others, for the same reason. The new store Galeries Lafayette *Décoration et Maison* (Decoration and Home) is not a store like any other, either: it says 'fashion' on every floor, in every department.

As a just reward for this effort of thinking and acting like a brand, Louis Vuitton decided that it could no longer *not* be seen at Galeries Lafayette. The fashion brands now jostle one another to get a mention there.

What can we draw from this example? The generalist brand must of course occupy all segments, always assuming that it can exercise its own personal brand imprint there. Will it be able to imprint its strong, aspirational central values there? If not, then it should not go there. Figure 11.4 shows clearly that, even if the base of the pyramid representing the generalist brand is larger by definition, all of the models must be ruled by a strong common vision and conception. Of course the models must have personality, in order to be intrinsically boosted by added values, but there must be a *leitmotif* between them that cannot only be purely formal.

Peugeot is a model of a generalist brand that has understood how much thinking like a brand means imprinting its difference, and therefore its values, on all its models, all its acts and client relationships. From the little 106 to the splendid 607, all have the feline design that has become so characteristic of the brand: but let no one be deceived, the Peugeot brand is not Swatch, where the differentiation essentially comes down to design. The feline design merely expresses with personality the values found in the brand: audacity, dynamism, aesthetics and reliability. Citroen has also understood how the generalist brand is managed: not like a rake that catches everything, but as a precise, differentiating, aspira-

tional automobile project. Then in each segment the models must each embody each of the three values of the brand's identity kernel. This is non-negotiable. The brand must also respect, in each segment, the price deciles that correspond to its positioning.

The relationship between brand and products also differs between the two cases. The specialist is by its nature highly typified, identifiable and exclusive. The reverse is true of the generalist. In this way we recognise a BMW immediately from its design, but also from a unique driving experience. BMW expresses the virtues of German engineering. Conversely, a Volkswagen is harder to recognise at first glance. This is not to say that its models do not have common traits: they must do, or they could not all carry the same brand. However, there are many more differences between the models in the Volkswagen range than the BMW range.

Volkswagen, like any generalist brand, sees itself as ecumenical: the car that will attract people looking for a small city car (the Lupo) is not the car that must steal market share from the Mercedes C-Class (the Passat). At BMW, between the 1 series and the 7 series, there are differences of degree only. They are almost all 100 per cent BMW. Each model

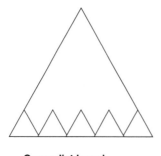

Generalist brand

- Multiple targets
Products are sub-brands

Specialist brand

- Monotarget
Products are variants

Figure 11.4   Generalist and specialist brands

reproduces and embodies the essential facets of what we mean by BMW, therefore what we expect from a BMW!

As a specialist brand, BMW is consequently intransigent regarding the conditions that decide whether a model may be called a BMW or not: there are a series of *sine qua non* characteristics. The generalist brand is more flexible: the Renault range went from Twingo and even Dacia Logan to Vel Satis. It is not, however, open to all models. The Renault brand also has its criteria for inclusion and exclusion, but they are designed to enable greater openness towards different types of car buyer: there are sporty Renaults and softer Renaults, estates and minivans, and so on. Volvo is also a specialist brand. Of course it wishes to grow but remain the model, the referent of cars where security, comfort and reliability come first. This also applies to trucks, cranes, public works equipment and so on. By doing this, Volvo cuts itself off from all those customers who do not have safety as a priority. To brand is to choose.

Building the brand through coherence

All brands grow through multiplication. The brand begins by introducing variants of the initial new product or service that founded its success. This policy of product differentiation makes it possible to increase the brand's relevance, enlarge its presence and therefore its visibility, whether online, among distributors, or on the shelf, if applicable. This also increases sales.

Growth also comes from enlarging the initial target market, and the regular concomitant adaptation of the brand's products. The adoption of new distribution channels often introduces a variation in the offer in order to avoid conflicts between channels, despite the thorny problem of price disparities. Finally, the conquest of the international market, for example via commercial

agents, importers or even subsidiaries, may lead to a loss of control, and therefore to a local reinterpretation of the brand, not to mention the many demands for new products that will inevitably arise under the cover of better meeting the demands of consumers in the country in question.

Growth therefore introduces diversity. Hence the challenge: how to manage this enlivening diversity without losing identity? How to introduce variety without losing the brand's specificity, without diluting it? This is the problem of the necessary coherence of the brand. What is, for example, the coherence between Chanel No 5, and all the brand's recent perfumes such as Chance or Egoïste? What coherence is there between Calvin Klein's 'wicked' perfumes Obsession and CK One, aimed at adolescents, and Eternity, a hymn to the family, and Truth?

Since the brand only exists via its products or services, only overall coherence makes it possible to communicate what they have in common: that is, the brand identity. Curiously, the brand coherence criterion is rarely taken into account when evaluating new product projects. These are selected on the basis of their potential sales and profitability, their chances of success in the channel or country in question. The resources available for launching them are also taken into account. The link with the parent brand is a secondary criterion, not perceived to be strategic. The short term is therefore favoured over the long term.

Why brand coherence?

Why worry about coherence? After all, if products are selling well, the company will grow, as will its profits and the brand recognition. However, this is to forget that the company is pursuing another task: increasing its own financial and share valuation, which is affected by the strength of its brands. It is also necessary nowadays to build defences against the cheaper copies that will inevitably emerge on the market. So how does one build a strong brand? Through the total coherence of everything it does, which enables it to emerge from the group of competitors.

For managers, the brand is constructed in stages, from top to bottom: first of all the brand platform is written (the identity of the brand to be created), then the products, services and in-store experiences that best embody them are created. For consumers or customers, it is the other way around: the experience precedes the essence. Their perception of the brand is built through the coherence of their repeated experiences over time. This is why the first contacts with the brands are determining factors in the formation of a long-term image: in which products/services will the brand be embodied? In what channels? By which retailers, department stores or distributors? In which price quartile? Through which marketing communications? Managers must know in advance what perception they wish to create, and must hold fast to it over time, eliminate any action or product/service that does not conform. There is no brand without strong internal policing and without a strong external coherence as well.

Building the brand involves constructing the perception of the specificity of that brand, its exclusive and motivating added value. In perception, as in teaching, repetition and coherence over time are indispensable. Consumers must be exposed to messages and products that, through their diversity, tell perceptibly the same story, each in its own way. After all, if the products have the same brand name, it is necessarily because they have something in common. Admittedly Renault Trucks operates on the worldwide truck market and belongs to the Volvo Group, but it carries the Renault brand and therefore cannot have a clashing discourse.

It is clear therefore that to build a brand, the brand must have coherence, and paradoxically, it is the source of its own coherence. This is why good brand management requires

a brand platform: that is, a very short document specifying what makes the brand unique (see Chapter 7). This base is integrative and normative: it must be upheld in order to introduce a necessary coherence if the market is to have a clear, readable perception of the brand.

Of course, repetition should not mean uniformity. Repeating oneself too much is boring: there is not enough innovation, and there are no surprises. Variety, diversity and surprise are ingredients of the modern brand that should permanently stir up interest in it. Too much diversity, however, leads to inefficiency, dispersal and a fuzzy perception of the brand (see Figure 11.1).

The challenge of coherence essentially relates to generalist brands, since their business model is precisely that of encompassing and integrating the ranges of various specialists. They increase in size by doing so, but may lose the perception of uniqueness, both internally (the managers no longer know) and externally (among clients). Thus in 2006 when Orange replaced the specialist mass internet brand wanadoo, and the Equant brand, a specialist in telecommunications for large companies, the internal managers did not perceive the coherence: they saw a dilution of what used to be the strong coherence of each of these two brands, their uniqueness. An intensive internal programme was necessary for them to grasp the new strategy, and the single Orange brand.

No brand without family resemblance

To understand the notion of brand coherence, it is useful to proceed with an anthropomorphic analogy: that of a family. Two things characterise strong, large families: a strong common ethos (shared values or personality traits) and a certain physical resemblance. We recognise a member of the Kennedy clan at a glance. Admittedly, each member is also different from all the others in terms of personality, but they have a common ethos, and physical elements that identify them.

The same must be true of brands. Growth is normal, as long as the identity is maintained: the basis, and the identifying elements. The family membership must be seen and not merely read (the name common to all): in the end, it must be possible to recognise that a member belongs to the family without reading the name.

A brand name is a point of reference: a sign of added value. The fact of putting a product under this name, to categorise it as such, itself confirms that it is a full member of this family, of this brand. It is therefore necessary to visualise it: hence the importance of packaging, labels, design, and everything that is seen on office fronts, factories and distributors. This makes it possible to install the common visual elements that will point to a family relationship. This would seem to be self-evident, but often the first efforts of many managers when extending a range are to introduce a high degree of differentiation between its members, reducing their common elements as much as possible.

Family resemblance cannot be reduced to appearances. As the proverb has it, it is not the cowl that makes the monk, but his religion. It is therefore necessary to ensure that all the brand's products do indeed have the same religion, share the same values, even live them, and express them in their own way.

The objective of family resemblance is not only to create internal coherence and order; it is also a key factor in differentiating a brand from the competition. Of course each product has its own characteristics, but in carrying a name it inherits the promises of this name, which thereby constitute its genuine differentiation amongst its competitors. The main difference between Renault Trucks and DAF or Iveco or MAN is Renault. The same is true for Mercedes trucks.

Take Danone as an example: the central value of the Danone chilled products brand is 'active good health'. Danone likes the active life-style and contributes to it. This is not a hospital or a diet brand (like Weight Watchers). The extremely broad Danone range from Activia and Actimel, through to the double-cream gourmet dessert Danette. It could be considered that this constitutes brand incoherence. The gourmet product Danette does not spontaneously evoke 'active good health'. On the contrary. it is rather the halo attached to the Danone name that differentiates Danette (derived from milk) from its competitors (Cadbury's, Mont Blanc cream desserts, Mars bars and so on). This halo of active good health, carried by the parent brand, is the lever of difference.

Coherence is not uniformity. In mature markets, an excess of uniformity kills desire. The growth of the brand via an extension of its product range nevertheless occurs by upholding the brand's central values, or it will run the risk of diluting its specificity. At the same time, too great a resemblance between the models and versions of the brand damages the impression of renewal, and makes it impossible to indicate a clear differentiation within the range. This double requirement is almost contradictory: this is the challenge of brands today.

What cognitive psychology tells us: there are degrees of coherence

How, then, can we manage both resemblance and diversity? How can we include coherence without creating uniformity? In order to move forward on the operational level, a detour through theory will be useful. The questions above are precisely the subject of what is known as cognitive psychology, the study of how people think and form categories. The notion of coherence is not binary: there are degrees of coherence. To return to the brand, this means that not all the products represent the brand in the same way and to the same degree, in the same way that the members of a family do not all have the family resemblance to the same degree.

One of the central subjects of cognitive psychology is understanding the way in which we categorise real objects. In fact, the human mind is constantly sorting, classing objects together in order to reduce diversity and render reality simpler and more comprehensible. This task is known as categorisation. We invent categories.

The modern, polymorphous brand, spread over several markets in different guises, cannot be considered simply as an example of a single category. Danone is not a kind of yoghurt. It is yoghurts, of course, but it is also bottled water, and dried biscuits in Asia. Nestlé gives its name to coffee, and to orange juice in Brazil, to chocolate, baby products, ice creams, iced tea and so on. The modern brand is itself in reality an abstract category, and thus a concept, which is manifested through products. The question of the inclusion/ exclusion of these products under the umbrella of the 'brand' supposes an understanding of the laws of categorisation. This analysis will be based on the major works of psychologists such as Lakoff (1987) and Boush (1993) in order to fuel the practice of brand management with their key contributions.

Mention is often made of the 'brand concept'. It is necessary to take this declaration literally: the brand is, and indeed works in the same way as, a concept. It is a concept in the same way that 'bird' is a concept, or 'game'. A concept is an abstraction that determines what goes together, and what could possibly be brought together under the same denomination. A concept is therefore a fantastic tool for inclusion and differentiation. We can begin to see the link with the brand here.

Let us take the concept of 'bird', which makes it possible to consider that things as different as a hummingbird and a parrot or a hen belong in fact to the same category (bird), whereas a butterfly (which also flies) cannot. However, an ostrich – which does not fly – is also a bird. The concept is therefore a classification mechanism, for bringing things together that may be very different in appearance.

In order to classify and bring together or exclude objects, the concept must have a content and a rule for admissibility/exclusion:

- Certain concepts class things according to the presence or absence of characteristics: for example, a bird is an animal that lays eggs and has feathers, and which can usually (but not always) fly. We see therefore that certain characteristics are essential (egg-laying, feathers), but others are not necessary for inclusion (flight). Either it is, or it is not, a bird. The frontier of the 'bird' concept is relatively clear-cut. A butterfly has no feathers and is therefore not a bird.

- Certain concepts bring things together on the basis of a group of factors, linked less to the object than to the effect of the object. Take 'game' as an example. What is a game? Thinking about it, the definition is a tricky one: what relationship is there between poker and hopscotch? Between chess (called a game of chess) and a game of hide and seek? Probably the answer lies in the motivations and gratifications that cause us to spend time on these activities, rather than the innate characteristics of the different occupations called 'games'.

- Finally, certain concepts bring things together in a symbolic manner: what is 'good'? Under the umbrella of 'good', we must be able to include some very disparate examples, provided that they symbolise 'goodness'.

This detour via cognitive psychology does not deviate from the question of brands.

- The first type of concept is typically that of specialised brands, with a highly typified product. A Saab, for example, is recognised through its design, its sounds and the driving experience. Porsche is too, but not Toyota.

▌ The second type of concept would involve a brand such as Volvo. Volvo is summed up in a word: safety, an advantage for users. Volvo is synonymous with security, even in very different markets: public works, cranes, trucks, cars and so on.

▌ The third type of concept is called 'metaphorical'. Take Nivea: when asked, the managers of this brand repeat *ad infinitum* that the Nivea concept is summed up by 'Love and care'. Its expression in cosmetic products is of a metaphorical kind as regards 'love'. The notion of care can be taken at both a physical level (skin care) and a psychological level (self-care).

Comparing these three types of concept, R van der Vorst (2004) has rightly emphasised that their capacity for integrating variety differs widely. Concepts of the first type (known as taxonomic) are highly specific about their inclusion criteria. As such, they allow very little product variety. The frontiers of the brand are precise.

At the other extreme, certain concepts are relatively vague on the nature of their members. Saying, as France Telecom does, that it is 'the brand of relationships' was fairly non-specific, but consequently rendered the brand open to variety. Its frontiers, however, were not clear.

At this point, a return to cognitive psychology is necessary. It teaches that a category may be defined either by its frontiers, or by its members. In fact, if we take the concept of 'game', it has no frontiers. At its furthest limit, anything could be a game as long as one took pleasure from it. You might think this is overly confusing, and taking it too far.

Cognitive psychology teaches that these categories are however ordered: not all members have the same status, the same representativeness. Some are very good examples of the category, others are less good

examples. For example, each person spontaneously thinks of a particular game on hearing the word 'game'. For children it may be hopscotch; for adults, card games. All games can be classed in this way according to their perceived degree of representativeness of the concept 'game'. The most typical game, the best example, is called the 'prototype' (McGarty, 1999). The concept may not have clear frontiers, but its core, on the other hand, is precise, typified by the best example (the prototype).

To return to brands, the psychology of prototypes proves enlightening. What are the frontiers of the Nestlé brand? The brand regularly pushes them back by putting its name to more and more different products. Consumers, however, have no difficulty in classing the products marked Nestlé in order of representativeness, from the most typical to the least typical. Everything works as though they compared each product to the prototype of good Nestlé baby milk. The prototype is not necessarily a product: it can be a person. Richard Branson is the prototype of the Virgin brand: daring, fun and very friendly. This was also the case for Steve Jobs. He embodied 'Apple know-how', and the dwindling brand found a second wind when he returned to take charge. He is also symbolic of Apple values: simplicity, conviviality and creativity.

Relationships between concepts and examples, brand and products

As it is with concepts, so it is with brands. Two levels must be distinguished. The abstract level specifies the meaning of the concept (the brand meaning, the essence of its identity). The second level is that of the brand's embodiments, its products or services.

At the conceptual (brand) level, it is also necessary to distinguish between those facets of its identity that are essential, and those that are not necessary, which can be called 'peripheral'. This distinction is based on the contributions of social and representational psychology. Working on social stereotypes, researchers such as Asch (1946) and more recently in France Abric (1994), and in marketing Mischel (2000), have emphasised the need to sort those facets of identity without which the brand is no longer itself from the other, more peripheral facets. The first group are 'core facets'. For Apple, these were summarised as creativity, simplicity and conviviality. Design for Apple would be a more peripheral trait, specific to the iPod or iMac.

The product level is that of the embodiment of the brand identity. Placing the same name on several products is to tell or promise consumers that there is a certain equivalence between these products. Nevertheless, not all products represent the brand to the same degree. R van der Vorst (2004) recalls that products are constantly in competition. From this point of view, it is important to distinguish those facets of a product that are distinctive and differentiate from their competitors in that segment, and those that are not. Thus colour was highly differentiating for the iMac, not its memory capacity.

It is therefore possible to identify four types of relationship between brand and products, between the distinctive facets of the products and the essence of the brand (the facets of its core identity). (See Figure 11.5.)

▮ The 'typical example' relationship. In this case, the facets of the core identity of the brand are also the distinctive facets of the product, and vice versa.

▮ The 'similarity' relationship. In this case, the distinctive facets of the product are the same as those of the core identity, with one or two additional facets specific to the product (colour, for the iMac).

▮ The 'transformation' relationship. In this case, one of the facets of the core is not found in the product's distinctive facets. This is the case with iTunes for Apple.

▮ The 'contradiction' relationship. In this case, not only is one of the identifying values not embodied in the product, but it is contradicted by a specific facet of the product in question. The Mac Quadra, a computer created by Apple and intended for company executives, might be thought to be such a case.

Throughout the development of a brand, it is expressed through examples. The primary best-seller becomes the brand's 'prototype', that which shapes the identity of which it is the living and recognised symbol. The small blue tub of Nivea is the 'prototype' of Nivea. In fact, Nivea breaks into all countries through this universal product, which sums up the essence of the brand (love and care) and its associated values (accessibility, universality, simplicity, closeness). This is the first contact for most families throughout the world: everyone uses Nivea moisturising cream with its pleasant smell. Then the brand develops other self-care product lines, or other examples of the brand that are very similar to the prototype, aimed at a specific target or a particular use: for hands, against sun damage, for children and so on. Of course each one of these must have a specific element, in order to take into account competition in the segment. Their fatal weapon of differentiation, however, derives essentially from the respect for the brand's values and the status that the fact of carrying this brand name confers.

Then Nivea enlarges the circle of its product lines by introducing lines that are transformations of the brand (a key facet may be absent from the product's differentiating elements): deodorant lines, alcohol-based products for men, not to mention Nivea Beauty, where care is absent since it is a wide range of beauty products, of pure seduction (mascara, lipstick, eye shadow and so on). It might be asked whether Nivea Beauty was not in fact a contradiction from this point of view: not only was the care value missing from the distinctive

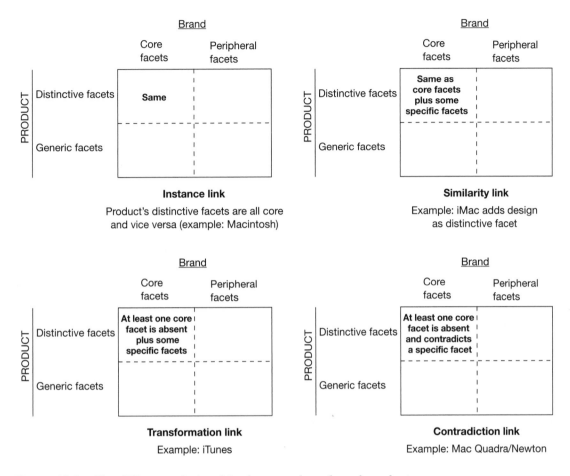

Figure 11.5   The different relationships between brands and products
Source: adapted from R van der Vorst (2004)

facets of these products, arguably their sales arguments (seduction, artificiality) were contradictory to the brand's essence.

Growth, diversity and managing coherence

Brand coherence is rarely instilled from the beginning. The need for it is only felt when sales stabilise, when margins are reducing and price competition intensifies. Then it becomes necessary to close ranks and hunt down any inefficiencies in order to rededicate financial resources to innovation and communication. The multiplication of products without coherence leads to enormous waste of energy and money. Instead of building a strong, distinctive, unique brand, products are scattered widely under a single name. The first step is therefore to begin again from the name.

Defining the core identity of the brand

At Mars, a fundamental debate divides the company. What are the key facets of the Mars brand? For some, the answer is purely the taste and the sensory experience. For others, the uniqueness of the brand relates to the taste and the energy provided (physical and emotional). This discussion is not a matter of splitting hairs. Depending on Masterfoods' choice of one or other of the two visions of the essence of its Mars brand, certain product lines may or may not be in contradiction with the brand, and therefore incoherent.

Thus, from the first perspective (taste and sensory experience), Mars with almonds is a mistake. Yes, it sells. But nothing is more contradictory to the famous Mars sensory experience than the dry, crunchy aspect of an almond. In fact, many consumers like Mars less once they have tasted a Mars with almonds. The same is true for Mars drinks and the Mars chocolate egg.

From the second perspective, based on taste and energy, Mars with almonds is not contradictory, nor is a Mars drink, but the Mars egg remains so (it was created to counter the Kinder egg, so strong on the notion of the parental gift). Note that the two visions of Mars do not offer the same prospects in terms of variety, and therefore of the inclusion of new products and new consumers (van der Vorst, 2004).

Defining Mars as a 'taste and sensory experience' is to define inclusion according to the product's character. This is a concept with clear borders, linked to the characteristics of the product. On the other hand, it leaves open the consumer benefit and the targets. Nothing in this schema prohibits the creation of new products, coherent with Mars of course, but also with the added benefits of energy here, of indulgence there, of a gift there, of sharing there. Moreover, this brand perspective makes it possible to aim at very different targets: men with a chocolate bar, women with Mars Delight, children with Mars Mini and so on. This brand essence categorises the products, but less so the clients (van der Vorst, 2004).

Defining Mars as 'taste and energy' opens up a multitude of organoleptic formats (bar, drink, biscuits, ice creams and so on) but is much more restrictive in terms of consumer

benefits and clients. Here a choice has been made: to address those clients and situations where energy is a key expectation. This brand essence categorises the clients, but less so the products.

How is the brand's core identity identified? Recall the central precept: the truth of a brand lies in the brand itself. By studying the heritage, roots and history of the brand (its DNA), potential facets of its core can be identified.

However, the evaluation of the clients themselves must be sought on this, in order to avoid a gap between an exhumed past identity, and the present reality (the market opinion): identity is not a point of view. For example, 'radical progress' is certainly in Citroen's DNA, but is it still attributed to the brand today? It is therefore also necessary to integrate the perception of consumers or industrial clients themselves. In addition to the image study that identifies the traits associated with the brand, another study must be carried out, to identify which of these traits are critical to the brand, the others being peripheral. G Michel (2000) has contributed to this by transposing the methodology of social psychology to marketing.

To find the answer, it is enough to ask interviewees whether a new product that does not have one or other of the brand's image traits could nevertheless carry the name of said brand. If the majority say no, it is a non-negotiable trait: it belongs to the core identity. The peripheral traits may be present or not, according to the segments and the products of the range that correspond to them.

However, if the core identity is subjected too much to the judgement of consumers who are constantly evolving, a deviation is created. For the directors of BMW, a BMW will always have rear-wheel drive, since this is the necessary physical signature of the unique driving experience of the cars of this brand. This would be true even if certain potential customers expressed the opinion that, for them, a front-wheel drive would not change

Question: what traits are necessary to the brand?

Out of the brand territory

Below 60%

Peripheral traits

60% to 70%

Kernel

Traits judged by more than 70% to be necessary to the brand definition (invariants)

60% to 70%

Below 60%

Out of the brand territory

Figure 11.6 How to identify kernel and peripheral traits

their love of the brand. Managing is not about following, but about having a vision.

Confirming the presence of brand core facets in each product

There is no brand: there are only expressions thereof. These expressions shape the representation. For the brand to be strong and distinctive, every expression must carry the brand's identity facets, and these must be clearly visible. Therefore each of the products or each of the daughter brands will be analysed – their packaging, their physical product, their communication, their price, their merchandising and so on – in order to identify whether the key facets, those of the core identity, are all well represented and active in these products and daughter brands. Figure 11.7 illustrates how the different Lacoste lines activate the three facets of the core identity (elegance, comfort and naturalness) and provide specific touches here or there (more technique, more fun, more

luxury, more fashion). If this were not the case, the product would have to be brought into line with the brand, or dropped.

Identifying the role of each product line in the construction of the brand

At this stage it is necessary to understand the link that each product line and daughter brand has with the parent brand. Is it a prototype? Should it become tomorrow's prototype? Is it a typical example? Is it similar? Is it a transformation? Is it contradictory?

According to the link that each line must have, a greater or lesser degree of distance in the expression of the line itself will be accepted. First of all, signs of strong cohesion are expected: the distances can only be a function of the link identified above. This also has an impact on the decision to give the product line its own name (giving it the status of a daughter brand) or not. Finally, this will determine the parent brand's posture towards

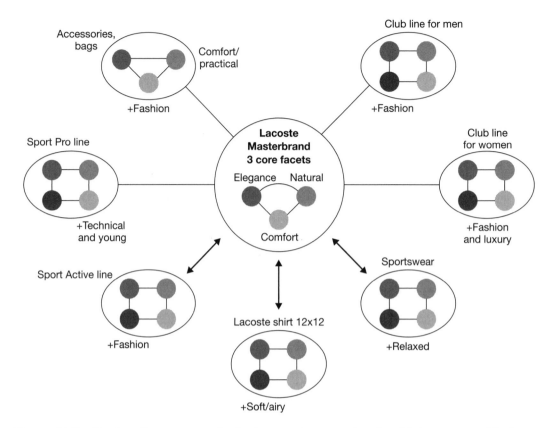

Figure 11.7   Product lines must embody the core facets and each adds its own specific facet

its products: this will be examined further on through what are known as the umbrella, source, endorsement and maker's mark architectures (see Chapter 13).

The marketing function of each product line or daughter brand will also be specified: of course it must absolutely observe and activate the central values, but also bring a new contribution. This might be, for example:

▌ modernising the brand by becoming its new prototype (Activia is the new Danone prototype, and has replaced its old prototype of natural yoghurt);

▌ rejuvenating the brand by opening it up to younger clienteles;

▌ bringing a new facet to the brand, such as technical expertise or a pleasure dimension;

▌ strengthening certain identity pillars of the brand: for example, the tennis lines strengthen the identity of Lacoste, the eponymous brand of the famous Musketeer René Lacoste, at the moment when its global competitor Ralph Lauren invented a tennis legitimacy for itself by sponsoring the 2006 Wimbledon tournament and launching a line of Wimbledon clothing.

Graphically representing the overall system of the brand

The brand must therefore be thought of as a concept, whose meaning unifies the products and distinguishes them from the competition. It is only expressed through its products, communications and activities in stores and

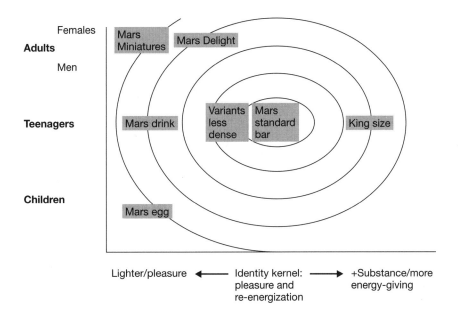

Figure 11.8   Organisation of Mars masterbrand and products
Source: R van der Vorst, 2004

other aspects. It is important to understand the overall system set-up, by mapping all the products seen as expressions of the brand, placed according to their distance from the central values of the brand. In Figure 11.8, we have mapped out the current Mars system. This exercise is necessary to avoid a common pitfall: a system that is empty at its centre.

It is possible, in fact, for everyone to be conscious of the values of the parent brand (also known as the masterbrand) but for no product of the range to assume these values 100 per cent and become the prototype. What is often found is a situation where the brand has three distinctive facets A, B and C; certain products carry value A, others B, and the third group facet C. This situation, however, does nothing to build the brand up with values A, B and C.

The brand is not an average, the sum of disparate discourses. It is built up in image and sales through successive products. These must be bearers of all the core values. Admittedly it is possible to place a stronger emphasis on this or that facet, but all the

facets must be well and truly present. Thus the premium line 'Club de Lacoste' does indeed emphasise elegance, but also activates the two other central brand values, comfort and naturalness.

Checking the coherence worldwide

The exercise described above should be carried out by geographic region. Here it may then appear that the same product does not have the same link to the parent brand on different continents, or the same role, or the same positioning. These situations lead to inefficiencies and should be corrected if necessary. It is nevertheless possible for local specificities to require adaptation. For example, in Germany, a country whose car-making pride is well known, the 'prototypes' of the Peugeot brand are the CC models of the 206 and 307. In fact, these represent a type of car that German car makers were not offering at the time: a convertible coupe. They represent more than 35 per cent of Peugeot sales in Germany, and

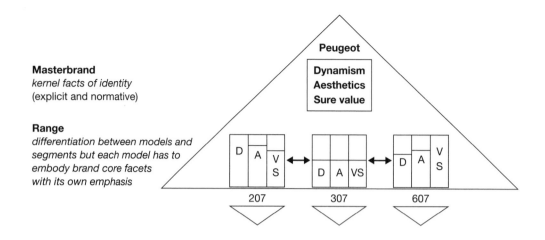

Figure 11.9   How the brand is carried by its products, each with its own emphasis

carry the central image of the brand (dynamism, aesthetics and value), with emphasis on the first two facets.

Brand globalisation therefore requires a double coherence: as discussed above, of the products in relation to the central facets of the masterbrand (masterbrand central or core facets), but also of each region of the world in relation to the identity of each product itself. (This point is developed further in the chapter on globalisation.) Figure 11.9 summarises our statement. The BMW 1 series expresses the core identity of its masterbrand BMW in its own way, and each region of the world must respect the identity of the BMW 1 series if there is a desire to construct a truly global perception of the masterbrand.

The three layers of a brand: kernel, codes and promises

The evolution of a brand needs a direction. Considering the brand as a vision about its product category, it is important to know in which direction it is looking. The brand being a genetic memory to help us manage the future, we must know what drives it, what is its prime reason for existing.

All these concepts (source of inspiration, statement, codes and communication themes) work together in a three-tier pyramid that is useful in managing the balance of change and identity.

▌ At the top of the pyramid is the kernel of the brand, the source of its identity. It must be known because it imparts coherence and consistency.

▌ The base of the pyramid are the themes: it is the tier of communication concepts and the product's positioning, of the promises linked to the latter.

▌ The middle level relates to the stylistic code, how the brand talks and which images it uses. It is through his or her style that an author (the brand) writes the theme and describes him- or herself as a brand. It is the style that leaves a mark.

Of course, there is a close relationship between the facets of the identity prism of a brand and the three tiers of its pyramid. An

Figure 11.10   Identity and pyramid models

examination of advertising themes reveals that they refer to the physical nature of products or to customer attitudes or finally to the relationship between the two (particularly in service brands). They are the outward facets of identity, those that are visible and that lead to something tangible. The style, as with one's handwriting, reveals the brand's interior facets, its personality, its culture, the self concept it offers. Finally, the genetic code, the roots of a brand, inspires its whole structure and nurtures its culture. It is the driving mechanism. There is, therefore, a strong relationship between stylistic codes and identity. In Volkswagen's case, its sense of humour is the consequence of solidarity because it demonstrates the rejection of car idolisation, the cult which leads to a hierarchical ranking of drivers and therefore to their animosity towards each other.

This idea of levels or tiers within the brand provides a tool which allows freedom for the brand in the sense that the brand no longer has to define itself by repeating the same themes. The choice of the theme has to integrate the needs of the times. It is founded on the reality of products and services. It corresponds to a concern or a desire of a particular market segment. Alongside these criteria, one must respect the brand's identity.

Brand communication can thus vary in its facets. Over time it seems first to start with the physique, goes through the reflected image and ends with the cultural facet. Benetton first launched its colourful sweaters, then modernised to appear more dyamic, before identifying with a set of universal values (friendship, racial tolerance, the world village). This evolution is normal: the brand goes from tangibles to intangibles. It starts as the name of a new product, an innovation and later acquires other meanings and autonomy. Benetton is now a cultural brand and addresses a range of moral issues. Nike moved from product communications to behavioural values (just do it!).

The pyramid model leads to a differentiated management of change. The brand's themes (its positionings) must evolve if they no longer motivate: it is obvious that Evian had to move from balance to youth. All themes tend to wear off and competitors do not stand still. The stylistic code, the expression of the personality and culture of the brand, has to be more stable: it enables the brand to gently pass without disruption from one theme to another. Finally, the genetic code is fixed. Changing it means building another brand, a homonym of the first, but different. This is how, even if the positioning of Evian has changed with time, from being the water of babies, to that of the Alps and that of the strength of balance, there is a strong sense that the basic identity has been preserved. Evian never was a water against something, but a water for something, natural and loving, a source of life. It is not for nothing that its label has always been pink: this colour is linked to the brand's kernel, its essential identity, those traits that are necessary to the brand. Without them, it would be another brand.

Finally, the idea of different tiers within the brand gives particular flexibility to those brands which embrace many products. In managing these products one must respect their individual position in their own markets. They may carry different promises for each product, provided they appear to emanate from a common source of inspiration. In this respect, brands work as a superstructure.

Taking into account the importance of this genetic code, how do we recognise it? All brands do not always have this identity basis. Some of them have only communication codes, or a style. When one says that Cacharel is romantic, one talks about a common style and source of coherence between Anaïs-Anaïs, Eden and Gloria. Its products carry within them a very precise and hidden driving principle.

Consumers, clients and even managers are rarely aware of the brand's pivotal guiding force. They readily talk of its visible facets and of its codes, but without penetrating the brand's programme. Nor is the brand's creator aware of it, but carries it subconsciously. He transmits it through his actions and his choices. Thus when Mr Robert Ricci died in the summer of 1988, his successor commissioned an analysis of the identity of the Nina

Ricci house alongside its worldwide best-selling perfume L'Air du Temps. The death of a creator signals the birth of a brand: respect for it demands understanding. An analysis of identity lies more in the history of the brand than in opinion surveys. The most typical products of the brand are closely examined throughout time: from what unconscious programme do they seem to emanate? Why does Nina Ricci haute couture sparkle with its dazzling evening dresses? Why did Mr Robert Ricci find in the photographer David Hamilton's 'fuzzy' style a sort of revelation, to the point of signing a long-term and exclusive contract with him? What is the link between the dresses, L'Air du Temps and Hamilton? Once the highest point of the Ricci pyramid is known, the problem of the necessary replacement of David Hamilton's style becomes less acute. We know what he was expressing. Other means of expression will achieve this without using fake Hamiltons. Long-established brands seeking such an overhaul should undergo an inner search before projecting themselves into the future.

Respecting the brand DNA

Each brand should be seen as a contract. It binds, promises and engages each side: the company and its clients. The brand expects loyalty from consumers but it must in turn be loyal to them. With time, it is normal that the brand should seek to widen its client base by offering other products and services. In doing so, it communicates more and more on its margins and less and less on its core, on the basic contract.

The source of the current problems of Club Med, which feels it has lost its identity, may also find their source in the forsaking of the founding principles of the brand. However, it was not without reason that the product range was differentiated to fit a particular market segmentation which, as customers were growing older, expected more comfort in the rooms and sometimes wanted to withdraw from the group and not sit down at mealtimes at the famous eight-people tables. What aged in Club Med's offer is the value system portrayed in its advertising, and which a part of the population no longer identifies with, in particular its opinion leaders. The concept of 'happiness' in groups is a cliché and no longer corresponds to the intense need for meaning expressed by our society. What made the inspired strength of Club Méditerranée was forgotten when the brand was restructured to make it international and renamed Club Med. Indeed, the Mediterranean Sea is not, as one would think, just a reference to the original location of the vacation villages or to some water sports. It is, on a symbolic level, a source of life. The intense need for Club Méditerranée lies in its brand kernel: to replenish, to find one's self again. This drive, remarkably transposed in its time by the famous advertising campaign coined by the FCA agency (love, live, play, talk...), has disappeared and does not seem to inspire the current brand any more, as Club Med has become a vacation club like all others, only more expensive than most, and no longer promotes a particular vision.

The pressures that lead a brand astray from the initial contract by little nudges are numerous and create the risk of identity loss. The management of the Paloma Picasso perfume brand is a good example of this. Through the roots of the brand and the creator whose name it bears, this brand symbolises a violent Latin character, the South, a haughty, self-asserting pride. Its codes of red and black are Latin codes, signs of a strong character, but such an identity creates territorial boundaries for the brand. It is strong in South America, in the Sunbelt in the United States (Florida, Texas, California), and in Europe in all the countries where Spain exerts an attraction (Germany, Great Britain, France). On the other hand, it has not been able to penetrate the Asian market (where the preference is for pastels, tenderness, softness),

or in Oceania, Australia and Scandinavian countries. Hence the question that arose at the launching of the third perfume: should one respect the brand contract – what it has stood for up until now, the basis of its success – or put on the market a softer version?

Revitalising brands also implies the rediscovery of one's roots. With time, we tend to forget the founding principles accumulating compromise after compromise. The Novotel management called the programme which redefined the orientation of the brand 'return to the future'. The aim was not to reconstruct the Novotels from the good old days but to take up again the historic mission of the brand, updated to meet the needs of its clients in the year 2000.

Managing two levels of branding

Managing both change and identity is helped by a double level of brand architecture. This is how Calvin Klein, Chanel and Volkswagen are organised. How does one consistently manage such brands? They are called source brands in the sense that they include products that have their own individual identity and brand name. In this sense we talk of mother brands and daughter brands, or first-name brands. Thus, there is Renault but there are also the personalities of Clio, Twingo, Megane and Val Satis, each with its own identity. The Renault brand is not content just with endorsing, it adds its own values and creates a coherent environment. It is no longer an umbrella brand because there are two levels to the brand (the family name and the first name), whereas an umbrella brand includes products without first names (such as a Philips TV, a Philips razor, a Philips coffee machine ...). The problem that surfaces is that of the balance which has to be struck between coherence and freedom, family resemblance and individuality. This concerns, beyond the examples just cited, all industrial groups that maintain the strong identities of corporate brands, and that do not want to be considered as merely a holding company. The key lies in a systematic approach to the source brand, analysing what each daughter brand brings to or borrows from the whole.

One should always start with understanding the whole (the masterbrand or house brand) and how this impacts on its products.

12

Growth through brand extensions

Brand extension is on the increase. When they wish to enter markets from which they have been absent, more and more companies do so using the name of one of their existing brands, rather than using a new brand name created for that purpose. Yet brand extension is not a recent phenomenon (Gamble, 1967). It is inherent in the luxury goods sector: the luxury brands originating in haute couture have extended to accessories, fancy leather goods, jewellery, watch-making, even tableware and cosmetics.

In the same way, the first distributors' brands (Migros in Switzerland, St Michael in Great Britain) covered several differentiated categories of products. Industrial brands themselves were extended beyond their initial product type to cover a range of diversified activities under the same name: Siemens, Philips and Mitsubishi have been using brand extension for a long time. Indeed, brand extension is even used systematically by Japanese conglomerates: Mitsubishi includes shipyards, nuclear plants, cars, high-fidelity systems, banks and even food under the three-diamond brand (the visual symbol of Mitsubishi).

Brand extension has become common practice. What was reserved for luxury goods is becoming a general managerial procedure: Mars is no longer only the famous bar but an ice cream, a chocolate drink and a slab of chocolate; Virgin covers everything from airlines to soft drinks; McCain covers French fries, pizzas, buns and iced tea; Evian now endorses cosmetics. For all those executives brought up on sacrosanct Procterian dogma according to which a brand must correspond to one, and only one, product, the present situation leads to thorough rethinking; even Mars, for so long the typical example of a product brand, has become an umbrella brand covering very different segments and products. Such development is the direct consequence of the recognition that brands are the real capital of a company and a source of competitive advantage.

Brand extensions are one of the hottest topics in brand management. They have spawned a rich and intense body of research. Some experts keep claiming that brand extension should be avoided (Trout and Ries, 1981, 2000). However, today, most companies, even those that were culturally the least prone to engage in brand extensions, have extended their brands. In fact, as we shall demonstrate, brand extension is a necessary strategic move at some point in the life of a brand. It is an essential way to sustain the brand's growth, once other approaches have been explored. Let us remember that growth should be built:

▌ First, by increasing the volume of purchase per capita of present customers of the present product (see Chapter 9).

▌ Then by new product development and line extension to increase the brand's relevance and address the needs of more specific targets or situations. Line extensions are, in fact, proliferating in modern supermarkets.

▌ By the globalisation of business in countries offering high growth opportunities (see Chapter 17).

▌ By innovating to modify the competitive situation, create new competitive advantages or open new markets, thus benefiting from the pioneer advantage. At this time the question of naming the innovation becomes acute. Should one extend the brand portfolio by adding a new brand (as when the Coca-Cola Company added Tab to its portfolio) or call it instead by the name of an already existing brand (Diet Coke, for instance)?

When an innovation is not in the core market of the brand, it means that the brand will extend out of this core, a process also called brand stretching. This is why brand extension is such an important topic: it is about the redefinition of the brand meaning. It is not possible to grow the business indefinitely without changing some facets of the brand. Hence the question, is the essence of the brand intact? Does the extension preserve the kernel? Also, what does the extension bring to the brand equity, to the brand image, beyond growing the business? These are indeed strategic questions.

Beyond branding itself, extensions are often diversifications, entries into unknown markets, with a different product from previously (see Table 12.1). As such they are a strategic move.

What is new about brand extensions?

Why has brand extension become such an important topic? In fact, most companies have discovered the virtues of brand extensions only recently. Certainly most luxury brands have thrived through extensions, and so have Japanese brands, and indeed Nestlé, but in North America and Europe most marketers have been trained in a 'Procterian' vision of marketing. At Procter & Gamble, since its foundation, a brand has been a single product with a benefit. As a consequence, the rule has been that new products should form a new brand. P&G's Ariel (known as Tide in the United States) is a specific low-suds detergent. Other detergents have other brand names such as Dash and Vizir. This practice is thoroughly product-based.

The brand extension perspective introduces two radical modifications. First, it maintains that a brand is a single and long-lasting promise, but this promise can or should be

Table 12.1   Relating extensions to strategy

	Products	
Markets	Present	New
Present	Intensive growth	Market development
New	Market extensions	Diversification

expressed and embodied in different products, and eventually in different categories. 'Palmolive' represents softness, and from this perspective it makes sense to have Palmolive hand soap, dishwashing liquid, shaving cream, shampoo and so on.

Second, it asks us eventually to redefine the historical brand benefit by nesting it in a higher order value. Brand extension exemplifies the move from tangible to intangible values, from a single product-based promise to a larger brand benefit, thus making the brand able to cover a wider range of products. Is Gillette simply the best shaving product, or 'The best a man can get'? as it says in its advertising baseline? This latter brand definition easily backs up the Gillette Sensor, or Mach 3, aimed at continually increasing the quality of a man's shave. It allows also the brand to grow by leveraging its reputation and trust to introduce a line of male toiletries, a profitable, growing market.

Brand extensions are an emotional topic because they are the first occasion on which the identity of a brand is redefined, when all the unwritten assumptions that may have been held for decades about the brand within the company are questioned. In addition, unlike mere line extensions, brand extensions are associated with diversification, so there is a sizeable impact on the company as a whole. Research on brand extension has been so obsessed by the brand itself that this has tended to foster a tunnel vision in marketing circles. The only focus of that research was to determine consumers' attitudes to various possible extensions for a specific brand (Aaker and Keller, 1990). This is why so many companies have gone through a phase where they extended their brands in all directions, just because the consumers said they could do it. This phase has ended; this early research neglected the company. It is a form of tunnel vision to focus on the brand only and exclusively. Diversification is a strategic concept, which has implications for the whole company. Will it be able to learn all the new

competences required to meet competition in the new market? At what price? With what delays? At what cost? Is it worth it? Is it sustainable? The brand and business perspective promoted by this book calls for a reinsertion of brand extension issues into the context of corporate strategy.

Finally, it is an involving topic because it is generally tied to a new product launch, which as for all new products commands time, energy, allocation of resources, and creates a situation of risk. This risk is increased by the fact that unlike line extensions, brand extensions lead the brand into new and unknown markets, which may be dominated by entrenched competitors. There is not only a straightforward financial risk should the extension fail, there is also potential damage to the image of the brand, in the distribution channels, among the trade, and among end users. A good example is the problems encountered by Mercedes when it launched its new Class A, a radical downward extension, after it decided to go where the market was and compete against Volkswagen. The car could not pass the 'elan test', thus destroying the sacrosanct image of Mercedes as one of the most secure cars in the world. The whole conception of a Mercedes car had to be redefined. One does not move easily from a high historical competence in manufacturing large sedan cars with rear wheel drive to making small compact cars with front wheel drive. Also for the first time, one could buy a new Mercedes for around €20,000.

This example illustrates the fact that brand extension decisions should not be looked at only through consumer research. As a rule, when expensive brands stretch downward, their existing clients are frustrated. They feel less exclusive, therefore their attitude to the extension is negative (Kirmani, Sood and Bridges, 1999). However consumers are in that respect quite conservative. They do not have a full picture of the Mercedes situation, and finally they do not have a long-term view. Very few people knew, for instance, that the average age of purchasers of the Class C, at that time the entry-level Mercedes, was 51. Also, very few people knew that unless the company was able to produce more than a million cars rapidly, its production costs would be too high to sustain modern competition even in the premium segments. Higher production costs provide no value to consumers.

Managing brand extensions is about identifying the growth opportunities. It aims also at maximising the chances of success of the new product launch, while increasing the value of the parent brand. This entails managing the whole product range: to maintain its equity. Mercedes reinvested to innovate in the high-end segment of its market through the new Class S and now a spectacular top-end model. On this occasion a naming problem arose: it was not called 'Class Y' but received a name, a brand: Maytag.

Since the first edition of this book in 1991, the brand extension field has changed. Companies have all gained experience in extending their brand. Some have made timid but successful extensions (Mars ice cream), others have experimented with at least 10 extensions, which may have all failed, as did Becel extensions, Unilever's anti-cholesterol margarine (Kapferer, 2001: p 222). All acknowledge the necessity to reintroduce more focus, and more corporate parameters into the process. The decision to extend the brand is a strategic one, and relying on consumer's attitudes to possible extensions is now held to be seriously insufficient. Decision grids have to encompass other dimensions. In brief, because a brand could create an extension, it does not follow that it should do it. To a far greater extent than it has been said or written, it is necessary to assess the competitive status of the extension and of the company behind it. The question of what the extension really brings to the business and to the brand itself has also become more acute.

On an academic level, recent research is now revealing the limits of early studies on brand extension. Some of the models and rules presented in these pioneer studies should be questioned if not forgotten.

Brand or line extensions?

When should one speak of line or of brand extension? We developed the case for line extensions in Chapter 9. This is a necessary step in growing the brand through:

- An extension of the line to enrich the basic promise through diversity (like providing new tastes, new flavours for a jam brand or a crush brand such as Minute Maid).

- A finer segmentation of a need (like the many variants of each shampoo brand according to the type of hair, age of customer, or kind of scalp problem).

- Providing complementary products. As mentioned in the discussion on line brand architecture (Chapter 13), a brand might provide all the products involved in solving a specific consumer problem. A brand fighting hair loss would not limit itself to its first product, a shampoo for instance, but also provide a gel, a hair dye and so on.

What is noticeable is that through these line extensions, the brand aims at intensive growth. It deepens its problem-solving ability more or less to the same customers, for the same need and consumption situation. This is not viewed as a diversification (which involves different clients and different products).

At the other extreme no one would quarrel with describing as brand extensions, rather than line extensions, Virgin Airlines, Hewlett-Packard's entry into the digital photo business, the Mercedes Class A, the Porsche Cayenne (its entry into the 4 × 4 market), Yamaha bikes (from a company originally known for its musical instruments), the Caterpillar fashion line, Salomon new surfboards (for the Hawaiian and Australian beaches), Ralph Lauren domestic paint, Evian cosmetics, Merlin Gerin moving from switchgears to electrical distribution products, or GE extending from electricity to capital investment. Typically in such brand extensions, the brand moves to another remote category, in which it is open to question whether it has the ability to deliver the same benefit, and therefore to stay the same. The buyers may be different, or the same: the first to buy the Porsche Cayenne were existing Porsche owners who now have two Porsche cars. In fact most of the early research on brand extension has focused on remote extensions, far from the prototypical product. Some of these brand extensions are more than simply brand extensions: they are real diversifications. The company wants to develop itself in new categories that may become dominant in its future sales. Certainly this is not the case for Caterpillar, but it could be the case for HP, stuck between Dell and IBM in its core activity. Few people recall that Findus, the name for frozen food, comes from 'Fruit Industry', the core original business of that Scandinavian company.

Where does line extension end, and where does brand extension start? Perrier is a case in point. To grow its sales the brand has launched three new products in three years:

▌ In 2001 it launched its first 'Pet' bottle, nicknamed 'rocket' because of its specific shape. It was the first time since the brand creation (in 1847) that a non-glass bottle had been created. It was aimed at mobile consumers and out-of-home consumption situations (such as stadiums and offices).

▌ In 2002 Perrier Fluo was created: it is an aromatised water in a plastic fluorescent-coloured small bottle. It is aimed at the young and competes in the soft drink market.

▌ In 2003, Eau de Perrier was launched to try to achieve better penetration in the table water market. The famous Perrier bubbles, which are the essence of the brand, prevent the brand from appealing to those who like to drink less bubbly water with meals. This extension had finer bubbles (like San Pellegrino) and a finer and more elegant bottle.

How should these extensions have been described? At Nestlé Water, the owner of Perrier, they are called line extensions for the sake of simplicity. However, despite the fact that all these new products are basically water, the soft drink entry qualifies as brand extension more than the others. It aims at a market dominated by other competitors, which is subject to other success factors, and is aimed at different consumers.

The ability of any product given the Perrier name to meet the demands of the soft drink market is surely a long-odds bet. Here promotion and place are essentials. Also, the brand evokes less fun than any other soft drink brand. This is why the decision was taken to have Perrier only endorse the product, the big name on the bottle being 'Fluo'. This refers both to the very odd colours of the bottle and to the fact that it is fluorescent in the darkness, a typical situation in discotheques and late-night bars. However the main question will be the ability of Nestlé Water to cater to these new circuits of distribution and consumption.

For Aaker and Keller (1990), brand extension refers to the use of the name of a brand on a different product category. This was the case when Bic went worldwide from ballpoint pens to disposable lighters, disposable razors, and even stockings and hosiery in central Europe. One should then speak of line extensions when the brand launches new products in the same category. Therefore Diet Coke should be called a line extension. Interestingly, at the Coca-Cola Company, Diet Coke is called the second 'brand' of the company, which says it has two worldwide leading brands: Coke and Diet

Coke (called Coke Light in Europe). These differences in perception are not an academic problem. They hint at the fact that, although the product may be the same, the market, the 'category' may be different. Since the emergence of 'category management' we know that category does not mean product (Nielsen, 1992). Therefore, Perrier Fluo would be considered as a line extension by those who focus on the physical resemblance with the core product of the parent brand: basically it is the same water. For us, it qualifies as a real brand extension, for it aims at a different category of need, and of usage situation, and of users, and of competition. The same would hold true *a fortiori* for Evian spray, which vaporises water onto the face. The product, created in 1968, holds the same water as any Evian bottle, but the need and usage are very different as the channel of distribution.

As for all concepts, the best tactic is also to realise that they are relative, and that they cannot obey simple yes/no cut-off points. One should acknowledge that there are both highly continuous extensions, which apparently capitalise on the real or perceived know-how of the brand (as with HP's entry in the digital market), and highly discontinuous extensions, which do not capitalise on this know-how but on a mission, a set of values driving all the behaviours of the brand whatever the market it decides to compete in. We analyse the Virgin case below.

This scale of discontinuity has a lot of implications. It is a measure of the risk taken by the corporation itself. The current brand literature focuses heavily on the intangible facets of brands, probably because they are treated as intangible assets in accounting terms. But this is a semantic confusion: a performance-based brand is also an intangible asset. Overlooking the performance source of brands leads us to underestimate the weight of corporate abilities. Some companies just do not have the know-how or resources necessitated by the extension of the brand into specific categories. Certainly they can use

licensing as a way of circumventing the problem: for example Evian Affinity (a cosmetic line) is managed by Johnson & Johnson. The other possibility is to outsource. It is a classic way of moving more quickly and benefiting from low import prices. However this often means reducing the perceived difference between brands, if most of them outsource to common OEM suppliers.

Another implication concerns the branding strategy itself. Should one give a brand name of its own to the extension, thus moving to a double-level branding architecture (that is, an endorsing or source brand architecture)? It is noticeable that Perrier is very discreet about Fluo, as all endorsing brands tend to be. Experimental literature shows that giving the product a different name prevents dilution of the parent brand image, especially in the case of downward extensions (where the product goes from a premium price to a mainstream price) (Kirmani, Sood and Bridges, 1999). One should therefore distinguish 'direct extensions' (without a specific name) and 'indirect extensions' (with a specific brand name in addition to the parent brand) (Farquhar *et al*, 1992).

The limits of the classical conception of a brand

Most brand limitations are self-imposed. This is why brand extension took so long to emerge as a normal practice of brand management. This is also why some authors still hold it in disrepute. These prejudices are based on a classic conception of brands, which reigned over marketers and all business schools for almost a century. However, it cannot resist the conditions of modern markets.

The classic conception of branding rests on the following equation:

$$1 \text{ brand} = 1 \text{ product} = 1 \text{ promise}$$

For instance, in the Procter & Gamble tradition, every new product receives a specific name, which is totally independent from the other brands. Ariel corresponds to a certain promise, Dash to another, Vizir to a third. Mr Proper is a household detergent, and nothing else. Let us compare this policy with that of Colgate-Palmolive: Palmolive is a toothpaste, a soap, a shaving cream and a dishwashing liquid; Ajax is a scrubbing powder, a household detergent and a window cleaning liquid.

The classic conception of branding leads to an increasing number of brands. If a brand corresponds to a single physical product, to a single promise, it cannot be used for other products. Under this conception it is a rigid designator, the name of a product, a proper noun, just as Aristotle is the name of the famous Greek philosopher (Cabat, 1989). It names a specific reality, as a commercial name is linked to a specific company.

Under this conception of the brand, few extensions are possible. The brand is in fact the name of a recipe. All that can be done is range extension, that is a variation around the central recipe either by:

- ameliorating the quality of its performances. The brand then gets a series number: for example Dash 1, then Dash 2 and Dash 3;

- increasing the number of sizes in order to adapt to the changing practices of the consumer (packet, tub, mini-tub);

- increasing the number of varieties (Woolite for wool and Woolite for synthetics).

The classic conception of branding is actually limiting. It does not differentiate the history of the brand from the reality of the brand. Of course, a brand originally begins with a new single product which is better than the competition, thanks to the know-how of a firm.

With time, and through communication, packaging, advertising, etc, the brand becomes rich with features, images and representations which give it its style. The brand thus has personality along with know-how. After designating an origin (the manufacturer's brand), or a place of sale (the commercial name), the brand conveys after some time the signs of non-material elements, which take root in physical production (the products) and iconic production (advertising images, logos, symbols of visual identity). The relationship between the brand and the product is therefore reversed: the brand is no longer the name of a product, but the product itself carries the brand in a sense that it reveals the exterior signs of an interior imprint. The brand has transformed the product, endowing it with both objective and subjective features.

In this reversed perspective, there is no other limit to brand extension than that of the ability of the brand to leave its mark on a new category of product, ie to segment it according to its own attributes. Bic, ignoring the dissimilarity of products, left its mark by creating sub-segments of simple, cheap and efficient goods wherever these attributes are valued. Bic failed where these were not valued – in the perfume segment.

The classic conception of branding is nominal: the brand is the name of an object. If one looks beyond this object, and wonders what project it conveys and what vocation it embodies, one can grasp the full meaning of the brand, its etymological meaning (the brandon), the exterior sign of an internal transformation, on behalf of a key value (the brand essence).

Thus, the classic conception of the brand takes the history of the brand for its long-term reality. But, although the brand originates from a product, it is not the product. The brand is the meaning of the product.

Products cannot speak for themselves. The consumer is perplexed in front of a tin of brandless frozen lasagna. How can he or she foresee the satisfaction that will be derived from this tin? The brand reveals the intention of the maker: what values did they try to put into this tin? What did they want to introduce in this product: the love of tradition, an example of work well done, a respect for modern tastes, the will to find a compromise between fat and light food?

Extensions cannot be made in all directions. The direction is defined by the brand itself. A brand works as a genetic programme. It carries the code of the future products which will bear its name.

What does this new conception of branding change for brand extension? According to the classic conception, brand extension barely goes beyond very similar products. The key concept is product or usage similarity. This does not explain how perfumes by jewellers – Van Cleef, Bulgari, Boucheron, etc – are successes. It reduces brand identity to one single facet, the physical. This logic would exclude the idea of a Swatch car.

The larger conception of branding leads to extensions out of the initial category. The brand is different from the original product. It is a way of dealing with products, of transforming them, of giving them a common set of added values, both tangible and intangible: this way, a Swatch car is possible. An alliance with a company which has the technical know-how (Mercedes for example) suffices. This alliance, eventually made explicit through co-distribution, will give reassurance as to the car's quality and free consumers' desires.

The case of Lacoste helps to compare the operational consequences of each of the two conceptions of branding. Lacoste gained its reputation in 1933 through its tennis shirt made out of knitwear (called the 12 × 12), so a logical extension of Lacoste could be made not only toward other knitwear products, but also to other polo-shirts, sportswear and textiles in general. Under this conception, shoes and leather items are excluded (apart from tennis shoes), since they do not use the same know-how as textiles and knitwear. Under Lacoste's broader brand conception, the crocodile signals a typical attitude: with Lacoste, one is casual when smartly dressed, and smart even when dressed casually. Lacoste is beyond fashion: it is a classic. From this perspective, Lacoste can brand shoes or leather goods as long as they preserve the brand's originality; it must not brand products that have already been seen. The other condition is to brand only products which embody the values of the brand: flexibility, casualness, extreme finish, durability, distance from fashion, unisex use, etc. What enables Lacoste to brand a product is not the physical fit, but whether the product belongs to the Lacoste culture and high standards.

This new perspective opens new sources of growth for brands. Instead of looking at themselves as product brands, they become concept brands, defined by a set of values and not by a single instance (Rijkenberg, 2001). Indeed, brand logic is additive. The brand is the sum of its attributes: it is revealed by the products that it covers. The case of McCain is typical. The brand generally penetrates new countries through its frozen fries (it is actually the main supplier to McDonald's). They later introduce a frozen pizza ('deep pan', typical of the American way of life and of eating). They then launch buns to aim at the snack market. McCain also launched an iced tea to penetrate this high-growth market. Brand identity is actually uncovered by the sum of all these products. McCain's identity in Europe is that of 'American fun and generous food'. Generosity is both a relationship trait and a physical trait: all portions should be bigger when signed by McCain. Hence the surname 'deep pan pizza' or the higher cap of its iced tea (surnamed Colorado to refer to a mythical view of America). Future products may come from anywhere as long as they embody this enlarged identity of the brand, and fall within the territory of legitimacy the brand has created step by step, through each of its product launches.

History should not determine the future. In order to remain up to date, the brand must also be able to evolve; this is achieved through extension towards products which lead it in new directions and modify its meaning. Nestlé, known for dry foods (its prototypical products are instant milk and chocolate), did not enter the ultra-fresh market of yoghurts just to increase its turnover. The move was also intended to nurture its image thanks to this more modern segment, capable of updating its traditional and classic image traits.

Why are brand extensions necessary?

Brand extensions are necessary. They are a direct consequence of competition in mature markets and of the fragmentation of media. The only justification for brand extension is growth and profitability.

Brand extension is not new: it is the core of the business model of luxury brands (see page 95). It can increase the power of the brand and its profitability. Typical margins in the ready-to-wear premium market are 53 per cent, but the average is 71 per cent for bags and 80 per cent for watches. This is why fashion brands extend so quickly to these categories. As to perfumes, sold under licence by l'Oréal, Procter & Gamble or Unilever, they provide royalties, and a considerable boost in international visibility to the extended brand. This is why extensions are strategic in the fashion and luxury sector. No name can survive without them. The first thing a capital investment fund does after having bought a name is to extend the brand. What would Armani, Ralph Lauren or Calvin Klein be without their licences and extensions?

Often, perfumes become the most visible part of the fashion brand, because of the high advertising budgets involved. In addition the perfume increases the brand awareness and dream value, a prerequisite before other extensions. In fact, without a perfume, can a designer brand succeed and be profitable? Success in modern competition means the ability to access a critical size and visibility. Although not always successful, launching a perfume under one's name is a classic, if not the only, way to build the brand and business. Interestingly, this is the argument used by an as yet little-known designer brand that sued P&G for damages when the latter decided to stop its plans of launching a perfume under its brand name. Without this expected boost, would the brand meet its growth and profitability objectives?

As long as growth and profitability can be achieved through the present customers and products, or through minor variations in these products and their benefits (also called line extensions) there is no need to extend. Globalisation in search for the new areas of consumption in the world is also a natural route, but this does not solve the problem of growth in domestic markets, which are often saturated. Brand extensions allow brands to compete in less saturated markets, with a perspective of growth and profitability, as long as the brand's assets are assets in these markets. That is to say, the brand image must be able to act as a driver of purchase in the other market.

Brand extension relies on the ability to create a competitive advantage by leveraging the reputation attached to the brand name in a growth category, different from the brand's present categories. This bold move, which often surprises the competition in the category of extension, makes five crucial assumptions:

- The brand has strong equities (strong assets): it is strongly associated with a number of customer benefits (tangible or intangible) and it inspires a high level of trust.

- These assets are 'transferable' to the new and attractive destination category, that of the extension. Its buyers will still believe and acknowledge that the new products (that is, the extension) are endowed with the benefits associated with the brand.

▌ These benefits and brand values are very relevant to that new category (extension). In fact, they should segment it in a previously unforeseen way, and leave the competition unable to react rapidly.

▌ The products and services (extension) named by the parent brand will deliver a real perceived advantage over the competition, both consumers and the trade.

▌ The brand and company behind it will be able to sustain competition in this new category over the long run. This refers to the question of resources needed to acquire leadership in the market in order to remain in it profitably.

As a consequence the most important part in the brand extension process is the selection of the destination category. This requires the company to assess various strategic parameters: the intrinsic attractiveness of the new category, the company's ability to acquire leadership in this category, and its ability to segment it profitably. These factors are to be found in the brand image, but also in the company's more general abilities and resources.

A second set of reasons that has pushed corporations to extend their brands is more defensive, or tied to efficiency and productivity factors:

▌ Facing higher media costs, companies have felt the limits of their former brand architecture and wish to create more encompassing brands, so called mega-brands, in which a larger product portfolio can be nested. Most companies that started with a product brand architecture have realised the impossibility of sustaining growing advertising allowances behind each product or brand. They have transferred some of these formerly independent products or lines to a single mega-brand, which acts either as an endorser (Kraft or Nestlé) or like a source brand (l'Oréal Paris),

as a quasi-branded house. This is why brand transfers have become so frequent. The goal is to capitalise on a single name and to nurture it by a constant flow of innovations.

▌ The fight against distributors' brands that themselves are mega-brands and are practising extension (as is, for example, President's Choice) has called for the reorganisation of products and innovations under a small number of banner brands.

▌ In 1995 Nestlé decided to extend its name into the yogurt market. Until then the group had been present in this market through a regional brand, which was Chambourcy in Europe. However, the competition with Danone was leading to rising marketing and advertising investment. As a result it was decided to leverage the Nestlé name, thus enabling the products to benefit from all the trust and equity attached to this name, and from the advertising investment in other product categories where the group was already competing under its house brand. All products were transferred from Chambourcy to Nestlé. In the meantime this extension provided the opportunity to nurture the brand image, by adding important facets that had been lacking up to then. Born in the larder, in the realm of dry goods, Nestlé as a brand was not associated with modern chilled and fresh products. These represent the future of modern food. It was necessary to reassociate the brand with these values, in order to avoid losing some relevance and equity.

▌ Some brands are in declining product categories. To avoid disappearing with their product they must move to another category. Why did Porsche enter the 4 × 4 market in 2003? As we shall see later, there is a danger in resting always on the same product, even if it is continually face-lifted, revamped and renewed. All over the world, data show that the share of the coupé in the overall car market is decreasing. If Porsche stayed in that niche without reacting to this trend, it would be competing in a shrinking market. In addition, the 911, Porsche's keynote product, was coming to look at odds with the trend in values among elite and niche car buyers worldwide. Some of their newer values are captured by the 4 × 4 category. It remained to Porsche to build a 4 × 4 which would be a 'real' Porsche at an acceptable price. The only way of producing one at a realistic cost was to capitalise on the platform of the Volkswagen 4 × 4.

Another example is that consumption of brown tobacco is strongly declining, a sure threat for Gauloises, the prototype of dark cigarettes. After decades of uncompromising battle against blond tobacco, the company had to make a hard choice. Should it let its banner brand die? It decided to extend it into the blond category, creating Gauloises Blondes, which now represent the largest part of its sales.

In the business-to-business market, the logic of continually increasing customer value leads in itself to brand extension. Take a service provider, say a company providing cleaning services for hospitals. How can it increase its sales to its core clients? Rooms cannot be cleaned two times or three times a day. There is no other avenue than to propose extended services, for instance supplying flowers for hospital rooms, lobbies and offices. This is another competence, an extension.

British Gas faced the same problem after the deregulation. How could it defend its business against all the new gas providers? It realised that its strength was its customer proximity: its engineers actually visited millions of households. It was time to leverage that competence and competitive advantage, and provide an extended set of home services including insurance and financial services to the customer base. This naturally entailed a change in name to facilitate consumer acceptance.

Labeyrie is a brand that originated in the 'foie gras' sector. This is a very cyclical market, where most sales are made in three months of the year. To be able to advertise and gain a competitive advantage, Labeyrie decided to enlarge its scope and extend to other luxury foods such as smoked salmon and caviar. The resulting increase in its sales volume made television advertising a realistic investment.

Many companies make a brand extension because they do not have the resources to sustain two brands nationally and internationally. This is why in Spain Don Simon sells wine, gazpacho and orange juice under the same name. This small company invests all its resources in productivity and quality. It fights head on against Tropicana in the juice sector, and has now extended its market throughout Europe. We shall see later that although they are governed by necessity, such decisions may prove later to be a real blessing.

Some sectors are under growing advertising constraints: cigarettes, spirits, beers and wine are all limited by law in their types of advertisement and sponsorship. They have to create brand extensions to circumvent these limitations. Such extensions actually act as surrogate brands. The most known and successful is Marlboro Classics, an offshoot of the cigarette brand, which has become a real outerwear fashion brand worldwide. It has a very specific design, and exclusive stores and concessions. This is a typical case of a successful licensing approach.

The Camel Trophy did not survive the introduction of laws forbidding any association of cigarette brands with sports sponsorship. Pharmaceutical laboratories are another typical case where extension makes it possible to increase competitiveness even though the core product is tightly constrained. In all countries, pharmaceutical laboratories have to make a choice: whether to produce freely available over-the-counter (OTC) products, or products that are only available on a doctor's prescription. OTC products are allowed to be advertised, but they are generally not prescribed and they tend to be expensive. Part of the cost of prescription drugs is usually reimbursed through the national security system or by health insurers, so they can cost less to the end-users. However, manufacturers are generally not allowed to advertise prescription drugs to consumers (although there are some exceptions: specific types of direct-to-consumer advertising are often permitted for asthma products, for instance). In France, the market leader for paracetamol is called Doliprane. This is a prescription drug, so consumers can be reimbursed for its cost, but in addition it can be bought freely without a prescription. As a prescription drug, however, Doliprane is not allowed to advertise. To circumvent the regulations it launched two extensions, Doli'rhume and Doli'tabs ('rhume' means catching a cold in French). These two variants could be advertised, because they are only sold in the OTC market. The heavy advertising campaigns not only boosted the sales of the two new products, but had a positive spillover effect on the core product.

What should one think about the Caterpillar line of shoes and clothes aimed at the youth market? Was it necessary for the tractor brand to extend itself in this way? Of course not. What then was the rationale? When asked that question, the CEO answered that it was intended to increase the share value by giving more visibility to the brand name, beyond the trade circles in which it had previously been known. Many small investors now buy shares, and familiar corporate names act as symbols of value to the lay investor. In addition,

Caterpillar clothes and shoes were able to express the exact values for which the Caterpillar was known: tough work, reliability, security and so on.

Similarly, why did Michelin extend its brand from tyres to guidebooks, over a century ago? The first Red Guide was produced to tell readers where to find a garage in the event of a breakdown. Soon it came to be aimed at inducing car owners to travel more, with tips about hotels and good restaurants. It was a great example of relational marketing before the word was ever invented.

Recently, Michelin, working with a partner, The Licensing Company, has created a dedicated company, Michelin Life Style Limited, based in London. It is marketing snow chains for cars, a product with obvious marketing synergy with tyres. There are plans to extend the brand into sport equipments such as ski shoes and running shoes, areas in which the use of rubber can increase comfort and security. These are the two key benefits of Michelin tyres.

In a slightly different way, My First Sony and My First Bosch are tactical extensions, designed to create early familiarity with the brand among soon-to-be clients.

Building the brand through systematic extensions: Nivea

In 2003, the three giants Procter & Gamble, Henkel and l'Oréal bid against each other to acquire Nivea, putting in very high offers – a sign of their extraordinary confidence in the growth potential of the company and its brand. What an astonishing outcome for a German company founded in 1912 in Hamburg on a single product: a little round, blue metallic box containing skin moisturising cream, which was treated almost like a medicine.

However, the company and its brand were split up after the war, and like other German brands (such as Persil), its assets were given to other companies across the world as war damages. This is why the brand had to be rebuilt with great patience, with the assets being bought back whenever and wherever possible, such as in the United States in 1974. In 2003 Nivea was the world's leading skincare brand, with a turnover of €2.5 billion and an average growth of 15 per cent per year. The brand's growth has been achieved entirely through progressive, carefully planned extensions repeated in country after country. As we shall see, each extension constructs a specific facet of the brand while penetrating new markets or new needs, all the while remaining faithful to the brand's heritage and key values.

Nivea provides a good example of well-managed systematic extensions. The lifespan and growth of this world-leading skincare brand can be explained through two key factors: the modernisation of the prototype product, Nivea cream, in its round blue box, and systematic brand extension via daughter brands (which Nivea calls 'sub-brands').

The little round box is the prototype of Nivea, and carries the brand's values. In every country it is introduced first, and made available at all sales points, explaining its penetration into all social environments. Next come the extensions, in a pre-established order, to build the brand: first care products, followed by hygiene, then hair products, and lastly make-up. The daughter brands expand these categories, with their specialisation based on age (Nivea Baby), purpose (Nivea Sun), gender (Nivea for Men), and so on.

However, if it is to maintain itself, the brand must work tirelessly to recapture its relevance, and this is why it must innovate. Each advertisement for a Nivea daughter-brand now places the emphasis on innovation. But even the prototype has needed an update: this has been the role of Nivea Soft, with its white box, as modern generations look for a cream which is less greasy and penetrates the skin more quickly. Nivea Soft is bringing the brand's foundation up to date.

Extensions very soon came to form a part of Nivea's business model. An analysis of its brand launches in all countries – from the United States to Russia and China – reveals a fixed, well-planned pattern of development. The brand is launched in each country using

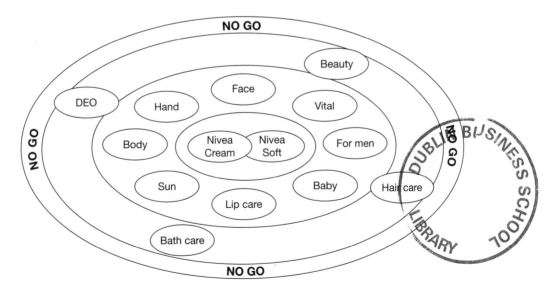

Figure 12.1   The Nivea extensions galaxy

its cornerstone (founding, prototype) product, portraying itself as a healthcare brand. Next follows Nivea Visage, a sub-brand which is key to its long-term business development. Nivea Visage is the perfect symbol of care: we entrust our faces to it.

After that follow the daughter brands judged to be most relevant for each different country, deepening this role and mission: Nivea Hand, Nivea Body, Nivea Sun, Nivea Lip Care, and three brands that are segmented by customer type: Nivea for Men, Nivea Vital (for the older market) and Nivea Baby (formerly known as Babyvea). The next to arrive are hygiene products, via the Nivea Deo and Nivea Bath Care daughter brands. Finally, these are followed by Nivea Hair Care and Nivea Beauty.

Thus, the order of entry in each new country is always carefully planned: care products first, followed by hygiene, then hair products and lastly make-up. Similarly, women's care products come before men's: Nivea Visage is always launched before Nivea for Men. Nivea's philosophy is that each country organisation is free to choose to launch a daughter brand, depending on the available potential in that market. However, Nivea Visage is of key importance. For example, although the care products market in Brazil is small in comparison to hygiene products, the brand construction order is still maintained. After all, Nivea is not Dove. The latter (Unilever) brand is based on hygiene (with as its core product a soap containing 25 per cent moisturising cream), but is now successfully expanding into the entire hygiene and beauty market worldwide.

The brand architecture is an umbrella, in the sense that each daughter brand is named descriptively, and thus represents a statement of the brand's values as they pertain to that category. However, note that the logos of each daughter brand are not uniform. This tiny difference makes the brand open, living and non-monolithic. Furthermore, each logo reflects a personality and values specific to the

daughter brand. In this respect, the Nivea brand is also a sort of branded house (source brand) with two clear brand levels, even though the mother level is dominant in this case.

Indeed, each daughter brand has its own personality, and this is a deliberate decision. Furthermore, the aim of each extension is to provide not only a deepening of the core competence (loving care for the skin) and greater penetration of the category, but also specific components of the overall image. For example, Nivea Sun is where the family and protection aspect is communicated, and so advertising for Nivea Sun shows mothers and children, and fathers and children, together.

Likewise, the final extension – the one farthest from the core of the brand – is Nivea Beauty. By now we have come a long way from long-lasting products, simplicity and harmony. In this category, the key words are accelerated range renewal (four per year), the game, fun, seduction and so on. However, in highly developed, sophisticated countries this extension is necessary. It brings young girls to Nivea who would not otherwise have come, and who will subsequently try out other products from the range. It also adds a necessary touch to the brand image: more modernity and 'fashion'.

We can therefore see that under this system, daughter brands are not extensions in the iterative sense, as they would be for a hypothetical brand X asking itself what else it could do. In reality, they are the means through which the brand's 'big plan' takes shape. Extension presupposes the existence of a long-term vision. Before sinking the pillars for a bridge across a river, one must first have picked a clear destination point on the other side. These extensions are not extensions in the traditional sense, but rather components of a pre-planned whole which accumulates its meaning, coherency and scale through them.

As with any new product launch, the key question is that of perceived distinctiveness from the existing competition. Of course, the brand brings its own intangibles and image equities, but they are not enough on their own: a physical basis for differentiation is needed. This is, therefore, where innovation comes in:

▮ Nivea Visage launched Patch in Europe (the fruit of an alliance with the Japanese firm Kiaoré).

▮ Nivea for Men provides more care during shaving.

▮ Nivea Vital is developing the concept of mature skin.

Lastly, as with any system, there are certain no-go areas – such as, for example, anti-cellulite products. This is not because no market exists: it does exist, and it is a thriving one. Rather, it is because none of the existing products work well. To enter this area with another product that did not really deliver its promise would therefore be to break the link of consumer confidence in Nivea –and more than any other brand in its sector, Nivea wants to be the brand of confidence.

There are many examples of companies that have built their meaning around successive extensions. For example, the Canadian company McCain has three divisions, frozen fries, pizzas and soft drinks. In high-potential countries, it enters by means of frozen fries, then after three years launches its pizzas, and lastly soft drinks (for example, Colorado iced tea). McCain is thus no longer a fries, pizza or soft drinks brand, but instead symbolises North American cooking (rich, plentiful, playful, modern, relaxed) in the eyes of non-American consumers. This process of scope enlargement takes time, and presupposes that the brand is able to carry it off, as we shall see below.

Extending the brand to internationalise it

As world leader in cosmetics and beauty, l'Oréal has to create barriers to entry against a major source of threat: pharmaceutical laboratories. These have the potential to innovate in cosmetics, thus endangering l'Oréal's market share. This threat was exemplified by Johnson & Johnson launching a new active ingredient Retinol in a number of its brands (such as Neutrogena and Roc).

L'Oréal bought a niche brand called La Roche Posay (LRP), named after a town known for its dermatological water and spa. The town hosts more than 10,000 patients per year, including about 3,000 children as young as five months. LRP's business model was based on medical expert prescription. When working with dermatologists, it takes two or three years before any new product can safely be introduced to the shelves of pharmacies. But the brand faced growth problems:

▮ It was imprisoned in its therapeutic niche, and limited to patients rather than the general public.

▮ It was remote from the public. A user might be satisfied by the performance of, say, Antelios XL (an LRP product prescribed by dermatologists), but without another prescription, he or she would not buy a different LRP product.

▮ As a consequence the brand was below the minimum critical size. LRP sold 560,000 units in 1998, while it needed to sell at least 1 million units.

L'Oréal's strategy is to build its growth on truly global brands, and this requires a minimum sales level of €150 millions per brand. LRP was intended to be the eleventh global brand of the l'Oréal Group, but as it was, it was not easily exportable. To thrive against modern competition it is necessary to move quickly in global markets with promising growth potential. L'Oréal's target markets were Europe, Brazil and Argentina in 2000, Scandinavia and Asia in 2001, and India in 2002. It needed the brand to have a presence in four market segments: hygiene, facial care products, solar protection and make-up. These last two categories were intended to release the first two sources of limitation in the brand's growth, and make it truly attractive to pharmacists all around the world.

In some markets pharmacists' shops were not appropriate outlets. The strategy here was to create another form of outlet, such as a concession in a department store (the solution in Canada), with a qualified pharmacist in attendance.

Because LRP did not have existing products in the solar protection and make-up categories, strategic extensions were planned for these. This was done by means of a brand transfer. LRP took over the products sold under another l'Oréal brand, Phas, which had been positioned on non-allergenic products (see Chapter 15 for the brand switch description).

Identifying potential extensions

It goes without saying that before making any brand extension it is imperative to know the brand well. What are its attributes? What is its personality? What identity does it convey to its buyers and users? What are its latent associations or traits? The answers to these questions are based on both quantitative studies (to discover the popularity and the image of the brand) and qualitative interviews of the target public. A simple listing of the image characteristics does not give a full picture of the brand. Defining the prism of identity requires qualitative investigation.

Armed with this information, the second step of the investigation procedure involves the extrapolation of the brand's distinctive features in order to assess their consequences. If Dove is personified by gentleness, then what other products need to be gentle? If Christofle is a brand for knives, forks and spoons, could it, by metonymy, be extended to glasses, plates or other tableware in general? Since Rossignol is active in one area

of sport (skiing), could it not also extend into tennis rackets and golf clubs?

Luxury product brands often find the reason and the inspiration for their extensions from within their own history. Thus René Lalique, founder of Lalique, made jewels, scarves and shawls. The extension of Baccarat into small items of furniture, jewellery, perfumes and lamps is also symbolic of the reconquest of unexploited areas.

Whatever the source, a long list emerges from this process of introspection and investigation into brand identity and extrapolations based on it. It is then subject to internal feasibility filters. Brand extension is a strategic choice that is also accompanied by other changes: in production, know-how, distribution channels, communication, corporate culture. These have to be financed either internally or by forming alliances. Thus, Boucheron sold 22 per cent of its shares, not those of its core business (high-fashion jewellery), but those of the company that managed the so-called 'first circle' extensions (jewellery, watches, spectacle frames, pens and perfumes) in order to increase its resources.

This shortlist is then tested with the target public. Opinion surveys are often used to achieve this. For every extension proposition consumers evaluate the product on a scale of interest to them such as 'very interesting, so-so, not interesting'. This leads to a popularity rating of the possible extensions.

This method is advantageous in that it is simple and that the grading is done by numbers. Its one drawback is that it is conservative. When a series of questions about a multitude of products are thrown at them, interviewees tend to comment only on the basis of the most striking features of the brand. Therefore, this technique is biased and conservative. Thus, when Bic was only making ballpoint pens, this strategy would have ended up by exhausting all the possibilities in stationery and completely rejecting the idea that Bic should sell razors.

Davidson (1987) distinguishes a number of concentric zones around an inner core: the outer core, the extension zones, and finally the no-go areas (see Figure 12.2). Close-ended questions in surveys provide information on the immediate vicinity of the brand (the outer core). In-depth qualitative phrases explore the remote extension zones.

Once again, it is necessary to proceed with a qualitative investigation to bring out the latent potential of a brand and to see how it can or cannot adopt each of these extensions. Through this same investigation we can also tell whether the resulting refusals were due to a conservative attitude linked to the actual situation, a lack of imagination on the part of the interviewee, or due to incompatibility with the brand.

The qualitative phase is a constructive one. Bearing in mind that a brand has to bring some added value to the product category, one would also like to know under what conditions the envisaged product would be legitimate for the brand. What attributes – objective and subjective – would be necessary for it to be able to bear the brand name? How is the product superior to the present market offer?

Thus, it is not enough to say that Lacoste could make jackets. One also has to describe what the characteristics of a Lacoste jacket would be and those of a 'non-Lacoste' jacket. The Lacoste identity prism encompasses the following characteristics: knit, finish, durability, discretion, harmony, social aptness, conformity and adaptability. The reputation of the original Lacoste product is that of a second skin: it induces a distancing effect which constitutes the central value of the brand. It nurtures an image of supple transition

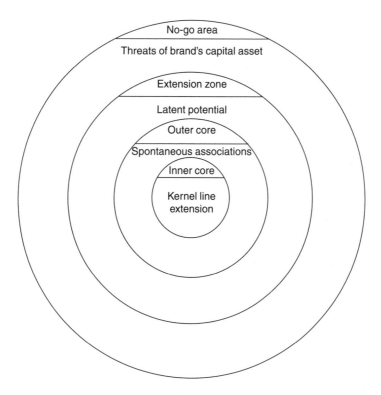

Figure 12.2   Perimeters of brand extension

between the personal and social – personal ease and social ease. The aerated knit is analogous to the skin and its pores. This identity prism defines the territories which are not Lacoste and which should be avoided for fear of losing the very meaning of the brand:

▮ since it conforms to a sporting ideal, Lacoste is transversal and cuts across all barriers of age and sex, thus it should not put its name to products which are exclusively feminine (in fact, the Lacoste aerobic line was a big failure), or hyper-masculine (eg hunting);

▮ Lacoste does not sell either garish colours or short-lived 'in' products;

▮ being a 'second skin', Lacoste does not make either heavy knitwear or shiny leather clothes.

One understands why there are no Lacoste leather jackets. They are very masculine, virile and fashionable, and they do not last. Only the suede jacket is capable of possessing Lacoste characteristics.

The qualitative stage also permits an understanding of the functions of the brand for its users. Is the brand a sign for itself or for others? Where would consumers like to see the brand signed? This information is essential for branding. On the pocket of a Lacoste blazer should the signature be Lacoste, the crocodile or Lacoste Club?

Fundamentally, the testing phase should not only find out whether the success factors of the extension category are coherent with the brand, but also whether the product is superior to its competitors when deprived of its brand. In spite of the many explications about image failure, many extensions fail simply because they are inferior to existing products and are more expensive. Above all, an extension is an innovation and its added-value should be considered. Finally, these projection techniques allow the tricky question of the boomerang effects on the brand capital to be dealt with.

The economics of brand extension

By capitalising on the brand awareness, the esteem and the qualities attached to an existing brand, the practice of brand extension can help to increase the chances of success of a new product and lower its launch costs. These two alleged consequences have been verified.

As shown in Figure 12.3, only 30 per cent of new brands survive longer than four years, whereas the rate is over 50 per cent for brand extensions.

How does extension increase chances of survival? First, distributors themselves will allocate more space to an already well-known brand than to a newcomer. But brand extension also has an impact on the consumer (see Figure 12.4):

▮ in the trial rate, inducing a higher rate (123 vs 100);

▮ in the conversion rate (17 per cent vs 13 per cent);

▮ in the loyalty rate (index of 161 vs 100 for new brands).

Thus, for an equal facing and an equal unweighted distribution/weighted distribution ratio, consumers have a higher probability of trial, conversion and loyalty when the product bears an existing brand name, as this second OC&C analysis shows.

As far back as 1969, Claycamp and Liddy had measured the impact of a 'family name' (extension) on the trial rate of the new product. Their forecasting model, known as Ayer's model, rested on a database of 60 launches in 32 categories, half of these being in the food sector. The basic structure of the model is presented in Figure 12.5.

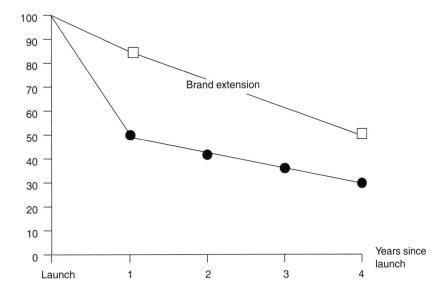

Figure 12.3 Rate of success of new brands vs brand extensions (OC&C)

The estimate of the parameters of the model (through double regression) resulted in a very positive weight for the 'brand extension' variable. A previously known name directly and strongly induces the consumer to try the product. Moreover, Liddy and Claycamp noted that this variable was not correlated to advertising recall or even to weighted distribution. This last point is surprising: perhaps American distributors do not act as barriers to entry as much as their European colleagues.

What conclusions can be drawn from these studies? It would be wrong to think now that all new products must be launched under a known brand. This would mean forgetting the usefulness of multi-brand portfolios in the maximisation of market coverage. Moreover, as will be discussed later, some brand extensions can hinder the success of a new product, or be detrimental to the brand capital itself. Thus Hermès refused to lease its name, in exchange for royalties, to the Wagons-Lits Group, which wanted to launch a top-of-range service of individual or package holidays. The service risks of hotels in exotic and far away countries were too high for Hermès to be willing to associate its name with that venture.

These figures also reveal that the consumers' view of the product is generally far less conservative than that of management

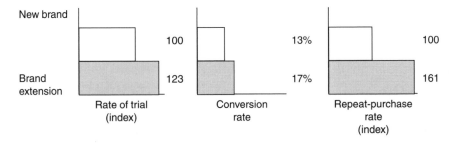

Figure 12.4 The impact of brand extension on the consumer adoption process (OC&C)

Figure 12.5 Ayer model: how a family name impacts the sales of a new product

itself. Quite often the latter is too blinkered by the origin of the brand and considers the manufacturing history of the brand as its definition. For management, Mars could not mean anything else but the chocolate bar. And yet the Mars ice-cream bar has been a success and the Mars biscuit launched in 2003 was also a hit. This proves that consumers distinguish rather well the brand from the product, or at least that they do not associate them irreversibly.

The second economic argument put forward to justify brand extension has to do with cost: launching a new brand would cost more than launching a new product under a well-known brand. Indeed, for consumer goods one estimate is that, as a result of lower expenses in 'push' and in 'pull', in promotion (to consumers and above all to distributors) as well as in media advertising, the savings due to the choice of brand extension amount to 21 per cent. Since the trial ratio is higher, the

strategy of brand extension proves economical as far as cost per trial is concerned (see Table 12.2).

However, another study from Nielsen based on 115 launches gives apparently contradictory results: the new products launched under new names get market shares twice as high as those of the products launched under known brands (except for health and beauty products, for which the results are identical: 2.7 per cent vs 2.6 per cent) (see Figure 12.6). The reason for this difference can be seen in the second column. The extension strategy would not in fact be less efficient: the lower market shares are due to the fact that management uses smaller communication budgets in cases of brand extension, which lowers the share of advertising presence.

For an equal percentage of advertising presence, brand extension results in equivalent or even greater market shares in the field of health and beauty where, the risk perceived

Table 12.2   Brand extension impact on launching costs

	New brand	Brand extension	%
Launching budget:			
– pull	100	78	–22
– push	30	24	–20
Total	130	102	–21
Trial rate	100	123	+23
Cost/trial	1.3	0.83	–36

Source: OC&C

by the consumers being higher, there is a preference for known brands.

What can be deduced from these two studies? Are they contradictory? The first one concludes that extension is more efficient even with a lower budget. The contradiction could be solved by considering the fact that many managers, confident in the productivity of brand extension, reduce the advertising budget dedicated to the extension launch (thus the results of the first column of Figure 12.6). For equal budgets, the extension strategy has a slight advantage which is not significant in the cleaning products and food sectors but significant in the health and beauty sector (0.46 vs 0.39). In addition, the fact that OC&C analyses efficiency in terms of

trial rate (very tightly linked to the familiarity of the brand name) whereas Nielsen's is based on market share over 24 months, which reflects the marketing mix and product quality as a whole, may have some bearing. Finally, this low launch budget of the extension may be linked to a desire to keep the bulk of advertising on the core product of the brand to preserve its sales (a mistake since it underestimates the reciprocal spillover effects of advertising a new product on the sales of the core product (Balachander and Ghose, 2003).

A hidden factor in each of these two studies is the moment of entry on the market. A risky, new market cannot be approached in the same way as the same market at a more mature

Figure 12.6 Comparative sales performance during first two years (Nielsen)

stage. Sullivan's (1991) analysis of 96 launches in eleven categories of products gives interesting descriptive results (see Table 12.3).

First, this analysis noted that companies preferred to penetrate new markets with new brands. Of the 48 launches studied that had taken place on emerging markets, only 13 were brand extensions. However, in mature markets, 40 out of the 48 launches analysed were brand extensions. Sullivan also noted that the brands which used their own names in order to penetrate a young market were rather weak brands. For example, in the United States, Royal Crown Cola was the first brand to penetrate the diet cola segment under its own name. It was followed by Pepsi-Cola with Diet Pepsi. Coca-Cola had preferred to launch Tab and not to put its brand capital at risk. It introduced Diet Coke last. The survey shows that the brands which have become leaders in these markets were almost always new brands (Diet Coke is an exception).

Why do strong brands hesitate to penetrate young markets? Of course, they would benefit from the fact that there is no competition yet. But creating a market entails more risks for the creator (Schnaars, 1995) and a negative effect on the brand and its capital. In a young, badly defined market, a brand must be flexible in order to find the best positioning. Brand extension does not permit such flexibility. The attributes of the brand must be respected. Furthermore, launching a brand which is specific to a new market enables the brand to become the reference on that market, by benefiting from what is called the pioneer advantage (Carpenter and Nakamoto, 1990). Finally, many new markets are created in reaction to old ones. For example, the snow surfing market is a counterculture against alpine skiing and its competition-oriented values; its proponents have their own brands and have refused the surfboards of Rossignol, the established brand.

Apart from the case of weak brands trying to dominate a new market, it can be attractive to be the only known and reassuring reference on a market where neither the offer nor distribution is structured, and where the consumer perceives a high risk. The consumer will appreciate the presence of a famous brand, even if it is far from its original market. Only its fame and serious reputation count. That is why Tefal penetrated the fledgling market of domestic appliances under its own name.

Finally, the analysis of success rates of the two launch strategies, depending on the degree of maturity of the markets, reveals a slight advantage for the new brand strategy in the market creation phase. But with time, the brand extension strategy seems more successful (see Table 12.3).

What research tells us about brand extensions

Since 1990, extension has attracted the attention of all marketing researchers and

Table 12.3   Success rate of two alternative branding policies

	Market development	
	Growth	Maturity
Launches of new brands	57%	43%
Launches of brand extensions	46%	68%

Source: Sullivan (1991)

academics. This barren ground was seducing, and in addition the stakes were high. This research, mostly experimental and quantitative, has focused on identifying the determinants of consumers' attitudes to an extension. Would they find the concept attractive or not? It has also looked for the conditions where the brand equity could be diluted by an extension, which is generally true when an extension fails to bear the 'brand contract'. What is the impact on the parent brand image or on the sales of its core product?

This research has thus focused on only a small part of the brand extension process, which involves eight key steps:

1. Assessment of the brand equities (its image, or emotional assets, its key competencies among various segments of the population).

2. Assessment of the intrinsic attractiveness of likely extension categories.

3. Assessment of the transferability of the brand assets in the chosen extension category.

4. Assessment of the relevance of these assets: are these assets real benefits in this category?

5. Assessment of the ability of the company to deliver the expected benefits subsumed by the brand name.

6. Assessment of the perceived superiority of the extension to existing competition.

7. Assessment of the ability of the company to sustain competition in the extension category and to acquire leadership through time.

8. Assessment of the feedback effects on the parent brand and on the sales of the core product. What does the extension bring to the brand (new clients, new image traits, new sales?)

Academic research mostly addresses issues 1, 3 and 8. It aims at answering such questions as: When is brand equity transferable? What causes positive consumer reactions to extension proposals? When can brand equity be damaged by an unsatisfying extension? Its dominant paradigm is experimental research, using consumer evaluations (I like it, I do not like it) as the variable to be explained. Only recently have researchers analysed back data, and the historical sequence of market entries, to focus on sales and segment leadership and try to understand the determinants of success and failure. (See Figure 12.7.)

Early experimental studies on brand extension

The first study was presented in 1987 during a symposium on brand extension at the

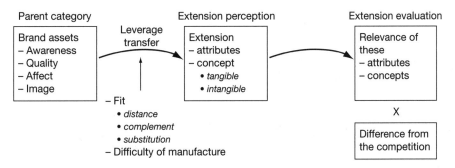

Figure 12.7   The brand extension decision

University of Minnesota. The attitude towards a fictitious brand of calculators (Tarco) was manipulated through the presentation of the results of tests evaluating six Tarco calculators. These tests concluded, according to the experimental group, that none of the six calculators were of poor quality, or one out of six, two out of six ... up to six out of six. Naturally, the general attitude towards Tarco was much influenced by this manipulation. Then a list of new products to be launched by Tarco was presented: these ranged from a new calculator and 'close' extensions (microcomputers, digital watches, cash registers, etc) to 'distant' extensions (bicycles, pens, office chairs). The interviewees in each group were asked to state their feelings about each of these new Tarco products before having even seen them. The correlation between the attitude towards Tarco and the attitude towards these extension products of Tarco was measured. The correlation was stronger when the extension was close. In short, the transfer of attitude is facilitated by the perceived similarity between the category of brand origin and the category of the product extension.

Naturally, the bases of 'perceived similarity' vary with the individuals. As another study has shown, experts and non-experts use different indexes to evaluate the degree of similarity between two products. For example, the two following types of extension were shown to two groups of individuals, non-experts and experts:

▌ one was a superficial extension, using superficial similarity and relatedness (from tennis shoes to tennis rackets);

▌ the other was a 'deeper' extension, using the same know-how (that of carbon fibre, enabling a brand of golf clubs to introduce tennis rackets).

When asked about their perception of similarity between the starting category and the final category (tennis rackets), non-experts found the superficial extension very similar, but the experts not as much. On the other hand, an explanation of the process and material used convinced the experts more easily of the fact that tennis rackets and golf clubs are close products, while for non-experts they remain quite dissimilar. Thus, identical composition is not a factor of perceived similarity for non-experts: they base their opinions on more superficial signs. They are sensitive to extensions based on relationships of complementarity or substitutability between products, which this creates a sense of 'fit':

▌ Uncle Ben's sauce is complementary to Uncle Ben's rice;

▌ Nesquik cereals are substitutes for Nesquik milk chocolate.

Experts are not satisfied with these peripheral cues. They need a stronger rationale, such as that of Look's extension. This brand, famous for its ski bindings, was extended to the upper-range mountain-bike market, for it could apply here its mastery of the automatic grip pedals and of new composite materials.

In the first study, the fact that Tarco was a fictitious brand was intentional. This way, the brand had no capital – no particular trust and emotion were associated to the brand. This explains the importance of the criterion of similarity of products to facilitate the transfer of attitudes. In a normal situation, if the brand is a strong one, the relevance of its key values in the product class it wishes to enter is what determines the attractiveness of the extension even if the categories of products are very different (Broniarczyk and Alba, 1994). The success of Bic in pens, razors and lighters illustrates this fact.

The first sign of awareness of a mechanism independent from the product and stemming from the brand itself appeared in 1991, among Park and his colleagues. Two lists of products were given to the persons interviewed: functional products and expressive products:

Functional products	Expressive products
TV	perfume
compact disc	shoe
cassette-player	wallet
radio	shirt
videotape	bag
VCR	pen
walkman	ring
car radio	watch
video camera	belt
record-player	crystal
headphones	tie

Two questions were asked:

1. the traditional question about the degree of similarity between the products within each column;

2. a question about whether the products of each column 'fit' together.

The researchers asked these two questions in two ways:

▮ blindly, as above;

▮ using a brand, here Sony for the first list and Gucci for the second.

What were the results?

▮ For the expressive products, the fact that the brand was mentioned or not did not modify the judgements of low perceived similarity between the products. However, the presence of the Gucci brand name created a considerable fit between products which did not seem to fit much without the brand (3.68), but suddenly fitted together (4.74) under the brand.

▮ For functional products, the presence or not of the brand did not modify the judgements of perceived similarity and of 'fit'.

In short, the authors hinted at two processes by which consumers build an opinion on an extension:

▮ If the brand is mainly functional, the extension is evaluated from the bottom up, according to inherent links between the category of the original product and that of the extended product. The consumers' evaluations rest on the degree of perceived similarity between product categories.

▮ If the brand is symbolic, the concept of the brand creates a link between products which otherwise would not have one. In this case, the judgements on extension are independent of the physical characteristics of the products. Each extension is evaluated according to its belonging to the brand concept and to its coherence with the value system of this brand. This is a top-down process.

Some extensions bear the risk of dilution of the brand. Like an elastic band that has been pulled too much, the brand can become weak. Many factors explain the weakening of a brand by excessive extension. Evaluating this risk is no mean task: what would be the impact on Tuborg if a sparkling mineral water were introduced under this brand (such an extension does exist in Greece)?

A study demonstrated the existence of this risk. It focused on a well-known health and beauty brand, Neutrogena. Two extensions were presented to the consumers, one very unusual for Neutrogena, the other very typical of Neutrogena. The experiment consisted of informing the consumers that both extensions did very poorly in the two dimensions that make Neutrogena famous, softness and quality. What would be the impact of such a statement on the image of Neutrogena itself (Loken and Roedder, 1993)? Would the image of softness and quality of typical Neutrogena products be affected, too? The study considered product A1, the brand prototype associated with Neutrogena by 83 per cent of consumers; product A2, associated by 61 per cent; product A3, by 55 per cent; product A4, by 39 per cent; and product A5, by 5 per cent. Here are the conclusions:

▌ Although of poor quality, the remote extension did not stain the image of the brand, nor the image of its other products. This phenomenon is well known to researchers on stereotypes: the exception does not harm the rule. The extension is atypical, therefore without influence on the heart of the brand.

▌ The situation is different for the more typical extension of Neutrogena. Its poor quality had a negative influence on both the image of the brand in its key attributes, and that of products typically and spontaneously associated to the brand. (A1, A2 and A3 had a statistically significant poorer softness image after exposure to the extension.) There has, indeed, been a negative impact on the brand and on its most significant products, but only in the case where the extension is typical of the brand. The danger concerns line extensions much more than brand extensions.

How attitudes about extensions are formed

Much research has been carried out into brand extension. As with any field of research, the pioneer articles are followed up by endless variations on the theme, exploring contextual aspects such as other products, countries, and interviewee types along with in-depth analyses (Leif Heim Egil, 2002), summaries, and then – much later – reanalyses and meta-analyses. Meanwhile, the results of the initial research have done the rounds, and have assumed the status of intangible truth. Only later do their limitations become apparent. This is why, it is possible to sort through the results of these summary analyses and critiques.

For example, Bottomley and Holden (2001) reanalysed data from all research that faithfully adhered to the basic Aaker–Keller paradigm (1990) to explain attitudes with regard to an extension. In this pioneering study, consumers were asked to evaluate ideas for extensions (a good idea/not a good idea; good/bad). The aim was to gain an understanding of the determining factors behind these evaluations from among a series of suggested values, such as the parent brand's reputation for quality, the perceived fit between the extension and the category of origin, and the perceived difficulty of constructing the extension, along with a number of other variables, without considering the interactions between variables. The perceived fit is the main variable to emerge from this pioneering research. It measures the psychological – and thus subjective – gap between the extension and the brand's typical product (its prototype). Traditionally, the fit is measured in three dimensions: the degree of perceived synergy between the extension and the prototype, the degree of perceived substitutability, and the perceived transferability of know-how.

Bottomley and Holden's reanalyses of the initial study and seven repeat studies produced conclusions somewhat different from those that were circulated following the initial research:

▌ Consumers' evaluations of an extension are in the first place influenced by the perceived quality of the parent brand and the perceived degree of fit. Clearly, extensions are not a way of saving weak brands: they must have a reputation for quality before it is possible to attempt brand stretching. With regard to the dimensions of fit, 'synergy' and 'transferability of know-how' are more important than 'substitutability'.

▌ These evaluations are also influenced by the interactions between the brand's perceived quality, the degree of synergy and the transferability of know-how, as well as by the interaction of the brand's perceived quality with the perceived difficulty of manufacturing the extension. (In short, the importance of the brand's perceived quality grows along with the perceived difficulty in carrying out this extension.)

▌ Last, there is a small direct influence produced by the perceived difficulty of manufacturing the extension: when this rises, the evaluation rises. Consumers do not like brands that are happy to put their names to excessively trivial products. However, this result is not confirmed in all cases. It is true that the success of brand licences among children casts doubt on the extent to which they are influenced by this variable: the Harry Potter name has appeared on some of the most banal products (exercise books, erasers, pencils, pens, clothing and so on). However, perhaps the effect does apply to parents, helplessly watching the tidal wave of demand for licensed products bear down on them. It may also apply to technical brands, which would explain their reluctance to move down-range by manufacturing oversimplified products.

The Aaker–Keller paradigm has provided an initial step in brand understanding. However, as can easily be seen, it has its roots in a traditional, cognitive view of the brand defined by its competence, objective attributes and know-how. To evaluate an extension, consumers are thus supposed to analyse the proximity of the extension product to the product that in their eyes most accurately represents the brand (its prototype). This is a bottom-up approach: the consumer's starting point is the similarities between products as a means of evaluating the brand extension. This applies well to so-called 'functional' brands.

But how much proximity is there between fries and pizza? Or between fries and buns, or fries and iced tea? There is little in a physical sense, and yet these products constitute the McCain range. In fact, the common factor behind the unity of this brand and the fit between its products is not the products themselves, but the brand concept, American food. In the future, McCain could start to sell brownies or ice cream. We may thus suppose that there is another way of evaluating fit other than just the three dimensions examined above: the evaluation of the fit with the intangible concept of the brand itself. In this case, consumers would use a top-down approach. Starting with the concept, they would ask themselves whether the product extension conforms to the concept.

Furthermore, extension serves to move a brand from being product-based ('McCain makes excellent frozen fries') to being concept-based ('McCain makes delicious American food products'). Becoming a concept brand enables preparation for future expansion via other new product introductions, thus increasing the brand's market power, turnover, profile and visibility: it becomes a mega-brand.

In acquiring an intangible dimension on which its identity is founded, the brand thus gains access to expansion. For as long as it stays a product brand, it remains confined to a product segment: if what you sell is Bic biros, how much further can you go than, say, erasers, marker pens and pencils? But when perceived as 'the brand of cool, simple, practical and plastic products', Bic can put its name to ballpoint pens and disposable razors and become a world leader in both these markets, as well as in the disposable lighter market.

The research can thus be summarised as in Figure 12.8: extension is based on physical fit and concept fit.

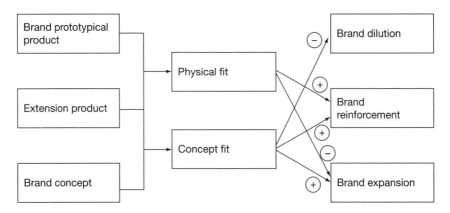

Figure 12.8   The consequences of product and concept fit and misfit
Source: Michel, 2000

The limits of early research on extension

Who knows Genichi Kawakami? He was the CEO of Yamaha for 52 years, and died in 2002. When he succeeded his father as CEO in 1950, Yamaha was a harmonium and piano company. In 1954 the company made a radical diversification into motorbikes. In parallel, it also created synthethisers and acoustic and electric guitars. Then it extended its activity to skis, tennis rackets and carbon-based golf clubs. Later it was to enter the hi-fi market, positioned as a premium product, followed by extensions in the video market and now multimedia. At the heart of all these strategic moves lay the belief that product innovations are the only way to enter markets and to remain profitably in these markets. They were also underwritten by a genuine vision of this CEO, that of the leisure society. Of course, it never came to the mind of Genichi Kawakami to call any of these innovations by any name other than Yamaha.

The problem is that, according to early brand extension research (Aaker and Keller, 1990), these extensions should have all failed. This casts doubts on the theory.

The prime factor for consumer acceptance of an extension, stemming out from this research, is 'the fit', the feeling of perceived similarity between the core product and the extension. This result has been amply confirmed by subsequent research (Leif Heim Egil, 2002; Bottomley and Holden, 2001). What fit or resemblance is there between a piano and a motorbike? None. However, Yamaha is the world's leading brand for musical instruments and the world number two manufacturer of motorbikes. What fit is there between a ballpoint pen and a lighter, or a lighter and a disposable razor? None. However, Bic is the world leading brand in these three markets. It successfully managed its very dissimilar extensions under the same name. According to its CEO, having the same name was precisely one of the factors of their success. Certainly, consultants told him not to launch the lighter in 1973 under the same name as the ballpoint pen (launched in 1950) or the disposable razor, launched in 1975. But the management had another vision. These three products now make 53 per cent of their sales in North and Central America.

Why are the findings of this early research so far from this reality? In fact, this pioneering work (Aaker and Keller, 1990) rested entirely on laboratory research. In this special context, consumers were presented with ideas about extensions and had to make an immediate evaluation. In the real world, the extensions are launched as all-new products, with information about the intrinsic value of the extension and trust relayed by publicity and word of mouth. In the laboratory research setting, the interviewees had none of these, and this is why they relied on perceived fit, a measure of 'global sameness', or similarity between the extension and the brand. In brief, the conclusions of that research present the consumer as very conservative. Recently, Klink and Smith (2001) confirmed that the results were determined by the method. The interviewees have too limited information, are exposed only once to the concept (in contrast to the multiple exposures of a real advertising launch campaign), and typically are not the risk-taking innovators who try new products first. Klink and Smith demonstrated that the effect of fit diminishes when consumer innovativeness increases, and that multiple exposures increase the perceived fit between an extension and the brand.

After 20 years of academic research it was time to make a meta-analysis of all the articles or studies focusing on the overt discrepancies between generally held beliefs stemming from research and the reality of brand and business. It now appears that laboratory research produced conservative statements about brand extension. In the real world consumers are more informed and can better evaluate the extensions.

The new perspective of typicality

Above, we have spoken of typical and atypical extensions. This raises the question of how to judge whether the product resulting from an extension is at the heart, at the limit or outside the territory of a brand. This question is one more application of a more general question at the heart of research on cognitive psychology: according to what criteria is an object considered part of a category?

Indeed, the psychological study of classification by categories aims at identifying the processes by which we form categories, and assigns certain objects to one category rather than to another. The brand is, in that sense, a category.

For decades, the dominating, or 'classical', theory answered this question in the following way: a product or an object belongs to a category if it has the necessary and sufficient features of this category. This leads one to question 'the' definition of the concept (or the category), ie about the nature of these features determining the belonging or non-belonging. This model works well for certain categories (for example the category of 'even numbers'), but it seems less reliable for others. Specialist or niche car makers such as BMW or Saab have definite image and physical traits, which can qualify a new car as belonging or not to the brand. This is not the case for the generalist brands such as Ford, Opel, Vauxhall and Nissan. The same holds true for Braun vs Philips.

Indeed, in this classic model, all examples of the category are equivalent since they all have these necessary and sufficient traits: two is an even number as much as 18 or 40! All BMWs are BMW.

Experience proves that the situation is different for many categories: for example, some birds are more 'birdlike' than others, and even a butterfly is more 'birdlike' than an ostrich. Belonging to a category does not seem to be a clear-cut binary function (yes/no) but a probabilistic one. The frontier between the 'bird' and 'insect' categories is unclear. This does not nullify these two categories: indeed, we all have in mind the prototype of a bird and that of an insect, and these two prototypes cannot be mistaken one for the other! However, the frontiers of each category are not that separate. (see also Chapter 11.)

Thus the new tendency of research on categorisation, led by Rosch (1978) and Lakoff

(1987), admits that categories can also be groups with unclear boundaries which are not defined by a series of necessary and sufficient features but by a prototype, the best exemplar.

Basically, an extension is considered acceptable if it 'fits' the idea that consumers have of the parent brand. This feeling is based either on a high perceived similarity to the most typical product of the brand (also called the prototype), or on the coherence between the extension and the brand contract (also called its concept or identity).

When the extension is distant from the mother brand, which attributes of the latter are transferred to the extension product, and which are not? As the notion of distance is linked to a comparison with the prototypical product – or products – of the brand, the objective characteristics of the brand are the ones which will be transferred the least to remote extensions. On the contrary, the intangible, more symbolic characteristics ignore distance and have an influence on all extensions. The doctoral thesis of Gali (1993) under supervision of the author, demonstrates this. Consumers were asked to evaluate the Miele brand according to various image dimensions, then to evaluate according to the same dimensions the most typical product of Miele (the washing-machine) and two extensions, one slightly atypical (a television) and one very atypical (a microcomputer).

What did the research reveal?

▌ First, the very atypical extension receives very little of the Miele functional values.

▌ Generally speaking, objective qualities are not transferred as well as symbolic qualities. Thus, typical physical features of Miele – quality, innovation, reliability – are weakly transferred to the image of the two extensions. On the contrary, the extensions receive the following features: for the young, to show off, for innovators. For that

reason, in a different context, luxury brands have little difficulty in practising extension even into dissimilar categories. Their primarily symbolic qualities ignore the distance between concrete objects. They can be transferred more easily.

How extensions impact the brand: a typology

Brand extension is a leap out of the category of origin to grow the business. Here again it is necessary to see the difference between close extensions, also called continuous extensions, and discontinuous or remote extensions. A brand of spark plugs for automobiles can undertake a close extension into other automobile accessories (batteries, windscreen wipers, etc), as is the case for Bosch and Valeo. A brand that masters optics can extend into photocopying: this is the case for Canon, Minolta, Ricoh, Kodak and Agfa. A sports brand can cover other sports goods (Adidas, Salomon). Discontinuous extensions eliminate technological synergies and physical links between products: they are real diversifications. For example Yamaha sells both motorbikes and classical pianos. The Carrefour distributor's brand covers the entire field of mass consumption goods and even quality goods.

Thus, there are extensions which are far from the original territory of the brand, and extensions which are close. This leads to brands with a narrow spectrum of products – specialised brands – and brands with a wide spectrum (such as Philips or General Electric). Is it better to be a specialist or a generalist? Both strategies are valid. A brand is arbitrary, in theory it can go wherever it wants to. Nothing can stop Bic from deciding to brand windsurfing equipment. If the corporate strategy puts forward synergies of brand awareness and savings on advertising, it will adopt a wide spectrum strategy. As a general rule, it can be stated that beyond the growth of sales and profits, brand extensions influence the brand and its capital in six different ways:

1. Some extensions exploit the brand capital: the new product sells thanks to its name. This is what happens when the product receiving the brand is no different from the existing competitors on the market: the brand has not entirely played its transformation role, but it enables the product to benefit from its image. By using this practice too frequently – through a loose licensing policy for example – the brand capital wears out as the brand becomes associated with these now commonplace products, and with their unjustified price premium. Industrial brands often fill up the gaps in their lines by buying the missing items from their competitors. This is typical of the copiers' market.

2. Other extensions destroy the brand capital, for instance when the extension is downwards. Porsche has cancelled its 924 range, cars which only justified their considerable price difference against their competitors (the Golf GTi) by the prestigious name. None of the objective or subjective values of Porsche could be found in the 924 model: neither masculinity, nor technology. This model seemed to announce the end of the Porsche myth. Since at that time the brand no longer took part in Formula 1 racing and was losing in the Le Mans 24-hour endurance race, the only communication element of the brand was advertising, of which a large part was dedicated to the 924. To return to its source, the brand ceased to manufacture the 924 and reinvested in the 911.

3. Some extensions have a neutral effect on the brand capital. The product is not out of place but is in tune with what is expected from the brand. Significantly, in the field of home appliances, some brands are thought to offer many more types of products than are actually produced, but if they decided to actually penetrate these markets, their image would not suffer. This shows that consumers have a perception of the brand which is different from that of those who manufacture it. They attribute to the brand areas of competence which are larger than and not limited to just the existing products.

4. Some extensions influence the meaning of the brand: when Rossignol added branded tennis rackets, the status of the brand changed. It is now less specialised and is characterised by a wider range of interests. Yet the two sports covered by Rossignol were not chosen randomly: the brand is still offering the equipment which extends the individual's body to help gain access to pleasure and performance. Nestlé increased its modernity by competing upfront under its own name with Danone on the ultrafresh market (ie yoghurt).

5. Some extensions are regenerating. They revive the brand and its core, and re-express its base values in a new, stronger manner. Thus, the classic green blazer is a regenerating product for Lacoste. It represents a rare symbiosis between the features building the Lacoste brand: conformity, discretion, sociability but also a certain distance on fashion. As for the green colour, it is more casual than the blue blazer (too uniform for Lacoste) and refers to the green grass of the original tennis courts at Wimbledon. The green blazer brings Lacoste up to date and at the same time expresses its roots. The 'Marlboro Classics' line allows the brand to recommunicate its history, its roots and founding values.

6. Finally, some extensions, although not desired by the brand, are necessary to

defend the brand capital: their purpose is, above all, to prevent the use of the brand name by another company in another category of products. Thus, Cartier may not want to develop along those lines, but they have to in order to prevent another company from registering the brand name Cartier on an international scale in the textiles category.

Avoiding the risk of dilution

In our many brand extension consulting missions, the recurring question concerns the risk of diluting the image capital. Could the business extension harm the brand's assets: its reputation, and the traits that comprise its value in the eyes of the market? For example, what will be the long-term effect on Danone's image if it starts selling Danone water too? What will be the long-term effect on Mercedes' image when it produces its A-Class range? What will be the long-term effect of Chanel's decision to start selling glasses at Afflelou, a discount franchise chain of opticians? What will be the long-term effect on the image of a brand that has sold only to professionals, but now starts selling to the general public too? What will be the long-term effect of an extension towards lower prices? What will be the long-term effect of selling not only pens but also cigarette lighters and razors under the Bic brand?

As these typical questions show, the problem lies in estimating the long-term effects. No study can predict the future. Second, the answer will depend to a large extent on the ability to perform the extension successfully and well. After all, an extension is more than just a brand extension: more importantly, it is a departure from the brand's tried and tested sphere of competence. Some learning will be necessary, and this may take time. For example, the little A-Class car revealed that Mercedes had not sufficiently mastered the engines and stability issues for this chassis type, thus reneging on the brand's traditional basic

contract and its three essential attributes: reliability, safety and standing.

Extensions also entail taking risks other than just image-related ones. A brand extension generally brings about changes in target markets, distributors (and perhaps even buyers, from a mass retail perspective), prices, manufacturing and logistics. These changes may be a source of annoyance to the brand's historical distribution channel, opinion leaders or existing customers. There is thus a genuine business risk – and this may affect sales of the current flagship product which constitutes the main sales platform.

An example of brand dilution: Vichy

Vichy is an example of a brand whose changes over its history have led to a loss of identity and value. It started out as a cosmetics brand that promoted itself as the dermatologists' brand. However, in an attempt to increase sales, it dropped this label and began developing products with a strong cosmetics base. Freed of its dermatology tag, the brand was able to advertise on television and develop products which, in accordance with women's wishes, had a much more cosmetics-based slant – as well as bigger margins. The brand was able to launch more new products every year, as the whole clinical tests process was no longer necessary. In just a few years, it became just another run-of-the-mill pharmacy product.

Vichy's sales increased very rapidly, as did its margins. However, at the same time its image was being eroded. This policy, although a winner in the short term, had caused a loss of identity in the eyes of consumers who could no longer perceive the brand's distinctiveness or added value. It was no longer what chemists wanted either, at a time when the pharmacies channel as a whole was attempting to re-establish its legitimacy against new distribution channels also seeking the right to sell so-called 'para-pharmacy' products.

It was back to the drawing board for Vichy's business model and brand mission. Vichy, the dedicated chemist's brand, needed to bolster its distribution channel. The brand was repositioned around the theme of health, and thus the brand slogan became *La santé passe aussi par la peau* ('Health is vital. Start with your skin'). Most importantly, all items and products that did not fit this philosophy were axed.

Such losses of identity are common: large groups often seek to make a profit out of their acquisitions and force small brands with a strong identity to move quickly into other distribution channels and categories. Neutrogena, for example, is facing this threat: it is expanding its presence in the worldwide food channel, but at the risk of losing the key values that make the brand truly distinctive.

Is the consumer bookkeeping or subtyping?

Academic research furnishes important information on the risk of image dilution. Unfortunately, however, it focuses exclusively on the misfit with the brand image: it does not consider risks arising from the fact that an extension is usually also accompanied by strategic changes in distribution and targets.

The foremost paradigm in research on dilution is a failure to honour the basic contract. What happens when the expectations created by the brand's name are dashed by the brand extension? Apart from this failure in itself, is there not a risk to the brand's image, or even to the sales of existing products? Basic research (Loken and Roedder John, 1993) has shown that any failure to honour the basic contract has a negative impact on the brand and its image for each image aspect that is ignored. A brand is constructed out of the sum of all of the impressions accumulated in consumers' memories. The only exception to this is if customers find themselves asking the question, is the unsatisfactory extension typical or atypical of the brand? If the extension is perceived as being atypical, the brand's image is safe. However, extensions that are fairly typical of the brand are the ones that dilute its image the most if they disappoint with regard to the brand contract. The problem is that there is no guarantee consumers will ask themselves whether the extension is typical or not. In the aforementioned study, researchers put the question to half the sampled group. The question did not spontaneously occur to the other half. It would therefore seem that consumers adopt a 'bookkeeping' approach in which the brand is responsible for everything it does, whether good or bad.

A second, more recent piece of research considered the question of the effect of breaking the brand contract during an extension on sales of the current flagship product (Roedder John, Loken, Joiner, 1998). Disappointment with the performance of a Johnson & Johnson brand extension did indeed impair the brand image with regard to the attribute that constituted its differentiating value: gentleness. However the sales of the prototype, or flagship product, was not affected. This suggests an 'experience effect'. Consumers who have already used the product are confident about qualities. They might view a brand extension negatively but this will not alter this confidence about the flagship product. However, J&J's flagship product (baby shampoo) *was* affected when the disappointment stemmed from a line extension (a simple modification to the basic product). Such very closely linked extensions are the ones that cause the most collateral damage to sales of the flagship product.

The risk of downward stretch

It is a well-known fact that price is an indication of quality, and can on its own create the image of a product with a high standing. In their extensions, some top-of-the-range prestige brands have been prompted to sell cheaper products in the search for a client base that is more numerous but less willing to pay a high price. This is the approach taken by brands such as Mercedes with its A-Class and Cartier with its Must de Cartier range. What effects do such acts have on the brand's existing clients?

Given that an expensive brand derives its value in part from the fact that it indicates the buyer has the financial means to afford expensive products (consumers' reflected image), it is hardly surprising that there is a negative reaction: their status has to be spread more thinly, and thus reduced. This has been confirmed by a study on 'The ownership effect in consumer response to brand stretches (Kirmani, Sood and Bridges, 1999). People who do not buy the prestige brand (BMW in this study) are pleased by its more accessible price extension; existing buyers are much less impressed. Current buyers, however, appreciate price-increasing 'upward-stretch' extensions far more than non-buyers do. With brands that are not of high standing (for example, Accura cars), there is no effect of this kind. This study also confirms that the act of using a sub-brand protects the top-of-the-range brand from image dilution in the event of a price-lowering 'downward-stretch' extension. This is what Cartier did with Must de Cartier, selling pens, cigarette lighters and leather goods in large retail stores to reach a wider clientele and increase its recognition, which until then had been restricted to a well-off elite.

Another interesting piece of research (Buchanan, Simmons and Bickart, 1999) analysed the risk of devaluation if a prestige brand adopts a less selective channel when entering a non-prestige market. For example, the luxury hairdresser J Dessange granted a licence to l'Oréal to use its name on a shampoo to be sold in supermarkets. The findings of this study were that it all depends on merchandising, and – in this case – on three factors. What is the brand's relative visibility, price gap and distance from one or more lesser known or lower prestige brands? If its relative visibility,

distance from the competition and price gap tally with the consumer's impression of the brand's standing, the risk is reduced. If they do not, the consumer mentally lowers the brand's standing. For example, it is crucially important for a brand of standing to have a clearly separated display which is distinct from competitors'. If it does not, and the display is mixed, the consumer interprets this as a signal from the (supposedly expert) retailer that the brand of lower standing placed alongside the brand of high standing is just as good.

What can we draw from this research on the risk of dilution? First, we can conclude that customers of prestige brands are happy where they are: they form a conservative lobby. In so doing, they demonstrate a lack of awareness of the economic conundrum faced by the brand or company. As Jürgen Schremp, the CEO of Daimler-Benz, observed in 1998, Mercedes could either stay where it was and – like Rolls-Royce – go bankrupt; or it could change, and sell over a million cars. Conscious of the risk of losing the attachment of its existing customers, the brand has to take precautions:

▌ Even in its lower cost extensions, the brand contract must be honoured – and the first consideration is quality.

▌ The brand should manage its downward extension while at the same time continuing to nourish the legend that ensures its high standing. After the A-Class, Mercedes relaunched the S-Class – voted by experts as the best car in the world – and announced Maytag, an even more luxurious model.

▌ The brand can use a sub-brand for its downward stretch.

▌ It can also split its distribution into segments. Chanel boutiques concentrate on products with a minimum price of €1,000, while Chanel sunglasses and cosmetics are intended for wider channels.

▪ Current buyers benefit from a greater level of attention and distinctive signs of recognition, following the model established by credit cards. There is a basic card for everyone, but also far more exclusive Gold and Platinum cards which provide a way of re-establishing the differentiation from other cardholders.

The brand is extended to grow through changing its scope of influence. It is not possible to grow while at the same time keeping everything intact and unchanged.

With regard to non-prestige brands, the risk of dilution can often be exaggerated internally. For example, all spirit brands have asked themselves what the impact would be if they were to enter the ready-to-drink (RTD) pre-mix/alcopop market. Would this not have an effect on their image among the buyers of their basic products – Smirnoff, Ricard, Johnnie Walker, Bacardi and so on? In fact, company studies reveal that this is far from the case. Buyers of established but somewhat elderly brands are delighted to see that the brands are consumed even by today's young people, albeit in a very different way, a fact that is flattering to their parents. This is not to suggest that such extensions are entirely without risk, but the risks are business-related. The first of these is that the new product launch will fail. The second is that older buyers with a high volume potential will be replaced by younger buyers who – at least initially – will consume less. The trick will be to encourage them to migrate at a later date from an RTD-type product to the far more profitable 'real' product. Even if Bacardi Breezer is a genuine worldwide success – like Smirnoff Mule or Ice before it – and even if the products are high-margin on account of their low actual alcohol content (5 per cent), it is still a fact that Bacardi-Martini is a spirits group that expects the high profits commensurate with the spirits sector, not the lower profits of the RTD sector. The challenge is therefore to migrate current RTD customers in future to the proper Smirnoff

and Bacardi products. We should add that the real risk would have been to do nothing and watch as young people deserted the brand as a result of its failure to adapt its products, consumption methods, sales and consumption locations and prices to new consumers. Extension is a necessity.

The traditional problem faced by professional brands is their desire also to address a less professional audience. Modern management techniques advocate talking to the customer's customer. By communicating with the general public to publicise the merits of aluminium verandahs, Technal – at that time a subsidiary of Alcan – increased demand from its actual clients (craftspeople and businesses that make aluminium verandahs for their customers). Somfy, the worldwide manufacturer of tubular motors for household automation products, did something similar: it produced advertising for automated blinds, even though its actual customers were the blind manufacturers themselves. Will such a strategy tread on professionals' toes? Such questions overlook the main issue: these extensions are strategic because they seek to maintain the domination of the channel, ensuring that the company does not become a mere OEM, parts manufacturer and subcontractor. Not to take such an extension risk is to take a much more serious medium-term risk instead. This is certainly one way for a leader to increase its recognition, and thus its brand's status. More importantly, it is the way to increase the size of the market, by directly influencing downstream demand from its own clients – who have a natural inclination to go on selling whatever sold well last year, and not to promote innovations. However, only innovations can make the market grow: this is why they must be 'pushed' by the distribution channel. If they are not, demand has to be 'pulled' instead.

Business-to-business brands start out as specialists, and grow via integration. The delicate phase comes when they stop being single-product specialists and expand their range to include another speciality. For example, could a company that has made its reputation in high-voltage switching gear also manufacture medium-voltage or low-voltage switching gear? More importantly, could it also distribute electricity distribution hardware (plugs, cables, conduits and so on) without losing its status? After all, switching gear is a key component of any industrial installation: safety comes first, especially in high-voltage equipment. The same cannot be said for electrical distribution hardware. But it also seems obvious that while we continue to look at the problem from the sole angle of brand extension, we are viewing things the wrong way around. The real question is one of leadership. Clients and distributors want more integration, because it makes their business life simpler. Furthermore, in emerging countries, the pursuit of critical size is vitally important. Can this be achieved with a single line of products? No.

However, it is important to maintain the image capital, which can be achieved in two interlinked ways. The first is by entering the new market (electrical distribution) with a differentiated range based on the attributes for success in this market, with an additional 'plus' as insurance (even if this is not a determining expectation for this new market), in the interests of brand identity and commercial success. The second is the pursuit of innovation and communication in the switchgear market to reinforce the brand's leadership in this sector.

By way of conclusion on the risk of dilution, let us remember that all extensions are a form of change whose aim is to ensure growth and profitability. It is impossible to expect both growth and a lack of change at the same time. Of course, the basic values and attributes of the brand's kernel of identity must be preserved. However, the extension is certain to add new attributes, which start out as being peripheral but may one day become part of the kernel themselves.

Balancing identity and adaptation to the extension market segments

Brand extension capitalises on the brand's 'assets'. It hopes that there will be a transfer of these 'assets' between the parent category and the extension category, given the perceived subjective proximity between the two categories. It is therefore a question of capitalising on identity: the intended result is an identity-based brand.

However, the success of an extension depends on its ability to deliver value to the client. In what way are these assets relevant? What makes them superior to the competition? This presents the problem of the extension's ability to exploit a genuine opportunity or real consumer insight in its market.

There is therefore always a balance to be struck between these two (equally legitimate) requirements. Since a name is a promise, the brand cannot make different promises with different products; but at the same time, unsuitability for the target market is the number one reason that new products fail: each market has its own 'drivers' and customer preference levers.

An extension category may be chosen for its contribution towards building the future brand. Nivea, for example, owns a raft of daughter brands, each positioned on extensions that have a highly specific role in building the Nivea brand over time (see page 306). The hygiene and beauty market – as the name suggests – consists of hygiene and care on one side, and make-up on the other. Why would a brand such as Nivea, positioned on skincare and having successfully offered all possible skincare permutations worldwide, use Nivea Beauty to enter the world of seduction, play and appearance against such well-established giants as Maybelline, Max Factor and Bourjois?

As always, the answer has to be growth, image and profitability. After all, the make-up market is a rich seam of double-figure growth.

Furthermore, it attracts new young customers. This fashion aspect lends the brand image a very modern appearance. And lastly, it is a profitable category.

However, Nivea still had to acquire legitimacy in this unexpected area. The first advertising campaign of Nivea Beauty was a failure; during extension, brands are often (naturally enough, perhaps) more preoccupied with their brand identity than with the customers in the target market. Nivea relied on bad insights. The sub-brand's positioning was 'All the colours of care' – but to a young target audience in the mass retail channel, this is not a relevant promise. At a chemist's it would have been a different story, hence the existence of La Roche Posay and Roc cosmetics. The brand repositioned its beauty line on the market expectations and the long-term weaknesses of the competition. The new promise was, 'The most beautiful me'.

As we can see, this promise is no longer a straightforward translation of the essence of the brand (loving care for the skin), but neither is it inconsistent with the brand's equities. Nivea Beauty's promise is that it preserves a woman's natural beauty. This capitalises on Nivea's fundamental intangible values: respect, humanity, love, naturalness, simplicity. The promise derives from a consumer insight as a reaction against the totalitarian line taken by many make-up, cosmetics and beauty products brands, urging women to look like top models and stars. This time around, the relaunch was a success. In terms of extension, the challenge lies in the balance between market appropriateness and faithfulness to the brand's identity: it is created through successive adjustments.

The McCain example provides another illustration of the difficulty inherent in brand extension. McCain is a Canadian company, operating worldwide, with three branches: frozen fries (it supplies McDonald's throughout the world), frozen pizzas, and soft drinks. In 1998, noting the rising popularity of tea-based drinks in the soft drinks market, it decided to launch an ice tea, Colorado by McCain. The firm justified its choice of an endorsing brand architecture by the over-prominence of the 'raw' product's image (in light of the previous launch of McCain fries and pizzas in the relevant countries). Consumers were therefore intended to ask for the Colorado tea drink, with its intangible youthful Tex-Mex connotations, thus fitting it into the overall American brand identity.

The marketing team was not limiting itself to image. Mindful of the competitive nature of the market, it also created a highly differentiated product embodying an essential McCain identity trait: generosity. As a result, the can of tea contained 33 cl instead of the competitors' usual 25 cl. This decision was based on sound logic: it differentiated the extension in terms of the brand's equities, both intangible and tangible. Sadly, this was also one of the causes of the extension's failure. In reality, this differentiation, embodying the brand's spirit of generosity (and thus larger portions, as befits the stereotypical American), proved to be a problem. The can, being taller than other standard cans in the category:

- was unsatisfactory to retailers, who like to keep storage issues as simple as possible;
- was rarely drunk in full by customers, who thought it contained too much;
- appeared more expensive in terms of its retail price, even though the per litre price was the same.

Paradoxically, then, this differentiation generated long-term dissatisfaction – a fundamental error in the cut-throat environment of this double-figure growth market.

The most serious problem faced by this extension was probably the fact that it was up against Lipton, the world's number one in tea products, aggressively pushing its two mega-brands (Lipton Ice Tea and Liptonic), with their associated promotional expenditure, to capture this market. Not even Nestea could compete, despite a strategic alliance with the Coca-Cola Company which ensured the distribution of its drink in all Coca-Cola vending machines. In the hypermarket – and thus the home consumption market – Nestea was powerless against Lipton.

At this point we should take another look at why strategic analysis is a higher priority than marketing analysis for the extension.

Assessing what should not change: the brand kernel

All extensions are real products or services, and real decisions have to be made concerning their attributes and characteristics. Typically the first extensions are very conservative. Then bolstered by success, extensions gain their degrees of freedom (from the prototype). This is the time when the issue of what should be left intact, unchanged, and what can change is asked.

Extension and respect for physical identity

One of the first questions raised in extensions is how far the brand can go from its physical basis. This is especially true for brands whose identity rests heavily on their physical facets. Dove positioning for instance is based on its moisturising power, and the claim of 25 per cent moisturising cream content. This claim is maintained across extensions. All Orangina's extensions respect the ratio of 10 per cent real juice and 2 per cent real pulp in the bottle or can.

Typically, first extensions are very close to the original: Mars introduced a Mars ice-cream bar, for Mars looks like a bar. Only later would it dare to move to other formats and shapes. However, growth can only be found by gaining more degrees of freedom: self-imitation cannot suffice. In addition, extension is an extension of the same benefit elsewhere: it accentuates the move of the brand from pure product to concept, from pure tangible values to intangible

values as well. Taillefine/Vitalinea is a leading yoghurt brand based on good taste with 0 per cent fat. It made a successful extension in the biscuit market, but with a promise of 'less fat'. Finally it was extended to purified water, a product with no taste but with slimness benefits.

At some point in time, it is then possible and even necessary to forget the tangible root. Smirnoff is a vodka. However, Smirnoff Ice, the world's number one ready-mixed drink, is based on not vodka but malt whisky. Skyy Blue also is not vodka but whisky-based. Of course, this is not a guaranteed way to success. In the United States everyone knows that Captain Morgan is a brand of rum. To grow the business it too introduced Captain Morgan Gold, a ready-mixed drink. Instead of rum, it too used whisky as a basis. This ingredient switch created a number of strategic advantages:

- lower taxes;

- access to greater distribution than is possible for rum, for instance through beer distributors;

- access to television advertising (not permitted for spirits in the United States).

The new product however failed. Consumers did not like the taste enough, a classic in food and drink new product failure.

In brand management, identity plays a key role – and this is doubly true in extensions management. If consumers reject the very idea of an extension, it is either because they cannot see what benefits it offers that the competition does not (the number one reason for the failure of extensions), or because they cannot see the logic of the extension under this brand. In other words, the extension is in conflict with their concept of the brand's essence and kernel of identity – that is to say, the handful of attributes without which the brand ceases to be the brand. So how can we gain an understanding of identity as perceived by consumers?

To return to basic theory for a moment, the

brand – like any concept – is defined by essential and less essential traits. The former are identifying traits, and are thus crucial. The latter are variable: they may be prominent in some brand products and less prominent in others. In his work on the perception of stereotypes, Salomon Asch showed that some traits had a considerable impact on overall perception, while others could be absent (or even contradictory) without affecting overall perception. Abric (1994) extended this theory to include social perceptions, and Mischel extended it to brands (2000). According to the theory, the brand changes over time by incorporating traits into its kernel which had until then been peripheral, featuring only in some of its products. These traits form the heart of the brand's vitality, the source of its ability to adapt to its ambient environment.

Preparing the brand for remote extensions

Not all brands lend themselves to extension. Some brands are defined only through their prototypical product or know-how. This is the case with cosmetic brands such as Clarins, Roc and Vichy. Their field of extension has to be limited within appropriate boundaries which combine both science and beauty.

Other brands are almost like sects and have quasi-religious principles: St Michael, the brand owned by Marks & Spencer, covers everything from food to clothes, from toys to para-pharmaceutical products and furnishing. Through its signature it imparts legitimacy to all that is in conformity with the Marks & Spencer ideology. Like a patron saint (etymologically, patron means pattern, ie model to be followed), the brand transforms and elevates all the products that it sanctifies.

If the brand is to remain intact in the eyes of the consumer and not be fragmented into disconnected units, the prerequisites of a remote extension must be taken into consideration. For the extension of one brand into various remote categories to look coherent, one has to draw upon the deeper meaning of the brand. This supposes that the brand either has such meaning or has the potential to acquire it. The Swiss brand, Caran d'Ache, built its reputation through upmarket pencils and writing tools. Its extension into scarves, wallets and leather items failed. The brand was missing the necessary deep meaning.

Figure 12.9 demonstrates the demands arising out of brand extension. Every degree of product dissimilarity changes the meaning and the status of the brand. Close extensions (B) are compatible with product or know-how brands: Heinz can market not only ketchup, but also mustard sauce. Extension one degree further (C) corresponds to brand benefits: Palmolive softens all that it embraces and Bic simplifies everything from pens to razors to lighters, making them disposable and cheap. A further extension (D), in order to be coherent with the initial product (A), assumes a brand defined by its personality. In the beginning, Sony was a brand exclusively for hi-fi systems. But in a few years it has acquired fame in the field of television sets and videos and has therefore modified its image and its significance, but its core values still remain technology, precision and innovation with a specific elegant and refined personality. The last extension (E) assumes a brand that is defined by deep values. Virgin is a good example.

Thus, the only way for a brand to give a single meaning to a collection of extensions is to regard them from a higher viewpoint. To make distant extensions fit, the brand has to distance itself physically and serve more as a source of inspiration and a value system that can embed itself in different products. This is the case with Nestlé, a brand with a very large spectrum of offers. The distance helps to maintain the angle between the brand and its capacity to lend itself to different products. The steeper the angle, the greater force it exerts on the products (from A to E). The flatter this angle, the less is the force available

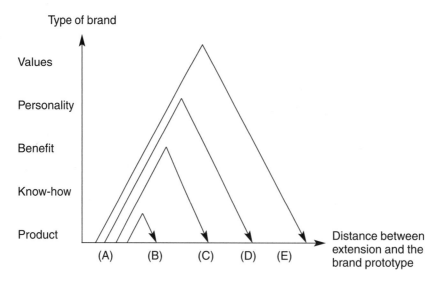

Figure 12.9   Type of brand and ability to extend further

to the brand to unify the products. Like an overstretched rubber band, the brand becomes weak, loses its grip and finally breaks.

More concretely, brands having only a physical facet (a product, a recipe) and no intangible identity do not lend themselves to remote extensions. They become diluted and are no more than numbers. This is the case with Mitsubishi. It no longer operates as a unifying brand but is only a corporate name and a factory trademark. It carries no signification other than the generic characteristics of Japanese technology and the image of industrial power that is associated with the group. Mitsubishi cars do not seem to embody any particular ideal and neither do Mitsubishi televisions or tools. This was also the case with Philips to a certain extent.

At the other end of the spectrum are the underexploited brands. These cover a very narrow product field but have an inner meaning which makes them legitimate over a large range of products. The brand Dole was a typical example of under-exploitation. This brand underestimated its growth potential for a long time. Management

considered the brand as a product and confined it to pineapple juice. But for consumers, Dole signified much more. Beyond its attributes (good taste, freshness and naturalness), lay a deeper core: sunshine. Dole was actually the sunshine brand and in this capacity could cover not only other fruit juices, but other products, eg ice creams. Very well known for a long time as a shoe brand, Salvatore Ferragamo has now successfully diversified into ladies' handbags, cardigans and ties.

As shown in Figure 12.9, the further a brand wants to move from its origins, the more it needs to have acquired a relevant intangible meaning.

Research does, indeed, demonstrate that the order in which intermediate extensions are made affects consumer reaction to the final extension. Thus, in an experiment, consumers were presented with a sequence of five extensions for a number of brands. These extensions were chosen to represent five degrees of perceived distance or fit with the brand. In one case, consumers viewed an ordered sequence of extensions (from the closest to the farthest); in the second case they

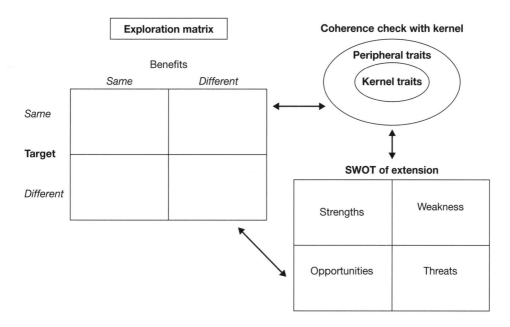

Figure 12.10   The managerial process of extension evaluation

saw an unordered sequence of extensions (Dawar and Anderson, 1992). Two results emerged from this laboratory experiment.

As expected, there is a decrease in perceived coherence due to the distance between the extension and the brand's present product. However, the decrease in perceived coherence due to the distance is less steep when consumers saw the remote extension after a series of prior extensions presented in order of increasing distance. Each one may have acted as a stepping stone and prompted a category (brand) extension mechanism known as 'chaining' (Lakoff, 1987). The same result held true for the purchase likelihood for extensions.

Interestingly, it took less time to evaluate the farthest extension's coherence with the brand when that extension was seen at the end of the ordered sequence (4 seconds vs 4.34). Actually, the ordered sequence had itself modified the meaning of the brand, making it clear that it was not a product brand but a larger brand with a wider territory.

Again, a real-world illustration of this process is that of McCain. This brand entered the market with its frozen fries. After two years, it moved to large American pizzas, then to buns and recently to the fast-growing iced tea market. The meaning of McCain is now clear: American food, simple products, generous portions, fun to eat and innovative in their category. This brand territory will determine McCain's future extensions.

A second experiment demonstrated another basic rule of brand extension: only the coherence between extensions can create a brand territory. Two extensions may be equally remote from the core of the brand but not in the same direction. When a remote extension is presented to consumers after an intermediate extension in the same direction, this sequence increases the perceived coherence of that remote extension and its purchase likelihood (compared to the case where the intermediate extension is not in the same direction) (Dawar and Anderson, 1992).

Figure 12.11　Framework for evaluating extensions

Keys to successful brand extensions

What advice can one give to increase the probability of success of brand extensions? Based on both research and consulting, there do exist key steps and questions in the extension process which require particular attention. Extensions must be evaluated in relation to the brand, consumers and the competition. (See Figure 12.10.)

Think of the big plan first

Extensions used to be managed too much on an ad hoc basis. Every new idea was screened and evaluated, then eventually implemented. Now this era has ended. Brand management entails a long-term vision for the brand itself. There should be a clear statement of where the management wants to lead the brand. The brand wants to be a leader of what? How should we define its leadership – by product? by category? by need? by target? One thing is sure: the ambition must be to construct some kind of leadership.

　This long-term vision can be compared to a stairway. It shows the direction of the stairway and the steps to get to the desired position. Each proposal is then evaluated in relationship to this objective. A brand cannot just stretch in all directions, but strategy should guide it. There is for instance a big difference in stating that Tide (Ariel) wants to lead the low-suds detergent market, and that it wants to be the brand for those who take trouble over the care of their textiles.

The limits of consumer research for managing extensions

The role of consumer research is to assess the level of risk. It indicates what difficulty may arise when using the same name on an extension. But research is not management. Brand management needs to integrate all dimensions of the decision. This is the fundamental rationale of this new edition of this book. Decisions about extensions will take into account production, financial, strategic and competitive factors, beyond the immediate reaction of consumers. Management is risk taking, a source of competitive advantage. Let us recall that consumers' reactions to brand extensions are reflections of the past. They rest on prior learnt associations. They are also short-term oriented. Management of brand extensions is based on a long-term vision. Prior to any extension, one question must be asked: what do we want the brand to look like in the future? Each extension is a step up the stairway to this goal. Consumers have no idea of the stairway.

Are our values here really valued there?

Many extensions fail because someone has overestimated the value of the brand assets in the extension category. Are they really assets there? Do they really have a motivating value? Do they deliver an unprecedented array of benefits? Too often someone overestimates this point, making the assumption that the brand assets are relevant. For instance, most perfume brands are tempted to launch cosmetic lines, but very few have succeeded. The drivers in the latter market are focused on confidence and hope in research, and this is not what a perfume brand can provide. It has no credentials.

A second key question concerns competition. Does the proposed extension really beat its competition? Too much of extension research is concept testing: it asserts the attractiveness of the concept. However, in stores customers compare offerings, and assess their relative attractiveness. Certainly an extension may be welcomed in research exercises, but that does not mean it will win out in the purchasing decision. Customers may be reluctant to change their existing purchasing patterns for the new brand and product. At the moment of truth, is curiosity enough? There has to be a strong incentive (perceived difference) or a pioneer effect (acting first).

It is noticeable that Nestea, Nestlé's entry in the iced tea soft drink market, has not been successful in Europe, despite its strategic alliance with Coca-Cola, which distributes the product and offers it in all the vending machines it controls. However, there is one country where Nestea is leader: Spain. There and only there, Nestea was launched before Lipton's Ice Tea, and so benefited from the pioneer advantage.

Think of the full marketing mix of the extension

An extension is not simply a new product or service, it entails a full new marketing mix. It requires in fact that the organisation think more about the consumer than the brand. When Nike launched its Nike Women extension, its management was so infatuated with the brand itself that it forgot consumers. This is why it was a failure: the products (shoes and clothes) had the same design as their male counterparts, and only the sizes were adapted to women. Nike Women was not really a line for women at all. Soon it was discovered that to succeed in this extension, it was first necessary to create relevant products. Female designers were hired to rethink the product offerings.

In Europe, Perrier has always been hampered by its most differentiating attribute, its strong bubbles. This is why Nestlé (which owns the brand) has restored it to growth via two innovations/extensions. The first, called Perrier Fluo, targets young people who perceive Perrier as being the brand of their parents. It offers a sophisticated taste (for example, peppermint) and finer bubbles, making it easier to drink than the original Perrier. Perrier Fluo also has lower production costs, because the packaging is plastic (rather than glass), and the water used is not taken from the Vergèze spring, the brand's historic source. The second extension, called Eau de Perrier, targets adult mealtime drinking. To this end, a finer, more elegant bubble was created, and the sparkle of the product was adjusted to make it lighter.

As we can see, extension often takes the form of the adaptation – indeed, sometimes the radical modification – of the product or entire marketing mix. The main and only real reason for extension is growth. Often, the brand needs to go beyond a mere range extension to achieve a significant leap. Thus, in the United States, Smirnoff – currently the world's number two spirits producer – decided to enter the store multiples channel in addition to its traditional channel (liquor stores). To do this, it launched a new ready-to-drink (RTD) product, Smirnoff Ice, with a low alcohol content, backed by an advertising investment of US $70 million. It has sold more than 30 million cases and produced 'a positive spillover effect on Smirnoff's image'. The extension also led to the acquisition of competence in this new distribution channel.

When Ricard launched its own RTD in order to penetrate the nightclubs, discotheques and night bars it had failed to enter with its core (and till that point, only) product, did it think enough of the new consumption situation associated with these places? After midnight, this simple RTD competes with all kinds of cocktails. It should therefore have been aromatised to better answer the needs of that situation. This extension is consumed in a specific place, at a specific time, and this had implications for the product itself. The same holds true for distribution. Extensions are often ways to get out of the classic distribution channels and become closer to the public's need.

Extension should meet trade expectations too

In its desire to maintain its dominant share of market in the UK, Smirnoff has shown the way by following a dual strategy. One part is aimed at adults, its present target market, with the introduction of Smirnoff Blue, Smirnoff Lemon and Smirnoff Black for instance, to compete with Absolut and Finlandia. The other is aimed at the youth market through Smirnoff Mule and later Smirnoff Ice, two ready-mixed drinks which gained high success and were soon imitated. The success of Smirnoff Mule demonstrates that all good innovations must provide value to the distributor *and* to the consumer.

The strategic goal was to establish these new products among young people for on-premise consumption. On Friday or Saturday nights, many pubs are literally full up and people gather outside them. Smirnoff Mule brings bartenders a faster way to serve clients than a draught beer, with a better margin:

they just have to hand the bottle over to customers, without the need for a glass. Meanwhile, the bottle with its highly visible branding acts as a badge, an identifier for customers, unlike a glass of beer which generally does not carry a brand name. This is a very important motivation for 18–24-year-olds who are insecure about their image. In addition, advertising reinforced the modern status of the new drink. More than £4.5 million was spent on Smirnoff Ice to launch it among young males (Mule having been mostly chosen by females).

The question of resources

The main source of failure of extensions is a lack of resources for the launch. Companies should remember that if an extension is aimed at a different market, its launch should be treated as a new product launch. Unfortunately many companies extend their brand, thinking that it is a way to save money compared with launching a new brand, and that a simple mention at the end of the regular 30-second television ad will suffice. It might do for a simple line extension, a variant, but not for a brand extension.

Companies also hesitate to divert investment from core products to finance an extension. They feel that by doing so they will put their core product at risk from competition. As a consequence, they decide at the last moment not to support the extension with the required budget. This reasoning underestimates the reciprocal spillover effect. Communicating the benefits of a new product has an effect on the sales of the core product (see Chapter 9). This is one of the virtues of mega-brands covering multiple products: they get re-energised through communication about their new products.

How will the competition react?

Some extensions attack the core market of a competitor. It will react fiercely and at any cost. This is rarely taken sufficiently into account when planning extensions. To sustain long-term competition supposes a long-term commitment, not only at head-quarters level, but at the local subsidiary level where budgets are tailored to innovations.

Extending the brand extensions

After a successful line or brand extension is created, one major question that soon arises concerns its geographical extension. In what countries should it be developed? In answering it is important to remember that extensions are often created in response to a specific market problem. For instance Orangina Red (with red oranges and guarana energising ingredients) was created to challenge Coke's appeal among the major soft drink gulpers, the teens. Coke's appeal is based on thrill and mystery: it is a black drink with a secret formula that can be mixed with forbidden (to teens) alcohols. Orangina Red was created to be the more thrilling and adventurous extension of Orangina. However, this logic only applies in countries where Orangina is in fact competing across flavours. In the United States for instance, it held a niche position within the 'new age' segment of orange-flavoured drinks. Orangina Red would make no sense there, while Orangina Light would.

Nivea's sub-brands are not present equally in all countries. The fashionable Nivea Beauty is not sold in the United States, for instance, although in this case it is because the sub-brand roll-out strategy has not reached this point.

Another reason for differences between countries is based on the potential of the country and the status of the parent brand within it. For instance, should Evian launch Evian Affinity in Japan or Korea? This extension is in line with the latest Evian positioning based on health, aesthetics and eternal youth, and Evian water is certainly known in Korea and Japan, but it commands a very low market share.

What name for brand extensions?

Why is Chanel's entry in the cosmetics market called Precision, and why does Biotherm call its entry in the male market Biotherm Homme? Obviously the question of the name cannot be separated from that of the chosen brand architecture (see Chapter 13). If it is decided to follow an umbrella brand architecture there should be no specific names. Architectures based on source brands and endorsing brands allow for another name.

The naming decision must satisfy two demands. First, it should help the extension succeed. By a name one can underline specific traits or benefits of the extension, or counter-balance possible negative thoughts. Second, it should not dilute the parent brand equity.

Fashion and perfume brands are not that legitimate in the highly scientific cosmetic market, where women are looking for innovative ingredients, not just dreams or fashion. Chanel's choice of Precision helped bypass the negative prejudice against this type of extension for perfume and couturier brands.

Many years ago, when there was still a lot of male prejudice against cosmetics, Vichy decided to name its male line Basic Homme de Vichy. Men were just not ready to buy Vichy for Men. In fact, at that time Vichy had not repositioned itself on effectiveness and health, but was a mid-range cosmetics line. Now its message is that health is tied up with skin condition. This message, this vision, has no sex, and is extendable directly to men. In addition the market has changed, and men are more open to buying cosmetic products. Basic Homme de Vichy was renamed Vichy Homme.

The name should also not dilute the parent brand equity. Too often, just because the parent brand is old, or seen as such in public surveys, the extension receives a new brand name, and the parent brand is hidden, in a typical endorsing architecture. This creates a self-fulfilling prophecy: hidden, the parent brand gets older and older in the public perception. The role of new products and brand extension is always to take from the brand equity but also to give to brand equity: imbalanced exchanges should be avoided.

As a rule, and as will be discussed with reference to the multicircular model (see Chapter 13), the more remote an extension from the brand core values, the more it should have an endorsing architecture and as a result a brand name of its own. The closer it is to the core, the more it should adopt an umbrella architecture, and receive a generic or descriptive name. For instance a prepaid card for mobile phones could be called Mobicard or BT Nomad Card, but surely not Nomad ... by BT.

Checking what the extension brings to the brand, its feedback effect

An extension uses brand capital. This is not surprising, since it was created to do so: the brand is a business development tool. It is therefore logical that we should seek to exploit this capital by putting it to productive use in new growth categories. However, we must also ensure a win–win outcome. After all, what does a brand extension really deliver? Sales alone are not enough. The benefits to be derived by the brand from this extension must be clearly specified.

Each extension from Kinder confectionery is aimed at a particular target, age segment or situation of use. Each also gives the brand widened relevance and less of a narrow image. This must be specified clearly in advance, and then measured afterwards.

Of course, we must be all the more careful to avoid any risk of dilution, as can happen when the values associated with the extension category contradict those of the brand, or when it is known that implementing the extension will be risky. After all, the implementation is the part customers see.

Is the market really attractive?

The first thing to evaluate in a brand extension is not the extension, it is the market attractiveness of the category. The key question in evaluating a brand extension is the intrinsic value of the category. Later, we examine this from the point of view of the business and the brand. This presupposes that we are considering not only the present but also the future of the category. An extension is not an overnight affair, it marks the beginning of a desire to invest in a new market. The extension itself is no more than a bridgehead. A realistic analysis of existing strengths, threats and opportunities is therefore required. Clearly, this corresponds to the traditional SWOT model (Figure 12.10).

Opportunities derive from the relationship between the factors for success in the category and the organisation's key competences, both tangible and intangible. They also derive from the brand's ability to segment the category according to its own values, or in other words to create genuinely relevant differentiation. Strategic analysis also analyses the future of competition and the organisation's relative strengths. Will its entry into the market trigger a competitive reaction, and if so, how big? To answer this question, it is necessary to evaluate the importance of the category to competitors.

To repeat, the fact that a brand *can* be extended does not mean it *should* be extended. One must take into account future competition and the costs of remaining a significant player in the category (the rate of innovation, rate of launches, marketing and sales investment and so on). Extension is not an inside feat: it must deliver a sustainable advantage. For instance, many food companies have thought of launching a frozen pizza, but what would they do next to capture shelf space from Buitoni or McCain, or to defend their own shelf share? In the middle term, who is in the best position to innovate most often? Table 12.4 presents a multi-criteria strategic evaluation grid.

Table 12.4 Extension strategic evaluation grid

	Extension 1	Extension 2	Extension 3
Is it a growing market?			
Are its success factors close to our strengths?			
Are the brand assets transferable?			
Are the brand assets still assets in this market?			
Will it impact positively the brand equity?			
How entrenched are competitors?			
How fast can they copy?			
Does the product have a clear differentiation?			
Is it a motivating difference?			
Can the company produce it?			
Can it produce at a normal cost?			
Will distribution accept it?			
Is it consistent with brand or company identity?			
Does it capitalise on the brand or company's present customers?			
Is it consistent with the brand or company's positioning?			
Does it capitalise on the company's expertise in:			
– production?			
– advertising?			
– logistics?			
– sales forces?			
– retail location?			
– pricing/promotion?			
Does is meet the company's profitability objectives?			
Can the company sustain competition (does it have the financial resources needed to compete)?			

The question of resources

As mentioned above, the main source of failure of extensions is the lack of resources for the launch, and later to defend them.

Should we implement it alone? Partnerships and licences

It is difficult for a company to master the many new competences needed for an extension at the same time, which is why so many companies prefer alliances:

▌ Nestlé won the battle in Europe against Kellogg's once it decided to find a technical partnership with the American General Mills.

▌ Weight Watchers' expansion in the pre-cooked meals category was made possible through a co-branding agreement with Fleury Michon, a leader in this field.

▌ Evian asked Coca-Cola to distribute it in the United States, where its core brand urgently needed to be made more available. It also asked Johnson & Johnson to develop and market Evian Affinity (its cosmetics line) worldwide.

One of the criteria in the strategic matrix for evaluating extensions concerns the company's ability to produce this extension. Of course, we are not suggesting that extensions should be restricted to categories that the company is itself capable of producing. Mars had no expertise in ice cream, nor did it have any knowledge of the buyers in this category, and hence it subcontracted production of Mars ice cream, its first major extension outside the chocolate bar market. All Cacharel extensions are based on licences: Playtex for hypermarket lingerie until 2004, l'Oréal for perfumes, household items by Arnolfo di Cambio and so on. In total, of a turnover of €35 million last year, royalties (extensions) accounted for €7.6 million.

Licences can enable extensions to move quickly into categories in which the brand has no experience of production, logistics or distribution. Some famous brands have never produced or even distributed their own products, but have instead operated on the basis of production and distribution licences throughout their existence, along with regional sub-licences, while retaining control over design, creation, strategic marketing and communication.

An extension-based business model: Virgin

Most brands conjure up an image of a product or service: shoes for Nike, yoghurt for Danone, ballpoint pens for Bic, a holiday village for Club Med, and so on. This is not surprising: before they became brands, they started out as a simple product or service, driven by marketing and sales. Virgin is an exception: who associates that brand with only one product or service? Indeed, Virgin now comprises 200 companies and 25,000 people working for the brand worldwide. It has a turnover in excess of €7 billion, and has become one of the world's top 50 brands. Even in countries in which it does not operate, it is still a famous brand.

It all started in 1969, when Richard Branson decided to launch a direct record-selling operation, enabling many groups without distribution by the 'majors' to gain access to the general public. The brand's DNA is already apparent in this founding act: Branson seeks out opportunities in markets choked by 'false' competition. He asks himself how he can operate differently from the leaders – who have usually frozen the market to their advantage. The Virgin name was chosen because it was friendly and modern, and could be applied to sectors other than just music. This last consideration alone presaged the business model that would follow.

Virgin's originality lies in the fact that it is held together by one entirely intangible 'glue', its brand. This is why the brand architecture is umbrella branding. Every year, Virgin launches itself into new businesses and pulls out of others. In under 20 years, Richard Branson has extended the brand to the following sectors (and subsequently pulled out of some of them):

- First business: mail order (1969).

- Records: Virgin Records (label created in 1973 and sold to EMI in 1992).

- Radio: Virgin Radio.

- Video games: Virgin Games (1983).

- Distribution: Virgin Vision (1983), Virgin Megastores (1988) and Virgin Bride (1996) for brides-to-be.

- Cosmetics: Virgin Vie.

- Drinks: Virgin Cola, Virgin Vodka (1994).

- Computers: PCs manufactured by ICL Fujitsu (1996), Internet terminals manufactured by Internet Appliance Network (2000).

- Air transport: Virgin Atlantic Airways (1984), Virgin Cargo (1984), Virgin Express (1996).

- Rail transport: Virgin Railways (1997).

- Tourism: Virgin Holidays (1895), tour operator, Virgin Sun.

- Hotels and pensions: Virgin Hotels, Virgin

Pensions (for senior citizens).

▌ Financial services: Virgin Direct Financial Services (by telephone, 1995), Virgin Bank.

▌ Internet: Virgin Net (1996).

▌ Utilities: Virgin Power House (2000): water, gas and electricity.

In a sense, Virgin is like the Japanese *keiretsus*, horizontally structured conglomerates consisting of independent companies that share one name and one set of values. How can a brand spread itself in so many directions without specific competencies and with minimal investment? Of course, the more widely the brand spreads itself into apparently dissimilar extensions, the greater the need for an intangible link (see Figure 12.12) – and this link consists of the Virgin brand's values. Its extensions actually form a family of independent companies that share the values of the Virgin brand.

To finance his expansion, Branson usually seeks support from appropriate partners in order to minimise his own investment, even if this means not being the majority shareholder. The partner thus provides the sector know-how, the money, and its own energy as an entrepreneur. For example, Virgin Megastores in the UK are 75 per cent owned by the W H Smith group. Similarly, Virgin Vodka was manufactured and distributed by William Grant in a 50/50 partnership with Branson.

Virgin allows start-ups to begin with a world brand as their 'birth gift', significantly reducing their necessary advertising expenditure – particularly as Branson is well aware of the financial benefits of repeated public relations exercises such as his balloon trip around the world, or riding down Fifth Avenue in a Patton tank to celebrate the launch of Virgin Cola. Branson also resells his businesses, but only after having added what makes them valuable in the eyes of the public – his brand. For example, the French Megastores were sold to Lagardère, and Virgin Atlantic Airways went to Singapore Airlines. Of course, the Virgin brand remains the property of Virgin Enterprises, a company of which he is the sole owner.

Virgin's extensions are remarkable in that they are truly based on a strategic analysis of the sector. But in addition, like any healthy extension, they deliver far more than just a name to customers: they represent true innovation which remains consistent with the brand's values. As its name so prophetically suggests, Virgin aims to take a brand new,

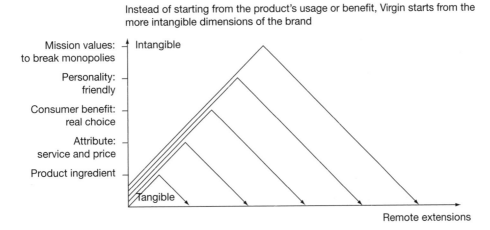

Figure 12.12   The Virgin extension model

'virgin' approach to markets and operate in a different way from the 'majors'. Virgin has a rebellious, extraverted personality. Its ambition is to 'unblock' markets and liberate consumers from meaningless choices between dominant market leaders. Its commercial proposition is innovation, quality and fun. The result is a product range totally different from those of its competitors, targeting a younger audience and better value for money, all under the aegis of an aspirational brand.

After all, in order to succeed, innovation is required at every stage, even if it means being copied: Virgin Atlantic Airways was the first company to offer a Volvo-chauffeured collection service for its business class clients from their offices, and a bathroom at the arrival airport. On board, Virgin innovated with the first personal video screens, followed by relaxing massages and the like. Another example is Virgin Cola, which innovated by offering an excellent taste, produced by the Canadian firm Cotts (bought out by Virgin in 1998), at a price nominally 10–15 per cent lower than that of Coke, with widespread distribution.

However, the system has its limits: extensions do not always work (a fact that applies to Virgin just as it does to any other firm, of course). The further you get from the British zone of influence, the weaker and less emotive the Virgin brand becomes. This makes the high visibility associated with the Megastores' music and entertainment brand a prime tool for generating recognition and empathy among young people from all countries.

Paradoxically, Virgin's failures do not seem to have damaged its business model. In situations where many brands would have packed up and gone home, Virgin simply continues to expand elsewhere. After all, should we criticise David if he loses to the Goliaths every now and then? At least he tried. But can this brand and business model last forever? Not if the extensions fail too frequently. An analysis of the failures readily shows when an extension has been inappropriate:

■ When it adds nothing other than just competition. This was what happened with Virgin Clothing, abandoned in 2000. London already buzzes with creators, rebels and anti-conformists. In a fragmented market with extremely wide price variations, what could Virgin add?

The same is true of Virgin Cola. In Europe, Pepsi already plays the role of the fly in Coca-Cola's ointment. Furthermore, the multiples' purchasing centres chose not to stock the brand, thus starving it of access to the public. A question mark also hangs over Virgin Express: despite the fact that Virgin Atlantic Airways and its battle against British Airways assumed emblematic status, the act of starting yet another low-cost airline to compete with Ryanair failed to connect with the brand's mission. There are no dominant leaders in this sector, and customers do not feel trapped.

■ When the scale of investment required pushes the fulfilment of the promise back into the long-term future. This is what has happened to Virgin Rail. In the UK, the brand's entry into commuter railways has not made any real difference to commuters' daily life: it has not been able to deliver a better experience. True, the dilapidated state of the rolling stock and infrastructure, handed over to the firm 'as is' under privatisation, ensured there could be no miracle: a network cannot be changed that quickly. Similarly, profitability issues concerning the MGM cinemas taken over by Virgin in 1995 prevented any real price reductions – one of the terms of the brand contract.

Without Richard Branson himself, could the Virgin group succeed? Given its founder's aura, and his ability to attract the attention of the media and to concentrate energy and investors around him, it must be concluded that Virgin is Branson himself. This is the brand's strength, but also its weakness. As with luxury brands, we should remember that a brand only truly begins with the loss of its founder.

How execution kills a good idea: easyCar

EasyJet's success is well known; the failure of its brand extensions is less so. We examine here how an ostensibly good extension idea (easyRent car hire) led to major financial losses.

EasyJet and RyanAir are the two best-known 'low-cost' companies in Europe. They have both picked up the clever idea of Herb Kelleher, the founder of the world's first low-cost airline: Southwest Airlines, in the United States. The strategic idea is to aim at the market of all those people who have never flown before, rather than fight over those who take planes on a regular basis. The first market is enormous, and has never been seriously explored, whereas the second is a sea of blood as a result of intense competition and high operational costs. It was therefore possible to speak metaphorically of a 'blue ocean'. They needed to find a way to liberate this potential demand. The only brake was the price of an air ticket, and the opportunity existed provided that it could fall below a psychological threshold, the cost of the taxi that takes you to the airport.

To achieve this price, they had to invent a new business model, a new economic equation, in order to offer a brand value proposition of a type never seen before, a type that would revolutionise demand. This was achieved first by suppressing all costs, other than safety, that inflated the price. Therefore they removed or reduced:

▮ All selling costs, by making it obligatory to buy exclusively over the internet.

▮ All on-board service costs: there is very little available to eat or drink, and everything must be paid for. Consequently, customers consume very little on board, and use of the toilets is reduced. This makes it possible to remove one toilet and replace it with seats, which in turn bring in money and increase passenger numbers.

▮ The cost of cleaning the plane during stopovers: the crew do the cleaning.

▮ Parking costs during stopovers: every minute that a plane is on the ground costs money. This time was therefore reduced to a minimum by maximising flying time and rotations per day. RyanAir was also able to exploit small, unknown, empty airports (such as Amiens, which is 142 km from Paris, as opposed to Roissy-Charles de Gaulle, which is only 30 km away). These smaller airports charge airlines much less, and there are grants available from local chambers of commerce for these low-cost airlines, which bring hundreds of tourists and create a regional economic boom.

▮ Plane maintenance costs, through a single-supplier policy. By buying only the same plane, and only from Boeing, all processes and costs can be simplified.

▮ Staff costs: these companies pay their staff much less than other airlines, and offer very few company benefits.

▮ Advertising costs: the founding directors were able to create regular media events through accusations against British Airways, for example, or fabulous offers (free flight for 10 people, etc). Anything became the pretext for staging an event.

▮ Costs linked to the lack of service: these companies try to avoid paying any compensation for (frequent) delays, or for lost luggage and the like, arguing that people cannot expect the lowest prices *and* compensation. After-flight service is defective, often non-existent.

Flushed with this success, Stelios Haji-Ioannou, the founder of easyJet, decided to extend the business model to many other activities, thereby imitating the approach of Richard Branson with his Virgin brand. He created the easy group, and launched products such as easyMoney, easyValue, easyInternet Café and easyCar.

It is true that the car rental market is an oligopoly, controlled worldwide by two giants, Hertz and Avis, whose margins and procedures showed that it should be easy to drastically reduce costs, and therefore prices. Furthermore, what could be more natural than to take advantage of travellers disembarking the easyJet plane by offering them a similar type of service to reduce the prices of car rental? Having paid just €30 for their plane ticket with easyJet, these travellers would choke at the notion of paying €100 for a day's car rental at Hertz or Avis. The idea was to offer managers travelling by plane an attractive car (Mercedes A-class) at €9 a day.

However, there are many differences between a plane and a car. On easyJet, the customer is required to have – non-negotiable – iron discipline from reservation to disembarkation. Moreover, the asset is not entrusted to the customer. The reverse is true for the car; customers refuse all constraints, and they are the ones entrusted with the asset (the car), the ones who manage it. Furthermore, customers arriving late (as they often do, since air travel is rarely punctual) find a queue at the easyCar counter, which is understaffed, thereby extending their wait: recriminations break out on all sides. On their return, they are in a hurry to return the car, and therefore mess up the formalities. This only multiplies the problems when the bill is received, since rental customers take less care of a hire car than they do of their own. EasyCar quickly crumpled under the complaints of customers, furious at finding themselves charged for repair costs.

In order to grow, easyCar opened agencies in town centres, which attracted a clientele particularly eager to get a bargain and try a Mercedes for €9. This led to an abnormally high number of damaged or dirty cars. It is difficult to immediately hire out a dirty or damaged car. The company could ask its flight crew to clean the cabin, but not its car rental clients. This therefore affected car rotation and created logistical complexities, leading to unforeseen costs that dragged the figures into the red, in addition to the ill will spread by aggravated customers. Finally, the Mercedes A-class was a brilliant choice of car, but an expensive one to maintain – and the buy-back price of the cars (in poor condition) was lower than anticipated.

13

Brand architecture

A brand has only one need: to grow, while maintaining its reputation and profits. Capitalising on the success of its founding product or service, it does so by means of successive extensions, which deepen the relationship with existing customers, or which make it possible to enter into new customer segments, or new distribution circuits. These extensions may be narrow to begin with (product line, range) or broader in scope (entry into new product categories, such as when the jeweller Bulgari also became a hotel brand).

When this extension of the perimeter of the brand's offer occurs, strategic questions arise: they concern the brand architecture. The answers to these will have a considerable effect on the value creation and the construction of brand capital. This is not a problem of aesthetics, but of efficiency.

The key questions of brand architecture

There are five types of question:

▌ What to call new products? Should they be given a descriptive name or a brand name?

When Lafarge invented a revolutionary, fluid and therefore extremely smooth concrete, should it have called it simply fluid cement, or Agilia? In the latter case, how should the link be made between this so-called daughter brand, Agilia, and the so-called parent brand, Lafarge? Should one say Lafarge Agilia or Agilia by Lafarge? Does the same rule apply for all daughter brands? How should it be expressed on the packaging of cement sacks, on the products themselves, on distributors' shelves, or on the stands at trade shows?

▌ How many brand levels to adopt? Should there be only one brand name within the company? This is the choice for most Asian groups. This means naming the products in a descriptive manner in order to have one single brand. Thus, we talk about Samsung televisions, Samsung mobile phones and Samsung digital cameras. In the same way, there are Braun coffee machines, Braun razors, Braun electric toothbrushes and Braun hairdryers. Conversely, for decades Philips razors have been known by the name Philishave, and we talk of the Apple iMac and now the iPod.

How much visibility to give to the corporate name, group name and the company name itself? Should everything be brought together under this one name, as Siemens and Axa have done, or should the name be given a role as a guarantee of daughter brands, as 3M and Danone have done? On all 3M products (such as Scotch and Post-It) we find a visible 3M signature. Conversely, you have to turn the Evian water bottle round to find the Danone Corp logo on the label at the back. As for Procter & Gamble's products and brands (Ariel, Tide, Dash, Always and so on), it takes a sharp eye to spot the name of the local subsidiary in the small print. Pharmaceutical laboratories answer these questions in different ways, depending on whether they operate in the prescribed products sector, or in over-the-counter (OTC) medication, or even manufacture generic medicines (Moss, 2007).

Within groups, should the brand be situated at the corporate level (Accor), or at the divisional or business unit level, as with the Accor Casino or Accor Hotels brands, alongside the well-known product brands (Formule 1, Motel 6, Red Roof, Etap, Mercure, Novotel, Sofitel, Suite Hotels and so on)?

More generally, should there be a different name for the company and the commercial brand? Thus, France Telecom is still the name of the institution, and Orange is now the only commercial brand, now that the Equant (which was dedicated to businesses) and wanadoo (previously the only international France Telecom brand dedicated to the internet) brands have been suppressed.

Should the same architecture apply around the world? For example, in the country of origin, in Europe, in the United States and in Asia?

These are necessary, even crucial questions, which need to be answered in order to make the continually renewed product offer easy to read, while at the same time building the brand's reputation through this offer.

The term 'branding strategy' is used for decisions on:

- the number of brand levels to be implemented (one, two or even three?);

- the role of the corporate in the product value communication: should it be absent, strongly present, or hardly present?

- the relative weight of these brands, and the graphic arrangement of their coexistence on all the documents, packaging, and products, but also industrial sites, offices, and business cards of salespersons and managers;

- the degree of globalisation of the architecture.

There are a few typical responses to these questions: these models are called *branding strategies*. They are discussed in detail below. First of all it is necessary to return to the key questions of brand architecture. Brand architecture is therefore a strategy: it may be ideal, or may lead to losses of efficiency, even to paralysis. In any case, what is expected is a coherent and well-founded response, even if it must change as competitive conditions evolve, rendering the previous choice of architecture null and void, or inefficient and too expensive. In fact, groups never cease to change their brand architecture, as the examples below illustrate.

In 1990, l'Oréal Paris, which had previously limited itself to endorsing its brand ranges worldwide (Elnett, Elsève, Studio Line, etc) by discreetly signing them, overturned this state of affairs, henceforth giving l'Oréal Paris a key role, under which all these so-called star brands had to fall into line, thereby displaying a community of values and communications style.

In the B2B sector, Henri Lachmann undertook the reverse change when he took over from Didier Pineau Valenciennes as managing director of the Schneider Electric Group. The latter was responsible for taking Schneider from a fragile status as ironmongers to that of a global high-tech company specialising in industrial electrical equipment, thanks to the acquisition of companies famous throughout the world (such as Merlin Gerin, Telemecanique, Yorkshire Switchgear, the Italian company Modicon and the American Square D). Pineau Valenciennes' goal was to achieve a unique corporate brand as quickly as possible, which would also play the part of a commercial brand: as its competitors Siemens, ABB, GE and Legrand and Hager do, Schneider Electric became the keystone of the whole offer. This involved the progressive disappearance of the specialised companies such as Telemécanique and Merlin Gerin, relegated to the rank of daughter brands, then to names of ranges. Taking over management of the company, Lachmann had a different vision. It was necessary to do the opposite, revitalising the daughter brands to worldwide recognition, since they were the capital of the emerging company Schneider Electric. This resulted in an architecture with two brand levels (that of the corporate name and that of the daughter brands).

In 2005, all products manufactured anywhere in the world by Unilever, a leading group in mass-market products, had to carry the U logo in a highly visible and identifiable way. Until then the company had been hidden, or at least not identified on product packaging, except for the legally required mention of the legal name of the local subsidiary (such as 'Lever Industan Ltd' in India). This emergence of the corporate brand is a fundamental tendency, but Unilever's competitor, Procter & Gamble, still hides its identity on its packaging. It is true that the company has had to cope with a particularly persistent and unpleasant rumour (Kapferer, 1987).

In 2006, Veolia, the world leader in environmental services (water and waste treatment, energy, delegated public transport) decided to remove its three trade brands, through which it had communicated since their creation: Connex for transport, Dalkia for energy and Onyx for waste treatment, substituting them with the unifying name Veolia: so the brands became Veolia Transport, Veolia Energy and so on.

Clearly brand architecture is not a technical or tactical problem, but a strategic one. The choice of one leads to a commitment that lasts several years, and it may become a source of cost cutting or of expensive inefficiencies. What is under discussion is not a formal problem of graphic organisation, but the concomitant construction of turnover, growth and a real brand capital, a source of competitive advantage. Brand growth implies increased complexity, and therefore the risk of loss of image coherence, and of dilution of the brand capital.

Type and role of brands

Let us look at a roll of adhesive tape. At the top and in large letters we find the name of the general public commercial brand name Scotch. Down and to the left we find 3M, or the company's corporate brand. Finally, under Scotch, comes the name of the product itself: Removable Magic™ Tape.

As we can see, there are three brand levels here, and a descriptor (or designator):

▌ the company's corporate brand 3M;

▌ the commercial brand Scotch, which acts as an umbrella brand for all the mass or general public products;

▌ the brand of the product line Magic™ Tape;

▌ the designator specifying what kind of Magic Tape it is: 'removable'.

3M is familiar with this three-level strategy. Many remember the advertising nickname of 'Gratton' ('scratcher' in French) on all the products of the Scotch-Brite line (scouring pads), under the commercial brand Scotch, from 3M. The *raton laveur* (raccoon) had appeared in Scotch-Brite advertisements, and suggested the nickname '*Gratton laveur*', which then appeared on its packaging.

The strategy of Nokia appears much simpler: here there is only one brand level. Everything is Nokia, followed by a serial number or code name that serves only to identify a reference, a code name that will be null and void in six months, given the speed at which the ranges in the field of telephony are rotated. Moreover, it is common to say, 'I'm going to buy "a Nokia"', without giving any other name. Then people specify which model they want to the salesperson by recalling the particular characteristics desired ('the one with this and that function and a very flat design' and so on).

As for Apple, the company has opted for two brand levels, Apple itself and iPod or iMac, named after the famous Macintosh. Apple's star products have all had their own name (sub-brand), except of course for the early ones that made the company's reputation. They were called Apples (1, then 2 then 3) and then a variant name. At l'Oréal also, the policy is not to mention the group name but to build the brands on star products (also called franchises) with their own names. For example, Garnier (the other global general public brand of the l'Oréal group) has built its reputation on the Fructis range, or the Recital line. Renault has built its reputation on brands that all have a name (Twingo, Clio, Megane, Espace, Vel Satis).

What explains the choice of architectures with one, two or even three brand levels? It is principally the market, its level of segmentation and the option of whether or not to lean on the corporate brand for support.

Products with very rapid rotation make it impossible to use anything other than a single brand name (Nokia, Samsung, Sony Ericsson, Sage and so on). It takes time to install a particular product brand.

In big industry, work is done by project: the name summarises the company's competence, stature and power, the professionalism of its men and women, the underlying culture. This is why big industrial companies like to capitalise all their shares on a single name. Nevertheless, taking public works for example, as invitations to tender are done through trade bodies, the groups have a two-level brand policy. Vinci suggests the power of a leading group, Via is the reputed global brand in road construction.

In the mass market, where products are largely similar, it is necessary to help create perceptible differentiations. Brand names contribute to this. Pepito by Lu was aimed at children from 6 to 10 years, then Prince by Lu took them on to the age of 15. The first name also makes it possible to confer an intangible personality on the product, an added value in comparison to the distributor's copy.

Which role for which brands?

In the above example of the removable Scotch Magic™ Tape from the 3M company, it is easy to understand how each level plays a specific role. The manner in which the consumer talks about the product indicates which of these levels plays the leading role, that of seller (the motivator), the one in which the perceived value resides. The consumer rarely says 'I want a 3M.' On the other hand, the manager of a clinic or hospital, hospital attendants and doctors will find it easier to emphasise 3M. In their eyes, all the professionalism of a company that, through its innovations, has been able to create products so useful to surgeons at the most critical moments of surgery resides at this level.

When you buy a KitKat Chunky from Nestlé, you are buying first and foremost 'a KitKat' in its larger version (here called

Chunky to increase the perception of volume and size), under the obvious auspices of the 'better living brand' Nestlé. If you turn over the product, you will see the corporate brand Nestlé itself (with its characteristic nest), which acts as a supreme guarantee, morally responsible for all the products made by its factories around the world, a kind of manufacturer's brand. Let us note that this manufacturing brand Nestlé is also present on the back of the regional European commercial processed meats brand Herta.

Through these examples may be distinguished the roles of:

▮ Motivator, the anchor point for value. My American colleague David Aaker speaks of the 'driver'. From a certain point of view, this is the true brand: the one that most symbolises the differentiation and creates the desire.

▮ Source of value for products. The commercial brand Nestlé applied as the aegis above all products indicates that these carry its values of taste, health and family.

▮ The producer's moral endorsement and responsibility, where the company supplies a telephone number that customers can call to report any deviation that they consider unacceptable, anywhere in the world. This is a manifestation of the demands of corporate social responsibility (CSR). Yesterday we said, 'Big is beautiful'; today we say, 'Big is responsible.'

▮ The designator of the specificity of the reference in question – when we say KitKat Chunky, to specify which one we wish to buy.

▮ An identifier of the origin: this is the role of the manufacturer's brand.

The accumulation of levels damages clarity, and appropriation by the client. It should therefore be combated, and only the indispensable levels should be kept. The debate on the presence or absence of the corporate brand on mass-market products cannot be decided only by questioning consumers. Of course, if they were asked whether they see any reason to keep the name 3M on the packaging, the majority would say no: they don't know 3M. Since the logo evokes nothing for them, they regard it as useless. However, the strategy cannot be based on this point of view alone. The legitimate ambition of enhancing the group's value on the stock exchange implies an awareness that cannot be built up through colossal advertising budgets, the money for which must necessarily be taken from the brands' operating budgets. It is therefore better to profit from the millions of stealth contacts offered by the products and the communication they make.

For this same reason, the Accor symbol appeared in the lobbies of all the group's hotels, regardless of brand. This made it clear that all of these hotels, previously presented as independent or even competitors, were in fact members of the same family. There was a loss in differentiation and probably in emotion, but Accor rapidly gained from it recognition as the leader in hotels and services in Europe.

A major alternative: branded house or house of brands?

The brand architecture is the coherent response given to the three questions examined above:

▮ How many brand levels should be used? One single level, or two? In other words, should brands be created to designate the activities or the professions or the products themselves?

▮ What linkage exists between these brand levels? This goes back to the question of the respective roles of the brands: where is the value located, who endorses whom, and so on?

What visibility should the corporate brand have? And what role?

The answers to these questions are not independent. In reality they form six types of overall response, with precise impacts that go far beyond the descriptive (what name or symbol is in large font, or in small, at the top or the bottom) and concern the offer itself. They affect its content, its values: that is, the degree of variety that a brand can offer under its name. These overall responses or branding architecture types number six in total. From this point on we shall distinguish the following architectures:

- the product-brand strategy and its variants, the line and range brands;

- the flexible umbrella strategy;

- the masterbrand strategy;

- the maker's mark strategy;

- the endorsing brand strategy;

- the source brand strategy.

These strategies are responses to the market. They may be structured along two axes (see Figure 13.1), according to whether the value sought by the brand relates more to power and stature on the one hand, or personalisation, differentiation and identity on the other.

At one extreme, the strategy known as the *corporate masterbrand* is characterised by a single and unique brand level, often the corporate name, and that of the company itself. The whole of the company that adopts it must then fall into line with the brand's values, and be the carrier of these values. Either something is IBM, or it is not. Brands in the industrial and public worlds and the services sectors (banks, insurance, consultancies and so on) typically follow this strategy. Here, reputation is linked to reassuring size and power.

At the other extreme we find the *product-brand strategy*. In this strategy, the company is

Figure 13.1 Positioning alternative branding strategies

not identified at all. This is the case with brands of LVMH and Procter & Gamble, which does not strongly identify itself on each of its brands (Ariel, Tide, Pampers, Always, Dash, Swiffer and the rest). This makes it possible to function in the same market, for example washing powders, with a portfolio of apparently competing brands. The car manufacturer PSA also functions via a product-brand strategy: you can buy either a Peugeot or a Citroën, but not a PSA.

Architectures with two or more brand levels represent a compromise between the power requirements that push for a single dominant name (masterbrand) and the personalisation requirements that push for segmented daughter brands, each having a clearly differentiated identity. In fact, generalised automobile brands attempt to capitalise on their name (Volkswagen, Toyota) but boost the attractiveness of the models themselves by means of a name that acts as a brand (Golf, Passat, Yaris, Prius).

It is also possible to classify these architectures according to the degree of constraint that they impose downstream, at the business, product and market levels. In this respect, the Americans distinguish between two basic alternatives: 'house of brands' or 'branded house' (that is, a basket of different brands or activities brought together under a single aegis) (see Table 13.1). These alternatives lead back in fact to the degree of constraint and coherence imposed on the products and markets. We will see that behind these basic alternatives can be found architectures that in practice are very different.

Table 13.1   'House of brands' or 'branded house'

House of brands	Branded house
Product-brand	Source brand
Line brand	
Range brand	
Maker's mark	
Endorsing brand	
Flexible umbrella brand	Masterbrand

The first option (house of brands) relates to a situation of extreme freedom of management for the brands, subsidiaries, activities and divisions. This is typical of Japanese groups. For example, there is no coordination between the Mitsubishi Motors division and the Mitsubishi Electric division. It may be the same name, and the same company in legal terms, but each division, like a silo, acts as it sees fit. It carries out its own advertising, with its own arguments, its brand values and so on. The important things are commercial success, and the growth in recognition of the Mitsubishi name.

As we can see, 'house of brands' does not relate solely to the product-brand architecture, as my American colleagues David Aaker (1995) and Kevin Lane Keller (2007) write, but also applies to umbrella-type strategies (a single brand for the whole company) where in fact the decisions made downstream, in contact with the market, are very free, and seek only to reach the objectives linked to that specific market, without coherence as a whole at the image level. Michelin has acted in this way for decades. Michelin's Truck Division did not coordinate with Michelin Private Vehicles or with Michelin Aviation. There was no desire to create variations on a common, specific and normative brand platform in each of these markets.

The 'branded house' expresses the desire to give coherence to the whole under the auspices of a brand with central values that find embodiment at the market and product level. This path brings together the masterbrand and also dominant (source) brand strategies, giving a strongly normative structure to the daughter brands on the second level. This strategy is pursued by Nivea for example, l'Oréal Paris and Kinder. This second level must express the values of the parent brand. In this way the necessary coherence can be instilled, as dealt with in Chapter 11. The 'branded house' is a family with a high degree of internal unity.

Figure 13.2 The six main brand architectures

This is why we can structure the strategies according to a matrix that classifies them. They are classified by the number of brand levels (one or two) and according to the degree of freedom allowed downstream, at market level, for decisions on product and service positioning. These will be examined here in turn.

Branding strategy and brand valuation

Branding strategy should not be seen as a formal design problem but rather a matter of deciding on the value flows to be created between the different parts and products of a company. The central issue is therefore the valuation of the offering, through the agency of the company itself.

The business angels and investment funds have got it right. For example, in the cosmetics sector, there is more to be gained from the resale of a 'branded house' than a basket of mixed brands, however well known, grouped together within a 'house of brands'. For example, Garnier has become a 'branded house', a house with a house spirit and house values that in return influence the positioning of the brands under Garnier. In fact, Garnier is itself a brand with a specific identity. SCAD, on the other hand, is a 'house of brands' that groups together brands as diverse as Dop, Vivelle, Dessange and J L David. SCAD is merely a commercial and marketing organisational structure.

In the cosmetics sector, a 'house of brands' is valued at six times the profits, while a 'branded house' enjoys an overvaluation that brings the P/E (Price-Earnings) ratio to 7 or 8. Similarly, as soon as a company is quoted on a stock exchange, all internal separatist tendencies – such as sub-brand logos protected jealously from the corporate brand – must cease. What had previously been of little consequence becomes unacceptable. All value flows must converge on the stock brand, since the market valuation of the company presupposes that the company capitalises on all sources of value created by its subsidiaries and sub-brands. Everyone and everything in the company contributes to this, including branding strategy.

Industrial companies are only just beginning to appreciate the importance of brands in terms of their profitability.

Brand architecture and corporate internal organisation

The brand architecture also has a strong influence on the functioning of the company. There is no masterbrand or source brand without a brand master, a guardian of the temple, someone who will ensure the necessary coherence, not only at the level of the logo or of the formal identity, across all countries and divisions. That would be to view this person as more than a guardian of policies – on character, on typographics, or on respect for graphic charts – (what is often referred to as a logo cop).

In reality, the more a company moves towards the 'branded house' type of architecture, the more it becomes necessary to install coordination and power structures. Hence at Schneider Electric, and also at the core of the Seb group, there exists a brand committee, made up not of communicators but of the managers of the business units and the divisions themselves. The profile of the participants in this brand committee is moreover symptomatic of how seriously or otherwise the company takes the notion of branding.

Japanese companies have recently become aware that their typical silo organisation, although it certainly had advantages, was damaging to the emotional quality of the brand and its coherence. Each division pushes a functional characteristic of its product, and nobody takes responsibility for the brand values themselves. This is why, in 1999, Toshiba decided to name a 'Mr Brand' in the person of the previous worldwide director of research and development for the Toshiba group. It should also be noted that Korean groups such as Samsung, and in particular LG, did not take so long: they were quick to name brand guardians, with transverse and global authority.

If we examine the architectures in detail, the apparently banal fact of moving from two brand levels to one is in reality a message on the company's methods of organisation and the distribution of power. In its beginnings, Veolia followed a house of brands strategy. Veolia was born from the splitting up of Vivendi Universal's public utilities division, but the value was located at the level of its business activities. In this way Connex brought together all the private trains, buses and subways throughout the world, Onyx was the global brand for waste management and Dalkia the brand for the energy branch. This marked a group where power coordinates, but the markets dominate. Veolia was more a group name than a brand carried by unique and differentiating values. This is somewhat like Suez nowadays. Moving to Veolia Transport, Veolia Water and Veolia Waste Management was a revolution in the methods of governance. This therefore gives us a single, central Veolia, which varies according to the market it is operating in.

Removing the division brands sends a strong message of integration, externally to clients and prospective clients, but also internally. The client may legitimately expect to see the organisational and IT silos disappear, and genuinely networked managers appear. When this is not the case, there is a gulf between the brand and the organisation.

The main types of brand architecture

Let us now examine the individual characters of the principal brand architectures. We shall begin with those architectures that allow great freedom in terms of products and communication: the link between the company values and those of the divisions, activities and product is lax. They are brought together under the term 'house of brands'. Then we examine strategies that are more restrictive downstream, since the latter should reflect central values, of which the brand is the concrete expression.

The product–brand strategy

It is widely known that a brand is at the same time a symbol, a word, an object and a concept: a symbol, since it has numerous facets and it incorporates figurative symbols such as logos, emblems, colours, forms, packaging and design; a word, because it is the brand name which serves as support for oral or written information on the product; an object, because the brand distinguishes each of the products from the other products or services; and finally, a concept in the sense that the brand, like any other symbol, imparts its own significance – in other words, its meaning.

The product–brand strategy involves the assignment of a particular name to one, and only one, product (or product line) as well as one exclusive positioning. The result of such a strategy is that each new product receives its own brand name that belongs only to it. Companies then have a brand portfolio that corresponds to their product portfolio as illustrated in Figure 13.3.

This brand strategy can be found in the hotel industry where the Accor Group has developed multiple brands for precise and exclusive positions: eg Sofitel, Novotel, Suit' Hotel, Ibis, Formule 1 and Motel 6. The company Procter & Gamble has made this strategy the symbol of its brand management philosophy. The company is represented in the European detergent market by the brands Ariel, Vizir, Dash and in the soaps market by Camay, Zest, etc. Each of these products has a precise, well-defined positioning and occupies a particular segment of the market: Camay is a seductive soap, Zest a soap for energy. Ariel positions itself as the best detergent in the market and Dash as the best value for money

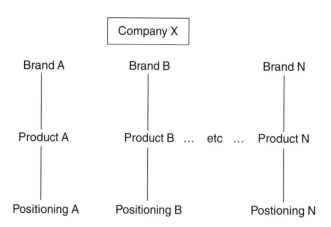

Figure 13.3   The product–brand strategy

in the intermediate price range. Both have developed a product line including powder, liquid and tablets.

Innovative companies in the food sector create new speciality products which are then distinguished through individual names and therefore these companies have a large brand product portfolio. The cheese company Bongrain markets more than 10 brands, such as St Moret, Caprice des Dieux and Chaumes. The mineral water market is composed of only product brands: one asks for Vittel, Evian or Contrex, knowing very well that there will be no ambiguity and one will get the product asked for. Here, the brand, the name of a product, becomes a strict indication of identity.

In an extreme case, the product is so specific that there is no equivalent, and the product is not only a product, but an entire product category of which it is the sole representative. This phenomenon has been described by some through the neologism 'branduct' (Swiners, 1979), an abbreviation of brand product. These products are so unique, so specific that they have no other name than their brand name. We see this in 'Post-it', Bailey's Irish Cream, Malibu liqueur, Mars, Bounty, Nuts, etc.

How is the strict relationship between one name, one product and one positioning maintained over a period of time? First, the only way to achieve brand extension is by renewing the product. To keep the product at its height and original positioning, the Ariel formula has often been improved since it was launched in 1969. Ariel receives the best technological and chemical inputs from Procter & Gamble (like its competitor, Skip, from Lever) (Kapferer and Thoenig, 1989). Often, to emphasise an important improvement to the product, the company adds a number after the brand name (Dash 1, Dash 2, Dash 3). To keep up with changing consumer habits, the brand name is applied to various formats (for example, in packaging: packets, drums, in powder or liquid form).

What, then, are the advantages of the product brand strategy for companies? For firms focusing on one market, it is an offensive strategy designed to occupy the whole market. By indulging in the practice of multiple brand entries in the same market (Procter & Gamble has four detergent brands), the company occupies many segments with different needs and expectations and therefore has a greater consolidated share of the market: it becomes category leader. However, this remains inconspicuous, for the corporate name is kept discreet if not hidden.

Some companies do wish to remain at the back and focus the lights exclusively on their brands. The cases of Procter & Gamble, Unilever, Masterfoods and Bestfoods are well known, that of ITW is less so. ITW stands for Illinois Toolwork. It is a billion-US-dollar corporation, very acquisitive: it owns more than 500 companies throughout the world. Its brands aim at the construction professional: they are called Paslode, Duo-Fast for wood products, Spit and Buidex for steel and concrete. The goal is to provide very specialised tools to specialised workers: a policy of niche brands, addressing segmented needs, craftspeople and channels is a direct consequence of this goal. People working with wood want to be reinforced and differentiated from people working with other materials. ITW does not wish to hurt this desire, and AS resisted all temptations to grow the ITW brand itself, for instance as an endorser. ITW's success rests precisely on the exact contrary.

When the segments are closely related, choosing one name per product helps customers to perceive better the differences between the various brands. This may also be necessary when the products resemble each other externally. Thus, one sees that although all detergents are composed of the same basic ingredients, the proportion of these may vary according to the factor that is being optimised: stain removal properties, care for synthetic materials, colourfast control or suitability for hand washing. The association of a specific name for a type of need underlines the physical difference between the products.

The product brand strategy is one that is adapted to the needs of innovative companies who want to pre-empt a positioning. In fact, the first brand to appear in a new segment, if it proves to be effective, has the advantage of the first player in the market. It becomes the nominal reference for the thus innovative product and maybe even the absolute reference. The brand name patents the innovation. This is particularly important in markets where the success is likely to induce copying. In the pharmaceutical world where copies are a certainty, every new product is registered under two names: one for the product, the formula, and another for the brand. Even if they have the same formula, future copies appear different because the originality of the brand name (Zantac, Tagamet) provides an aura of exclusivity and of legal protection. On the other hand, where the law cannot provide protection, forgeries and copies attempt to exploit the potential of the brand name by imitating it as closely as possible. That is why large mass retailers often use product brands or, to be more precise, counter–product brands. Thus, Fortini copies Martini, Whip copies Skip, etc. Scared of having their other brands cast out of favour manufacturers have, until now, hesitated to legally challenge the distributors for forgery or illegal imitation. (See also page 79.)

Product brand policies allow firms to take risks in new markets. At a time when the future of the liquid detergent was still uncertain, Procter & Gamble preferred to launch a product brand: Vizir. Launching it under the name Ariel liquid would have threatened Ariel's brand image asset and launching it under the name Dash would have incurred the risk of associating a potentially powerful concept with a weak brand and thereby overshadowing it. Coca-Cola did just the same when it first launched Tab to test the diet market.

Product brand policy implies that the name of the company behind it remains unknown to the public and is therefore different from the brand names. This practice allows the firm considerable freedom to move whenever and wherever it wishes, especially into new markets. Procter & Gamble moved from the creation of the soap, Ivory, in 1882, to the culinary aid, Crisco, in 1911, Chipso in 1926 and the machine detergent, Dreft, in 1933, Tide in 1946, Joy, the dishwashing agent in 1950 and then Dash in 1955, the toothpaste, Crest, in 1955, the peanut-butter, Jif, in 1956, Pampers in 1961, the coffee, Folgers, in 1963, the antiseptic mouthwash, Scope, as well as household paper rolls, Bounce, in 1965, Pringle chips in 1968, sanitary napkins, Rely, in 1974, Always (Whisper) and Sunny Delight later on.

Since each brand is independent of the others, the failure of one of them has no risk of negative spillover on the others, or on the company name (in cases where the company name remains relatively unknown to the public and different from that of any of the brands).

Finally, the distribution parameter also favours this strategy heavily: the shelf space accorded by a retailer to a company depends on the number of (strong) brands that it has. When a brand covers many products, the retailer stocks certain products and not others. In the case of product brands, there is only one product per brand, or one product line per brand.

The drawbacks arising from product brands are essentially economic. Thus multi-brand strategy is not for the faint-hearted.

In fact, a new product launch is often a new brand launch. Considering today's media costs, this involves considerable investments in advertising and promotions. Furthermore, retailers, unwilling to take risks with new products whose future is uncertain, stock them only when reassured by heavy listing fees.

Multiplication of product brands in a market due to the increasingly narrow segmentation weighs heavily on the chances of a rapid return on investment. The volumes required to justify such investment (in R&D, equipment, and sales and marketing expenses) make the product brand strategy an ideal one for growing markets where a small market share could nevertheless mean high volumes. When the market is saturated, this possibility disappears. On the other hand, in a stable market it is sometimes more advantageous to nurture an existing brand with the innovation in question rather than attempt to give it product brand status by launching it under its own name.

The role of fire curtains between product brands is certainly important in times of crises, but in other times it prevents the brand from benefiting from the positive spillover effect created by other products under the same name. The success of brand A will not help other products because their names, B, C, D, etc are different and do not bear any relation to A. As we can see, in this strategy, the firm gives the brand a completely distinct and exclusive function and almost no hints about its origin. New products do not benefit from the renown of one of the already existing brands nor from the economies that one could derive from it. On the other hand, this advantage has no role among distributors who are well aware of the company name behind the brand and its reputation for success or failure.

The case of 'branducts' is even more marked. Since they represent an entire category of products on their own, they have to invest twice as much in advertising. While a brand of whisky only has to associate itself with the whisky category for the customer to recall the brand when he wants to buy a whisky, other products such as Sheridan, Malibu or Bailey's cannot fall back on the cushion of a product category. They therefore need a permanent spontaneous awareness: either one thinks of Bailey's or one does not (in which case the probability of a sale is zero). Furthermore, isolated due to the lack of a category shelf, branducts suffer from a lack of prominence and visibility on the shelves. This makes their fame their only strong point. In times of recession, they are the first to undergo budget reductions.

The line brand strategy

Deglaude Laboratories launched a product brand, Foltene: a single product associated with a single benefit, the regrowth of hair. A strong TV advertising campaign made the market explode and Foltene became the leader with a single product and a 55 per cent market share. They should have remained thus, but consumer logic prevailed. Bald people were not looking for a single product. They wanted an all-encompassing service, a total care routine. They wrote asking that shampooing be combined with the Foltene treatment. In 1982 Deglaude launched a mild shampoo (which was later subdivided according to hair type) followed by a daily-use lotion. All this was by way of response to customer demands.

Christian Dior launched Capture, an anti-ageing liposome complex for the skin. Following its success, a first spin-off was soon launched: 'Capture, eye shaper', followed by lip shapers and then other products for the body. The Capture line was born.

Thus, to take up Botton and Cegarra's definition (1990), the line responds to the concern of offering one coherent response under a single name by proposing many complementary products. This goes from variations of the offer, as in the case of Capture or with the fragrances of an aftershave, to the inclusion of various products within one specific effect, as in the case of Foltene. This is also the case with Studio Line hair products from l'Oréal, which offers structuring gel, lacquer, a spray, etc. Calgon (a Benckiser brand) markets a dishwasher powder together with a rinsing agent and limescale inhibitor. That these products are completely different for the producer makes no difference to the consumer, who perceives them as related.

It should be clear that the line involves the exploitation of a successful concept by extending it but by staying very close to the initial product (eg Capture liposomes or the Foltene principle). In other cases, the line is launched as a complete ensemble, with many complementary products linked by a single central concept (for Studio it was allowing youngsters to do their own hair and give themselves a 'look'). The eventual extension of the line will involve only the marginal costs linked to retailers' discounts and to the packaging. It does not need advertising. It should be compared to the marginal number of consumers that could be won. As one can see, the line brand strategy offers multiple advantages:

▍ it reinforces the selling power of the brand and creates a strong brand image;

▍ it facilitates distribution for each line extension;

▍ it reduces launch costs.

The disadvantages of the line strategy lie in the tendency to forget that a line has limits. One should only include product innovations that are very closely linked to the existing ones. On the other hand, the inclusion of a powerful innovation could slow its development. Thus, even though Capture was the result of seven years' research in collaboration with the Pasteur Institute, received three patents and brought with it a revolutionary anti-ageing principle, Dior decided to attach it to a currently existing anti-ageing line. This did not prevent the success of Capture, but unnecessarily delayed it initially.

The range brand strategy

Campbell's Soup, Knorr, Bird's Eye and Igloo all propose more than 100 frozen food products. But not all range brands are this extensive. The Tylenol range now covers a number of different products. Range brands bestow a single brand name and promote through a single promise a range of products belonging to the same area of competence. In range brand architecture, products guard their common name (fish à la provençale, mushroom pizza, pancakes with ham and cheese in the case of Bird's Eye). In the Clarins cosmetic range, products are named 'purifying plant mask', extracts of 'fresh cells', multi-tensor toning solution, day or night soothing cream, etc.

Range brand structure is found in the food sector (Green Giant, Campbell, Heinz, Whiskas and so on), equipment (Moulinex, Seb, Rowenta, Samsonite) or in industry (Steelcase, Facom). These brands combine all their products through a unique principle, a brand concept, as is shown in Figure 13.4. The

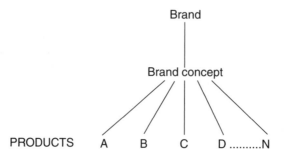

Figure 13.4 Range brand formation

advantages and disadvantages of the structure are as follows:

▌ It avoids the random spread of external communications by focusing on a single name – the brand name – and thereby creating brand capital for itself which can even be shared by other products. Furthermore, in such a structure the brand communicates in a generic manner by developing its unique brand concept. Thus, the range brand of pet food, Fido, covers many products but in its advertisement it only has a taster dog who marks his approval on a product with a paw print. This commercial transfers the brand focalisation and its pre-eminence to the animal. Another approach consists of communicating the brand concept by concentrating only on certain of the most representative products through which the brand can best express its meaning and convey consumer benefit. This can then be shared by other products of the range which are not directly mentioned.

▌ The brand can easily distribute new products that are consistent with its mission and fall within the same category. Furthermore, the cost of such new launches is very low.

Among the problems that are most frequently encountered is one of brand opacity as it expands. The brand name Findus covers scores of savoury frozen products. It is a good brand – high quality, modern, a specialist in frozen products and a generalist as well because it makes all kinds of dishes. For years, product names were the names of the recipes. But these names are banal. Any brand can claim that it has the same recipe. To enrich the brand and to express its personality on one hand, and on the other hand to help the consumer choose from the mass of products that are on offer, an intermediate level of categorisation must be created between the brand

name and each actual product name. This is the role of specific lines such as:

▌ 'Lean cuisine' that regrouped 18 dishes all recognisable by their white packaging;

▌ 'Traditional' covering nine dishes with maroon outers;

▌ 'Seafoods' comprising nine kinds of dishes and assorted products (previously simply called hake cutlets, whiting fillets, etc) in blue packaging.

Such names for a line throw light on the products and also help to structure the range in the same way as retailers organise their shelves. The criteria for segmentation and for the creation of families of products depend on the brand. Thus, should we make the distinctions according to the content (poultry, beef, pork etc, as in a butcher's shop) or according to consumer benefits (light, traditional, exotic, family orientated ...)?

The line structures the offer, by putting together products which are undoubtedly heterogeneous, but all of which have the same function. Thus, in the Clarins cosmetic range brand, the offer is also made more clear and structured by way of lines. To assist the consumer in deciphering the scientific terms used on the products, the brand proposes lines as one would a prescription. For example:

▌ the 'soothing line' for sensitive skins includes a mild day cream and a mild night cream as well as a restructuring fluid in capsules;

▌ the 'slimming and firmness' line regroups an exfoliating scrub, a slimming bath, a 'bio-superactivated' reducing cream and an 'anti-water' oil.

The Clarins offer ceases to be a long list of creams, serums, lotions, balms and gels and now forms structured and coherent groups as seen in Figure 13.5.

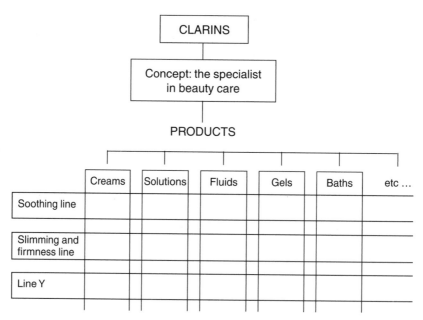

Figure 13.5   Range brand structured in lines

The maker's mark strategy

For many years the Bel logo has been systematically marked on the packaging of cheeses produced by this company: Laughing Cow, Kiri, Port Salut, Mini Babybel, Sylphide and other brands. But what does Bel mean? Nothing else was done to explain the brand. It was the maker's mark, the maker's seal, a proto-brand in the sense that it did not seek to build itself a territory of meaning, of emotion. The Bel company added its seal to authenticate the product and guarantee its provenance. The function of this maker's seal was to create a recognition sign identifying the industrial group that made it. Consumers are not worried about this, but this sign is aimed essentially at distributors and department heads. It is also important internally, for all the international cheese-making companies acquired, who see in the application of this seal to their products, the sign of their full integration into the Bel family.

In formal terms, in relation to the previous architecture where the corporate brand is completely absent, this strategy is characterised by a discreet corporate logo, giving preeminence to the commercial brand. In a certain way, the presence of 3M on all its mass-market products must be a mystery in the eyes of its consumers, if they notice it at all. From this point of view, the architecture is close to that of the 'maker's mark'. In the United States, where 3M is better known, the application of the 3M logo plays more of an endorsing role.

Endorsing brand strategy

Everyone recognises famous car brands such as Pontiac, Buick and Chevrolet in the United States or Opel in Europe. Next to their logos and to the signs of the dealers of these brands we always see the two letters: GM. It is obviously General Motors, the endorsing brand. Again, what is the link between the cleaner Pledge, Wizard Air Freshener and Toilet Duck? They are all Johnson products. The endorsing brand gives its approval to a wide diversity of products grouped under product brands, line brands or range brands. Johnson is the guarantor of their high quality and security. This having been said, each product is then free to manifest its originality: that is what gives rise to the different names seen in the range.

Figure 13.6 symbolises endorsing brand strategy. As one can see, the endorsing brand is placed lower down because it acts as a base guarantor. Furthermore what the consumers buy is Pontiac or Opel: they drive choice. General Motors and Johnson are supports and assume a secondary position.

The brand endorsement can be indicated in a graphic manner by placing the emblem of the endorser next to the brand name or (when signed above, it acts as maker's mark) by simply signing the endorser's name.

The advantage of the endorsing brand is the greater freedom of movement that it allows. Unlike the source brand, the endorsing brand profits less from its products. Each particular product name evokes a forceful image and has a power of recall for the consumer. There is little image transfer to the endorser.

The endorsing brand strategy is one of the least expensive ways of giving substance to a company name and allowing it to achieve a minimal brand status. Thus, we can see the initials ICI (Imperial Chemical Industries) on Valentine or Dulux paint pots, the name Bayer on packets of garden products and Monsanto on Round Up. The high quality of these brands is guaranteed by the names of these major organisations. On the other hand, through their presence in everyday life these companies become more familiar and close to the people, as in the case of ICI in Europe. Since the scientific and technical guarantees are assured by the endorsing brand, product brands can devote more time to expressing other facets of their personality.

Therefore, as one can see, there is a division of roles at each stage of the branding hierarchy. The endorsing brand becomes responsible for the guarantee that is essential for all brands and, today, these guarantees not only cover areas such as quality and scientific expertise, but also civic responsibility, ethics and environmental concerns. The other brand functions are assumed by the specifically named brands: distinction, personalisation and even pleasure (Kapferer and Laurent, 1992).

Figure 13.6   Endorsing brand strategy

Umbrella brand strategies

Under the term 'umbrella brand', we find in fact two modes of implementation in companies, the first relatively liberal towards products and subsidiaries, the other exercising real control. We shall examine both in turn: the first is in reality a house of brands, the other a branded house.

The flexible umbrella brand

The umbrella brand strategy is characterised by a single brand level: the products are not given a daughter brand. They may possibly be given code names, but only with the aim of identifying them in catalogues or price lists. Philips televisions are known as 'televisions' (whereas Sony's is known as a 'Trinitron'), Philips razors are known as 'razors', and so on.

Unlike the product brand, where a brand relates to a single product and vice versa, the case of Philips underlines that here the umbrella brand covers several product categories, both figuratively and in reality. This is the principal advantage of this strategy, moreover: offering a common umbrella, a common name, to a highly diversified range.

It is important in these analyses to distinguish between two types of umbrella brand, according to the degree of freedom accorded to the products, divisions or branches. This flexible umbrella strategy is currently typical of Japanese, Korean and Chinese brands. Mitsubishi sells cars, electrical products, lifts and nuclear plants under its name, but also food products under the Three Diamonds brand (the Mitsubishi symbol is made up of three diamonds). Toshiba is only known in Europe for its laptop computers, but you only have to visit the Tokyo department stores to see Toshiba sewing machines and frying pans. There, Toshiba is rather like Philips in Europe.

In fact, the umbrella brand has been typical of Japanese organisations, where sales subsidiaries of these Japanese companies had a high degree of freedom. What was required of them was to establish themselves in the country, not to make waves, and to conquer the markets. Historically, the penetration of the United States and Europe by Japanese equipment products (radio, hi-fi, television, photography, reprographics, telephones, IT, games and so on) was carried out via the exportation of products made in Japan. The distribution subsidiaries were tasked only with selling them; they were managed by local people, since the Japanese did not like working abroad. Moreover, the emphasis placed locally on sales was convenient for subsidiaries essentially made up of in-country managers. Besides the sales objectives, and respect for corporate ethics, there were few constraints on the managers. There was a point on the brand map, if not the graphic map, but no value platforms. The Japanese

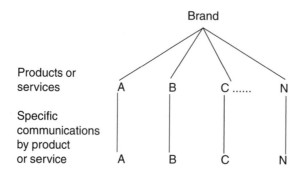

Figure 13.7   Umbrella brand strategy

global success was achieved on the basis of the advantages and the low prices of the products themselves, carried by quality commercial organisations, under the umbrella of a brand whose dispersion also contributed to building its recognition. The umbrella brand was a name, not a vision finding embodiment in services and products. This name was generally the corporate name, that of the industrial group.

This is why the subsidiaries had a high degree of freedom: their marketing communications were carried out by country. Within the same country, over several years, the advertising campaigns of Toshiba hi-fi, Toshiba lo-fi, Toshiba televisions, not to mention microcomputing, were not at all coordinated. Each had its own brand slogan and emphasised different values, and even worked with a different advertising agency.

It is known that brand strategies have organisational implications. The supple, flexible umbrella architecture gives the subsidiaries a great deal of autonomy, which can motivate them and make it easier to recruit bosses with entrepreneurial profiles, which is very useful during the phase of conquering market shares. The international unity is through products, imported from Japan.

Another advantage: since the name is more a corporate name than a brand, there is no hesitation in placing it on products that are highly disparate from a Western point of view: sewing machines, saucepans and microcomputers. This is rather like the now-dead Thomson brand. In Asia, however, the more powerful a group, the more it is respected. From this point of view, manufacturing everything helps to increase power.

On the communications level, the emphasis is placed on the specific qualities and advantages of the products. Therefore there is little intangible added value, which would be very useful once the conquest phase is over. When the markets mature and the products become equivalent, it is then

necessary to turn to other levers of attraction and attachment. On the other hand, it does build the country brand.

The disadvantages of this approach make themselves felt later in the brand's life. It is devoid of emotional content: it is not a source of aspiration, of tacit agreement, of affective attachment. Admittedly, it is perceived as a source of quality products, but it is also seen as cold and distant. As the global director of the Toshiba brand (a post newly created precisely to remedy this state of affairs) told us one evening, the brand could be compared to a highly technically skilled work colleague, whom you might ask for help, but whom you would not invite home for dinner.

In the West, the notion of a brand was forged on the notion of speciality. Procter & Gamble founded a school of thought that was taught for years in business schools the world over, where a brand does only one thing; a single product rigorously produced and varying according to its formats or forms (washing powder, washing liquid, tablets or pearls). We now know that this vision is restrictive. Of course a brand can only have one value system and make one central promise, but these may be applied to different products. The global success of Bic testifies to this, as does that of Nivea, l'Oréal Paris, Virgin and Amazon, not to mention distributor brands such as the Carrefour brand, which by its construction covers multiple product categories. The problem with the flexible umbrella brand is that the value system is not perceived; and it is through these values that the tacit agreement and the affective relationship are developed, beyond the satisfaction linked with the product or the excellence of the service. There is therefore a double rupture: no value link expressed between the corporate and the products, or between the products/categories themselves.

By signing its products without explaining why, the brand is diluted. Like an elastic band, it stretches and breaks. In the chapter on brand extension we saw that the brand may indeed bring together intrinsically different products, on condition that it gives them a common meaning. This is the case with luxury brands, but also Virgin, for example, or Apple. We know that the brand functions as a concept, and therefore has power to integrate objects that are different at first glance. Signing products from the ballpoint pen to the razor, to cigarette lighters, and to kayak canoes, with the name Bic is to say that there is Bic in each of them. Therefore, the common name presents a group of common values embodied in these different categories. The flexible umbrella structure offers none of this, other than generic propositions such as 'making quality products'. To achieve this, it is necessary to move to the encompassing umbrella, or masterbrand, strategy.

The aligning umbrella brand (masterbrand)

This is the second version of the umbrella brand. At first glance, in formal terms, nothing distinguishes it from the previous version: the company still accepts only a single brand for the whole, and consequently imposes descriptive names for the products and services or divisions and branches. Here we find sub-brands.

In practice, however, a gulf separates these two outworkings of the umbrella brand. Here the parent brand is mistress: it provides not just a name, but a frame of reference behind which everything should align, in order eventually to become the embodiment of it, the living spokesperson. Here the brand is the surrounding framework. This is the clearest example of what we call a 'branded house'.

The masterbrand prototype is Nivea. A Nivea product or communication can be recognised at a glance. Nivea is active in a large number of categories: moisturising creams, sunscreens, deodorants, shampoos, beauty products and make-up. Everywhere, in each of its categories, it faces specialist brands. It counters these with products embodying its

two central values, 'love and care'. This embodiment begins with the composition of the products themselves, their harmlessness, their softness, and extends to the manner in which they are communicated. Everything is codified in a centralised manner. The masterbrand is strong because it brings together a broad offering of products under highly differentiating common values. At Nivea, the categories are each sold under a variant of the name Nivea and a descriptor of the function or target. In this way, we have Nivea Body, Nivea Sun, Nivea Hands, Nivea Visage and so on.

Other examples of this strategy are found in B2B, where there are strong brands such as Legrand and Hager for low-voltage electrical appliances.

The encompassing umbrella architecture is also known as masterbrand. The name 'masterbrand' implies a guardian of the temple: a person, judge or authority capable of policing, not dissident logos but projects, innovations and even advertisements that do not fully embody the brand's central values, since these are what dilutes its promise. The brand is only as strong as its weakest link.

The brand power conferred by this architecture, when properly implemented, is remarkable. It offers economies of scale linked to the variety of products and markets that the brand can cover while creating a brand identity (that is, a group of values that are highly differentiating and relevant in each of its markets).

Korean companies, which 20 years ago were content to imitate Japanese groups, even to their practice of the flexible umbrella brand, have acquired a strong global image by changing their brand architecture. LG has a clear brand platform that is imposed on all divisions and countries. The same is true for Samsung.

In Europe, since 2004, Philips has been attempting to become a masterbrand, a strong surrounding framework. The new managing director has installed a new 'One brand' motto for all the divisions of this global group. It is difficult to imagine the cultural revolution created in this company by such an apparently simple declaration. Let us consider how it will differ from the situation before 2004, as I learnt in the Netherlands on a consultancy trip:

▥ Philips is active in many countries under another brand name. Thus, Philips razors are sold under Norelco in the United States. This is why Philips is unknown in the United States. It is therefore necessary to replace the best-known razor brand in the United States with an unknown name.

▥ Philips does admittedly act under its name alone in televisions and medical equipment and light bulbs, but everywhere in the world it goes by the name Philishave for razors. Therefore, Philishave must be abolished.

▥ Moreover, the division of small household appliances functions with first-name brands in order to differentiate its products from the competition and make them stars. It would therefore be necessary to cease this practice: and this division is the most profitable in the group.

However, one cannot build a mega-brand by balkanising it. It needs a platform (central values, core identity), and support at the highest levels of management. The products, divisions and branches must reposition themselves in order to present the central values of the brand at home and abroad. Hence a study was carried out to define the platform of the Philips brand (see Chapter 7) and consider its consequences both at the level of the new products and services to be created, and at the communications level.

Source brand strategy

This is identical to the umbrella brand strategy except for one key point – the products have their own brand name. They are no longer called by one generic name such as eau de toilette or eau de parfum, but each has own name, eg Jazz, Poison, Opium, Nina, Loulou, etc. This two-tier brand structure, known as double-branding, is shown in Figure 13.8.

Since this strategy is often confused with the endorsing brand strategy, it is important to specify the differences at the beginning. When Nestlé puts its name on the chocolate

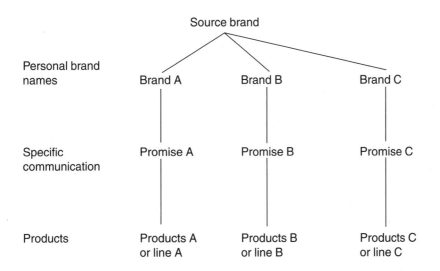

Figure 13.8 Source brand or parent brand strategy

Crunch and Galak, on the bars Yes, Nuts and Kit Kat and on Nescafé, Nesquik, etc, the corporate brand is endorsing the quality of the merchandise and acts as a maker's mark. The Nestlé name dispels the incertitude that certain products can create. Nestlé takes a back seat position. The product itself is the driver of the consumers' choice; it is the hero to the extent that few customers of Crunch attribute it to Nestlé. On the contrary, when we see the Yves Saint Laurent name on a perfume such as Jazz, this name is more than a simple endorsement. Here, it is the brand name which holds sway and which accords Jazz the seal of approval and the distinction which it would not otherwise enjoy. Yves Saint Laurent is the driver of purchase, not Jazz. Jazz is another key to the door of the Yves Saint Laurent cultural universe. The problem with many brands is that they have converted from source brands to endorsing brands. Within the source brand concept, the family spirit dominates even if the offspring all have their own individual names. With the endorsing brand, however, the products are autonomous and have only the endorsing brand in common. Today, where do Nestlé, Kellogg's or Kraft stand? What about Du Pont or Bayer, Glaxo or Merck?

The benefit from the source brand strategy lies in its ability to provide a two-tiered sense of difference and depth. It is difficult to personalise an offer or a proposition to a client without any personalised vocabulary. The parent brand offers its significance and identity, modified and enriched by the daughter brand in order to attract a specific customer segment. Ranges having 'Christian names' allow a brand which needs to maintain its own brand image to win over newer consumer categories and new territory.

The limits of the source brand lie in the necessity to respect the core, the spirit and the identity of the parent brand. This defines the strict boundaries not to be infringed as far as brand extension and also product communication are concerned. Only the names that are related to the parent brand's field of activity should be associated with it. All product aids should share the same spirit. If greater freedom is sought, then the endorsing brand strategy is more suitable.

Garnier for example wanted to become a source brand and abandon its previous endorsing brand strategy. This is a delicate process for it means moving from patchwork to unity.

Creating a source brand: from patchwork to unity

Companies need to improve their efficiency on a regular basis. One way of doing this is to put an end to the natural dispersion of brands and identities, and reorganise supply under proper parent brands that fulfil more than an endorsing function. These parent brands would be a source of strong, differentiated and unique values shared by all products and sub-brands, which also have their own particular personality based on their target group, product territory and specific function. What the present work refers to as a 'source brand' partly corresponds to what some people have called a 'branded house' (as opposed to a 'patchwork' or 'house of brands'). It should be remembered that, unlike the umbrella brand, the source brand is a strategy with two layers of branding.

So how does a company convert a 'patchwork' into a real 'house'? The first thing it has to do is define the identity of the brand for the future. The real identity of a brand lies within the brand itself, while its future lies in its ability to adapt to the markets. It is therefore by analysing the roots and origins of the brand, its early products and performance that it is possible to isolate its core, its key values, the source of its influence and legitimacy. But this analysis must then be considered carefully within the context of the development of tomorrow's markets and consumers.

Garnier provides a good illustration of this

process. Until 2002, this internationally renowned brand was known as Laboratoires Garnier. Its task was to become the other international brand of the mass-market network, alongside l'Oréal Paris, which was positioned as a more glamorous, more expensive product within the same shelf ranges. It was a question of finding values that were positive, aspirational, internally and externally motivating, and had popular appeal since the brand had been allotted a more accessible market position.

Historically speaking, the origins of Laboratoires Garnier date from 1904, when M. Garnier first invented a herbal hair tonic. This original product already had some of the key attributes of the brand – naturalness and beauty care. Some time later, after the Second World War, a hugely successful shampoo called Moëlle Garnier not only revitalised the 'genes' of the brand but also boosted business. Relaunched in 1986, the brand was extended by its sub-brands – Synergie (cosmetics), Ambre Solaire (sun care), Graphic (hair care), Ultra Doux (skin care) and Lumia (hair colour).

The brand achieved international renown and established a strong position on several European markets. However, its sub-brands declined in popularity and remained regional. All except one, that is, which had already been extremely successful outside Europe and appealed to the younger generation in countries throughout the world – Fructis, the first strengthening shampoo with active fruit concentrates. Fructis was a direct descendant of the Garnier line but with a more modern image. The real reinvention came with Fructis Style, a range of revolutionary styling products containing fruit wax and characterised by a complete range of strong, tactile sensations – the colours, consistency and aroma of fruit. With Fructis, a new generation of sensual products was born.

But to conquer the world market the brand needed a new identity that, while respecting its origins, would nevertheless make it an aspirational brand for modern young people worldwide. Fructis and especially Fructis Style would be the new prototype for the brand, while their casual and ironic tone would provide the basis for its reinvention.

What were the consequences for Garnier? In order to be attractive and accessible to young people in countries throughout the world, the brand had to change its name from Laboratoires Garnier and simply become known as Garnier. It was no longer a scientific or a French brand, it was accessible and international. Furthermore its brand contract, its values, were now written in English.

How does Garnier define its aims? 'Garnier believes in beauty through nature. Scientifically developed and enriched with selected natural ingredients, our products help you look healthy and feel good every day.' This contract is outlined in six core values:

- Natural high tech (which distinguishes it from Yves Rocher, which is not high tech, and l'Oréal Paris which does not focus on the natural element).

- Healthy beauty: Garnier is a healthy brand, which does not use top models, but unknown models who look and feel good (like the girl next door).

- Total experience: Garnier is not selling just a product but a complete experience that appeals to all five senses.

- Universal: it is multi-ethnic, multiracial, multigeneration.

- Accessible, as evidenced by price and distribution.

- Positive irreverence: this is a distinctive personality trait, found in all Garnier advertisements.

How was this new identity projected across all Garnier's daughter brands?

- The first stage was one of identification.

Apart from modifying the name, a new logo was created in green, orange and red, the colours of fruit but also traffic lights.

▌ The next stage involved bringing the sub-brands portfolio into line with the source brand. Since Garnier is a source brand, the sub-brands must reflect its core values. So the Neutralia sub-brand (shower gel) was abandoned because its clinical purity no longer corresponded to the Garnier 'house' image, while the Ultra Doux brand was extended to replace Neutralia. Similarly, the Synergie sub-brand (cosmetics) became Skin Natural which was much more in line with Garnier's values.

▌ The third stage consisted of developing business by organising an attack on growth markets, that is, deciding which sub-brands would target which countries and which segments. What would be the consequences in terms of range and adaptation to multiple niching (universality value)?

▌ The fourth stage involved defining how the advertising was to be handled. What distinguishes a Garnier advertisement? They all begin with a light-hearted statement of the problem, followed by the presentation of the solution, and involve a wide range of different people, all looking and feeling good and reflecting the cultural and racial diversity of the country in question. The slogan says 'Take care of yourself'.

▌ In the fifth stage, the promotional principles were established – an accessible brand that offers a full experience – and Garnier developed massive sampling and street marketing initiatives involving direct contact with consumers in all countries.

It is significant that the website is called GarnierBeautyBar.com. Visually, it is presented like a real 'house' where you can visit each room and discover and/or personally experiment with one of the Garnier sub-brands. The 'branded house' has constructed a 'virtual house' in which all the brands in the family are brought together with a view to offering an intense product experience. Garnier's (male and female) customers enter via the Garnier Hall from where they can go to the Beauty Lounge, Style Room, Tonic Area or Game Zone and try out their future looks, carry out personalised diagnostic tests or simply experiment and develop their customer loyalty.

From this it can be seen that the source brand is a structure that restructures all its parts. Many groups use this type of brand architecture to give greater impact to their diverse product ranges by making them converge on a common image. For example, all Danone products and brands now focus on health, the core value of the source brand, in the knowledge that there are seven types of health, and therefore seven different ways of presenting it. Danone has also changed its status from an 'endorsing brand' to a 'source brand'.

Mixed approaches

The six branding strategies presented here are models, typical cases of branding. In reality, companies adopt mixed configurations where the same brand can be, according to the product, range, umbrella, parent or endorsing brand. For example, l'Oréal is a range brand of lipsticks. It is a source brand for Studio, Elsève or Plénitude. The hybrid character of the usage of the brand l'Oréal and the strategies adopted reflect its willingness to adapt to the decision-making processes of consumers in different sub-markets (hair care products, perfumes or cosmetics) or according to the distribution channels (ie self-service or specialist stores). In certain cases, l'Oréal guarantees reliability and technical capacity. In others, it wants to achieve recognition (ie in cosmetics) and therefore needs to place itself to the forefront. And finally, in still other cases, l'Oréal has to be invisible – either to avoid being associated with a low-price segment or to avoid hurting one of its prestige products. Nevertheless, many hybrid situations result out of the series of small decisions that are taken as and when a new product is launched. Due to the lack of an overall plan for a brand's relationship with its products, a number of non-coherent branding decisions often exist side by side.

3M provides an interesting example of the accumulation of separate branding policies, with as many as five denominational stages (quintuple branding). This is shown in Figure 13.9. 3M is a company focused on high-tech research into industrial and domestic applications of adhesives. This covers a vast area which includes glues, obviously, but also films, cassettes, medical plasters, transparencies and overhead projector products, etc. The 3M name is synonymous with seriousness, power and heavy R&D. But this also leaves an image of coldness. Thus, to humanise the contact with the general buyer, the umbrella brand Scotch was created. Video cassettes, glue sticks and sellotape are all branded Scotch directly. But for the scouring pads, on the other hand, a line brand called Scotch-Brite was created. To counter the challenge of a rival product from Spontex (who simply call them scouring pads) Scotch replaced the generic name by a particular name, the 'Raccoon' (just like the Volkswagen Beetle). This differentiated its product and explained its advantages in a unique manner and gave it a closer and more friendly image.

The 'Raccoon' itself has been expanded into many versions – green, blue, red – depending on its shape and use. For its general consumer products, such as sponges and glues, 3M was used as an endorsing brand with a signature in small print. Curiously enough, 3M is scarcely in evidence on Scotch cassettes. Is this to distinguish better from the video cassettes marked clearly and exclusively 3M and targeted at professional use? In fact, while 3M provides a guarantee of good performance and an endorsing brand for general consumer products, it serves as an umbrella brand for professional products: all the power and significance of the 3M name is reflected in products

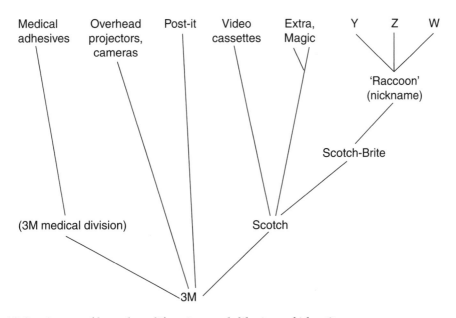

Figure 13.9   A case of brand proliferation and dilution of identity

such as cameras, overhead projectors and dental cement (coming from the 3M health division). Post-it, the famous 'adhesive notes that serve as a memory tool or a message carrier', is also signed 3M. In order to patent this invention in a better way and to define it in a better manner than the long description used above, that it be given a proper name was to be expected.

Thus, depending on the level of professional end-use that a product has, or the need for an up-to-date image of excellence and performance, it is either signed 3M in a prominent manner or even perhaps exclusively. If not, 3M is present through the brand Scotch. Perhaps this is why the sellotape, Scotch Magic, used the name 3M only as a recall tool. On the other hand, aerosol glue for communication professionals bears the Scotch name in small print and 3M in large letters. There are also differentiated product advertisements for the 'Raccoon', general-use sellotape, Scotch cassettes and Post-it. Beyond the endorsing brand, there are no common codes of expression which appear independent in form and intent.

Choosing the appropriate branding strategy

Which is the best branding strategy? Procter & Gamble are firm supporters of product brands; are they right and l'Oréal, their more flexible competitor, wrong?

Each type of brand strategy has its own advantages and disadvantages, as has been described. However, a simple list of the pros and cons does not provide a procedure for making a choice in a given company in a given market. The choice of brand policy is not a stylistic exercise, but more a strategic decision aimed at promoting individual products and ranges as well as capitalising the brand in the long term. It should be considered in the light of three factors: the

product or service, consumer behaviour, and the firm's competitive position. Brand policy is a reflection of the strategy chosen by a particular company in a specific context.

What parameters should be taken into account when choosing a branding strategy? The first is *corporate strategy*, of which branding strategy is in fact the symbol. For example, in 2003, Schneider Electric, one of the leaders in the field of electrical distribution and industrial control, decided to revitalise its Merlin Gerin and Telemecanique brands, which were well known to research departments and electrical integrators and installers throughout the world. In so doing, Schneider ended an initiative launched some 10 years previously with a different aim in mind, namely to replace individual brands with a single, group brand. The company's new director, who had come from Steelcase, outlined the strategic positioning of Schneider Electric against GE, ABB and Siemens. Compared with these general electrical and electronic giants, Schneider Electric is not a small general electrical company but rather likes to see itself as a multi-specialist company. In fact, because it sells intermediate products, its customers are looking for a specialist company. On the other hand, when compared with its many single-specialist competitors, Schneider Electric is more of a general electrical company. So if it wants to position itself as a multi-specialist company, the specialities must be offered by specialist brands, united by a group brand, a single entity, which facilitates customer relations. This is why it was decided not to follow the single-brand path, but to bring the range of 50 product brands together under three integrated international brands – Merlin Gerin, Telemecanique and the US company Square D, in 130 countries. There is therefore a Schneider Electric front office and a Schneider Electric sales force organised by type of customer, and these customers are able to purchase products under different product brands.

Another consequence is that distributors will once again become the official distributors of Merlin Gerin or Telemecanique without there being any obligation, as in the past, to automatically reference both brands.

Similarly, Groupe SEB, world leader in small household appliances, decided to form itself into a multi-brand group, with four international brands – Moulinex, Tefal, Krups and Rowenta. Why not follow the tempting single-brand path, like Philips? Precisely because of Philips. The strategy lies in the art of being different. The single brand is an advantage if you are already a single brand like Philips, one of the few international brands whose reputation is based on the fact that it is distributed throughout the world – even, via its light bulbs, in the depths of the Amazon basin. It is basically too late to try to emulate Philips. In today's fragmented markets, with their aggressive distribution networks and consumer segments, it is far better to exploit the targeted reputation (in terms of product and values) of the brands that people have bought precisely because they were brands.

The second parameter is the *business model*. In this respect it is interesting to compare companies within the same sector, since their brand policy is often a reflection of their business model, the driving force of their competitive edge and their profitability. This can be illustrated by comparing three giants of the European cheese industry – Bel, Bongrain and Lactalis. Bel develops range brands around a central innovative product, thereby giving rise to an entire range of products with The Laughing Cow, Kiri or Mini Babybel signature. Bongrain develops product brands – Chaumes, Vieux Pané, Caprices des Dieux, Haut Ségur – while Lactalis uses a single brand (Président) as an umbrella for all its cheeses and butter, and even milk in Russia and Spain. So why the different brand policies?

In fact, the business models of these companies are not the same, hence the different brand strategies. Bel likes to see itself as the inventor of modernity, anti-traditionalism, accessibility and everyday values. It does not deal in those speciality cheeses bought as a weekend treat. As the inventor of modernity, it must therefore create brands, with their own particular shapes and characteristics, that can subsequently be offered in a variety of forms to capitalise on the investment in promotion. Bongrain decided to develop processed AOC (*appellations d'origine contrôlées*) cheeses to make them more accessible in terms of taste, price, preservability and usage. Vieux Pané is a processed version of the AOC cheese category called 'Pont l'Evêque' but, as such, does not have the right to use the name of the appellation. Bongrain therefore has to give each of the specialities it creates a new name – hence the product-brand policy. The disadvantage of this is that it has to promote each new brand, meanwhile supporting through advertising many small volume brands.

The business model of Lactalis is to segment generic categories in order to bring them up to date and into line with everyday life and the modern life-style. This model gives rise to an umbrella-brand policy – under a single brand (Président), there are descriptive names for each of the varieties, each of the various forms, with low-fat butter remaining a quality butter, Emmental a real Emmental, and Brie a real Brie.

The third parameter for choosing a brand architecture is *cultural*. The United States has developed the culture of the product brand – a brand that produces a single product. Ivory, the founder brand of Procter & Gamble, is and continues to remain a soap, which explains the company's reluctance to extend the brand and even the ideological opposition of such authors as Trout and Ries who have berated it in their work for the past 20 years. But the US domestic market favoured this product-brand policy. On the other hand, it also explains why Europe and Japan have been the main exponents of the umbrella-brand policy. Nivea and Nestlé are just two of the many

European examples. In Japan, apart from the size of the domestic market, the concept of the company has also counted for a lot in the sense that, the more products and sectors a company covers, the greater its reputation. It would simply not occur to the director of a Japanese company not to use the corporate name to promote all kinds of brand extensions. Yamaha is a typical example, putting its name to such widely diverse products as motorcycles and pianos.

The fourth parameter is the *pace of innovation*. How do you develop product brands in a sector that updates its offer on an annual basis? In this instance, a single-brand policy covering the entire range is preferable, as in the case of Nokia, Sony-Ericsson, Alcatel, Samsung and even Whirlpool and GE.

A fifth parameter is the a*dded-value lever* on which a product is based. This point is illustrated in Figure 13.1, giving the relative positioning of these different strategies. When the added value in a particular market is linked to reassurance, reputation and scale, a single-brand umbrella strategy is recommended (in the world of industry, this is often the corporate brand), although a source-branding strategy with two levels – a real 'branded house' like Garnier or l'Oréal Paris – can work equally well. However, the more segmented the market, with top-quality, personalised products, the more one has to favour either a portfolio of l'Oréal product brands or an endorsing brand strategy that sanctions the sub-brands (the logic of Danone or Nestlé in dairy products).

Next there is the problem of *resources*. In the absence of sufficient funding, a company should concentrate its efforts on a single brand, especially if it is international. The need to achieve a visibility threshold comes before all other considerations. However, in case of co-branding, it is impossible to do so: this is why Philips and Douwe Egberts (a leading coffee company) created a separate name (Senseo) to designate their joint innovation in coffee machines.

Finally the *brand vision* impacts the choice of architecture. In the cosmetic market there are thousands of products and many scientific terms, and innovations are essential. This is what leads to an opacity in the market. Brands serve as milestones and a question that is frequently asked is which naming strategy should be used? There is no single answer to such a general question: it depends a lot on the brand's conception of itself.

Lancôme prefers a mono-product policy with only a small range derived from the leading product (Progress for the face, eyeliner, anti-wrinkle cream, etc). Thus, recently the brand chose to launch mono-products for body care, each with its own brand instead of a line under one name. There was Cadence for the body (moisturiser), Exfoliance (scrub) and Sculptural (slimmer). Lancôme is not an endorsing brand. It wants to be a source brand and therefore the creator of a precise vision, that of French elegance. The brand wants to serve as a vehicle to express:

- the product's technological level and its performance;

- luxury as perceived in a French manner, that is to say natural sophistication; Lancôme makes laboratories appear charming.

Lancôme expresses itself through its products and the services that surround them (the dialogue and the advice of salespeople). They want a brand policy that is coherent and easily understandable on two levels: the consumer and the seller. But, consumers actually respond badly to brand policy in this sector: they do not usually memorise brand names and may simply ask for the 'moisturising cream from Lancôme' when they enter the shop. The sales assistant then explains that there are two: Hydrix and Transhydrix. The two names help the assistant explain the existence of multiple products. Through these different product names, the customer understands the different products and the assistant can subsequently promote each one by stressing their individual functions, use and specific characteristics. Thus, at Lancôme, they try to give each product a different name to reflect a function (Nutrix nurtures the skin, Hydrix moisturises it and Forte-Vital makes it firmer) or the main ingredient if it is something new or revolutionary (eg Niosome contains niosomes, Oligo-Majors has oligo elements). This naming policy makes the sales pitch clearer because it explains the differences between the products and other closely positioned products and therefore avoids the confusion that could have occurred had they been in the same line and under a single common name.

This would appear to close the argument clearly between product brands and line brands in favour of the former as far as cosmetics are concerned. But, at Clarins, as a general rule, there are no mono-products and their 70 products are all grouped into lines. Since Clarins is not Lancôme, it does not have the same image, the same identity or the same conception of itself. It projects itself as a Beauty Institute and the profession of beautician is very important to them. This concept implies the use of many products belonging to the same line, just as in a prescription. A mono-product cannot do everything and from this arises the preference for product lines that act in synergy. Clarins wants to create stable lines that can last for years and are in conformity with its identity, personality and brand culture. Finally, it prefers objective product promises rather than a plethora of slogans for mono-products that all play on one factor, presently 'victory over ageing'. From this arises the names for their products, which are always in the beauty sector. The names are always descriptive of the product's actions and do not play upon dreams and fantasies as did Christian Dior when he launched 'Capture'. At Clarins, names are constituted of two or three words, for example, 'Multi-Repair Restructuring Lotion'.

In the past, the creation of any new product was usually also accompanied by the creation of a new name. In christening the new product, the product manager gave it life. Without a name, the product had no real existence. Once branded, it had a life. In 1981, at 3M, 244 new brands were created and registered. In 1991, only four new brands were created. The same thing happened at Nestlé: in 1991, the company created 101 new products but only five new brands. The age of brand multiplication is over. What has led to this change in practice?

The realisation that brands are the true capital of the company has led to this revolution. By capitalising on fewer brands, companies had to sustain their equity by nurturing them through constant innovations and line or range extensions. Therefore, the question 'what name do we choose?' becomes 'which new product should we put under which already existing brand?'

Companies with decentralised management are particularly susceptible to brand proliferation. Thus, 3M, in spite of its high rank in the Fortune 500 companies and its 60,000 products, remained relatively unknown. One part of the explanation for this was the excessive number of trademarks with which it was burdened: over 1,500. In order to solve this problem, 3M decided to take the cat by the tail and created a branding committee at the highest level (Corporate Branding Policy Committee) whose mission was to establish a precise doctrine regarding brand policy. Its approval was necessary before the creation of any new brand. To make 3M become a real corporate brand, it was decided that from then on 3M would be used to sign or guarantee all products (except the cosmetic line). The second decision was the banning of the use of more than two names on one product (as was the case with Scotch Magic) in order to abolish brand pile-ups, as is shown in Figure 13.9. In order to facilitate the integration of the new brand policy that capitalised on a few mega-brands (also called primary or power brands), 3M distribute to all its subsidiaries a guide explaining the policy to be followed in case of branding when faced with a new product. The creation of this guide led to a drastic fall in the requests for new brand creation: be it parent brands (like Scotch) or daughter brand (like Magic).

The decision tree shown in Figure 13.10 puts each innovation through four questions which serve as filters to limit the creation of a new brand to certain very specific circumstances (like Post-it). The first filter question asks if the innovation satisfies one of the following four criteria: Is it a top priority innovation? Does it create a new kind of price/quality relationship? Does it create a new product category that did not exist until then? Is it the outcome of an acquisition? The second filter question asks whether the brand could not be used to nurture an already existing parent brand in 3M's primary brands portfolio. The third filter question seeks to discover whether the new product can provide the occasion for the

creation of a new parent brand. The last filter question evaluates the capacity of the new product to justify the creation of a new secondary brand (daughter brand). From the decision tree emerge six exhaustive branding possibilities that are based on measurable market parameters. They go from the extremely simple (slides for overhead projectors from 3M) to multiple level branding (Scotch Magic, the sellotape from 3M). As expected, the creation of a new brand (primary or secondary) became the exception rather than the rule. A number of restrictive conditions had to be fulfilled first: mainly, that the innovation creates new primary demand and that none of the existing primary brands are suited.

New trends in branding strategies

Companies do evolve in their branding strategies. An analysis of their international behaviour reveals significant trends.

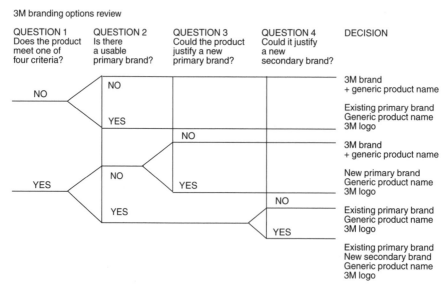

Figure 13.10   3M branding options review

Why the rise of branded houses?

An interesting classification of branding architectures is that of 'branded house' versus 'house of brands'. As it names indicates, the 'house of brands' refers to a company which operates through well-known brands but itself remains discreet if not hidden: this is the case of the ITW (Illinois Tool Works) operating with such brands as Paslode or Spit, and well known in professional circles. Procter & Gamble and Georgia Pacific also operate that way.

The branded house is the inverse case: the company itself is the one and single brand, acting as a banner and a federating force. For Aaker and Joachimstahler (2000), the models of such architecture are GE (GE Capital, GE Medical and so on) and Virgin. In fact, it is over-restrictive to assimilate the branded house to this type of case. The branded house is a strategy by which the corporation is the source of reputation and the federating force. This can be achieved by two branding architectures: the *corporate umbrella brand* (Sony, Philips, GE and Virgin are examples), and the *corporate source brand*, where there exist sub-brands or branded subsidiaries, but the leader is the parent company. This is typically the policy followed by HSBC, which puts its name or logotype before that of all subsidiaries, as long as these subsidiaries keep their name.

Two brand architectures correspond to the so-called 'house of brands': naturally what is called the *product brand* approach, and also the *endorsing brand* approach. When 3M puts its name at the bottom of all its products, is it really driving customers' perception of value? No. Although present, visibly it remains discreet: this is the sign of a 'house of brands'. The brands of the portfolio act very independently.

Paradoxically some corporate umbrellas are also very close to being quasi houses of brands. This may look as a contradiction with what has just been said. In fact, the whole issue is that of power and organisation. Take Toshiba for instance. This conglomerate is organised in business units: computers, hi-fi, television, cookware (in Japan) and so on. Not only are the business unit directors totally independent, the country managers are also very independent. Their role is to sell the products coming from Japan. As a consequence, there is no desire at all to coordinate the communications between business units, and for a given business unit between countries. The result is that although they wear the same name, Toshiba hi-fi products do not have the same image as Toshiba computers, Toshiba television sets and so on. The Toshiba corporation up until now never thought of itself as a brand that needed to be managed globally as such. It is only recently that a VP was named with that objective, with worldwide responsibilities and authority. His or her first task will be to establish the Toshiba brand platform and to enforce it throughout all communications of any product in the world. Philips is itself now acting under the 'one Philips' internal motto.

Why do so many organisations move towards this branded house architecture to recreate identity where there is diversity, fragmentation, if not a patchwork? In modern developed markets, unlike the emerging ones, it is no longer sufficient to be known. One must also consistently evoke a set of values and stimulate emotional resonance. This supposes some discipline and less autonomy. Sales-oriented organisations, such as those of Korean and Japanese companies, assign high sales objectives to their country managers. In exchange they have a lot of freedom. This is why their communication is generally managed at the local level. Creating a branded house will meet resistance because one source of autonomy, and not least, advertising freedom, will be affected. However, a branded house does not automatically mean a global campaign: the spirit of the brand may emerge through different and even localised communications.

Loyalty and the rise of transverse brands

There is another reason for changing brand strategy – when the emphasis shifts from product logic to customer logic, from a desire to conquer new markets to developing customer loyalty. Accor Hotels, the European leader in the hotel industry, is a good example of a company that was able to react and modify certain fundamental principles of its brand policy. Accor owes its success to the creative brilliance of its two founders who invented the product brand in the hotel sector. Novotel, their first hotel chain, was based on the concept of total standardisation – whichever hotel they stayed in, businessmen and women felt at home, down to the very layout and decoration of the rooms. Then they covered the different market segments with other product brands: Formule 1, Etap Hotels, Ibis, Mercure, Novotel, Sofitel and Suit'Hotel in Europe, and Motel 6 in the United States.

According to the original logic, Accor – the name of the holding company – was limited to that single function and was therefore invisible. Then, in view of the requirements of stock exchange valuation, it was decided to make the corporate brand more visible. It began to appear in small print on the hotel brochures, before being incorporated as the trade name – Accor Hotels – in the actual logo of each product brand.

The growth of the group's market share recently led to another reassessment: the decision to move from individual loyalty programmes for each brand to a corporate loyalty programme (Accor Hotels Favourite Guest).

It was this same need to develop loyalty that led l'Oréal Paris to break with its historic brand strategy in 1995. The decision was made in response to Nivea, whose simple strategy maximised brand loyalty within an increasingly broad portfolio of sub-brands that were in direct competition with the brands in the l'Oréal group. L'Oréal realised

the limitations of a flagship-brand strategy in which l'Oréal Paris merely endorsed a large number of independent sub-brands – Elsève, Elnet, Plénitude and so on. Apart from the fact that the publicity budget was fragmented, there was no effective capitalisation. The group therefore switched from a 'house of brands' logic (with l'Oréal Paris as the endorsing brand) to a 'branded house' logic, a source brand with a basic unity and a very distinctive form. This is when the so-called 'dream team' appeared on the international scene – a collection of internationally renowned top models and stars, each promoting a sub-brand from the l'Oréal Paris house, using the same creative platform and publicity signature ('because I am worth it'). At the same time, the l'Oréal Paris brand name became larger, more visible, and more prominent for such sub-brands as Elsève, on the packaging and in-store merchandising. Finally, the denominative logic was applied to brand extension categories that were not yet sufficiently attributed to the brand (due to its historic associations with hair products). Plénitude, the brand then in competition with Nivea, was abandoned in favour of Dermo Expertise, Pure Zone and Solar Expertise, whose more descriptive names immediately suggest competence in the area concerned.

By doing this, l'Oréal Paris was also aiming to develop real customer loyalty across the different sections of the brand and thereby make up the time lost to Nivea in this respect. In 2002, in an extension of this customer loyalty objective, l'Oréal Paris launched its first advertising campaign with a view to creating a relational database.

Industry discovers the importance of branding

When branding policy is considered, the industrial sector does not immediately spring to mind. Paradoxically, since promotion in this sector is not done through costly publicity but through catalogues, the sales force and trade exhibitions, companies do not hesitate to register trademarks. Air Liquide, for example, has registered a total of 880 trademarks (effectively, brand names).

As well as representing a considerable cost, these trademarks also create confusion and opacity further down the line, at sales team and at catalogue level. The problem is that they are specialist names which it is hoped will be passed on by word of mouth and recommendation: 'I want some X.' But this is quite clearly impossible as there are far too many, which is why the industrial sector is beginning to incorporate the concept of the endorsing or source brand, and even the mega-brand, which creates an umbrella for a series of specialist products.

Internationalising the architecture of the brand

Should companies globalise their branding architectures? Should they just duplicate them when entering new countries and continents? It is a fact that most branding architectures have been created slowly, through time in the domestic market. They benefited from low media costs, and a lower competition. This is why we so often find 'product brand' architectures. They resulted from the acquisition of a company by its main competitor: to avoid losing market share, the acquirer decided to keep the brands apart. Can the same portfolio architecture be applied when entering Russia or the United States?

In Russia, as in many former communist countries, there is a unique opportunity to rapidly take a dominant position by investing fast and heavily as long as western competitors are not there, and media costs remain low. This is what Frito Lay did. This means capitalising on one brand, used as source brand or endorsement, and rapidly pushing new products into new segments.

In the United States, the challenge is the media and distribution costs. The consequence is the obligation to nest products under an umbrella brand which remains to be created. As a result we see what can be called a 'vertical crunch' of brand architectures. There are in fact two types of 'vertical crunch'. The first is a bottom-up crunch, when a mere descriptor becomes a driver (the way consumers name what they buy). For instance in Europe, the whole shampoo line of l'Oréal Paris is sold under the brand Elsève: its many products have names such as Color Vive and Energance. In the United States, Elsève has not been launched. Instead of three levels, there are only two levels (l'Oréal Paris and a wide range made of names like Vita Vive, Nutri Vive, Hydra Vive, Curl Vive, Color Vive and Body Vive).

The other is a top-down crunch, when a mere endorsing brand becomes the driver. For instance in Europe the famous biscuit speciality Pim's is called Pim's by Lu. In the United States, it is Lu Pim's.

Companies also exploit local equities to carry international brands. For instance, all Unilever's global ice cream concepts (Magnum, Solero and so on) are endorsed by a local house brand, acting as reassurance by its long-established proximity and familiarity in the country.

Some classic dysfunctions

Brand architecture, like any plan, is one thing. Implementation is another. In practice, we find four classic branding dysfunctions.

The case of the parent brand swallowed up by a daughter brand

Sometimes, in fact, one of the daughter brands can prove remarkably successful, attracting to itself all the advertising investment. The result is that the parent brand has been taken over by the image created by this exclusive communication. It can no longer play its role as parent brand and create new daughter brands. This is the price of success: not only does the star product hide the others, but it drags the parent brand with it. For years the Nina Ricci brand was associated with a single perfume, its global success L'air du temps. This created a fundamental problem for licences: a luxury brand makes its profits through these. However, Nina Ricci no longer had its own identity, and potential licensees did not want to be licensees of L'air du temps, but of the parent brand. It was necessary to reconstitute the identity of the latter.

Volkswagen was swallowed up in image (and sales) by the Golf, a car which has known glory but which symbolises the 1980s!

Company–product disconnection

Essilor is the worldwide number one company in corrective optical lenses. When a consumer goes to an optician in the United Kingdom with a prescription, this optician sends the prescription to Essilor UK, which manufactures the lenses during the night in its very automatised and modern factory in Portugal and has them sent back by Fedex to the optician the next day. What a gigantic service provided to the opticians : this is a B2B winning-business model.

One exception is Varilux, the worldwide name for Essilor's brand of progressive multifocal lenses. It has been quite well advertised at the end-user level, so that people ask for Varilux lenses. What is changing is the distribution: huge multiple chains of dispensing opticians are developing, such as Grand Optical and Afflelou. Their innovation is to be able to produce directly in the store a large number of lens prescriptions, in one hour only. As a result Essilor is threatened. As a company it is not known by the end users. It is only known and respected by opticians: but some of them are grouping together and starting to limit Essilor's role to the difficult prescriptions that cannot immediately be made in the shop.

In the B2B sector Sage is an illustration of this problem. It is a giant in terms of market sector (number three in the world in management software) and a dwarf in terms of image, whereas everyone recognises SAP, Microsoft, Oracle and Cegid. It is true that the company has a decentralised structure: communications are paid for by market, therefore by the products sold in each. This has two consequences: tomorrow's promising products are not communicated enough, and the communication places emphasis on the products, and not enough on the Sage brand. This may place a brake on organic growth. The Sage brand is well known to accountants (who buy its best-selling accounts software) but not people from other corporate functions, where tomorrow's growth segments are located.

Brand shadowing results from an excess of endorsement or of emphasis on the umbrella

Sales of the product suffer as a result of this. When Ricard, the true pastis of Provence, launched an alcohol-free pastis called Pacific, it called it Pacific de Ricard, with packaging whose codes and label were resolutely Marseillais and similar to that of a traditional aniseed liqueur. Over the months, and following consumer analysis, the visibility of the Ricard brand was reduced. Nowadays it is seen as having the status of a maker's seal. Pacific was given specific symbols that seemed disconnected from pastis: those of the Pacific Ocean and its islands.

Balkanisation of the brand

If segmented, differentiated brands are created under its aegis, the parent brand is impoverished and becomes simply an endorsing brand. Diluted, it no longer imposes a framework, an individual vision, its identity or its values. It is a known name, with a story, but one that is now overtaken by the stories written in the media by its autonomous daughter brands.

For example, the segmentation of Dim products with daughter brands ended at one point by turning them into stars. Dim became a name on the packaging of tights and stockings, minor in comparison to that of the daughter brands (Macadam, Dim'up, Diam's and so on). Moreover, the coherence of a great brand was nowhere to be found. However, it is the parent brand, Dim, whose job it is to survive. In order to do so, it must remain intrinsically attractive, a source of desire. It does so, admittedly, through its daughter brands, who ensure its relevance today in growing market segments. Nevertheless, the daughter brands must be dissolved when they lose their relevance, and new ones must be created. It is therefore necessary to ensure the pre-eminence of the parent brand. To do this, it is necessary to:

▮ redefine the identity of the parent brand;

▮ redefine a true source brand strategy, ensuring the pre-eminence of the parent brand;

▮ align the daughter brands within the framework defined by the parent brand.

The parent brand, after all, is the surrounding framework. It is worth looking at this process in detail, since it should be implemented regularly in order to correct the effect of centrifugal forces.

What name for new products?

A company grows through its new products: they make it possible to gain a differential in products and services over the competition. They also make it possible to focus advertising on news that will interest the market. Finally, they provide the springboard for a revitalisation of strategic image features of the brand. For every launch of a particular innovation,

the same question arises from the parents of the project: what shall we call it?

The question of naming new products is important: it is not at all a euphonic problem (does the name sound nice?), but a fundamental one. In reality, the first question should be: do we need to call it anything?

Why, in fact, did 3M give the name 'Post-It' to something it could have called 'removable Scotch tape'? Scotch is 3M's well-known brand and the name indicates 'adhesive products'. Isn't Post-It an innovative variant of Scotch tape? Now a brand – in this case, Scotch – is only supported when it is nourished through innovation. Let us take another, B2B, example: an innovation by Lafarge. It is a revolutionary, ultra-fast, fine cement that makes it possible to obtain an extremely smooth surface. Should a new name be found for it, with the potential for turning it into a Lafarge product or range brand later, or should it simply be called 'the new Lafarge ultra-smooth cement', opting for a descriptive name, as it would be in a master-brand or umbrella strategy? The name therefore poses the underlying question of the brand strategy (the number of levels and the links between them, between the corporate and the products).

When should you create a sub-brand?

When a new product arrives, there is too great a tendency to opt for the creation of a specific brand. This is understandable; the inventor reacts like any parents who, proud of their child, seek to give it a first name. However, a first name is an identity, and a lasting commitment of a marketing budget in order to forge this identity and achieve recognition for the daughter brand. Moreover, in practice, by focusing on the so-called daughter brand, there is a tendency to let the parent brand take a step back, into the background, something that is quickly translated into the periodic monitoring studies of brand equity. The parent brand declines in spontaneous recognition and in image.

Figure 13.11 Which brand architecture is suitable for brand innovation?

The reaction then is to change the status of the daughter brand, to turn it into a simple product. For example, the prepaid card from Bouygues Telecom was initially treated as a relatively autonomous daughter brand: Nomad! It later became the Bouygues Telecom Nomad card.

When, then, should one create a sub-brand?

▌ Chapter 11 on brand coherence presented the four figures of the relationship between product and brand: variant, similarity, transformation and contradiction. The closer one is to the variant, the more natural it becomes to give the product a purely descriptive name, or even to invent the descriptive name in question. Is a walkman a brand, or did it quickly become the generic word to describe this new piece of equipment created by Sony? People talk of the 'new Philips television'. Conversely, the further we move from the strict reproduction of the central values of the brand through the new product, the more a daughter brand is justified.

▌ A first name is necessary in order to create a category: iPod! It could have been called the Apple MP3. But there was a need in the mass communication to strongly signal the technological, sociological and cultural breakaway. Therefore, capitalising on the pioneer's advantage, the category is structured around the pioneer, here iPod. The new entrants position themselves in relation to the iPod.

▌ A first name is necessary, albeit supported by a long-term investment in communication, when the protection of the innovation must be improved. When Candia, the milk brand, invented milk with a guaranteed vitamin content, it could have been called 'milk with guaranteed vitamin content' or 'vitamin milk'. After all, people say semi-skimmed milk or flavoured milk. However, it is necessary to account for the competitors' reaction. Carrefour, noting the success of the major brand's innovation, would not be slow in launching its copy under its own distributor's brand: Carrefour milk with guaranteed vitamin content. By launching its milk with guaranteed vitamin content under the name Viva, underpinned by long-term advertising campaigns, the Candia brand was able to create a halo of exclusivity, of differentiation. Viva not only created the segment: it is its referent. The consumers buy Viva with all its evocations of active good health. It is more than a product; it is a true (daughter) brand.

- A first name is necessary in order to correct the negative induced effects of an innovation. The sausage company Aoste (now acquired by Sara Lee) innovated by inventing the first industrial sausage: each of them had exactly the same weight and the same length. This was a complete break from the age-old practice of sausage-making, all slightly different in appearance, weight and length, but one that responded to the major expectation of large-scale distribution: economy of cost. In fact, there was no longer a need to weigh each product, hence there were savings in time, personnel and money. However, it was necessary to give it a name that would correct, even remove, the immediate evocations on seeing the product (it's an industrialised product, standardised to the maximum). It was launched under the name 'Shepherd's Stick' by Justin Bridou, in order to create a rural, rustic imaginary background for this industrial product. The 'Shepherd's Stick' became the leader of the segment it had created.

- With services, a first name is often necessary in order to give flesh to an innovation. In 2004, Gaz de France, a distribution company, wanted to provide a modular, global offer to its 10 million subscribers. It was a personalised diagnosis, a proposal according to the desired comfort level. Told in these terms, readers might ask themselves how this proposal was in any way revolutionary. After all, isn't all that part of the minimum client focus? The fact is that ordinary words make innovative proposals sound banal. This is why Gaz de France named their proposal 'Dolce Vita' and based all its advertising communication on this name, which became a daughter brand, with an emotional dimension. In contrast, when Orange, the French leader in mobile telephones, launched landline/mobile convergence on 5 October 2006, it named it simply 'Unix', a descriptive name to get the concept across: clients could receive calls made to the landline on their mobile. In Great Britain, British Gas created a daughter brand in services: Goldfish.

- When the parent brand does not (yet) have the image suitable for the targeted market, a relay or an intermediary is required. This is the goal of the first-name brand. Venus by Gillette made it possible for this very macho brand to target women. Peugeot motorcycles and scooters have used many first names: young people seeking emancipation need a badge. Buying 'a Peugeot' 15 years ago did not fulfil this function sufficiently, even if the product itself was remarkable; hence first names such as Booster.

The maternal identity of Nestlé did not legitimate its presence in coffees. Nestlé is historically, and first of all in everyone's lives, baby milk. It was not possible to launch a 'Nestlé coffee'. Nescafé made it possible to say both 'instant, powdered', giving reassurance through the confidence linked with the name, while distancing the maternal image, and to say 'coffee'. The word café brought Nestlé an element that it had previously lacked. Conversely, the identity of Philips was already technological: it was enough to endorse the razor. Choosing to call the razors 'Philishave' rather than Philips razors brought nothing new: the activity descriptor 'shave' did not bring any added value and contributed to distancing the salience of Philips. In fact, Braun simply calls its razors – Braun razors.

Taking into account the tendency to think up a first name too quickly, several warnings should be heeded before launching into the choice of a daughter brand:

- No first names without a major, long-term advertising investment. Otherwise, the product will appear on shelves or in cata-logues, with a mysterious name, and the customer will be unable to grasp what the new product has to offer. All too often there is a time lag between the decisions on the name, taken very early, and the fixing of the budget, which may change at the last moment.

▎ The second question concerns the future: will this daughter brand be able to provide an umbrella for other products? Will it be possible to put other future products under Agilia by Lafarge, for example, that will be coherent with this name? This criterion is essential and too rarely used: if it is not respected, the company plunges ahead into an economic impasse. In fact, it is difficult to support a single product in advertising and communication. Only the arrival of a genuine range, and other new products, will make it possible to acquire the critical mass that generates a sufficient size of marketing communications budget.

▎ Is the parent brand sufficiently well known to move on to the stage of having daughter brands? It is the parent brand that gives meaning to the daughter brand. How were the first Apple products known, for over 10 years? Apple 1, 2 and 3. Only later, in the place of the Apple 4, to clearly show the discontinuity, was the name Macintosh used. What did the low-cost telephone operator Free call its convergence offer? Free Box! Orange called its unique landline/mobile offer Orange Unix! The first Danone products were all called Danone or a variant thereof (Danette, Danessa, Danino, Dan'up and so on).

In the industrial domain, Veolia Environment removed all its daughter brands, since the problem for Veolia is that it is an unknown group: it therefore has an urgent need to make itself known worldwide. Therefore, its global daughter branch brands, Connex, Dalkia and Onyx, were de-christened and renamed Veolia

Transport, Veolia Energy and Veolia Waste.

▎ Before creating a daughter brand, would it not be better to launch the innovation under an existing daughter brand? For every daughter brand has to ward off its own obsolescence through innovation. Systematically placing innovations under new first-name brands handicaps the older ones. We will see below how 3M created a multi-criteria grid to manage this real risk.

A case in point: names in the automobile industry

The car fascinates us. Innumerable reviews and magazines are dedicated to it. This sector only lives through innovation, giving us the desire to change cars. Different constructors have different policies regarding their new models. Renault gives them all proper names (Vel Satis, Megane, Twingo, Logan and so on). Peugeot follows its three-digit logic with a zero in the middle (which forced the first Porsche known as 901 to become the 911 in order to avoid legal proceedings). Citroen opted at one point for proper brands (Citroen Xsara, Saxo, Xantia) before returning to the initials C1, C2, C3, C4 and so on. With BMW you buy a series number: series 1, 3, 5 or the top-of-the-range 7. What is the logic to these choices?

The first structuring factor of the decision concerns the maker's status: a generalist or a specialist? Generalists target all segments of the market, all consumers. Since they promote the car for everyone, their image is consequently not as strong as the specialists. As a result, their image is less in a position to dynamise new models, to bring them a strong emotional added value. These are reassuring brands, brands with guarantee and proximity through their network, not desire. The reverse is true for the specialists, who have segmented their market to a high degree and made their choice. The name alone of the specialist is the stuff of dreams: BMW, Saab, Volvo, Morgan,

Mini and so on. According to their means, buyers take away a little or a lot of the dream: the 1 or 3 series, or later on the 5 or 7 series. As with Mercedes, one always buys 'class', A, B, C, M, E, S and so on.

There is no dreaming with generalists: it is therefore necessary to boost the model itself with imaginary added value, with emotion. Hence the need for a highly evocative individual name. Remember the Golf Gti! From whom? Volkswagen. In order to compete with Mercedes, Volkswagen concentrates on the Passat, since Volkswagen means 'people's car'.

Other parameters, however, come into play. Why, in fact, does Peugeot opt for numbers rather than model names, when it is a generalist? Before we answer this, let us recall that a number can play the part of a brand, like Chanel No 5, or 007, or number 23, the number of the football star David Beckham at Manchester United. Each of these numbers has an emotional potential. Likewise 205 or 911 in cars, through their association with a cult model, the first of which marked an era, the second of which marked several generations of men.

Peugeot's approach is explained by the specific positioning of the brand: it wants to be 'the most specialist of the generalists', as A Saint Geours, its managing director, has said. This is why the brand, although generalist, accentuates its differentiating traits and the radical design that makes it palpable.

As for Citroen's policy shift, it can be explained as a result of the costs incurred by a daughter brand policy. If a model lasts six years, it is therefore necessary to invest over this time period to give it recognition and an image before turning these into profits and losses. Moreover, Citroen's objective is to strengthen its image. The emphasis placed on first-name brands, in addition to being slow and costly, does not rebound strongly onto the parent brand. Hence the decision to group the portfolio of models around Citroen, a single brand. We then buy a variation on the theme according to segment: C1, C2, C3 and so on.

Group and corporate brands

Since 1990, there has been a basic tendency for corporate brands to be as visible as possible on the products themselves. For example, Pharmaceutical Laboratories now regard themselves as a brand in their own right and take much greater care to ensure that their brand name is clearly visible on the packaging of brands of medication. In the professional electrical equipment sector, the name Schneider Electric appears on the packaging of products from the Merlin Gerin, Telemecanique and – in the United States – Square D brands. The back of all Nestlé products bears the Nestlé corporate brand name and the customer service phone number. It is the same for Danone, which has taken great care to create a logo for its Danone corporate brand, as distinct from the Danone commercial brand used for chilled products, and water and biscuits in Asia.

This tendency is part of a basic trend – the demand for responsibility and transparency. The company presents itself as the ultimate endorsement and no longer hides behind its brands. This also has the effect of increasing its visibility, and therefore its attractiveness to students, executives and the employment market in general. In Asia, television ads for Procter & Gamble and Unilever brands bear in the last seconds the signature of the companies themselves. This is not the case in the United States or in Europe, although – influenced by this Asian experience – Unilever is looking for some kind of higher public visibility to boost its corporate brand profile. In Asia, however, these two companies do not enjoy any reputation and this must therefore be established.

Finally, once a company is quoted on a stock exchange, it must try to influence the share price since, over and above the financial results published on a regular basis, market predictions are influenced by the company's name and reputation. So anything that makes people dream a little adds to its goodwill.

Companies regularly change their name and take the name of their flagship commercial brand. For example, the company formerly known as BSN changed its name to Danone Corp (it nearly became Evian Corp), while the Volkswagen group and l'Oréal group have both taken their name from their flagship brands. Mars, on the other hand, changed its name and became known as Masterfoods, as other companies are called Bestfoods (Unilever) or General Foods. So what are the reasons for these two diametrically opposed attitudes?

Capitalising on a flagship brand by applying its name to the group makes it possible to take advantage of the halo effect, even if this involves two clearly distinct sources, since the image of the one influences the perception of the other. For example, the press regularly refers to Volkswagen as Europe's number one brand when it was not the brand but the multi-brand group that earned the title through the cumulative sales of each of its brands. In fact, at the beginning of 2003, Europe's number one group was PSA Peugeot Citroën.

The l'Oréal group does not advertise a great deal. However, its brands use heavy advertising, along with research and development, as one of their main weapons. By sharing the name of its glamour ('l'Oréal Paris') brand, the l'Oréal group benefits from the impact of an international image that inspires confidence in shareholders and defines what they do.

It was for entirely opposite reasons that Mars took the less transparent name of Masterfoods. Apparently, it was difficult to sell brands of pet food such as Pedigree and Whiskas under the Mars corporate or group name, particularly since Mars conjures up the image of a single product, a legendary chocolate bar, which has growth limits in an extremely segmented market. There was also a risk of a negative halo effect on financial predictions. LVMH, the initials of Louis Vuitton Moet Hennessy, uses both strategies. On the one hand, the experts are familiar with

the significance of the acronym, which refers to internationally renowned luxury brands. On the other, by retaining the acronym, the group demonstrates its intention to remain discreet by placing the emphasis at brand level rather than corporate level, and leaving the brands to develop through their own creativity, publicity and the quality of their distribution. From this, it can be seen that the position of the corporate brand in relation to its subsidiaries is in fact a reflection of the group's internal organisation.

This essential part of group strategy is developed below.

Group and subsidiary relationships

In the industrial sector where external growth is the norm, the question of the status of corporate brands that have been acquired crops up again. Should they be left independent? Should they disappear? Should they be endorsed with a simple visual symbol of the parent company? Or joined to the name of the parent company? If they behave as mere holding companies such firms should not be surprised by their low public recognition. For instance, although it was founded in 1969 and was one of the largest chemical companies in the world, Akzo remained largely unknown. No wonder: all the companies acquired had kept their own company names and brand names (Warner Lambert, Stauffer, Montedison, Diamond Salt, etc). Akzo thus acquired a poor image in terms of technology because of its lack of visibility. It had become the biggest unknown company in the world.

General Electric has defined four brand policies and specifies the conditions for their application. These policies range from:

▪ The so-called monolithic approach where GE behaves like an umbrella brand and replaces the corporate brand which has been bought (either immediately or after a transitional period of double branding). The brands GE Silicons, GE Motors and GE

Aircraft Engines have all emerged from this process.

▌ The endorsement approach where GE signs its name beside the name of the product or the company that has been acquired.

▌ The financial approach where GE behaves like a holding company and is only discreetly mentioned (X, member of the GE group).

▌ The autonomous approach where the acquired company or product makes no reference to GE.

To decide upon a policy, GE uses six selection criteria:

1. Does GE control the company?

2. Does GE have long-term commitments in this company?

3. Does the product category have an image value? Dynamic or not?

4. Is there a strong demand for GE quality in this industry?

5. Is the corporate brand which has been bought strong?

6. What could be the resultant impact on GE?

Group style and branding strategy

At regular intervals, the major industrial groups ask themselves whether their branding strategy is as effective as it could be. There are three formal types of strategy that can be implemented within industrial groups. Although the terms 'subsidiaries', 'holding companies' and 'companies' tend to be used in this context, structurally speaking they represent the typical figures of branding strategy – source brand (A), endorsing brand (B) and umbrella brand (C). But beyond these terms, the impact on level-one subsidiaries (sub-brands) is self-evidently not the same.

Above all, each branding architecture has organisational repercussions, with each playing a different role for the group in relation to its subsidiaries and sub-subsidiaries:

▌ The strategy in which the group is a source brand can be likened to the role of an orchestra conductor or band leader.

▌ The strategy in which the group is an umbrella brand makes it a unifier.

▌ The strategy in which the group is an endorsing brand makes it a coordinator.

It is obviously not up to the branding decisions to determine the management style of a particular group – that would be a reversal of roles – but it should explain management choices and the criteria on which these choices are based.

Internationalising the group/ subsidiary architecture

The world is complex. Groups must face the fact that their different branches have a very different competitive status in different countries. In addition, in some regions high equity brands/companies were purchased as a means to penetrate the channels of distribution. This creates a question as to the longevity of these brands.

Architecture has a connotation of something nice, square and fixed. In fluctuating and fragmented modern markets, one should be careful not to harness operations under too many constraints that would prove to be counterproductive. This is why it may not be ideal to have the same branding architecture across all products/services and regions of the world.

Let us analyse the Lafarge case. This worldwide company is known for its core business: concrete and cement. Less known is the fact that Lafarge has many other branches: roofing systems, plaster, granular products and paints. If internally the goal of creating a feeling of belongingness to the group is justified, the same does not necessarily hold true as far as branding is concerned.

As for all brands, two criteria need to be taken into account. First, is the activity core or not? If it is not, it could be sold in the future. For instance, in the plaster business, if BPB (British Plaster Board) takes over Knauf, then Lafarge would become stuck in the number three position in this market. There is no reason to stay in a business where one is number three: resources might more profitably be invested in other businesses. Second, are there strong local brands in the portfolio and are they key drivers to customer loyalty?

As a consequence Lafarge has not chosen a uniform, monolithic umbrella brand architecture. It is definitely umbrella on the core activity: after acquiring the Korean Ala Cement company, this local leading company soon became Lafarge Ala Cement, or in India Lafarge Tata Cement. For non-core activities, Lafarge acts as an endorsing brand when there exist strong local names in key mature markets. This is the case for Redland in the UK, Braas in Germany and Klaukol.

Should Redland have become Lafarge Roofing UK or Lafarge Redland? Here a distinction must be made between the legal name of the company and the commercial brand. Marketing research has shown how much these names conjured emotional attachment among local professionals: the company became dual named, and the local brand became endorsed by the branch (Lafarge Roofing). However, in Malaysia from the start it created Lafarge Roofing Malaysia.

This shows that the question of the name of societies, branches and brands needs to be well understood as implying different criteria. Not all societies are brands, or divisions that are organisational classifications subject to change. Brands are made to convey values to one or many targets.

Corporate brands and product brands

For years, companies have hidden behind their brands. Through prudence and fear of being affected in case of brand failure, company names have been separate from those of the brands. Thus Procter & Gamble remain unknown to the public while their brands are the stars (Ariel, Pampers). In fact, it is this that allowed the company to keep its turnover stable when the rumour of it being linked to a sect raged through the United States. The brands, autonomous from the company itself, suffered no setback. Nevertheless, such instances are rare and the tendency is more towards transparency due to communication obligations. Also, the public wants to know, in larger numbers than before, who are the actors behind the brands. Journalists want to disclose who is the 'brand behind the brand'. This also explains why so many companies have taken on the names of their most famous brands (eg Alcatel-Alsthom, Danone). They get more visibility and acknowledgement. This helps the stock exchange investor also, in cases where he is not an expert or very well-informed, to understand better what he is buying. It may also create a beneficial confusion for the brand itself. After it bought Audi, Seat and Skoda, Volkswagen Group is now co-leader in Europe on a cumulative basis. However, many people mistakenly speak of Volkswagen as a brand being the number one in Europe.

The trend towards greater visibility of corporate names also has other causes. Distribution is one of them. Distributors, multiple retailers and hypermarket chains are not very interested in brands. Their fundamental relationship is with corporations, not with brands. It is a business to business relationship. The name of the powerful corporation is therefore a potent reminder of that relationship.

Only corporate names can endow brands with stature, an extra dimension calling for respect. Would Audi have succeeded in its remarkable recovery had it not been known that Audi belonged to the Volkswagen Group? The same holds true for Seat and Skoda. Nissan's status will change because it is now part of the Renault group. As long as car makes are only brands and not part of a larger and more dynamic corporation, they arouse perceived risk among consumers and do not guarantee a long-term presence.

Many companies sell in industrial and commercial markets at the same time. Here, there is the problem of having to choose between the use of product brands or the use of the corporate reputation to support the products. This depends on the quality of the company's endorsement and the degree of visibility that it wants to acquire. In practice, the respective weight to be attributed to the product brand and the corporate brand depends on a case-by-case analysis of the returns brought by each of them on the many targets concerned. Table 13.2 presents the outline of such an analysis.

At ICI three kinds of brand policy were used (see Figure 13.12):

▌ The first policy is the classic umbrella brand where the products keep their generic names and are signed with the corporate name. Most often this concerns raw materials and undifferentiated products where the company guarantees a certain quality and the differentiation is essentially commercial (ie special conditions offered to the client on a case-by-case basis). An example would be ICI polyurethanes.

▌ The second policy is that of the endorsing brand. The company puts its name beside the product brand and this confers a status of high technology and reliability to the product. Thus, Dulux paints are accompanied by the ICI logo.

▌ The third policy makes exclusive use of the product brand. Tactel is one of the most widely sold fibres but it never mentions ICI. The product is sold to the textile industry and to the fashion world, and it is feared that the mention of the ICI name may alter the positive images linked to Tactel. Similarly the insecticide, Karate, which is sold throughout the world, also does not make any mention of ICI. Does this have anything to do with not wanting to step on ecological toes and avoid the possibility of blame regarding the harmful effects of pesticides on ground water? This situation is not only changing through time, but it also changes according to the company. Decis, the world leader in pesticides, makes a reference to Roussel Uclaf (Agrevo division)

Table 13.2 Shared roles of the corporate and product brand

Targets	Product brand	Corporate brand
Customers	+++++	+
Trade associations	++++	+
Employees	+++	++
Suppliers	+++	+++
Press	+++	+++
Issues groups	++	++++
Local community	++	++++
Academia	++	++++
Regulatory authorities	+	++++
Government commission	+	++++
Financial markets	+	+++++
Stockholders	+	+++++

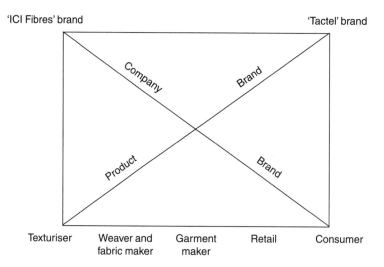

Figure 13.12 Corporate and product branding at ICI

on its packaging. Similarly, to benefit from its innovations, Du Pont de Nemours mentioned clearly 'Lycra by Du Pont' on all its communications for Lycra, the fabric that has revolutionised women's lingerie.

Product innovations generally provide an ideal occasion to ask fundamental questions about the branding policy. How to name these innovations? Let us suppose that the Lafarge Roofing Division decides to launch a radical innovation in roof maintenance and rebuilding, associated with a guarantee for 10 years or more: an 'all in one approach', service oriented instead of technology oriented. How should it be called? Would a name like Lafarge Roofing Total Solution be better than a new specific international name for that innovation?

It is surely an occasion to demonstrate the ability of the group to deliver more than cement, its core symbolic product and star (which in this sense means offering high growth and high profitability). However, roofing is a high involvement decision, with both a high perceived risk and dimensions of emotion. It may be hard for the corporation ego to recognise it, but would a Lafarge name be able to evoke the sufficient emotion needed in all real brands within a realistic timespan? Wouldn't it be better to use it as a guarantee, and let a specific good commercial name foster the benefits, tangible and intangible, of this total solution, against the small local companies with which it will be competing?

14

Multi-brand portfolios

Although the main function of a brand extension is growth, there are limits to what a single brand can achieve. Each brand is targeted. Even if psychographics are substituted for demographics, a brand is not a catchall. BMW values attract only 20 per cent of the premium car buyers worldwide. BMW refuses to dilute its brand and in order to grow it went international. It also bought the Mini and Rolls-Royce brands.

The other way in which a company can grow is by creating new brands to meet the demand that existing brands cannot satisfy. But it takes courage to launch and position new brands.

It takes courage because, at a time when extensions are the order of the day, it is difficult to admit that even a mega-brand has its limits. Companies prefer to attribute failure to production problems so that they can try – and fail – again. Thus Mattel is facing the challenge of the 'tweens' (see Lindstrom, 2003) who are no longer really children but not quite teenagers or adolescents. There is a saying in the business that today's kids are getting older younger.

In concrete terms, this means that the company's business model for the 1970s, 1980s and 1990s is defunct. In the past, Mattel treated children in the 4–10 age group in exactly the same way, as a homogenous group. This had a major advantage in terms of cost (economies of scale) – they were all sold the same Barbie doll, which represented 40 per cent of the company's sales.

Mattel's first response to the tweens challenge was to segment the target group and create a special Barbie for 8–10-year-olds, the Barbie Generation Girl with the single Barbie signature. Then, to counter the success of MGA's Bratz dolls for 8–12-year-olds, Mattel relaunched My Scene Barbie, still with the Barbie signature but smaller. However, the company had to make up its mind to take the plunge and create a genuine new brand rather than a brand extension, and in 2003, the multinational launched Flavas to succeed Barbie. After all, there comes a time in every little girl's life when she no longer wishes to play with Barbie.

Levi's had already taken the plunge by launching Dockers after initially trying a simple brand extension – Levi's Tailored

Classic. But the same brand cannot be simultaneously rebellious and classic. In the car sector, brands seem to represent progress up the social ladder. Thus, Honda created the Accura in the United States, just as Toyota created the Lexus and Nissan Infinity, since customers worldwide seem to equate changing the brand of their car with proof of financial success. This is why Renault really needs to buy Volvo or Jaguar to add some top-of-the-range brands to its portfolio.

This same rationale applies to the distribution networks. For example, Hanes – the largest apparel brand in the world – is sold in the big department stores but could not be sold in supermarkets, so Eggs was created for this network.

Basically, therefore, the purpose of multibrand portfolios is to better meet the demands of segmented markets, and any reassessment of the portfolio raises the question of the segments to be retained. So when Procter & Gamble decided to dispose of a number of brands in Europe, in 1999, it was because they did not fit into the group's European segmentation – premium, smart buyer and low-price.

Inherited complex portfolios

The question of how many brands should be kept in each market has become a primary concern of all senior marketing managers. The fact is that, due to historical reasons, most firms have to manage a large portfolio of brands. The natural tendency during the growth of firms has been to add new brands each time they wanted to penetrate new market segments or new distribution channels. This was done so as not to create conflicts with former segments and channels which could have endangered their old brands. The vogue of company mergers and acquisitions brought additional brands that managers were reluctant to dispose of or merge with other brands. The size of brand portfolios, therefore, just grew and grew, with increased complexity and waste.

Times have changed though, and now the trend is to reduce the size of portfolios as quickly as possible. There are several reasons for this reverse in trends:

▌ Although it is easy to maintain several brands simultaneously in industrial markets where different brands are sometimes used for the same product to ease relations with distributors, in the retail market it is nearly impossible. The direct consequence is that only a few brands in a portfolio will be promoted, to gain a significant market share. The others will be abandoned.

▌ The concentration of the distribution trade has reduced the number of retailers and has even almost suppressed certain retail channels and small businesses. Brands that were previously uniquely handled by specific distribution channels and sold only in certain stores may now be found in a single wholesaler or purchasing group. This tends to lead to the reduction in their numbers. The trade has also pursued a policy of creating distributors' own brands. This, coupled with the fact that supermarket shelf space is limited, leads to the reduction of space allocated to the other brands, another factor causing a reduction in the number of references or brands themselves.

▌ Industrial production has also become concentrated. International competition has put the emphasis on high productivity and low costs and has led to the regrouping of production units and research and development activities. There is less justification for large brand portfolios when the products, however varied, come from the same factories, and even the same production line.

▌ Consumers, however, still have the last say and despite the fact that the objective of a brand is to clarify the market, their most frequent complaint is that they are confused by the growing number of brands. A company is fooling the consumer if it sells two identical products under two different brand names. Manufacturers respond by rationalising their brands.

▌ The last point, but not the least, concerns brand internationalisation. In many areas today, national barriers no longer make sense. In Europe, for example, class, lifestyle and consumer needs are no longer exclusive to a single country. The luxury goods industry has long been targeting the world market, as indeed have most industrial companies. Not all brands are suited to the international arena, however. The investment required to establish a significant global presence means that firms can only maintain a small number of brands, or indeed just a single one for a mono-brand strategy such as that of Philips, Siemens, Alcatel, Mitsubishi or ABB.

How many brands, therefore, should be retained in a portfolio? It is obvious at this stage that there does not exist any magic formula or number. The question of the number of brands to retain is closely linked to the strategic role and status of the brands. In keeping only a single brand, we are assuming that an umbrella brand policy is possible and indeed pertinent in the market being considered. For decades, the Philips brand included both brown and white products, yet they parted with the latter markets, selling them to the American company Whirlpool. The decision regarding the number of brands to be retained should therefore be closely linked to an analysis of the brand's function in its respective market. Every market can be segmented, by product, customer expectation or type of clientele. This does not mean, though, that a market divided into six segments, for example, should necessarily call for six brands. This depends on their function (do we need endorsing, umbrella, range or product

brands?). It also depends upon the long-term corporate objectives, the degree of competition and the resources of the company. The appropriate number of brands results from a multi-stage, multi-criteria decision process whereby various scenarios are presented and evaluated. A good example of this approach is Michelin.

From single to multiple brands: Michelin

Companies' attitudes to brands are changing – should they adopt a single-brand policy or penetrate markets from several different angles (multiple entries)? Some have decided to concentrate on a small number of international brands, which does not prevent them from promoting strong, local brands in their countries of origin – as l'Oréal did with Dop. Some have concentrated on a single brand (Philips), while others have changed from a single-brand policy to a real portfolio – as in the case of Michelin, the world's leading tyre manufacturer. This last case is extremely interesting.

Initially, Michelin found it difficult to accept the need for a brand portfolio. The company's success was based on the fact that it focused on research in the interests of quality, under a single name – the name of the family that had created a set of values and the means to achieve a valid long-term policy. Culturally speaking, everything at Michelin revolved around the Michelin name. Of course other brands existed, but they were often found in the basket of factories bought locally to penetrate the market – there are 80 Michelin factories worldwide. These factories did not receive any form of innovation or marketing support – they were purely tactical brands.

The problem with this is that the market is segmented. In the US automobile market, for example, there are certainly customers who want the best quality in the world, but there are also customers who want a major brand that offers good value for money, and those who only have US $100 to buy a set of tyres. There are also the 4 × 4 and pick-up drivers who are conscious of changing fashions and want customised tyres. For these drivers, the Michelin brand is too staid. A single brand cannot meet such a diverse demand, whereas a group can. This is why BF Goodrich is positioned as a sports brand in a flourishing market that pays little attention to price, namely the 4 × 4 market.

In the United States, Uniroyal targets the cost-conscious customer and is referenced by General Motors. This market segment is serviced by the Kleber brand in Europe where, following a series of mergers and the restructuring of groups, Uniroyal is still managed by Continental, Michelin's German competitor. In China, the role is fulfilled by the local brand Warrior, which has the largest market share. Distributor requirements also have to be taken into account since distributors are now demanding a quality tyre with their own brand name. Michelin has two policies in this respect. The first is to supply a tyre with the distributor's brand name, according to the latter's specifications. Thus, Michelin manufactures tyres for the Liberator brand, sold exclusively by Wal-Mart in the United States, and for Norauto in Europe. The second is to supply the distributor with a brand that belongs to Michelin. Thus Warrior, positioned as a middle-range brand in China, is used as the name for low-cost tyres in the United States and Europe. The same applies to the Japanese brand Riken, the Hungarian brand Taurus and the Czech brand Kormoran.

Michelin's global strategy aims to encourage customers to move from mass-produced products to middle- and then top-of-the-range products, with the different brands making it easier to emphasise perceived difference. Second, it involves adapting to the market. For example, the Chinese market was for a long time small and elitist because of the high proportion of top-of-the-range vehicles.

Michelin's major share in this market was aided by the ill will created by accidents in Formula 1 racing that were linked to quality defects in the tyres produced by the Japanese group Bridgestone-Firestone. As the Chinese car market becomes increasingly democratic, there is a need to offer new buyers quality tyres, since those produced locally are dangerous at the speeds that can now be reached on the new Chinese motorways. The Michelin group must therefore provide a response to the middle range and the economical segments (if not it will be marginalised), but without endangering the reputation of Michelin as the world's number one brand for quality. The acquisition of the leading local brand Warrior has enabled it to complete its brand portfolio in this segment. In Japan and Korea, there is also a segment of clients demanding products 'made in the United States'. This demand has been satisfied by the acquisition of the US company BF Goodrich.

The last aspect of Michelin's global strategy, required to complete the picture, is that, because tyres are relatively inexpensive to transport, the tyre market is truly global (unlike the car market). Today, the group's Chinese factories manufacture tyres for distributors' brands (private labels) in the United States, and will soon be producing Uniroyal and BF Goodrich tyres for Michelin North America. One day, they will also be making Michelin tyres. Furthermore, the globalisation of production makes it possible to circumvent customs barriers. For example, Japanese car manufacturers cannot export cars to the United States unless they include a minimum percentage of parts made in the United States, which is why these manufacturers fit their cars with Michelin tyres made in US factories. This has enabled Michelin to penetrate the reputedly nationalistic and closed Japanese market through this, as yet, fairly low-key distribution.

This example illustrates the flexibility and adaptation made possible by a brand portfolio – from local brands through middle-range brands to life-style and top-of-the-range brands, not forgetting the connection with the distribution networks via distributors' brands. All this adds up to global segmentation and the logic of globalised product platforms. Even so, as has been seen for the Michelin group, the branches are totally independent and the positioning of the brands is completely different in aviation, agriculture, the truck division and the car industry.

The benefits of multiple entries

At the beginning of this chapter, we looked at the practical reasons why the number of brands had to be reduced, sometimes even to a single brand. They all correspond to a strategy of domination and competitive advantage via low cost. While recognising the market segmentation, it has been decided not to take it into account at brand level, but only in terms of products.

The multi-brand approach, on the contrary, is the logical consequence of a differentiation strategy and as such cannot coexist with a low-cost policy, in view of reduced economies of scale, technical specialisation, specific sales networks and necessary advertising investments. Nevertheless, with the exception of exclusive luxury brands, pressure remains. In order to take advantage of productivity gains, there is a tendency to fragment the production chain in the cause of differentiation at the last possible moment, thus exploiting the benefits of the learning curve. This is the case in the domestic appliances industry, making industrial regrouping a necessity, as well as in the food processing or automobile industries. The policy of having general car brands makes the most of all possible production and corporate communication synergism, and breeds the loyalty of the customer who progresses from one model to another within the same make.

With all the advantages of a mono-brand policy, what makes it necessary to have several brands on the market at the same time?

To start with, market growth. No single brand can develop a market on its own. Even if it forms the sole presence at the outset, once the brand has created the market, its development requires a multiplication of players, each investing to promote their respective differences. The collective presence of a number of contributors helps to promote a market. Beyond their differences, their combined advertising accentuates the common advantages of the product category. A multiple presence is necessary to support the market as a whole. It would not be in Philips' interest to see its competitors in the electric razor market disappear. This would only decrease the number of messages praising the merits of electric razors, which could only benefit Gillette and Wilkinson Sword. Philips should acquire a brand and maintain it as an active brand in the market. In the pharmaceutical industry, a laboratory discovering a new formula could certainly profit from 'co-marketing' it with other laboratories in order to accelerate its impact. An example of this is found in the case of aspartame.

Multiple brands allow for best market coverage. No single brand can cover a market on its own. As a market matures there is a need for differentiation and it becomes necessary to offer a wider range; the market is becoming segmented. A brand cannot be targeted at several different qualities at the same time without running the risk of losing its identity. In any case, consumers and retailers themselves will object to further brand ascendancy. This dual process is illustrated by the case of Rossignol. The company Rossignol followed a dual brand policy:

▌ a mono-brand multi-product policy: the hallmark Rossignol covers its skis, ski suits and ski boots (those coming from its acquisition of the Le Trappeur Brand, since then de-baptised);

▪ a multi-brand mono-product policy, with the Dynastar brand on skis, Kerma brand on sticks and Lange brand on boots.

With 20 per cent of the world ski market, Rossignol is the leading manufacturer. Its share in the upmarket ski sector is thought to be even greater, of the order of 40 per cent or more. This is an area where the company should not offend people's susceptibilities by expecting them to dress from head to toe in Rossignol products. If the world leader wants to grow even bigger, it should be the one increasing the choice, rather than its competitors. In this market, the distribution is still handled by a large number of small independent retailers, who fear the control of a single supplier. This is why each company brand has its own sales force. In the United States the Rossignol company presence is assured by two separate companies, Dynastar Inc. and Rossignol Inc. In the industrial sector, Facom and Legrand, two dominant leaders, successfully increased their hold on their market by creating apparently separate and autonomous brands. This enabled them to find new distributors, who were only too happy to have at their disposal a near exclusive brand, different from those of other retailers in that zone.

Multiple brands offer a tactical flexibility which also enables one to limit a competitor's field of extension. In this way Delsey, the leading European luggage manufacturer, cornered Samsonite. They created a new brand, Visa, positioned to undercut Samsonite prices, while at the same time Delsey restrained them from moving into the top-of-the-range market.

A multi-brand policy can stop any new competitors entering a market. A strong entry barrier to a market can be created by offering a complete range to retailers, with a brand name for each sector of the market. This is why in on-premises in the European market, soft drink companies create barriers to entry by providing the full range of products needed (Coke, Fanta, Sprite and so on).

A multi-brand policy is necessary to protect the main brand image. This partly explains why the Disney Corporation uses a number of brands in film production, for example Buena Vista and Touchstone. This enables them to produce films of every type without endangering the revered Disney name. Similarly, when the success of an innovation is not certain, it would be foolish to risk associating it with a successful brand. This is why Procter & Gamble launched their first liquid detergent under the brand name Vizir and not under the name of the leading market brand, Ariel. The inverse policy was adopted by the Cadbury Schweppes group when it decided to launch its new fizzy drinks not under the brand Wipps but as Dry de Schweppes. This was not only because Schweppes' name helped the sales but because it was thought that the new brand Wipps would reinforce the slightly old and stuck-up image of Schweppes, and would have, in the long term, threatened the value of the brand. In order to avoid having to lower the prices of its leading products, 3M created the sub-brand Tartan which only covers the products where 3M is the dominant leader. This minimises the risk of unwanted cannibalisation. Where 3M is not dominant but a challenger, retailers might be tempted to move directly to the lowest priced alternative from 3M.

Linking the portfolio to segmentation

The brand portfolio is indicative of a company's desire to better meet the demands of the market, not only through differentiated products but also through different brands and therefore different identities. The organisation of the brand portfolio reflects the type of market segmentation chosen by the company. Ferrero (Kinder) bases its market segmentation on narrow age groups and user status, l'Oréal bases it on distribution channels, Legrand on types of consumer motivators, Procter & Gamble and Volkswagen on price brackets, SEB on consumer populations and value systems, Evian on the benefits sought from the water, Guinness on occasions, and so on.

The following sections illustrate how portfolio brands and segmentation are linked.

Socio-demographic segmentation

Although certain people regard socio-demographic segmentation as an outmoded concept, it is still a useful tool when it comes to understanding consumer behaviour and preferences, and as such, can be used to establish a brand portfolio. Ferrero (Kinder) is Europe's leading confectionery company. Unlike the Mars bar, Kinder has developed a portfolio that adheres rigorously to segmentation by age, with the development of needs and situations corresponding to each age group – from Kinder eggs for the very young to snacks for adolescents. All magazine editors produce different titles based on age and gender. Their magazines target extremely narrow age groups and reflect progress at school or rather the child's cognitive development according to Piaget. Lego also has a brand portfolio based on different age groups, from the very young to pre-adolescence.

Psychographic segmentation

To whom should Pernod-Ricard sell Ballantines in China? And to whom should it sell Chivas? Both are some of the best products of Scotland. Clearly socio-demographics do not help. But the general life-style values, the attitudes about heritage vs modernity of the new rich in Shanghai, are not all the same.

Benefit segmentation

A key criterion for segmentation is the main benefit looked for by consumers. Companies can organise their brand portfolio by positioning each brand on one single motivation/benefit, as long as of course it is a profitable business. This is the basis of Danone Waters brand portfolio in Europe. Recent marketing research revealed the following motivations to purchase: status, good life (13 per cent); health (57 per cent); and price (30 per cent). The macro motivation for health needs to be sub-segmented: for 16 per cent it refers to an aesthetic vision of health, for 15 per cent it means vitality and for 26 per cent this refers to specific problems. Danone Waters reorganised its brand portfolio of non-carbonated waters as follows:

- Evian targets 29 per cent of the consumers (those seeking status and aesthetic health).

- Volvic is positioned on vitality (15 per cent of the market), against Nestlé's Vittel.

- New brands were created on physiological needs: Taillefine against Contrex (Nestlé), both on remaining slim, and Talians, another new brand.

- A host of source waters to fulfil distribution expectations of a low-cost brand.

In this portfolio, Evian's role is to be the referent of the market, and to valorise water as much as possible (in addition, this is consistent with the fact that Evian's supply is not unlimited: it takes time for the Alps to create this water). As a consequence, some brand extensions are forbidden, such as the growing area of aromatised waters. The second brand of the group, Volvic, priced 10 per cent below Evian, has the ability to stimulate the market through such extensions. Taillefine (known as Vitalinea in other countries) is actually an extension in the field of water of a dairy brand positioned on 0 per cent fat. To compete in the weight-conscious segment, against Contrex (segment leader, from Nestlé), instead of launching from scratch a new brand, it was decided to extend this global franchise to water.

Attitude segmentation

Unlike most automobile manufacturers, which organise their portfolio along a vertical price line, PSA has chosen to develop two parallel generalist brands, Peugeot and Citroën. In 2007 PSA is the second largest European car manufacturer. What is the basis then of the segmentation? Peugeot has in its roots, its identity, a number of core values (reliability/quality but also dynamism and aesthetics) which address primarily the consumers who like to drive, to master their car, deriving pleasure out of it. Citroën, although its cars share 60 per cent of their hidden parts with the Peugeot models, delivers a totally different driving and living experience. Once a brand with character, ingenuity, innovativeness, it went bankrupt twice before being bought by Peugeot. Reinventing Citroën, PSA has made it a car brand for people expecting their car to foresee the evolution of life-styles (Folz, 2003).

There are strong gains in having two parallel brands, beyond sharing the same platform for manufacturing. Aiming at the same price segment, when one model of a brand starts declining in its life cycle, the other brand launches its own model. As a result, the rate of innovation of the group within each price segment is exceptionally high compared with competitors, a key success factor in modern markets. Also, with only two brands, one avoids the problems of Volkswagen with its four brands largely overlapping, a factor that negatively affects the profitability of the global portfolio. Salespeople trade consumers down by suggesting they consider Skoda or Seat cars, entry brands, which are essentially the same as Volkswagen cars. In addition, these two entry brands now face growth problems: where should Skoda and Seat go? To capitalise on their recently built brand loyalty, they wish to trade their own consumers up with higher-priced models, but run the risk of increased cannibalisation, and of a still larger lack of differentiation from Volkswagen's lower lines.

Channel segmentation

This is a growing mode of segmentation and organisation of brands. The rationale is that channels are fighting against each other. An allocation of different brands to each channel avoids conflicts, price harmonisation problems, and maximises the adaptation of the brand to the motives of channel patrons. In addition, taking the small appliance business for instance, being sold exclusively at Wal-Mart prevents brands from having a presence in the selective distribution channels, which still represent more than 55 per cent of the market in the United States. This is why a portfolio is very helpful in allocating brands to channels.

The paradigm of this approach is l'Oréal: all its brands have to be sold in one and one only channel:

- There are brands for selective premium distribution and department stores: Lancôme, Helena Rubinstein, Biotherm, Kiehl's and Sue Emura.

- There are brands for mass channels: l'Oréal Paris, Garnier and Maybelline.

- There are brands for pharmacies: La Roche Posay and Vichy.

- There is a brand for direct sales by mail order: CCB (Club des Créateurs de Beauté) although this name is really a handicap for the globalisation of the brand.

- There are brands for the professional hairdresser channel: l'Oréal Paris Professionnel, Redken, Matrix, Kerastase and Inné.

The first segmentation criterion is the channel. When this channel is not already present, it is reconstructed thanks to the presence of two or more brands in the channel so that costs can be shared. For instance, if pharmacies in Canada do not sell cosmetics, a specific counter can be developed in department stores, with a pharmacist to assist consumers, selling both La Roche Posay and Vichy.

Of course there is another segmentation criterion: price. In each channel, there is a premium brand and a mainstream brand. Finally each brand epitomises one universal model of beauty. In the mass channels, everywhere in the world, l'Oréal Paris symbolises Paris, and Maybelline the American style of beauty.

L'Oréal's profitability rests largely on this systematic channel-based brand portfolio organisation. It gives this group the ability to price the same product very differently from one channel to another, capitalising on the fact that consumers' price sensitivity is not at all the same across channels and purchase situations. For instance, a hair fixing gel sold to consumers at a hairdressing salon for €9 under the brand Tecniart (l'Oréal Paris Professional) is bought by the hairdresser for half this price, that is to say for more or less the price at which a consumer would find the product under Fructis (Garnier) or Studio Line (l'Oréal Paris) in mass distribution. Kerastase shampoos are sold at €8 to the consumer in a hair salon, but the same product is sold at €2.5 under the Elsève brand at a multiple retailer.

The same holds true for an industrial group like Saint Gobain. This group has created a portfolio of stores aiming at building and construction:

▊ from Platform du Bâtiment, a cash and carry for small general contractors;

▊ to the mass multiple retailer Point P aimed at craftspeople;

▊ to Lapeyre aimed at the DIY expert, able to buy a window and install it without professional help;

▊ and K par K (literally, case by case), a chain of mini-stores selling tailor-made new windows, fully installed.

Of course, the last option is the most expensive (€1,000 for a replacement window, with everything included), but in most of the cases, the windows that need replacing are standard in size and design. It is therefore a standard window that is bought (not a customised one), essentially the same product as could be found at Lapeyre for instance at a fraction of the price, but without any service. The same reasoning applies to the other brands in the portfolio.

Occasion segmentation

An increasing number of companies have become aware of the importance of occasion segmentation (see also Chapter 9). All products are in fact purchased or consumed on a particular occasion. The real issue is therefore to influence the occasions affecting consumption rather than the consumers themselves. In fact, the same person can consume a product in different ways during the course of the same day if he or she has encountered several clearly differentiated occasions. Each occasion gives rise to clearly differentiated expectations, and therefore to a specific type of competition for the brand since, on each occasion, the brand does not encounter the same set of circumstances.

In the case of Guinness, the occasion not only forms the basis of the brand portfolio but also structures the organisation of sales and marketing. Today, there are occasion managers, just as there used to be brand managers. Thus Guinness is positioned on the so-called 'affiliation' occasion typical of the pub environment, while Carlsberg corresponds to the 'release' occasion in nightclubs and Budweiser targets the 'relaxing at home' occasion.

When dealing with occasion segmentation, the first thing a company should do before developing several new brands is to consider whether line extensions could enable a particular brand to expand by gaining a foothold in situations or places that have so far been inaccessible. However, there are limits to this extension, which is where the brand portfolio comes in.

Price segmentation

This is a most classic organisation of the portfolio. The whole Group Volkswagen brand portfolio is based on it, with entries ranging from the low-end Skoda or Seat to Volkswagen itself, Audi and luxury brands like Rolls-Royce. Accor, Europe's leading hotel group, has achieved its success by launching a set of product brands, all positioned at a specific price. The Chanel-Bourjois company has two entries, the luxury brand Chanel, and Bourjois for the mass market.

In the construction market, Velux is one of the most global brands: it stands for roof windows in 40 countries all around the world. It has just introduced Roof Light as a low-cost alternative, targeting the price-sensitive market segment. The price gap with Velux is 30 per cent, less expensive than Velux's main competitors (Roto and Fakro), which are sold with a 20 per cent price gap. It is also sold as a private label of large multiple retailers in the DIY market.

In fact, very few brands have successfully managed to cover substantially different price ranges. It is true that generalist car manufacturers like Renault build a wide range of cars,

from the Twingo to the Val Satis. But they cannot really enter the top-of-the-range market, even when they add a flattering extension to their brand name such as Avontime. This was also one of the aims of their association with Volvo, a brand more easily associated with top of the range cars. Toyota took the approach of creating a separate brand, Lexus. A brand portfolio makes it possible to cover the different price sectors without affecting the reputation of each brand. The Sanford group, having taken over Parker, Waterman and Paper Mate, can specialise its brands in terms of price and style. By reputation, Parker represents the top of the range in each product segment, from the ballpoint pen to the ink pen. Waterman represents the middle of the range. The Whirlpool group allocates to each of its brands a price bracket. The average price of the Whirlpool brand itself must be that of the middle of the market. The average price of the Laden brand corresponds to the lower quartile of the market price range and that of Bauknecht the higher quartile (see Figure 14.1).

A multi-brand portfolio only makes sense if, in the long term, each brand has its own territory. This is not always the case – companies hang on to brands whose images are not different enough to justify the economies of the multi-brand policy.

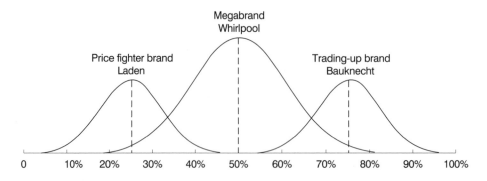

Figure 14.1   Segmenting the brand portfolio by price spectrum

Linking brand portfolio to prescription segmentation

In the business-to-business sector, the type of key influencer targeted constitutes a strategic criterion for segmentation. The market can in fact be segmented according to the decision-making process. Along the value distribution chain several participants play a key role, and brands have different ideas of what they consider to be a key role.

For example, in the aluminium systems market for the residential and service sectors, the leading European company HBS (Hydro Building Systems) has three brands – Wicona from Germany, Domal from Italy and Technal from France – all represented to varying degrees in Europe, depending on the level of maturity and development of the markets. In reality, each brand targets a different operator-prescriber:

▌ Wicona targets architects, research departments and engineering companies.

▌ Domal targets installation companies, general companies that win tenders associated with building sites. It supplies flexible and inexpensive extruded aluminium systems manufactured in its small plants.

▌ Technal aims directly at the end-users via television and a network of well-known registered installers who also co-finance the advertising.

Legrand, Europe's leading electrical appliance company, uses the same type of organisation. Legrand's expansionist policy is based on external growth. In the electrical equipment sector, standards vary significantly from country to county in order to prevent access to national markets. There is also a great deal of intense lobbying by operators who want to perpetuate a situation that creates a network of local markets. The only way to penetrate these markets is to buy the leading local company, which is why Legrand acquired the

Italian company Bticino. It then specialised the brands, allocating Bticino to the prescribers, engineering bureaux and research departments, while Legrand became the installers' brand, offering them a broad and totally integrated range of products in which ease of installation is the cardinal virtue.

Another example of this type of brand portfolio organisation was provided by the UK company Arjo Wiggins, formerly a leading manufacturer of top-quality paper for companies and professionals. This company reorganised its basket of brands to create mega-brands, whose size is critical, bringing together what were previously small product brands under the umbrella of each one. The new organisation is structured as follows:

▌ AW Curious Collection targets creators and designers in advertising and design agencies, since they are the key influencers for projects and creations in which innovation and creativity count for a great deal. For example, the Curious Collection ranges include aluminium and steel paper.

▌ AW Impressions targets the printers who are the key prescribers for a great many of the jobs they are asked to do by companies – for instance, letterheads.

▌ Conqueror targets the general public, the end-users who want a quality paper to reflect their company or their personal image.

Global portfolio strategy

For the last few years big groups have been carrying out a policy of stuffing their portfolios with additional brands, either through acquisition or partnerships, at the same time as extending the product range of some of their brands. Nestlé has become the world's number one food processing company thanks to its acquisition of Carnation and Stouffer in the USA, Rowntree in the UK,

Buitoni-Perugina in Italy and Perrier in France. Philip Morris is another busy company; its foodstuffs division is made up from Kraft (cheeses), General Foods (coffee, cornflakes, confectionery, chocolate) and Jacobs-Suchard (coffee, chocolate).

In the mineral water market, outside Evian and Badoit, the Danone group, which already owns Volvic, has bought La Salvetat, a sparkling mineral water spring. Kraft General Foods owns three strategically important chocolate brands: Milka, Suchard and Côte d'Or.

This trend towards company size growth is partly motivated by the gains that can result from joining forces in research and development, logistics, manufacturing, distribution and sales. Another reason is due to the levels of financial and human resources that are now necessary to compete on the world market. A third reason is the desire to buy a dominant position and be able to restrict the market to a duopoly or an oligopoly. A final reason is to be able to resist the pressure exerted by the concentration of distributors.

It is worth remembering that besides this quantitative aspect, the idea of a portfolio implies a global vision of the competition in a market or category. A portfolio also forces the relationships between one brand and the others in the portfolio to be considered, the idea being that a brand's value can be enhanced by belonging to a larger portfolio. There are several decision grids, the most famous being the Boston Consulting Group's. Hence at Pernod-Ricard one speaks of growth products (Clan Campbell, for example), contributors (Ricard, Pastis 51, Orangina) and the famous cash cows. To these can be added the concept of a 'strategic brand': Pacific, a non-alcoholic aniseed drink, may not be financially interesting but is vital for the long-term prospects as it accustoms future customers to the aniseed taste. Unisabi (Mars) control half the cat food market thanks to a portfolio that is made up from the following

brands: Ronron, Kit-e-Kat, Whiskas and Sheba. These can be classified into strategic, value and tactical brands. Whiskas is strategically aimed at being the invincible brand in the market, with the biggest range, large profits, central consumer benefit (best nutrition) and the most expensive advertising campaign. Sheba is a value brand: its market share in money is three times as much as its market share in volume. Sheba, a high-quality product, is targeted at the most dedicated owners. Ronron is a buffer brand, low in price and hardly given any advertising support; it is there to counter-attack the distributor own brands. Strategic, niche and tactical brands can also be distinguished in the Heineken Breweries.

The case of industrial brand portfolios

In the industrial world, multi-brand strategies either have very few constraints, or there is a multitude that is very often underestimated.

The first case is illustrated by the chemical industry in the agricultural market. As each herbicide brand is associated with one unique active principle, a single company often stocks 500 trademarks or even more!

When a brand is strategic and the portfolio corresponds to the segmentation of the final market, the brand must mean more than a mere difference in name or logo on the product. In this way BASF used to sell paint to coach builders worldwide under two brands, Glasurit and RM. They are, in fact, the same product. In the car world there is a difficulty with the idea of two different qualities – no one would buy the inferior one. The two brands are thus supplementary and not complementary.

Glasurit is aimed at the technically minded coach builder. As its international slogan points out, Glasurit is the 'Preferred Technology Partner'. As its slogan indicates, RM is the thoughtful coach builder partner, 'The key to your success'. It is aimed at the other segment of coach builder who expect service to increase their activity. They see themselves rather as company directors than as painters.

To maximise their chances of success, BASF gave each brand the necessary means to defend itself. Dictating who did what would only weaken both brands and give the advantage to their competitor Akzo. Instead BASF decided to:

- create two separate management teams (as opposed to a common marketing department, which was for a long time the case), based in two different countries;

- have two separate sales forces in charge of the distribution, so as to minimise cannibalisation from the inside;

- avoid all references to the parent company BASF, in order to increase the perceived difference between the two brands;

- develop services in line with the positioning of each brand;

- have different advertising campaigns on a worldwide scale.

This is how BASF maximised its cover of the market. It adapted itself to the two distinct segments of the car refinish market and to the psychology of the constructors. Mercedes, for instance, would not like the idea that its paint supplier also supplied Lada!

The constraints associated with multi-brands are often underestimated in the industrial world, where a brand is considered just a name or a reference in a catalogue. When a brand corresponds to a strategic segmentation this underestimation can undermine or even break the strategy. In the industrial electrical equipment market, the manufacturers have to decide whom to favour, the installing company, the wholesaler/distributor or the end-user. It is impossible to favour all three at the same time. Merlin-Gerin, who concentrated on the distributors, were losing touch

with the fitters. For the latter, the Sarel company was created. This increased the proportion of the market that could be reached, provided that all links with Merlin-Gerin were hidden. In practice, in the various countries they operated in, because of the different turnovers of Merlin-Gerin and Sarel the constraints of their multi-brand strategy were soon forgotten for the sake of saving costs.

- Sarel could sometimes be found in the same office block as Merlin-Gerin's local headquarters.

- The published organisation charts did nothing to hide the Sarel–Merlin-Gerin link. Sound management on the organisational front could instead dictate that, despite its small size, Sarel be directly linked with Schneider's, their common parent company, and not Merlin-Gerin's local manager.

- On occasions, in order to save money, both Sarel and Merlin-Gerin shared the same trade exhibition stands.

The organisation of brands in the business-to-business sector poses specific problems that need to be addressed as such. For example, industrial groups whose growth typically involves the acquisition of companies soon begin to wonder whether or not to keep the brand name of the newly acquired company, and how much independence it should have in relation to the purchasing group.

Furthermore, the engineering culture might make the product central to the group or company identity, while the brand is little more than an appendage and is often the name of a reference. This explains the increasing number of references, registered throughout the world, that preoccupy companies' legal departments and give rise to regular complaints about the excessive number of brands. However, although there may be a brand name in legal terms, there is every reason to believe that these names are not in fact real brands with real market power.

It is therefore a question of reducing the number of brand names in the portfolio, and reorganising them around a few valid mega-brands that serve as an umbrella, a central point of reference. From this it can be seen that the task of rationalising the brand portfolio is in fact indicative of the need to reorganise the business. How do you manage multi-product mega-brands within a structure of business units, knowing that the mega-brand may well cover several business units? Do you need to create a brand committee, from across the business units, that meets on a regular basis with a view to making decisions about problems of coherence in the development of the brand – coherence in terms of products and services, price positioning on the various markets, advertising and catalogues? At this stage, large-scale industry begins to consider how other more 'lowly' sectors – the mass-consumer market and FMCG market – have resolved this type of problem.

The role of the sales force in designing the portfolio organisation

In business-to-business contexts, it is essential to include sales in any consideration of brands since it is ultimately the sales force, the technical and commercial engineers, and the front office who represent the brand. It is therefore important to distinguish four types of brand:

1. The *integrating brand* is usually the corporate brand when it is used to sell a global service to a single client. It is client-centred. To this end, it brings together the skills and synergies of the different business units. The front office and sales force represent the name of the group. Typical examples of this are Vinci, Schneider Electric in its promotion of global services, and Suez Industrial Solutions.

   The integrating brand (usually the group) also ensures the transversality of the product brands at the level of the catalogue, invoicing and shared vision (for example, when the brand/group issues a communication on 'security').

2. The *integrated brand* is usually the name of an acquired company, internationally renowned for a particular application, a particular need or a particular area of expertise. However, the front office and sales force operates under the name of the group

3. The *endorsed brand* only uses the name of the group as an endorsement (as with, a company that is a member of XXXX) and has its own name and front office. This is typically the case when the brand uses a business model that is different from the group's area of expertise.

4. The *independent brand* is presented as completely independent, with no links to the group, which in theory implies separate offices in the different countries concerned. It therefore has its own name and front office and there is no visible relationship with the group. This type of brand makes it possible to overcome the problem of expanding market coverage when a brand is already dominant. Thus, when a brand in the group already covers more than 50 per cent of a particular market, it is logical to launch an independent brand for all those who do not want to work with the first. Furthermore, the independent brand is often used to advocate a policy that contradicts the official policy of the group, in order to increase market coverage without placing the group in a precarious position. The US group Rockwool is a typical example of this type of portfolio organisation.

Linking the brand portfolio to the corporate strategy

So how many brands does a company put on the market? Does it adopt the single-brand or the brand-portfolio model? These are the type of questions asked by modern company and group managers. And this is how group policies evolve, based on the lessons learnt from the development of their market shares and from the diagnosis of the causes of a possible upper limit on profits.

As has already been seen, Michelin is a typical example of a group whose global market share reached an upper limit in spite of the widely acclaimed excellence, not to say superiority, of Michelin tyres, including Formula 1 versions. After years of using a virtually single-brand model, the Michelin group decided to change its policy. Michelin certainly remained the flagship, but it was no longer the only brand to be the focus of innovative ideas and new advertising. In the private car market, Michelin realised the advantages of double segmentation – the first linked to price, the second to the fashion for status tyres. There are customers throughout the world who want value for money but, while recognising the superiority of the Michelin brand, are not committed enough to want to buy Michelin tyres. But should they simply be left, as in the past, to turn to the competition in the form of Bridgestone? The demands of this segment of smart buyers needed to be met, and this was done via Kleber in Europe – an old brand in the portfolio that has been revitalised through innovation, such as the non-puncturing tyre – and Uniroyal in the United States.

But there is also a segment of drivers, usually drivers of pick-ups and 4 × 4s in the United States and Europe, for whom tyres are a kind of status symbol. They want their tyres to be flashy and ostentatious and are not attracted by Michelin because, in their eyes, a brand that focuses on safety, performance and long-term development is too staid, not fash-

ionable enough, not different enough. It is to these drivers that the group dedicated its US brand Goodrich, with a policy of offering a regularly updated range of large, custom-made tyres. However, while Kleber is cheaper than Michelin, Goodrich is positioned in the same price bracket.

SEB, world leader in small household appliances, decided to concentrate on four major brands (Moulinex, Tefal, Rowenta, Krups) to compete with Philips on the international market, while for the moment retaining certain local and regional brands such as Calor, SEB and Arno. However, there was a strong temptation to emulate Philips and its single-brand policy on the domestic market. But this would have been a mistake since there is no point in imitating a market leader on a smaller – and therefore less visible and less successful – scale.

The growth of Legrand, the market leader in small electrical appliances for the residential and service sector, was achieved through the acquisition of specialist brands. Then Legrand picked up 80 per cent of its catalogue and 'Legrandised' it, making it simple, ergonomic, user-friendly for installers and electricians, and above all compatible with the rest of the catalogue (based on the Lego model). Legrand became the reference catalogue for the sector – a business model that is repeated worldwide. So what does Legrand do with the brands it buys? It keeps them to create a protective barrier, using them in a preventative capacity to ensure its domination of the market. The electrical installation market is no different from other markets and Legrand, like other market leaders, creates the desire to be different among certain customers, making sure they do not want to have the same brand as their colleagues and competitors. So, rather than leaving them to turn to its competitors, Legrand keeps their custom by offering – albeit much reduced – specialist brands. As already stated, these brands also create a protective barrier for Legrand so that a newcomer trying to penetrate the market could not replace Legrand in the eyes of wholesalers. It would be offered the place of a small specialist brand.

There are also parameters linked to the distribution strategy that explain why the Volvo truck division that bought Renault Trucks has maintained the Renault brand name. But this can only be understood by taking account of the general strategy of manufacturers in response to the liberalisation of the European car and truck market. Agents are now no longer obliged to deal exclusively with a single brand so, if they want to prevent another manufacturer from filling the breach, it is better to offer two fairly well differentiated brands, but which belong to the same group. And this is exactly what Volvo did. To prevent the risk of any drift towards the lower-priced models (as is happening in the Volkswagen group), the price of Renault Trucks was re-evaluated, which helped to greatly increase the profitability of the division.

The l'Oréal group continues to buy new brands and thereby extend its portfolio. In fact, it is moving out of Europe, is currently targeting the United States and has plans for Asia where it is still a modest player.

To accompany this expansionist strategy, the group buys strong local brands either because they are the leaders in their market segment or because they anticipate the trends of the future. This is why it bought the US mainstream brand of make-up, Maybelline, as well as Softsheen Carson, which specialises in haircare for African-Americans. It has also bought the US brands Redken, a very fashionable haircare brand for professionals, and Kiehl's, a 'long-term development' and 'niche' brand of cosmetics. In Japan, it has bought the Sue Uemura brand. One interesting fact that will be examined in the chapter on globalisation is that l'Oréal subsequently globalised these local brands.

Key rules to manage a multi-brand portfolio

There are a few principles to be followed to optimise the results of multi-brand entries in a competitive market. Although simple to express, they pose implementation problems to organisations built and organised on other principles than brand logic.

Portfolios need strong coordination

Brand portfolios do not manage themselves, they need some form of coordination and even a coordinator above brand level. Experience has shown that companies are 'porous', with ideas passing between departments, across corridors and even between buildings. This gives rise to an – albeit involuntary – tendency to duplicate brands within the same portfolio. The allocation of innovations also gives rise to difficulties, with each brand wanting the innovation before the others. This is why companies have either a brand coordinator or a brand committee responsible for addressing these problems.

Allocate innovations according to each brand's positioning

It is a well-known fact that innovations are the lifeblood of a brand, since they renew its relevance and differentiation. This is why it is essential to have clear and precise platforms (a charter of identity) for each brand – a tool for clarifying the main lines of development and innovation of the brand. This makes it possible to allocate innovation according to brand values and not under pressure from the sales force, which wants each brand to enjoy the same advantages. In fact, it should be quite the opposite – it is through innovation that the brand reveals its identity. It is therefore important to distinguish between exclusive innovations (such as coupés for

Peugeot) and innovations that will be introduced over a period of time (phased innovations), and also to establish the order in which these innovations will be allocated to the brands.

Apart from brand values, positioning and market share also influence the allocation of innovations. For example, there is no point in allocating a specialised innovation (targeting a small number of households) to a mass-market brand. It is far better to reserve an exclusive innovation for a top-of-the-range brand which, by definition, targets a more limited clientele. This is how Elcobrandt manages the allocation of innovations between its mass-market brand Brandt and its top-of-the-range brand Thomson.

However, the rule for allocating innovations as a function of brand identity comes up against another type of logic, the logic of cost reduction. For example, the logic of platforms where an increasing number of parts are shared between different brand models totally contradicts the principle of allocating innovations according to brand value. Nothing could be more a function of identity than Citroën's hydro-pneumatic suspension, which reflects the identity and very essence of the brand – overcoming technical constraints to increase passenger comfort. This suspension – the historic attribute dating from the famous DS models – is only found at the very top of the Citroën range. But if it had to be invented today, what industrial group governed by the logic of production platforms would agree to create and develop such an innovation for a single brand, let alone a single model?

Conversely, to increase the relevance of the Peugeot 607, it could be necessary to adopt the rear-wheel drive option typical of the German top-of-the-range models that set the international standards. The 607 is constructed on the top-of-the-range Citroën platform which, as everyone knows, is a front-wheel drive. Given the design issues and costs of a production line for a rear-wheel drive, it is easy to understand why an industrial group might hesitate to commit itself to this option for the only top-of-the-range model of a single brand. The future lies in partnerships with other manufacturers.

Do not 'rob Peter to pay Paul'

Since the aim is to create a portfolio of strong brands, you must avoid making this mistake. Although it is standard practice to position brands clearly in relation to one another in order to maximise their appropriateness for the segments targeted, a brand should not be prevented from becoming strong. Thus innovation is an integral part of the key values of PSA's two general brands Peugeot and Citroën. Limiting this value (innovativeness) to one brand would destroy the other. There is simply no future for non-innovative brands in the car market.

A brand portfolio is not an accumulation of independent brands but the reflection of a global strategy of market domination

This makes the procedures and intervention of the US Federal Authorities and the European Commission rather paradoxical since, for these bodies, the fact of maintaining a sufficient level of competition is essential to accept or refuse a proposed merger or an acquisition. But there is no point in hiding the naked truth. Corporate mergers and brand acquisitions are largely determined by a single objective – market domination – over and above the synergies and cost reductions achieved by pooling resources. Why did Coca-Cola want to buy Orangina and pay US $1 billion for this predominately local brand? Quite simply because it would have enabled the group to force Pepsi-Cola out of the market. Since it did not have a fizzy orange drink in its portfolio to offset Coca-Cola's Fanta, Pepsico had in fact signed a strategic distribution agreement with Orangina.

A portfolio is therefore a global approach on

the chessboard of competition, with a precise role allocated to each brand. Brand managers should therefore receive a set of instructions so that they understand their role and do not deviate from the global plan by carrying out a series of independent initiatives over a period of time.

A portfolio is not a simple collection of brands that just happen to be there as a result of the vagaries of history, but a well-structured and coherent group in which each brand has a place and clearly defined role:

▊ For example, this may be a financial role, in which the brand contributes to the financing of another brand. This is typically the case of local brands which are leaders in their own market. These brands are and must remain important contributors to enable the portfolio under construction to develop as a whole.

▊ The role of a brand may also be to defend the brand leader. For example, Colgate Palmolive, thinking that a price war was about to be declared on its leading fabric softener Soupline, was prepared to lower the price of its 'flanker' brand Doulinge to avoid lowering the price of its brand leader. Legrand successfully covered the market and rendered its general brand impervious to attacks from competitors by a precise allocation of roles between the Legrand general brand and the specialist brands it had bought and maintained (Arnoult, Planet Watthom and so on). These brands formed an outer barrier at wholesaler level in the event of foreign competitors trying to enter the market. If the wholesalers were disloyal to Legrand and referenced a newcomer, at least they only affected the escort ships and not the flagship.

▊ A brand can also fulfil the role of group banner brand, especially if the brand has the same name as the group.

▊ It is worthy of note that this rationale is equally valid for daughter brands and their role in the construction, reinforcement and defence of the parent brand. It has already been seen that, apart from their specific positioning relating to a particular need or clientele, the 14 daughter brands of Nivea all had a specific role to play and made their contribution to the Nivea 'house' in terms of a specialised area of competence as well as an input of innovation, sensuality and fashion. There is no doubt that they are all very much Nivea brands but nonetheless each adds a personal touch, which is why, in spite of a very strong 'Nivea-ness' and very precise guidelines on how the brand should be presented, it does not come across as monolithic.

▊ The consequence of the portfolio logic is that it is dangerous to acquire a brand leader without the smaller brands that go with it. If Schneider had succeeded in merging with Legrand, it would have been crucial to preserve the network of more modest, more specialised brands maintained precisely because they created an effective barrier that protected the star brand, Legrand. All too often, company rescuers, especially if they are investment funds, do not have this long-term vision. They resell the small brands without taking account of their collective role.

Within all large companies, there is an inevitable tendency to replicate

Take the Seb group, managing four global brands of small appliances: Krups, Rowenta, Moulinex and Tefal. How do we prevent ideas and designs from being known by another and adopted, hence diluting brand identity?

This must be combated since it destroys the competitiveness and imagination of the brands concerned. It is partly because there is always an underlying competition based on prices, since the basic function of groups is to reduce costs by pooling as many resources as possible. The main danger of groups is that, in the interests of making economies (which is quite natural), they tend to erode the identity of their brand in their portfolio by giving the common areas too much prominence when they should be concealing them, or by publicising too much information on the fact that the different brand models come from the same platform. It is crucial to ensure that all the visible parts of these brands are different. Now 'visible' does not only refer to design: companies that buy trucks look at the engine and some key hidden technical parts of the truck, especially for long-haul models.

It will be a challenge for Volvo AG to keep enough differentiating competencies between long-haul Volvo Trucks and Renault trucks. The brand positionings should be the guiding force.

Focus each brand of the portfolio on a specific external competitor

This is one way of preventing the brands in a portfolio from replicating each other, apart from permanent surveillance by the brand committee or brand coordinator. This reminds managers that the best way to cover the market is via the logic of multi-brand portfolios and not by 'narrowing the focus'. Choosing a target competitor for each brand increases the chances of achieving this objective.

A classic risk of brand portfolios is their complexity

This is true since exaggerated fragmentation does not allow each brand to achieve its critical size. This is what business-to-business companies look out for since, for them, a brand – even registered – is merely a name and not a long-term publicity and promotional medium. This is why their legal departments are gradually collapsing under the cost of registering and monitoring trademarks (brand names), and it is what led Air Liquide to reassess its entire portfolio of more than 700

'brands' in 2003. Distributors are also susceptible to the same risk when they rethink their portfolio of distributors' brands (private labels). Decathlon managed to avoid this pitfall; when it changed from the single Decathlon brand to the so-called 'passion brands' portfolio, as many as 13 brands were envisaged before some were merged and the company decided on 7.

The Volkswagen group is currently subject to this risk. Although Seat and Skoda should, in theory, have been separated geographically, the four brands Seat, Skoda, Volkswagen and Audi are still found in several countries, each with its own network of agents. Sustaining an independent commercial network requires a large product range and the ability to create customer loyalty. This means that Seat and Skoda have to move upmarket, but where do they stop and how are they to be differentiated from the very similar newcomers from Volkswagen and Audi? Price is one solution, but the publicity based on the fact that these four brands come from the same factories and even the same platforms has created the ideal conditions for internal cannibalisation. The agents selling Seat and Skoda use it as a sales argument.

The growing role of design in portfolio management

Design plays a crucial role in the battle for differentiation. It is design that structures customer expectations, design that evokes brand values, creates visible differences and develops new favourites on mature markets. This is why it has to observe several key principles:

▮ The principle of radicalisation. Design cannot be vague – since the strategy is to attack the market with a small number of brands, they must be clearly defined, with a specific design, all the more so since organisations have a natural tendency to soften the hard edges, which leads to a resemblance on the shelves that has a dramatic effect on perceived differentiation. Radical design must also compensate for the increasing lack of differentiation due to the industrial logic of platforms. There is no place on today's mature markets for half-hearted designs. If there is a brand identity, it must be clearly visible.

■ The principle of externalisation. If the company is responsible for defining the story to be told by each brand, that is, creating its identity, it is important to seek outside help for the design itself by appointing a designer for each brand who is totally committed to that brand. Thomson did the opposite and entrusted the design of its four brands, Thomson, Saba, Telefunken and Brandt, to the same designer, Philippe Starck, who was a brand in his own right. This is why, within an organisation, design must be positioned at brand level, not corporate level, even if this requires robust coordination to avoid replication between brands, a tendency that is all too frequent. But this risk is avoided if the company appoints an external designer, for each brand, who is inspired by its strategic platform.

■ The principle of business. The function of design is to promote and develop business, not art. Design should not become self-absorbed. For example, the aim of designing a coffee pot is not to enable consumers to invite their friends round to admire their coffee pot, but to offer them a good cup of coffee. In short, the purpose of design is to enable the brand not just to look good but to function efficiently.

■ The principle of courage. The key question in design is whether a design can be properly tested. Certainly, the ergonomics and functionality of a product must always be tested at user-status level. But apart from that, what is the relevance of a few individuals' (interviewees') opinions of a design when it is, by definition, the

opinion leaders (the press) who decide whether or not a product is in good taste when it is launched in a few months' or years' time? Design is a risk. In the car sector, for example, how can you predict which design will be perceived as avant-garde in another four years, in the event that the brand could be said to be a trend setter? Renault took the risk with its audacious (some will say over-audacious) design. But four years ahead of its time, it is difficult to forecast perceptions with any degree of accuracy.

Does the corporate organisation match the brand portfolio?

A brand is only successful if the factors governing its production work together in a coordinated and motivated manner. The success of a group logic and a brand portfolio cannot be assessed without analysing the conditions of its development and, above all, the type of organisation. Since this is not widely publicised, or may even be deliberately played down, it tends to be overlooked as a key factor in the success of a brand portfolio policy.

The main risk of a brand portfolio is the gradual de-energising of the brands, reduced to the state of increasingly undifferentiated 'outer casings' that are little more than publicity devices. This is exacerbated by the fact that the economic press only talks in terms of groups and therefore publicises the fact that brands that were once different are now produced by the same group. Its readers, often opinion leaders, are within their rights to ask certain questions, behind the bodywork, what remains of the brand identity? Do Jaguars still have a Jaguar engine or do they have a Ford engine? Will the specificity of Saab disappear with its integration within the GM group?

The essence of a brand is differentiation. Anything that detracts from this is a threat –

within the context of a favourable economic equation, of course.

To a certain extent, over-centralisation is responsible for the loss of differentiation. At Fiat, the different brands are managed within the same department, with Alfa Romeo alongside Lancia and Fiat, a type of organisation that leads one to wonder whether the company still believes in its brands. Conversely, PSA – Europe's second largest car manufacturer, almost on a par with Volkswagen – may use the same factories but Peugeot and Citroën remain separate organisations with their own product plan, marketing, design, publicity, sponsorship and, of course, distribution network (Folz, 2003). Volkswagen has abolished the VAG (Volkswagen Audi) network and given each brand its own distribution network. It has to be said that the sales force in the VAG network had a strong tendency to push the Volkswagen models rather than the very similar Audi models, which were 10 per cent more expensive.

Part of Seagram's problems can be explained by the over-centralised organisation of its international brands. The development of international campaigns at all price levels is a classic tendency among all centralised organisations. It is significant that the first thing the buyer of Seagram did was to decentralise the organisation of the brand portfolio. Thus the management of Martell, the flagship of cognac worldwide, was relocated in Cognac where famous brandy is produced, while Chivas was returned to London.

LVMH, world leader in the luxury market with such famous brands as Christian Dior, Christian Lacroix, Vuitton, Moet, Hennessy and Tag Heuer, has an interesting business model. The group manages 45 international luxury brands. When asked about the upper limit on the number of brands in such a portfolio, the group's CEO, B Arnault, replied that there wasn't one. In fact, success in the luxury sector depends on there being three types of people able to work together – in design, management and marketing – but

this is impossible to achieve at a centralised level. At LVMH, however, each brand is a 'house', a mini-company, and this makes it possible to create the optimum conditions under which extremely talented people from these three areas of competence are able to work together. As heads of their 'brand-company', they are more motivated and their remuneration is directly proportional to their financial results and the international reputation of the brand.

Although it not as widely known, l'Oréal functions in the same way. It is significant that within the l'Oréal group, reference is made to the Garnier 'house', the Lancôme 'house' and so on. These 'houses' are autonomous operational units that manage their business with an international approach.

In the field of distributor brands, changing from the single brand – usually a store brand – to private labels also affects the organisation. The recent transformation of Decathlon (the world's fifth largest retailer of sports clothing and equipment), from the Decathlon brand to the so-called 'passion brands' portfolio, had far-reaching repercussions for the organisation – is it in fact possible to develop 'passion brands' within a centralising structure? The first people who have to be inspired by this passion are those within the organisation, the managers and the teams, then the co-designers, the fans and the opinion leaders. There is a need to recreate a formal autonomy.

Auditing the portfolio strategically

Companies regularly reassess the relevance of their brand portfolio. Numerous matrices have been devised to help them do this – all derived from matrices used for the evaluation of the activity portfolios created by consultants such as the Boston Consulting Group, McKinsey and Mercier. These matrices incorporate profitability, the competitive situation and the potential for growth. But can matrices for the analysis of an activity portfolio be simply converted into matrices for the evaluation of a brand portfolio?

There are two possible levels of analysis. The first is the intra-brand level which evaluates the portfolio of brand products (sub-brands or daughter brands) according to the criteria mentioned above – are they in declining or non-cash generating segments, what are the growth vectors for the future? The second level asks the same questions at multi-brand level, on the global chessboard of actual and predictable competition. The lines and columns of the matrix are growth and profitability. The markets are then shown as circles whose size reflects the actual size of the market. Brands are represented as portions of these circles (markets) where the portions reflect their market share.

The most classic way of structuring a portfolio is to divide the brands into groups according to attractiveness and function. This makes it possible to identify:

- Global brands, which should theoretically be the largest source of growth in the brand contribution, and as such should receive the lion's share of investment in advertising and promotion.

- Local or regional growth brands, which have the potential to one day become global brands.

- Local or regional brands that can be qualified as 'fortress' brands and which are often the historic market leaders, 'entrenched', and therefore very profitable. There is therefore a strategic interest in maintaining these 'fortress' brands since they in fact finance the development of global brands in their own country. They are often brands in mainstream segments.

- Local or regional 'cash-cow' brands, which have a low growth rate but a strong contribution margin.

Another form of audit consists of regularly evaluating the ability of the current portfolio to ensure the profitable coverage of future markets. Is the current portfolio the right response to market developments and competitive logic?

Thus, in the insurance sector, everyone is familiar with the growth of new distribution methods, like the telephone and the internet. An insurance company cannot afford not to be represented in this way. However, since the conditions offered are so very different from those offered by the network of general agents and brokers, they need to be represented by a specialist brand. This is how UK insurer Aviva structured its brand portfolio. Eurofil was created to cover the growing segment of low-cost car insurance without creating conflict with Aviva's other insurance distribution networks.

The segmentation of a market by user status (linking volumes, expectations and competitors to the use made of the product) also makes it possible to identify unexploited pockets of growth in the current portfolio. The first question to be asked is whether a range extension would offer an opportunity to gain a foothold in these areas. In this respect, all Nivea's sub-brands reflect this determination to exploit all the potential sources of growth on the beauty-care market by capitalising on the single Nivea brand.

When this cannot be done, a company must have the courage to launch a new brand. For instance, in 2003, after trying everything under the global Barbie brand, Mattel decided to launch the new Flavas brand.

Auditing the portfolio can also reveal that it does not constitute enough of a barrier to prevent competitors entering the market, or even an incitement for them to leave. For example, it is impossible to find Orangina on the French TGV (high-speed train) network or in many airports and stations, even though it is the second largest soft-drinks brand in the country. The logic of the operators of the café-hotel-restaurant network is to choose a soft-drinks distributor offering a complete portfolio – from cola to lime and fruit juice. So clients of the Coca-Cola Company receive Fanta (a fizzy orange drink) and Minute Maid (fresh orange juice) but not Orangina. This therefore creates a local monopoly and prevents free choice among end consumers.

A local and global portfolio – Nestlé

How do the multinationals organise their brand portfolio to improve the efficiency of their brands simultaneously? Nestlé is an interesting example of this.

The Nestlé portfolio of 8,500 brands is organised by geographical status and role. Together they create a 'hierarchy of brands' in which each product is associated with at least two brands, at different levels in the hierarchy (not to mention brands of ingredients). The geographical criterion allows three groups of brands to be distinguished – international, regional and local brands.

These brands fulfil different functions and roles, depending on the customers, and represent the principal families of brand architecture. There are 'family brands' (or source brands), range brands, product brands and endorsing brands. Eighty per cent of the Nestlé Group's activity is brought together under six strategic corporate brands – Nestlé, Nescafé, Nestea, Maggi, Buitoni and Purina. Seventy strategic international brands, designating either ranges or products, come under – or even outside – the umbrella of these six corporate brands. They include Nesquik (an extensive range of chocolate milk products), but also product brands such as Kit Kat, Lion, Friskies and the mineral waters Perrier, San Pellegrino, Vittel and Nestlé Pure Life.

A third category of brands groups together 83 brands known as 'strategic regional brands', which are regional rather than international, such as mineral waters like Aquarel and Contrex, the Nuts bar, and Herta cold meats. Finally, there is a fourth category of local brands sold only in their country of origin.

Thus the Nestlé brand refers to several levels and roles:

- It is a corporate brand and as such acts as an endorsement for all the products and brands in the group. This endorsement function means that the corporate brand usually appears on the side of the packaging or on the labelling on the back.

- The Nestlé brand is also one of the six strategic corporate brands, with the status of a family brand or source brand. It covers categories as diverse as baby products, products for children, chocolates, ice cream, chocolate bars and fresh dairy products.

- The Nestlé brand is sometimes simply a product or range brand, as for example Nestlé chocolate or Nestlé condensed milk. These are the basic products, the symbolic products that lie – both literally and figuratively – at the heart of the Nestlé galaxy.

To help identify the different extensions of Nestlé the commercial brand, according to category, the categories have a different symbol. This means that, beyond the unity, there is recognition of the fact that what customers expect from a yoghurt is not the same as what they expect from baby food. Similarly, there is also a logo and symbol for Nestlé the company, that is, the corporate brand.

It is worth pointing out that 20 per cent of Nestlé's turnover is not produced under the six famous 'strategic corporate brands'. This is the case with mineral waters, for example. Perrier, which is classified as a recreational drink for adults, is indeed managed within the Nestlé Water division. But this division does not have a brand – its identification is a matter of internal organisation. For clients the world over, Perrier is simply Perrier.

15

Handling name changes and brand transfers

One of the most spectacular aspects of brand management, but also one of the most risky, is the changing of brand names. Some cases immediately spring to mind: Philips–Whirlpool, Raider–Twix, Andersen–Accenture, Pal–Pedigree, Datsun–Nissan. The industrial world is now used to external growth by company acquisitions and to the creation of large groups such as Novartis, Zeneca, Alcatel and Schneider by the fusion of identities which were previously separate and independent.

This growth in brand transfers is normal: it is the consequence of capitalisation, the key to modern brand management. The reorganisation of multi-brand portfolios and the reduction in the number of brands has meant that the products under brands due to disappear will have to be transferred to one of the remaining brands. The same applies for companies themselves. This approach is risky: the abandonment of a brand means that the market is going to lose one of its benchmarks, one of its choices or even one of the loyal customers' favourite choices. The risk of losing part of your market share is high. This is why the transfer of a brand is a strategic decision

that is not to be taken lightly. To this day, empirical studies on the question are either scarce (Riezebos and Snellen, 1993), or private and confidential (Greig and Poynter, 1994). It is possible though, thanks to the accumulated experience of ten or so cases, to define the conditions for successful name changes on a local level or multinational plane.

Brand transfers are more than a name change

Brand transfers are too often thought of simply as name changes, though admittedly this is the most risky facet of the change. In the customers' minds a well-known name is linked with mental associations, empathy and personal preferences. However, a brand is made up of many components, which cannot be reduced to just one, the name. In fact, when you examine the numerous examples that have occured both in Europe and the United States, the situation is far from simple. Many of them involve other changes in the marketing mix.

Some brand changes are also product

changes. What disturbed Treets fans, apart from the loss of a product they loved, was that M&Ms included two different products: peanuts covered in chocolate and a sweet similar to Smarties. It was therefore a transition from a simple and familiar situation to a totally confusing one where all references had changed, as, indeed, had the product itself. When Shell changed the name of its oil from Puissance to Helix it also modified the characteristics of the product. However, the fact that these characteristics are 'hidden', hardly perceptible by the customers, meant that this was not a risky move for Shell. The change of the oil formula could be used as an alibi for the introduction of the new name.

As regards name changes, the risks associated vary immensely depending on whether we are dealing with product brands, umbrella brands, endorsing brands or source brands. Examples of the first two cases are Raider/Twix and Philips/Whirlpool respectively. The change only affects the one and only nominal indicator of the product or products. Conversely, Puissance has become Helix but still remains under the mother brand Shell. Changing a name when the product is defined by a hierarchy of brand names is far less problematic.

With self-service, visual identity has become crucial as an aid to customers to quickly pick out their brand. Distributors' own-brands capitalise on this: their imitations, which aim at confusing the customer, rely less and less on similar names (for example Sablito against Pépito) and more and more on near identical copies of colour codes of the national brands that are targeted on the shelves (Kapferer and Thoenig, 1992). In this way, in the UK, a fierce conflict arose between Coca-Cola and the retailer Sainsbury, whose colas totally imitated the Coca-Cola colours: red for classic cola, white for sugar-free cola and gold for sugar- and caffeine-free cola. Conversely, some brand changes are accompanied by profound modifications of the colour codes. Thus, the brown Shell Puissance 5 oilcan became the yellow Shell Helix Standard oilcan. The long and gradual change from Pal to Pedigree was accompanied by the adoption worldwide of a new colour, bright yellow, striking and eye-catching, to reinforce the impact on the shelves. Since colour is the first thing that consumers notice in a self-service situation, how risky such modifications can be is all the more evident.

The shape of packaging is the second most important visual recognition factor. This is why, despite the savings that could have been achieved by adopting a unique European oilcan, Shell immediately refused to abandon its easily recognisable and very practical 'spout' can. Part of Shell oil's added value comes from this can. Finally, brand transitions can be accompanied by changes to the logo or trade mark as well as to visual symbols. As regards this last point, the impact of the disappearance of visual brand symbols shouldn't be underestimated. Replacing Nesquik's gentle giant Groquick by a rabbit in some countries for reasons of international coordination is playing with the relationship children have with Nesquik. The same applies to people associated with a brand. The disappearance of emblematic figures can have drastic consequences for a brand.

Finally, with written and musical slogans now under copyright, it has to be realised how important they are, as they are what people will remember. When Raider was changed to Twix, Mars hesitated but decided not to keep the same brand music. Music is one of the vehicles of a brand's personality. A slogan is also, in the long run, an integral part of a brand and can now be put under copyright. The famous slogan 'Melts in your mouth not in your hand' was lost when Treets became M&Ms.

Reasons for brand transfers

What are the aims behind the numerous brand changes that we are witnessing? The reasons are numerous:

▍ Many local brands are bought with the intention of transferring their activities to the buyer's international own brand. In this way, the latter becomes truly global. This is what Electrolux is currently doing.

▍ The creation of worldwide companies leads to the same results. Ciba-Geigy and Sandoz merged under the new name Novartis. Alcatel was born out of the joint venture between CGE and ITT. In a few years all the company brands of both companies and even a few product brands (such as their telephones) were given the Alcatel name.

▍ Firms decide to transfer brands when they decide to stop some of their activities. So when General Electric wanted to withdraw from the small domestic appliances market, Black & Decker took over with the agreement that they could only use the GE name for a limited period. No brand would want part of its image to be controlled by another company. It was the same for Philips and Whirlpool: the takeover of the former's 'white goods' activities by the latter included the agreement that the Philips name could only be used for a limited period. Looking to concentrate only on its 'brown' products and small domestic appliances, Philips only conceded its name to Whirlpool temporarily. Whirlpool bought the white activities for the European market share it immediately gave them, as well as the chance to be the world's number one domestic appliances manufacturer.

▍ The search for the critical size also provides an explanation for brand transfers. The Mars group abandoned its European brands Treets and Bonitos to merge them into the global brand M&Ms. To compete against McDonald's, the European Quick bought Free Time and changed its trade name.

▍ Brand transition is a common tactic used when trying to access a foreign market. It is basically the same ploy as the 'Trojan Horse'. The local industries in a country are often highly protected using all kinds of domestic regulations to prevent foreign product invasions. The electrical equipment market is a typical example. Desperate to grow internationally, Merlin-Gerin bought the famous Yorkshire Switchgear company as a way to penetrate the British market. The transfer was carried out progressively. Yorkshire Switchgear received the endorsement of Merlin-Gerin, then the names were switched round before finally being replaced uniquely with Merlin-Gerin UK, now Schneider Electric.

▍ The fact that international markets are now more homogeneous than ever before is also an explication for the number of brand transfers. Companies that favour global brands are replacing all their local brands with global ones. This is why Raider in continental Europe became Twix, Pal changed to Pedigree, and why the paint brand Valentine will be transferred to Dulux, the worldwide brand of ICI. In order to make sure European motorists can spot their products in all European countries, Shell gave their lubricant a unique name, Helix, and where possible used the same colour codes.

▍ With time, the name attached to a brand can become a burden to the brand's development, for example when wanting to access new activities, international markets or simply when wanting to rejuvenate a brand. Corporate names that attract bad will have to change: Philip Morris became Altria Group, Vivendi became Veolia. BSN became Danone in order to instantly gain international recognition, which would have been lengthy if not impossible with an acronym.

▍ Brand transfers can also be the result of lost court cases. For example, Yves Saint Laurent had to abandon the name of its brand of perfume Champagne in several countries, turning it into Yvresse. The sportswear brand Best Montana lost its case against the luxury brand Montana and had to become Best Mountain.

Moving local names to a single one, such as an US name, allows the organisation to delocalise plants easily under this foreign name. This also has fiscal reasons. The foreign name can receive royalties from the subsidiaries, reducing local tax liabilities.

The challenge of brand transfers

Brand transfers are everywhere. This is hardly surprising since this is the age of mergers and acquisitions, which always give rise to the rationalisation of ranges, products and brand portfolios. Companies have to choose between brands that have hitherto been competitive with parallel ranges. On mature, low-growth markets, the need to make economies, create synergies and increase efficiency has the same result. Finally, globalisation brings its share of brand transfers to the advantage of the global brand. For all the above reasons, reducing the number of brands is the order of the day.

This explains the wealth of publicity announcing – if you know how to read between the lines – an imminent brand transfer. For example, the Swedish company Electrolux, the world's leading manufacturer of household appliances, prepared the worldwide transfer of its local brands – the historic leaders of their market, acquired country by country. It acted as the endorsement for these local brands – Zanussi Electrolux in the UK, Arthur Martin Electrolux in France, Rex Electrolux in Italy, and so on – and appeared as such in the promotional publicity. It has to be said that, in 2003, only 15 per cent of sales were made under the brand name of this international group. The aim was to increase this figure to between 60 and 70 per cent by 2007, so that 55 per cent of

consumers would include Electrolux among the 'three brands they have in mind when entering an electrical appliance store' – what is known as an 'evoked set' or 'consideration set'. In 2001, this could be said of only 21 per cent of consumers. In 2007 the local names became Electrolux.

Berated by financial analysts the world over for not having enough global brands with a turnover of more than US $1 billion, the Unilever Group made the decision to reduce drastically the number of these brands in a process known as the 'path to growth'. The group's Elida-Fabergé division played a pioneering role – by reducing the number of brands from 13 to 8, growth increased from less than 2 per cent to 11 per cent.

But this objective of reducing the size of brand portfolios also creates challenging problems in certain product categories. This happens when the brands to be merged are well established and do not have the same positioning on the market. For example, the famous detergents category is not particularly profitable compared with other categories since distribution costs are extremely high and the market is fragmented. Many of the smaller brands no longer justify the promotional support. Throughout Europe, Lever has organised its portfolio in three price-related segments – the premium segment with Skip (in competition with Procter & Gamble's Ariel), the smart buyer segment with Omo for example, and the economy (or low-price) segment with Persil (except in the UK where, for historical reasons, Persil replaced Skip). The question therefore arises, given the market shares and Lever's declared intention of concentrating its business around strong brands, how to unite the brand in the smart buyer segment with the brand in the economy segment. The difficulty becomes all the more apparent since in many countries, these are well-established brands that, over time, have forged a very specific bond with a section of the public. The issue should involve the distributors who, throughout Europe, are wondering about the future of the low-price segment, positioned just above their distributors' brands. Should this segment in fact be allowed to survive?

Another illustration of the risks associated with brand transfers is provided by the example of Phas and La Roche Posay, two brands of cosmetics in the l'Oréal Group that were merged in 2000. Each represented approximately 15 per cent of the market share in a sector that was losing momentum, namely pharmacy. This should make it possible to begin internationalising the brands under a single banner, with critical mass. Named after a thermal spring used to treat skin disorders, La Roche Posay is associated with a guarantee of proven effectiveness in the treatment of skin conditions. Its business model was based on recommendation by dermatologists. Conversely, Phas was a brand of cosmetics – with no dermatological endorsement – for skins that were extremely sensitive to ordinary make-up. Its strength was hypo-allergenic tolerance rather than effectiveness. It is easy to understand why this – albeit necessary – transfer ran the risk of diluting the brand capital for La Roche Posay. The brand was going to have to put its signature to products formerly under the Phas label and which had no guarantee of effectiveness.

When the risks are too great, it is better to avoid them and choose another strategy.

When one should not switch

The internationalisation of companies raises the question of the globalisation of brand portfolios. This involves changing the name of the products or services of a well-known and very popular local brand to that of a less well-known and less familiar international brand. However, before considering how a company goes about making such changes in order to effect a brand transfer, the following caveat should be borne in mind. There are occasions when this transfer

should not be made, if it presents too great a risk for the business and the brand capital. Thus, when BP bought the German Aral service stations in 2003, it decided not to change the brand name as it had done in California when it bought Arco. In the same year, Shell bought the other major German service-station group, DEA, but decided to bring it under the Shell banner. So who was right – BP or Shell?

In fact, they were both right. Aral is a very strong local brand, almost a national symbol, rather like the Continental tyres fitted on all Mercedes manufactured in Europe. So why would BP run the risk of severing this extremely rare bond that generates customer loyalty, in a sector already threatened by 'commoditisation'? Conversely, although DEA has a good customer service record, it does not inspire the same emotional attachment and its transfer would therefore be less risky. Customer service relations are created by the people who work for the company. So, if these people remain in situ, the continuity of satisfaction is maintained and customer loyalty guaranteed.

There are other instances when a brand transfer should not be made to the advantage of a new, global brand and when it is better to retain the local name, for example when the meaning of the name to be internationalised proves problematic in the other country. Procter & Gamble's German competitor Henkel could not extend its product brand 'Somat' – designed to make glassware shine – in the UK since the word 'matt' is the opposite of shiny.

There is no shortage of examples where, to an outsider, the local brand seemed little more than a legacy from the past but was regarded locally as an icon. This happened in the case of many leading Eastern European brands, which the multinationals decided had to be replaced by the global – European or US – brand. But they had not taken account of the consumers who are often extremely emotionally attached to the local brands that are part of their everyday life and past memories. The Danone Group had to reverse such a decision in the Czech Republic. After abandoning the Opavia brand in favour of the global Danone brand, it had to reintroduce Opavia – famous for its biscuits and the country's favourite food brand – because it was a national symbol.

In this respect, the Bel group was well advised not to pursue a potential brand transfer which involved replacing the German brand Adler, famous for its processed cheese portions, with the international mega-brand, The Laughing Cow, whose prototype is also processed cheese portions. However, the symbol of the Adler brand, familiar to all Germans, has long been the imperial eagle. It is hard to imagine the juxtaposition of two more paradoxical animal logos.

L'Oréal is pragmatic when it comes to brand transfers. In line with its expressed intention of developing mainly via its 17 global brands, the group bought Maybelline, a brand of make-up sold on the US mass market. In the space of a few years, it launched the brand in 80 countries but to do so had to effect a transfer with the local brand in the principal countries concerned. The problem was that the local brand was often a strong brand that was popular with both distributors and customers – Jade in Germany, Colorama in Brazil, Missiland in Argentina, Gemey in France – while Maybelline means nothing in these countries. The group has carried out a deliberate policy of double branding for five years, introducing an increasing number of US concepts and innovations but, even so, there is still no question of setting an exact date for phasing out the local brand. Yet, as far as the financial analysts and major multinational distribution groups are concerned, l'Oréal has achieved the desired effect – by increasing the sales of co-branded products in each country, the group can say that Maybelline is the leading international brand of make-up in the mass-market sector.

When brand transfer fails

Companies that are overconfident in themselves often underestimate the emotional attachment created by local brands, long since written off by the advocates of globalisation. In so doing, they do not realise to what extent brand transfers can destroy value and, above all, the value of the market share. This is illustrated by the example of Fairy in Germany. In 2000, the buzzword at Procter & Gamble was 'globalisation' at all costs. In Europe, the group introduced global segmentation and all the brands that did not fit within the framework were eliminated (Kapferer, 2001, p 52). Furthermore, local brand names were to be replaced by the global brand name corresponding to each segment.

In Germany, Procter & Gamble had been successfully marketing a washing-up liquid under the name Fairy for years, with the brand reaching 12 per cent of the market share in terms of value. In the middle of 2000, the Fairy brand became known as Dawn, the name of Procter & Gamble's international brand. Nothing had changed except the name, which is a good measure of the power of the brand. However, in spite of colossal investments to inform people that Fairy was now called Dawn, the market share plummeted and, in the last quarter of 2001, stood at just 4.7 per cent, whereas it was still at 11.9 per cent on the day before the name changed. It was estimated that, in 2001, Procter & Gamble sustained a loss in turnover in Germany of US $8 million (Schroiff and Arnold, 2003). The group made the same mistake in Austria when it tried to replace Bold with Dash. In view of the destruction of value caused by these two costly mistakes, it was decided to return to the previous brand names.

What was the reasoning behind these two brand transfers? Because Fairy used the same consumer benefit as Dawn, the ability to cut through grease, Procter & Gamble thought that the brand transfer would be easy. However, this transfer was not even attempted in the UK, possibly because Fairy was positioned according to a different consumer benefit from Dawn. But the brand can also be much more than a name – it can be the sign of a certain product guarantee. Local brands inspire customer loyalty through their origins, their being a part of everyday life, their proximity, their confidence (Schuiling and Kapferer, 2003). There is a real emotional dimension in the attachment to certain brands, as has been shown by Fournier (2001).

So what lessons can be learnt from this example? A transfer must first of all take account of consumer opinion. A transfer must offer some form of benefit and create value for consumers. This is the key to successful transfers. Second, in the process of convergence implemented within the multinationals, the principle source of productivity is the product platform. But people tend to focus on the visible part of the product, the actual change of name, whereas this is not in fact the real issue – far from it. In globalisation, the homogenisation of names should be the last problem to be solved. There are also a great many fringe benefits to be gained by unifying and reducing the number of different packages, non-standardised parts and product plat-

forms. Furthermore, productivity is vastly improved by the convergence of brand platforms, which makes it possible to use a single agency and employ the best designers. It is not important if a product has to have a different name in different regions. To quote just three examples, a leading line of male toiletries is known as Axe in Europe and Lynx in the UK, a brand of washing powder as Skip in Europe and Persil in the UK, while the Opel brand in Europe is Vauxhall in the UK.

Analysing best practices

There is not much academic research on brand transfers. It is however possible to draw on some brand and business models to clarify the conditions of a successful transfer. We selected them because they illustrate very different market situations and brand role, from mere impulse to highly risky purchase decisions, from products to services.

From Raider to Twix

In the autumn of 1991, continental Europeans were informed by a massive advertising campaign that the chocolate bar Raider was to be henceforth called Twix, Twix being the name used everywhere else in the world from New York to Tokyo and London. The difference

Figure 15.1   When rebranding fails: from Fairy to Dawn (P&G)

from the Mars group's previous brand transfer (from Treets to M&Ms) where everything had changed, including the product, was that this time, great care was taken not to disturb the customers. Nothing was changed apart from the name. It was a success.

Why was the brand change necessary? Philippe Villemus, the marketing director of Mars, explained (for more details see Villemus, 1996) that Mars was a worldwide group with six brands each worth more than a billion (US) dollars, and that it wanted only to have mega-brands which satisfy the five following conditions:

▪ is able to meet an important, durable and global need;

▪ represents the highest level of quality;

▪ is omnipresent all over the world, and within every one's reach both physically and financially;

▪ creates a high level of public confidence; and

▪ is the leader in their segment (when this is not the case the brand is simply removed, like Treets and Bonitos).

For legal reasons it can happen that a trademark cannot be registered in a particular country or region. This was the case with the Twix name in continental Europe. As soon as the legal aspect had been dealt with by the acquisition of legal rights in certain countries, the group did not hesitate to rename Raider and to give Europe the global name.

What were the objectives behind this change of brand? In the first instance, it was to gain more market share and increase sales, otherwise, according to Villemus, there would have been no point to the operation. It is important to remember that a brand transition is not an exercise in style, but a unique opportunity to increase the share of the market. It is a competitive move. A second objective was to have a global brand. A third objective was to reduce production, packaging and advertising costs. A fourth objective was to make its management easier. Finally, it was desirable to have one brand name so as to make the preparations easier for the intended brand extensions towards new sectors such as ice creams.

Raider had a strong brand equity in Europe so the transition was no small matter. It was the second most popular chocolate bar after Mars and it had an annual volume growth rate of 12 per cent. This was thanks to its specific concept and its slogan, which included a physical description of the product as well as its benefits for the customer. In France, for example, spontaneous recognition was 43 per cent, assisted recognition was 96 per cent and that of the slogan was 88 per cent. Eighty-five per cent of all adolescents had tried Raider and 44 per cent bought it on a regular basis. Knowing this, Twix was marketed as the ideal snack for adolescents and young people between the ages of 15 and 25.

Even though the customers thought that the transition was rapid, in truth it took over a year. From October 1990 to October 1991, the Raider's wrapping carried the words 'known globally as Twix' and for six months after the transition, 'Raider's new name'.

The communication objectives given to the campaign by the marketing director were:

▪ to communicate clearly and simply that only the name was changing;

▪ to transfer all Raider's values to Twix;

▪ to quickly obtain a high brand awareness within the target group of young people (30 per cent unaided, 80 per cent assisted);

▪ to make the change popular using the alibi that the new name was in tune with the rest of the world, and that Twix was a global brand for young people all over the world.

The key elements of the success of the operation were due to the flawless implementation of the strategy:

it was very rapid: 15 days to change every-thing in one country (the whole transfer in Europe took three months);

Mars made a big event of it, which maximised its visibility and the awareness created;

promotional activities at sales outlets contributed to the impact and trial of Twix;

finally, great care was taken to ensure good coordination with field activities. It was decided that, even if it meant buying back stock, on the day of the transfer no stocks of Raider should be left in any shops.

Looking more closely at the different means of communication that were used, we see that the packaging was the first medium. It was used for one year before the transfer to warn customers of, and to familiarise them with, the new name. It was used for six months after that to explain the transfer. In order to meet the communication objectives the advertising campaign was characterised by:

a strong emphasis on the pack-shot to maximise the recognition;

the interruption of all communication of the Raider brand six months before transfer day to hasten the drop in its awareness;

a high-impact European commercial starring David Bowie;

a strong concentration of means: in three weeks as much as the total advertisement budget for two years was spent on tele-vision advertisements alone (it is now easy to understand why it was absolutely vital that all Raider packets were removed from all sales outlets).

In shops, Twix was given prominence and was put on visible display. Twix was the focal point of all the sales force, and all other brands were sidelined in terms of priority. Supermarkets had, of course, been informed

well in advance. The bar code was kept the same so that supermarkets did not take Twix to be listed as a new brand and hence claim a listing fee.

Six months after the operation, Twix's market share was the same as Raider's had been. But from then on there was only one brand name, one factory and far less complexity. Due to its young and interna-tional status, Twix's image was more modern than Raider's.

Looking back, all the decisions taken seem logical. All successful operations give the impression of being easy. But the decisions were not taken without debate. For example, some people recommended improving the recipe and announcing 'even better'. In the end it was decided, after reflection on the opposite approach of Treets/M&Ms, to change the product as little as possible. It might also have been a good idea not to change the Raider music in the change-over film to Twix. Was the modification necessary? It is said to have disturbed some customers, which goes to show just how much the brand's music is an integral part of its identity and personality.

From Philips to Whirlpool

On 1 January 1989, Philips and Whirlpool joined together to create the world's biggest household appliances group, Whirlpool International, owned 53 per cent by Whirlpool and 47 per cent by Philips. This partnership was formed with the intention of attaining a significant global size which would enable and ensure the development of a long-lasting manufacturing firm. Besides, Philips wanted to concentrate on its core activity. Finally, both companies were highly complementary, in their plant layout and industrial capacity, in innovation and in their geographic market coverage. Philips was the most important domestic appliances brand in Europe. Whirlpool, for its part, was the number one in the United States, Mexico and Brazil. With 11.1 per cent of all the goods manufactured, Philips Whirlpool overtook Electrolux (9.6 per cent) to become the world leader in the household appliances market. In 1990 the Philips Whirlpool brand was launched in Europe by a spectacular advertising campaign (US $50 million). In 1991, Whirlpool bought the remaining 47 per cent held by Philips. In January 1993, the Philips Whirlpool brand became Whirlpool in all communications, but the dual brand was kept on its products. In the last countries to make the switch, Philips was removed from all products in 1996. Via this brand transfer Whirlpool became the world number one domestic appliance brand. The importance of what was at stake and the risks involved during the brand transition become evident when one looks at the significance customers put on a brand when buying durable goods which are perceived as high-risk investments. According to a study carried out by Landor, in Europe Philips was the second-most powerful brand over all sectors. In France, another study showed that when customers were asked to mention names of brands from any sector off the top of their head, Philips was placed fifth after Renault, Peugeot, Adidas and Citroën (Kapferer, 1996). Nevertheless, it is worth noting that Philips' market share and its public brand recognition differed from country to country. This is why it was quickly apparent that it would be impossible to carry out the change in different European countries simultaneously. In the same way, the guarantee role of brands in the domestic appliances market rules out a sudden, quick transfer as was the case with Raider/Twix.

In January 1990, the assisted brand awareness of Whirlpool in Europe was non-existent. This was why a stage-by-stage progressive approach was decided upon. This included a Philips Whirlpool stage before Philips was abandoned. The case is different, therefore, from that of Black & Decker's takeover of General Electric's domestic appliances activities in the United States where both names already had a good reputation.

Another reason favoured the stage-by-stage approach. In order to ensure global coherence, Philips' products left in stores would have had to have been bought back, as Twix had been for the transfer to Raider. But this of course would have been impossible for both practical and financial reasons.

So what was Whirlpool's transfer strategy and why did they choose it? In the first instance early research had shown that customers perceived favourably the Philips Whirlpool partnership. Both companies had very different images. Whirlpool had potential, it evoked change, fluidity, movement and dynamism. It had the ideal qualities required to give the brand transfer a positive image. The fusion of both companies gave the Philips Whirlpool brand an ideal image, the dynamism of one was tempered by the solidarity of the other. Research showed that the Philips Whirlpool couple was perceived as 'sure and dynamic, solid and robust, classic and stylish, reliable and innovating'. In Europe, the arrival of Whirlpool was seen by consumers as bringing new impetus to Philips, a touch of high tech to a reliable classic brand, imagination to a brand characterised by experience.

The first thing that needed to be done was to decide upon the nature of the dual brand and its visual form. To start with, should it be called Whirlpool Philips or Philips Whirlpool? Tests revealed that the first option did not inspire confidence and that it evoked a confused perception. People associated it with jacuzzis and all 'water equipment'. On the other hand, Philips Whirlpool evoked a healthy equitable partnership or even a slight predominance of Philips. Only a minority thought that it referred to a Philips product range like that of the Philips Tracer razors. The second question regarded the graphic trademark. Should both names be written on the same line or one on top of the other? The first choice was adopted because it inspired an image of partnership and looked better.

With regard to the communication, what target should it be aimed at? Obviously the priority was the distributors. Only 20 per cent of domestic appliance customers visit a shop with a specific brand in mind, and only 10 per cent, ie half of them, actually buy that brand. This shows the importance of sales outlet staff in the sale of these products. Whirlpool started in 1990 a considerable communication effort aimed at retailers – this is a little known facet of brand transfers. This, of course, was addressed to the big European or national retail bosses, but it was also used by Whirlpool's sales force with customers, shop owners and sales staff whose opinions were so influential on consumers. Moreover, Whirlpool's image was that of an innovating leader, so merely confining oneself to innovations in products and services would have been limited. Whirlpool brought about a revolution in producer–distributor relations, a new approach that distributors weren't accustomed to, which not only touched on services but market information and more besides. As regards the consumers, the plan was to reassure them as quickly as possible by the rapid acquisition of brand awareness and a strong image of quality and innovation.

These communication objectives had several important operational consequences. On the one hand, wanting to associate with Whirlpool an image of quality and innovation implied that the brand transfer on the products themselves had to take place progressively, in line with the launch of new products and the rejuvenation of Philips' old ranges. If this had not been the case the project would have suffered from the Talbot-Chrysler syndrome, where the only thing that was changed on the vehicles was the name on the bonnet. The Whirlpool brand on its own was not to be found on an old product. Launching a new brand implies taking great care over the early impressions the brand would create among the European audiences. Giving Whirlpool a quality image involved prohibiting all promotional advertising of any sort in the media during the first years of establishing the brand in Europe. Finally, as it

is impossible to pursue an image objective and an awareness objective at the same time, it was obvious that to the classic advertising a media action had to be added so as to quickly reach the required level of brand awareness before the final brand transfer, ie two-thirds of the assisted awareness of Philips. It is certainly true that, in the case of durable goods, the involvement of consumers is low when they are not actually engaged in the buying process – which is most of the time. When the consumer is not considering a purchase, the means of persuasion that should be adopted are very specific. When consumers' attention disperses, a multiple contact approach should be privileged, even if received incidentally. This calls for a high number of (gross rating point) *GRP*. Consumer resistance can become weak; in this case contact should be received in an agreeable ambience to benefit the effect of the affective transfer to the brand. Finally, when the consumer is not ready to make a cognitive effort one must repeat the consumer benefits of the brand rather than point out the difference between specific products.

This is why, in some countries, Whirlpool invested large amounts of money sponsoring prime-time TV programmes. This choice was no coincidence; they represent viewers' favourite moments on the most popular channels, and are often associated with a relaxed family atmosphere. Thanks to this strategy, the brand awareness made considerable progress. In all the countries where only traditional commercials were used, the awareness reached was less significant.

It was indeed important to separate the treatment of the Philips brand in the media and in sales outlets. In the media, it was necessary to stop mentioning the brand as quickly as possible, otherwise the brand would only have been reinforced when the objective was to see a decline in its spontaneous awareness. This is why, during the short period when the dual brand existed, Philips Whirlpool adverts finished with the dual brand but the signature tune only mentioned

Whirlpool. This was to ensure that only this brand was associated with the innovations.

As early as January 1993, it was decided to remove Philips from all TV adverts. This put an end to any reinforcement of Philips' awareness. What is more, it sent the message to retailers that Whirlpool, the market leader, no longer needed the Philips guarantee and that the transfer programme was ahead of schedule.

On a European level, how was the multiplicity of countries to be dealt with? Taking into account the differences in the market shares and the brand equity that Philips had from country to country, all monolithic approaches were ruled out. Some countries wanted to pass to the single brand, Whirlpool, quickly. Others would have liked more time: where Philips' reputation was excellent, it could not be removed overnight if the objective was not only to maintain market share but also use the transfer to increase it. The order in which each country was to have the Whirlpool brand transfer was decided using a multi-criteria analysis, which took into account, for each country:

▌ Philips' market share;

▌ the presumed reaction of the distributors (based on an ad hoc survey);

▌ the strength of the brand in the eyes of consumers (brand recognition, evoked set, preference);

▌ the influence of retailers on the customers' decisions;

▌ the feeling that the management in the country was ready for the abandonment of the Philips brand.

Recent research on the transfer from the local brand Libertel to Vodafone seems to indicate that a dual branding phase does not in fact transfer values from the former to the latter. In fact brand values must be built, they are not simply transferred by this tactic of dual naming for a while. Attaching two names is creating a third one. In the Philips–Whirlpool case, the dual naming gave saliency (brand awareness) to Whirlpool, but did not transfer the values of Philips onto Whirlpool. Its first objective was to maintain the consumer or customer loyalty and the trade franchise, which would have deserted if the name Philips had not been maintained as an endorser of the totally unknown American newcomer.

Transferring a service brand

Services need to be analysed separately. On the one hand, unlike product brands, service brands have nothing to show: they are intangible. Their name is the proof of their existence. Brand awareness and saliency is of vital importance. On the other hand, their nature can make brand transfers easier, because they are often tied to a place (the specific geographical location of service delivery, of 'servuction'). In addition, the driver of loyalty is the direct relation with the salesperson, agent or staff. This is not too say that the brand is of no importance: when BP and Shell took over two German networks of petrol distribution, much care was taken in handling the situation. Not recognising the name and visual identity of the gas station they have historically, if not ritually, used acts as a deterrent for many German consumers.

However, global brands are created by replacing local leaders by global names. This is how Axa built its global worldwide brand recognition, acquiring local leaders and instantaneously moving them to Axa, as a way of immediately indicating internally what the strategy was, namely to become the local arm of the first worldwide insurance brand. In the service business, hesitations and dual brandings may create some internal doubts about the future strategy, and lead people to defend their former identity instead of thinking of the new future. As a result, the internal phase comes first and foremost in service brand transfers. A lot of discussion groups must be created, for the sake of communication and release of tensions, whereby all parts of the company that has been taken over can express how they see the future and concretely build the pathways to become the quality arm of the new global brand. Two recent cases are interesting in that respect, Accenture and Orange.

The Accenture case

On 7 August 2000 the International Arbitrage Court, in the case between Andersen Consulting (AC) and Arthur Andersen and Andersen Worldwide, ruled that among others things, AC would not be allowed to use its existing name after 1 January 2001. It had less than 145 days to transfer its intellectual, technological and reputational capital to a new brand.

The first step in this process consisted of an internal wide-scale and in-depth interrogation on what was expected from the new brand:

▎ What new values should it foster?

▎ It should attract what types of new consultants?

▎ How could it contribute to the development of business?

▎ How could it reinforce differentiation?

▎ What changes could be suggested?

The process of name choice was also internally managed by means of a 'brandstorming' process. All employees were asked to participate. On 1 September 2000 various names were proposed by Landor, a globally known design agency. On 21 September, 2,677 proposals were made internally, for such names as Future Creation Group, Global Already, Deep Thought, Mind Rocket and

Global Curves. On 5 October, 68 names were screened for legal registrability, international semantic connotations, availability of the domain name and so on. On 12 October, 29 finalists were submitted to a vote at the firm's Miami Congress, and 10 of these were discussed by a brand steering committee on 23 October. Finally, on 25 October, Accenture was selected. This name had been proposed by the Norwegian senior manager, to convey putting the accent on the future. To help fulfil the mission (reinventing the business to win in the new economic context), the key words linked to this brand would be agile, visionary, well connected and passionate.

As a rule, communicating a new brand aims at creating an immediate boost of unaided awareness and suggesting the new values of the brand. To regain its status within the very closed club of the big five accountancy/ consulting firms, a blitz communication strategy was chosen in this case. US $175 million was budgeted to reach these two objectives worldwide, and the goal was to reach 30 per cent awareness in three months.

Here again, the emphasis of service brands is on employees. For the sake of an efficient brand alignment, 50 work groups were created to manage the name change in 137 countries. This involved creating a new internet site, internal communication kits, communication with 20,000 managers in client companies, communication with thousands of potential candidates, and of course communication for introducing the name on stock exchanges. As the global campaign put it, the company was renamed, redefined, reborn.

Moving to Orange

On 30 May 2000 the UK's third largest mobile phone operator, Orange, was acquired by FT, the incumbent national French operator. As with all former monopolies, FT needed a commercial brand to carry its offer and eventually extend it to other services internationally. British Gas had created a precedent with the creation of a commercial brand to offer services to households, including its traditional utilities but also insurance and financial services. The goal of FT was to make Orange the second largest operator in Europe, after Vodafone. In 2005, the objective was to be present in 50 countries.

In each country, the strategy was to rename the local operating company as Orange, exploiting this opportunity to capture the high-consumption-rate young consumers segment. Up to then the former monopoly telecomms organisations had not looked very attractive to them. The success of Orange in the UK had been based on a disruptive approach to the mobile phone business, epitomised by the simplicity of its name. In fact, its six brand values were dynamism, modernity, simplicity, transparency, proximity and responsibility. These values contrasted strongly with those of the UK's former monopoly telecomms company, BT. Orange in the UK had been a challenger brand, proposing a true relationship with consumers, an innovation after decades of monopoly offerings.

In the countries in which Orange would now operate, the challenge became to make a local former monopoly, often still the market leader, acquire the brand and adopt its values. The goal of the brand transfer was first and foremost to get across the 'Orange attitude'. The difficulty was to align the company itself, the employees and the newly acquired brand values in each country. The process was divided into three steps: 'Let's build Orange' (defining the brand's values, and understanding them), 'Let's live Orange' (understanding how to put these values into action), and 'Let's launch Orange' (the communication launch itself).

The second phase involved an in-depth immersion of each employee in the new values, both individually and within his/her functional team. Scores of focus groups, internal meetings, and global sessions would slowly build up that understanding over a period of one year.

The director of human resources would naturally be part of the process of 'Let's live Orange'. For instance, an evaluation grid was created, to help measure how each participant stood in achieving the brand values. In addition, to foster group adhesion, this form was to be completed by all the members of the individual's team, as a measure of how others saw each person's performance. Two other regular features, 'all in store' and 'all on line' were intended to help employees understand in practice the challenges of selling the Orange way.

The 'Let's launch Orange' phase was designed to provide the opportunity to make a strong impression, accentuating the idea that a radical new offer was now present in the marketplace. The media were key in conveying this impression and helping to immediately capture new consumers. Employees were also involved, and each one was sent a cassette and CD-ROM outlining the full launch process. Finally, all existing clients were to be contacted individually to tell them about the name change and what it would mean for them.

How soon after an acquisition should transfer take place?

There are two paths to growth: organic, internal growth, or the acquisition of brands and products from elsewhere. Companies are increasingly coming to rely on external growth. In fact, we are used to hearing that one company has bought another: Google buys YouTube or MySpace. In industrial electrical equipment, Hager grows in Europe through buying out local leaders (such as Ashley and Klik in the United Kingdom) – leaders that have market share, reputation, a loyal client base and the respect of distributors. The question then arises of whether these brand names, with their reputations at the local or technical specialist level, should be retained.

Four factors explain the enthusiasm for external growth:

▨ It is a consequence of saturated markets: growth is achieved by buying the market share of another company, linked to a headline product, an innovation and a brand.

▨ We can also note a degree of dissatisfaction with internal innovation. Spotting external tendencies and snapping them up is the faster route.

▨ It is the end result of the tendency to fall back on the 'core business', on what the company is best at and where its competitive advantage is greatest. This is why groups sell their so-called peripheral businesses. Thus Bel (Laughing Cow, Kiri, and so on) sold its 'regional' cheese business (for example le Rouy) to Lactalis (Président and Société) in 2003. During these acquisitions, the question of names and architectures raises its head. For example, should le Rouy be called le Rouy by Président?

▨ Finally, these acquisitions are often part of a strategic plan consisting not only of buying market share, but also of developing a European or world brand.

The question of architecture immediately arises for innovations stemming from external growth. Can the acquiring company impose its name from the start, without losing customers – in both senses of the word 'lose'? For example, Philips bought the Sonicare company (no relation to Sony), a specialist in oral hygiene the world over. Sonicare sold an innovative product under its name, a revolutionary electric toothbrush, which had become the reference among dentists. What should this innovation be called once it had entered the Philips fold, and what brand(s) should it have? Sonicare has a good reputation in the United States and Japan, but less so in Europe. The reverse is true for Philips.

Should it then follow the same architecture, in accordance with the dogma of globalisation? Or should it adapt to the markets?

Fundamentally, three phases of the decision process can be identified:

▨ First is the question of coherence. Is this innovation coherent with the brand the organisation hopes to build? Imagine that Philips wished to reinvent its brand worldwide around the values of sense and simplicity. Philips wants to be recognised – to a greater extent than current image studies show – as a leader in innovation with sense, innovation that is close to and simplifies daily life. This kernel identity of two values allows it to carry out an initial sorting of innovations that do or do not follow this direction, and of companies to buy and not to buy. Sonicare was in fact coherent with Philips' new desired identity. In contrast, when we worked with Citroen on its repositioning, the brand's executive director reminded us that since the products designed three or four years ago had not yet been launched on the market, it was impossible to enact a public repositioning. It would have been immediately contradicted by the models to be launched, themselves the fruit of a previous vision of what Citroen would become.

▨ The question of strategy: should the product be launched alone, or should it be part of a strategic alliance? In the case of an alliance, the daughter brand is almost obligatory, since with co-branding neither brand can innovate graphically.

For example, Philips allied itself with the Dutch coffee giant Douwe Egberts to create Senseo, a coffee-maker that makes the best coffee at home, without having to pay the high prices for Nespresso. Note that in the latter case, Nestlé appears to have retained mastery over the project, since the daughter brand is a variation on the word Nestlé, combined with the generic word espresso, whereas the coffee maker is made by Krups, part of the Seb group.

▌ The third question is that of acceptability to the market. In short, there may be a difference between the brand's 10-year vision and its current situation among particular targets. One must not mistake desire for reality. In this case, the brand cannot act alone. It needs an ally, an intermediary: this is the role of the daughter brand. For example, in order to penetrate and dominate the feminine shaving market, Gillette uses a worldwide daughter brand, Venus. Furthermore, it follows the endorsement brand architecture. Venus is written in large type, with Gillette mentioned in small letters at the bottom of the packaging.

In truth, Gillette is a masculine brand – some might even say macho. 'Masculine perfection' is the brand's international slogan. This image profile is hardly likely to generate value among the majority of women. They insist on maintaining their self-concept – even though there are genuine advantages to the product. Gillette remained pragmatic and discreet, and emphasised Venus, a reassuring hymn to femininity. This example shows clearly how the choice of a name arises from the choice of an architecture. The product is indeed Venus – by Gillette.

Depending on the gap that exists between the brand's current profile and the expectations of the target of the innovation in question, different architectures will be selected. The more the image is a handicap, the more likely it is that reduced visibility will be selected (maker's mark architecture). Otherwise, it is possible to go as far as dual branding architecture, or source branding.

▌ The fourth question is planned evolution. In fact, the architecture selected in the first phase is only provisional. Remember that one of the functions of the innovation is to provide the brand's identity kernel with traits that it had previously lacked. Once these traits have been acquired, and the gulf that existed between the brand and the target has been reduced, the architecture originally chosen no longer has any reason for existing. It needs to evolve. This is expressed in Figure 15.2, showing a decision-making model developed with the Dutch consultancy agency VODW.

If everyone is in agreement with the final objective of a brand transfer, the timetable and the phases of the operation are crucial. As the schema shows, as the brand becomes more coherent with the market's expectations, under the effects of communication and time, the brand can take greater visibility on the product and move from a discreet endorsement or maker's mark to that of the unique source or masterbrand in the final phase.

The decision-making tree is based on the image diagnosis among the targeted clients – whether and how much the overall brand (later to become the only brand) is in step with the specific category expectations in the country in question. If it is already at 100 per cent, then a rapid brand change is desirable. If it is low, then the image of the generalist brand risks causing offence and damaging the product's sales, making the competing sales forces' job easier. This is typically the case during the takeover by a generalist of a highly specialised brand, fetishised by a particular segment,. It is important to not forget the final objective (to finally arrive at a single name), but to proceed in stages.

We have sketched out the stages to indicate the different phases to be followed in the graphical relationship between the product-brand and the global brand. Through the different stages, an evolution of perception occurs, bringing the global brand's image closer to the expectations of the category's or segment's customers in the country, or the segment in question. This makes it possible to

$t_1 \longleftarrow t_0$

100/0

Present image   66/33
of the brand
to be transferred   50/50

33/66

Brand	→	Brand
Brand First name	→	Brand
First name by Brand	→	Brand First name
First name	→	First name by Brand

← →

% of perceived values similar   % of values contrary
with those of the brand to   to the values of the
be deleted (first name)   target and category

Figure 15.2   A stepwise approach to brand transfers (relating the type of transfer to the image gap) (Kapferer/VODW)

move to the final stage, above. This process should be undertaken at a regional level: even for global brands, business is always local. Therefore, these progressive transfers should be implemented along a local timetable, determined according to the local image diagnostic.

Managing resistance to change

It is a fact that brand changes arouse hostility, which can be a real danger in terms of the effect on market share. The source of the opposition can be found with consumers, with distributors and also internally. From the clients' point of view a brand change is not a superficial act, but it affects the very identity of the product. There is therefore a perceived risk of altering the implied contract. This is especially the case in emerging countries. A change of design is interpreted as a sign of a counterfeit product. It is also the case in the service industry. When there is a lack of any tangible element the brand becomes the heart of all contractual relations. Besides, we have already

seen that a brand can only be successfully extended to cover a new category of products if it is seen to be legitimate (Chapter 9). This was Black & Decker's principal challenge when it took over General Electric's domestic electrical appliance activities.

A successful brand transfer also has to deal with distributors. In the industrial world with long distribution channels, retailers tend to choose a few complementary brands that they stick with. Having promoted these brands, they have inevitably linked their reputation with them and their customer loyalty derives from them. To change a brand is therefore like questioning 10 or 15 years of good and loyal service. A retailer loyal to a brand expects something in return from the company. A simple presentation of the strategic reasons why a company should replace brand X by brand Y is not enough, even if the products remain identical. There must be some compensation. The situation is completely different when dealing with supermarkets who care far less about brands apart from their own. Here their analysis is much more down to earth: is this an opportunity to receive a listing allowance for the new brand or a contribution to the temporary hassle incurred by the transfer? Also, distributors will not hesitate to criticise any operations aimed at placing a weak brand under the umbrella of a strong one in order to improve its shelf prominence.

Finally, one must not forget the internal and human elements of resistance. Generally speaking, all brand changes have to pass through managers who will inevitably be attached to their own brand. When l'Oréal decided to give Ambre Solaire a modern technological dimension by placing it under the umbrella brand Garnier, the division came up against numerous pockets of resistance in Europe. In the UK, where Ambre Solaire had a good name and Garnier was unknown, the partisans against the change pushed forward the fact that the future signature brand Garnier had little recognition. The opposite was true in France: the Garnier management argued on the basis that Ambre Solaire suffered from a bad reputation, and that the change might devalue their brand. In the end the operation did take place and Ambre Solaire sales increased from €4 million to €20 million.

The precautions taken by the British group ICI when it made an apparently insignificant brand change, transferring the leading paint brand in the French market Valentine to 'ICI Dulux Valentine', illustrate the need to take into account these three stumbling blocks. The precautions aimed solely at the personnel showed just how much they were involved. The personnel at Valentine were attached to their brand so much that they saw themselves as its trustees and looked after it as if it were their own. This is why they took any brand modification to heart, and the dividing line between evolution and dispossession was very fine. The importance of internal communication during this brand change was therefore absolutely crucial if feelings of loss of identity were to be avoided and all thoughts of disappearance kept at bay.

As a result, one of the first things to be done was the setting up of a selective information policy. Only the people who worked closely on the project were informed of progress. The project itself was given a code name rather than a title which would have given the game away. Afterwards, when the deadline date was imminent, the personnel were told. The operation was presented as a step forward and not as the end of the Valentine company once bought by the ICI giant.

The sales force was gathered for a big presentation on the evolution of the European market, on ICI and on its Dulux brand. Particular attention was given to the worldwide importance of Dulux, to its long history (founded in 1930), to its sympathetic and relaxed communication strategy (projection of advertisements), to its content and to its corporate values. The change was presented not as a big event but rather a natural evolution which would bring real and important benefits to the customer.

This gathering was held six months before the brand change. A notable consequence of this date was that all internal rumours were avoided, at least on a large scale.

Some of the distributors were informed very early on of the name change. It is worth remembering that they were part of the cause of the decision to change, because they also favoured a European extension and therefore wanted a European brand. They could not therefore oppose the principle of a brand change. All that was needed was to show them that everything would be done to assure a smooth transition.

Some retailers were informed a whole year before the name change directly by Valentine managers, when internally only the people responsible for the project knew about it. On the other hand, shopkeepers were forewarned by Valentine sales representatives only three months beforehand. Finally, department or shelf managers were informed by mail, just before the change, that on 23 March 1992, ICI Valentine was to become ICI Dulux Valentine. The letter was accompanied by a free luxurious badge of the Valentine mascot, a panther. And when the Valentine sales force next came by they distributed an ICI Dulux Valentine watch (blue background, 12 yellow stars for the 12 hours of the clock and a black panther in the middle) which was such a great success that some people still wear it.

In fact, if this brand transfer was carried out without any hitches, it is because it was presented as an adaptation to meet the constraints of the retailers, and therefore more for their benefit than a revolutionary brand change. What is more the new packaging was intended to make the distributors' life easier and the product clearer and more comprehensible for the consumer, and it permitted a more homogeneous organisation of the shelves.

It had already been established that it was more practical, from the clients' point of view, to organise shelves according to purpose (paint for floors, for ceilings, for wood, for steel, etc), rather than according to brands. Thanks to the new packaging, customers could easily find all the information they needed, paint for the kitchen, for the bedroom, etc.

What is more, Valentine made sure that the brand change would not upset the shelf layouts and that no extra work was needed by the distributors. They also decided that at no point should there be the two different brand names on the same shelf. This is why 180 people carried out the necessary relabelling when the transfer took place in each of the 620 shops concerned. What is more, a freephone number was made available to the retailers should any kind of problem occur.

Tests to measure consumer reactions were also carried out before the brand change. Tachytoscope tests (successive presentations of the old and new packaging) revealed that both versions of the packaging were equally well associated to the brand.

Another benefit for the customer was the opportunity to quickly reorganise the whole range of paint products into sectors according to the main kinds of uses. In normal circum-stances this would have taken three years. This makes the customers' choice much easier when they do not know what kind of paint to use in the room or on the surface that they are repainting.

Factors of successful brand transfers

Although the cases looked at and their particular situations vary a lot, it is still possible to draw an overall lesson from the principal experiences in this domain. For fast-moving consumer goods a good summary is by Philippe Villemus, former marketing director of Mars, who remarks:

> Above all, this kind of operation requires a combined effort from all the company departments: production, logistics, sales force, marketing and general management. All will be concerned and any false note will be a source of problems.
>
> Second, it is vital that this event be considered an opportunity and not a constraint. The transfer must be an occasion for reappraisal, when the strengths and weakness of the brand can be rethought, and an occasion to gain new market shares by profiting from the extra attention that the new brand will have for a while. In this respect the transfer has to be seen positively by the personnel, the distributors and the consumers, so the benefits that the new brand will bring for each of them must be specified.
>
> A brand transfer cannot be improvised, it must be well prepared. The retailers, prescribers, opinion leaders and the personnel must all be warned well in advance.
>
> The time factor is crucial: one must wait until all the customers are aware of the change, and if the operation has to be carried out quickly, one must have, at one's disposal, the communications means necessary to be able to let them know.
>
> You cannot force a brand change on retailers. Not only should they be informed but everything possible should be done to facilitate their work. That means no double stock. The same product codes should be maintained. This approach not only reduces demands for listing allowances, it makes the rotation of the new brand easier. In the case where a new code is

introduced, the chances are that the optical check-outs will not be able to read them because the new reference has not been registered at a central level nor in the shop's computer system.

Even when the transfer is to take place in transitional phases, like a double brand phase before the actual inversion, one should still opt for the quickest time frame. It is true that the average purchase frequency should be taken into account; the frequency of paint purchases compared to that of ultra-fresh produce leads to very different minimal transitional periods. To linger too long only results in being bogged down and losing one's way. This was the case of the Pal to Pedigree transition which took several years. Retrospectively, the process would have benefited if it had been shorter, or even, as in the Raider/Twix case, instantaneous and accompanied by a strong advertising campaign.

Nothing is more shocking to the customer than the strategy of 'fait accompli', imposed without warning, information or explanations. The loyalty to the brand is dented by this sudden disaffection and lack of consideration. Lessons have been drawn from the Treets/M&Ms mishap.

(Villemus, 1996)

A typical 'fait accompli' is the sudden change from Coke to New Coke on 8 May 1985. That event was called the marketing blunder of the century. In fact the brand change nearly created a revolution in the United States that forced the return of the classic Coca-Cola to the shelves and the disappearance of New Coke. After having advertised during more than a century that Coke was the real thing, it was odd to force consumers to change without any warning. Consumers need to be respected: they want to understand how a change will create value for them. A brand transfer is always an act of violence, unlike mere extensions which preserve the consumers' freedom of choice. A brand is much more than a name, it is an emotional link (Fournier, 2000). One does not lose a friend without harm and pain, even resentment.

Today, most brand transfers are explained to clients or consumers. They are forewarned and reassured. They learn how the new brand intends to provide more value to them. Also, in order to not lose consumers at the point of purchase, the former brand recognition signs are maintained for a while. Finally, a tag line can be added on the packages, after the shift, reminding that 'this the new name of …'.

Last, but not least, to achieve successful brand transfers it is important to know what characteristics the customer identifies with the brand and where its equity lies. The Shell Helix case is revealing in this respect. Having decided to replace all its local lubricant brands with one European brand, Shell left the coordination of the transition to its subsidiaries. France was a particular problem in view of the share of the automobile oils market enjoyed by the self-service supermarkets (more than 50 per cent). The strategy that was adopted consisted of the launch in September 1992 of a top-of-the-range oil called Shell Helix Ultra. It was added to the local Puissance range of products, keeping its characteristic can with a practical spout, but in a different colour, grey. Shell Helix Ultra was launched in the automobile press and sold only in Shell service stations. The print advertising campaign slogan, aiming at making Helix the market reference, was: 'One day all oils will be like Helix.' In the meantime the name Helix Plus was added in small letters to Puissance 7 and Helix Standard to Puissance 5. In October 1993, in order to follow the European transition, all the 'Puissance' brands were replaced by Helix. A small mention of Puissance under Helix survived for a few months. The Puissance 7 blue can became the Shell Helix Plus blue can, but the Puissance 5 brown can became the Shell Helix Standard yellow can. The advertisement campaign put the old Puissance 7 can and the new Helix Plus can side by side under the slogan: 'It may have changed its name but the spout remains.' The problem was that the advertisement agency focused on the name change while the clientele paid more attention to the colour of the can. Yet nowhere in the advertising campaign did the yellow can appear. The customers looking for their brown can could not find it: instead they could only find a yellow can the name of which they had never heard of. In reality, despite the brand awareness scores of the name Puissance, the strength of the brand was in fact associated not with its name but with its colour! The customers should have been informed of a transition from brown to yellow rather than soley a name change from Puissance to Helix.

In durable goods sectors and in service sectors, in fact in all sectors with high perceived risk, it is important to stress the role of internal communications. Brands are not abstractions, they are literally carried by people who identify with them. To changing the brand is to change their identification. They need to adhere. This is of paramount importance for corporate brand changes.

Changing the corporate brand

On 1 January 1991, CGE became Alcatel 'to have a brand with a higher profile'. It had up till then been handicapped by the confusion that was occurring due to its similarity with General Electric. In 2000 CGEA became Connex because its name, unpronounceable in international markets hindered expansion and the effectiveness of all communication. To the precautions to take when changing a brand name a few more can be added when dealing with company names. These are based on the fact that there is always a strong internal public and a multitude of external micro-publics.

The first problem that should be avoided is that of rumours, which will always portray a different picture of the change than the reality. The internal public is quick to interpret any change in terms of a crisis, serious problems or shareholder pressure, especially when new majority shareholders have arrived. A big effort is therefore needed to explain the situation. As regards the external public, they generally under-evaluate internal problems. The name change does not bring them any specific advantages so there is no reason for them to pay too much attention. But if they did understand they might go along with the decision, so the name change must be made relevant to them. Finally, each micro-public demands a specific action. In this way, with regard to the transfer to Connex, the first problem that had to be resolved was that of the stock market traders. The company was quoted in about 10 markets around the world, so they had to be certain that right from day one all financiers would be looking for the letter A and not C in the finance sections of their newspapers.

In July 1999 a small energy company, Total, took over the large Elf company, thus creating the fourth largest energy company in the world, and the only one that was not Anglo-Saxon in origin. Naturally, the success of such corporate mergers goes far beyond the topic of the present chapter. Reducing it to a name change would be looking through a tunnel. However, names do play a role in such mergers. In this case the names were not changed immediately to increase the chances of success of the whole operation.

According to the general management of TotalFinaElf, the merger was a success because of the following factors:

▌ It was well prepared by the company taking over. For instance, they had already analysed all the personnel of the target company. Just one month after the takeover, a new organisation chart was issued, so all the employees in the former Elf company learned quickly where they would now stand.

▌ The company taking over had the courage of respecting a 50:50 equilibrium in all assignments, teams and staffs and did not act as a victor.

▌ Hundreds of committees were created to discuss all types of topics, so that yesterday's enemies became less hostile, learnt to know each other and eventually became friends.

- After the takeover the group took as its name TotalFinaElf and kept it for three years. This name was chosen for internal purposes. It indicated that no one was defeated. Keeping the name of the companies that had been taken over was a sign of respect. Externally it was a sign of power.

- Only in 2003 was the group name changed to Total, after an intense probe of the internal climate. However, the Total logo did change at this occasion. The new Total is not the same as the former Total: the new logo conveyed the new values of this leading European fuel company. A merger is a unique opportunity to create a leap forward. Why come back to a former name, and not start with a clean slate as Novartis (formerly Ciba Sandoz) or Aventis (formerly Hoechst Rhone Poulenc) have done? These laboratories have brands as assets, their medical and pharmaceutical product brands. The assets of an energy company are found in its petrol reserves. They depend heavily on the reputation the company has built up under its name in all oil-producing countries over 50 years of activity. Total was a key asset: it meant trust all around the world. In addition, the international financial community expect the Total financial management team to continue in place, and the continuity was intended as a way of reassuring them.

16

Brand turnaround and rejuvenation

Because brands are assets, companies try to make them produce earnings as long as possible. They do not believe in the brand life cycle. This is why even though their sales may have come to a minimum, or even after a number of years of inactivity, it is frequent to witness efforts to relaunch this activity. Investment funds and business angels are fond of sleeping beauties, brands whose name still evokes resonance in our memory. There are good reasons for that. As assets, these brands are still endowed with brand awareness, attributes, beliefs: it is less costly to start from these premises than to restart from scratch. This is why, for instance, in 2003 Unilever relaunched Sunsilk shampoo for the third time in Europe.

Second, as old brands they capture a value enhancing emotion, nostalgia. Part of the past of many consumers in our ageing societies, they evoke the ebb of life and good times past. Some of these consumers may want to recapture these emotions, as a symbolic way to stop the passage of time (Brown *et al*, 2003).

It is necessary to differentiate clearly between a number of close and related concepts: an old product relaunch, a reinvention, an old product facelift and a brand revitalisation:

▌ An old product relaunch consists in taking a product from the past and selling it as it was. In 2001, Wal-Mart listed a new and unknown brand, Lorina. This brand comes from a small company selling lemonade. For all distributors, lemonade is a commodity: the cheapest is the better. One litre of standard lemonade is sold at around a quarter-euro. Lorina sells it for €4. It has recreated the exact lemonade people used to drink in the 1950s, with a typical glass bottle, a very specific cap and a recipe from that time. Who are the buyers? People of 50 and older.

▌ An old product reinvention is the new VW Beetle. No one, except collectors, would be prepared now to drive an old Beetle: it is too insecure and uncomfortable by modern standards. This is why Volkswagen decided to reskin it a little while keeping its unique design, and to completely revise all its functionalities to match a modern consumer's bottom-line expectations. Who are the buyers? Old consumers and those younger people who are willing to adhere to the brand community.

▮ Brand revitalisation in the narrow sense consists of recreating a consistent flow of sales, putting the brand back to life, on a growth slope again. When the brand is made up of many products, we shall see that this typically entails two actions in parallel: keeping the old typical product globally as it is (to keep its franchise) and reinventing it for new and younger consumers (that is to say asking the question, what would this product be today, if we had to invent it from scratch for the needs of modern consumers?).

▮ Brand facelifts (Lehu, 2006) are part of the revitalisation process. They refer to an upgrading of the performance and/or design of the brand to keep up with the competition.

A lot of people are interested in brand revitalisation:

▮ Young investors or venture capitalists who buy an ailing brand at low price, often an old brand, with the objective of reselling it in a few years at a profit, after revitalising it.

▮ Small businesses that will never have enough money to create their own brand, but are willing to buy the name of a formerly active brand for a reasonable price. For instance, 10 years after having stopped selling the European yogurt brand Chambourcy, Nestlé thought it could sell it. A small company bought it, but the fact that the name was still known did not guarantee the success of the revitalisation, and it soon went out of business. A brand alone without a viable economic equation is of no use. (Nestlé had, of course, put a number of restrictions on the use of the brand, since it did not want to find it competing against itself). In addition, the sales of a brand are the result not only of the attractiveness of

that brand to consumers, but also of the muscles of the corporation operating it. Modern mass retailers also tend to value much more the capacity of a company to sustain competition, and to deliver products efficiently to their storage facilities, than its possession of a known but old brand.

▮ Large companies are also interested in revitalising old brands, but only if these brands are not perceived as old, that is to say as brands with no relevance for today, associated exclusively with older consumers. This is how Ford bought Jaguar and had to invest as much again into putting it back to use as a marque for quality cars.

▮ Global companies might buy a leading local brand in order to ease and finance the local development of their international stars. The local brand is a door opener with local distribution. However, it is often found that these so-called local leaders present the clear symptoms of ageing (no innovation, too few younger clients, little challenge of the past practices, no systematic upgrading of packages, designs and communication).

The decay of brand equity

Although they may have ceased their commercial activity, brands do not immediately lose their assets. Learnt through time, their brand image is not erased from consumers' long-term memories. Indeed, after many years a brand can still evoke a number of positive or negative associations. What is lost however is the key brand asset: brand salience, the capacity of the brand to be evoked spontaneously in consumers' minds as soon as the need to buy the product type appears. This is why belonging to the consumer 'evoked set' (or consideration set) is a key measure of brand equity, signifying both brand presence and its perceived unique relevance for that need.

Table 16.1 illustrates how brand equity decays over time. Brand X is a FMCG food brand in a very popular category (with almost 100 per cent penetration). Until recently, this brand was the number two in its market. Then it was bought by market number three, which immediately sold all Brand X's factories so that the acquisition of the brand paid off immediately. Most important, it discontinued its activity and as a result became the market number two in volume and number one in value. Eight years after the end of any kind of commercial activity, the brand equity had not disappeared. Top-of-mind awareness had dropped from 13 per cent to 5 per cent and aided awareness from 86 per cent to 55 per cent. Interestingly, there are still 13 per cent of consumers who declare that they have bought it at least once over the preceding 12 months. This latter figure casts doubts on the validity of such indicators of brand equity in this FMCG category: it seems to be a mere reflection of spontaneous awareness.

How much would this brand be worth if its owner decided to sell it? Not far from zero. The owner would never take the risk of selling it so that it could be revived in its own market. Out of this market, it is just a name with faded remote credentials: there will be no buyer. Could the owner itself revitalise that brand? Probably in specific segments or niches. As far as the mainstream market is concerned, a return to the shelves would be impossible. They are now overcrowded, first by private labels, and second by the few remaining producers' brands, which have become mega-brands. Typically, a shift of channel would be possible. For instance, a drink brand might be sold via on-premise distribution (for consumption in canteens and business restaurants), if this were a channel where it could add value without meeting fierce competition. Channel and use changes are a classic form of revitalisation for this very reason.

This example illustrates a fact too often overlooked: the value of a brand does not lie in its assets, but in the ability of a company to make a profitable business with these assets. After eight years of inactivity the whole commercial environment will have changed. Nature abhors a vacuum, and business does too. As soon as the brand disappears from the stores, the shelves are filled with other products from other brands, including the distributors' own brand. In order to sell the original again, they would need to be displaced. It costs a lot to induce the modern distribution to reallocate space for a comeback, with very little guarantee of success. A brand is not enough to stage a comeback, one needs an innovation.

It is clear why it is essential to prevent decline, and how a brand loses value after a period of inactivity. But what are the factors of decline?

The factors of decline

Following the analysis of the factors of a brand's longevity in Chapter 10, one could

Table 16.1   How brand equity decays over time

Years after the end of the brand's commercial activity							
1	2	3	4	5	6	7	8
Top of mind (saliency)	13	12	7	7	6	3	1	5
Total unaided awareness	26	28	20	29	15	14	11	16
Aided awareness	86	83	76	73	68	50	55	55
Bought last 12 months	27	29	17	19	12	15	10	13

FMCG food brand; sample size 450/year; all figures are percentages simply say that in contrast, brands decline when they are not respected. In fact, their decline always comes from mismanagement. When a company ceases to be interested in its brands (thus creating a lack of innovation, advertising or productivity), it can expect the consumer also to lose interest. And if the brand loses dynamism, energy, and shows fewer and fewer signs of vitality, how can one possibly hope that it will arouse passion and proselytism? Apart from these rules, which are so basic that it is astonishing that they can be forgotten, there are some factors that accelerate decline. These will now be studied.

When quality is forgotten

The first and surest road to decline is through the degradation of the quality of the products. The brand ceases to be a sign of quality. Economic factors oblige companies to cut corners with regard to quality, albeit in minor steps, and unfortunately, far too frequently. For instance, when l'Oréal bought out Lanvin, its leading perfume Arpège was a mere shadow of its former self. The fragrance had originally been made up of natural oils but by then included a fair amount of artificial ingredients. The bottle had even lost its round shape. Consumers around the world were conscious that they were no longer respected since Arpège had been so badly mistreated. L'Oréal's first step was to give back to this perfume the case, the bottle and the ingredients of the quality that it deserved. This task, which was not spectacular but was expensive, was absolutely necessary. It enabled contact to be re-established with the consumers who had been forsaken, and the rebuilding of acceptable foundations for the brand.

Beware of non-significant differences

The change in the level of quality of a product is rarely abrupt, but results from the insidious logic of statistical tests. Each change is tested against the product's previous version: if consumers have a lower opinion of the changed product but statistical analysis reveals that the difference is not significant, the company will not hesitate to carry out the change to provide a source of financial savings. The problem entirely rests with the expression 'significant difference'. All the decisions are based on the so-called 'alpha risk threshold' (generally 5 per cent). As long as the difference observed in the sample, just due to chance, affects less than 5 per cent of the cases, it is declared non-significant. In sciences, the aim of this high-risk threshold is to avoid taking for real a phenomenon which would not exist in reality. The problem is that in marketing, it is the 'beta risk' that should be taken into account, the aim of which is to avoid considering as false a hypothesis that is in reality true. For, through modifying a product even by the smallest amount which each time has been declared 'non-significant', a considerable risk is taken. Consumers are not fooled. They avoid the product, then abandon it, even sometimes spreading by word of mouth a very negative opinion. From then on, any modification of the product must be approached with caution if it is rated below the standard product, even if the difference is said to be non-significant.

Missing the new trend

The third factor of decline is the refusal to follow immediately a durable change. Thus Taylor Made, for a long time the world reference for golf clubs, did not believe the gigantic head launched by the Callaway brand under the suggestive name of 'Big Bertha' would catch on. By clinging to a different conception that was more demanding for the average player, ie for the majority of the market, Taylor Made suddenly lost its leadership. In the same way, Banga orange juice continued to believe in glass bottles when the market, following the market leader Oasis, turned towards plastic.

In 2001, according to Zandl, a specialised US marketing research company, the jeans was still number one in the youth clothing preference. However, young people now quote 112 different brands as being their 'preferred brand for jeans'. The market has become fragmented, a challenge for Levi's, whose image and sales are very much associated with a mono-product, the 501.

Fragmentation led tribes, small groups to prefer new types of jeans, more adapted to new usages, and new brands. A lot of new competitors filled niches. Pepe and Diesel addressed the urban rebel, 'For us by us' and underground streetwear. Gap also became a major player. Levi's had expressed disbelief in streetwear and neglected the rappers and gliders, who are in fact the opinion leaders of the new youth. Tight 501s are totally unadapted to skateboarding and roller-skating. Skaters wish to wear an XXXXL rolled up their knees, and rappers like multi-pocket trousers. On the other end of the spectrum, girls desired Tommy Hilfiger and Polo jeans, not to speak of Armani and Versace jeans. It was clearly the end of the mass market. Levi's had not foreseen it, and worse, it had not reacted when the trends were there.

The mono-product syndrome

Still at the level of product policy, the brands associated with a single product are more vulnerable. They risk being carried away by the decline of that product. This again is part of what happened to Levi's, with its too-long association with the mythical 501. Wonderbra is another clear instance of a brand that fell into the mono-product trap.

Who has never heard about Wonderbra? Very few, either women or men. Although the product is in fact comparatively old (it was invented in Canada in 1953 by Canadelle Corp), its real launch in Europe was quite recent (1994). Sara Lee had bought the company and gave Playtex the responsibility of launching the Wonderbra in Europe. The fantastic advertising campaign ('Hello boys') and accompanying publicity made this innovation famous. The brand helped women who felt they had small breasts look more sexy and gain self-assurance as a result. It created a new segment. In 1995, 5 million units were sold in Europe, and 86 per cent of its consumers were less than 35 years old. Now where is Wonderbra? Still trying to find pathways for growth, if not prevent decline. Despite an aided awareness level of 70 per cent, its goodwill has come close to bad will in some countries, in the trade channels.

After the peak sales of 1995, sales started to decline. Competitors with known brands entered this segment too.

The problem was that Wonderbra became associated not with a brand but with a product, and its brand name became a generic name: people spoke of 'the wonderbra'. This highly technical product (it had 42 parts, and needed a specific manufacturing technology) was much adored inside the company. Everyone was very proud of it. Where to go next? If innovation is the key to market penetration, a brand has to become more than a name of a product. But Wonderbra did not innovate sufficiently, and consumers did not repurchase its products. Today, 61 per cent of Wonderbra consumers possess only one Wonderbra. They wear it for special occasions, and rarely on weekdays. Wonderbra might instead have capitalised on its sexy positioning but offered new products based on different reasons for purchase. The very same benefit could have been expressed using different materials or shapes. Instead it remained too narrow, preventing the consumer from moving freely within the brand.

Another difficulty was the global management of the brand. New models were designed essentially for the UK, its leading European market, because of an excess of centralisation at Playtex (Sara Lee). The management did not recognise that the tastes and wishes of Italian, French and Spanish women were not those of English women. As a result European sales became one-country sales.

Distribution factors

The relationship with a distribution channel can be a factor of decline if the brand does not live up to the new expectations of it. Because companies such as l'Oréal developed particular brands for supermarket distribution, such as Plénitude for cosmetics, Vichy's status in the field of pharmaceuticals is under threat. Consumers who go to a chemist shop to buy such products expect from them a higher level of quality as befits the laboratory guarantee. But over time, Vichy had become a generalist brand more focused on life-style than scientific quality. It found itself, in 1995, carrying products which no longer corresponded with the products which consumers wanted to buy in a chemist shop. Vichy's survival was contingent upon a qualitative upgrade of all its products and its repositioning on the benefit of better health through the skin.

Other brands have collapsed because they have allowed themselves to become trapped in a declining distribution network. The recent rise of large liquor stores in Japan, at the expense of small convenience outlets, has caused the immediate decline of all the brands lacking a sufficient level of public awareness. In small outlets, they did not need it: the store owner pushed the brand, sold it to his clients. In modern distribution the brand has to sell itself, it needs market pull.

Weak communication creates a distance

Finally, communication can accelerate the decline of brands. Beyond the obvious fact that ceasing to advertise means ceasing to exist in the market and ceasing to be a key actor, the sensible management of communication consists of modernising the signs, but keeping the essence.

If the daughter brands are too much in the spotlight, the mother brand can be adversely affected and give the impression that it is in decline. This happened with Dim, a Sara Lee hosiery brand. Although the brand was by far the main advertiser in its hosiery market, and even in the textile market in general, it seemed to be declining, less active. Such an imbalance between the actual share of voice and the feeling of loss of energy felt by the market worried the management of the Sara Lee group. In fact, the diagnosis was clear: the promotional tactics of the daughter brands had been carried so far that they had fragmented Dim's image. Indeed, it was appropriate to clarify Dim's wide range by attributing names to different products which did not propose the same customer benefits, hence the appearance of Sublim, Diam's and other lines. On the other hand, this measure produced a dispersion of the Dim image, even the disappearance of Dim to the benefit of the daughter brands.

The first symptom of this condition was the packaging. There was no longer any homogeneity between the different packagings, and the mother brand appeared in a minor endorsing role in variable places. Moreover, in the context of the organisational change, further divisions had been introduced (tights, lingerie, men's items). Unfortunately, there was no longer anybody in charge of coherence between the divisions and of the defence of the Dim mother brand's capital. Finally, since the Dim logotype only appeared clearly on bottom-end products and was concealed on advanced products, this increased the perception that its quality had declined. At the same time, the market was moving towards opaque tights, a more durable and more top-end product, which could easily make Dim the symbol, not of today's woman, but rather of a poor quality.

In order to correct these dangerous impressions, Dim undertook to increase the added value of all its products, including the basic product, to upgrade all its packagings, to return the status of source-brand by replacing the first-name brands under a visible umbrella, and to clearly advertise 'Dim presents the new

Diam's' instead of 'This is the new Diam's by Dim'. (This example illustrates, in passing, a tendency which is fatal for a brand: its systematic distance from the best new products, thereby confining it to an offer which is static, obsolete or old-fashioned.) To complete the story, it should also be mentioned that, in parallel with the excessive exposure of the daughter brands, the Dim brand had been extended to leisure and indoor clothing. This created an added danger for the brand, that of dilution. By leaving its field of competence (everything which is worn close to the body) to enter the sector of regular clothes, its added value became less tangible. The existence of clothes with a Dim label without any tangible added value could only raise doubts about the brand's actual contribution, not only in this new market, but also in its basic markets: tights and lingerie. So, in the context of Dim's renewal plan, an end was put to this extension, which was causing the dilution of the brand's capital. The priority was to return Dim to the field in which it was recognised to have expertise. The history of ready-to-wear clothes contains too many examples of brands which have abandoned their initial concept to experiment with new extensions and so lose their identity. This has been the case with Newman, which can no longer be associated with a typical product, of Marlboro Classics which has moved away from its founding style, and so on.

When the brand becomes generic

The highest degree of dilution of the brand's added value occurs when the brand becomes generic. The brand is considered a descriptive word, part of everyday vocabulary with no distinctive properties. The classic examples are well-known: Scotch, Kleenex, Xerox, Nylon, Velux. What causes a brand to be reduced to the point of becoming generic? The abandonment of any communication on the brand's specific nature and purpose can

cause its decline. Thus, any dominant brand of a new product risks becoming a generic name. This can be prevented by taking certain precautions, for example:

- create a word to designate the product of the brand;

- never mention the brand's name alone, but together with the product's generic designation;

- never use the brand's name as a verb (in the United States, for instance, to xerox means to make a photocopy) or as a noun, but as an adjective;

- systematically protest whenever the brand's name is used as a common noun by third parties and the media; for instance, request that an erratum be published. Through not having reacted strongly enough, Du Pont de Nemours lost the ownership of Nylon and Teflon, which have since become generic terms;

- nurture the perceived difference between the brand and competitive products, either with tangible attributes or with intangible values. In any event introduce new products.

Preventing the brand from ageing

It is frequently said that a brand is ageing, shows signs of ageing or seems aged. This impression may be felt by customers, non-customers, suppliers, distributors or employees themselves, who acknowledge a difference between them and their competitors. Ballantines, Martini, Black & White, Club Med, Yves Saint Laurent and Guy Laroche have all been described as ageing.

The concept of ageing has in fact two different meanings:

- The general meaning suggests a slow but systematic decline over a long period of time. The brand is not destined to end rapidly but seems likely to be inevitably phased out with time. Yesterday strong and active, it appears today much more mundane, as if it no longer had anything to say or to propose to the market and lived exclusively on its loyal clients. One symptom of this is the widening gap between the spontaneous awareness and the assisted awareness. The brand still rings a bell, but it is not one of the brands which has an impact on the market. It does not launch new products as often as the category actors. It does not surprise. It repeats itself. There is only a small difference between repetition and boredom.

▌ The second meaning refers to the reflected image of the customer. Everything points to the typical customer being older. And even in the case of a company whose marketing is deliberately targeted at older customers, it is never advisable for the image of a brand to be too closely associated with an older clientele. Although it is aiming at the flourishing older customer market (that is, customers over 50), Damart must make sure not to be associated with the clientele who are 60 or 70. Without going to that extreme, the Yves Saint Laurent label appears to young people to represent a clientele older than that of Dior's and Chanel.

What is it that produces these impressions of ageing? Most of the time these impressions are well founded: the brand no longer seems to belong to its time and has lost its inner energy.

Many brands allow themselves to be associated with the products of another age. With the acceleration of time, the notion of another era now refers to a close past. In all markets dominated by technology, obsolescence can occur very rapidly. Little can be done for brands linked to a dated technology, or those which seem not to have kept up to date with progress or with the internet.

A brand can be 18 years old and threatened with ageing. The challenge for the eau de toilette Eau Jeune (ie Young Water), launched by l'Oréal for supermarket distribution, is to be still considered Eau Jeune by the next generation of 18- to 25-year-olds, but who are so different. If this brand had remained a single product, it would have disappeared. What symbolised youth in 1987 no longer symbolises it in 1997.

The point of view expressed by the brand on its market can also sometimes seem to be suddenly behind the new dominant values. As long as decisions regarding Playtex in Europe were taken in the United States, the brand never seemed to take into consideration the role of femininity in women's choices. Even though the products were of high quality, they were purely functional, that is based on the tangible problem of breast support. What was relevant in the United States was totally opposite to the way European women related to their bodies. In its tone and inflexibility, Playtex seemed to be addressing the mothers, not the daughters.

Although it was still the world's leading brand for shoes and ski bindings, Salomon recently realised that it was in great danger of ageing within a few years. In fact, Salomon, in the same way as Rossignol does, has represented the values of alpine skiing for half a century: effort, order, competition, gaining one hundredth of a second, beating all others by a microsecond. The new generations no longer subscribe to these values: a counter-culture, originating in the surf, is dominant on the slopes, bringing with it new sports and new values. What has been called the 'glide generation' has not learnt alpine skiing and probably never will. They instinctively practise snowboarding on the slopes in winter and roller-skating or rollerblading in the streets. They put as paramount values friendship and emotion: they eschew competition and the brands associated with yesteryear. They have elected their own gods: Burton, Airwalk, Quiksilver, Oxbow. All these brands are new and symbolise another vision of sport.

The lack of evolution in a brand's outward signs indicates its present lack of interest in attracting new customers.

Certain brands also come to a standstill because they remain associated with the same images. The fact that Yves Saint Laurent seems more dated than Dior or Chanel is connected with the omnipresence of the ageing creator himself and association with Catherine Deneuve. Lancôme was sensible enough to bring in younger and international stars.

As for the clientele, the loss of direct contact with young people is the surest symptom of ageing. This is what differentiates Johnnie Walker from Jack Daniel's or Martini from Bacardi.

Without necessarily having to appeal to young people between the ages of 20 and 25, the brand should always be attractive to tomorrow's consumers. The buyers who are today in their forties will modify their functional expectations when they reach their fifties. But they will also like to show that they have not changed by staying with their usual brands. They will refuse to support the ghetto brands which signal their entry into old age. This is why Damart's future depends on its image among 45-year-old men and women even if its marketing is rather targeted at the 55-year-old senior consumer. Damart has to work on the evolution of its image, not of its target clientele. To do so, they must improve their image so as not to appear a last-frontier brand. This is why, besides the modernisation of their main product, underwear, they have left behind their old methods of distribution: some department stores now have a Damart lingerie department next to Playtex, Rosy or Warner. Damart also advertises products that cross the generation barrier, allowing them to dissociate their image from one based merely on age: thick and coloured tights are just as appropriate for a young girl in a short skirt

riding a motorbike as they are for skiers and autumn hikers. Through these significant actions, they address their future customers and put an end to the stagnation of their clientele, for in 1990 Damart was attracting hardly any new buyers, but was selling more and more to loyal customers.

As has been noted, keeping in touch with young people implies a cultural revolution among management. The efforts to be made may seem huge to an older internal team who often do not appreciate the danger they are facing as their own reference points always seem secure. Finally, with consumers living longer, the effects of the clientele's ageing may pass unnoticed. The decline is slow and never spectacular. But unfortunately, as with a cancer, without an obvious sign of decline to react rapidly to, it may sometimes be too late.

To make the radical internal changes required to energise an organisation which has aged with its own reference points, there should be no hesitation in rejuvenating the entire management with younger people. The revitalisation of brands always starts with a major work of internal rejuvenation.

Rejuvenating a brand

How should one rejuvenate a brand? How can a declining or a past brand revive? How do you recreate a durable growth for a brand that has for long been declining? Although there exist a wide variety of situations, the goal is the same: to bring a brand back to life. This leads to the core question, what life? Whose life? As a rule, it will rarely be the same as formerly.

There is a big difference between respecting one's roots and cultivating the past. Revitalisations, revivals are based on an updating of the overall offer of the brand while staying true to part of its identity. Revival means aiming at a new growth market. The brand must find a new relevance and differentiation. The term 'revival' of a brand is not quite accurate since it always implies a change in the product, or in the market, or in the target market. It is a relaunch but not necessarily among the same people as before, or in the same distribution channels, for the same uses, or whatever. With time the consumers, the markets and competition will have changed.

Redefining the brand essence

Even forgotten brands have an internal meaning, a domain of legitimacy to be exploited. The first task in a brand revitalisation is to understand which values of this brand still have a high relevance, and which have lost meaning. Burberry rediscovered its DNA: the ability to epitomise the classic eccentric dandy in English fashion. Old brands have disseminated bits of associations in people's memories, even among non-customers or newer generations. These weak memories act as a 'humus'. It is important to analyse this humus. What is left about the brand essence? What are the potentialities emerging from it? What market opportunities could be met? It is useful to analyse this as shown in Figure 16.1.

As a rule, declining brands have few positive salient evocations, or these evocations are generic and lack differentiation. The real potential usually lies in the latent associations. It will be the role of marketing to choose the right set from among these buried positive associations. Then the brand will have to embody them in new products or services and channels aimed at the new target.

Revitalising through new uses

The revitalisation of a brand usually follows new paths that are very different from those that led to its initial success. If there has been a decline, it is because these paths did not lead to any new demand or pocket of growth.

Revitalisation involves establishing new parameters for the brand. Since its original consumers are no longer able to ensure its success, it has to attract a new clientele, develop new user occasions, new distribution channels and new consumer networks.

Brandy is a classic example. It is typically

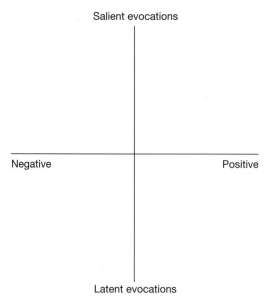

Figure 16.1   Analysing the potential of an old brand

associated with the 'after-dinner' and 'connoisseurs enjoying a brandy together' type of occasion, an image and occasion that have been responsible for a massive decline in the volume of brandy sales worldwide. After years of decline in the face of competition from white spirits, which are much easier to drink and much trendier (Bacardi, Absolut, Seagram's Gin and so on), brandy sales have recently soared in the United States. But with one major difference – 50 per cent of the volume of brandy currently consumed in the United States is consumed by the black community, which represents 12 per cent of the population. It has become the favourite drink of African-American males, within the context of a lively social situation, where status value is essential. They ask for Martell or Hennessy, as well as Thackeray (gin) and Crystal Roederer (champagne).

To target a new consumer group, a company must be ready to call its traditional marketing into question and define an optimum marketing mix for its new target group. The process begins with new customers, their life-style and new occasions on which the product is consumed or purchased. Innovation is therefore central to the revitalisation of old brands.

Revitalising through distribution change

In fact, it seems that a classic revitalisation strategy is to use known brands in different distribution circuits. For instance, a supermarket food brand could be moved to a channel that rests on 'push' marketing rather than 'pull' marketing. This is why one sees many formerly famous brands in canteens, or office restaurants for instance. It creates value in the eyes of the clients (more than an unknown brand or a private label) and these brands are cheaper than well-known leading brands. The obverse is also true. One company has specialised in purchasing old medical products, with 100 per cent aided awareness, that are little prescribed these days. Some of them have become generic names. The strategy consists in selling them on the shelves of supermarkets, where their name triggers immediate recognition and trust.

Revitalising through innovations

Barely 10 years ago, Mercedes was under threat. The brand had certainly gained international acclaim, but the signs were nevertheless worrying. In California, where new consumer trends are created, Mercedes was no longer an aspirational brand. It had been replaced by Lexus, the top-of-the-range brand from Toyota. And in Europe the average buyer of the smallest Mercedes of that period, the C-Class, was 51 years old.

Clearly Mercedes was becoming a brand for older people. The company's CEO made a harsh but accurate diagnosis: either the brand remain as it was and the company would go bankrupt (like Rolls-Royce) or it would have to evolve.

The first step was to re-establish the conditions that would create a favourable economic equation – the company would have to produce 1 million vehicles to lower production costs to an acceptable level. The second was to attract a younger clientele – they could not be left to the competition until they reached 51! To do this, the company had to break with the standard design of all Mercedes cars for the previous 60 years.

This is why the event that revitalised Mercedes was the launch of the A-Class. This little car, which was in direct competition with the Volkswagen Golf, was the brand's new 'prototype' in Europe. It departed from the traditional Mercedes image on two counts – it had front-wheel drive and a completely different design. However, it still had the interior space of the C-Class and the safety of the E-Class. In fact, it currently accounts for 30 per cent of Mercedes sales in Europe. Above all, it has attracted a younger clientele (with an average age of 37), more women and the style conscious.

In the United States, the new Mercedes prototype is the luxury 4 × 4 M-Class, which has re-established contact with the trendy set of California and elsewhere.

To target even younger consumers, the beautiful CLK Roadster was deliberately positioned at an attractive price. Its beauty, sensitivity and design are now part of the new Mercedes brand contract. Of course, any form of extension modifies the original brand, and Mercedes is no longer an exclusively luxury brand. The new Mercedes management is more segmented, more attuned to the needs of its consumers and their life-style. The brand regularly renews its status as the world's leading car manufacturer via its top of the range models, of which the S-Class is the symbol.

Revitalising through segmentation

To revitalise Burberry, Rose Mary Bravo knew she had to segment the lines and sub-brand them. Burberry London is a modernised offering for the classic clients. Burberry Prorsum is very fashionable and modern. Thomas Burberry is aimed at teenagers. The first segment ensures cashflow and makes it possible to take a risk on cash-demanding fashion stores.

Revitalising by contact with opinion leaders

Why did Hush Puppies become fashionable again in the United States in 1993 (Gladwell, 2000)? Because East Side Manhattan fashionistas found them cute and appropriate for their quest of permanent differentiation.

Ageing brands have generally lost contact with the trendsetters in their category, the tribes that prefigure change. Advertising and product innovation will be of no help without the active support of these trendsetting tribes. It is not easy to make friends again with people one has not called for years, during which time they have been seduced by the competition,

including new entrants. In addition the ageing brand is held as an icon of the past, and may attract bad will, not goodwill.

The task of recreating proximity through direct contacts and shared emotional experiences will be difficult, but it is an essential part of any comeback. Salomon, which had lost contact with the surfers who were its future market, had to create an internal cultural revolution, changing its management and hiring young people who were likely to be able to recreate the lost connection.

Apple had lost contact with today's new trendsetters, who are no longer advertising agencies, but the kids seduced by Napster and whose use of the internet is now mostly to exchange music within their virtual tribe. Ballantines, formerly at Allied Domecq, realised recently that it too had lost all contact with youth. Managers more concerned with their own fate in the midst of mergers and acquisitions in their sector concentrated on the brand's core clients, not the future clients. They forgot that sustaining brand equity means addressing current and future business alike. For instance, in 1995 brand equity monitoring showed that in some European countries, brand spontaneous awareness among 18–24-year-olds had dropped from 47 per cent to 13 per cent in seven years.

It is not possible to get out of this dramatic problem just by changing one's advertising. Sometimes creating a new product is needed, because in between, everything has changed: consumers, their habits, the competition, places of consumption and so on.

Regaining contact is a preliminary. A brand is not a product with a name, it is a relationship. After years of indifference, not to say neglect by Ballantines, the brand had to reconquer the lost relationship. It might still have been number one in some countries, but that was because of a core of frequent buyers, all ageing. Benchmarking the best practice of Pernod-Ricard, the brand decided to invest massively in Europe, and also in South America, to reconquer proximity by contact. Targeting is crucial: what key tribe? The management identified snowboarding as representing the core values of the new generation.

In cooperation with the International Snowboarding Federation, which was fighting against the International Ski Federation, it sponsored all alpine snowboard events, and created a night event in discos. However, to be effective today at regaining contact, sponsoring must go far beyond just stamping the event with the brand name everywhere. The brand must be at the centre, or a key ally of the event.

Step two entailed recognition that urban youth was the target. Ballantines decided to bring snowboarding to cities through the 'Ballantines Urban High' Tour. In the middle of capital cities from Berlin to Rio de Janeiro, or on their beaches, Ballantines had a huge ramp built, covered in artificial snow, to host three-day national contests to find the best freelance snowboarders. The contest was preceded by country-wide selection phases, thereby creating a mounting buzz through word of mouth. The event fuelled involvement. The first event of the series took place in October 1995 in Berlin, symbolically at the Brandenburg Gate (which used to be the only gate in the Berlin Wall where people from the former East Germany could come through to the free West). Because among young people everything goes together, during the contest there were an open air concert (with the group Prodigy), grunge fashion shows, and night-time promotions in all the city's discos around snowboarding themes. In addition for the cream of the cream, Ballantines created Ballantines orbit, a huge mobile tent, with restricted invitation to those perceived as style leaders to listen to live techno music. After Berlin the tour went on to Prague, Milan, Moscow, Rio de Janeiro – it still goes on.

The lessons that can be drawn from this case are that proximity today means bumping into the lives of the target group, not just being there. A multidimensional event was created, merging fashion, sport, music, dancing, entertainment and video games, showing a high level of investment, and a very good understanding of the target audience's desires. A special logo was created, Ballantines Urban High, which could eventually become a label for licensed products (a clothing line, T-shirts, music and so on), certainly a website, and why not a franchised store chain in the future?

The event was well prepared for through the selection phases and brand presence across the country,. The budget commitment was high (about €600,000) for the Berlin event, which was attended by 100,000 young people (so it cost €5 per person for a contact that should create a long-lasting emotional memory and involvement with the brand).

Revitalising through 360° communications

When Chivas was declining worldwide, its advertising said defensively, 'When you know'. In a major turnaround, Chivas 18 now promotes the 'Chivas life'. Its identity is rich and generous, its positioning sells an appetite for life. This new platform is expressed through 360° via global advertising, but also major events, parties with celebrities, partnership with luxury resorts worldwide, not to mention product placement which contributes to making brands 'cool'.

Changing the business model

Once in a while daring entrepreneurs buy an old and ailing brand and decide to revitalise it. It also happens that big groups do so. What is often presented as a brand revitalisation is actually a change in the business model. In Chapter 1 we emphasised that a brand that cannot provide benefits has no real value. By benefits is meant financial benefits, economic value added (EVA) once the cost of capital had been paid (see also Chapter 18). What makes an ailing brand more valuable is the new business model on which it will rely.

For decades l'Aigle, a former subsidiary of Hutchinson, was known for its rubber boots. Its name was also its symbol: it came directly from the American Eagle. It had become a cult brand among fishermen, hunters, nature lovers and country landowners. But Chinese imports and modern distribution created too many problems, the company went broke, and it was bought in an LBO. Now there are Aigle stores opening everywhere in the world. Has the brand changed? In name terms it has lost a letter, moving from l'Aigle to Aigle, gaining simplicity and internationality. Most important, it moved from a boots brand to a leisurewear brand, whose prototype (most symbolic product) has moved from the rubber boots to a parka, a solid product, as the main value of the brand commands. The vintage rubber boots are still there to nurture the myth, but business grew through the new prototype. There are a lot of benefits in this change of business model:

- Brands that rely too much on a mono-product are always in danger, as they cannot smooth out a drop in sales. Boots sell less when climate becomes dryer. Also, since the rubber boots were of excellent quality, they lasted a long time. Brand loyalty was high but the time between purchases was too long.

- Extending the line to leisurewear made it possible to free the brand from the grip of modern distribution and build its own selective distribution network. The extended line made it more than possible to fill each store.

- Leisure wear is fashion conscious: people buy new garments each year even if they already own similar ones. It is also a less price-sensitive sector.

This example is a reminder that too often the success of the revitalisation is attributed to 'the brand' as a short cut, because there is a lack of information on the company itself, the strategy, the back office. Certainly the brand reputation was an invaluable asset, but that asset was worth nothing as long as it was not supported by a valid business model.

Growing older but not ageing

Louis Vuitton is 150 years old! It is also the most fashionable luxury brand in Asia. One way of understanding revitalisation is to consider brands that have not 'aged'. How have they done it? Typically, the brands that have defied the passage of time have adopted a dual logic, as illustrated by Nivea and Lacoste. To follow their example and stay young, a brand must implement three types of initiatives towards the product. These can also be used as a model for relaunching a brand.

Facelifting, reinventing and innovating

The management of a brand involves maintaining the present (what the brand is now) while at the same time working for the future. It is the present that constitutes the source of income and therefore allows the development of the growth products of the future. As shown in Figure 16.2, in order to stay young, a brand must implement three types of initiatives at the same time:

- It must continually modernise the 'prototype' in the same way that Nivea introduced Nivea Soft to modernise its basic in the famous metallic blue jar. Nivea Soft is lighter and less greasy, and is marketed in a white jar. Lacoste regularly improves its famous 12 × 12 polo shirt in terms of the quality of the wool, the colours, the sleeves and so on.

- It must also reinvent the 'prototype', just as

Figure 16.2   Sustaining brand equity long term: dual management in practice

Lacoste produced a tight-fitting shirt with Lycra since this is how the woman of 2005 liked to dress. It was an immediate hit. For example, imagine a brand of haircare products whose basic product is a lotion. It would certainly have to modernise it in terms of the packaging, and update the formulation. But it should above all consider how today's customers would want to apply the product. It is quite possible that rubbing a lotion into the scalp is something that is no longer done, even though the product itself is extremely relevant. In this case, another method of application would certainly be the best form of innovation. You only have to think of Nivea, which invented the first spray-on sun lotion.

▌ Finally, it must innovate by actively seeking out the trends and behaviour that currently dominate the younger consumer segments, since these are the segments that will generate customer loyalty in the future. To return to the example of the haircare brand, it simply cannot afford not to create new products – which are of course in line with its brand contract. Young people are mad about hair gels, styling products and hair colour. These markets certainly exist already, but the brand can create new segments within these markets that work in its favour.

Actively seeking out new types of behaviour means opening up to the idea of exploring new distribution channels, since new behaviour is often linked to new places and situations. These innovations also provide an opportunity to launch new and truly groundbreaking publicity campaigns, both in terms of their basic structure and especially their style. In this way, the brand sends out clear signals that it is reinventing itself. At the same time, these campaigns aim to launch the business of these innovations, just as they would for any new product.

Detecting the symptoms of ageing brands

Brands are built by the sum of all their behaviours creating value at contact points with customers. This is why brands should regularly monitor their behaviour. There are many sure symptoms of a brand dropping off, and they can be grouped into seven main types.

Insufficient preparation for the future

▌ Insufficient rate of new products in the yearly sales.

▌ Low rate of patent registration.

▌ Low rate of trademark registration (a sign of little need to name new products and services).

▌ Insufficient investment in R&D, in market sensing, in trend spotting.

▌ Insufficient knowledge about new uses and new emerging situations of use.

▌ Date of the last executive committee meeting to address these issues.

Insufficient dual management

▌ Insufficient knowledge about non-consumers, modern consumers, tomorrow's consumers.

▌ More and more sales to a reduced number of clients.

▌ Following the demands of existing clients, not foreseeing the changes in the market.

▌ Slow but regular increase of the average age of clients.

Insufficient capacity to capture growth pockets as they emerge

▌ Thinking the brand only through its historical product, without being ready to capture emerging new materials and demands.

▌ Excessive vision of what is called brand coherence, thus limiting the types of extensions to be made by the brand.

Insufficient relevance

▌ Weakening of the present positioning and values.

▌ Weakening of the way values are materialised.

▌ Date of the last customer satisfaction questionnaire.

▌ Date of the last interview with lost customers.

▌ Increase in proportion of customers declaring they are 'moderately satisfied'.

▌ Date of the last blind test.

▌ Lowering rate of repeat purchase.

▌ Decrease in spontaneous awareness (saliency).

▌ Decrease in number of spontaneous press quotes.

Insufficient vitality at contact

▌ Lack of regular updating of the quality of the logo and visual symbol of the brand.

▌ Date of last change or facelift for the packaging (design, ergonomics).

▌ Lack of regular facelifts for stores or concessions.

▌ Lack of organised merchandising, lack of plans to regularly rethink it.

▌ Lack of service (call centres, websites and so on).

▌ Lack of brand proximity marketing.

▌ Lack of advertising.

Insufficient self-stimulation

▌ Lack of curiosity.

▌ Lack of desire to surprise.

▌ Lack of PR events.

▌ Lack of contacts with new opinion leaders, with the press.

Insufficient staffing

▌ Lack of young managers.

▌ Sex imbalance among executives (100 per cent male or 100 per cent female).

Back to the future

Often a brand's decline is tied to forgetting the brand's mission. Little by little small adjustments have been added to the strategy, and cumulatively they have led the brand astray. This is how heavy discounters become less heavy discounters, luxury brands become less luxurious, feminine brands become less feminine and so on. 'Back to the core' is a classic revitalising strategy. It does not mean being obsessed with the past, but if the early vision and mission are still valid, trying to come back to it while acknowledging that the product itself may need to be updated.

Many groups act preventively by regularly checking the relevance of their identity and the fact that the operations are actually in line with this strategy. For instance, at Decathlon, as soon as operating margins get higher, the alarm bell rings. Decathlon's deep culture focuses on making people happy through sport and physical activities. This is achieved through a remarkable policy of providing own brands with the best performance/price ratio on the market. Higher margins seem to indicate that this ratio is becoming less exceptional than it should be.

This is also very typical of hotel management. Regularly at Accor Hotels, each brand holds a seminar called 'Back to the future'. The goal is to assess if the strategy is being followed or if in fact it has subtly changed. If it is the case, what services should be deleted or added in order to once more fulfill the brand's mission?

17

Managing global brands

Geographic extension is the necessary fate of brands. On it depend the brand's growth, and its ability to innovate and to sustain its competitive edge in terms of economies of scale and productivity. As such, marketing directors are no longer questioning the principle of international expansion, but are preoccupied with the means by which this can be accomplished. They ask themselves: Where should we go? What balance do we maintain between a global brand which shuns linguistic and national frontiers, and one which makes provision for local requirements and context? Which brands are destined to have global significance and which should remain on a national footing? Finally, how do we rationalise the portfolio of national brands into a small number of global brands? Any such transition must be carefully managed.

The debate between advocates of brand globalisation and those of a sound adaptation to local markets was set in an academic fashion in the 1980s through the articles of Levitt (1983), and Quelch and Hoff (1986). One had to choose sides almost ideologically. Twenty years later, we are able to learn from past experience which was more or less

successful. If on a global scale we cannot deny the existence of certain factors that bring together countries and cultures, we must not forget that the speed of this coming together is sometimes slower than reckoned. Moreover, if at a certain level of generality or social and cultural trends consumers in many countries declare the same motivations and expectations, a closer look reveals slight differences that must be taken into account. This chapter urges us to a pragmatic approach. The empires built by Marlboro or Coca-Cola will not be replicated, as they benefited from particular historical and time factors. The international expansion of Coca-Cola was fostered in great part by two world wars and the presence of GIs in Europe and Asia. It took Marlboro 35 years to conquer the world and McDonald's 22 years! A contemplation of these models, however agreeable it may be, is quite useless for Danone, for example, whose brand image varies from one country to the next because the products through which it penetrated these countries cannot be the same: creamy desserts in Germany, plain yoghurts in France, fruit yoghurts in Great Britain. How do you then create a uniform image around the concept of health if in concrete terms the brand does not have the same products in each market or country? This is the reality for most brands today. They are not much helped by the models of brands that have created a new category (Coke, Amazon, IBM, Chanel). They need other models, more relevant to the situation most companies and brands are facing, when they operate in already existing categories.

The latest on globalisation

In 2003 the G8 summit coincided with an anniversary that went unnoticed. Twenty years earlier, in May–June 1983, an article entitled 'The globalization of markets', by Professor Theodore Levitt was published in the *Harvard Business Review*. The direct and simple nature of its argument was to make it one of the most quoted and influential articles in the field of business management. According to Professor Levitt, national differences and preferences would no longer carry any weight in the face of the progress and reduced costs associated with international products and brands. With everyone in the world travelling either physically or, in most cases, via satellite television, the desire to buy products and brands sold in other countries would also greatly increase.

In short, while recognising that the world was indeed round, companies had a vested interest in regarding it as flat, and treating it like a single market. This was the strategy adopted by Coca-Cola, McDonald's and Microsoft, and by the many companies that followed in their wake. The main obstacle to the globalisation of markets was decentralised organisation and its symbol – national marketing directors who, by their very nature, could not help but promote the opposite argument, the one that justified their position.

Twenty years later, how far has this prediction of globalised markets been fulfilled? Anyone who travels knows that the same brands are found in countries throughout the world, whether it is Philips, Michelin, Sony, Hugo Boss, Nike, HSBC or Axa. However, beneath the surface, what do companies really think of globalised brands? Is it still what they want? Is it still their ideal?

It should first of all be pointed out that Professor Levitt's prediction was based essentially on factors associated with production and on the unmistakable competitive advantages of economies of scale. In fact, most globalisation has taken place at production level, which is why it has been the target of some of the criticisms levelled by the anti-globalisation lobby. In her very interesting book *No Logo* (1999), Naomi Klein berates the companies that do not have factories and, as a result, wash their hands of anything that goes on in the archaic factories of their Asian subcontractors. Nike is a good example of this. By contrast, when Jean Mantelet, the creator of Moulinex, tried to keep employment in Upper Normandy at all costs, it ultimately cost him his company (but not the brand). The movement towards globalisation of the upstream (production) stage is therefore unavoidable. Successful companies have globalised their factories and supply chains to bring them closer to their markets and/or take advantage of lower costs. The car industry is a typical example.

It should, however, be recognised that this is a movement that has affected products more than services. While the circulation of the flow of money and information no longer encounters any barriers and is instantaneous, the movement towards the relocation of, for example, the processing of financial information, data files and bank databases is only just beginning. UK banks and insurance companies have taken the initiative by finding in Bangalore, the Indian equivalent of Silicon Valley, a well-qualified but much less expensive workforce. Call centres serving

French customers are often based on the island of Mauritius.

There is one point on which the forecast of globalised markets can be challenged – the downstream stage of brands and products that are a long way from the predicted standardisation. Of course, you find Porsche and Jaguar worldwide, but these are exported brands, like Chanel. They are the standard bearers of a particular country or culture, and appeal to an international clientele. The car industry provides a good illustration of why the concept of the global product is in fact a myth. Paradoxically, the most global product that ever existed in the car sector was Ford's famous Model T – it was totally standardised, with 20 million cars manufactured and sold worldwide. Even though the domestic market was by far its principal market, the Model T was a truly universal product. In 1981, the launch of the famous Ford Escort in the United States and Europe appeared to be a sign of globalisation. In fact the US and European models only had one part in common – the radiator cap. Hardly a global product! More recently, the Ford Focus was launched in Europe (1990) and the United States (2000), and this time the models from these two world regions had 65 per cent of parts in common. But Ford does not think it can go much further – there are too many structural and long-term factors against it. So what are they exactly?

■ The first is that energy is very cheap in the United States, which it will never be again in Europe. Low-energy innovations that have an enhanced value in Europe are regarded as irrelevant in the United States. This is why the engine type cannot be the same in both regions.

■ The second is that vehicle standards and testing remain primarily national and in any event regional. Manufacturers therefore have to adapt their vehicles to suit the specifications and requirements of local test centres. Safety standards in the United States are less stringent than in Europe and Asia.

■ The third factor concerns structural differences such as the type of roads, climate, humidity and the resulting use of vehicles. This therefore involves very different drivers of preference on either side of the Atlantic.

■ The last factor is the customers themselves. Everyone knows that the Germans like a certain type of comfort, the British and French another. Today, manufacturers are flocking to China which alone will shortly represent 25 per cent of the growth of the world car market. They are opening factories and establishing joint ventures like PSA Peugeot Citroën, but not with the aim of slavishly duplicating European models. It is impossible to appeal to a market of 300 million Chinese who now have the financial resources to access the market without taking account of the customers themselves.

The time has in fact come to recognise the post-global brand – the brand that no longer tries to adhere unreservedly to the model of total globalisation, which is no longer perceived as ideal. Of course, globalisation at the upstream or production stage remains a priority in many sectors. Like the car sector, which has reduced costs by sharing production platforms, companies can still save more money by creating a smaller number of product platforms that are able, if the need arises, to produce differentiated models. The service sector could also benefit from upstream globalisation.

However, the further you go downstream and the closer you get to the customer, the more obvious it becomes that the global concept tends to be replaced by the regional or local concept in the case of a large country. There will therefore never be a car that is truly global, but a more American type for the

United States, and other types that are characteristically European and Chinese. This has already happened on other mass-consumption markets. For example, the strategy of the US company Procter & Gamble is based on regionalisation, with the US flagship brands Tide, Whisper and Clairol becoming Ariel, Allways and Wella in Europe. The company has a factory in Europe for all its detergents.

It is becoming more and more common for companies to develop products for specific geographical regions, in the way that Hennessy created Pure White for Europe. Dannon (USA) could not sell its drinkable, low-fat yoghurts in Europe since they neither correspond to local taste nor meet the current food standards requirements. It is however true that initiatives designed to open up regional markets, such as the EU, Mercosur and Alena, help to make the region, in the broader sense of the term, a relevant market segment. Furthermore, it is at regional level that the world's markets, and even its historical and cultural communities, are at their most permeable.

Finally, even when a brand appears to be global, when it is distributed and well known in countries throughout the world, closer examination reveals that the product is often far from standardised – it is more of a composite, hybrid or highly adapted product. For example, l'Oréal differentiates between the cosmetic products of its so-called global brands by basing them on the four types of climates in China, since they determine four skin types.

The idea of a global market and the standardisation that it implies, has usefully served to start a basic movement in all companies. But over-globalisation leads to loss of relevance, a lesson that companies have often learnt to their cost since 1983. This is why today's brands are post-global – they have assimilated the myth and distanced themselves from it without exactly renouncing it. Today, it is more appropriate to refer to selective globalisation.

Why are American brands ideogically more global, and the European ones less so? We hypothesise that the American globalised brands were exports of successful brands that had taken many years to find their optimal functioning and positioning in the United States. The idea that this equation of success would simply apply elsewhere seemed to be taken for granted, for the United States themselves constitute a non-homogeneous market. As an example, it is noticeable that Wal-Mart's first store outside the United States, in Mexico, was created 30 years after the creation of Wal-Mart (Bell, Lal and Salmon, 2003). Its worldwide competitor Carrefour opened its first foreign hypermarket in 1969, only six years after it created its first store. Unsurprisingly Wal-Mart applied the rules that made its success in the United States, but in some countries, more remote from the United States than Mexico, such as Brazil, the golden rule of everyday low price does not seem to work. The average Brazilian consumer is instead eager to capitalise on special bargains. Carrefour, being unsure about its optimal formula, was more open to the specificities of the new countries.

The same holds true for Nestlé, number one food company in the world. How can Nestlé be sure that the situation is the same everywhere when it comes from a small country like Switzerland? In fact Nestlé internationalised to four countries its first-ever product, powdered milk, four months after it was launched in Switzerland.

We tend to favour extreme solutions (to be or not to be global?), for they are rhetorically more provocative. Real life is in the middle, but it is more complicated. People have to collaborate in the organisation. Then the question becomes how to build a collaborative organisation (Hansen and Nohria, 2003).

What is new then? Realism in globalisation, the mark of the post-global brand.

Patterns of brand globalisation

Before we move forward, it is important to specify the meaning of global. For most managers a brand is global when it is sold everywhere in the world. Finding ads in all airports about Nokia, Dell, IBM or Alcatel seems to be a living sign of real globalisation. However, this may be a superficial vision.

We know from Chapter 1 that a brand is a system relating three facets, a concept, a name, and a product or service. It can be pictured as a triangle. As a consequence, when one speaks of globalisation, one should specify of what?

We saw that there are strong compelling economic reasons to globalise products or platforms. There are also good reasons to use the same name, for the sake of capitalising on one single name and exploiting the extra value of global perception. Finally, some concepts are reflections of the existence of global segments. Actually, the combination of these three poles creates eight possible alternative strategies as far as the continuum from globalisation to localisation is concerned (see Table 17.1).

When people refer to globalisation, it is generally in a loose sense, a feeling that the brand is known, visible and distributed everywhere. When we travel abroad some brands do seem global: we see them on billboards as soon as we land at an airport. It is this vision that creates negative attitudes about globali-sation, the feeling of an inescapable loss of country differences. All commercial centres sell now the same stuff, the same brands, throughout the world. Human richness and diversity now seem dangerously eroded by the law of economies of scale. Of course, those who do not travel are pleased by the possibility of accessing the brands and products they see on television while watching the world.

What are these eight structural types obtained by combining the two possible answers on each part of the brand system?

- Type 1 is the fully global model. Here there are very few adaptations, except for details.

- Type 2 recognises the need for different positioning strategy: Mars is a meal substitute in UK (have a Mars a day), but an energiser in Europe. Cars follow the same approach. What is a small car for the German market is seen as a family car in Portugal.

- Type 3 acknowledges the need for important product adaptations. Different countries have different tastes for coffee. The skin and hair of Brazilians are not the same as those of Argentinians. In China, according to the l'Oréal Group, because of the differences in climate, sun, and humidity, there are four types of skin balance to be respected from north to south, east to west. Connex is a world

Table 17.1   From global to local: eight alternative patterns of globalisation

(Yes = global, No = localised)

Type	1	2	3	4	5	6	7	8
Name	Yes	Yes	Yes	Yes	No	No	No	No
Positioning	Yes	No	Yes	No	Yes	No	Yes	No
Product	Yes	Yes	No	No	Yes	Yes	No	No
Examples :	Coke	Mars	Nescafé	Persil	Ariel/	Volks-	Cycl-	Pure
	Chanel	Martell	Garnier		Tide	wagen	europe	local
	Amex				Vauxhall Opel	(Group)	(Group)	
	Sony					Benckiser		

ground transportation brand: it operates railways, buses and metro systems wherever municipalities want to create concessions for this public service. However, the same concept, 'security', means very different things in Stockholm, where Connex operates the metro, and in Rio de Janeiro. Thus, obedience to the same brand values cannot mean providing the same secure product everywhere. Local expectations are not as high in South America as they are in Scandinavia for instance, or the capacity to pay the price.

- Type 4 is the result of brands being split between companies. This is the case of Persil: this brand is operated by Unilever and by Henkel. The same holds true for Gervais, an ice cream brand at Nestlé, and a range brand of dairies at Danone.

- Type 5 results when the company cannot use the same name for legal reasons everywhere. For instance Vauxhall in the UK is Opel in Europe.

- Type 6 results when almost similar products are sold under two world brands with different price positionings. It is what is currently happening at the high end of the Volkswagen range, where the cars are very close even in design to the Audi entry models.

- Type 7 is the business model of Cycleurope, leader in the bicycle market. Cycleurope is a Swedish company, which has bought the market leading bike brands in other countries. These are typical local names, with high recognition and proximity. There are strong differences in the bike standards expected by the Dutch, Swedes, Germans, French and Italians: the size of the wheel, the gear, the height of the bike are different. Standardisation can only concern the frames.

- Type eight is the fully local model.

Looking more specifically at two of these variables, the brand name and the product platform (is it common or are there widely different products?), there are four strategies.

Danone for instance, like Unilever, is not obsessed with common names, but with the creation of products/concepts that reach an annual turnover worldwide of €1 billion. The CEO, Frank Riboud, states that 'our ambition is not to develop brands that are number one in the world, but brands that are number one locally with global world concepts/products'. For instance 'Taillefine' (literally, slim waist), whose name changes according to the country (Light'fit in the United States, Silhouette in Canada, Corpus in Brazil, Ser in Argentina, Vitalinea in Spain, Vitasnella in Italy, Vitaline in Greece), is a concept of adult tasty food aimed at those maintaining a low-fat diet. It is stretched over the three divisions of Danone group, dairies, water and biscuits. As such one finds the products of this concept either as purified water, or as biscuits under Lu source brand, or as dairies under Danone source brand. But in Argentina the group has kept the endorsing local brand Serenissima, with its 65 per cent market share, to reinforce its competitiveness. This local brand, number one in Argentina, now endorses the global concepts.

Another global concept is Actimel, a specific yoghurt designed to reinforce the body's natural defences. It is sold in 22 countries, with a sales turnover of half a billion euros, and a sales growth of 40 per cent in 2002. A final example of a world concept is the aromatised water sold as Danone Activ'Aro in the UK, Volvic Magic in France, and Bonafont Levite in Mexico. On the whole more than 60 per cent of the Danone group sales are made by concepts that are the market leader in most of the countries where they are sold.

Unilever has been criticised for having more than 1,400 brands, none of which reach the critical size (US $1 billion) to become a world mega-brand. It is now engaged in a fierce reduction of the number of brands. However, to take the ice-cream business, it is operated under the endorsement of the well-known names of the former local market leaders (Walls in the UK, Miko in France and so on), all presenting a common international logo. But their sales are made through power products that are sold globally and managed as real brands: Magnum, Solero and so on. In the margarine business, trust is very important. Local names have been maintained, but the whole company operates four typical product platforms for the whole European market.

The matrix in Table 17.2 reminds us that most companies started in quadrant A. They were international in sales before they thought they had an asset called a brand, and by default before they realised they had to globalise their business. Mostly operating in existing categories, and they do not consider Coke or McDonald's as a valid benchmark for them.

From A they can move either to B or C. B entails rationalising the products: it is the main source of profits and synergies. C means creating brand transfers to reduce the number of brands. The output is less strong and the risks higher. However, for all disruptive new products such as Actimel, the quadrant D strategy should be adopted.

Why globalise?

An economic necessity

Very few people dispute the need to internationalise business. World commerce has existed since caravans brought spices from all over Asia to Europe. The great naval explorers of the 15th and 16th centuries were also motivated by the prospect of opening new routes to merchandise. Colonisation had economic motives: access to raw materials, to gold, then wheat, then oil.

Production was the first business function to be delocalised. Finance is international. It is the time of marketing. Why then global brands? Why not simply international or multi-local brands?

In the competitive race, economies of scale provide a strategic lever in that they contribute to competitive pricing. A company designing a car with worldwide market potential in mind has a competitive advantage over the manufacturer who only sets his sights locally. Even though the latter may produce a car which better reflects the tastes of his own country, the difference in price from that of a Japanese or a Korean car designed from the start with a worldwide market in mind will naturally make even the most patriotic motorist hesitate. This is why Renault's Twingo, whose low price is a key element of positioning for the easy-to-live-with car, was designed from the start for a whole continent: the same product everywhere.

Table 17.2 Globalisation matrix

	Different brands	**Same brand everywhere**
Same products or concepts	Different brands, identical platforms (Unilever, Danone) **(B)**	Global brands, no adaption of product (Coca-Cola, Chanel, Sony) **(D)**
Different products or concepts	Sum of local tastes Franchises **(A)**	Nestlé (Nescafé) Yoplait President **(C)**

The local company – even if it is positioned in a niche – has no other way of overcoming the price handicap than to extend its outlets while innovating. Geographical extension is an essential condition in the race for survival.

If the brand is to remain competitive, its innovation must be offered immediately to all at the lowest possible price. The marginal cost of each progressive feature rises day by day. Hundreds of researchers are needed to even hope to innovate. Industrial investments and research costs must now be set against low unit margins. Using the awareness and public confidence which it has acquired, the brand provides the firm with access to outlets on an ever-widening scale. Without these, such investments could not be economically justified. The manufacturer's brand opens the way to progress and, at the same time, makes it available for all.

To summarise thus far, globalisation particularly affects products by allowing overall savings and leaps in the experience curve. But a global product does not necessarily signify a global name, in other words moving from a single product to a single brand needs further discussion on the subject of economy of signs and symbols.

The global name: a source of advantages

In certain market areas, the global brand is a necessity, whereas in many other cases it is a means of exploiting and taking advantage of new opportunities in communication.

The single brand is a necessity whenever the clients themselves are already operating worldwide. Firms using IBM or Dell in London would see no sense in having the same equipment in their Bogota or Kuala Lumpur offices under a different brand name. The same applies to most technological industries. Caterpillar, Sumitomo, Schlumberger, Siemens and Alcatel are of necessity world brands – quite apart from the fact that they are global enterprises.

It is also necessary to retain a single brand when the brand itself corresponds to the signature or *griffe* of its individual creator. Take the luxury trade – Pierre Cardin is Pierre Cardin wherever his products are found, just as Ralph Lauren is Ralph Lauren. Their creations are bought around the world because their signature bears witness to the values of their creator. Whether or not the creator lives on in body or in spirit does not change the rule: from a single source comes a single name.

These cases apart, the single brand permits the exploitation of new international opportunities:

- As tourism develops, for instance, it is a disadvantage that certain products have different names in different countries. If this were not the case, tourists could find their brands. Seeing the queues of comforted tourists from all countries in front of McDonald's instead of Quick is enough to convince anyone. This argument applies, however, more to some sectors than to others: to food more than lingerie and to car oil more than cooking oil. But the main advantage is linked to the synergy: the exposure of an American executive to DHL in Europe will benefit the renown and the reputation of DHL in the United States. Brands acquire additional credibility when they prove to have international appeal. This is why in 1989 Ariel brought out the first advertising commercial featuring testimony from housewives from different European countries.

- The more international media develop, the greater the opportunities they provide for the single brand. This has long been the case with traditional media; it now concerns satellite, cable and the internet. Real opportunities for worldwide coverage are provided by such events as Grand Slam tennis tournaments, the Tour de France, the World Soccer Cup, the Olympic Games, Formula 1 motor racing, etc. Through its sponsorship of the Roland Garros tournament, the BNP Bank is known as far afield as California where they speak of the tournament as the 'BNP Tournament', just as there is a 'Volvo Grand Prix'. These programmes reach an international audience and therefore in practical terms exclude on-the-spot local brands, since the costs involved in appealing to only part of the audience would be prohibitive. Only global brands can be present in worldwide events such as the Olympic games or Formula 1 motor racing. Only the global brand can justify the cost of sponsoring such worldwide stars as Tiger Woods, or Michael Schumacher.

From single name to global brand

How far do we push the global idea? To what extent do we continue to make marketing decisions on a national level? Should we globalise positioning, creative concepts and even the ads themselves? The fact is that, though no one denies that a single name is often an advantage, there is some dispute over the brand strategy to be adopted, together with the form it should take. For some, the essence of marketing is to stick close to customers, while for others, the advantages offered by homogeneous marketing on a global scale offer no alternative.

Before dealing with the respective arguments, it is important to be precise about the terms used. Global marketing implies the wish to extend a single marketing mix to a particular region (eg Europe or Asia), or even to the world. It also denotes a situation in which a firm's competitive position in one country can be significantly affected by its position in other countries. The global approach sees the role of individual countries as only part of a wider competitive action.

The global approach considers countries and their roles in a widened competitive field. The aims of marketing in each country are no longer determined by the local subsidiary, but

are decided upon according to the global competitive system. Thus, whereas traditionally each subsidiary planned their activities based on their own resources and the domestic market, within a global strategy the following is the case:

- Certain countries have the task of developing a marketing mix for a new product, testing its capabilities in their home markets before its extension to other countries. This therefore constitutes a test, not of the best marketing mix on single national lines but of a global marketing mix prior to extension. As a consequence, nowadays it is insufficient to keep an eye on the competition in one country alone – every country should be included.

- Certain countries are assigned to develop know-how on a particular brand or a type of product brand so that they can act as a precursor and coordinator for others.

In contrast to the global approach, many multinational firms follow a 'multi-local' philosophy, preferring to follow specific trends in each country's market. Not only will the same brand differ from one market to the next both in positioning and in price level, but it is also supported by its own specific advertising campaign. Coca-Cola follows a global marketing policy, while Nestlé prefers multi-local marketing. Thus Maggi ready-snacks were launched:

- in Germany under the name 'Maggi, 5 Minuten Terrine' and positioned as a practical nutritious food for men and women and between 30 and 40;

- in France under its own name 'Bolino' (with Maggi in small print) and positioned as an instant snack for the young single person;

- in Switzerland under another name, 'Quick Lunch', and positioned as a quick meal approved by mothers.

In these three countries, the product achieved its sales objectives. Manichean comparisons should, therefore, not be made between global and multi-local policies in terms of either customer appreciation or sales. However, a company's ultimate aim is not simply to achieve maximum sales – marketing globalisation leads to profitability.

▮ In the first place, it cuts out duplicated tasks. For example, instead of bringing out different TV advertising for each country, the firm can use a single ad for the region in mind. Bearing in mind the high cost of producing these ads (up to US$1 million), the potential for savings is considerable. The McCann-Erickson agency was proud of the fact that they have saved Coca-Cola US$90 million in production costs over 20 years, thanks to producing ads with world appeal. Even if production costs are, from now on, low compared to the investment in the media themselves, rendering the economy argument less forceful, it is still worthwhile for middle brands used to developing one campaign per country!

▮ By launching a product in several countries simultaneously, it eliminates the problems which arise when a new product appears at staggered intervals from one country to the next, depending on the local situation. This has the drawback of allowing competitors time to pre-empt certain ideas in one country which they have seen in another.

▮ Globalisation allows a firm to exploit good ideas wherever they come from. Since good ideas are rare, they must be made maximum use of. By getting representatives in several countries to put their minds to a particular question, there is a better chance of coming up with a strong idea that can be used on a global plane. This is how the global idea 'Put a tiger in your tank' came to be used around the world. The Timotei shampoo was developed in Finland and spread to other European countries to benefit from the emergence of a trend towards natural goods. The worldwide drink Malibu was created in South Africa.

▮ A global policy allows a firm to slip the stranglehold of the major retailer, whose commercial demands are closer to a systematic toll than to a payment for real services to the producer. A national brand may have few means of extricating itself; such is the intensity of distribution concentration that it is forced to use a small number of major retailers in order to reach the consumer. The global brand is fortunately less susceptible to local pressures.

▮ When a brand goes international, it can however benefit from the internationalisation of its main domestic retailers. Thus Wal-Mart acts as bridgehead to many North American brands, and Carrefour to many European brands.

The emergence of global segments

All sociocultural studies underscore the convergence of life-styles. There are fewer differences between top executives in Japan and in Germany than between executives and employees within Germany. In addition identification models act on a worldwide basis: some Chinese women identify with American woman, others with the French, and a growing number now identify with Korea's style of beauty. The same may be true in Holland or in New York. This is why l'Oréal has developed a wide array of global brands: far from pushing towards uniformity, this group diffuses heterogeneity. This is why it takes much care in offering brands that symbolise not one single type of beauty but all of them, from Softsheen Carson for the black community worldwide, to Sue Uemura or Maybelline. The group takes much care in leaving each of its brand's headquarters in its home country to preserve its specificity.

However, they must globalise their concept and products and communications. Global segments should each have a global brand corresponding to their needs.

Pricing issues

Finally, the price factor will be a key component of the homogenisation of brand strategies in the future. Indeed everything points to reducing the price span within which the same brand can evolve from one country to another, from one area to another.

▌ The existence of a concentration of distributors on a regional or international level creates a major destabilising threat to brands that optimise locally their price policy. There is nothing to prevent the distributors from demanding the lowest price to be seen in Europe, which may be in Portugal for instance, or in a country that has lowered its prices as a means of competition.

▌ The emergence of parallel markets needs to be avoided as these would destabilise the normal distribution channels of a country and therefore the relationship between a brand and its distributors.

There is indeed a close relationship between price positioning and market positioning. A brand cannot be the most expensive on the market in one place and in the mainstream in another. The price level situates the brand in terms of perceived quality, performance and prestige. In the market for special vintages of champagne, for example, to be the most expensive, on a par with or cheaper than Dom Perignon, does not position its challenger Veuve Clicquot in the same way. Reducing the international price variance of a brand is a factor which encourages uniform positioning and, by extension, affects the whole brand policy. Unless a policy is explicitly chosen that allows optimum prices locally and strong

price differences from one country to another, identical products need to be sold under different brand names in each country. This is the strategy followed by Benckiser, which buys strong local brands. R&D are indeed by necessity European, using the principle of a 'lead country' for the development of new products and the definition of the marketing mix.

Fighting the grey market

A classical consequence of economic heterogeneity is the grey market. To reach public accessibility, brands must align their prices on the local economic level. However, when a gap exists among countries not too far apart in distance, a grey market grows, disturbing the sales and trade goodwill in the country invaded by parallel imports. Of course, in the case of luxury goods with selective distribution agreements, the first reaction is to install some form of trace, in order to identify those commercial agents that break these agreements, reselling outside their zone.

A second approach is to change the brand. Thus in Northern Europe Viakal, an anti-limescaling household product, became Antikal to stop the grey market of Italian Viakal products, which were sold there at a price 30 per cent lower. Without going to such extremes, Hennessy cognac decided to stop selling its VSOP product in Western Europe, and instead created a customised product called Fine de Cognac. Europe was in any case drinking less and less VSOP, but it had become a source of a grey market for Russia. In fact, throughout the world, global brands are developing more and more regional products for these commercial reasons.

A final approach of course is to create a price corridor across all countries of a region or continent. This cuts the risk of a grey market growing, but handicaps the sales where the brand is overpriced for the sake of respecting the international corridor. As an example, the net trade price of Absolut vodka in Europe is around €5.5 on average as evidenced in Table 17.3.

The benefits of a global image

A great deal has been written on the subject of global brands, but what exactly do we know about them? In fact very little, until recently when the subject was further clarified by the three studies outlined below. Two of these studies focus on the benefits of having – that is, being perceived as having – a global image. But how does perceived brand globalness (PBG) create value? There are a number of reasons for creating a global brand – economies of scale, synergies between countries, the speed with which innovations created worldwide can be brought onto the market, the existence of exploitable global segments and finally, as has already been suggested, the benefits of having an international image. Today, in the age of cultural integration, modernity is expressed via internationalism. The perception of globalness would therefore increase perceived value. It is symptomatic that, in countries throughout the world, young people's favourite brands are usually international, whereas the reverse is true for adults.

One of the studies (Alden, Steenkamp and Batra, 1999) set out to validate this hypothesis. In a quantitative study carried out in the United States and South Korea, the authors demonstrated that perceived globalness (the fact of being perceived to be selling products worldwide) exerted a strong influence over purchase decisions. But contrary to expectation, this influence was not because perceived globalness enabled consumers to participate in a global culture. In fact, perceived globalness primarily influenced the perceived quality, and second the perceived prestige, of the brand. These effects were however not quite as strong for ethnocentric consumers, that is, those who were more focused on national values. These results needed to be extended to other countries and include other criteria for consumer segmentation, since the cultural connections between South Korea and the United States are well known.

This was done by Holt, Quelch and Taylor (2003) when they studied how global perceptions drive value, using a sample of 1,800 respondents in 12 countries. According to the study, perceived globalness influences brand preferences via five levers:

- As an indicator of quality (higher quality due to perceived globalness). This effect is in fact the most important, and explained 34 per cent of the variance in preferences observed by the study.

- The second effect is the increased status conferred on the brand by its perceived globalness. This explained 12 per cent of the variance and coincides with the results of the previous study.

- The third lever is linked to the images and special characteristics attributed to individual countries. Global brands are often associated with a country of origin and therefore a stereotype of competence, such as clocks and watches (Switzerland), TGV high speed trains (France). This accounted for 10 per cent of the variance.

- Increased responsibility, fostered by perceived brand globalness. Because they are represented worldwide, global brands

Table 17.3 How Absolut copes with the grey market: corridor pricing

Country	Germany	France	Spain	Italy	UK	Greece	Portugal
Net price	5.21	5.81	5.16	5.35	5.97	5.66	5.77

Prices are estimates of net/net trade retail prices in Europe in euros have a higher profile and therefore have to be more environmentally and socially aware than other brands. Being big is equated with being more responsible. This effect only explained 8 per cent of the variance. However, it was extremely important for 22 per cent of respondents, and important for 41 per cent of this group.

▌ Finally, the American image, or the American dream, is associated with a number of global brands. This effect did not explain the variance in preferences between brands when consumers were taken as a whole. However, as soon as these international consumers were segmented, the American image was a dream for 39 per cent, which made it a factor of preference, while it was anathema for 29 per cent and therefore a negative factor and rejection.

To their credit, Holt *et al* segmented the consumers. In the seven segments that resulted – from 'pro-west' to 'anti-globalisation' – the hierarchy of the five levers was completely different. How people understand and value global brands is very segmented. Countries are also heterogeneous. China, for instance, is both pro and anti American values: it has consumers belonging to both groups. Muslim countries such as Indonesia, Turkey and Egypt are very influenced by the perception of globalness. However, one should recall that the interviewees were not laypeople, but well off ones, probably with a westernised life-style. People in India, Brazil and South Africa were not very much influenced by perceptions of globalness; is it because they have a strong local culture they are proud of? Finally, those least influenced by the perception of brand globalness are US consumers.

This should not be a surprise: the Americans do not consider that the choice of other countries is relevant. It is an ethnocentric country. Also, since many of the so-called global brands are American in origin, their status is ambiguous. They are selling everywhere in the world but they seem to be deep local brands.

Schuiling and Kapferer (2004) have compared the distinctive properties of local and international food brands, separating, however, international brands in their home country from the same brands in other countries. In fact, their data show that the best brand profile is that of the international brands in their home country. No wonder: countries export their best in class brands. The data also show how global brands really differ from local ones. Working on a database of 507 brands in four countries, and 9,739 respondents, Schuiling and Kapferer have isolated the discriminant properties of each type of brand: local (that is, sold in one country, whatever its perception by the public) and international (sold in all countries, whatever the perception of the public). The authors first notice that on the whole local brands that have been present for a much longer time in the country are endowed with a higher brand awareness score than more recent international arrivals. Since brand awareness is correlated with image (see page 21), are the so-called differences of image only an outcome of this brand awareness gap? When the data are adjusted for awareness, there do remain differences in image, some negative, some positive, as evidenced by Table 17.4.

It is noticeable that, compared with local brands, global brands have a significant deficit on:

▌ health value (–3.29 per cent);

▌ reliability (–3.05 per cent);

▌ trust (–1.88 per cent).

On the other hand, they outperform local brands on the following levers:

Table 17.4 How global and local brands differ (in percentages, after adjusting for brand awareness level)

	Local brand (B. Aw = 85%)	Global brand (B. Aw = 85%)	Global–local
High quality	25.29	27.07	+1.78
Trust	22.11	20.23	−1.88
Reliable	22.11	19.06	−3.05
Fashionable	14.04	15.50	+1.46
Original	13.57	14.64	+1.07
Distinct	12.56	13.70	+1.14
Sympathetic	11.74	13.19	+1.45
Funny	9.76	12.90	+3.14
Pleasing	7.08	12.90	+5.82
Healthy	15.56	12.27	−3.29
Innovating	6.08	11.50	+5.42
A leader	8.07	9.33	+1.26
Unique	4.40	7.61	+3.21

(Base 9,739 respondents , 507 brands)

Source: Kapferer and Schuiling (2004)

▌ pleasing (+ 5.82 per cent);

▌ innovativeness (+5.42 per cent);

▌ uniqueness (+3.21 per cent);

▌ fun, thrill (+3.14 per cent);

▌ high quality (+ 1.78 per cent);

▌ fashionable (+ 1.46 per cent);

▌ sympathetic (+ 1.45 per cent).

Conditions favouring global brands

Certain situations make global communication and brand policy easier. They are linked to the product, to the markets, to the force of brand identity and also to the organisation of companies.

Social and cultural changes provide a favourable platform for global brands. Under these circumstances, part of the market no longer identifies with long-established local values and seeks new models on which to build its identity. Turning its back on prevailing national values, it is open to outside influence from abroad. In drinking Coca-Cola, we are drinking the American myth – in other words the fresh, open, bubbling, young and dynamic all-American images. Youngsters form a target in search of identity and in need of their own reference points. In an effort to stand out from the rest, they draw their sources of identity from media-personified cultural models. Levi's are linked with a mythical image of breaking away down the long, lonely road – the rebel. Nike encourages them to strive to surpass themselves, turning its back on the national confines of race and culture. Women also constitute a clientele looking for new models; Estée Lauder could portray the free, independent and seductive woman, and use this image for its own globalisation. Brands corresponding to new eating habits also have to impose forcefully their view of the world in order to rally consumers in search of change. In this way, the brand is seen as a new flag-waver.

New, unexplored sectors have not, by definition, inherited a system of values.

Everything is there for the making, and it's up to the brand to do it. This is why there is nothing to prevent the global marketing of high-tech, computer, internet, photographic, electronic and telecommunications or service brands. Dell can, and must, spread its brand everywhere, because brands themselves are the only point of reference in these markets. Only the themes of the campaigns will change to take into account the country's level of economic development, hence its preoccupation. Globalisation also applies to new services: Hertz, Avis and Europcar globalised their campaigns by portraying the stereotype of the hurried businessman – and in any event an Italian businessman wants to identify more with being a businessman than with being an Italian. The argument of novelty works also for McDonald's, Malibu or Corona!

The world has been standardised by the increasing and levelling power of technology – this is Levitt's point (1983). Its products no longer stem from local culture but belong to our times. They are the fruit of science and time. They therefore escape the local cultural contingencies that hinder global communication.

In general terms, globalisation is possible – and indeed desirable – in markets which revolve around mobility. This applies to multimedia, the hotel industry, car rental, airlines, and also the transfer of pictures and sounds. When the brand is perceived as being international, its authority and expertise are automatically accepted. Again, brands have a clear opportunity to organise and structure those market sectors which symbolise the disappearance of time and space constraints. It is their role to deploy their system of values, which can only be unique faced with mobile clients.

Globalisation is possible when the brand is totally built into a cultural stereotype. AEG, Bosch, Siemens, Mercedes and BMW rest secure in the 'Made in Germany' model, which opens up the global market, since the stereotype invoked is a collective symbol breaking national bounds. It conjures up a meaning of robust performance in any country. The Barilla name is another stereotype built on the classic Italian image of tomato sauce, pasta, a carefree way of life, songs and sun. Volvo, Ericson, ABB and Saab epitomise Sweden.

Finally, certain brands represent archetypes or 'universal truths', to paraphrase Zaltman (Wathieu, Zaltman and Liu, 2003). Snuggles fabric softener not only arouses the same notion in every country – that of gentleness (which is not in itself original) – but also the image of reliance, love and security as in one's childhood, as symbolised by the teddy bear. This is why, in order to express the notion of 'snuggling, caressing, cajoling', the brand name is translated as Cajoline in France, Kuchelweib in Germany, Yumos in Turkey, Mimosin in Spain and Cocolino in Italy. La Vache-Qui-Rit, which corresponds to the archetype of the generous mother, is likewise translated (Die Lächende Kuhe or The Laughing Cow). Marlboro embodies the archetype of the macho man – alone and untouched, authentic, yet modernised and popularised throughout the world in Western sagas of the conquest of America. Maybelline expresses American beauty. Lancôme expresses the French woman.

Several of the above factors explain why luxury brands and *griffes* have gained a worldwide appeal. In the first place, they bear a message – each creator is expressing his or her own personal values. They were not conceived as a result of any market study or consumer analysis from one country to the next. It is the creator's identity and his or her desire to express his or her own values that form the automatic basis of the brand's identity, in no matter what part of the world. Second, behind every luxury brand there is a guiding standard – sometimes even an archetype. Cacharel and Nina Ricci represent the dawning of femininity, a dawn tinted with shyness and modesty. Yves Saint Laurent stands for female independence, even rebellion. Finally, the 'Made in France' label and the myth of Paris imbue these brands with definitive cultural undertones. All these are reasons why such brands are able to impose their own vision of the world on national outlooks. Like any religion, brands that set out to convert must believe in their message and spread it unerringly among the multitudes.

On the whole, brands whose identity focuses on the product and its roots can more easily go global. Jack Daniel's whiskey builds the pivot of its brand identity from its distillery and its tradition, which leads to advertising which has been remarkably stable throughout time and similar in all countries. Even though it is working with different agencies, the articles and conditions are such that each one produces commercials or announcements that are typically Jack Daniel's.

Certain organisational factors also ease the shift to a global brand. One-man companies and brands that bear the name of their creator who is still alive are from the start more global. Countries have less ability to modulate locally the identity of Ralph Lauren since the head of the company is precisely Ralph Lauren. It is also true for Bic or Paloma Picasso.

American companies are more ready to globalise because marketing on their domestic market is in essence global, considering the social and cultural diversity of the American melting-pot. Organisational factors also point in the same direction. When expanding towards Europe, these companies created European headquarters from the beginning, based most often in Brussels or London. Individual countries therefore had to account for their results to these European centres. As seen from the US, there was very early on the need for a centre for 'European operations', for considering Europe as a single and homogeneous area.

Finally, a single centre for production in Europe or South America is also a strong factor for globalisation, at least for products. The fact that one factory centralises the production of detergents for Procter & Gamble in the whole of Europe leads to a standard product offer throughout and to the spread of technical innovations to all countries at the same time. In markets where the product advantage is key in the positioning of the brand, this centralisation of production and of R&D leaves little room for differentiation on a local basis.

Disruption versus optimising products

Apart from factors linked to the market or to the organisations themselves, the same company may have to follow two different policies according to the status of its products. One analysis that explains the differences in observed behaviour is linked to the type of marketing. Certain products are the optimisation of an existing offer. Others are complete breaks from what is on offer, innovations even to the extent of creating a new segment that did not exist before. This distinction has an impact on the chosen international policy. Optimisation marketing leads to more flexibility when there is a need to adapt to local conditions. Strong innovation, however, that which conveys new vision, tends to impose itself on all countries and hardly needs any adapting.

Generally speaking, a strong new concept is capable of breaking the rules and borders. For example, alcoholic beverages are generally promoted using local strategies. What is more cultural than alcohol? Moreover, it is drunk by adults and as we get older our tastes and preferences solidify (unlike with soft-drinks for teenagers). However, very new concepts in this field are able to have a worldwide impact: Corona, Absolut, Bailey's, Malibu. It is the same for cheese: La Vache-Qui-rit is a global concept.

The excess of globalisation

Arguments against globalisation are, in fact, arguments against a strict and rigid monolithic international marketing policy. In fact, there are plenty of examples of failure resulting from undue haste in adopting a global marketing policy without certain precautions. These examples have been analysed by corporations. They have learnt their lessons.

Globalisation has become associated with deafness or blindness. Naomi Klein (1999) has called the attention of global brands to the fact that some of them have become businesses without any production facilities. They outsource all their production. However, the absence of plants does not mean the brand can feel unconcerned by what takes place in the plants of its suppliers: working children, sweatshops and poor conditions of work all impact on the brand image. Today, big means responsible: ethics will be part of the evaluation by the financial markets (see Chapter 18). In the present chapter we address another issue, strictly managerial: the lack of adaptation to salient differences between markets.

Arguments against globalisation are in fact arguments against a strict and rigid monolithic international marketing policy. There are plenty of examples of failure resulting from undue haste in adopting a global marketing policy without certain precautions. Thus, in January 1984 Procter & Gamble launched in France the anti-dandruff shampoo Head and Shoulders relying on exactly the same marketing mix and positioning which had led to its success in the UK and the Netherlands. At the end of 1989, Head and Shoulders still had only 1 per cent of the French market. The problem was that they had not taken sufficient account of a feature particular to the French market and present nowhere else. Consumers either buy anti-dandruff shampoos in pharmacies, the pharmacy being a guarantee for efficiency and treatment, or they pick up the line extension of their usual brand in their hypermarket (Palmolive dandruff shampoo, etc) for everyday use. In between these two brand groups, there is scarcely room for a brand positioned on efficiency, sold in hypermarkets and much more expensive than usual brands. The adopted communication mix in no way bettered the situation of this shampoo:

▮ Procter & Gamble had decided not to translate the name, relying on the evidence that it had been well accepted in Holland as it stood. However, outside the UK, Holland is the EU country that speaks the best English, so there is a considerable inherent risk in extending a policy tested in Holland to a country such as France.

▮ For its launch, Procter & Gamble used their British film showing a face divided in two so that the results could be seen. The punchline was 'Dandruff talks behind your back'. In France, however, dandruff is seen as a social problem – one should not point the finger in blame, but should sympathise with the problem. The tone adopted in the British approach was perhaps in keeping with Dutch levels of sensitivity, but scarcely applicable to the French.

Head and Shoulders illustrates the harsh realities of different levels of sensitivity and competitive forces in the marketplace, both of which make a monolithic global policy a perilous strategy.

Such reverses do not, as such, amount to a rebuttal of global policy, since we have such universal successes as Dell, Sony, McDonald's and Volkswagen. The idea of global marketing has an inescapable draw, even though its implementation has been seen to vary considerably in speed according to the markets, the public and the companies themselves, and in spite of the fact that certain idiosyncratic brands are destined to remain on a local footing.

Barriers to globalisation

What are the strongest barriers to globalisation? What are the parameters that, according to managers themselves, make difficult, even impossible, brand globalisation? Table 17.5 is particularly revealing in this regard.

The first and only factor that justifies for most people interviewed (55.2 per cent) the non-application of a global strategy is legal differences. It is true, for example, that laws which deal with the definition of products, the right to sell, the authorisation and manner of advertising of alcohol and the use of children in advertising vary considerably. However, because of the Single European Act, Mercosur in South America or the GATT, these differences in legislation will have to be evened out, thus suppressing the major obstacle to globalisation. The second factor is linked to the local competitive situation (number and strength of competitors, levels of brand awareness, type and level of distribution, stage in the product life cycle). Taking the example of Orangina once more, it is not possible to approach the market where Orangina is a close second to Coca-Cola in the same way as the English market, where it occupies a niche in the premium segment of carbonated orange soft drinks and competes with Fanta, Sunkist and Tango, the local dominant brand. This has a deep impact on market strategy and positioning, but the Orangina identity is nevertheless the same. Moreover, since they are known in advance, these very different market situations can be integrated when filming commercials. Some commercials destined for countries where Orangina is not known will need longer sequences on the product and on shaking the pulp. At the other end of the scale these sequences can be reduced in other countries. The significance of this factor concerning the local competitive situation explains in some measure global success of brands such as Mars, Gillette, McDonald's, Coke, Bailey's, Dell, eBay, Ryanair, Somfy and so on. They didn't really have any competitors in the market, and they were new products, creating new segments or revealing the start of a latent transnational demand. They were driven by

Table 17.5 What differences between countries would compel you to adapt the marketing mix of the brand?

Type of difference	Necessary adaptation (%)
Legal differences	55
Competition	47
Consumption habits	41
Distribution structure	39
Brand awareness	38
Brand distribution level	37
Media audience	37
Marketing programme success	34
Consumers' needs	33
Media availability	32
Brand images	30.5
Norms for products manufacturing	27.5
Brand history	25.2
Life-style differences	25
Cultural differences	25
Subsidiary sales	23
Consumers' buying power	22
Consumers' age differences	12

Source: Kapferer/Eurocom pan-European survey

the feeling that they had an excellent product and extended their programme to all countries. The third factor hindering globalisation is the differences in consumer habits: these are, as we have seen, fatal for products such as Ricard that are deeply rooted in a particular culture. Moreover, to become truly global, a brand must play down its ethnic component. As long as Bailey's was an 'Irish Cream' its potential was limited. An 'exotic' beverage coming from afar, its 'strangeness' relegated it to small sales volumes, to fans of Ireland who would sip it in the evening by the fireplace. But how many people know Ireland throughout the world? Who will still drink alcohol as a liqueur? The globalisation of Bailey's consisted of breaking away from the association with the liqueur set ('The Bailey's moment is whenever') and the promotion of Ireland as a tourist destination, and promoting instead 'Baileys on ice' (see page 239).

Table 17.6 presents the facets that are most easily globalised for pan-European brands.

As we can see, the percentage varies from 10 per cent to 93 per cent. Such a variance is linked to the fact that the phrase 'brand globalisation' refers both to identity and to action (the marketing mix). It is the fixed image of the brand (its fixed logo) that is the most globalised, a sign that image precedes sound. What counts is that the exclusive typography and the red colour of Coca-Cola can be found throughout the world, even if it isn't written 'Coca-Cola'. Unilever does not use its Motta brand of ice cream everywhere, but its local equivalents use the same colour and signal codes. The brand name comes in second. It is true that most companies have inherited some odd situations where what is called Dash in Italy is called Ariel in Europe and so on. When brands are local strengths it is not a good idea to risk standardising too fast. The operational facets of the marketing mix are naturally adapted to local markets, all the more so as we approach below-the-line activities or local financial optimisation regarding the price. In the era of television and multimedia, image wins over word. All the more so in Third World countries where illiteracy is common. Colour codes and graphics must be global: Coke is red, Heineken is green. However, even the strongest brands hesitate when the question arises of what to call them in the enormous Chinese market (see below).

Let us analyse in depth how these barriers impact the internationalisation of brands.

Table 17.6 Which facets of the brand mix are most often globalised? (Kapferer/Eurocom)

	%
Logotype, trademark	93
Brand name	81
Product features	67
Packaging	53
After-sales service	48
Distribution channels	46
Sponsoring (arts)	32
Sponsoring (sports)	29
Advertising positioning	29
Advertising execution	25
Relative pricing	24
Direct marketing	18
Sales promotion	10

Coping with local diversity

How do global brands integrate the true diversity of the world, economic, legislative and cultural? How do they build a global brand in such heterogeneous conditions? Can the brand be in fact truly global?

Coping with economic heterogeneity

How should the global brand cope with the reality of widely differing levels of development of markets? This certainly concerns emerging countries, but also the very advanced countries when a new category is concerned.

The first approach is, of course, by adapting the product lines to the markets. One does not sell the same cars in China and in Europe. Car manufacturers use more entry-level models in China. Interestingly, since they want to build a global brand, which means a global perception and not only a global name, care must be taken in launching these models under the same brand values as any upper model of the range sold elsewhere in the world. This causes difficulties in creating a homogeneous concept.

For instance Wyborowa, probably the most exquisite vodka (made in Poland, the homeland of vodka), has to expand in two widely different markets: the most advanced and largest market for international brands (the United States), where there already exists a premium and super premium segment, with very sophisticated brands as Skyy, Belvedere, Grey Goose and Ketel One, well above the prices set by Finlandia and Absolut, not to speak of Smirnoff; and Europe, which is just discovering the category, and in comparison many consumers hardly know what vodka is and why they should drink it. Clearly, to succeed in the United States the brand needs to launch a super premium version, used as the prototype of the brand, but this is not needed in Europe. How then can a brand present a united concept with two different prototypes?

A second approach is by segmenting the product line. For instance Arc International, the leading group in the world for glass tableware, has recently rationalised its brand portfolio, concentrating on four brands, along a double market segmentation by channel of distribution and by price level. Luminarc is to be the unique mass market brand. The whole range has been subdivided into three subsets, casual, modern and formal, and each of these families has a positive name. In developed countries, many people would not consider buying products from the 'casual ' family, but these same products are used as gifts in many developing countries.

The third approach is by a phased introduction of innovations. Thus, Danone as a group is totally positioned on 'active health'. However, this concept is a broad one, and cannot mean the same thing in India and in Scandinavia. As a matter of fact, Danone distinguishes three stages of development corresponding to three levels of market maturity: quality /security, health and nutrition, and active health. Markets at each of these stages will see the launch of products that correspond to their meaning of this large concept, 'health'.

Interestingly, although it is very much centralised, Absolut adapts its advertising to the level of maturity in relation to its category of each country. Thus the consumer benefit used in advertising varies according to a fixed ladder of market development and sophistication, from purity (Absolut Perfection ads) to closeness, topicality, taste variety (such as Absolut Lemon) during the growth phase, and creativity/originality in the maturity phase.

A fourth approach is to stick firmly to the brand values through different levels of operationalisation. The best example is Connex. This world brand of public ground transportation was launched in 2000. Its market comes from the growth in the privatisation of former public transport services. Connex has been promoted on a number of added values – regularity, safety, comfort – but because of wide differences in the level of economic development and cost constraints, it is impossible to operationalise each value the same way all over the world. Expectations of service regularity are not the same in Lagos (Nigeria) and Perth (Australia), for instance. Connex could have decided to restrict use of its name to circumstances that met the highest service delivery standards, but this would have created a very elitist and restricted brand, and would have been contrary to its global strategy: Connex's future growth potential is mostly found in countries that want to accelerate the level of satisfaction attached to public services by outsourcing them.

As a consequence, it was decided to stick to the brand values but to define locally how they are operationalised. In addition, since a brand represents a permanent search for added values, in each city or region where Connex operates, these operational standards must be upgraded year after year, and the result made public.

Coping with differences in legislation and norms

Best practice seminars and books are replete with examples of globalised brands such as Coca-Cola, Mars and Microsoft. Certainly they are interesting examples. However, they also have their limits, imposed not least by differences in taste, in legislation, in norms. Thus none of the yoghurts sold by Dannon USA could be described as yoghurts in the EU, because they contain too high a proportion of starch and stabilising agents, and their taste too is unlikely to meet with public acceptance in Europe. Why? Because Dannon USA, since its creation in 1942, has tried to build its business in the United States.

In the United States there was no custom of eating yoghurt when Dannon began, unlike in Holland, Germany and France. Moreover, the fact that it is eaten with a spoon gave a childish personality to the category. As a result, the whole market started as a niche market, mostly aimed at women, promoting the health benefits, a little like Slimfast. Also, unlike in Europe, Dannon yoghurts actually compete in the snack market, and US consumers typically drink a cola (diet or otherwise) while consuming the product. As a consequence, the yoghurts needed to be sweeter and thicker.

Coping with category differences

Although products may have the same name, they do not mean the same thing from one country to another. Thus, the same apparent product needs to be positioned in accordance with the significance of the category in the different countries.

The example of yoghurt is relevant. At first glance it would seem possible to sell plain Danone yoghurt to everyone in Europe in the same way, whether it be flavoured Danone Kid or Danone Activia. However, despite appearances, yoghurt is a typical case of non-transversality because of the different circumstances in each of the markets when yoghurt was first introduced. In France, the market is still influenced by the fact that yoghurt was first introduced as a health product and therefore was sold exclusively in pharmacies (in much the same way as mineral water). Though this is no longer the case and most younger consumers would not be aware of it, this has a deep and unconscious impact on attitudes in the market. Thus, in France the product reference is a plain yoghurt, a symbol of good health, while fruit and flavourings were only added a long time afterwards. In Anglo-Saxon countries, on the other hand, where there weren't any pharmacies in the French sense, yoghurt was first introduced as a low-fat product containing fruit for enjoyment, and in this sense it was a product for adults. The motivation to purchase in the yoghurt market therefore comes from very different impulses in different countries because of the way the market was first created in those countries. Moreover, as a result of these differing motivations, the same product will be regarded in a different light in the various countries involved.

For example, in the UK, the origins of the yoghurt market mean that the product is regarded as being one for pleasure, for the enjoyable experience of eating. Flavoured yoghurt, ie yoghurt without the fruit, is therefore a lesser product, and also means it cannot be positioned in the market for children. Moreover, plain yoghurt without either flavouring or fruit – and therefore without pleasure in the eating – is thus a boring product only for those on a diet. In Spain and Portugal, on the other hand, where fruit is abundant, the fruit yoghurt does not have the position of product reference in the market. Indeed, there, where the standard of living is lower than in other European countries, flavoured yoghurt constitutes the main segment, and is eaten as much by children as it is by adults: it is a family product and does not need a first name (such as Kid). Again, in Italy, the reference is blended yoghurt with a different texture, and flavoured yoghurt is positioned for very young children. Yet again, in France, flavoured yoghurt is regarded simply as a plain yoghurt with added flavouring, so the logic of the health benefit prevails, as testified by the slogan 'Petit à petit on devient moins petit' (literally 'Little by little we become less little'). To emphasise this promise and to differentiate it from competitors, Danone chose to give the first name 'Kid' to this type of yoghurt, thus identifying it with a child reaching a later stage of development.

In a similar way the reaction to Activia is different depending on the country. In France Activia is perceived as the rebirth of plain yoghurt, conveying health and pleasure. In the UK Activia was the first to introduce the health aspect of the product to the market. In Italy, on the other hand, cultural morality frowns upon the taking of pleasure in the taste of food and it is not considered possible to taste good and and be healthy at the same time. This is reflected in the related commercials – the internal body clock of the UK commercial instead of the nude woman chosen in France.

Thus by considering one of the few food markets that does not have a long history but is actually an industrial product, we can clearly see that the conditions under which the market was created in each country have determined the long-term perception of that product in each specific market. Only Yop crosses these borders. Positioned for teenagers like a soft drink around the concept of freedom, Yop has a European commercial that works well in all countries, provided of course the market understands the concept of a drinkable yoghurt.

Coping with differences of segment

The same product may belong to different segments in different countries. It then faces different competition and aims at different targets. In the car industry, the small car segment represents 38 per cent of cars on average in Europe, with extremes reaching 59 per cent in Portugal and 18 per cent in Austria or Germany. In Italy, the small household car is nevertheless the main car, in which the whole family fits. This determines a stream of structural expectations (five doors for example) very different from France where the segment corresponds to the second or even the third car. Another problem arises when Germany is considered: in this country the segment simply does not exist. Here it is the Golf that is considered the small car, when it is in the middle range segment everywhere else in Europe. It was, therefore, difficult to speak of the Peugeot 106, for instance, in the same way in all countries. In France, in order to compete with the Renault Clio and not to poach sales from the Peugeot 206, the amount of interior space was emphasised, despite the small size of the car (hence the slogan 'la surprise de taille' – 'the size surprise'). In Germany, the 106 was positioned like the Austin Mini, as a second car, small, feminine and urban, and after that as the most environmentally friendly because it was the smallest. In the countries of Southern Europe the interior space was again emphasised to make it a good first family car. In the UK the 106 was positioned as a feminine car which was small but which allowed escape through its comfortable and dynamic aspects – two qualities that make Peugeot a valued brand in this country.

Coping with differences in meaning

The danger with international communication is that there may seems to be a common understanding of words, where in fact there is not. Simple words as ' nature' and 'well-being' do not mean the same thing across countries. If they did, it still remains to be proven that the best way to communicate the concept is similar across countries. Often it is not.

According to the country, the same idea must be expressed through different symbols. This established fact has the paradoxical consequence that it is not by using the same brand name from one country to another that one stays closest to the initial brand concept. The concept behind Jif is better expressed by Viss in Germany and Cif in France. One can change a local name to a global name when the former has little intrinsic meaning and the name precisely encompasses the concept of the product. Otherwise, a fundamental element of the identity is shattered. The diversity of names draws the product closer to its consumers in each market. This is why Playtex applies a modular policy: the Playtex name is worldwide. On the other hand, the company adapts the names of individual products to the markets. Indeed, Playtex only launches new product concepts if they are international. The marketing strategy is homogeneous within large geographic areas (Europe for example): thus the 'Cross Your Heart' range has the same positioning, the same consumer benefit, the same advertising theme and the same execution in all countries. Cross Your Heart adapts to local markets in terms of fabric (cotton in Italy for instance) or of packaging (to take into account differences in distribution circuits). As for the name, it is 'Coeur Croisé' in France (a direct translation), but 'Crusado Magico' in Spain (a slight shift to a 'magic cross'). To stick to the common concept and convey it as best it can, Playtex does not hesitate to change the name of the products if necessary, to provide a more appropriate translation.

▌ Thus the line of bras without underwires is called 'WOW!' in the US ('WithOut a Wire'), but 'Armagiques' in France.

▌ The line of girdles that feature long-lasting comfort is called '18 hours', which can be translated in each country.

▌ A line of bras is called 'SuperLook', a name which in this case needs no translation. Wonderbra itself was launched untranslated.

Despite the legitimate willingness to globalise, we must not overlook real cultural differences and differences in perception. This is why Procter & Gamble has created different versions according to the country for the Mr Clean brand, while nevertheless remaining within the limits of a common strategy (shine). Indeed, the symbols of 'shine' change with the culture. In France, it is expressed by the idea of the mirror ('You can see yourself in it'), while in the USA, the emphasis is on reflection off water ('Is it water? No it's the shine!'). Throughout the world, Camay is the soap which implies 'seduction'. This is the line which Procter & Gamble have always taken. However, though customer habits and expectations are the same the world over where soap is concerned, cultural blocks call for different approaches when speaking to a woman about intimate moments.

▌ In France, the seductive power was portrayed by a woman beautifying herself in her bath for her husband. The success of this commercial tempted the Japanese to introduce it in their market where it caused fury when the advertisement was screened. In Japan it is considered an insult for a man to enter the bathroom while his wife is performing her ablutions.

▌ In Italy, they preferred to show a fawning wife and her macho man.

▌ The Austrians just use Paris as a backdrop to signify seduction.

▌ In Greece, they added a more sensual note, bringing in the proverbial vamp.

Flexibility at the creative stage not only satisfies local cultural requirements, but also allows Camay to establish its own status in different countries.

Building the brand in emerging countries

Today, all eyes are turned towards the East, where companies are keen to compete in countries that were once part of the Soviet bloc. Beyond lies Asia – the five 'tiger economies' and China. Pioneer managers sent into the field are faced with the task of achieving major sales objectives within a short space of time. There is a great temptation to use an internationalised version of the flagship brand as far as possible, for example the Kraft, Müeller or Campina dairy brands. In fact, everything encourages managers to do so:

▨ Their managerial freedom – in these distant countries they feel less restricted by the constraints of head office.

▨ The pressure of sales and objectives, combined with a lack of resources.

▨ The pitfalls of market research – since the brand is weak and not yet crystallised around a prototype, it seems able to be used anywhere.

▨ It is therefore tempting to actually use it anywhere, on all products, all the more so because this type of initiative proves effective at sales level. As a symbol of quality, in countries that are not used to quality, a brand is reassuring and boosts the sales of anything it endorses. Any new initiative works.

It is a well-known fact that the first thing multinationals do in these countries is to rationalise production. The skill of manufacturers lies in their ability to significantly increase the quality of production, which gives local consumers access to levels of quality worthy of the name. Is not the primary function of a brand to guarantee quality? The brand therefore serves to endorse production and symbolise the newly acquired quality and reliability. By adopting this logic, the international brand becomes a strong umbrella brand from the outset, a source of reputation and power. The way to creating a strong brand appears to be clearly mapped out.

It should be pointed out that most examples of globalisation cited in managerial literature written in English are in fact 'product globalisations' based on a model of geographical extension from the country of origin, as with McDonald's, Mars and Coca-Cola. In many cases, however, this model is not applicable since companies are not seeking to impose specific tastes on the inhabitants of other countries, but to recreate their brand (Kraft, Müeller or Président) at local level. For example, while it is reasonable to assume that most Russians would not want to eat Camembert, it is quite legitimate for Lactalis to try to globalise its flagship brand Président. But this can only be done via large-volume local products to get the business off to a good start, otherwise it is not worth investing in a sales force or advertising.

The first problem is that, by covering all segments in a new country, the brand may deviate from the strategy (positioning) that has been fixed for it, in Europe or the United States for example. What is not a problem for Thailand or China can be a serious issue in Russia. But the strategy is global and has to be reflected in each country. Creating an umbrella brand that covers all segments in a country from the outset may favour short-term sales but does not really prepare for the future.

The second problem is that establishing an umbrella brand quickly from the outset may fill the brand catalogues but does not really create a strong brand for the future. So what will happen exactly?

It will not take long before all the brand's western competitors will be in the country as well. The levels of quality between these competitors will therefore be comparable. So what will differentiate the brand from all the others? It will be a general brand, with no real identity, no prototype, no strong differentiation.

How long can you go on introducing new initiatives that keep working? This type of success can be short-lived if a competitor also decides to launch an innovation. Taking the easy option does not lay foundations for the future. It is essential not to lose sight of the long-term objective and to bear the middle and long term in mind when considering short-term initiatives, for example when promoting difference(s) to create preference over future competitors.

It is therefore essential to build firm foundations at the outset and extend the brand later. This means making choices and selections, despite the temptation not to do so. But this is the way global brands are constructed.

Naming problems

The ultimate symbol of successful globalisation is the ability to use the same name worldwide. However, a brand name often poses problems for globalisation. The main ones are outlined below:

▮ First of all, there is the problem of prior registration by a local company. For example, the name Eurostar had already been registered by a service company and had to be bought from that company, a solution that is not always possible. Less straightforward was the problem of the Crocodile brand, registered by a Chinese company and rapidly reinforced by a vast network of stores known as The Crocodile Shop, just as the global brand Lacoste accessed the Asian market. Lacoste's logo is a crocodile.

▮ Second, the name can be a problem in terms of its meaning in a specific language. There is no shortage of anecdotes about brand names that have sexual connotations in other countries.

▮ A less common problem is the translation of descriptive names. Traditionally, the Americans do not translate their descriptive brand names – Pampers are Pampers the world over, as is Head & Shoulders. But for an international brand of cheese such as La Vache Qui Rit (The Laughing Cow), the name is important because it conveys a message and permits the correct interpretation of the brand symbol (a cow's head). Without it, the cow could appear stupid, smiling or mad. In this case, there is a link between the brand name and brand symbol. The question therefore arises as to whether or not to translate this descriptive brand name for each country, and if so, whether to keep a reference to the brand name in French. If this is done, should this reference be above or below the local translation? Finally, should the answers to these questions be different for each region, since the answers depend on the added value desired?

In certain areas, there is a real problem of counterfeited goods and therefore a need to reassure consumers that the product is in fact the real thing. In some areas (such as Saudi Arabia, the Middle East and Germany), the added value comes from the reference to France, while in others, the 'made in France' label can be a negative factor due to changing economic circumstances, for example in the United States in 2003.

▮ Finally China poses a specific problem because of its very different regional dialects.

Naming in China

Naming in China often forces managers to face a choice: should they name semantically or phonetically? (Schmitt and Zhang, 2001). The dilemma is as follows: should one respect the sound of the name even if it has no local meaning and is therefore difficult to pronounce and to memorise, or should one respect the concept even if it means parting from the international sound of the brand name? Ideally of course, one would say both. The Chinese sound should resemble the international pronunciation, but the meaning should also be appropriate. Microsoft's semantic name would be Wei Jua, which means micro flexible and soft. In addition it is a pleasant sound to a Chinese ear. Coca-Cola and Carrefour found both a semantic and phonetic appropriate translation: Keu Ko Keu Leu means 'good to drink and makes happy', Tia-leu-Fu means something close to 'the house of happiness'. The leading worldwide brand of insecticide, Decis from Aventis, is pronounced Di-Cha-Seu which luckily means 'at them until death'.

Others are less lucky. Peugeot is said as 'Piao Je', but in Cantonese, it evokes a prostitute. Orangina starts with an O: in Chinese there are no nice words starting with an O.

There is a danger however in localising the name too much in China. Foreign brands are now valued much more than local brands. All signs which accentuate the perception of being a local brand may erode brand equity in the long term. The size of this market requires that all due precautions be taken.

Achieving the delicate local–global balance

Each company has to find its own balance between localisation (the adaptation of its products to local markets) and the deep-rooted *raison d'être* of globalisation, the pursuit of a competitive advantage through reduced costs. It is therefore possible to say that there is a contradiction between the need to create value – via the adaptation of products and symbols to suit a particular country, market segment and even ethnic groups, communities or individuals on a one-to-one basis – and the economic requirement of reducing costs. As with any dilemma, every company knows there is no single solution, just progressive adaptations and even policy reviews when they have placed too much emphasis on localisation or standardisation.

Cosmetic groups (such as Estée Lauder, Shiseido and l'Oréal) and car manufacturers are in the throes of this dilemma since they are both 'high-tech' and 'high-touch'. It is a well-known fact that globalisation was born of technology, and aids the diffusion of research via the ever-decreasing costs of that technology. However, because cosmetic brands target the beauty of individual women, they must be ultra-sensitive and therefore 'high-touch' and, as such, adapt as far as possible to specific physiological characteristics, as well as to the basic and cultural characteristics of women in countries throughout the world. There is no longer an overall concept of beauty, but an acceptance of the diversity of different types of beauty within the same country and between generations. The dilemma is equally acute for the car industry when a car is not simply positioned as a low-priced vehicle. A car has a special significance for individual consumers, and since each consumer is different, there is not only an expectation of diversity at brand level, but also in respect of models, line extensions and even the personalisation of the relationship with the brand.

Each to his own balance?

To take one category, cosmetics for example, it is significant that the brands positioned as 'mass market' have to develop their proximity much more than the so-called elitist brands. As such, they not only make greater use of direct-contact marketing but also tend to adapt products and publicity much more within the well-defined framework of the brand identity, on the one hand, and the brand's economic equation, on the other. Thus Garnier and Maybelline adapt much more than Lancôme, and in the case of Garnier, this adaptation is automatic and built in from the outset. For example, Garnier offers the most extensive range of cosmetics to meet the demands of all skin and hair types in Europe and the United States. Depending on the country, its subsidiaries select the products best suited to their requirements, since each country develops its own market. The same applies to the format of the packaging and labelling. The differentiation is situated at national level and not at the level of the region or zone, since the women of – albeit geographically close – countries such as Korea, Taiwan and Japan in fact have very different expectations. The Lancôme customer, on the other hand, is widely travelled and expects to be able to buy the same products in Tokyo or Paris – by being over-adapted, these products would lose their status. Naturally, Lancôme develops specific skin-whitening products to meet the very strong demand among Asian women in these countries.

So how do companies reconcile this fine-tuned adaptation and the economic equation? By making the economic equation the criterion for the acceptance of the adaptation. Thus for l'Oréal, innovation assumes the status of a religion, with over 500 patents registered each year. This innovation can come from one of three sources:

▌ one of four basic research laboratories – two in the United States, one in Europe and one in Japan;

▌ from brand marketing teams throughout the world;

▌ from any of the various national retail distribution subsidiaries.

Sometimes there is a strong local demand in a particular country. For example, in 1997, Brazil expressed a desire for a specific haircare product since Brazilian hair – the result of the country's ethnic melting pot – is characteristically dry and unmanageable and needs a moisturising conditioner. Brazilian women are proud of their hair, which they regard, even more than their faces, as the symbol of their sensuality. They therefore want it to be long and flowing, to move with their body, what the Brazilians call *cacheado*, or curling and wavy. So the European laboratory developed a unique formula and then l'Oréal considered the economic equation. Could enough of this new product be sold in Brazil and, of course, elsewhere in the world? It was called Elsève Hydramax and soon became the most popular haircare product in Brazil before being extended to other countries.

Maybelline provides another example. Although it is a US brand and its teams are based in New York, the Japanese laboratory discovered an innovative active ingredient that was able to meet the very specific demands of very trendy and 'hip' young Japanese women, typical of Tokyo's Shibuya district, for a particular type of lipstick. These are young women with small mouths, and in Japan mother-of-pearl is very popular. This molecule created the effect of water, giving the lipstick a 'wet look'. After careful economic analysis, the product was developed in Japan under the name Maybelline Watershine Diamonds. In the space of a year, it made Maybelline the best-selling mass-market make-up brand in Japan, and was subsequently extended to the United States and Europe where it enjoyed a similar meteoric success.

In both these cases, the local innovations were only accepted when they were considered 'globalisable' with the potential for global successes. This is a far cry from the 'think global, act local' business model. It is more a case of 'think local, act global'.

Competitive advantage through adaptation

Globalisation at all price has a cost: failure. On the other hand, some examples, not much publicised, show how market adaptation helps in developing a profitable business and slowly gaining market leadership.

Year after year, Nestlé has tried to compete against Kellogg's in the cereals market. This is normal: cereals are close to the core product of Nestlé, milk. They address the same target too (children), and the same benefit: growth.

As long as Nestlé copied Kellogg's it was unsuccessful. In addition, Nestlé had no know-how in cereals. It needed an alliance. General Mills in the United States was itself looking for a way to enter Europe, after Kellogg's, Quaker Oats, and the private labels of strong or even dominant multiple retailers. To compete against a leader one needs an innovation. Because of Nestlé's decentralised culture, local subsidiaries have some autonomy. The French subsidiary identified a need so far untapped by Kellogg's: children love chocolate. They wish to have chocolate for breakfast. Why didn't Kellogg's identify this need? First, it was a local need, and centralised global companies are not fitted to adapt to local needs. Second, it did not fit with the ideology of cereals for growth and health. Finally, leaders tend to defend their acquired position instead of looking for new markets (Christensen, 1997). Also, as a chocolate brand, Nestlé had more insight into this market. The result was the launch of a local new product, thanks to the know-how of General Mills, marketed and distributed by Nestlé: Chocapic, the first cereals in chocolate. Soon this product became the market leader with a share of 11 per cent: all multiple retailers had to distribute it. This is how Nestlé fought back successfully. It innovated in a high-volume market, then Chocapic was rapidly extended to other European and world countries.

Everyone has heard about Malibu, a white rum and coconut light drink. What about Soho or Ditta, which recently passed Malibu in volume and value sales? Soho and Ditta are the two names of the same product, a mixer based on lychees. Why are there two names?

Because it is not possible to sell a lychee mixer drink the same way in Japan (where it is now the number one brand) and in Europe. In Japan, Ditta is aimed at young women who typically go to bars to chat together, a classic of Japanese social behaviour. The communication target was the bar staff who promoted imaginative new cocktails. In Europe, the brand called Soho is mostly sold off-premises, in multiple retailers, thanks to in-store wet trial campaigns. The target market is women as a basis for cocktails (with grapefruit for instance). Here again, leadership came from adaptation.

Adaptation: a necessity for growth through time

A final example is Barilla, a mainstream popular pasta brand that is number one in Italy. It decided to extend geographically in Europe, by means of a positioning very different from its own domestic positioning: it created the premium pasta market in Europe. Barilla was introduced almost as a luxury brand (see Table 17.7). This was implemented through cartons with a specific design and the launch of a collection of forms of pasta unknown in most countries. Naturally the price was 25 per cent higher than the local leader, which itself often had an Italian name but did not play on this image dimension, having lost all links with Italy a long time ago.

Barilla's goal is not to remain a niche player in all foreign countries, but to become the number two if not the number one. This necessitates addressing the local habits of average consumers, not elitist ones. As a consequence, the brand has to widen its range and lower its prices on new lines adapted to children and family consumption, even if this means producing products that are hardly typically Italian but represent a large part of local consumption (like noodles). This also entails packaging these lines in a far less premium style (no more cartons). Finally, the advertising itself should bring the brand closer to the markets: it has to stop being perceived as the brand of Italians. Positioning a brand on export markets as the one preferred by consumers in its domestic market contributes to reinforcing an alien image. Some consumers may like to imitate the choices of foreigners, but becoming a local leader means addressing the needs of this market, the first one being to be relevant for that market.

Being perceived as local: the new ideal of global brands?

A curious turnaround appears to be taking place. In multinationals the world over, CEOs are proudly producing figures proving that their brand is perceived as 'local'. In fact, brands that have been very successfully 'globalised' for some time are now perceived as local brands, a phenomenon that is just as true for Nivea and Kodak as it is for brands of medication (Aspro and Rennies), washing powder (Ariel and Omo) and even Shell, which the Swedes firmly believe to be their national brand. Is this desire to appear local a concession to fashion, a concession to the World Social Forums against capitalist globalisation, or does it reflect a deeper awareness?

It should first of all be pointed out that this trend does not affect all brands, only those that want to be accessible, popular brands reaching a wide public in countries throughout the world. By definition, 'high-tech' is not local – if it is, it is perceived as 'low-tech'. It is technology that unites the world, which is the essential factor of globalisation and the attendant standardisation, by creating the same desire for a particular piece or pieces of new equipment in consumers the world over. Thus, the big technological brands are clearly perceived as global, a perception that invests them with additional perceived quality and prestige. Similarly, 'high-touch' brands are also global – their customers are, in part, buying a value based on the idea that, if they travelled to Paris, New York or Tokyo, they would find exactly the same product. This is why luxury goods and top-of-the-range cosmetics do not try to appear local – their added value stems from their global image and their foreign origins. Finally, this basic trend does not affect brands whose added value stems from their association with a particular country. For example, Coca-Cola and Levi's are universal symbols of the United States, while Lacoste symbolises French sporting elegance. Today, young consumers worldwide, who have grown up with mixed cultures, tend to favour brands with a strong national identity which allow them to experiment with their own particular identity.

However, the search for popular success on the world market forces companies to recognise that being close to consumers is a key factor of this success. L'Oréal was quick to realise this and, within its very diverse brand portfolio, the name of the typically French brand Laboratoires Garnier was changed to Garnier in 2001. The change of name was not accidental – it was designed to facilitate the brand's acceptance by countries on all five continents. In spite of a 'brand identity' platform that is the same in all countries, Garnier readily adapts its products and ingredients to suit local hair and skin types, as well as adapting its packaging to suit local practices (large formats in Portugal, tiny formats in Korea) and its advertising (using local models) to appeal to local consumers. This strategy is therefore the direct opposite of that used by the group's top-of-the-range brand Lancôme, which is extremely globalised in all aspects of its marketing mix. Thus, the higher up the range the brand, the less it has to adapt.

If brands are seeking to maximise their integration within a country, it is because companies have realised that the global brand was above all a consequence of the pursuit of economies of scale and the competitive advantage they provide. Consumers have never been known to ask for global brands. There is, therefore, a difference between being a global brand that is represented on all continents because it meets a universal need, and proclaiming a global brand from the rooftops. Furthermore, our recent research has shown that the key asset of local brands is confidence, and in these times of doubt, food scandals and capitalist crises (like Enron), the confidence factor is a distinct advantage.

This is why groups like Danone say they want to be 'a local global company', but in Danone's case the brand is actually – and legally – a local brand in several countries.

Being relevant before being global?

The global brand results from a deliberate will to rationalise its management and less from a demand from the market. The typical consumer does not buy a global brand *per se*, but on the contrary, individualistic brands that correspond exactly to his/her specific needs. Even when it is global, the brand is bought in an individualistic fashion. The buyer of Mr Clean in France compares it to Ajax and to other local competing brands: he/she has no notion of the existence of Mr Clean in another country, with the same positioning and the same promise of shine. The buyer is sensitive to the latter and to the personality of the brand, just like the buyers of Mr Clean in these other countries. Thus, when in several countries, groups of buyers appear sensitive to the same advantages and expect the same features, there is an opportunity for a global brand. We should speak here of 'coincidence of globalism', referring to the fact that globalism expresses a corporate view, whereas at the consumer's level in each country, in spite of so-called similar needs, their choice remains individualistic and egocentric (Buzzell and Quelch, 1988). The brand must therefore often be a chameleon and seem 'just like back home'. This does not apply to international high-tech, service, luxury or alcoholic beverage brands. But

Kodak and Philips are considered French by a third of the French population, as Bic is thought to be an American brand in the USA.

Integration factors

How does a company speed up perceived integration and acquire the desired level of assimilation in a country? This is an issue that even involves high-tech companies if they do not want to be perceived as cold, distant and indifferent to public concerns, simply content to sell and therefore a symbol of the predatory multinationals. The first thing is to tune into local needs and then implement a local marketing campaign – on the streets, in sports stadia, as part of local life. Media advertising should be balanced by direct contact and involvement in a country's everyday life. It was not by chance that Garnier launched its new Fructis Style product on, among other things, more than 100 buses in each country – buses that would travel back and forth across towns and cities, in direct contact with the general public.

Last but not least, and bearing in mind that the brand and company are one and the same thing in the eyes of the general public, it is a distinct advantage to have factories and produce the product in the countries in question. This not only helps the brand to put down roots but also increases its status, since it provides employment. If the company also has a well-developed social policy, people will talk about it and it will gain respect and confidence. Far from behaving like a coloniser or a predator, the brand will be seen as seeking to share its success. The local publicity given to the social initiatives of Danone (the company) in Mexico greatly helped to speed up the brand's assimilation in this key country. As can be seen, in the age of the responsible and ethical brand, companies no longer hide behind their brands (quite the opposite, in fact) in their penetration of foreign markets.

Local brands can strike back

The criticism of local brands has therefore been exaggerated (Kapferer, 2001) and their strength underestimated. Because they tried to replace local brands with global brands too quickly, Procter & Gamble and Danone were forced to back-pedal and try to win back the customers they had lost. It should be remembered that pro-global propaganda was a one-way street and did not brook any form of opposition. However, it is worth considering how many leading brands are in fact not local. The leading brands on a number of markets – fruit juices, beer, cooking oil, butter, cheese – are all local brands. It could be argued that these are traditional products, but it is significant that in Korea and Japan, the number one hamburger is not McDonald's or Burger King, but Lotteria (an offshoot of the Lotte department stores). The same is true in Belgium where Quick is still the market leader, more than 10 years after the US giant penetrated the Belgian market. The paradox is explained by the 'first mover advantage'. In these countries, it was the local brands that established the hamburger restaurants and the market for which they became the referents. There is no difference in the structures of these competitors, but the key factor of the success of any restaurant is its position – when McDonald's arrived in Korea and Belgium, the best sites were already taken.

Today, many global brands affirm that they try not to appear global. This is certainly true in the case of Danone, which is in fact legally the local brand in four different countries. The Danone brand, the result of an innovation, was created in Spain in 1919 by Isaac Carasso, who named it after his son (Danon is the Catalan diminutive for Daniel). Danone was registered in France in 1929, while Dannon Milk Products, Inc. was created in New York in 1942 by Daniel Carasso, who had emigrated to the United States. The brand was subsequently extended to Mexico. In each of these four countries, Danone or Dannon is

regarded as a local brand. Strangely enough, according to its directors, the German brand Nivea also aspires to be perceived as a local brand even though it is one of the most widely distributed brands in the world. The same applies to the Danish brand Velux, the number one roof window manufacturer, Bic, Garnier and others.

In 1998, the trend was for globalisation at all costs, and having bought the Czech company Opavia, the Danone group decided to replace this local brand with its own global brand. However, Danone had seriously underestimated the strength of the local brand and had to back-pedal. Opavia had more than 70 per cent of the market share in the Czech Republic. During the communist era, the only 'treat' available to the Czechs was biscuits, and Opavia had become their friend and ally. Last but not least, Opavia was also the name of a Czech town, which made it a patriotic brand. All these factors were difficult to appreciate when legislating from a distance. Each country has its own icon brands and globalisation simply cannot afford to ignore the consumer.

The international study referred to earlier (Schuiling and Kapferer, 2004; see page 468) identified the levers specific to local brands – confidence and proximity. These are key factors of success if the local brand also knows how to market its products effectively.

Developing local brands

Since many brands are and will continue to remain local, how can they be developed in the face of international competition? The strength of local brands has already been demonstrated (Schuiling and Kapferer, 2004) and their strong points compared with global brands. But confidence and proximity will not provide indefinite protection – they have to be maintained, and the strategies that maintain them are therefore particularly important. But it is equally important to address the weaknesses of local brands – a lack of innovation, fun and fashion, according to the new, younger generation of consumers. Local brands also suffer from a number of weaknesses and limitations at management level, and these are outlined below:

▪ The first is often inertia – too used to simply being there, because of their history rather than their ambition, local brands often lack energy because they lack ambition. The brand therefore needs to be revitalised from within, and its aims, mission statements and advantages clearly redefined.

▪ Local brands are often too widely dispersed. It is therefore crucial to refocus resources on certain markets or market segments in which they can hope to dominate or at least be joint market leaders. They also have to accept the need to part with some of their business in order to concentrate on the segments with the potential to dominate the market. Alternatively they can target niches, small but profitable markets, in a way that the multinationals are unable to do.

▪ Local brands often lack innovation – they rely too heavily on loyalty as a driver of preference and have therefore lost their relevance because their products are no longer modern enough or sufficiently well adapted to meet present-day demands. It cannot be said often enough that innovations are the lifeblood of a brand. There are several types of innovation. Some demand huge investments in R&D and are beyond the scope of local brands, while others are more closely identified with the user values of the products and are therefore more accessible. A third type is related not so much to basic research (new active ingredients) as to the search for new concepts that are linked to a consumer insight.

▪ Local brands tend to have an established form of management. There is a need to bring in new managers who relate to and therefore understand the new markets and segments, who can identify consumer insights and convert them into ideas.

▪ Local brands are too self-restricting. In an age that glorifies globalisation, there is little in the way of advice or articles to support local brands (Kapferer, 2001). They therefore run the risk of being too self-restricting, as in the case of the Norwegian company DBS, a local market leader in the bicycle sector. DBS did not think it would be able to sell modern mountain bikes under its own name, in the face of competition from Giant or the US company Cannondale. In fact, it was a huge success – consumers were delighted to be able to buy quality products throughout Norway (due to the extended distribution of the brand), under the national brand name. Of course, there are always people who will only buy international brands, but it is important to take account of the less obsessive majority.

▪ There is another form of geographical self-restriction. There is no reason why a local brand should not seek opportunities for growth in neighbouring countries, which are often familiar with the brand or have cultural similarities that favour its assimilation. Thus, it is quite natural for local Estonian brands to be sold in Lithuania and Latvia, or for Polish brands to be sold in Hungary and the Czech Republic. But the geographical area can extend further afield. One of the key factors of the success of small and medium-sized enterprises is their assimilation at international level very early on in their development (Simon, 2000). It is significant that in the case of Wal-Mart, the world's leading distributor, a development team travels the world in search of innovative products that will differentiate the store's ranges from those of its competitors and add an element of surprise for customers. This was how the micro-company Lorina, which had relaunched the 'orange crush' drinks popular in the past, was spotted at a trade exhibition for new products and then referenced in the United States a year after its creation. This referencing with a mega-distributor is often tied to an exclusivity agreement that guarantees a certain continuity for a brand's international development.

- Finally, local brands must not appear local. Except in the case of ethnic or traditional craft products linked to a particular region, modernity is expressed via cultural integration. Who knows whether or not Hollywood chewing gum is a local brand? Or Gemey, Dop, Tango or Wall's ice cream? The top three brands in the world's largest market in terms of volume (France) for Scotch whisky are all local brands. Certainly these whiskies come from Scotland, where whisky is produced to excess, but these brands were created by wines and spirits merchants – two low-price brands, based essentially on trade marketing (William Peel, Label 5), and a mainstream brand (Clan Campbell). It was these brands, less expensive than the big international brands, that enabled the French market to double in size in the space of 15 years.

A good example of management of local brands against increasing international competition is Amore Pacific, Korea's dynamic and leading cosmetics company, and strong market leader thanks to a wide brand portfolio. How did Amore Pacific strengthen its brand proactively?

- First, the brands are allocated by distribution route: one brand, one channel. This includes the very dominant direct sales channel (door to door or through customer-led parties), a channel imported brand cannot penetrate for it requires a know-how and resources it will not possess.

- Second, small brands have been merged into larger ones, to create mega-brands and reach a higher critical size, a condition of higher marketing investments.

- Third, brands are permanently nurtured by innovations.

- Fourth, local brands do not look at all local. La Neige for instance aims at the youth market, with a French looking name and capitalises on its proximity to French customers. Hera (the name of a Greek goddess) is a direct competitor of Lancôme and Estée Lauder: as such it is strongly visible in all premium department stores as in the duty free zone of Korean Airports.

- Finally, Amore Pacific has extended its best brands to other countries. La Neige has been successfully launched in Hong Kong and Shanghai, as Hera. There is a growing demand in Asia for Asian brands that understand Asian women better than western imported ones.

The process of brand globalisation

While there is no shortage of examples of globalisation in books, articles and at conferences, most focus on product brands such as Coke, Marlboro, Starbucks, McDonald's, Amazon, eBay and Intel. However, these examples are centred around unpredictable and/or radical innovations which, after becoming leaders in the United States (a domestic market that is equal to 50 per cent of the world market), were able to be exported on the basis of their reputation. They do not correspond to the reality of most global groups and brands, which often have a small country of origin and have to become global from the start. This was true in the case of Nestlé (the world's leading food company), which originated in Switzerland, Unilever (the Netherlands), Absolut (Sweden), Grey Goose (the Netherlands), Finlandia (Finland) and Velux (Denmark). It is significant that, four months after the launch of the first product ever manufactured by Nestlé (baby cereal), it was already being sold in five different countries. Nestlé made diversity part of its strategy from the outset and still continues to do so today – Nescafé currently offers a range of no less than 32 different coffee-related products in Europe. This is a far cry from the single Coke-style product. Whereas US brands promote the 'American way of life', this does not apply to other brands and groups throughout the world. The object of this chapter and indeed the entire book is to try to re-establish a certain balance and to suggest alternative, and sometimes more relevant, models.

Key stages in the process of brand globalisation are:

▮ defining brand identity;

▮ choosing regions and countries;

▮ accessing the markets;

▮ choosing the brand architecture;

▮ choosing products adapted to the markets;

▮ constructing global campaigns.

Defining brand identity

Brand globalisation presupposes the definition of the brand to be globalised. That is, the brand must have an identity that will serve as a medium for its globalisation, in both tangible and intangible terms. The company must therefore start by defining and writing the parameters of the brand's identity. This is essential for coherence, all the more so since globalisation will greatly increase the brand's centrifugal tendencies, with everyone wanting to interpret it in their own particular way. To limit these tendencies, there must be a clear and concise platform with salient points and flesh.

It should be remembered that the modern brand is no longer a simple 'product plus' (a mere definition of a product with a plus

value, like 'the best toothpaste for helping prevent tooth decay'). It is a source that has to be defined. To avoid problems of understanding and translation, globalisation very often involves the choice of all-purpose words that have the advantage of creating consensus the world over, such as 'high quality', 'client focused', 'dynamic' and 'competent'. But it is important to be wary of international consensus since it usually reflects a certain weakness in the brand definition and therefore the brand identity.

Brands are based on differentiation. They have to have character, salient and original points. But would Marlboro dare to launch its brand today using the symbol of a solitary, macho, craggy, outdoor figure?

Global brands are universal stereotypes

As a rule each brand should be based on a consumer or customer insight. An insight is literally an insight into the consumer or customer, a short sentence encapsulating the state of mind or expectation or attitude the brand is responding to.

As a consequence, global brands tend to address universal truths, global insights. Taking the spirit market, what are the universal truths of alcohols? Here consumption is conspicuous: by drinking, men try to enhance their male status. By its symbolic character, and the values it promotes ('keep walking', that is to say persevere) Johnnie Walker represents the adult male achievement. It is about effort and masculinity, about being a real male throughout the world. J&B is about social success. Chivas encourages joy and conspicuous consumption. Bacardi is an escape to paradise.

Give flesh to your identity

There are several ways of preventing the salient points of the brand identity becoming lost in the globalisation process:

- by accompanying the facets of the brand identity with a comparison, saying what the brand is and what it is not;

- by accompanying the words with images (brand concept board);

- by reinforcing the facets through training initiatives and creating local brand relays (keepers of the flame);

- by not delegating strategic implementation (such as advertising and the web) to the local level.

At this point, it is important to distinguish between exported brands and global brands in the strict sense of the term. Jaguar, Porsche and BMW are exported brands – Jaguar's brand values have not been redefined for globalisation, while BMW and Porsche certainly incorporate the characteristics of the global market (in fact the US market) in order to define the specifications of their future products. The Porsche 928 was designed for the United States, its broad highways and style of driving, and the design of the latest BMW Series 5 was developed entirely with the United States in mind. But what you are buying is Coventry, Stuttgart or Munich – the brands have not changed in the slightest in respect of their identity and core values. The same is true of Chanel. These are brands exported worldwide.

The brand to be globalised must think about its identity. Will the identity that has ensured success in its country of origin guar-antee success in the rest of the world, or at least the key countries in which it is to be marketed? There is therefore an interaction between the first (defining brand identity) and second (choosing regions and countries) phases of brand globalisation. When a brand is exported, it immediately acquires the added values associated with its international perception, and it enjoys the 'spillover effects of international perception'. Absolut is not highly rated in Sweden, but in the United States – where it is perceived as an imported vodka, while Smirnoff (the local leader) is produced in the United States – it has created the premium segment.

Separate the domestic and the international positioning

When it leaves its country of origin, a brand is transformed, and changes its nature. For example, Barilla in Italy is a popular 'mainstream' pasta brand that offers good value for money and inspires confidence. As shown by Table 17.7, in other countries it is positioned as the ultimate Italian 'must have', top quality, traditional and fashionable, but loses its 'value for money' and 'confidence' – it takes time to build up confidence.

Generally speaking, exported brands must be positioned at the top of the range since they have to support transport costs and customs duties. Furthermore, it is an opportunity to take advantage of the spillover effects of perceived brand globalness (PBG). In this way, the Swedish vodka Absolut

Table 17.7 Barilla's international and domestic image

Percentage perceiving the brand to be:	Italy	France	Germany
High quality	34.9	56.9	40.6
Trustworthy	56.6	44.8	17.4
Good quality/price	33.8	26.8	17.2
Fashionable	11.0	19.6	26.1
Authentic	8.9	16.0	13.7

Source: Kapferer and Schuiling (2004)

created the top-of-the-range (premium) segment in the United States, where it is sold for 20 per cent more than the local market leader (Smirnoff), which has factories scattered throughout the region.

Choosing regions and countries

An examination of the so-called global brands reveals that they are far from being as widely distributed throughout the world as we are led to believe. Of course, this could be because conquering world markets is a gradual process and a company must first of all establish itself as the leader in its domestic market. For example, the first Wal-Mart was not established outside the United States until 1991, 30 years after the creation of the first store in this famous US chain, while McDonald's accessed other markets gradually, one by one.

However, there is another explanation – not all countries are potential customers for the brand in question. For example, dairy products are not part of Asian culture, which is a handicap for Danone. Similarly, yoghurt is not a part of US culture and this is a handicap for Dannon USA which, although created in 1942, has not managed to impose itself as a major brand. The Japanese do not like their perfume to impinge on others, which is a handicap for all brands of strong perfume. This is why brands such as Paloma Picasso, with its characteristically Spanish values and strong essences, sell better in Texas, California and of course southern Europe, but also in countries (such as Germany) whose tourists visit southern Europe.

At this stage a strategic analysis should be carried out to assess the potentials of each country and the barriers to accessing their markets. This analysis should incorporate:

- the size of the existing market;
- indicators of growth and/or the latent potentials of this market, and its 'segmentability' – sociocultural develop-

ments and the growth of purchasing power;

- consumer insights on their prospects for rapid development;
- the nature of any competition and its ability to react – does the brand in question have the potential for strong differentiation, or a 'plus value'?
- the existence of a rudimentary brand equity in the country or region (via tourism or the international media which transmit brand images into homes throughout the world);
- the existence of adequate distribution channels likely to promote the brand concept;
- the existence of a media network;
- the existence of adequate commercial partners at local level;
- the non-existence of barriers to market access – customs, formal and informal regulations;
- the potential for registering or buying the brand name (a check that it is not already owned locally).

The presence of trade barriers was why countries like India, fearing a sort of neocolonialism through the intermediary of companies, for a long time remained closed to imports. It would have been theoretically possible, for example, to manufacture a major brand of car in that country, but this would require all the subcontractors who are a necessary part of the production process to do the same thing. In the absence of subcontractors and adequate partners, there is a risk of departing from the brand contract in that particular country – its cars will sell but will be of inferior quality. This was also a problem in Brazil for a long time.

As has already been stated, the key issue in brand naming is the globalisation of product platforms – for example, Unilever defined five platforms for margarine. It is not a major problem that one of these platforms is Becel in Portugal and ProActiv elsewhere – since global economies and synergies must first of all be achieved at production and concept/positioning level, the name becomes a secondary problem. As the focus of media attention, a name that is the same everywhere is of course desirable, but it is not the central issue because it is not the principal source of increased profitability.

The result of the strategic analysis of the countries in question sometimes explains the distribution of sales of international brands. Thus, the three key countries for The Laughing Cow brand are of course its country of origin but also Germany and Saudi Arabia, where temperatures are so high that processed cheese is the only way to provide the daily milk intake for both adults and children. The creation of factories in Morocco and Egypt has also reduced the problem of customs barriers.

Within the context of globalisation, the order in which countries, regions and continents are 'conquered' is also a strategic issue. For example, Amore Pacific is the international flagship brand of the Korean company of the same name – it embodies its know-how, values and ethics. It is also a modern brand that seeks to ally itself with the concept of western beauty without rejecting its Asiatic origins. In 2003 the question arose as to which it should penetrate first, the US or European market. Apart from the issues addressed above, the company was concerned whether it was in its best interest to advertise success in Europe then the United States, or vice versa. Given that perceived brand globalness is not a driver of preference in the United States, or at least less so than in Europe (Holt, Quelch and Taylor, 2003), it was decided to penetrate the US market first. In addition, the United States seem geographically, socially and culturally much closer to Korea than Europe, which is not only distant and fragmented, but also has strong well-established brands.

It will come as no surprise that, today, all western brands are looking towards the East:

- Eastern Europe and Russia are two of the long-awaited growth regions for brands battling it out on saturated western markets. They also offer a competitive advantage for Scandinavian brands that have long-established ties with these regions, and for Germany whose area of influence has always historically been Eastern Europe. But given the present low purchasing power, it is also an area of expansion for brands positioned according to price, such as the Korean brands LG, Samsung, Daewoo and Khia, and the Turkish brands targeting Romania, Bulgaria and Albania.

- China is another growth region – today, one-third of its billion inhabitants are creditworthy. It is significant that barely two years ago, l'Oréal was achieving 49 per cent of its turnover in Western Europe, 32 per cent in the United States and only 19 per cent in the rest of the world. Given the considerable needs of Asia in general, due to the size of its population and its improving standard of living, it is easy to understand that l'Oréal's priorities now lie in this direction. This is reflected by the fact that one of the group's basic international research centres was established in Japan, and also by the group's acquisition of Japanese brands. Gone are the days when Chinese women only looked at western brands. Today they are very much aware of their Asiatic origins and are now turning to luxury and top-of-the-range Japanese and Korean brands – as evidenced by the success of the Korean brand, La Neige, in the department stores of Hong Kong and Shanghai. This is why l'Oréal bought the Japanese brand Sue Uemura, whose global brand portfolio reflects cultural diversity. Finally, the 11 global brands in the l'Oréal portfolio are to be launched in China.

India, which is slowly emerging from a protectionist phase in respect of its identity and the desire to preserve its independence, will be the other growth region of the future. The competitive positions are already being taken up. The same applies to Brazil.

Accessing the markets

A brand is not a simply a name on a particular range of products – it is what distinguishes those products, and a source of added value in the eyes of the target market. A brand is established over a period of time, and nothing is more important than a brand's first initiatives in a country, since these are what determine its long-term representation. The mainstay or basis of this representation is the 'prototype'. It should be remembered that this key notion was identified by the psychology of abstract concepts (see Chapter 11) – the prototype is the 'best exemplar' which embodies the brand identity.

Today, in response to the demands of rationalisation and efficiency, many brands have two levels of branding – the parent brand and the daughter brand. A typical brand architecture is that of the source brand, a branded house with two levels. Frito Lay, Garnier, Dannon, Müeller, Campina, Ford, Toyota and Renault are all typical source brands. The brand can only be globalised via its daughter brands, which themselves cover a range of products. The key to globalising these parent brands is therefore a good daughter brand.

It is significant that Garnier was able to begin its globalisation in 2001 when it realised that it finally had a suitable prototype, one that could embody the brand's modern values (see Chapter 13). This prototype – Fructis Style, created in 2000 – was the most recent of all the Garnier daughter brands, but it was the one that enabled Garnier to be launched in the United States, the Republic of South Africa, Brazil and China. It is now the segment leader in all these countries.

Globally speaking, there are two major strategies for accessing national markets, by creating a new category or segmenting an existing category.

Creating a new category

Garnier is a typical example of this. The parent brand establishes itself by launching a daughter brand that becomes the reference, the pioneer of a new category which has the benefit of the 'first mover advantage', little or no competition and easier negotiations with distributors who are eager for creative innovations and value rather than a mere change of brands between competitors. The downside of this strategy is that it requires a greater investment in marketing and advertising. Its success also establishes the meaning of the parent brand, which enables it to launch its other daughter brands at a later date.

Nivea uses the same strategy even though it has an 'umbrella brand' architecture. It launches Nivea Cream before the lines that establish its competence in the facial and body care sector, the keys to creating a long-term bond of confidence.

Segmenting an existing category

The alternative strategy involves the immediate creation of a significant volume of business by launching a differentiated product, based on the brand values, but in a large-volume local category. For example, in Lebanon Yoplait began by launching two traditional local dairy products, Laban and Labneh. The aim was to quickly become the referent for traditional fresh dairy products by giving the country what a large industrial company can give – superior and consistent quality, more hygienic products, a more subtle taste, products with a longer shelf life, and more practical packaging.

Lactalis, an international giant of the cheese industry, globalised its umbrella brand Président in the same way. The Président business model is the segmentation of generic categories. Created in 1968, it became the leading brand of France's leading cheese (Camembert) and then the leading brand of butter, before extending to other products such as Brie and Emmental. By segmenting the generic category, Président introduces modern quality, practicality, adaptability to new uses and so on. The mistake would be to try to globalise Président by exporting Camembert – for example, why would the Spanish, Russians or Kazakhs want to eat Camembert? At best it would appeal to a tiny minority (a niche). This is not how a leading brand is recreated – and this is the key issue.

It is the business model of the brand that has to be globalised. For Président, this involves recreating – in Russia, Kazakhstan, Spain or any other country – the initiative used to successfully create the original brand, by segmenting a large-volume traditional local category.

It is worth noting that Danone, unable to create a new category of dairy products in Asia, decided to establish itself by segmenting an existing category to embody its key value, health. Throughout the world, Danone is famous for its yoghurts and mineral water. In Asia it puts its name to biscuits – that promise health (growth and vitamins) to parents and children – via global daughter brands such as Prince and Pepito, or by endorsing an ultra-popular, leading local brand such as Jacob's in Indonesia, Thailand and Singapore, and Tiger in China.

Adapting the brand architecture

Should the brand architecture be the same in all countries? Maybe it 'should' but can it in fact be the same? The gradual globalisation of a brand with two levels of branding (including a source brand or endorsing brand) automatically raises this type of question. Also, adaptation is governed by practical considerations – it is impossible to recreate what was achieved without the pressures of time and

profitability in other markets, including the country of origin. Depending on the country, the type of brand architecture used will be the 'horizontal crunch' and/or the 'vertical crunch'.

The 'horizontal crunch' involves reducing the horizontal range of brands and 'nicheing' certain brands below others. Thus, in the United States, it is possible to find a Mini Babybel cheese with a taste of Bonbel, the whole being endorsed by The Laughing Cow, whereas in France and Germany these three names correspond to three different brands. But when a company moves into the United States, the problem is not so much ensuring greater market coverage with a portfolio containing a range of speciality products as surviving by capitalising. What was an independent brand becomes a daughter brand or an additional item under the same brand name (line extension).

The 'vertical crunch' has the reverse effect – vertical brand architectures with three levels of branding are reduced to two levels for reasons of efficiency and practicality. This type of crunch is subdivided into the 'top-down crunch' and the 'bottom-up crunch'.

The 'bottom-up crunch' helps to reduce the number of levels by suppressing the one in the middle and raising the one at the bottom. In Europe, l'Oréal Paris is represented in the shampoo market by the Elsève brand, whose products have names (such as Color Vive) that describe the function of the product. They are therefore referred to as Elsève Color Vive by l'Oréal. The driver (what the consumer actually buys) is Elsève, while l'Oréal Paris acts as an endorsement.

In the United States, it was decided to do away with Elsève but to give all the products in the range the suffix 'Vive': Nutri Vive, Vita Vive, Color Vive, Curl Vive, Hydra Vive, Body Vive. This makes the relationship between l'Oréal and its products much stronger and more direct, which in turn promotes a reciprocal regeneration. The brand now has a co-driver since US consumers are not buying l'Oréal shampoo or Color Vive, but a combination of the two – l'Oréal Color Vive. This also avoids the fragmentation of publicity in a country where media costs are extremely high.

The 'top-down crunch' occurs when an endorsing brand becomes a driver and relegates the daughter brand to the role of descriptor. It is significant that in Europe, the European brand of biscuits Lu is sold by speciality brands. According to the packaging, Lu comes under the aegis of its daughter brands Prince, Pim's and Mikado. Below the names, each specific product may even be described as an 'energy added' biscuit, for example.

In the countries to be 'conquered' by the brand (like the United States), Lu has been upgraded from an endorsing brand to a range brand, while the other names are less prominent on the packaging and become descriptors.

Choosing products adapted to the markets

Managing the growth of business and the establishment of the brand simultaneously means constantly adapting the marketing – and therefore the product ranges – to the market, but within the framework of a well-defined and coherent strategy. As has already been stated, the 'prototypes' must be chosen as a function of the image to be created. Gone are the days when importers decided which products would be allowed into a country on the basis of purely short-term requirements. These importers were merchants and intermediaries, not shareholders in the company, and therefore had no long-term objectives. This was why many brands were launched via different products in countries that were in fact quite close to the country of origin. Within the space of a few years, this led to discrepancies in the product image and therefore to significant discrepancies in the price premium.

Products must be a source of rapid growth and yet comply with the sphere of influence that the brand wants to establish over a period of time. Product campaigns, especially in the initial stages, can help to achieve this. The different ways in which products are adapted to suit different countries, areas and regions were examined earlier as part of the localisation-globalisation dilemma.

Constructing global campaigns

Not all brands want to globalise their communication. Japanese companies typically allow their subsidiaries, in all their branches, a great deal of freedom at local level. Of course, this creates an impression of disunity since the images projected by the various branches within the same country tend to be very different. But from a cultural point of view, large Japanese – and more recently Korean – groups seem to want to offset the extreme standardisation of their global products (the source of economies of scale) by allowing this freedom at local level. These local subsidiaries are mainly sales subsidiaries whose purpose is to optimise the sales of global products in a particular country. Their local managers are judged on these results, not on the attendant creation of brand equity. Their marketing structures are essentially operational marketing structures, with the exception of Sony, which has developed its brand concept in other countries, and Toyota in the United States.

Another brand that favours a local approach is Bonduelle, a leading company on the European vegetable market, where it has to confront an amazing diversity of situations. In Spain, for example, the brand had to access the market via the frozen foods sector, in Russia via tinned sweetcorn. Peas, its flagship product, vary greatly from country to country. The Germans and Dutch like large, green peas, while the French prefer small, sweet, extra fine peas. In Italy, Germany and the Netherlands, peas are mainly used for decoration (as in a salad), which gave rise to the launch of Bonduelle's 'Crea Salad'. Faced with such diversity, the company has centred its globalisation initiatives around internal values and company dialogue. Furthermore, the name, logo and packaging are the same for all products, although advertising remains very local.

An increasing number of brands want to control their global image. While it is important to start by creating a brand identity platform, this serves no purpose unless it is presented coherently throughout the world. So, if a brand has decided to conduct a voluntarist policy of globalisation, it needs to develop its own procedures for constructing its global campaigns. The most typical are outlined below.

Globalising communications: processes and problems

Today, brands want to globalise their advertising, although this may not be possible in certain situations for practical reasons. There is no shortage of questions on this score. How do brands construct global campaigns without damaging promotional creativity? How do they avoid demotivating the countries concerned? How do they inject a positive spiral into the company, throughout the countries concerned, to destroy the not-invented-here (NIH) syndrome? The great progress made in this field provides benchmarks from which lessons can be learnt. In the following analysis, it will be noted that, first and foremost, these campaigns identify what unites the brand, which is what it wants to globalise:

▌ the brand spirit, the parameters of brand identity;

▌ the brand's visual identity;

▌ the strategic product (prototype);

▌ the executional codes of the campaign.

These must be identified before moving any closer towards an identical copy strategy, a common creative concept or even a global campaign. Companies also vary depending on whether they impose a certain discipline or encourage the search for standardisation.

Contrary to appearances, McDonald's is not particularly prescriptive when it comes to brand advertising. Of course the marketing is global, like the product. With a few exceptions and adaptations (which are the focus of media attention), the concept is strong because it is standardised the world over – even though McDonald's is organised according to national subsidiaries that are virtually independent. With regard to advertising, the company's corporate headquarters run the Ronald McDonald films and charity initiatives, and offer guidelines without seeking to impose any form of obligation or control. This is explained by the McDonald's business model – the form of the advertising cannot be imposed upon those who pay for it, the franchisees in each country who pay 4 per cent of their turnover for the franchise. Once a month, a vote is taken at the country's executive headquarters in respect of future campaigns.

Even so, an incredible impression of 'commonness' emerges from the television ads in all the franchise countries. But this is not the result of any form of constraint – at McDonald's, informality is the unifying principle. It is due to the high level of understanding and sharing, by the group's advertising managers worldwide, of the following elements:

▌ the state of mind of the brand, its concept (food, family and fun, simple human truths) and the essence of the brand (the child within us);

▌ the brand promise expressed according to a traditional 'laddering' (features, functions, rewards, values, personality);

▌ the golden rules of advertising (tenets of Great McDonald's Advertising), such as 'every McDonald's ad is a brand ad' or 'show human relationships', 'stay current: understand me, the client' or 'woven into the fabric of local, everyday life', or 'always put emotion into it'.

As a result, the baselines vary greatly depending on the country, but they all represent the same source, the same identity, whether it is 'Mac your day' (Australia), 'Every time a good time' (Germany), 'Smile' (South America), or 'You know our products from the cradle' (Poland).

To promote even greater standardisation, without damaging the McDonald's business model, advertising films from all over the world are shown at the Creative Brand Seminars held on a regular basis. This encourages countries to use very creative films that, although produced in other countries, are still extremely relevant. The 'best practices' are posted on the intranet and discussed at McDonald's Hamburger University. Finally, incentives are offered for using other countries' films. Today, 50 per cent of McDonald's television advertising is based on the sharing and use of these 'best practices'.

The car manufacturing group Volkswagen is extremely centralised in respect of marketing, but when it comes to advertising, allows great freedom of expression within a strong brand framework. For example, each country can produce a different film (based on the same strategic and creative brief) for the market's most popular models, because creative advertising is not centralised. However, for less 'mainstream' products such as the 4 × 4 Touareg or the Phayton, a single film is produced by the German group's corporate headquarters.

The new Polo provides a good example of the creative process. It is based on the very strong Volkswagen brand platform. In the past, the brand concept was centred around reliability and the tone characterised by an implicit understanding (humour) with the consumer. Today, due to the presence of the

Skoda and Seat brands, the brand concept has evolved – it is now based on the democratisation of excellence. Then there is the platform of the daughter brand, the framework of the positioning of the model and the consideration of all the models in the 'Tone and Style of VW Advertising' framework. This framework is reminiscent of the principles used by the Tribal DDB advertising agency since 1960, which have created the exceptional distinctiveness of VW advertising and invested the brand with its unique personality. It includes such principles as: 'Do not exaggerate: call a spade a spade', ' Don't shout, he can hear you especially if you talk sense', 'Be authentic, honest, human, open, accessible', 'Make people think and smile', 'Be teasing, elliptic: one should understand only at the point of revelation' and finally and most importantly 'Be original'. In DDB ads, Volkswagen cars rarely move.

The positioning of the Polo that provided a worldwide framework was 'Polo inspires self confidence because you can feel it is the only car in its class that is built without compromise'. Then a creative brief was produced that summarised the advertising objectives, the advertising target and the consumer insight ('I feel I can take on the world'), the product range and the reason to believe. Using this brief, local DDB agencies set to work and came up with the creative idea that was finally used: 'Tough new Polo, careful it doesn't go to your head'. Then the films based on this creative concept were produced by the local teams in each country.

Philips was recently restructured as a centralised organisation for a global brand, with its headquarters in the Netherlands. The new 'unique' brand concept was established – 'A unique experience' – valid for all three market segments (home entertainment, personal expression and professional business products). The company's senior management now decides on the choice of transnational products that will form the basis of the brand's publicity. It centralises briefings and develops the advertising campaigns with local design teams. The pretest procedure is centralised, as is production, with additional items built in at the filming stage of the ad, to reduce the cost of line extensions.

Nivea uses a similar model, with very explicit guidelines on the brand identity, the personality of each sub-brand, and the strict provisos for handling the publicity that create the 'Niveaness' so typical of all the brand ads, in spite of their diversity. The director of Nivea's Worldwide Marketing, based in Hamburg, appoints three local marketing directors to work on a project, in partnership with the TBWA Hamburg advertising agency. They are chosen from countries throughout the world and their task is to define the creative platform. This is then sent to the local TBWA agencies of the three marketing directors which produce creative ideas and then campaigns. The campaign chosen is then imposed in all countries unless it has to be customised. This happened in the case of the campaign to relaunch Nivea Soft, for which the creative idea was 'soft as the morning rain'. But this had to be adapted for three countries – the UK, where it rains a lot, Saudi Arabia, where it hardly rains at all, and Indonesia, where rain is associated with the devastation caused by monsoons. The adapted ideas for each of these countries were:

- so light, soft sensation for beautiful skin (UK and Australia);
- it feels like under the trees (Indonesia);
- it feels like the summer rain (Saudi Arabia).

These case studies illustrate the typical processes of groups wanting to globalise their advertising. But it should be remembered that globalisation must be pragmatic and take account of strong regional differences (different competitors, different consumer needs). It is therefore advisable to:

- Start by globalising at regional level. For example, start in Asia and then incorporate the United States and Europe, or vice versa.
- Establish common brand platforms (identity) and share the spirit of the brand to create an implicit sense of affinity.
- Establish guidelines for the handling of advertising, which are either limited to using common symbols of recognition or go much further in order to bring out the personality of the brand.
- If necessary, admit that the angle of attack cannot be the same for all markets (positioning versus competitors, the unique compelling competitive advantage), depending on regions and/or continents.
- Remember that, while a single advertisement is of course economically justifiable in the pursuit of this objective, the objective of branding is not to save money but to boost business. Working at international level is expensive since it requires the creation of an international structure, the organisation of lots of meetings, and so on.
- Possibly be more prescriptive with regard to common strategic products than local tactical products.

In conclusion, it is important to define the relationship to be established with the countries concerned – is it a logic of supplier and customer or one of authority, between decision maker and subordinate? Depending on the possibilities, there is a choice between decentralised or centralised management. There are six types of relationship or different managerial functions, as summarised in Figure 17.1, that can be applied to all elements of brand marketing. The globalisation process of each company can be represented on this grid by marking (with a cross) the point of intersection between an element of the marketing mix and the type of relationship with the countries concerned, in respect of this particular element.

Function / Brand mix	Ignore	Inform	Persuade	Approve	Decide	Oblige
Product Concept Positioning Price Distribution CRM Web activity Activation Promotion Advertising – creative concept – executional guides – production						
	Decentralised			Centralised		

Source: TBWA

Figure 17.1 Managing the globalisation process between headquarters and subsidiaries

Making local brands converge

A classic strategy for globalisation consists of unifying the local brands inherited during the growth of the groups. Big groups have, historically speaking, often chosen a strategy of external growth through the buying up of strong local brands. The industrial sector typically uses this strategy: Schneider has never stopped purchasing local leading brands of electronics, for instance. In buying these well-established reputations, these companies were able to smooth their way through local markets. This approach also involves fast-moving consumer goods. The former BSN took over the famous Belgian biscuit brand, Beukelaer, the local equivalent of Lu. The Swedish group Molnycke bought Nana in France, which then joined the Scandinavian brand of sanitary protection, Libresse.

Given this patchwork type of situation where there is not much standardisation in the brand portfolio, companies proceed to regroup brands around the same positioning.

Two scenarios are then possible:

- The company changes the names of the local brands by substituting the name of its own brand.

- In the second scenario, the company decides to keep the local brand equities connected to the brand names. General Motor's branch in Europe is called Opel while in the UK it is known as Vauxhall. However, these brands do need to converge.

The harmonising process of a brand portfolio is quite tricky and should always be conducted on a voluntary basis, since the initial situations of each separate brand name are never the same. A systematic programme of unification according to the style, but above all according to the product basis, must be implemented. The example of Mölnycke is interesting from this point of view. In the female hygiene market, the intimate relationship which has slowly been built up with the client is a key factor in the capital of the brand, of course, there is the product benefit, but there is also the climate of a relationship within the brand identity. This relationship must be maintained. Having judged it necessary to preserve the brand capital attached to Nana in Southern Europe and to Libresse in Northern Europe, at the same time as Procter & Gamble was entering the market with Always, the Mölnycke group progressed in three steps.

The first step consisted of determining together what the unique positioning of these two brands could be. The positioning revolved around the concept of what is 'natural'. Deeper examination revealed that this concept gave rise to different readings, according to the country under examination. In Scandinavian countries, the home territory for Libresse, nature in its strictest sense was evoked, whereas in the home countries of Nana nature connoted spontaneity. The second step consisted of bringing the brand image of Libresse and Nana closer together as they were quite different to start with. Libresse had to develop a more feminine image and more humour, going so far as to include a man in the advertisement for the first time. As for the Nana woman, she had to evolve in her commercials, become more natural with less frivolity, more pared down to the essential, more thoughtful.

This second step was brought about by specific communications, but then having achieved a single concept for the brand, the third step consisted of launching new products shared by both brands with the same commercial.

In conclusion, analysis of this internationalisation strategy enables the definition of the typical pathway to follow in all countries with similar constraints. The process is made up of seven basic steps (see Table 17.8). A consensus of opinion about the kernel of the brand, the deep identity to which all subsidiaries must adhere, is the essential starting point of these seven steps. This adhesion is revealed through visible signs such as logos, codes, tone and style. The ultimate phase is the quest for commercials that resemble each other more and more, until a single commercial is possible for all.

The reader will have understood by now that whether or not to have common advertising is not the important issue. One cannot reduce the question of globalisation to knowing whether it is possible to produce a standard commercial.

Of much greater importance are the existence of one common invisible kernel and competitive positioning and economies of scale at the production level.

Table 17.8   How to make local brands converge

Step 1	Is internationalisation necessary? Pertinence of globalisation for the brand or brands?
Step 2	Which brand facets should be internationalised? Which ones should not?
Step 3	Agreed-upon description for the network of the common kernel, brand platform, identity prism and positioning
Step 4	Definition of the common visible facets, of the graphic charters, packaging charters, charters of advertising expression
Step 5	Definition of the common copy strategy
Step 6	Definition of the common advertising execution
Step 7	Global launching of common products

Source: Adapted from F Bonnal/DDB

Part Four

Brand valuation

18

Financial valuation and accounting for brands

In 2007 Fortune brands announced it wanted to sell the world-famous vodka brand Absolut. Rumours say Ford wants to sell Volvo and even Jaguar. What price for these businesses? What part of the price represents the value of the name itself and its power worldwide?

Financial evaluation and accounting procedures for brands have become subjects of considerable interest and debate, as can be seen by the numerous articles that have been published on the subject. This intense interest in the subject has several technical, economic and fiscal aspects, but especially reflects the discovery of the importance of intangible investments in modern companies, and of the growth that a brand can generate in certain cases. The debates are international, as they concern the IAS new norms of accounting as they affect large multinational corporations that they acquired and hence need to value fairly, and revalue regularly.

The reason for the sudden interest in this subject – it was hardly mentioned before 1985 – is the large increase in the number of takeover bids for companies with brands. The financial and tax implications of the new problems posed by goodwill were considerable.

When one company is bought by another, there is often a huge difference between the book value of the company assets and the price paid, especially if there are strong brands and positive forecasts of growth. This difference is called goodwill: it is actually a measure of the financial markets' positive attitude to the future of the company. For accounting purposes, the payment by the acquiring company must lead to the inclusion in its balance sheet of what has effectively been bought (assets minus debts) so as to get a perfect match between these elements and the price paid (see Figure 18.2).

In all modern accounting systems and norms, goodwill must be allocated to the specific items that have created it. Brands are one of these, as well as patents, know-how and databases. Hence, it can be said that the question of brand valuation has stemmed from the necessity to account for sometimes huge goodwill payments when major corporations were sold. There are other situations where brands need to be evaluated. For instance, when a brand is purchased, the value of this asset must be made explicit.

Accounting is governed by the principle of

Figure 18.1   What is 'brand equity'?

prudence. Its evaluations must be shown to be valid, coherent and reproduceable. This is why, paradoxically, only the brands that have been bought individually, or that were included in the price paid for a company, can be posted in the balance sheet of the acquiring company. The overall price paid gives an upper limit to their value. So far, all over the world, the principle of prudence has led national and international accounting norms and standards to forbid the posting in the balance sheet of internally grown brands. It is of course possible to propose brand valuations, but as long as the brands have not been bought and sold, there is too much doubt about the validity of these estimates. Brands acquire value through the market.

Accounting for brands: the debate

The debate on the inclusion of all of the brands, whether they be purchased or created, raises basic questions about the very essence of accounting. Why do balance sheets and company accounts exist? Is it to give an estimation of the true financial value of the company (which of course is very subjective) or, following the accounting prudence principle, to include only objective data and to assess only past and recorded transactions? Until now the second idea has been chosen in all countries: therefore only transactions involving external brands are recorded. If the internal brands were to be noted, the principle of reality would be respected at the expense of reliability and of the consistency of accounting. In fact, what would we think of a balance sheet which was based on non-uniform and sometimes subjective methods of evaluation? The inclusion of an acquired brand does not violate the principle of bookkeeping at historical costs, which is a fundamental accounting principle. How then can internal brands be valued? As we will see later on, the valuation methods, which are based on historical costs or replacement costs, are not good enough. The best methods are those based on projections of future income, which are highly subjective. A certain amount of uncertainty and heterogeneity, which are against the rules of caution, would be created if these were included in the balance sheet.

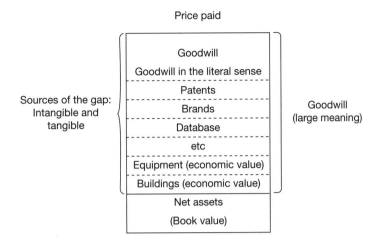

Figure 18.2 The issue of fair valuation of brands

But one may contend that the function of accounting is to present a framework to identify and deal with a company's commercial expenses which are accumulated in the form of intangible assets that are developed internally. For the moment, these outlays are treated as expenses and are deducted from the company's income for the year in question; this in turn reduces the amount of tax that the company has to pay. However, some tax authorities are beginning to clamp down on the payment of back taxes. For example, they now consider that the money spent to produce advertising commercials can no longer be classified as expenses but are rather investments and thus are no longer exempt from tax.

Accountancy, just like taxation, is interested in the recording of costs (as expenses or as investments). Financial analysis estimates the discounted value of certain assets as a function of the probability of the future income that they are supposed to generate. Thus, there will not be only one value of the brand because valuation methods depend on the goals of the valuation. The accounting principles already exist and can integrate with some reservations the costs accrued during the creation of a brand. It is for the finance people to estimate the market value of these assets according to their own methods. This reasoning already exists for buildings and thus can also be applied to brands.

Here, a first conclusion is taking shape concerning the monetary value of brands: ideally for a valuation method to be acceptable it should be possible to apply it equally well to brands which are to be bought and to brands that already exist within the company, with a financial aim as well as an accounting aim. However, this is not possible.

The notion of value is highly dependent on your position. Rowntree was worth £1 billion for its shareholders and £2.4 billion for Nestlé! For Midland Bank, Lanvin was worth £400 million; for Henri Racamier and l'Oréal it was worth £500 million. On top of this, accountancy is controlled by a principle of prudence, objectivity and coherence through time. By definition, in its own evaluation, a raider thinks and acts differently. He does not want to be prudent and is rather subjective. The valuation of brands in the context of mergers and acquisitions is a one-off operation: it aims to fix a price at the start given the intentions and synergies that can be expected by the potential buyer. Accounting for brands should obey different norms since their value derives from a different point of view. When there is no transaction involved, the internal brand is valued either as a function of accrued costs or as a function of its everyday usage (and not what another party could do with it). Therefore, there will definitely be a gap between the value of the brand which is bought and of the brand which is created. Moreover, the need to constantly revalue brand values either up or down, in a subjective manner, if they are legitimately noted in the balance sheet introduces fluctuations which undermine the reliability of company accounts. We can reply that the value of the inventory which, in Europe, is indicated annually in the notes to the accounts does not have this effect. It is understandable why the accounting experts at the London Business School who were studying the case for the inclusion of all brands on the balance sheet gave an unfavourable opinion (Barwise, 1989) concerning home-grown brands.

It is a paradox that those who support the most the argument of posting brand values are the marketing people. Perhaps they are hoping to find a method accepted by accountants and financiers of valuing the long-term effects of marketing decisions. However, even though everybody agrees orally that, for example, advertising has both short- and long-term effects, controllers analyse brand performance within a short span of time. Product or brand managers have to produce positive annual operating accounts, positive profit and loss accounts. Thus, evaluation and control are done on an annual basis. This type of behaviour encourages all decisions which are profitable in the short-term. Marketing people would like to have a way to counterbalance this short-term bias, which has the effect of ballooning annual earnings but of eventually undermining brand equity through rapid promotions and brand extensions which are

too far from the core activity. On the other hand, looking for gains in awareness at any price may not always add to the marginal increase in brand equity and thus should be halted, with the money put to better use.

More generally, the value of a brand can be measured if the sources of this value can be located, in other words to measure is to understand. Therefore the resulting figure does not interest marketing as much as the process by which it is acquired, that is, the understanding of how a brand works, of its growth, of its increase or loss in value. This understanding is a learning experience and introduces logical and analytical elements to areas where magical beliefs dominated. It also supplies the means for a real communication between people working in marketing, accounting, finance, tax and law. Finally, even if, for reasons linked to tax or respect for the principle of objectivity and accounting coherence, the inclusion of internal brands on the balance sheet is still not recommended and should not be practised by the company, brand valuation remains a worthy exercise to be carried out internally, for all the above mentioned reasons. Mergers and acquisitions are in the end exceptional events even though they do catch the media's attention. The valuation of brands should not be restricted simply to mergers and acquisitions, it is also needed for the benefits that can be obtained from the point of view of management: for help in the decision-making process, for management control, for information systems, for marketing training and for education of product and brand managers. At this time when much is being said about the decline of brands, it is healthy to wonder what the real value of their awareness, image and public esteem is. Brand equity is based on psychological indicators, which are measured from the consumers' point of view, and is only worth something if it results in extra profits. The demands which arise from the presentation of company accounts and from shareholder and investor information are one thing, those arising from a management control system are another. The two should not be mixed up because they do not have the same objectives nor are they faced with the same constraints. There is no single value.

The notion of value is ambiguous and a source of several misunderstandings. It is important to understand that there is no single value for a brand; in fact, there are several because the valuation will be different depending on its aims:

- the value of liquidity in the case of a forced sale;
- the book value for company accounts;
- the value needed in order to encourage banks to lend the company money;
- the value of losses or damage to the worth of the brand should an adverse event occur;
- the value in order to estimate the price of licences;
- the value for management control, which depends on the behaviour encouraged by managers;
- the value for the partial sale of assets;
- the value in case of a takeover or of a merger and acquisition.

For the last case the buyer only asks one question: by how much will actual income rise due to the acquisition of a company with a strong brand? In order to reply to this question the company will evaluate any possible synergies that may exist between the two companies, any resulting cost savings (due to production, logistics, distribution, marketing), any extra capacity to impose one's decisions on distributors or the possibility of brand extensions or internationalisation. The proposed price for buying the company will be shaped by these questions. However, none of these questions will have any influence on the book value of the company's brands.

What conclusions should be drawn at this stage? Financial valuation of brands allows for the multidisciplinary meeting of all the company's departments: marketing, audit, finance, production, tax, etc. A capitalistic perspective is introduced in the long run, counterbalancing the logic of annual valuation perspectives. It acts as a reminder of the fact that a company's wealth no longer comes solely from the land, plant and equipment but also from its intangible assets (know-how, patents, brands, etc).

The debate on the value of brands and the way to account for them as assets is essentially an accounting one. This is not the essential benefit, but rather the integration of brand value in evaluating marketing and advertising decisions, which have been up to now subject to one single criterion: the preservation of the annual operating statement of the brand. Before we start to talk about the different valuation techniques, it is important to remember that the real objective of a valuation (for an acquisition or for the presentation of company accounts or for management) modifies the criteria of valuation for these methods. Depending on this objective we will have to choose between these demands which are, unfortunately, not very compatible: more validity or more reliability? more subjectivity or more objectivity? more present value or more historical costs?

What is financial brand equity?

The 1990s witnessed the flourishing of the concept of brand equity (Aaker, 1990). The act of combining a financial concept (equity) with a manifestly marketing-based notion (the brand) is symptomatic of a growing awareness of the financial value of brands, which has emerged from the exclusive world of advertising and marketing to become a very serious factor which – given the importance of equity – has a major impact on overall management. (Figure 18.1)

It is worth mentioning again what is meant by 'equity' in financial terms, and thus what connotations emerge from the combination of the terms 'brand' and 'equity'. Literally, equity is 'the owner's claim on the business'. It represents an ownership interest in an enterprise. This equity (called equity securities) is opposed to debt securities, although both are sources of funds, hence liabilities in the balance sheet. The use of the term 'equity' when attached to a brand refers in fact not to a liability but to an asset, built over time thanks to the investment of the business in it. For the sake of precision one should speak in fact of brand assets, not of brand equity.

Curiously enough, although the term 'brand equity' represents an invitation to combine the marketing perspective with the economic and financial perspective, subsequent events have revealed a disagreement within the community of experts. When it came to measuring this brand equity and discussing what makes a strong brand, there was a split between what some called 'consumer-based brand equity' and others referred to as 'financial brand equity'.

The former school of thought (consumer-based brand equity) approaches the question of brand value by taking the customer's point of view. This in turn leads to several different theories. Some believe that brand value exists wherever the preferences expressed for a brand are greater than a simple assessment of the utility of the product or service's attributes would have suggested. We can see that this approach considers the brand as a surplus, a preference that cannot be accounted for by the product alone. It is measured as a residual:

BE = Declared preference – preference predicted by product utilities

As we can see, this theory sees the brand as the degree of influence that exists over and above the product itself: the brand is thus restricted entirely to an intangible, emotional dimension. However, BMW – one of the world's strongest brands – owes its strength and attraction as much to a product with special, unique performance as it does to the image of its owners that the brand conveys.

Others (Aaker, 1990) maintain that brand value incorporates all of the following variables: recognition, perceived quality, imagery, loyalty and patent quality. Note that according to this definition – and in contrast to the previous definition – the product is included in brand equity because of the patents that make it different or even superior.

Still others, taking a highly cognitive approach (Keller, 1998), see the brand as a collection of memory associations that generate a different reaction to the brand. Keller, for example, speaks of positive customer-based brand equity if identification of the brand produces a more favourable reaction than if the brand is not identified. However, he also defines negative customer-based brand equity as a situation in which such identification leads to a less favourable reaction. Note that in the financial context which produced the notion of equity, there is no such thing as negative equity. The latter school of thought is populated by financial analysts whose role it is to evaluate assets (which can sometimes include intangible assets, and thus brands). From their economic perspective, brand equity is the value today of profits imputable to the brand in the future.

An economic analysis of brand equity requires us to look more closely at the word 'imputable'. The question is, imputable by whom? In contrast to the consumer-based approaches, the economic analysis prompts a simple yet fundamental observation: the brand is a conditional asset (Nussenbaum, 2003). After all, without a product (or service) there is no brand. In order to produce a profit or EVA (economic value added), there must already be sales, and thus a tangible base for the brand and its distribution. Here, 'already' means in advance: spending and paying come before receiving. This gives us the basic equation:

Value = –I + R

This equation is exactly the same as the following, more fully developed, version giving the value of any asset. Since an asset is a factor with inherent future values, its value appreciates by the present sum of its future expected profits once the initial investment has been deducted.

$$V = I + \sum_{t=1}^{n} \frac{(R_i - D_i)}{(1+r)^i}$$

Imputation of added value to the conditional asset that is the brand presupposes the following:

1. That a value already exists to be shared.

2. That the tangible and intangible factors required for its production have been factored in.

3. That a residual or excess profit remains after paying for these advance assets, which make production and distribution possible.

We believe it is time to bring the two approaches to the concept of brand equity together. After all, the brand is a tool for increasing business: its value is linked to, and dependent on, this objective.

Economic analysis tells us that, irrespective of a brand's reputation, image, preference factors and loyalty, the brand has no value if the company does not produce an excess profit capable of paying off the existing assets (tangible and intangible). Reputation and image do not constitute value in themselves if they do not translate into a profitable product or service.

Seen in this way, it is an illusion to believe that a brand has value simply because it has 'magic'. Many entrepreneurs have bought brands on this basis, but have never been able to convert this value into a hard profit. A brand is only worth anything if a profitable economic formula can be built around it; which is something of a paradox, given that this is an entirely consumer-based concept. However, the economic realities are clear: even if a name has an attraction for consumers, it does not guarantee future profits.

This can be illustrated by an example. The now-defunct Ribourel (property development) brand was the subject of a debate on the exact theme of this chapter. How much was it worth? It was shown that it was worth nothing: the brand's image was associated with value for money, but there was no way of turning this into a profit margin. The Ribourel concept was founded on an idea that was strong and attractive, but economically unachievable. The brand had no economic value under such circumstances.

The reader may remember the terse, shocking statement issued by Daewoo in offering to buy Thomson for the symbolic price of €1. The point being made was that the brand had no value. One might retort that quite the reverse was shown to be true under the management of CEO Thierry Breton; but in fact, what Thierry Breton did was to bring about a change in the business model in order to return the company to added value.

Using the same logic, if a brand can induce the consumer to pay a price differential but the cost of creating the brand is greater than the price increase, the brand has no value.

We should therefore put forward a unifying definition of a brand that has value (strong brand equity): *a strong brand is a name that influences buyers through the value it offers and is backed by a profitable economic formula.*

In this definition, several points should be noted:

▌ Modern competition revolves around concepts and ideas. A name is associated with an attractive, unique value that provides the source of its purchasing influence.

▌ Strength can also refer to the number of

people who associate the brand with this idea. A brand is a strong shared idea; for example, everyone says that BMWs are the best cars.

▎ This must be turned into an economically profitable reality.

We can clearly see both the connection and the ambiguity between the purely consumer-based and purely economic approaches. It all hangs on the use of one common word 'value', which takes on two different meanings. From the point of view of the marketer, taking his cue from the work of the psychologist M Rokeach, a value is an ideal to be attained, mobilising our energies and directing our choices. For the economist, however, it is a balance: $V = -I + R$.

A strong brand thus focuses its efforts on attaining a value through the consumption of a product or service which is given its meaning by marketing and advertising. However, this same brand has no economic value if this approach does not result in EVA: it is useless.

An economic formula for the brand does exist: this is one of the two keys to its value.

From economic value added to the brand

Over the last 10 years, intense accounting debates have raged in the United States, mainland Europe and Great Britain over the evaluation of brands. These debates centre around questions with significant repercussions for companies and their profit-and-loss accounts:

▎ When can a brand be activated and recorded on the balance sheet? Does it have to have been bought? If so, this excludes home-grown brands.

▎ Should brands be depreciated? If so, over what period?

▎ How do you reliably assess the value of a brand?

These issues should not be perceived as being of academic interest only: in fact, they ask important questions as to the very nature of brands and their impact on the added value created by the company over the lifespan of the brand. This last point thus prompts the following question: do brands have a life cycle? We know that in retrospect, we can reconstruct the life cycle of a product, with its typical launch, growth, maturity and decline phases. We say 'in retrospect' because during the life of a product, it is always possible to maintain that the situation we know as the mature stage simply points to insufficient effort (too few line extensions, too little international expansion, and so on).

Now, by feeding on new products that replace the old, the brand 'surfs' product life cycles and acquires from them an apparently indefinite lifespan. Nevertheless, the debate on the depreciation of brands leads to very different conclusions depending on whether one believes that brands have a life cycle (and should thus be depreciated), or that they do not. If a brand's lifespan cannot be determined in advance, there is no justification for depreciation.

However, we should start at the beginning, with the question of the nature of brands. Remember that a brand cannot exist without a product (or service): a product or service is needed before the brand can perform its economic role, which is to add value through the differentiation it creates and the added values it promises. In this respect, a brand is a true conditional asset. Its value can take a tangible form only if the company has already made a capital investment in producing and deploying the brand platform – its products or services. The consequences of this point are crucial: the brand is an added value, and thus if we are to take financial advantage of it, we must have profits, but only once we have allowed (at a given rate, t) for the capital required for its production (Nussenbaum, 2003). The company must therefore already have produced EVA. Remember the EVA equation:

EVA = nett EBIT after tax – t (Tangible Assets + Working Capital Requirement)

Still following the basic theory which dictates that the brand is a conditional asset, we should also factor in the cost of other intangible assets that have contributed to the business; for example, patents (which are crucial in the high-tech or medical marketing industries). Once these directly evaluable assets have been factored in, the residual thus derived will create the envelope within which we find the economic value of the brand and of other intangibles that cannot easily be evaluated directly.

This once again raises the question of identifying these other sources of added value. It stems from an assumption which forms the basis of economic and accounting practice worldwide – that a brand has no value unless it is able to produce excess profit even after taking into account the factors that enable the production and distribution of the products and services, regardless of whether these factors are physical and tangible or non-physical and intangible.

This theory of conditional assets accounts for the progressive, steady process of evaluating brands by means of allocating successive residual balances: EBIT, nett EBIT (after the imposition of company tax), EVA, and EVA after the direct identification of certain intangible assets.

Theoretically speaking, then, the brand evaluation process is simple (it consists of a series of successive residual balance allocations). However, for reasons related not so much to methodology as to the company's information system, it is tricky to implement in practice. To put a value on a brand, we have to be able to identify its profits – yet a brand can span many markets governed by a variety of different economic mechanisms, or markets in which factors such as the relative value of the brand in comparison to other assets might not be the same. For example, the relative importance of the brand in sales of a hair products brand is not the same in all distribution channels: it is important in the modern channel (supermarkets and hypermarkets), but very weak when the same product is sold directly by hairdressers, on account of the strong influence of the hairdresser's recommendation to the customer. To develop this idea further: for any given brand in any given channel, the degree to which this brand influences the customer's purchasing decision will vary depending on whether the product is a shampoo or a hair colouring product. Analyses must therefore be conducted individually at the relevant level, not collectively at the overall level. The question thus becomes: do we have the appropriate reporting data that such an analysis requires?

The brand: an identifiable asset?

We know that according to standard accounting practices, an asset can only be entered in the accounts if it can be identified and clear future economic benefits can be attributed to it. Inter-country debate currently rages on the criteria for such identifiability.

Some countries implement a difficult criterion: transferability. It is a tough condition because before an asset can be transferable, legal rights for this asset must be held; not only this, but a market must also exist. An alternative criterion has a more economic basis: it is sufficient to be able to trace specific revenue back to this asset. How is this viewed in worldwide terms?

Under current international accounting standards (IAS), an asset is deemed to be identifiable if we hold rights over it: in other words, if these rights can be protected. Logically, therefore, according to this concept, the company can exercise no legal rights over market share or a client base. From the IAS standpoint, an intangible asset can be recorded if:

- the recorder controls, holds the aforementioned legal rights;

- it is transferable (separable);

- it is the source of specific future revenue extending beyond the yearly accounting period.

In other countries such as France, market share can be activated and posted in the balance sheet.

The US position is a pragmatic one: what conditions must be met here before an intangible asset can be entered separately into the consolidated accounts once a company has been absorbed or bought out? They are two-fold: separability (it can be transferred independently of the rest of the company) and the unambiguous allocation of specific revenues.

Pragmatically, to avoid ambiguity, the US standard supplies a list of intangible assets. In the Statement of Financial Accounting Standards no 141, (FASB), this list specifies exactly what can be allocated: no reference is made to market share. Nor is know-how included, as this is an abstract concept (except in the form of computer software). However, it does include the valuation of a customer database. The US position thus concerns itself less with legal property, instead taking a more economic approach.

The new draft IAS, which will become prevalent in stock-exchange-listed companies throughout the world, is similar in design to the US model.

However, a case does exist where the brand is, and remains, unrecordable: when it is an 'internal' brand, that is, one created by the company itself and thus not bought, or one found in a company that has been bought by or merged with the company. Accounting is subject to the principle of prudence: what is a brand worth? The price paid by a party buying the company already offers an indication in the form of an upper threshold, once all other assets within the company have been deducted at their economic value. When there is a market transaction, then, the value acquires a physical form. Until that time, it is merely a virtual, potential value. In all countries, recording unreliable information in the accounts is perceived as a much greater evil than that of failing to take an economic value (the brand) into consideration.

Value depends on the evaluation goals

Incongruous though it may seem, the brand contains not one value but many: everything depends on the evaluation goals. Thus, if the goal is to assess a contribution containing an intangible asset, to be checked by an auditor, a prudent approach should be taken.

Similarly, it is a universal truth that value is in the eye of the beholder. For example, only Coca-Cola could offer US $1 billion to buy the little round Orangina bottle. With its network of bottlers in all countries worldwide, it would instantly be able to multiply sales of the product – which was based on the same business model as Coke (selling syrup to bottlers) – ten-fold. Pepsi-Cola offered less, as did Schweppes: hardly surprisingly, since their brand development plan was simply not on the same scale as Coca-Cola's.

Lastly, we are bound to get different figures when evaluating for estimation purposes than when evaluating for balance sheet recording purposes. In producing an estimate, it is permissible to include future plans, new production factories and shops that may be opened, or brand extensions into other categories. This makes the brand's future potential look even brighter. However, when it comes to recording for accounting purposes, prudence is required. It is not possible to make use of such predictions, since the projected factories, stores and extensions do not actually exist, and therefore cannot be included. Under European accounting law, no allowance can be made for that which does not exist.

However, under IAS such possibilities could be taken into account, taking their cue from the more flexible US standards.

In the Coca-Cola/Orangina case, we therefore find ourselves in an odd situation: the value of the brand appears to differ depending on which company perspective we consider the question from. In the consolidated accounts of Coca-Cola in the United States, the value recorded for the Orangina brand would have taken into consideration the expansion potential from its new distribution. In the accounts of Pernod-Ricard, the company originally holding the Orangina brand, it would have had a different value as part of a transfer operation.

Evaluating brand valuation methods

A number of methods have been proposed to define the value posted in the balance sheet when a brand is part of the assets of an acquired company, or any other instance

when this valuation is needed. They can be positioned on a two-dimensional mapping. The horizontal axis refers to time (but do we base the analysis on the past, the present or the future?). This axis discriminates between valuations based on historical costs (those that helped build the brand), valuations based on present earnings, on market price, and those which rely on a business plan: that is to say, a forecast. The vertical axis is a real/virtual dimension. Some analysts rely on hard facts (historical accounts are facts, as well as present earnings). However, some methods rely more on estimates about the present (the replacement method), or about the future (the discounted cashflow method). We now analyse these methods in turn.

Valuation by historical costs

The brand is an asset whose value comes from investments over a period of time (even though accountants do not strictly regard this as a true form of investment). The logical approach would therefore be to add together

Figure 18.3 Positioning brand valuation methods

all the costs associated with a particular period: development costs, marketing costs, advertising and communication costs, etc. These costs can be determined objectively, and will have been in past income statements.

As we can see, this approach allows us to overcome the tricky problem of separability, by isolating the direct costs associated with the brand and also by attributing to it the indirect costs such as the sales force and general expenses. Even though this method is simple and logical, it nevertheless raises the following practical difficulties, which reintroduce a certain subjectivity:

▌ Over what period should costs be accounted for? Numerous brands are very old as we have seen: Coca-Cola dates back to 1887, Danone to 1919, Lacoste to 1933, Yves Saint Laurent to 1958, Dim to 1965. Should we include costs right from their beginnings? Everyone knows of old brands that no longer exist. Companies must go back in time and ask themselves if past advertising still has an effect today.

▌ Which costs should be taken into account? Investment in advertising has a dual marketing role: one part generates extra sales, which can be measured immediately, while the other part builds brand awareness and image which facilitates future sales. The practical difficulty is in estimating year by year the weight that should be attributed to each part. Also, how far ahead are we looking when talking about future sales? On top of this we have to look at the advertising wear-out curves over a given time period. If, as has been shown in studies on the persistence of attitude changes, such effects decrease in a linear manner over, for example, five years, it may be that expenses arising over this period, including only 20 per cent of those for year $n-5$, can be posted.

▌ It is not simply a question of adding up the costs, you also have to take into account an appropriate discount rate which has to be calculated.

On top of the subjective nature of the answers to the above questions, valuation by costs causes several basic problems which are linked directly to a partial understanding of the brand:

▌ When creating a brand, a large part of the long-term investment does not involve a cash outlay, and therefore cannot be posted to the accounts. These include stringent quality controls, accumulated know-how, specific expertise, involvement of personnel, etc. All of these are essential for encouraging repurchase, for the brand's long-term reputation and for word-of-mouth. There would be no trace in the accounts of brands like Rolls-Royce because there were no advertisements for it.

▌ One of the major strategies to create a strong brand consists of choosing a competitive launch price, which may be the same as that of competitors' even though the product is upgraded. Swatch is an ideal example of this. They could have opted for a slight price differential, or a price premium, to cover the costs of innovation and of upgrading the product. They decided, however, to set an aggressive price that was equal to that of their competitors, thus maximising the brand's price/quality ratio and enhancing its attractiveness. This is one of its key success factors. Unfortunately, this non-cash investment would not appear in a system where only cash expenditures are registered.

▌ The method therefore favours brands whose value only comes from advertising and marketing and which have a significant price premium. It would not apply to brands such as Rolls-Royce or St Michael (Marks & Spencer's brand) which advertise very little. It could also be said that past expenditure is not a guarantee of present value. There are several brands that are heavily advertised but of little value and are coming to the end of their life.

▮ This method is favourable to recent brands and *a fortiori* to internal brands that are in the process of being created, as we have already seen.

Valuation by replacement costs

To overcome the difficulties arising from the historical costs approach, it might be better to place oneself in the present and to confront the problem by resorting to the classic alternative – as we cannot buy this brand, how much would it cost to recreate it? By taking its various characteristics into account (awareness, percentage of trial purchases and repurchases, absolute and relative market share, distribution network, image, leadership, quality of the legal deposition and presence in how many countries), how much would we have to spend, and over what period, in order to create an equivalent brand?

Is it possible to remake Coca-Cola, Schweppes, Mars, Buitoni or Martell? Probably not. How about Benetton, Bang & Olufsen, Saab or Epson? More than likely. For a certain number of brands, the question no longer arises since it is impossible to recreate them. The context has changed too much:

▮ They were created in an era when advertising expenditure was negligible and the brand was nurtured over time by word-of-mouth. Today, it costs so much for a 1 per cent share of voice that it has become impossible to create a leading brand through unaided awareness. In any case unaided awareness is a restricted area and to gain access a competing brand must leave. This is because of memory blocks. There is no reason why today's well-known brands should allow themselves to be thrown out.

▮ It is difficult to imitate the performance level of brand leaders. Backed by research and development and an intangible but very real know-how, they enjoy a long-lasting competitive advantage and a resulting image of stability. Any challenger is taking a risk. Unless they have access to the necessary technology, their chances of encouraging repurchasing and loyalty are virtually zero.

▮ Major retailers have now become exacting gatekeepers. They give pride of place to their own brands, only selling one or two national brands that tomorrow will be international.

▮ Finally, considering the high failure rate of new product launches, it is easy to understand the uncertainty of the return on the large amount of money that has to be invested in the long term. If you are going to pay a lot you might as well buy certainty. Hence, the clutter of takeover bids, raids, mergers and acquisitions of firms with strong brands that are already market leaders.

On the other hand, when these factors which hinder market entry are no longer present, the market is more accessible. The possibility of creating tomorrow's brand leaders from scratch ceases to be theoretical, even though uncertainty and the necessary time element may still exist. Therefore, future Benettons will probably be created. Franchising allows wider market penetration without admitting defeat at the hands of major retailers. What is more, the fashion industry is open to new ideas. In this domain, style is more important than technology. Computer services and the high-tech world in general are also open to innovation. Generally speaking, the future will see the emergence of new international brands, each positioned in its own particular niche. They will thus no longer seek global awareness but will aspire to be leaders in particular market segments.

Brand valuation by replacement costs nevertheless remains very subjective. It requires the combined opinions of experts and ambiguous procedures. On top of this it should be remembered that the aim of the valuation process is not, in itself, to arrive at a value but to get an idea of the economic value of the asset in question – in this case the brand. Cost methods focus on the inputs, whereas the economic value is based on the outputs – what the brand produces and not what it consumes. Profit is not generated through investments but through market domination and leadership.

Valuation by market price

When valuing a brand why not start with the value of similar brands on the market? This is how property or second-hand cars are valued. Each apartment or car is inspected and given a price that is above, equal to or below the average market price of similar goods.

Even though this method is very appealing, it raises two major problems when applied to brands. First, the market doesn't exist. Although such transactions are often cited in the financial pages, acquisitions and brand sales are relatively few. Brands are not bought to be sold again. In spite of this, we can get an idea of the multiples applicable to each sector of activity (from 25 to 30) thanks to the number of transactions that have taken place since 1983. Thus, such an approach could tempt some wishing to value a brand.

However, there is a major difference between the real estate market and the market for brands, which is relatively small. On the real estate market the buyer is a price-taker, that is, the price is fixed by the market. Irrespective of the use that he or she will make of the property, the price remains the same. For brands, the buyer is a price-setter, that is, he or she sets the price of the brand. Each buyer bases his/her valuation on his/her own views, on potential synergies and on his/her

future strategy. Why did Unilever pay €100 million for Boursin, the well-known brand of cheese? It can be explained by the pressing need of this group to acquire shelf space in major supermarkets in which it had previously been absent. Having at its disposal a compulsory brand, they saw a way of opening the door to other speciality products. In April 1990 Jean-Louis Sherrer was bought for three times less than the price that Mr Chevalier paid for Balmain two months earlier. For Mr Chevalier, Balmain was a means of entry – or rather re-entry – into the luxury market. Hermès, which was already present on this market, didn't need to pay this price (Melin, 1990).

In abstract terms the purchase price is not the price paid for the brand but is the interaction between brand and purchaser. To use the price paid for a similar brand as a reference, without knowing the specific reasons behind that brand's purchase, ignores the fact that an essential part of the price probably included the synergies and the specific objectives of the buyer in question. Each buyer has his/her own intentions and ideas. The value cannot be determined by proxy.

This is what distinguishes fundamentally the market for brands from that for real estate, or for example for advertising agencies. In the case of the latter, norms and standards exist that are not dependent on the buyers' intentions (50 to 70 per cent of the gross margin on top of the net assets). Despite this, valuations in the luxury market frequently take into account recent transactions and use a multiple of the sales (1.5 for Yves Saint Laurent, 2 for Lanvin and for Balmain, 2.9 for Martell, 2 for Bénédictine).

Considering the difficulties which are inherent in the cost-based methods or in the referential methods on a hypothetical market, prospective buyers tend rather to look at the expected profits from brand ownership. Since the third type of approach relies on two major philosophies, we are devoting a special section to it.

Valuation by royalties

What annual royalties could the company hope to receive if it licensed the rights to use the brand? The answer to this question would form a means of directly measuring the brand's financial contribution and would also solve the problem of separability. The figure obtained could subsequently be used to calculate the discounted cashflows over several years. The difficulty is that this is not a very common practice in most markets. They are found in the luxury and textile markets.

From a conceptual point of view, it is not certain that this method properly separates just the value of the brand (Barwise, 1989). In fact, companies often use licences to reach countries where their brand is not present. However, the royalty fee does not include solely the use of the brand. The brand owner also undertakes to supply a package of basic materials, know-how and services, which allow the licensee to maintain the brand's appropriate quality level.

Valuation by future earnings

Since the brand aspires to become an asset, it is best to begin by a reminder of what an asset is. It is an element which will generate future profits with reasonable certainty. Valuation methods have been developed on the basis of expected returns of brand ownership. Naturally, these tie in fully with the purchaser's intentions. If he/she wishes to internationalise the brand, it will be of more value to him/her than to a buyer wishing to keep it as a local brand. The value measured by expected profits cannot be separated from the characteristics of the future buyer and from his/her strategies for the brand. This explains why the stock market value compared to a predator's value of a branded company will always be structurally lower. The former valuation is related to the existing business, taking into account current facts and figures provided by the firm. The latter comes from the overvaluation created by the prospect of synergies, complementary marketing processes and the attainment of strategic market positions.

The process of valuing the expected profits of the brand can be divided into three independent stages (see Figure 18.4):

1. The first step involves separating and isolating the net income associated with the brand (and not with the company for example).

2. The second step is to estimate the future cashflows. This requires a strategic analysis of the brand in its market or markets.

3. The third step involves choosing, by using a classic financial method, a discount rate and period.

This is the classic method of valuing all investments, whether tangible or intangible. The analyst calculates the anticipated annual income attributable to the brand over a 5- or 10-year period. The discount rate used is the weighted average cost of capital, which if necessary is increased to take account of the risks arising from a weak brand (that is to reduce the weight of future revenues in the calculation of the present value). Beyond this period, the residual value is calculated by assuming that the income is constant or growing at a constant rate for infinity (Nussenbaum, 1990). The following formula is used:

$$\text{Value of the brand} = \sum_{t=1}^{N} \frac{RB_t}{(1+r)^t} + \frac{\text{Residual value}}{(1+r)^N}$$

where:

RB_t = Anticipated revenue in year t, attributable to the brand

r = Discounting rate

$$\text{Residual value after year } N = \frac{RB_n}{r} \text{ or } \frac{RB_N}{r-g}$$

where:

g = rate of revenue growth

Figure 18.4   A multi-step approach to brand valuation

This is the classic model for valuation by the discounted cashflow method, even though analysts offer numerous variations of it (Mauguère, 1990; Melin, 1990). This method was used to value Cognac Hennessy at 6.9 billion francs, based on a capitalisation of its net revenue over 25 years at a rate of 6.5 per cent (Blanc and Hoffstetter, 1990).

This method was also used to value the Candia milk brand as part of a restructuring programme. The final figure, which was around 1.8 billion francs, was the result of a business plan within which two questions were discussed:

- Knowing that milk is a commodity, what percentage of Candia's future sales will be generated by products which are heavily marketed, differentiated and have a strong identity which justifies a price premium?

- At how much do we estimate the price premium that Candia can demand over more ordinary products? In such markets, even a tiny difference may amount to huge profits.

Sceptics of this method (Murphy, 1990; Ward, 1989) object to its three sources of uncertainty: the anticipation of cashflows, the choice of period and the discount rate:

▍ By definition any forecast is uncertain. This does not apply only to brands, but to any investment evaluation – tangible or intangible – which is calculated by the above method. For brands, cashflow forecasts could be ruined if a competitor launched a superior product which was not accounted for in the calculations. This argument overlooks the fact that these forecasts were made after an in-depth analysis of the brand's strengths and weaknesses (on the basis of the criteria presented earlier). It can be assumed that these were included when the anticipated cashflows were calculated. In any case the discounting rate takes into account the anticipated risk factor.

▍ A second criticism lies in the subjective nature of the choice of a discounting rate. However, on the one hand analysts test the sensitivity of their findings against variations in this rate, and on the other hand, this rate is fixed by taking into account stable company data, such as its average cost of capital. The only subjective factors are the risk premium and the future rate of inflation. Furthermore, very often the risk is zero from the purchaser's point of view as he or she feels that success is a certainty.

▍ Finally, there are those who criticise the choice of period for calculating cashflows. Why 10 years and not 15? What is the value of forecasts made so far ahead? On the one hand, the brand may disappear after only a few years and on the other, in certain volatile sectors three years is already a long time (eg laptop computers).

This is where certain valuations come from: brand value should be based on that which is certain, ie the net income of the brand at the moment. This is the basis of the multiple method (see Table 1.3). Brand value is calculated by applying a multiple to the current profits of the brand, measured over three years (t–1, t+1). This approach does not need internal data.

Valuation by present earnings

Who can predict the future? How can one be sure that the forecasts of a business plan will be matched? In fact, one of the reasons so many internet brands have been heavily overvalued is that they made no profit whatsoever (eBay excepted). The brand valuation process relied exclusively on forecasts and business plans which were created just to attract new investors, so the founders could resell before the collapse of the illusion.

Interbrand, a major brand valuation company, has promoted a specific approach to circumvent this problem. No business, no brand. Interbrand valuations rely exclusively on three years: last year, this year and next year. After partitioning each year's revenue to pay for the invested capital which made the business possible and other direct intangible assets, one is left with a global residue, made of a weighted average of the residues of each of these three years. This residue should be then multiplied by a figure called 'the multiple', hence the name of the Interbrand proprietary method: the multiple method. Although Interbrand seems to have moved now to the most orthodox method (discounted cashflow), we analyse this former approach on which many brand valuations have been based.

In the financial valuation of companies, it is typical to examine what is known as the price/earnings ratio (P/E). This ratio links the market capitalisation of a firm to its net profits. A high ratio is a signal of high investor confidence and optimism in the growth of future profits. Even though the brand is not the company, the same reasoning can be applied:

$$\text{Firm} : \text{P}/\text{E} = \frac{\text{Market value of equity}}{\text{Known profits}}$$

$$\text{Brand} : \text{Multiple} = \frac{\text{Value to be calculated}}{\text{Net profits of brand}}$$

The only difference lies in the fact that for a brand there are no data on its market capitalisation because it doesn't exist, therefore it is this that we are trying to calculate. This notional market value of equity is the price to be paid for the brand (before the effect of overbidding). In order to calculate this, it is necessary to determine M, the multiple which is equivalent to the P/E ratio specific to the brand.

There are four stages to this method:

1. **Calculating the applicable net profit**. Interbrand used the profits for the last three years (t–2, t–1, t), thus avoiding a possibly atypical evaluation based upon a single year. These profits were discounted to take account of inflation. A weighted average of these three figures was calculated in accordance with what we consider to be the most and least important years. This weighted average after-tax net profit which is attributable to the brand forms the basis of all calculations.

2. **Assessing the brand's strength**. This method uses a set of marketing and strategic criteria to give the brand an overall mark. Interbrand uses only seven of these factors and takes a weighted sum of the individual marks for each factor in order to calculate the overall mark, as can be seen in Table 18.1 (Penrose, 1989).

3. **Estimating the multiple**. A relationship necessarily exists between the multiple

(an indicator of confidence about the future) and this score for brand strength. If this relationship was known precisely, the multiple would then be predicted by the brand strength score. For this, Interbrand developed a model known as the 'S-curve' which plots the multiple against brand strength.

The model is based on Interbrand's examination of the multiples involved in numerous brand negotiations over recent periods – in sectors close to the one being studied. The P/E of the companies with the closest comparable brands are used. Interbrand then reconstructed the company's profile and brand strength. Plotting the multiples (P/E) against the reconstructed scores results in an S-shaped curve (see Figure 18.5).

4. **Calculating brand value**. This is calculated by multiplying the applicable net brand profit by the relevant multiple.

We can illustrate this method by an actual case. In 1988 Reckitt & Colman valued its brands in this way. They valued household and hygienic goods where they were market leaders, as well as food products (condiments) where they were also a leader, and finally pharmaceutical goods where they had an average position.

The specific situation enjoyed by those brands in the first group is as follows:

Table 18.1   A method of valuing brand strength

Factor of valuation	Maximum score	Brand A	Brand B	Brand C
Leadership	25	19	19	10
Stability	15	12	9	7
Market	10	7	6	8
Internationality	25	18	5	2
Trend	10	7	5	7
Support	10	8	7	8
Protection	5	5	3	4
Brand strength	100	76	54	46

Source: Penrose/Interbrand (1990)

Figure 18.5   The Interbrand S-curve – relation between brand strength and multiple

- world leadership;

- growing markets, with few new entrants except for distributors' own-brands;

- unaided brand awareness (eg Airwick) high in the UK and in Anglo-Saxon countries but less so in France;

- customers' brand loyalty;

- strong brand image and assurance of quality;

- for each of its brands, little possibility for diversification.

Reckitt & Colman estimated that 5 per cent of profits on these brands came from sales under distributors' own-brands. Interbrand considered that the remaining 95 per cent was the brand's gross profit. The income generated by the brand can be calculated by subtracting the expected return on investment from net assets. The net revenue was weighted according to the importance of each brand and discounted for the previous three years. The following results were obtained for each category:

- household and hygienic products: £53.8 million;

- food products: £24.7 million;

- pharmaceutical goods: £17.1 million.

What multiple should be applied? For the first group, the multiple used by Reckitt & Colman in 1985 when buying Airwick was applied. A multiple of 17 was used for food products and was based on recent transactions in the sector during the last few years, for example the BSN–Nabisco takeover bid. Finally, a multiple of 20 was used for the pharmaceutical group. In fact, recent transactions in the pharmaceutical industry had been using multiples which were closer to 30. A lower multiple was chosen in this case because of Reckitt & Colman's relatively weak position in the sector. By applying these figures to the net revenue in each category, the following brand values were estimated:

- household and hygienic products: 53.8 × 20 = £1,076 million;

- food products: 24.7 × 17 = £420 million;

- pharmaceutical goods: 17.1 × 20 = £342 million.

Comparison of the cash flow and multiple method

The multiple method, which was developed in the UK, is becoming a classic. It was, in fact, used by such companies as Rank Hovis McDougall and Grand Metropolitan whose decisions to post brand values to their balance sheets caused a controversy which is still not settled. It is also the method which communicates the most through books, articles and seminars. The simplicity of the method used is such that it is uncharacteristic of the stringent world of financial analysis. All this said, is it valid?

First, the multiple method is not all that different from the classic method of discounted cashflow. It is a particular example of it.

When a constant and infinite annual cashflow is expected, the present value of the brand is defined thus:

$$\text{Brand value} = \frac{RB}{(1+r)} + \frac{RB}{(1+r)^2} + \frac{RB}{(1+r)^3} + \dots + \frac{RB}{(1+r)^\infty} = \frac{RB}{r}$$

As we can see, the multiple is none other than the inverse of the cost of capital adjusted for risk $(1/r)$. If a constant growth rate (g) of annual income is expected, the multiple is:

$$B = \frac{1}{r-g}$$

Equations aside, the point to remember is that we cannot reproach the method of discounted cashflows for making certain hypotheses, since the multiple approach is itself a particular hypothesis, which is equally as questionable but not explicit. It draws its apparent validity from the fact that all its calculations are based upon:

▊ net known profits attributable to the brand over the previous three years;

▊ marketing data and the subjective opinions of managers regarding brand strength;

▊ multiples based on recent transactions by similar companies;

▊ an S-curve, using information from a database to plot these multiples (or P/E ratios) against brand strength scores.

However, face validity (or appearance) does not mean validity *per se*. In its present form, Interbrand's method poses various problems:

1. Market multiples, which were used as parameters for the S-curve, are not valid indicators of the strength of the brands even though they were the mainstay of these transactions. In fact the final transaction price includes both the estimated value of the brand and a certain amount which is due to overbidding. For example, in the fight between Jacob Suchard and Nestlé, the initial bid was 630 pence and the final bid was, 1,075 pence! Market prices include the effect of this overbidding and thus overvalue the brand. It is therefore rather curious that we are trying to link market multiples to a value for brand strength as this value ignores the effect of overbidding. For this reason a certain doubt arises about the applicability of this method to value and post to the balance sheet unacquired, internally created brands. The value attributed to the asset will be greater than the value of the brand as it will include an unspecified amount which is a result of overbidding! The fact that companies may nevertheless have used this method to represent their brands as assets in no way validates this approach.

2. Even in a market where there is no overbidding, the stated multiple measures the value of the brand from the point of view of the potential buyer. It expresses his vision, his strategies and any synergies that he may expect. The fact that in 1985 BSN did not buy Buitoni despite it being reasonably priced does not mean that Buitoni was worth less but means that it was worth less in the eyes of BSN. In 1988 Nestlé valued it at several billion Swiss

francs. It again seems strange to try to relate market multiples, which are closely linked to the buyer, to the scores for brand strength, which are calculated by an outsider and do not include the synergistic benefits. This poses a problem when internally created brands are posted to the balance sheet. They are valued in the context of a 'going concern' according to their current benefit to the companies who own them. On the other hand, multiples supplied by the market are calculated with the idea of using them for a totally different reason.

3. For the moment, no illustrations of the S-curve showing the variance around the curve have been published. This variance is a measure of the quality of the empirical relationship between the two variables. As it is, the curve would have us believe that there is zero variance, which is impossible. A single brand strength score probably corresponds to several multiples or at least to a range of values (within which the S-curve is found). Such uncertainty causes problems as in reality the financial value of a brand is very sensitive to even a slight change in the multiple. Going back to the Reckitt & Colman's household and hygiene brands, we see that a one point variation in the multiple results in either a £53.8 million increase or decrease in the value of the brand. This is a far cry from the principles of prudence, reliability and rational certainty which govern accounting practice and information.

4. The very validity of the S-curve is questionable. Interbrand uses the following argument: a new brand grows slowly during its early stages. Then, once it moves from being a national brand to being an international one, its growth is exponential. Finally, as it moves from the international to the worldwide arena, its growth slows once more. For example, the

difference between Buitoni's purchase and resale price signalled the transition of a national brand to a European wide one.

Experience shows that brands are susceptible to large threshold effects. Their strength with customers and retailers is developed in stages. Thus, today, a moderately known brand may be worth virtually the same as a little known one. However, beyond a certain threshold, it grows in value. Research on brand awareness has shown that, in markets with intensive communication, it is only once a brand has reached a certain level of aided awareness that its unaided awareness will start to increase. This is due to a memory block. Likewise, major retailers are replacing middle-of-the-range brands with their own products. These brands rely more on supply than on demand and they would cease to be sold if the retailers replaced them with their own brands. Thus their future is very unstable. This would lead us to believe that the relationship between brand strength and the multiple – provided that both are assessed by the same potential buyer – is better illustrated by a stepped graph (See Figure 18.6).

In conclusion, the widespread use of the multiple method is not proof of validity, as we have just seen, but testifies to its simplicity and handiness for non-specialists, and therefore its internal educational value. A small variation in the chosen multiple leads to important differences in the value of the brand. The present method of choosing the multiple is unsatisfactory from the point of view of reference multiples and of the brand strength scores. What can we make of a total score which is obtained after subjective weightings of factors which are sometimes redundant or in any case correlated? This wish for simplicity is to the detriment of the method's validity. Despite its claim to be accurate, the multiple method in its present form is just as subjective as that of discounted

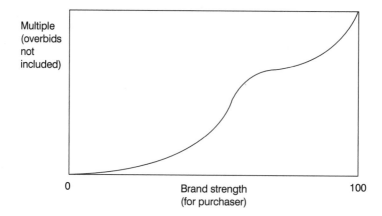

Figure 18.6   Stepped graph showing relationship between brand strength and multiple

cashflows. To use a hundred or so criteria instead of seven would change nothing. By doing this, we introduce a certain amount of redundancy between the criteria, which results in more weight being given to some factors. As long as the method is subjective, it should remain transparent. The multi-criteria method gains nothing from being summarised in a single score since there are many implicit hypotheses in the weightings. The brand profile should be used instead to make a realistic, valid business plan, materialising in discounted cashflows.

Last but not least, the multiple method is too sensitive to small variations of the multiple itself. Multiplying 800 million by seven or eight makes a lot of a difference. Such sensitivity is at odds with the principle of prudence. Brand valuation is not an exact science. It is not acceptable to obtain outputs that can vary by millions of pounds just by changing the multiple by 1 unit. This is probably why recently Interbrand moved unobtrusively towards the classic financial methodology, the discounted cashflow approach (Table 18.2).

Table 18.2   Another estimate of the financial value of brands (2007)

Rank	Brand	Value (US$ billion)
1	Coca-Cola	65,324
2	Microsoft	58,709
3	IBM	57,091
4	GE	51,569
5	Nokia	33,696
6	Toyota	32,070
7	Intel	30,954
8	McDonald's	29,398
9	Disney	29,210
10	Mercedes-Benz	23,568
11	Citi	23,443
12	Hewlett-Packard	22,197
13	BMW	21,612
14	Marlboro	21,283
15	American Express	20,827
16	Gillette	20,415
17	Louis Vuitton	20,321
18	Cisco	19,099
19	Honda	17,998
20	Google	17,837

Source: BusinessWeek/Interbrand, 6 August 2007

Brand valuation in practice

How do we evaluate the brand in practice using the discounted cashflow method? During a company acquisition, as soon as the target company has been taken over by its buyer, it becomes necessary to record its assets *at their true value* in the consolidated accounts of the buyer company or group. These assets include tangible and intangible assets; the brand falls into the latter category.

Given that the purchase price for the company is generally well above its nett accounting value, the difference (or gap) is known as the first consolidation difference, or goodwill in the wider sense of the term. It must be allocated to its various components, the company assets, evaluated at their 'fair value'. The non-allocated residual balance will be referred to as goodwill in the strict sense. How then do we determine the value of each asset and, in particular, the value of a brand? This takes the form of a nine-stage procedure:

1. The first key stage is to segment the brand into strategic units. In order to be able to isolate the share of added value imputable to the brand, we need to work from the bottom up, starting with the factors that produce the sales and profits: the 'cash-generating units' and 'reporting units'. We must identify the excess profit of each of these strategic units, which then allows us to establish what share of this excess profit is imputable to the brand, remembering that this share can vary from one unit to another. Furthermore, the individual profitability structures and growth potential for each unit may be very different.

    Thus, for a hygiene and beauty brand, the relevant unit would operate at product level for each distribution channel. Each product has its own individual profitability structure; and furthermore, the relative weight of the brand in the consumer's decision-making process varies from product to product. Lastly, sales and growth potential also vary from product to product and from channel to channel.

2. The second stage will be to build the forecasted profit accounts using the business plan. Like any asset, the brand has no value apart from the potential for future profit derived from its use. What will this use be? What sales do we expect? At what price? With what sales and marketing expenditure?

    This second stage aims to define the overall share imputable to intangible assets in the financial results forecasted for each of these units, and is known as the EVA (economic value added). This is obtained by taking the product or business's trading profit and subtracting company tax (which gives nett EBIT), then allowing for permanent invested capital and working capital requirement (which gives the EVA). Invested capital is entered at a 'normal' rate (t), the average cost of the capital. This produces the following sequence of residual balances:

    EBIT – Taxes = t (Tangible Assets + WCR) + t' (Intangible Assets)

    Nett EBIT – t (Tangible Assets +WCR) = EVA = t' (Intangible Assets)

    Remember that these calculations are based on a business plan: they are forecasts for future profits under a specific growth hypothesis.

3. The third stage is where we deduct from this EVA the contributions of other intangible assets once they become directly evaluable: for example, assigning a value to patents based on the usual rates applied in this area, or the virtual allowance made for a portfolio of customers or subscribers, a function of market practices. We should add that if the brand operated exclusively

through licences (as is the case with certain luxury brands), its contribution could then be evaluated directly. This deduction, made in order to account for other intangible assets required for business, reminds us that the brand is indeed a conditional asset.

4. So is this residual balance the share of the profit attributable to the brand? Not necessarily: this is where the allocations to the brand and to other potential candidates stage comes in. Here, we should ask ourselves what weight the brand carries in the customer's purchasing decision for each analysis unit (that is, each product in its distribution channel). This is a question for an expert jury to answer. Other methods exist. The customers themselves could be interviewed. A typical study consists first of identifying all the product choice criteria, then measuring the influence each one has in the customer's decision, and lastly evaluating the brand's share in the perception associated with each criterion. For example, we know that the brand has a strong influence on the perception of taste: in blind testings, consumers preferred Pepsi to Coca-Cola, but as soon as the brand is identified, they claim to have preferred the glass of Coca-Cola. Conversely, recognition of the brand has no influence on the perception of its presence in stores. By adding together the respective influence of each of these criteria and balancing these against the role played by the brand in evaluating each of them, we obtain an overall percentage which measures the brand's total influence in the purchase. A typical service station brand will score a 30 per cent rating, whereas a soft drink brand will be of the order of 70 per cent.

5. Once armed with this percentage, we can then calculate year by year, in the business plan, the share of excess profit attributable to the brand for each cash-generating unit or reporting unit.

6. Given that the ultimate goal is to produce a discounted sum of these revenues specifically attributable to the brand, we must first fix on the discount rate to be used. It will depend on our understanding of risks: in other words, are the brand's levers of added value durable in the long term? How is the market growing? Is it open to competition? Is it becoming commoditised? Is it becoming sensitive to price, and thus to distributor's brands? What is its state of innovation? What is its R&D potential, and so on?

7. The purpose of this seventh stage is to conduct a strategic audit of the brand and a 'risks and opportunities' audit, by examining (see Table 18.3):

   – the risks associated with the market;
   – the risks associated with the brand and the long-term status of its differentiating features;
   – the risks associated with the product itself;
   – the risks associated with the company, its staff and its finances for developing the brand;
   – the opportunities for geographical expansion;
   – the opportunities for brand extension into other product categories.

   This strategic analysis produces a risk evaluation, and thus a discounting rate for future use.

8. This stage is that of the discounted sum of profits attributable to the brand, based on the discount rate identified above, after the strategic audit of the brand. It produces the brand's value, which will in theory be taken as a deduction from goodwill and recorded on the balance sheet as such. It is a good idea at this stage to check whether the value obtained is especially sensitive to the discount rate used.

9. Finally, an evaluation should not be confined to one single method. The goal

Table 18.3   Assessing brand strength: strategic diagnosis

Risks associated with the future market	Growth of the market
	Profitability of the market
	Importance of competitor and retailer brands
	Expected technological innovations
	Changes in customer expectations
	Strength of barriers to entry
Risks associated with the sources of brand value	Quality of past advertising support
	Image and reputation
	Quality of trademarks and their registration
	Customer loyalty
	Distributor attitudes and loyalty
	Attitudes of opinion leaders
	Relative position in the market
Risks associated with the product	Life of patents
	Existence of 'me-too' brands and product copiability
	R&D perspectives
Risks associated with the business	Financial support
	Strategic coherence
Potential	Potential for geographical extension
	Licensing potential
	Potential for extension into other product categories

of reliable accounts and fair value evaluation demands cross-checking against other evaluation sources. It is true that only the discounted cashflow method is economically valid and accepted by official accounting and auditing bodies. But it is also true that other methods exist; these may not be accepted to the same degree, but they can be used for cross-checking results. Fair value has to be obtained through a narrowing-down process; it cannot be calculated directly.

For this reason, it is common to cross-check results obtained from the discounted sum of revenues imputable to the brand with an evaluation based on the royalties method. To do this, we calculate which royalty rate would, when applied to forecasted turnover, give the same overall current royalty value after discounting. It is reassuring if this rate matches standard figures for the sector. For example, in the haircare products

sector, l'Oréal would pay Jacques Dessange 3 per cent of its turnover for products sold under its licence name.

If the gap between the results produced by these two approaches is too wide, a complete rethink is necessary in order to identify the sources of the discrepancy and, if appropriate, to correct them. For example, in an evaluation, the value of non-directly-calculated intangibles works out at a royalty rate of nearly 30 per cent. This is impossible. After analysis, it is decided to impute one-third of the value to the brand and two-thirds to the market share (an asset that can be recorded on the balance sheet in some countries).

An alternative version of the above procedure exists. It consists of taking (during Stage 4) the discounted sum of the combined value of all intangible assets; that is to say, the EVA taken as a whole – after having used the strategic audit matrix to establish the discount rate to be used, of course. This overall intangible asset value is thus distributed between each of them afterwards. As we can see, this variation assumes that the basis for distribution remains more or less the same regardless of which cash-generating units and products are involved.

The evaluation of complex cases

The above method works well for most brands, and is the standard approach. However, there are cases where, in order to evaluate certain brands – or brands in unusual market situations – we have to use one of the other methods examined above.

The case of loss-making companies

The above procedure is based on the theory that the brand is a conditional asset, and hence its value is obtained after the deduction of an allowance for the capital invested in production. This poses the problem of how to value brands owned by loss-making companies.

According to the above approach – which assumes a profitable balance – if there are no profits then the brand has no economic value in its current sphere of activity. It acquires value only if a new business plan, with very different cost structures, can demonstrate not only that the company can generate a profit, but also that there will be excess profits even after an allowance has been made for the tangible and intangible assets required for the production and distribution of the product or service.

Financial valuation thus dispels any mirages surrounding the brand: regardless of its reputation and image, a brand acquires value only if it is backed by a profit-making business plan. The term 'mirage' is an apposite one, as many buyers allow themselves to be seduced by brand awareness and image statistics. The economic approach reminds us

that reputation and image are worth nothing unless they produce profit – with the help of other assets, which have to be factored in.

The case of abandoned and subsequently resold brands

Companies regularly kill off brands; in order for mega-brands to be created, business operations have to be contracted to just a handful of brands, and many must thus be disposed of. For example, Nestlé abandoned Chambourcy, and PSA abandoned Talbot. Nevertheless, brands can be sold on after several years of inactivity. How can we use the multi-stage approach shown above if there has been no economic activity, and therefore no profit or loss figures? How, for example, can we estimate the value of a brand which has lain dormant for years, such as Talbot, Simca, Studebaker or Plymouth? According to the successive residuals approach, we should assess it as part of the new business plan incorporating this revitalised brand; or in any event, this is what the buyer should do before buying.

Another evaluation method consists of measuring the additional price and margin that the use of the hitherto defunct brand would enable its new user to command.

We have to consider this in terms of the differential margin: although the brand might make it possible to charge a higher public price at the retail level, the retailer might well keep the majority of this increase and hand over only a modest proportion to the end-purchaser. In fact, this is often what actually happens: when the brand is weak, and returns to the marketplace after a long absence, retailers take advantage of the fact to increase the size of their cut.

It is in the interests of the seller to use a different valuation method. A good candidate is the replacement cost method (the amount that has to be spent now to rebuild the brand and its residual reputation, along with all of its copyright registrations worldwide, for example). As a last resort, there is always sale by auction.

How can weak brands be evaluated?

Some brands remain brands only in the legal sense: they have become mere names, and no longer influence buyers. How are these to be evaluated? This is a common scenario. Given that money was paid for these brands, the replacement cost method is advisable. For example, how much would need to be spent today to:

▌ create a brand in this sector: name research, name tests and so on;

▌ trademark it in all relevant countries;

▌ devise a graphic theme for a new logo and so on?

How can young brands be evaluated?

This case is similar to the previous one. Once a young brand has proven that it can be profitable (for example, in the fashion market), the commodity being sold is in fact the time and money saved in establishing the legal and image foundations of the brand (its name and visual identity). Going beyond this means indulging in the same sort of risks taken by all investors in the dot.com brands, often to their cost. Unlike our fashion example, these brands had provided no proof that they could one day make money. Without a business, and in any case without profits, they could not be evaluated in any reliable way. This was the cause of the internet boom: five-year business plans produced estimated revenues which, when multiplied by a factor of between three and seven, resulted in exorbitant valuations.

How can parent brands be evaluated?

Today, brand theory dictates a two-level architecture with a parent brand and daughter brands. For example, Garnier is a parent brand, while Fructis, Ambre Solaire, Feria and Graphic are daughter brands. So how can we calculate the value of parent brands such as Garnier and l'Oréal Paris?

Remember that the first essential stage in the process is segmentation into strategic units: cash reporting units.

It is this requirement that the analysis be conducted at the level of reporting units and cash generating units that provides an explanation of how to evaluate parent brands that contain several daughter brands. Typical examples are Chanel and Dior. For example, there is no such thing as a Chanel perfume; rather, there are products with brands such as Chanel No 5, and Chanel No 18. These are daughter brands. The same is true with Dior Parfum: the reason it has created a Fahrenheit unit, producing profit and loss accounts, is that value is being created at this point. By adding up our evaluations of individual daughter brands, we arrive at an overall cumulative value for them. The value of Dior itself, separated from its daughter brands, is thus a residual one.

What about the brand values published annually in the press?

Given the rigour and hard work required in an evaluation of intangible assets conducted by the company itself, which has full access to all relevant information, what should we make of the annual 'hit parade' charts which appear in the economics press, giving new values for the top worldwide brands (see Tables 1.3 and 18.2)? Why such big differences between valuations?

The Interbrand research company, which is overwhelmingly the main producer of such data, has used two methods over time. Historically, it has attempted to derive values for brand EVA from public information in the annual reports of stock-exchange-listed companies and a variety of other public sources. Not being able to work with a business plan, given the confidentiality of company plans, Interbrand instead analysed data from the last two years. So how does it make the leap from EVA to brand value? It used an estimation of the share of EVA attributable to the brand, multiplied by a figure (the 'multiple'), itself derived from a statistical model based on the analysis of the price/earnings ratio (p/e) for stock-exchange-listed companies such as Gillette. The price/earnings ratio is actually a multiple itself. It compares the stock value with the profits associated with that stock: this will indicate, say, that a stock is worth 10 times its dividend price.

Interbrand configured its statistical model using stock-exchange-listed companies. Knowing the multiple (p/e) for each company, it performed a strategic analysis of its brands, following a method similar to the one we have described for our strategic audit of the brand. The end result of Interbrand's strategic evaluation of the brand is an overall score for the brand, measuring the strength of the brand (the 'brand strength index'). This is the sum of the partial scores obtained from each of the individual audit criteria (see Table 18.1). The criteria are leadership, stability and so on. It is then easy to identify the statistical relationship between the recalculated strength of the brands and the virtual multiple approximated by the price/earnings ratio (p/e) on the stock exchange. This statistical relationship has never been published, but has been represented as shown in Figure 18.5.

Having produced an external estimate of the EVA for each brand, it was then easy for Interbrand to calculate the brand strength index which, when factored into the statistical model, identifies the virtual multiple. All that remained at this point was to measure this virtual multiple as the share of estimated EVA allocated to the brand.

Several remarks can be made about this external procedure, which is used to produce the published 'league tables' of global brand value.

The tables are based on this logic, except that they are not in possession of all of the relevant information (as opposed to, say, an auditor appointed by the company to value its brands). They are thus obliged to obtain an external estimation based on the accounts published by stock-exchange-listed companies, and the figures are subject to a wide margin of error. Furthermore, these league tables cannot measure the value of brands belonging to family-run companies such as Mars, Levi's and Lacoste, which do not release public figures. Nor can they include brands belonging to companies producing consolidated accounts that are not broken down by brand. Lastly, they exclude cases in which sales may be attributable to factors other than pure demand. Consider air transport, for example, where the policy of alliances means that it is possible to end up flying with Delta Airlines after having bought an Air France ticket. Also, a significant part of demand is influenced by exit barriers such as frequent flyer cards: this is not pure demand driven by customer preference.

Other critical remarks may be made about this approach, as we have already seen, including sensitivity to variations in the multiple, and the validity of the graph.

Recently, Interbrand has changed its method of producing its 'global brand value' league tables, moving towards a more conventional financial and economic approach. Although its methodology has not been explicitly published, reference has been made to 'net present value of future brand earnings', which would be more in line with our recommended nine-step process. However, questions must be asked as to the validity of estimating these future brand earnings, without internal access to the company in question, by 'experts' with no knowledge of the actual business plan or the real financial data. Yet it is on such fragile estimates that the annual brand table published by *Business Week* – and faithfully reproduced by the world's economic press – is based. The other source of brand valuation, Brandz, still relies on multiples.

Bibliography

Aaker, D (1990) Brand extensions: the good, the bad and the ugly, *Sloan Management Review*, Summer, pp 47–56

Aaker, D (1991) *Managing Brand Equity*, Free Press, New York

Aaker, D (1995) *Building Strong Brands*, Free Press, New York

Aaker, D (1996) *Building Strong Brands*, Free Press, New York

Aaker, D and Biel, A (1993) *Brand Equity and Advertising*, Lawrence Erlbaum, Hillsdale, New Jersey

Aaker, D and Joachimstahler E (2000) *Brand Leadership*, Free Press, New York

Aaker, D and Keller, K L (1990) Consumer evaluations of brand extensions, *Journal of Marketing*, Jan, **54** (1), pp 27–41

Aaker, J (1995) Conceptualizing and measuring brand personality, Working Paper no 255, Anderson Graduate School of Management, UCLA

Aaker, J (1997) Dimensions of brand personality, *Journal of Marketing Research*, **24**, Aug, pp 347–56

Abric, J-C (1994) Pratiques sociales et représentations, Presses Universitaires de France, Paris

Advertising Research Foundation (1995) *Exploring Brand Equity*, Advertising Research Foundation, New York

Agefi (1990) Le goodwill, objet de controversé en Europe, *Agefi*, 1 Feb

AhluWalia, R (2000) Examination of psychological processes underlying resistance to persuasion, *Journal of Consumer Research*, **27** (2), Sep, pp 217–32

Ahonen, T T and Moore, A (2005) *Communities Dominate Brands*, Future Text, London

Ailawadi, K and Harlam, B (2004) The determinants of retail margins: the role of store brand share, *Journal of Marketing*, **68** (1), Jan, pp 147–65

Ailawadi, K, Lehmann, D and Neslin, S (2003) Revenue premium as an outcome measure of brand equity, *Journal of Marketing*, **67** (4), Oct, pp 1–17

Alba, J W and Chattopadhyay, A (1986) Salience effects in brand recall, *Journal of Marketing Research*, **23**, p 369

Alden, D, Steenkamp, and Batra, R (1999) Brand positioning through advertising in a global consumer culture, *Journal of Marketing*, 63

Alden, D, Steenkamp, J-B and Smith, R E (1999) Brand positioning in Asia, North America and Europe, *Journal of Marketing*, **63** (1), pp 75–87

Ambler, T and Styles, C (1996) Brand development versus new product development, *Marketing Intelligence and Planning*, **14** (7), pp 10–19

Arnault, B (2000) *La Passion Creative*, Plon: Pocket, Paris

Arnold, T (1989) Accounting for the value of brands, *Accountant's Magazine*, Feb, p 12

Asch, S (1946) Forming impressions of personality, *Journal of Abnormal and Social Psychology*, **41**, pp 25–90

Azoulay, A and Kapferer, J-N (2003) Do brand personality scales really measure brand personality?, *Journal of Brand Management*, **11** (2), Nov, pp 143–55

Baillot, J (1990) La marque et l'automobile, *Humanisme et Entreprise*, **181**, June, pp 5–8

Balachander, S and Ghose, S (2003) Reciprocal spillover effects: a strategic benefit of brand extensions, *Journal of Marketing*, **67** (1), Jan, pp 4–14

Baldinger, A (1992) What CEOs are saying about brand equity, *Journal of Advertising Research*, Jul/Aug, **32** (4), pp 6–12

Barwise, P (1989) *Accounting for Brands*, London Business School

Barwise, P (1993) Brand equity: snark or boojum, *International Journal of Research in Marketing*, **10** (2), pp 93–104

Batra, R (2002) How brand reputation affects the relationship of advertising and brand equity outcomes, *Journal of Advertising Research*

Bedbury, S (2002) *A New Brand World*, Viking, New York

Bell, D, Lal, R and Salmon, W (2003) Globalization of retailing, Globalization of Markets Colloquium, Harvard Business School, May

Berard, C (1990) La marque: élément du patrimoine de l'entreprise, *Revue de l'ENA*, 202, May, pp 24–25

Berry, N C (1988) Revitalizing brands, *Journal of Consumer Marketing*, **5** (Summer), pp 15–20

Birkigt, K and Stadler, M M (1980) *Corporate Identity: Grundlagen, Funktionen, Fallbeispiele*, Verlag Moderne Industrie, Munich

Birol, J and Kapferer, J-N (1991) Les campagnes collectives, Internal document, Agence Sicquier-Courcelles/HEC

Blackett, T (1985) The role of brand valuation in marketing strategy, *Marketing and Research Today*, Nov, pp 245–47

Blackston, M (1992) Building brand equity by managing the brand's relationships, *Journal of Advertising Research*, May/Jun, **32** (3), pp 79–83

Blanc, C and Hoffstetter, P (1990) L'évaluation des marques, HEC Research paper, under the direction of J-N Kapferer, June, Jouy-en-Josas

Blattberg, R (2001) *Customer Equity*, Harvard Business School Press, Cambridge, Mass

Boddewyn, J, Soehl, R and Picard, J (1986) Standardization in international marketing: is Ted Levitt in fact right?, *Business Horizons*, pp 69–75

Bon, J, Michon, C and Ollivier, A (1981) Etude empirique de la demographie des marques: le rôle de la publicité, Fondation Jours de France pour la recherche en publicité, Paris

Bontemps, A and Lehu, J-M (2002) *Lifting de marque*, Editions d'Organisation, Paris

Bottomley, P P and Holden, S (2001) Do we really know how consumers evaluate brand extensions?, *Journal of Marketing Research*, **38**, Nov, pp 494–501

Botton, M and Cegarra, J J (1990) *Le nom de marque*, McGraw-Hill, Paris

Boush, D (1993) Brands as categories, in *Brand Equity and Advertising*, ed D Aaker and A Biel, Lawrence Erlbaum, Hillsdale, NJ, pp 299–312

Brandenburger, A and Nalebuff, B (1996) *Coopetition*, Doubleday, New York

Broadbent, S (1983) *Advertising Works 2*, Holt, Rinehart and Winston, London

Brodbeck, D and Mongibeaux, J F (1990) *Chic et Toc: le vrai livre des contrefaçons*, Balland, Paris

Broniarczyk, S and Alba, J (1994) The importance of the brand in brand extension, *Journal of Marketing Research*, **31**, May, pp 214–28

Brown, S, Kozinets, R and Sherry, J F (2003) Teaching old brands new tricks, *Journal of Marketing*, **67** (3), Jul, pp 19–33

Brown, T and Dacin, P (1997) The company and the product: corporate associations and consumer product responses, *Journal of Marketing*, **61** (1), Jan, pp 68–84

Buchan, E and Brown, A (1989) Mergers and acquisitions, in *Brand Valuation*, ed J Murphy, Hutchinson Business Books, London, pp 81–94

Buchanan, W, Simmons, R and Bickart, S (1999) Brand equity dilution: retailer display and context brand effects, *Journal of Marketing Research*, Aug, **36**, pp 345–55

Buck, S (1997) The continuing grocery revolution, *Journal of Brand Management*, **4** (4), pp 227–38

Burgaud, D and Mourier, P (1989) Europe: développement d'une marque, *MOCI*, **889**, pp 125–28

Buzzell, R D (1968) Can you standardize multinational marketing?, *Harvard Business Review*, Nov–Dec

Buzzell, R D and Gale, B T (1987) *The PIMS Principles*, Free Press, New York

Buzzell, R D, Gale, B T and Sultan, R G (1975) Market share – a key to profitability, *Harvard Business Review*, Jan–Feb, pp 97–106

Buzzell, R D and Quelch, J A (1988) *Multinational Marketing Management*, Addison Wesley, New York

Buzzell, R D and Quelch, J A (1990) *The Marketing Challenge of 1992*, Addison Wesley, New York

Cabat, O (1989) Archéologie de la marque moderne, in *La marque*, ed J-N Kapferer and J C Thoenig, McGraw-Hill, Paris

Carpenter, G and Nakamoto, K (1990) Competitive strategies for late entry into market with a dominant brand, *Management Science*, **36** (10), pp 1268–78

Carratu, V (1987) Commercial counterfeiting, in *Branding: A key marketing tool*, ed J Murphy, McGraw-Hill, London

Carroll, J M (1985) *What's in a Name?* Freeman, New York

Cauzard, D, Perret, J and Ronin, Y (1989) *Image de marque et marque d'image*, Ramsay, Paris

Chadha, R and Husband, P (2006) *The Cult of the Luxury Brand*, Nicholas Brealey, London

Chan, KW and Mauborne, R (2000) Value innovation, *Harvard Business Review*

Channon, C (1987) *Advertising Works 4*, Cassell, London

Chanterac, V (1989) La marque a travers le droit, in *La marque*, ed J-N Kapferer and J C Thoenig, McGraw-Hill, Paris

Charbonnier, C and Lombard, E (1998) Can multi-product brands support various personalities? Esomar Annual Conference Proceedings, Vienna

Chateau, J (1972) *Les sources de l'imaginaire*, Editions Universitaires, Paris

Chaudhuri, A (2002) How brand reputation affects the advertising brand equity link, *Journal of Advertising Research*, May-June

Chevalier, M (2003) *Pro Logo*, Editions d'Organisation, Paris

Chinardet, C (1994) *Trade-Marketing*, Editions d'Organisation, Paris

Chip, H, Bell, C and Sternberg, E (2001) Emotional selection in memes: the case of urban legends, *Journal of Personality and Social Psychology*, **81**, Dec, pp 1028–41

Christensen, C (1997) *The Innovator's Dilemma*, Harvard Business School Press, Cambridge, MA

Clarke, D G (1976) Econometric measurement of the duration of advertising effect on sales, *Journal of Marketing Research*, **13**, Nov, pp 345–50

Claycamp, H and Liddy, L (1969) Prediction of new product performance, *Journal of Marketing Research*, **6** (3), Nov, pp 414–20

Cohen, J M and Serog, P (2006) *Savoir Manger: Le guide des aliments* (*Knowing how to eat: a guide to food*), Flammarion, Paris

Cohen, M, Eliashberg, J and Ho, T (1997) An anatomy of a decision support system for developing and launching line extensions, *Journal of Marketing Research*, **34** (1), Feb, pp 117–29

Collins, J and Porras, J (1994) *Built to Last,* Harper Business, London

Conseil National de la Comptabilité (1989) La formation du capital commercial dans l'entreprise, 27.A.89.16, Sep

Cooper, M (1989a) The basis of brand evaluation, *Accountancy*, Mar, p 32

Cooper, M (1989b) Brand valuation in the balance, *Accountancy*, Jul, p 28

Corstjens, J and Corstjens, M (1995) *Store Wars: The battle for mindspace and shelfspace*, Wiley, London

Corstjens, M (1999) *Store Wars*, Wiley, Chichester

Corstjens M and Lal, R (2000) Building store loyalty through store brands, *Journal of Marketing Research*, **37** (3)

Coumau, J B, Gagne, J-F and Josserand, E (2005) *Manager par la marque (Brand management)*, Editions d'Organisation, Paris

Crimmins, J (1992) Better measurement and management of brand value, *Journal of Advertising Research*, Jul/Aug, **32** (4), pp 11–19

Cross, R and Smith, J (1994) *Customer Bonding*, NTC Business Books

Crozier, M (1989) *L'Entreprise à l'Ecoute: apprendre le management post-industriel*, InterEditions, Paris

Dacin, P and Smith, D (1994) The effect of brand portfolio characteristics on consumer evaluations of brand extensions, *Journal of Marketing Research*, **31**, May, pp 229–42

Danziger, P (2004) *Why People Buy Things They Do Not Need*, Kaplan, New York

Darby, M and Kami, E (1973) Free competition and the optimal amount of fraud, *Journal of Law and Economics*, **16** (1), pp 67–88

Davidson, J H (1987) *Offensive Marketing*, Gower Press, London

Davis, S (2000) *Brand Asset Management*, Jossey-Bass, San Francisco, CA

Dawar, N (2002) How brand reputation affects the relationship of advertising and brand equity outcomes, *Journal of Advertising Research*

Dawar, N and Anderson, P (1992) Determining the order and direction of multiple brand extensions, Working Paper no 92/36/MKT, INSEAD

De Chernatony, L (1996) Integrated brand building using brand taxonomies, *Marketing Intelligence and Planning*, **14** (7), pp 40–45

De Chernatony, L and McDonald, M (1994) *Creating Powerful Brands*, Butterworth-Heinemann, Oxford

Defever, P (1989) L'utilisation de la communication électronique sur les lieux de vente, *Revue française du marketing*, **123** (3), pp 5–15

Degon, R (l994) La marque et le prix, *Journée IREP La Marque*, Sep, pp 28–38

DeJean, J (2006) *The Essence of Style*, Free Press, New York

Dhalla, N K (1978) Assessing the long term value of advertising, *Business Review*, **56**, Jan–Feb, pp 87–95

Diefenbach, J (1987) The corporate identity as the brand, in *Branding: A key marketing tool*, ed J Murphy, McGraw-Hill, London

Donaton, S (2004) *Madison and Vine*, Crain Communication, Chicago

Dru, J-M (1996) *Disruption*, Wiley, New York

Dru, J-M (2002) *Beyond Disruption*, Wiley, New York

Dubois, B and Paternault, C (1995) Understanding the world of international luxury brands, *Journal of Advertising Research*, **35** (4), Jul–Aug, pp 69–76

Durand, G (1964) *L'imagination symbolique*, PUP, Paris

Durand, G (1969) *Les Structures Anthropologiques de l'Imaginaire*, Bordas, Paris

Duvillier, J P (1987) L'absence d'enregistrement à 1'actif du fonds de commerce, *Revue française de comptabilité*, October, **183**, p 36

Dyson, P, Farr, A and Hollis, N (1996) Understanding, measuring and using brand equity, *Journal of Advertising Research*, **36** (6), Nov–Dec, pp 9–21

East, R and Hammund, K (1996) The erosion of repeat-purchase loyalty, *Marketing Letters*, **7** (2), pp l63–71

Edwards, H and Day, D (2005) *Creating Passion Brands*, Kogan Page, London

Ehrenberg, A (1972) *Repeat Buying*, Edward Arnold, London

Ehrenberg, A, Barnard, N, Kennedy, R and Bloom, H (2002) Brand advertising as creative publicity, *Journal of Advertising Research*, **42** (4), Jul/Aug, pp 7–18

Eiglier, P and Langeard, E (1990) *Servuction*, Editions d'Organisation

Eliade, M (1952) *Images et Symboles,* Gallimard, Paris

Erdem, T, Zhao, Y and Valenzuela, A (2004) Performance of store brands: a cross country analysis of consumer store brand preferences, perceptions and risk, *Journal of Marketing Research*, **41**, pp 86–100

Etchegoyen, A (2004) *La Force de la Fidelité (Power and fidelity)*, Anne Carriere, Paris

Farquhar, P H (1989) Managing brand equity, *Marketing Research*, Sep, **1** (3), pp 24–33

Farquhar, P H (1994) Strategic challenges for branding, *Marketing Management*, **3** (2), pp 9–15

Farquhar, P H, Han, J, Herr, P and Ijiri, Y (1992) Strategies for leveraging master brands, *Marketing Research*, Sep, pp 32–39

Feldwick, P (1996) What is brand equity anyway and how do you measure it ?, *Journal of the Market Research Society*, **38**, pp 85–104

Feldwick, P and Bonnal, F (1995) Reports of the death of brands have been greatly exaggerated, *Marketing and Research Today*, **23** (2), May, pp 86–95

Feral, F (1989) Les signes de qualité en France à la veille du grand marché communautaire et à la lumière d'autres systèmes, *CERVAC*, Université d'Aix Marseille 3, October

Financial Times (1993) *Accounting for Brands*, London, FTBI Report

Firat, F and Dholakia, N (1998) *Consuming People*, Routledge, London

Folz, J-M (2003) Managing two brands for success: Peugeot and Citroen, in *Marken Management in der Automobilindustrie*, ed R Kalmbach and B Gottschalk, Auto Business Verlag, pp 341–62

Fombrun, C (2001) Corporate reputation, *Thexis*, **4**, pp 23–27

Fombrun, C, Gardberg, J and Sever, J (2000) The reputation quotient, a multi stakeholder measure of corporate reputation, *Journal of Brand Management* (7), pp 241–55

Fourcade, A and Cabat, (1981) *Anthropologie de la publicité*, Fondation Jours de France pour la recherche en publicité

Fournier, S (1998) Consumers and their brands, *Journal of Consumer Research*, **24** (4), Mar, pp 343–73

Frey, J B (1989) Measuring corporate reputation and its value, Marketing Science Conference, Duke University, NC, USA, 17 March

Friedman, T L (2000) *The Lexus and the Olive Tree*, Anchor Books, New York

Fry, J N (1967) Family branding and consumer brand choice, *Journal of Marketing Research*, **4**, Aug, pp 237–47

Fry, J N, Shaw, D, Haehling, C and Dipchand, C (l973) Customer loyalty to banks: a longitudinal study, *Journal of Business*, **46**, pp 517–25

Gali, J (1993) Does consumer involvement impact evaluations of brand extensions?, unpublished doctoral dissertation, HEC Graduate School of Management

Gamble, T (1967) Brand extension, in *Plotting Marketing Strategy*, ed L Adler, Interpublic Press Books, New York

Garbett, T (1981) *Corporate Advertising*, McGraw-Hill, New York

Geary, M (1990) Fusions et acquisitions: le problème de goodwill, in *Seminaire: Le traitement du goodwill*, 1 February, PF Publications Conferences, Paris

Gelle, T (1990) La comptabilisation des marques, HEC research paper, under the direction of L Collins, May, Jouy-en-Josas

Gladwell, M (2000) *The Tipping Point*, Schuster, London

Glemer, F and Mira, R (1993) The brand leader's dilemma, *McKinsey Quarterly*, **2**, pp 34–44

Greener, M (1989) The bomb in the balance sheet, *Accountancy*, August, p 30

Greig, I and Poynter, R (1994) Brand transfer: building the Whirlpool brand in Europe, *Esomar Conference Proceedings, 26–29 October, Building Successful Brands*, pp 65–78

Guest, L (1964) Brand loyalty revisited: a twenty years report, *Journal of Applied Psychology*, **48** (2), pp 93–97

Gürhan-Canli and Maheswaran (1998) The effects of extensions on brand name dilution enhancement, *Journal of Consumer Research*, **35**, Nov, pp 464–73

Hague, P and Jackson, P (1994) *The Power of Industrial Brands*, McGraw-Hill, London

Hallberg, G (1995) *All Consumers are not Created Equal*, Wiley, New York

Hambleton, R (1990) *The Branding of America*, Country Roads, USA

Hamel, G and Prahalad, C (1985) Do you really have a global strategy?, *Harvard Business Review*, Jul–Aug

Hamel, G and Prahalad, C K (1994) *Competing for the Future*, Harvard Business School Press, Boston, MA

Heather, E (1958) What's in a brand name, *Management Review*, Jun, pp 33–35

Heilbrunn, B (2003) The drivers of brand attachment, Working paper, EM Lyon

Heller, R (1986) On the awareness effects of mere distribution, *Marketing Science*, **5**, Summer, p 273

Hem, L (2003) Context effects in brand extensions: implications for evaluations, *Annual EMAC Conference Proceedings*

Henderson, P and Cote, J (1998) Guidelines for selecting or modifying logos, *Journal of Marketing*, **62** (2), Apr, pp 14–30

Hill, S and Lederer, C (2001) *The Infinite Asset*, Harvard Business School Press, Boston, MA

Hirschmann, E and Holbrook, M (1982) Hedonic consumption, *Journal of Marketing*, **46** (2), pp 92–101

Hite, R and Fraser, C (1988) International advertising strategies of multinational corporations, *Journal of Advertising Research*, Aug/Sep, **28** (4), pp 9–17

Hoch, S (1996) How should national brands think about private labels?, *Sloan Management Review*, **37**, Winter, pp 89–102

Hoch, S and Banerji, S (1993) When do private labels succeed?, *Sloan Management Review*, Summer, pp 57–67

Holbrook M and Hirschmann E (1982) The experiential aspects of consumption, *Journal of Consumer Research*, **9**, 2, Sep, pp 132–40

Holt, D B (2004) *How Brands Become Icons*, Harvard Business School Press, Cambridge, MA

Holt, D, Quelch, J and Taylor, E (2003) Managing the transnational brand: how global perceptions drive value, Globalization of Markets Colloquium, Harvard Business School

Hout, T, Porter, M and Rudder, E (1982) How global companies win out, *Harvard Business Review*, Sep–Oct

Hussey, R and Ong, A (1997) Accounting for goodwill and intangible assets, *Journal of Brand Management*, **4** (4), pp 239–47

Ind, N (2001) *Living the Brand*, Kogan Page, London

Ind, N (2005) *Beyond Branding*, Kogan Page, London

Interbrand (1997) *Brand Valuation*, Premier Books, London

Interbrand (1998) *Brands: The new wealth creators*, Macmillan Business, Basingstoke

IREP (1994) *La Marque*, Seminar on Branding, September, Institut de Recherches et d'Etudes Publicitaires, Paris

Jacobson, R and Aaker, D (1985) Is market share all that it's cracked up to be?, *Journal of Marketing*, **45** (4), Fall, pp 11–22

Jacoby, J and Chestnut, R (1978) *Brand Loyalty and Measurement*, Wiley, New York

Jaubert, M J (1985) *Slogan, mon Amour*, Bernard Barrault Editeur, Paris

Jensen, R (1999) *The Dream Society*, McGraw Hill, New York

Joachimsthaler, E and Aaker, D (1997) Building brands without mass media, *Harvard Business Review*, **75** (1), Jan–Feb, pp 39–52

Jones, J P (1986) *What's in a Name: Advertising and the concept of brands*, Lexington Books, Lexington, KY

Kapferer, J-N (1986) Beyond positioning, retailer's identity, *Esomar Seminar Proceedings, Brussels, 4–6 June*, pp l67–76

Kapferer, J N (1987) *Rumeurs: Le plus vieux media du monde* (*Rumours: the oldest medium in the world*), Le Seuil, Paris

Kapferer, J-N (1991) *Rumors: Uses, interpretations and images*, Transactions, New Brunswick

Kapferer, J-N (1995a) Stealing brand equity: measuring perceptual confusion between national brands and copycat own-label products, *Marketing and Research Today*, **23** (2), May, pp 96–103

Kapferer, J-N (1995b) Brand confusion: empirical study of a legal concept, *Psychology and Marketing*, **12** (6), pp 551–68

Kapferer, J-N (1996) Alternative methods for measuring brand confusion created by retailers imitation, HEC Research Report

Kapferer, J-N (1998) The role of branding in medical prescription, HEC Graduate School of Management, Research Paper Series

Kapferer, J N (2000) Why are we seduced by luxury brands? *Journal of Brand Management*, Nov/Dec

Kapferer, J-N (2001) *Reinventing the Brand*, Kogan Page, London

Kapferer, J-N (2003) Corporate and brand identity, in *Corporate and Organizational Identities*, ed B Moingeon, Routledge, London

Kapferer, J-N (2004) Building brands by rumors, in *Rumours as Medium: Facetten der medienkultur* (Vol 5), ed M Bruhn, V Kaufmann, W Wunderlich and A Haupt, Springer, Berlin

Kapferer, P and Gaston Breton, T (2004) *Carte Bleue, la petite carte qui a changé notre vie*, Cherche Midi, France

Kapferer, J-N and Laurent, G (1995) *La Sensibilité aux Marques*, Editions d'Organisation, Paris

Kapferer, J-N and Laurent, G (1996) How consumers build their perception of mega-brands, unpublished working paper, HEC Graduate School of Management

Kapferer, J-N and Laurent, G (1988) Consumers' brand sensitivity: a new concept for brand management, in *Defining, Measuring and Managing Brand Equity, Marketing Science Institute: A conference summary*, Report pp 88–104, MSI, Cambridge, MA

Kapferer, J-N and Laurent, G (2002) *Identifying Brand Prototypes*, HEC Research Report

Kapferer, J-N and Thoenig, J C (1989) *La Marque*, McGraw-Hill, Paris

Kapferer, J-N and Thoenig, JC (1992) *La Confusion des Marques*, Prodimarques, Paris

Kapferer, J-N, Thoenig, J C *et al* (1991) Une analyse empirique des effets de l'imitation des marques par les contremarques: mesure des taux de confusion au tachystoscope, *Revue française du marketing*, Jan, 136, pp 53–68

Kapferer, P and Gaston Breton (2002) Lacoste: the legend, chen Church Ridir, Paris

Kapferer, P and Gaston Breton, T (2005) *Renault Trucks, une autre idée du camion* (*Renault Trucks, another concept of a lorry*), Cherche Midi, France

Kapferer, P and Gaston Breton, T (2006) *Rungis: Le plus grand marché du monde (Rungis:the largest market in the world)*, Cherche Midi, France

Kapferer, P and Gaston Breton, T (2007) *HEC: Excellence Européenne, rayonnement mondial (HEC: European excellence, global reach)*, Cherche Midi, France

Keller, K L (1992) Conceptualising, measuring and managing customer based brand equity, *Journal of Marketing*, Jan, pp 1–22

Keller, K L (1998) *Strategic Brand Management*, Prentice Hall

Keller, K (2003) Brand synthesis: the multidimensionality of brand knowledge, *Journal of Consumer Research*, **29** (4), pp 595–600

Keller, Kevin Lane (2007) *Strategic Brand Management*, Prentice Hall, New York

Keller, K L and Aaker, D (1992) The effects of sequential introduction of brand extensions, *Journal of Marketing Research*, **29** (1), Feb, pp 35–50

Keller, K, Heckler, S and Houston, M (1998) The effects of brand name suggestiveness on advertising recall, *Journal of Marketing*, **62** (1), pp 48–58

King, S (1973) *Developing New Brands*, Wiley, New York

Kirmani, A, Sood, S and Bridges, S (1999) The ownership effect in consumer responses to brand line stretches, *Journal of Marketing*, **63** (1), pp 88–101

Kleiber, G (1990) *La Semantique du Prototype*, Presses Universitaires de France, Paris

Klein, N (1999) *No Logo*, Picador, New York

Klink, R and Smith, D (2001) Threats to the external validity of extension research, *Journal of Marketing Research*, **38**, Aug, pp 326–35

Knox, S (1996) The death of brand deference, *Marketing Intelligence and Planning*, **14** (7), pp 35–39

Kotler, P (1997) *The Marketing of Nations*, McGraw Hill, New York

Kotler, P (2002) *Kotler on Marketing*, Village Mondial, Paris

Kotler, P and Dubois, B (1991) *Marketing Management*, Publi-Union, Paris

Kotler, P and Gertner, D (2002) Country as a brand, product and beyond, *Journal of Brand Management*, **9** (4–5), Apr, pp 249–61

Kotler, P, Pfoertsch, W and Michi, I (2007) *B2B Branding*, Springer, Berlin

Kozinets, R (2002) Tribalized marketing: the strategic implications of virtual communities of consumption, *European Management Journal*, 17, June, pp 252–64

Krief, Y (1986) L'entreprise, l'institution, la marque, *Revue française du marketing*, **109**, pp 77–96

Krief, Y and Barjansky, M (1981) La marque: nature et fonction, *Stratégies*, 261 and 262, pp 37–41, 32–36

Kripke, S (1980) *Naming and Necessity*, Harvard University Press, Cambridge, MA

Kumar, N and Steenkamp, J-B (2007) *Private Label Strategy*, Harvard Business School Press, Cambridge, Mass

Laforet, S and Saunders, J (1994) Managing brand portfolios: how the leaders do it, *Journal of Advertising Research*, **34** (5), pp 64–67

Lai, K and Zaichkowsky, J (1999) Brand imitation: do the Chinese have different views, *Asia Pacific Journal of Management*, **16** (2), pp 179–92

Lakoff, G (1987) *Women, Fire and Dangerous Things*, University of Chicago Press, Ill

Lane, V and Jacobson, R (1995) Stock market reactions to brand extension announcements, *Journal of Marketing*, **59** (1), pp 63–77

Laurent, G and Kapferer, J-N (1985) Measuring consumer involvement profiles, *Journal of Marketing Research*, **22**, pp 41–53

Laurent, G, Kapferer, J-N and Roussel, F (1987) Thresholds in brand awareness, *40th Esomar Marketing Research Congress Proceedings*, Montreux, Sep 13–17, pp 677–99

Laurent, G, Kapferer, J-N and Roussel, F (1995) The underlying structure of brand awareness scores, *Marketing Science*, **14** (3), pp 170–79

Leclerc, F, Schmitt, B H and Dube-Rioux, L (1989) Brand name à la francaise? Oui, but for the right product!, *Advances in Consumer Research*, **16**, pp 253–57

Lehu, J M (2006) *Brand Rejuvenation*, Kogan Page, London

Leif Heim Egil (2002) Variables moderating consumers' reactions to brand extensions, Association for Consumer Research, European Conference Proceedings

Leuthesser, L (1988) Defining, measuring and managing brand equity, Marketing Science Institute, Report no 88–104, Cambridge, MA

Levitt, T (1967) Market stretching, in *Plotting Marketing Strategy*, ed L Adler, Interpublic Press Books, New York

Levitt, T (1969) The augmented product concept, in *The Marketing Mode: Pathways to corporate growth*, McGraw-Hill, New York

Levitt, T (1981) Marketing intangible products and product intangibles, *Harvard Business Review*, **59** (3), May/Jun, pp 94–102

Levitt, T (1983) The globalization of markets, *Harvard Business Review*, May/June

Levy, S (1999) *Brands, Consumers, Symbols and Research*, Sage, Thousand Oaks, CA

Lewi, C and Kapferer, J-N (1996) Consumers' preference for retailers' brands, *Esomar Conference Proceedings – The Big Brand Challenge*, Oct 9–11, pp 229–41

Lindsay, M (1990) Establish brand equity through advertising, *Marketing News*, 22 Jan, pp 16–17

Lindstrom, M (2003) *BRANDchild*, Kogan Page, London

Lindstrom, M (2005) *Brand Sense*, Free Press, New York

Lipowetsky, J and Roux, E (2004) *Le luxe (Luxury)*, Flammarion, Paris

Loden, D J (1 992) *Mega Brands*, Irwin, IL

Loken, B and Roedder John, D (1993) Diluting brand beliefs: when do brand extensions have a negative impact?, *Journal of Marketing*, **57**, July, pp 71–84

MacInnis, D J and Nakamoto, P K (1990) Examining factors that influence the perceived goodness of brand extensions, Working Paper no 54, University of Arizona

Macrae, C (1991) *World Class Brands*, Addison-Wesley, England

Macrae, C (1996) *The Brand Chartering Handbook*, Addison-Wesley, Harlow, UK

Maffesoli, M (1996) *The Time of the Tribes: The decline of individualism in mass societies*, Sage, Thousand Oaks, CA

Maffesoli, M (2007) *Le Réenchantement (Reenchantment)*, La Table Ronde, Paris

Magrath, A J (1990) Brands can either grow old gracefully or become dinosaurs, *Marketing News*, 22 Jan, pp 16–17

Marconi, J (1994) *Beyond Branding*, Probus, Chicago

Margolis, S E (1989) Monopolistic competition and multiproduct brand names, *Journal of Business*, **62** (2), pp 199–210

Marketing Mix (1987) Monter une gamme: un problème majeur, *Marketing Mix*, **17**, Nov, pp 40–6

Marion, G (1989) *Les images de l'entreprise*, Les Editions d'Organisation

Martin, D N (1989) *Romancing the Brand*, American Management Association, New York

Martin, Dick (2007) *Rebuilding Brand America*, Amacom, New York

Mauguère, H (1990) *L'évaluation des entreprises non cotées*, Dunod Entreprise, Paris

Maurice, A (1989) Enquête sur les contremarques: les apprentis sorciers, *References*, May, pp 16–20

Mazanec, J A and Schweiger, G C (1981) Improved marketing efficiency through multiproduct brand names? *European Research*, Jan, pp 32–44

McAlexander, J H, Schouten, J W and Koenig, H F (2002) Building brand community, *Journal of Marketing*, **66** (1), Jan, pp 38–54

McCartney, S (2005) *The Fake Factor*, Cyan, London

McGarty, Craig (1999) *Categorization in Social Psychology*, Sage, Thousand Oaks, IL

McKenna, R (1991) *Relationship Marketing*, Addison-Wesley, Reading, MA

McKinsey Corp (1990) *The Luxury Industry*, McKinsey, Paris

McWilliam, G (1989) Managing the brand manager, in *Brand Valuation*, ed J Murphy, Hutchinson Business Books, London, pp 154–65

Meffert, H and Bruhn, M (1984) *Marken Strategien in Wettbewerb Gabler*, Wiesbaden

Melin, B (1990) Comment evaluer les marques, Research paper, under the direction of J-N Kapferer, HEC, June, Jouy-en-Josas

Meyers-Levy, J (1989) Investigating dimensions of brand names that influence the perceived familiarity of brands, *Advances in Consumer Research*, **16**, pp 258–63

Michel, G (2000) *La Stratégie d'Extension de Marque (Brand extension strategy)*, Vuibert, Paris

Micheli, J A (2006) *The Starbucks Experience*, McGraw Hill, New York

Milligan, A (2004) *Brand it Like Beckham*, Cyan, London

Miniard, Sirdeshmukh and Innis (1992) Peripheral persuasion and brand choice, *Journal of Consumer Research*, **19**, Sep, pp 226–39

Moingeon, B and Soenen, G (2003) *Corporate and organizational identities*, Routledge, London

Mongibeaux, J F (1990) Contrefaçons et contremarques, *Revue de l'ENA*, Sep–Oct

Moore, E, Wilkie, W and Lutz, R (2002) Passing the torch: intergenerational influences as sources of brand equity, *Journal of Marketing*, **66** (2), Apr, pp 17–37

Moore, J (2006) *Tribal Knowledge*, Kaplan, Chicago

Moorhouse, M (1989) Brand accounting, in *Brand Valuation*, ed J Murphy, Hutchinson Business Books, London, pp 143–53

Moss, G D (2007) *Pharmaceuticals: Where's the brand logic?*, Haworth, New York

Muller, M and Mainz, A (1989) Brands, bids and balance sheets: putting a price on protected products, *Acquisitions Monthly*, Apr, **24**, pp 26–27

Muniz, A and O'Guinn, T (2001) Brand community, *Journal of Consumer Research*, **27** (4), March, pp 412–32

Murphy, J (1989) *Brand Valuation*, Hutchinson Business Books, London

Murphy, J (1990) *Brand Strategy*, Director Books, London

Nedungadi, P and Hutchinson, J W (1985) The prototypicality of brands, in *Advances in Consumer Research*, 12, ed E Hirschman and M Holbrook, Association for Consumer Research, pp 498–503

Nelson, P (1970) Information and consumer behavior, *Journal of Political Economy*, **78** (2), pp 311–329

Neuhaus, C F and Taylor, J R (1972) Variables affecting sales of family-branded products, *Journal of Marketing Research*, **14**, Nov, pp 419–22

Neyrinck, J (2000) *Les paradoxes du marketing*, Editions d'Organisation, Paris

Nielsen, (1992) *Category Management*, NTC Business Books

Nohria, N and Hansen, M (2003) Organising multinational companies, Harvard Business School Globalization Conference Proceedings

Norman, D A (2004) *Emotional Design*, Basic Books, London

Nussenbaum, M (1990) Comment évaluer les marques, *Option Finance*, 7 May, **113**, pp 20–2

Nussenbaum, M (2003) Juste valeur et actifs incorporels, *Revue d'Economie Financière*, 71, pp 71–86

Olins, W (1978) *The Corporate Personality*, Mayflower, New York

Olins, W (1989) *Corporate Identity*, Thames and Hudson, London

Oliver, T (1987) The wide world of branding, in *Branding: A key marketing tool*, ed J Murphy, McGraw-Hill, London

Parameswaran, M G (2001) *Brand Building Advertising*, Tata McGraw-Hill, New Delhi

Pariente, S (1989) *La concurrence dans les relations industrie–commerce*, Institut du commerce et de la consommation, Paris

Park, C W, Javorskey, B J and MacInnis, D J (1986) Strategic brand concept–image management, *Journal of Marketing*, **50** (Oct) pp 135–45

Park, C W, Milberg, S and Lawson, R (1991) Evaluation of brand extensions, *Journal of Consumer Research*, **18**, Sep, pp 185–93

Pastoureau, M (1992) *Dictionnaire des couleurs de notre temps*, Editions Bonneton

Pauwels, K and Srinivasan, S (2002) Who benefits from store brand entry, Working Paper, UCLA

Pearson, S (1996) *Building Brands Directly*, Macmillan, Basingstoke

Peckham, J O (1981) *The Wheel of Marketing*, Nielsen, Chicago

Pendergrast, M (1993) *For God, Country and Coca-Cola*, Maxwell MacMillan, New York

Penrose, N (1989) Valuation of brand names and trade marks, in *Brand Valuation*, ed J Murphy, Hutchinson Business Books, London, pp 32–45

Peppers, D and Rogers, M (1993) *The One to One Future*, Piatkus, London

Perrier, R (1989) Valuation and licensing, in *Brand Valuation*, ed J Murphy, Hutchinson Business Books, London, pp 104–12

Pettis, C (1995) *Technobrands*, Amacom, New York

Porter, M (1980) Choix stratégiques et concurrence, *Economica*, Paris

Pourquery, D (1987) Mais ou est donc passé Béatrice Foods? *Le monde affaires*, 7 November, pp 10–12

Publicis (1988) Advertising in Europe, *Publicis*, September, 1

Quelch, J and Harding, D (1996) Brands versus private labels, fighting to win, *Harvard Business Review*, Jan–Feb, **74** (1), pp 99–111

Quelch, J and Hoff, E (1986) Customizing global marketing, *Harvard Business Review*, May/Jun

Quelch, J and Kenny, D (1994) Extend profits, not product lines, *Harvard Business Review*, Sep–Oct, **72** (4), pp 153–64

Ramsay, W (1992) The decline and fall of manufacturer branding, *Esomar Conference Proceedings – The Challenge of Branding*, 28–30 October, pp 233–52

Rangaswamy, A, Burke, R and Oliva, T (1993) Brand equity and the extendibility of brand names, *International Journal of Research in Marketing*, **10** (1), pp 61–75

Rao, V R, Mahajan, V and Varaiya, N (1990) A balance model for evaluating firms for acquisition, Working Paper, Graduate School of Management, Cornell University, NY, Jan

Rapp, S and Collins, L (1994) *Beyond Maxi-Marketing*, McGraw-Hill

Rastoin, N (1981) Sortez vos griffes, *Coopération – distribution – consommation*, 5, pp 26–35

Reddy, S, Holak, S and Bhat, S (1994) To extend or not to extend, *Journal of Marketing Research*, **31**, May, pp 243–62

Rege, P (1959) *A vos marques*, Favre, Lausanne

Regouby, C (1988) *La Communication globale*, Les Editions d'Organisation, Paris

Reichheld, F (1996) *The Loyalty Effect*, Harvard Business School Press, Boston, MA

Reichheld, F (2006) *The Ultimate Question*, Harvard Business School Press, Cambridge, Mass

Resnik, A, Turney, P and Mason, J (1979) Marketers turn to counter segmentation, *Harvard Business Review*, **57** (3), pp 115–29

Revue Française de Comptabilité (1989) Le débat sur les marques en Grande-Bretagne, *Revue Française de Comptabilité*, Oct, **205**, p 19

Revue Française de Comptabilité (1990) Incorporels identifiables: le projet australien, *Revue Française de Comptabilité*, Jan, **208**, p 11

Ridderstrale, J and Nordstrom, K (2000) *Funky Business*, FT Publishing, London

Ries, A (2000) *Advertising is Dead*, McGraw-Hill

Ries, A and Ries, L (2004) *The Origin of Brands*, Harper Business, New York

Ries, A and Trout, J (1987) *Positioning*, McGraw-Hill, Paris

Ries, A and Trout, J (1990) *Bottom Up Marketing*, PLUME books

Riezebos, H (1994) *Brand-Added Value*, Eburon, Delft, Netherlands

Riezebos, H and Snellen, M (1993) *Brand Names Changes*, Erasmus, Management Report Series, no 149

Riezebos, R (2003) *Brand Management*, Prentice Hall, New York

Rijkenberg, J (2001) *Concepting*, Warc, New York

RISC (1991) *Brand Value and Management in the Luxury Industry*, Sep, International Research Institute on Social Charge, Paris

Roberts, K (2005) *Lovemarks*, Power House Books, London

Roeder-John D, Loken, B and Joiner, C (1995) The negative impact of brand extensions: can you dilute flagship products, Research paper, University of Minnesota

Romaniuk, J and Ehrenberg, A (2003) Do brands lack personality?, Marketing Science Centre Research Report no 14, May, University of South Australia

Rosch, E (1978) Principles of categorization, in *Cognition and Categorization*, ed E Rosch and B Lloyd, Lawrence Erlbaum, Hillsdale, NJ, pp 27–48

Rosch, E and Lloyd, B (1978) *Cognition and Categorization*, Lawrence Erlbaum, Hillsdale, NJ

Rubinson, J (1992) Marketers need new research tools to manage the complex brand portfolios of the 90s, *Marketing Research*, **5** (3), pp 7–11

Russell, A (2002) Investigating the effectiveness of product placements in television shows: the role of modality and plot connection congruence on brand memory and attitude, *Journal of Consumer Research*, Dec, pp 306–18

Rutteman, P (1989) Mergers, acquisitions, brand and goodwill, *Accountancy*, September, p 27

Rutteman, P (1990) Boosting the profits of the brands industry, *Accountancy*, January, pp 26–27

Samways, A and Whittome, K (1994) UK brand strategies: facing the competitive challenge, a Financial Times Management Report, Financial Times, London

Santi, M (1996) The determinants of profitability among suppliers of distributors' own brands, unpublished working paper, HEC Graduate School of Management

Sapolsky, H M (1986) *Consuming Fears: The politics of product risks*, Basic Books, New York

Saporito, B (1986) Has been brands go back to work, *Fortune*, 28 Apr, pp 123–24

Sappington, D and Wernerfelt, B (1985) To brand or not to brand? *Journal of Business*, **58**, Jul, pp 279–93

Sattler, H (1994) *Der Wert von Marken*, Research Paper no 341, Institut für Betriebswirtschaftslehre, Kiel University

Saunders, J and Guoqun, F (1996) Dual branding: how corporate names add value, *Marketing Intelligence and Planning*, **14** (7), pp 29–34

Saunders, J and Watters, R (1993) Branding financial services, *International Journal of Bank Marketing*, **11** (6), pp 32–38

Schechter, A (1993) Names changes increase, *Marketing News*, American Marketing Association, 1 March, p 1

Schlossberg, H (1990) Brand value can be worth more than physical assets, *Marketing News*, 5 Mar, p 6

Schmitt, B (1999) *Experiential Marketing*, Free Press, New York

Schmitt, B (2003) *Customer Experience Management*, Wiley, New York

Schmitt, B and Zhang, S (2001) Creating local brands in multi lingual international markets, *The Journal of Marketing Research*, **38** (3)

Schnaars, D (1995) *Imitation Strategies*, Free Press, New York

Schroeder, J E and Salzer-Mörling, M (2006) *Brand Culture*, Routledge, London

Schroiff, H-W and Arnold, D (2003) Managing the brand–product continuum in global markets, Globalization of Markets Colloquium, Harvard Business School, May

Schuiling, I and Kapferer, J-N (2004) How global brands really differ from local brands, paper under review, Université Catholique de Louvain, Belgium and HEC Paris, France

Schultz, M, Antorini, Y M and Csaba, F F (2005) *Corporate Branding*, Copenhagen Business School Press

Schwebig, P (1985) *L'identité de l'entreprise*, McGraw Hill, Paris

Schwebig, P (1988) *Les communications de l'entreprise*, McGraw-Hill, Paris

Scoble, R and Israel, S (2006) *Naked Conversations*, Wiley, New York

Seguela, J (1982) *Hollywood Lave Plus Blanc*, Flammarion, Paris

Selame, E and Selame, J (1988) *The Company Image*, Wiley, New York

Selden, L and Colvin, G (2003) *Angel Customers and Demon Customers*, Portfolio, London and New York

Sicard, M C (2003) *Luxe, mensonge et marketing*, Village Mondial, ParisSelden, L and Colvin, G (2003) *Angel Customers and Demon Customers*, Portfolio, London and New York

Silverstein, M and Fiske, N (2003) *Trading Up*, Portfolio Penguin

Silverstein, R (2006) *Trading Up*, Portfolio, London and New York

Simon, C J and Sullivan, M W (1989) The measurement and determinants of brand equity: a financial approach, Working Paper, Oct, University of Chicago

Simon, H (2000) *Hidden Champions*, Harvard Business School Press, Cambridge, MA

Simon, H, Bilstein, F and Luby, F (2006) *Manage for Profit not for Market Share*, Harvard Business School Press, Cambridge, Mass

Smith, D and Park, C W (1992) The effects of brand extensions on market share and advertising efficiency, *Journal of Marketing Research*, 29, Aug, pp 296–313

Steenkamp, J B, Batra, R and Alden, D (2002) How perceived globalness creates brand value, *Journal of International Business Studies*, 33, pp 35–47

Stobart, P (1989) Brand valuation: a true and fair view, *Accountancy*, Oct, p 27

Stobart, P (1994) *Brand Power*, Macmillan, Basingstoke

Sudovar, B (1987) Branding in the pharmaceutical industry, in *Branding: A key marketing tool*, ed J Murphy, McGraw-Hill, London

Sullivan, M (1988) Measuring image spillovers in umbrella branded products, Working Paper, Graduate School of Business, University of Chicago

Sullivan, M (1991) Brand extension and order of entry, Marketing Science Institute, Report no 91–105, Cambridge, MA

Sullivan, M (1992) Brand extensions: when to use them, *Management Science*, 38, Jun, pp 793–806

Swaminathan, V, Fox, R and Reddy, S (2001) The impact of brand extension introduction on choice, *Journal of Marketing*, 65 (4), pp 1–15

Swiners, J L (1979) Bilan critique du rôle de la copy–stratégie dans la pratique publicitaire actuelle, *IREP*, Jun, 19

Szymanowski, ? (2007)

Tauber, E (1988) Brand leverage: strategy for growth in a cost-control world, *Journal of Advertising Research*, Aug–Sep, 28 (4), pp 26–30

Taylor, R (1987) The branding of services, *in Branding: A key marketing tool*, ed J Murphy, McGraw-Hill, London

Tchakhotine, S (1952) *La Propagande Politique*, Gallimard, Paris

Terrasse, C and Kapferer, J-N (2006) L'engagement: une facette clé de la valeur de la marque. Doctoral thesis, HEC

Thil, E and Baroux, C (1983) *Un Pave dans la Marque*, Flammarion, Paris

Thiolon, B (1990) La marque et la banque, *Humanisme et Entreprise*, 181, June, pp 29–32

Thoenig, J C (1990) *Les performances économiques de l'industrie de produits de marque et de la distribution*, ILEC, Paris

Thoenig, J-C and Waldman, C (2005) *De l'Entreprise marchande à l'Entreprise Marquante (From market enterprise to brand enterprise)*, Editions d'Organisation, Paris

Thomassen, L, Lincoln, K and Aconis, A (2006) *Retailization*, Kogan Page, London

Touche Ross Europe (1989) *Accounting for Europe Success by A D 2000*, Internal Report, Touche Ross Europe, London

Trout, J and Ries, A (1981) *Positioning: The battle for your mind*, McGraw Hill

Trout, J and Rivkin, S (2000) *Differentiate or die*, Wiley

Turngate, M (2005) *Fashion Brands*, Kogan Page, London

Tuvee, L (1987) L'histoire du marketing global: bibliographic commentée, *Revue Française du Marketing*, **114** (4), pp 19–48

Twitchell, J B (2006) *Branded Nation*, Simon Schuster, New York

University of Minnesota Consumer Behavior Seminar (1987) Affect generalization to similar and dissimilar brand extensions, *Psychology and Marketing*, **4** (Fall), pp 225–37

Upshaw, L (1995) *Building Brand Identity*, Wiley, New York

Valette Florence, P (2004) La personnalite de la marque, *Recherches et Applications en Marketing*

Van der Vorst, R (2004) *Branding: A systems theoretic perspective*, Nijmegen University, Netherlands

Van Gelder, S (2003) *Global Brand Strategy*, Kogan Page, London

Van Riel, C (2001) Corporate branding management, *Thexis*, **4**, pp 5–12

Veblen, T (1889) *The Theory of The Leisure Class*, Macmillan, New York

Viale, F (1994) Faut-il inscrire les marques an bilan? *Les Echos*, 11 Nov

Viale, F and Lafay, F (1990) Les marques: un nouvel enjeu pour les entreprises, *Revue Francaise de Comptabilité*, 216, Oct, pp 92–99

Ville, G (1986) Maîtriser et optimiser l'avenir d'une marque, *Esomar Congress Proceedings*, pp 527–41

Villemus, P (1996) *La Déroute des Marques*, Editions d'Organisation, Paris

Vincent, L (2002) *Legendary Brands*, Dearborn, Chicago

Wansink, B and Ray, M (1996) Advertising strategies to increase usage frequency, *Journal of Marketing*, **60** (1), Jan, pp 31–47

Ward, K (1989) Can the cash flows of brands really be capitalized? in *Brand Valuation*, ed J Murphy, Hutchinson Business Books, London, pp 70–80

Warin, G and Tubiana, A (2003) *Marques sous licence*, Editions d'Organisation, Paris

Wathieu, L, Zaltman, G and Liu, Y (2003) Rooting marketing strategy in human universals, Globalization of Markets Colloquium, Harvard Business School

Watkins, T (1986) *The Economics of the Brands: A marketing analysis*, McGraw-Hill

Wentz, L (1989) How experts value brands, *Advertising Age*, 16 Jan, p 24

Wernerfelt, B (1988) Umbrella branding as a signal of new product quality, *Rand Journal of Economics*, **19** (Autumn), pp 458–66

Wernerfelt, B (1990) Advertising content when brand choice is a signal, *Journal of Business*, **63** (1), pp 91–98

Winram, S (1987) The opportunity for world brands, in *Branding: A key marketing tool*, ed J Murphy, McGraw-Hill, London

Yentis, A and Bond, J (1995) Andres comes out of the closet, *Marketing and Research Today*, **23** (2), May, pp l04–12

Yoshimori, M (1989) Concepts et stratégies de marque au Japon, in *La marque*, ed J-N Kapferer and J C Thoenig, McGraw-Hill, Paris

Young, R (1967) Multibrand entries, in *Plotting Marketing Strategy*, ed L Adler, Interpublic Press Books, New York

Young & Rubicam (1994) *Brand Asset Valuator*, Young & Rubicam, London

Yovovich, B G (1988) What is your brand really worth? *Adweek's Marketing Week*, 8 August, pp 18–24

Yovovich, B G (1995) *New Marketing Imperatives*, Prentice Hall, Englewood Cliffs, NJ

Zaichkowsky, J and Simpson, R (1996) The effect of experience with a brand imitator on the original brand, *Marketing Letters*, **7** (1), pp 31–39

Zareer, P (1987) De la valeur des marques de commerce, *CA Magazine*, Feb, p 72

Zhang, S and Schmitt, B (2001) Creating local brands in a multilingual international market, *Journal of Marketing Research*, **38**, Aug, pp 313–25

Zyman, S (1999) *The End of Marketing as We Know It*, Harper Business

Index

NB: page numbers in *italic* indicate figures or tables